Weisenberg, upon various difficult
subjects, and afterwards ------- off
Messengers with ------- &
private letters to Vienna, Berlin
Paris & Brussells. however
I contrived to get it all done by
about Two this Morning; and
now for my Consolation I have
staring me in the Face 13
Boxes full of Papers, which ought
all to be read forthwith, and
which have come to me since
Yesterday Morning. —
I am going to Day to dine with
Grey at Sheen with ye D. of
Richmond. Grey is Extremely
amiable towards me, and I
think is now pleased at my having
kept him stout on the Turkish

PALMERSTON

DAVID BROWN

PALMERSTON

A BIOGRAPHY

YALE UNIVERSITY PRESS
NEW HAVEN AND LONDON

For information about this and other Yale University Press publications, please contact:
U.S. Office: sales.press@yale.edu   www.yalebooks.com
Europe Office: sales@yaleup.co.uk   www.yaleup.co.uk

Set in Minion Pro by IDSUK (DataConnection) Ltd
Printed in Great Britain by the MPG Books Group

Library of Congress Cataloging-in-Publication Data

Brown, David, 1972–
    Palmerston: a biography / David Brown.
      p. cm.
    Includes bibliographical references and index.
    ISBN 978-0-300-11898-8 (cl: alk. paper)
1. Palmerston, Henry John Temple, Viscount, 1784–1865. 2. Great Britain – Politics and
government—1837–1901. 3. Prime ministers—Great Britain—Biography. I. Title.
    DA536.P2B75 2010
    941.081092—dc22
    [B]   2010020688

A catalogue record for this book is available from the British Library.

10 9 8 7 6 5 4 3 2

To Adeline

Contents

ILLUSTRATIONS

Endpapers: Letter from Palmerston to Lady Cowper, 31 December 1831. University of Southampton. By kind permission of the Broadlands Archive Trustees.

Plates

1 Drawing of the future Lord Palmerston, by Miss Mary Tate, 6 October 1801. University of Southampton. By kind permission of the Broadlands Archive Trustees.

2 *Professor Dugald Stewart*, by Sir Henry Raeburn, *c.*1810. Scottish National Portrait Gallery.

3 *Emily Mary, Countess Cowper*, lithograph after Sir Thomas Lawrence. Private Collection/The Bridgeman Art Library.

4 Watercolour plan of Mullaghmore Harbour, with a note to Henry Townshend from C.E. Donnel describing the work in progress etc., January 1825. University of Southampton. By kind permission of the Broadlands Archive Trustees.

5 *Arthur Wellesley, 1st Duke of Wellington*, by John Jackson, 1830–31. © National Portrait Gallery, London.

6 *Charles Grey, 2nd Earl Grey*, after Sir Thomas Lawrence, *c.*1828. © National Portrait Gallery, London.

7 *William Lamb, 2nd Viscount Melbourne*, by Sir Edwin Henry Landseer, 1836. © National Portrait Gallery, London.

8 *Lord John Russell*, engraving by D.J. Pound after a photograph by Mayall. Mary Evans Picture Library.

9 *Henry John Temple, 3rd Viscount Palmerston*, by John Partridge, 1844–45. © National Portrait Gallery, London.

10 'To the electors of the Borough of Tiverton', 23 July 1847. University of Southampton. By kind permission of the Broadlands Archive Trustees.

11 Broadlands, unattributed design in *Morris's Views*. Mary Evans Picture Library.

Maps

A Note on Quotations

Though Palmerston prided himself on the clarity of his handwriting, his grammatical style was idiosyncratic, and especially his use of capitalisation. As he grew older his writing employed more capitalisation, generally of nouns, though even in this he was inconsistent (and not unique). It may well have been used to signify emphasis but it is difficult to discern a uniform pattern or logic. Certainly those letters written in later life, produced in a bolder (that is to say, frequently larger, heavier and 'more flowing') hand, are characterised by the greater use of capitalisation and this may indicate a growing confidence in his form of expression. Studies of dialect and speech would employ analysis of such written emphasis for evidence of spoken style. However, as with all handwritten texts, there remains a high degree of ambiguity: in Palmerston's case, for example, the distinctions between capital and lower case letters 'e' and 's' are slight and cannot always be judged precisely. Therefore it has been decided on the grounds of consistency as well as readability to standardise quotations and to modernise such eccentric spelling (for all primary quotations used). The integrity of the original text has been preserved in all other respects, save for some minor modernisation of syntax, primarily of punctuation, where this removes ambiguity. Italicised text in quotations indicates emphasis in the original source.

ACKNOWLEDGEMENTS

In researching and writing this book I have incurred a good many debts which it is a pleasure to acknowledge here. Periods of leave and research trips have been generously funded by the Arts and Humanities Research Council, the British Academy, the Carnegie Trust for the Universities of Scotland, and the University of Strathclyde. I am grateful to them all for their support of this project.

I would like to express my gratitude to the staff of the libraries, archives and record offices in which the research for this book was conducted. For permission to quote from materials in their possession, or for which they own the copyright, I am grateful to: the Bodleian Library, University of Oxford; the Borthwick Institute, University of York; the British Library; the Trustees of the Broadlands Archives; Lady Clarendon; the Governors of Dunford House and the County Archivist, West Sussex Record Office; Durham University Library; Hampshire Record Office; the Controller of Her Majesty's Stationery Office; the Museum of London; the National Archives, Kew; the Trustees of the National Library of Scotland; the National Library of Wales; Manuscripts and Special Collections, the University of Nottingham; the Public Record Office of Northern Ireland; the Société civile du Val Richer; West Yorkshire Archive Service, Leeds.

While I have endeavoured to trace the owners of material used in preparing this book I apologise for any inadvertent infringement of copyright and trust that, in the event of such an oversight, a general acknowledgement of the value of being able to consult the papers I have used for this book will be accepted in lieu of more precise thanks. One resource more than any other has been central to my work and I would like to single out for special mention Chris Woolgar and everyone associated with the Archives and Special Collections at the Hartley Library, University of Southampton, for their help and assistance over a number of years as I worked through Palmerston's papers. Chris has long offered valued support of my work and good advice for which I am extremely grateful.

My colleagues at the University of Strathclyde have, on the whole, created an environment conducive to serious research. In particular I would like to thank Richard Finlay for his encouragement and friendship which have been unstinting ever since I arrived in Glasgow. I am also grateful to Ali Cathcart, Allan Macinnes, John Young, Arthur McIvor, Conan Fischer, Bill Wurthmann and former colleagues David Moon and Hamish Fraser, for various kindnesses. I have benefited from a number of stimulating discussions with David Bebbington over lunches in Stirling. I am also very grateful to those historians who have discussed nineteenth-century history with me over the years. John Charmley and Muriel Chamberlain share some responsibility for first interesting me in the period and keeping that interest alive, but I have also gained much from conversations with Michael Bentley, James Gregory (who was good enough to allow me to consult his unpublished paper on the writing of Palmerston's official biography), Angus Hawkins, Geoff Hicks, Tony Howe (who also very kindly supplied transcripts of Richard Cobden's letters), Andrew Lambert, Thomas Otte, the late Michael Partridge, Keith Robbins and Miles Taylor.

My greatest intellectual debt remains that to Paul Smith. He has encouraged, discussed and politely criticised my work, and with characteristic generosity read the whole of the first draft of this book and offered extremely valuable comments on it. Though it is an inadequate acknowledgement, I hope that he will see in what follows some evidence of his good advice having been acted upon. I should also like to thank Paul and his wife Yvonne for a number of very enjoyable evenings at their home when researching this book has taken me back to Southampton.

I am pleased, too, to have an opportunity to thank the following who have offered good company and sometimes accommodation during my many visits to Southampton: Nick Kingwell, Tony Kushner, Tom Lawson, John Oldfield, and Simon and Judith Payling.

I could not have asked for a more supportive and encouraging editor than Robert Baldock, nor a more efficient publisher than Yale. The process of turning the manuscript into a book has been a pleasurable one thanks in large part to the efforts of Rachael Lonsdale. Beth Humphries did a wonderful job of copy-editing the manuscript.

Writing can be, so the cliché has it, a lonely business. It has been a process enlivened, however, by the company of some very good friends and for that I should particularly like to thank Donald Bloxham, Richard and Anna King, Nathalie Lebret, Alison Mitchell, and Jim and Rebecca Mills.

My parents and step-parents have been unwavering in their love and support and I owe them a great deal. *La famille Cordier* has made life a lot of fun. My greatest thanks, however, are to my wife, Adeline, to whom this book is dedicated with all my love.

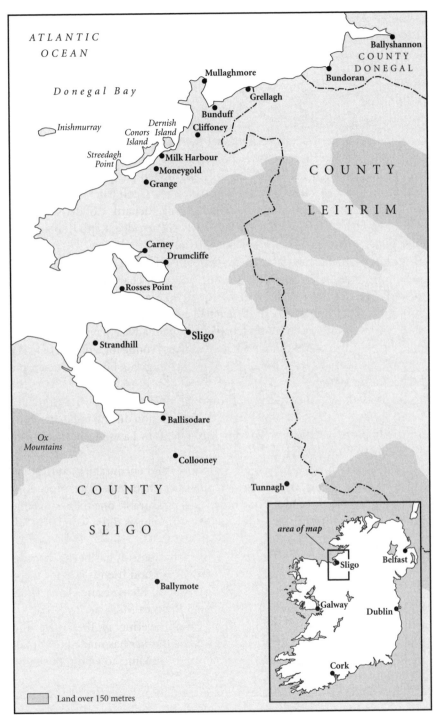

1 Places on or near the Palmerston properties in Sligo

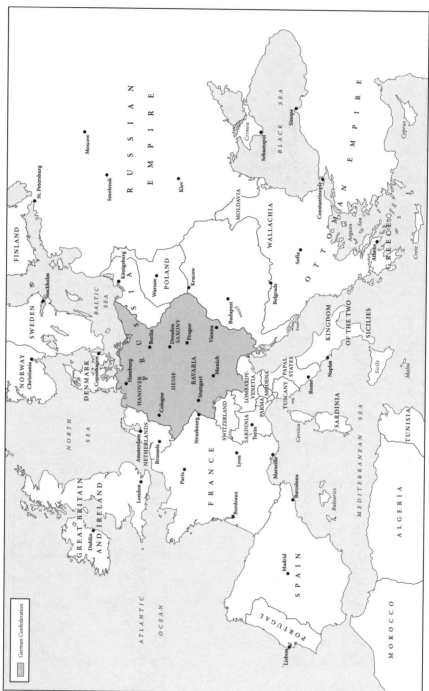

2 Europe in the early nineteenth century

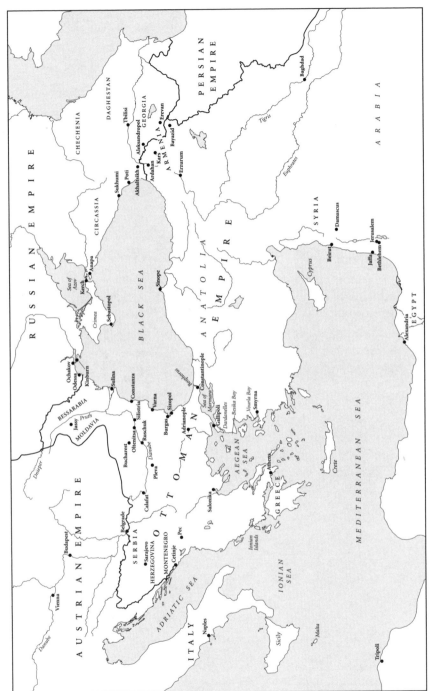

3 The Ottoman Empire and surrounding area

INTRODUCTION

O<small>N</small> 18 O<small>CTOBER</small> 1865 Henry John Temple, third Viscount Palmerston, died, two days short of his eighty-first birthday. He had just completed his ninth year as Prime Minister and as he lay dying at Brocket Hall in Hertfordshire he could, had he been in a nostalgic frame of mind, have looked back on a career spanning almost six decades and one that included, in addition to two terms as Prime Minister, almost nineteen years as Secretary at War, fifteen years as Foreign Secretary and two more as Home Secretary. It had been a good innings by any standard. As William Gladstone would observe, 'Death has indeed laid low the most towering antlers in all the forest'.[1]

It is striking, however, that Palmerston's public career took a long time to peak. He was already forty-five when he first entered the Foreign Office in which he was to make his reputation, and by the time he became Prime Minister, in 1855, he had already lived his threescore years and ten. In its obituary, *The Times* suggested that, 'Had he died at seventy he would have left a second class reputation. It was his great and peculiar fortune to live to right himself'.[2] Many had sought to write Palmerston off, politically if not vitally, when he was seventy. Disraeli, for one, sneered from the opposition benches, that Palmerston had become an 'old painted pantaloon', and was 'really an impostor, utterly exhausted, and at best only ginger-beer and not champagne'.[3] Yet, although increasingly frail and gouty,[4] Palmerston in 1855 was neither 'second class' nor 'exhausted'. Such a man would hardly have been able to press his claims to the premiership on the basis that his appointment was, quite simply, 'inevitable',[5] had he neither political backing nor physical stamina enough to substantiate them; Palmerston had both. It was precisely because he had impressed himself on the public stage so effectively by 1855 that opponents and critics were keen to undermine him.

Yet, the ambiguous nature of Palmerston's immediate posthumous reputation points to an important aspect of his life, which was long and varied, colourful and active, but while incontestably 'significant', it remained ambiguous in its apparent import and impact. Palmerston was born five years before the French Revolution of 1789 and yet lived to see the end of the American Civil War in 1865 and his death came only five years before

Bismarck united Germany and altered the balance of power in Europe for ever. Born into the genteel world of Georgian high society, Palmerston lived and eventually died at the head of a heavily industrialised, swaggering imperial nation. The Pax Britannica was also the age of Palmerston. Politically, at home, he lived through dramatic change too: he entered Parliament in 1807 by the rottenest of routes, accepting the seat of Newport, Isle of Wight, on the strict understanding that he never set foot in the place; he left Parliament, according to one recent account,[6] a much reformed and more democratic place and despite his well-known antipathy towards the working classes, believing them likely to kill their children for a drink (what then might they do with the vote?),[7] had emerged as a popular hero to rival any later charismatic leader: Palmerston was the 'People's Minister',[8] long before anyone thought to call Gladstone the 'People's William'.

Just as he lived through turbulent and changing times, Palmerston's reputation has similarly suffered the vagaries of historical fad and fashion and early biographers, determined to see him as 'something', created a variety of apparently contradictory portraits and images. Here was the Regency dandy who liked parties more than politics, and yet, standing at a tall desk so that he would not be able to fall asleep at his work, Palmerston happily attended to the minutiae of office, working from seven in the morning to one o'clock the next such that, as one bus driver was reported to observe, ' 'E earns 'is wages; I never come by without seeing 'im 'ard at it'.[9] The amorous and charming Lord Cupid was also the abrasive Lord Pumicestone who vexed Queen Victoria and Prince Albert to such an extent that they may well have been drawn to agree with those German conservatives who discerned in Palmerston signs that he was the son of the devil.[10] Politically, too, he defied neat categorisation. As Edward Whitty lamented, essaying a pen portrait of the new Prime Minister in 1855:

> The difficulty of daguerreotyping Proteus would be comparable with the perplexity of a biographer in attempting a sketch of the career of Henry John Temple, Viscount Palmerston. For, though the individuality is, at all stages, identical, there are four different personages to deal with – Palmerston, who was the raging young Pittite; Palmerston, the adolescing Canningite; Palmerston the juvenile Whig; and Palmerston the attaining-years-of-discretion Coalitionist. There is none of the Ciceronian symmetry in the career – beginning, middle, and end; it is all beginning.[11]

All of which has served, all too often, to create a portrait of Palmerston as a mixed bag of contradictions and a man frequently out of tune with his times. Yet it is not enough to dismiss Palmerston as a cynical opportunist, a dangerous politician (and lover) or a cavalier adventurer. If there is no obscuring the fact that this is a complicated life to unravel, then equally there is no avoiding Lord Palmerston. His life and career are interwoven with, and

profoundly affect, the course of modern history. As one of his early biographers noted, in reviewing the work of another:

> The route from the Napoleonic Wars to Queen Victoria's first Jubilee
> runs, so to speak, straight through Lord Palmerston. That astonishing
> career bars the whole course of English and, to a large extent, of European
> history between 1830 and 1865; and if you propose to take your passen-
> gers across the intervening years by an honest route which will enable
> them to see where they are really going, you have got somehow to nego-
> tiate the formidable slopes of the Palmerstonian *massif*. Poor-spirited
> persons may prefer to travel through this period by following the shady
> valley of Disraeli's early life or the comparatively easy gradients of
> Mr. Gladstone. But their unheroic choice is a mere shirking of difficulties;
> and if you steer an honest course, you are brought straight up against the
> massive silhouette of Lord Palmerston's official life. . . .
>
>   That means, to put the problem at its lowest, a truly terrifying accumu-
> lation of paper waiting to be reviewed by any investigator of Lord
> Palmerston's career, a mountain of material beneath whose frowning
> crags chicken-hearted scholars slink away to find circuitous routes round
> the obstacle and easier careers to write about.[12]

The accumulation of paper is indeed enormous. However, while many previous
biographers have been aware of that mountain of material, few have actually
attempted, or had the opportunity to attempt, to scale it. Henry Lytton Bulwer
and Evelyn Ashley's official *Life*, published in five volumes in the 1870s, did
make considerable use of Palmerston's private papers and provided a useful
introduction to their subject, but their approach was highly selective, and
narrowly focused on presenting Palmerston in a favourable light. Later scholars
would in due course come to a study of Palmerston with more searching questions but with due respect for the important work of those such as Herbert Bell,
and later Sir Charles Webster, Donald Southgate and Jasper Ridley, previous
biographers have sought to assess Palmerston from a selective perspective,
using Palmerston's private papers sparingly or not at all. Only Kenneth Bourne
in recent years attempted the task with full access to those papers, but premature death meant that Bourne's study remained incomplete. Yet as Bourne's
Early Years, a substantial examination of the first half of Palmerston's life
demonstrated, full access to those papers is in itself a mixed blessing: the sheer
wealth of detail in Bourne's account often, as reviewers at the time pointed out,
threatened to overwhelm and obscure the book's principal subject.[13] Seeing the
'Palmerstonian *massif*' in perspective is no easy task and past biographers have
regularly stated the difficulty of their undertaking. Donald Southgate opined in
1966 that 'no definitive life can be written until many have slaved at the galleys
over many years', while Kenneth Bourne, sixteen years later, thought there

'probably never will be' a 'satisfactory biography of Palmerston'.[14] Thus did Muriel Chamberlain suggest that although 'Everyone thinks that he or she knows Lord Palmerston', 'Contradictions meet the biographer at every turn'.[15] To make a claim to have produced a 'definitive' account is to give easy hostages to fortune, while to see the contradictions as problems is to miss the point. It is in his complexity that Palmerston is most interesting and it is his apparent adaptability or changeability that makes him a valuable medium for understanding the Victorian world. Palmerston himself suggested that the lives of others should be read for the purposes of improvement: 'In biography read the history of great & wise men avoid the details of the vices & crimes & depravity of mankind, which leave an unsatisfactory and humiliated feeling on the mind, while on the contrary the relation of great & noble actions pleases and elevates,' he wrote in late 1829.[16] It is necessary, however, to pay some attention to those vices (and crimes and depravity if they exist) if the subject is to be rendered with any accuracy.

Whether a satisfactory biography of Palmerston can be written remains something for others to judge. My intention in this study has been, as far as possible, to 'make sense' of Palmerston. He emerges here, I hope, as neither behind nor ahead of his times, but very much of them. I have attempted to understand the Palmerston mindset (indeed, perhaps it is necessary first of all to assert that I believe that there was one) but also to consider how Palmerston was perceived by his contemporaries. I agree with Jonathan Parry that Palmerston was 'the defining political personality of his age',[17] but this is not Carlylean 'great man' history; rather what follows is offered primarily as a prism through which to view (Whig-Liberal) nineteenth-century Britain while it is to be hoped explaining the life and career of one of its principal characters.

In January 1843, Palmerston's eye was caught by an article in the *Edinburgh Review*. The former Foreign Secretary, now sitting uncomfortably on the opposition benches, was evidently struck by what he took to be a distillation of the essence of good statesmanship and copied out an extract by hand:

> The statesman who in treading the slippery path of politics, is sustained & guided only by the hope of fame, or the desire of a lofty reputation, will not only find himself beset with incessant temptations to turn aside from the line of strict integrity, but the disappointment he is sure to meet with will probably drive him to misanthropy, perhaps even irritate him to tarnish by vindictive treachery a virtue founded upon no solid or enduring principle. But the statesman who looks in the simple performance of his duty, for consolation & support amid all the toils & sufferings which that duty may call him to encounter; who aims not at popularity, because he is conscious that continued popularity rarely accompanies systematic and unyielding integrity; who, as he is urged to no questionable measures by the hope of fame, so is deterred from none that are just

by the fear of censure such a man may steer a steady course through the
shoals and breakers of the stormiest sea; & whether he meet with the
hatred or gratitude of his countrymen is to him a consideration of minor
moment, for his reward is otherwise sure. He has laboured with
constancy for great objects he has conferred signal benefits upon his
fellow men. Nobler occupation man cannot aspire to, sublimer power no
ambition need desire; greater reward it would be very difficult to obtain.[18]

To many of his critics, this would have seemed the very antithesis of the
Palmerstonian approach to politics. Very often Palmerston was viewed as a
superficial politician, forging policies based on a crude appreciation of
national honour and power and justifying and grounding those policies in a
selective reading of a vociferous patriotic opinion. Yet there is a case to be
made for seeing the abrasive Lord Pumicestone, the amorous Lord Cupid and
the threatening 'devil's son', cavalier hero and anti-hero of Regency parties and
Victorian parliaments, as something more than the jaunty, irreverent and
opportunistic politician of popular caricature. Colourful though he might have
been, Palmerston was not sufficiently charismatic to sustain a parliamentary
career of almost half a century (more than thirty of those years in the highest
offices of state) by sheer force of personality alone. Remembered as the quin-
tessential gunboat diplomat, Palmerston resorted to such bullying in only two
cases of any great significance, against China and against Greece, and important though such episodes are, they do not define his foreign policy, let alone
his political character. Nor does his oft-quoted advice to George Goschen in
1864 when Prime Minister, that the government could not 'go on adding to the
Statute Book *ad infinitum*',[19] denote a domestic politician of narrow horizons
and negligible reforming spirit. By the same token, Palmerston has long
remained an elusive character: moving politically from Tory to Whig to
Liberal; from reactionary eighteenth-century throwback to enlightened
harbinger of late nineteenth-century democracy; the flamboyant and apparently disreputable society beau who was in fact a near teetotal workaholic.

Crucially, Palmerston was very much rooted in a clearly identified intellectual tradition. His exposure to the ideas of the Enlightenment during his days
as a student at Edinburgh University at the beginning of the nineteenth
century were to provide an intellectual framework within which he would
subsequently approach political life. It was not, therefore, mere hyperbole
when, sixty years after leaving the city, Palmerston returned to Edinburgh in
1863 and claimed that he was 'proud to acknowledge – that if I have been in
any way successful in public life, and if I have been enabled to steer my course
in a manner satisfactory to my own conscience, and meeting the general
approval of my fellow-countrymen . . . it has been that in these three years that
I passed in this city, I was furnished by able hands with charts and compasses
which taught me how to steer my course, to avoid many of the dangers to

which the voyage of life is exposed, and to pursue in safety the career which I was destined to fill.' Palmerston pointed, in particular, to the value of having been 'taught that liberality of sentiment which perhaps in those days was not so generally diffused as in the days in which we live', and stressed the progressive and forward-looking nature of those ideas. Though the liberal idealism of that period had now grown into mid-Victorian orthodoxy in matters of politics and 'social organisation', at the time, Palmerston said, those same ideas 'were struggling against prejudice and limited ignorance for ascendancy in the minds and actions of mankind'.[20] If his commitment to those ideals was sometimes questionable in practice, Palmerston should not be dismissed as a politician lacking principles. His belief in liberal progress, conceived within the carefully prescribed limits of moderate concession to responsible opinion, was sincere and informed his understanding of his political responsibilities and obligations.

Palmerston was also a flamboyant politician. This has, no doubt, affected historical assessments of his seriousness. Thus, as George Francis noted in an article in *Fraser's Magazine* in 1846, rather than crush opponents with well-worked arguments, he was just as likely to dodge difficult situations with mockery. Palmerston, he wrote:

Possesses himself of considerable power of ridicule; and when he finds the argument of an opponent unanswerable, or that it could only be answered by alliance with some principle that might be turned against himself, he is a great adept at getting rid of it by a side-wind of absurd allusion. He knows exactly what will win a cheer and what ought to be avoided as calculated to provoke laughter in an assembly where appreciation of what is elevated in sentiment is by no means common.[21]

Palmerston was serious in his approach to politics, but he was also acutely aware of the need to carry popular support with him. 'As Lord Carlingford used to say, the secret of Lord Palmerston's popularity lay in the fact that he was "understanded of the people".'[22]

CHAPTER 1

ABOUT HARRY, 1784–1800

'a young man of great promise . . . "of wit and pleasure".'
Augustus Clifford, a former school friend, on Palmerston's early character.[1]

HENRY JOHN TEMPLE was not obviously born to greatness. His early life would follow the well-worn path of a late eighteenth-century eldest son of the aristocracy, but in so far as that path had a final destination, it was probably thought to be entry into the diplomatic service, a route his younger brother William would follow, rather than to the highest offices of state. Unlike many of those among whom he would live his later life – the Russells, the Stanleys, the Cecils – the future third Viscount Palmerston's pedigree did not provide him with an automatic entrée into the elite ranks of the political establishment. The peerage which he would ultimately succeed to was an Irish one, and though an unequivocally aristocratic inheritance, it was not strictly an English one. Likewise, although he was born into a Whiggish household, the Temple family was not part of the 'grandmother-hood' of great Whig families so his veins were never thought to be filled with pure Whig blood. Yet the future Lord Palmerston would in time come to be described as 'the most English minister', a patriotic totem for many and emblem of Victorian power for many more. Perhaps because he had not been born into the confines of an established political and social heritage he was able to forge a role adapted (and re-adapted) to the demands of the age in which he lived.

Henry John Temple's family could claim to trace its origins back to the eleventh century, to Leofric, Earl of Mercia (and husband of Lady Godiva), something which the eagles on the family crest were said to commemorate. Nineteenth-century genealogists dismissed the descent from Leofric as a 'fabulous and modern' concoction and preferred to date the emergence of the Temples to the reign of Henry III (1216–72). There was, nonetheless, enough of a family history to satisfy Victorian appetites for heritable greatness in their leading figures and, since he died without legitimate issue, Henry came to be seen as 'the last fruit off an old tree'. 'The distinctive *ethos* of the Temples,' suggested one such observer, 'has been a union of more than usual of the kind of talent which makes men of letters, with more than usual of the kind of talent which makes them men of business.'[2]

Little of any significance is known about the family until the sixteenth century, by which time Peter Temple of Butlers Marston in Warwickshire and Stowe in Buckinghamshire stood at the head of a Midlands gentry family of some rank and wealth. Peter's eldest son, John, inherited Stowe and the Temples of Stowe thrived for four generations. They lived on, by marriage, when Hester Temple, the sister of Sir Richard Temple (created Baron Cobham in 1714 and who had died without issue in 1749), married George Grenville and became ancestor to the Dukes of Buckingham. The Palmerstons, however, were descended from Peter by his second son, Anthony who, it was judged, 'had acquired a less splendid position but a more brilliant name'.[3] Anthony's son, William, made a name for himself at Cambridge as a defender of the logical teachings of Petrus Ramus (Pierre de la Ramée) in the field of rhetoric and dialectic, but by the nineteenth century was better remembered for having served as secretary to Sir Philip Sidney, until Sidney's death in 1586, and later undertaking the same office for Robert Devereux, second earl of Essex, in the process using Essex's influence to secure for himself a seat in Parliament for Tamworth in 1597. Tarnished by association with Essex's plot to overthrow Elizabeth I in 1601, however, William spent the following eight years in relative obscurity before establishing the Temple family's enduring connections with Ireland, becoming in 1609 provost of Dublin College, a post he held until 1627, and an institution which he would represent in the Irish Parliament of 1614. He was knighted in 1622 and was still a Master in Chancery at the time of his death in 1627.[4] Sir William's son, John, rose to prominence in Anglo-Irish politics in the mid-seventeenth century. Educated in Dublin he moved to England where at court he became close to the second earl of Leicester and acted on Leicester's behalf in the latter's appointment as Lord Lieutenant of Ireland in 1641. Though not a universally popular choice Sir John (having been knighted in 1633) was created Master of the Rolls and a privy councillor in Ireland in 1641. His increasingly pro-parliamentary position during the wars became ever clearer and he was eventually imprisoned for opposing the cessation of hostilities in 1643. He was released a year later and in 1646 became MP for Chichester, although he remained closely associated and identified with politics in Ireland and was immediately appointed to the Westminster committee responsible for over-seeing Irish affairs. In 1646 he also published his account of *The Irish Rebellion; or, an history of the beginning and first progresse of the general rebellion raised in the kingdom of Ireland upon the 23 October 1641*, a partisan tract which did much to stir feelings in England in favour of Cromwellian subjugation of Ireland (and which, in 1689, James II's Irish Parliament ordered to be burnt by the public hangman). He was excluded from Parliament in 1648, however, for voting in favour of the King's proposals for peace and chose to live in 'retirement' in London until 1653, at which point he returned to Ireland, resumed his duties as Master of the Rolls and 'prospered' during the Restoration, extending the family's estate interests in Ireland to encompass lands in Carlow, Kilkenny,

Meath, Westmeath and Dublin, including under the Act of Settlement in 1666 confirmation in perpetuity of his lands in Palmerstown.[5]

Sir John Temple's eldest son, Sir William, was to become one of the most notable of the Temples in the years before 1784. As an opponent of the Commonwealth of the 1650s, William's public life began only in 1660 when he was elected to the Irish Convention for Carlow and subsequently for the same seat in the legitimate Parliament of 1661. It was in the diplomatic sphere that he was to become prominent, however, and William enjoyed a moderately distinguished career, though one which, characterised by a persistent Francophobia, was not universally celebrated. A well travelled and linguistically adept figure, he was granted a residency in Brussels in 1665 and developed a faith in the merits of an English alliance with the Netherlands against French expansionism. In 1668 he was ambassador to the Netherlands although a lack of political appetite for a meaningful alliance with the Dutch at home weakened his position and he spent the years after 1670 essentially in retirement back in England and occupied himself with writing works of history (of dubious merit) and political theory. In 1674, however, he returned to the Netherlands where, among other things, as ambassador extraordinary, he conducted negotiations which eventually led to the Treaty of Nijmegen (1678). He is also said to have been instrumental in arranging the marriage of the Prince of Orange and Princess Mary. Later he would serve as briefly as ambassador extraordinary to Spain (1680–81) before ending his public life as a commissioner for the remedy of defective titles in Ireland from 1683.[6] During his life, William added to the family's land-holding, gaining a grant of lands in Carlow in 1669. He also set about some modest estate reforms in Ireland, such as timber planting, and published essays on topics including 'the present state and settlement of Ireland', and 'the advancement of trade in Ireland'. William died in 1699 without an heir although his brother, Sir John Temple, had by this time also made his mark in political life, first as Solicitor-General for Ireland and later as Attorney-General (described by one source as 'one of the ablest and honestest lawyers in his majesties dominions') and as member for Carlow was also temporary Speaker of the Irish House of Commons. Reports that he would or did serve in England as Attorney-General seem inaccurate, the proposal scuttled, apparently, by Charles II's insistence that he 'would never trust any of the blood of a rebel' (such as Sir John *père*).[7]

Sir John died in 1704 and was succeeded by Henry, who would become the first Viscount Palmerston. Henry's public career was spent in England, as MP for East Grinstead (1727–34), for Bossiney in Cornwall (1734–41) and for Weobly in Herefordshire (1741–47), although he does not appear to have left much of an impression on parliamentary life, preferring distractions of a cultural to a political kind. In 1723 Henry Temple was created a peer of Ireland as Baron Temple of Mount Temple, County Sligo and Viscount Palmerston of Palmerston, County Dublin, an acknowledgement, apparently, of his illustrious ancestors' discharge of their public duties in Ireland with 'fidelity, prudence and abstinence'. Palmerston outlived his son and heir, also Henry, who died in 1740 and on his death in 1757 the Palmerston title, and estates, which included the recently purchased family seat of Broadlands in Hampshire, passed to his grandson, another Henry, who became Viscount Palmerston and in due course father to Henry John.[8]

The second Viscount Palmerston sat in the Irish House of Lords from 1761 but never participated in the business of that House. In so far as he entertained political ambitions, and he entertained very few, they were focused on English politics and he sat successively as MP for East Looe (1762–68), Southampton (1768–74), Hastings (1774–84), Boroughbridge (1784–90), Newport, Isle of Wight (1790–96) and finally Winchester (1796–1801). But the expense of buying these seats from their patrons (Boroughbridge, for example, had cost him £2,685 and Newport £4,200) was evidently unsustainable and by 1801 Palmerston told his wife that, having by that time sat in seven parliaments, he was no longer 'desirous of throwing away a great sum of money for the satisfaction of continuing any longer'. He had little enough interest in the daily grind of parliamentary politics and had clearly not been very much inspired by his tenure of relatively minor public office at the Admiralty in the 1760s and 1770s and at the Treasury Board in the 1770s and 1780s. It had perhaps been the proffered salary of £1,000 per annum at the Admiralty that had overcome his initial aversion to 'the attainment of any public employment', for Palmerston, though comfortably off, was never, by the standards of the time, especially wealthy. His annual income of around £7,000, derived from rents and the interest on stock holdings, was sufficient but was never the means to fund an extravagant life.[9]

What funds he did have were used in the pursuit of literary and scientific enquiry and travel in the best traditions of a Regency dilettante. He counted among his friends and correspondents such luminaries of the eighteenth-century scene as David Garrick, Edward Gibbon, Samuel Johnson, Sir William Herschel, Sir Joseph Banks and Joshua Reynolds. He devoted considerable time and resources to the improvement of his estates, notably at Broadlands which benefited from the expert eye of Lancelot 'Capability' Brown.[10] But Palmerston's abiding passion was travel. He spent weeks and months undertaking grand tours of parts of northern and western Europe and used the time to broaden his cultural horizons and expand his artistic collections. Only through experiencing the terror of revolutionary Paris at first hand did he appear to develop any meaningful political convictions, finding it harder after 1791 to sustain his Foxite Whiggism in the face of Pitt's promise of a firmer hand in dealing with cross-Channel dangers. Thus does his biographer observe that the second Viscount 'was an arch-typical Whig peer, even if the Irish title, membership of the House of Commons and his gravitation to Pitt serve to confuse the description. A bustling, hearty, cheerful man, he was a spectator rather than an innovator in political life, yet his range of acquaintance and catholic taste in the arts made him a person of consequence.'[11]

Palmerston's first wife, Frances Poole, died in childbirth in 1769 (the child, too, did not survive), less than two years after their marriage. It was a blow to the Viscount, who distracted himself with renewed travels, first in Wales, then a Grand Tour taking in much of Switzerland, northern Italy, the Rhine, Luxembourg and finally Paris. If his marriage to Frances had been a loving one, his subsequent courtship of Mary Mee, whose family had made its fortune in the City of London, was no less of a romantic engagement. In a riding accident in October 1782 the phaeton in which Palmerston was driving Sarah Culverden and her younger sister Mary Mee overturned, causing the dislocation of Mary's elbow. Palmerston's enquiries after Mary's health soon became compliments and within days a series of love letters. They were married on 4 January 1783 in Bath.[12]

Mary has been described as a lively and charming woman, and an elegant society hostess. Her home, as one visitor recorded, 'was a kind of enchanted castle, where there were regular reunions of the first society, entertained with amusements and splendid hospitality'.[13] Into this ebullient household, in the autumn of 1784 the Palmerstons' first child, Henry John, was born, at 4 Park Street in Westminster (now 20 Queen Anne's Gate).[14] Lord Palmerston noted in his diary on 19 October that his wife was 'ill' and on the 20th recorded that 'Mr Cholmondeley, Mr Mee, Mrs Mee, Mrs Culverden and Miss Whitworth dined. Lady P. brought to bed of a son at seven in the evening.' The following day Palmerston, by his own account, 'Walked into the City; dined at the Crown and Anchor; Play'.[15] Well might Philip Guedalla have remarked that after young Harry's birth, 'the world went on much as before'.[16] Palmerston was not, however, unaffected by the birth of his heir. A christening concert and a ball of 'great magnificence' were held a month after the birth, in November 1784 at Winchester, judged 'more convenient to the country in general' than Broadlands, near Romsey.[17]

The Palmerstons' home at Broadlands was a happy one. As one visitor observed, 'There you would have seen a very beautiful place, a comfortable house, a good-natured, poetical, stuttering Viscount, & a pleasing unaffected woman who, tho' she *did* squeeze through the City gates into a Viscountess, wears her blushing honours without shaking them at you every moment. There you would have seen waterworks by day & fireworks by night'.[18] It was a congenial environment for Harry who would later come to view London, by contrast, as 'that gloomy prison'.[19] Perhaps this was a reflection of the fact that his father, the second Viscount, according to one of his closest friends, 'has not got to his second childhood, but only as far as his second boyhood; for no schoolboy is so fond of a breaking-up as he is of a junket and pleasuring'.[20] Harry gained a sister, Frances, in February 1786 and very soon the house was filled with more noise. 'The children are perfectly well,' Lady Palmerston wrote to her husband in December 1786 during one of his many absences. 'Harry never ceases chattering and Fanny, like her Uncle Culverden, is "jig everlasting and dance without end", for she never will be quiet one moment.'[21] Harry, too, enjoyed dancing a jig 'with his knees bent and his shoulders up to his ears'.[22] To this merry party were added three more children over the next few years: William in January 1788, Mary in January 1789 and Elizabeth in March 1790. Boisterous the Temple children might have been, but health concerns were a frequent intrusion into the household. Harry had evidently been in dubious physical condition since his birth, although Lord Minto, a family friend and later one of Harry's guardians, could report in July 1785 that 'Harry is much improved, and is a fine, eager, lively, good-humoured boy'.[23] He was plagued throughout his early years, however, by recurrent bouts of 'St Anthony's fire', or erysipelas, a bacterial infection that caused sore red rashes, or 'eruptions', on his face. In November 1788 Lady Palmerston informed her husband that Harry had suffered another attack 'in the same place as usual', around his eyes and cheeks, which three grains of James's powder alleviated for the moment but did not cure completely. The 'old complaint' again returned in December 1790 and May 1792, though with diminishing intensity, yet the 'disagreeable remains of his disorder' were still apparent in early 1795. Harry was not born with the strongest of constitutions. He would fall 'extremely ill' again while travelling through Europe with the family in 1793, with a fever common to Verona and which only doses of quinine and bed-rest alleviated.[24] He had reacted badly, too, to the primitive smallpox vaccination administered to him and Frances by Baron Dimsdale in 1787 which, in the days before Dr Jenner's discovery of the efficacy of cowpox in resisting the disease, consisted of inoculation with a form of live smallpox. The preventive measure was evidence of the Palmerstons' progressive outlook, but when the other three children were similarly treated in 1791 the venture proved less successful and Mary died a month after the inoculation.[25]

Meanwhile, Harry showed himself a precocious child and willing student. A Mr Williams was engaged in July 1791 to tutor Harry for two hours each morning. 'I really felt it was a sad thing so clever a boy should waste all his hours,' wrote Lady Palmerston, 'and without some obligation to attend it is impossible to expect children will prefer learning anything to playing about.'[26] Harry demonstrated a particular aptitude for languages that would serve him well throughout his later life, but this came less from Mr Williams and more from the early tuition he received from a French governess, Thérèse Mercier, who had been appointed a couple of years before Williams, in 1788, and, thanks to his father's taste for travel, from the tutor the family picked up in Italy in 1792–94.

Palmerston had decided to take his family away to the continent in July 1792, having spent much of the previous year himself in Paris. It was perhaps in part a move to distract Lady Palmerston from the loss of Mary, and also from the financial embarrassment and personal disgrace of her brother Benjamin Mee, that Palmerston proposed a Grand Tour *en famille*.[27] It was perhaps also to broaden Harry's mind.[28] It was almost certainly to satisfy Palmerston's own restless desire for new experiences and it was to prove an eventful tour.[29] The Palmerstons travelled first to Paris and were received in August 1792 by Louis XVI and Marie Antoinette only days before the royal palace was attacked by the mob. In the heady atmosphere of revolutionary Paris the Palmerstons soon lost their appetite for sightseeing and on 7 August, not without difficulty, left the French capital and headed, via Lyons, for twenty-six somewhat calmer months in the Italian states. The journey through France had been a trying one. Leaving Paris one of the Palmerstons' coaches (carrying servants and the children except Harry) was waylaid by crowds in the Faubourg St Antoine while in Lyons the party was 'much incommoded . . . by crowds of people going to join the armies, who,' Palmerston recorded, 'being the very refuse of the mob and under no discipline, were unpleasant fellow travellers'.[30] It is too much to suggest that these experiences marked the seven-year-old Harry in any meaningful way, but the tour was vitally important to his intellectual development. The Palmerstons might have relaxed in the company of British communities abroad, and allowed the children to pass their time riding every day and sightseeing,[31] but they did not neglect the need to advance Harry's studies.

Gaetano Ravizzotti would become not only Harry's tutor, but a profound influence in the early fashioning of the future third viscount. M. Ravizzotti, or Mr Gaetano as Harry and the rest of the family usually called him, had joined the family entourage in Italy some time during the Palmerstons' tour in 1793,[32] and travelled back to England as tutor to the Temple children in 1794. Little is known about Ravizzotti's background, though Kenneth Bourne notes that he 'was later credited with being a refugee, presumably of radical inclinations', that he had taught in Naples and was thought to hail from Rome.[33] He became, however, a long-standing friend as well as tutor to Harry. By the time Harry had left for France and Italy in 1792 he had picked up the rudiments of French from Thérèse Mercier, and under Ravizzotti's guidance his studies advanced such that when Sir Gilbert Elliot (later the second earl of Minto) met the Palmerstons in Florence in October 1794 he was struck by how well Harry already spoke French and Italian.[34] Palmerston was keen that his son should not abandon these studies on their return (not least if he was to enter the diplomatic corps) and, as he wrote in late 1794, hoped the boy would 'not omit to apply himself in the afternoon to his French and Italian with Mr Gaetano as it would be a pity to neglect them'.[35] The lessons were conducted in the Book Room at Broadlands and soon Latin, and probably some Greek, were added to the curriculum. Harry proudly told his mother in February 1795 that 'I am now translating the deluge from Latin into English and almost out of the syntaxis',[36] and he was soon confident enough to send his first letter in French, writing to his mother, who was away, and enquiring after her and his grand-mother's health and reporting on the weather and his siblings' well-being.[37] Ravizzotti consolidated Harry's education in the further study of modern and ancient languages, history and literature, while his mother made sure that his cultural sensibilities were refined with visits to the theatre with Gaetano and his brother William.[38] However, by the time the family was back in England from the continental tour in late 1794 it had already been decided that Harry's studies would best be continued at Harrow.

Harry's arrival at Harrow was delayed by an outbreak of scarlet fever there in March 1795 (from which one boy is reported to have died). All boys were sent away from the school until April and Harry's mother, always protective of her son, steeled her earlier resolve not to send him until May. Given the schooling Harry received from Ravizzotti at home, that was judged 'soon enough as he will not be losing time in the meanwhile'.[39]

According to Philip Guedalla, 'Harrow in 1795 reflected accurately the educational ideals prevalent in the reign of Queen Elizabeth. An alarming Doctor dispensed stray fragments of Renaissance learning; scared prize-winners declaimed short, petrified portions of classical eloquence; and there was an exquisite aloofness from the vulgarity of contemporary ideas. To this pleasing retardation British institutions owe much of their stability.'[40] In fact, the school was emerging from a fraught recent past of pupil rebellion and disquiet under the headmastership of Benjamin Heath into happier and more prosperous times. Dr Joseph Drury, erstwhile assistant master at the school following a moderately successful Cambridge career, had taken over as head-master from his brother-in-law Heath in 1785 and under his 'eminently successful' guidance the school entered into what by common agreement seems to have been 'one of the most brilliant' periods in its history.[41] Drury sought to imbue his pupils with a love of literature and learning, and hoped to inspire a love of the classics and therefore 'spared his hearers any long philo-logical dissertations'; he encouraged the Harrow boys to read and declaim English verse, something no doubt of great benefit to future statesmen and politician-orators; but above all, Drury aimed to be their friend: 'the most distinctive feature of Dr Drury's training,' it has been observed, 'consisted in the friendly intercourse which he held with his scholars, not only by visiting them in their rooms, but by admitting them to walk and talk with him.'[42] It is said that 'the aroma of scholarship flavoured even his most ordinary sentences' and Harry admitted in later life that even to be reprimanded by Drury was a 'positive pleasure'.[43] However, while Drury set the tone for the school, it was the master of one of the school's boarding houses, Thomas Bromley, and his wife, who would most shape Harry's experiences there.

In April 1795 in advance of Harry's entry into the school, Mrs Bromley wrote to Lady Palmerston to make the necessary arrangements for the arrival of the new boarder. Two suits of clothes, a greatcoat, ten shirts, ten pocket handkerchiefs and six or eight pairs of stockings were judged a sufficient wardrobe and Lord Palmerston was soon able to reassure his wife of Mrs Bromley's sound judgement in such matters. 'She seems very intelligent and notable and I dare say will take very good care of Harry,' Palmerston noted on visiting the school on 18 May. To spare Harry ridicule at the hands of other boys Palmerston urged his wife not to send nightshirts, and having inspected the lodgings reassured her that the 'turn-up' bed in Harry's room would be a 'very convenient circumstance'. And so, on 26 May, Harry was carried to Harrow to settle in for the final two months of the year before the school broke up again in July. Palmerston left his son 'in very good spirits and perfectly happy in staying there'. Harry had a small bureau, some bookshelves and a couple of cupboards installed in his room, 'a very active and pleasant servant' to attend on him and, no doubt to everyone's relief, having discovered that some other boys also wore nightshirts, Harry, too, was allowed two of his own to guard against the cold.[44]

Palmerston returned to Harrow at the beginning of June to hear the speeches. Harry he found 'well and happy', in improved health and in the middle of a wide circle of friends, including the Ponsonbys and, all in all, 'quite at home'. Though the speeches were a disappointment ('I could not have believed so many boys could have been found who would have spoke so ill as most of them did,' said Palmerston), in all other regards Harrow was proving to be a very sound choice. Mr Bromley reported to Palmerston that 'he never saw a boy become a schoolboy so immediately' as Harry had done. 'Indeed,' Palmerston noted, Bromley 'spoke very handsomely of him before him in every respect and says that as he finds him very quick at his book and that he has made good progress, he shall keep him some time unplaced and under his more immediate inspection, in order to place him the better a little while hence and more according to his age and parts.'[45]

Meanwhile, Harry found his learning of modern and ancient languages stood him in good stead. In October 1795 he wrote to his mother explaining proudly that 'I have had an exercise read over, for which by rights, I ought to have had *half a guinea*, but it is the custom among the *big boys*, never to take it. But however at the holydays it will bring me in a prize-book, it was about *Nelson's Victory*, in Latin verse.'[46] In the same month, Bromley wrote to Lord Palmerston with an interim report on Harry's progress. 'I have the satisfaction to say, that he is going on in every respect as well as possible', he said, noting that Harry's progress in Greek and French brought 'the fourth form very distinctly in view'. Harry was, said Bromley, 'to say the truth, just what I think a boy should be'.[47] Accordingly, in February 1796, Harry was finally placed in the fourth form, much to his delight, as this meant that he escaped fagging and 'need not answer when anybody calls Boy!'[48]

If Harry had always seemed a sickly child, Harrow put paid to notions that he was really a physical weakling. A school song celebrating 'Temple's frame of

iron' is said to have paid tribute in latter years to one of the school's more enthusiastic sportsmen, and, if the rumours are to be believed, a plucky behind-the-
school fighter. Harry had been at the school barely a fortnight when he wrote
home enthusing about the fashion, particularly in his house, for crossbows. He
had already acquired one for his brother William to go with the two or three
that it was, apparently, *de rigueur* for any self-respecting Harrow boy to have for
himself at the time: 'some of us have two or three apiece and should have more
but that whalebone costs money, and shot are not to be found like stones, but
however that is a good thing for if they were, all the windows in Harrow would
be broken'. Mr Bromley's threats 'to make a collection of them' did not apparently diminish the rate of schoolroom production.[49] Shooting sports were
evidently popular at the time and by December Harry's ambitions extended to
gunmanship. A school friend by the name of Kingsley was due to visit
Broadlands (and bring his own gun) over Christmas, causing Harry to entreat
his father to allow him to take up shooting during the holiday, for he feared that
if it became known at the school that he was no marksman he would 'be most
terribly laughed at, as it is reckoned almost a disgrace not to shoot, and indeed
there is hardly another boy of my age here, that does not'.[50]

The eyes and cheeks that had previously been aflame with the red eruptions
of St Anthony's fire were now often of a blacker and bluer hue. It was not
perhaps an uncommon piece of intelligence that Harry sent to his mother
when he reported in early 1798 that he and his brother William, since March
also a Harrovian, were 'both very well in health tho' not in beauty'. William had
a swollen lip after a cricketing accident; Harry's 'two blue eyes' had been
'exchanged for two black ones in consequence of a battle'.[51] Certainly when
Augustus Clifford, a Harrow contemporary of Harry's, reflected back on his
schooldays in 1870, it was the late Prime Minister's even temper and plucki-
ness that stuck in his mind. 'I can remember well Temple fighting "behind
school" a great boy called Salisbury, twice his size and he would not give in, but
was brought home with black eyes and a bloody nose, and Mother Bromley
taking care of him.'[52] The story had lost nothing in the telling, and Harry, now
as tall as his father, was unlikely to have been so towered over by a classmate,
but Clifford's memory reveals much about how Harry was remembered both
as a schoolboy and, perhaps more significantly, later, as the third Viscount
Palmerston, the embodiment of noble English manhood.

Between 1795 and 1800 Harry took to Harrow and Harrow took to him. He
was popular with fellow pupils, not least the younger ones who found him the
most lenient of the older boys in his treatment of fags, and he left a favourable
impression on his masters. Mrs Bromley might have worried about Harry's
penchant for bathing in the sea,[53] but he was never a troublesome schoolboy.
Harry participated with enthusiasm in the competitive life of an English public
school. He wrote home for two pairs of cricket stumps and a good bat with
which to take up a fight with Eton 'not with cannon and balls, but with bats

and balls, eighteen against eighteen.[54] Whether or not Harry prospered at the wicket remains unknown, but towards the end of his Harrow career he gave an upbeat assessment of the school team's prowess. The Harrovians had accepted a tie with Westminster School in the summer of 1800 when two Westminster old boys ('both great blackguards') came down to the school on behalf of the Westminster team to scout the opposition. 'These two men saw us play, and told us they thought we should beat Westminster, and very kindly wanted to make a match with us, he [one of the two, an attorney named Barton] was to bring eleven players from town, not the Marylebone club he said, but some others, not very good players; or in other words he wanted us to play all England, which was *excessively kind* of him, but we begged to be excused, and told him we had no time to play a match.'[55] In addition, Harry trod the boards when the school staged classical plays and amused himself out of doors following the rabbit-chasing fortunes of the ferret in which he had a share.[56]

But Harry was becoming a serious young man. In 1798 Francis Hare, whom Palmerston had befriended in Italy during his time there, wrote from Bologna to enquire after his friend. 'I hope you take no part in those vices which are common to a public school, such as I suppose Harrow, as swearing & getting drunk, but I imagine the son of a gentleman so well taught cannot partake in things like these,' he wrote, adding, 'I still persist in my opinion of never marrying & I suppose you to think the same as you must have read as well as myself of the many faults & vices of women.' Harry wrote an equally precocious reply. 'I am perfectly of *your* opinion concerning drinking & swearing, which though fashionable at present, I think extremely ungentlemanlike, as for getting drunk I can find no pleasure in it. . . . I cannot agree with you about marriage though I should be by no means precipitate about my choice.'[57] Harry was far too conscientious a pupil to be overly distracted by drink, women, or even cricket. His letters home recorded his academic achievements with as much enthusiasm as his sporting ones. His Latin compositions continued to be rewarded with prize-books and his reading matter became more varied. In 1799 he had begun George Gregory's *Economy of Nature* which his father had sent to him in October and which he found 'gives one a very good account of things, without entering into too prolix details.'[58] By December he was to be found explaining his studies in science to his mother: 'I have got through the first volume of Gregory, which alone has taken me almost as much time as both the other two will; The chief part of it being about light and vision, optics, catadioptrics, and dioptrics, in which one is obliged to recur to the plates at every half page. My next volume is about metals and water.'[59]

Before he left the school in the summer of 1800 Harry was also initiated into the rite of public declamation from the classics at the school speech days. His first attempt, from Tacitus, in May of that year, met with parental approval, though Harry was quick to acknowledge the importance of his father's tutelage. For the June event, he was to read from Cicero's second oration against

Catiline. It was, judged Harry, 'a good speech, but rather difficult to deliver properly', and he feared that 'our set of speakers will not be better in June than in May', having suspected his father had not been especially impressed by them.[60] Harry was evidently sufficiently adept, however, for his father to press on Drury that he be allowed another turn in July when one of the speakers dropped out and so Harry ended his Harrow days with a reading from 'The Bard' by Thomas Gray.[61]

In 1800, at the age of fifteen, Harry, now a school monitor,[62] was thought to have exhausted what Harrow had to offer. He was developing mature interests in politics: his observations on such matters had evolved from the childish comment on seeing Charles James Fox in 1795 that he 'never saw a man so fat in all my life', to analyses of Napoleonic manoeuvres in the Netherlands four years later.[63] His father decided that the time was ripe for him to move on, to pastures new, this time north of the border. The University of Edinburgh had developed a high reputation among the educated Whig classes by this time and in June 1800 Harry agreed with his father 'that I shall learn much more by entering on a course of study at Edinburgh than I could do here'. He looked forward to studying under 'so respectable a man' as the eminent Dugald Stewart to whom Edinburgh owed much of its academic reputation.[64] Thomas Bromley bade Harry a fond farewell, confident of his former charge's promise: 'I cannot part with Mr Temple,' he told Palmerston, 'without troubling your Lordship with a line to express my sincere & cordial wishes for his future welfare and to hope that I shall frequently hear of his succeeding as well in his studies at Edinburgh, as he has done with us. We trust that William will make himself happy & comfortable without his brother, tho' he must feel the loss of him for some time at least. They certainly are both of them such boys as any instructor would be desirous of having; and of course cannot fail of proving a source of happiness & satisfaction to your Lordship & Lady Palmerston.'[65]

Harry himself held Harrow close to his heart throughout his later life. According to one history of the place: 'No school function of importance was complete without Lord Palmerston's presence. His opinion was sought when a knotty question stood for decision, or a point of monitorial etiquette required adjusting', while as a near-octogenarian Prime Minister, he would ride out from his Piccadilly home to Harrow to preside over a school function, and while there 'break a lance on behalf of his dear Harrow boys constantly in disgrace for the stone-throwing he himself declared that he and his compeers indulged in'.[66]

CHAPTER 2

NORTH AND SOUTH, 1800–1806

To distant orbs a guide amid the night,
To nearer worlds a source of life and light,
Each sun, resplendent on its proper throne,
Gilds other systems and supports its own.
Thus we see Stewart, on his fame reclined,
Enlighten all the Universe of mind;
To some for wonder, some for joy appear,
Admired when distant, and beloved when near.
'Twas he gave laws to fancy, grace to thought,
Taught virtue's laws, and practised what he taught.

Lord John Russell to Dugald Stewart, 1812[1]

GIVEN HIS FATHER'S fondness for travel, and the common expectations of the age that a young man be personally acquainted with Britain's neighbours, it was not surprising that a Grand Tour was considered an appropriate next step for Harry on leaving Harrow. Having evaded the worst excesses of revolutionary France in the 1790s, not even Napoleonic threats in 1800 were enough to crush the suggestion that Harry join his father's friend, Lord Minto, who was at that time in Vienna on a special mission. Minto had reassured the Palmerstons that there was 'no safer or better place for young men', but Harry himself was not encouraged by reports from Minto's children that rather than Viennese society being 'uncommonly good', it was, in fact, 'a bore'.[2] The Palmerstons decided against sending Harry at such a tender age anyway, though as he was not yet ready for Cambridge, to which it was assumed he would follow his father as an undergraduate in due course, some 'intermediate situation between school and an English university' was required.[3] Thus was Harry enrolled as a student at Edinburgh, but far from being simply an intermediate situation, this was to be a key staging post in the development of the future third Viscount. As he would put it himself when summarising his early life for the benefit of his future wife, 'I left Harrow at sixteen, and went for three years to Edinburgh. I lived with Dugald Stewart, and attended the lectures at the University. In those years I laid the foundation of whatever useful knowledge and habits of mind I possess.'[4]

By the turn of the century, Scotland, said Lady Minto, had 'arrived at the true pitch of comfort and happiness', such that social equality and educational opportunity had created a dynamic society, in stark contrast to that found in England. Scots were, she judged, 'very superior to the English, who are too far gone in luxury and dissipation to be agreeable or happy. *Morals* here are certainly very good, and yet the manners are much more free, and one scarcely ever meets with affectation and airs.'[5] Such a society, at the forefront of the European Enlightenment, with its overtones of rationality, progress and improvement, was increasingly attractive to English Whiggery. The Scottish university system was widely acknowledged to have surpassed what was on offer at either Oxford or Cambridge, academically if not yet socially, and the Scottish 'ancients' were increasingly recruiting the sons of the English Whig nobility; it was certainly a more attractive prospect than braving a 'grand tour' of a war-torn continent.[6] Edinburgh University, in particular, had by the turn of the century established itself as a leading institution and Palmerston was not alone in sending his son north of the border for the sort of serious education that was not to be had at the English universities. It was, it was said, difficult 'to conceive a university where industry was more general, where reading was more fashionable, where indolence and ignorance were more disreputable', and where 'every mind was in a state of fermentation.'[7] One of those fermenting minds was that of Dugald Stewart, Professor of Moral Philosophy since 1785.

Stewart had been born in 1753 into a high-minded family: his father, Matthew, was Professor of Mathematics at the University and his mother, Marjory, was the daughter of Archibald Stewart, a prominent Edinburgh lawyer. Dugald had studied at Edinburgh University himself where he had been heavily influenced by the teachings of Adam Ferguson on moral philosophy. At Ferguson's suggestion, Stewart followed Edinburgh with a period at Glasgow University where he profited from attending the classes of 'common-sense' philosopher Thomas Reid, who would become in turn another profound intellectual influence on the young Dugald. In 1772, however, Stewart returned to Edinburgh where, at the age of only nineteen, he replaced his father as Lecturer in Mathematics, a startling though not unprecedented rise through the academic ranks. Officially Matthew Stewart continued to hold the chair and receive the modest stipend that went with it (in lieu, effectively, of a pension) while his son cut his teeth teaching undergraduates and lived off their fees. By the later 1770s, Stewart was beginning to display his wide academic talents having also begun, in 1778, to stand in for his erstwhile tutor, Ferguson, in the teaching of moral philosophy. When Ferguson formally resigned his chair in 1785, Stewart became, at the age of only twenty-two, Professor of Moral Philosophy. His reputation as an engaging teacher grew and ensured that a steady stream of students would draw their inspiration from his lectures. He courted some controversy, however, by his perceived enthusiasm for the French Revolution (in fact he was alarmed by the violent turn taken by events there) and his published admiration for French deputy and philosopher Condorcet. He was not really so radical as his detractors suggested; attention to his Moderatism and respect for order and authority more accurately characterise his outlook.[8]

Palmerston had made enquiries into the curriculum at Edinburgh and found its provisions for tuition 'in various branches of science', including mathematics, algebra, natural philosophy, chemistry, botany, history and moral philosophy, satisfactory. The classics were, regrettably, neglected, but separate arrangements could always be made to consolidate Harry's studies in that area. Dugald Stewart was the only professor in the University known to take lodgers (although in fact others, such as John Playfair with whom Lord John Russell stayed, did the same) and for the considerable sum of £400 per annum, Palmerston hoped to place Harry there. It was a more expensive arrangement than might have been found elsewhere, Glasgow University rates being somewhere in the order of £80–£120 per annum,[9] and even in Edinburgh good lodgings for a student and his tutor were to be had for around a guinea and a half a week, but Stewart's rates were also, proportionately, less than they had been in the early 1780s when he had first taken students into his home.[10] The money was well spent, however, given that, as Palmerston noted, Stewart 'takes considerable pains with the young men under his care if they are disposed to be industrious and in that case they may by his assistance get much forwarder and draw much more advantage from the lectures of the other professors than they could otherwise do'. Palmerston was also pleased to find that Stewart arranged evening debates for recreational purposes and so even though the fees to Stewart would need to be augmented by further stipends to such other professors as were chosen to instruct Harry, it was deemed a sound investment.[11]

'My son, who was fifteen years of age last October, has risen nearly to the top of Harrow School and has given me uniform satisfaction with regard to his disposition, his capacity and his acquirements,' Palmerston had written to Stewart in the summer of 1800. 'He is now coming to that critical and important period when a young man's mind is most open to receive such impressions as may operate powerfully on his character and his happiness during the remainder of his life.' He looked, therefore, to secure for Harry 'such a course of studies as may give full exercise to his talents and enlarge his understanding', while at the same time making sure that he would have the opportunity to 'converse as much as possible with persons to whose opinions he must look up with deference, and in whose society his manners would be improved and his morals secured'. Consequently, Harry needed to rise above 'the common routine of classical instruction' of an English public school and broaden his education at a more rounded institution. Palmerston reassured the professor, who was known to be reluctant to take on boys older than sixteen, whom he feared were difficult to direct,[12] that his son was as yet an amenable and unaffected boy. 'You will find him perfectly tractable and disposed to conform himself with cheerfulness to all such regulations as you shall think fit to prescribe to him; and though he is forward enough in all good points, he is still a boy, and has not assumed the airs and manners of a premature man.'[13] Stewart, who had already heard good things about Harry from other sources, declared himself 'highly honoured' to accept Harry as a student and lodger in his own home. The Edinburgh term beginning in November, it was agreed that the Stewarts would receive Harry at the beginning of October.[14]

The Palmerstons, in company with their friend Count Rumford, left for Scotland in mid-September 1800, making a small northern tour of the journey encompassing visits to Burghley, Clumber, Worksop, Glasgow, the ironworks at Carron, Stirling, and Lochs Long and Lomond *en route*.[15] A month after leaving southern England, the party arrived at its destination. 'The first view of Edinburgh is very fine,' noted Harry in his journal, 'we saw Arthurs Seat[,] Salisbury Hills and the Castle with the firth on the right. The entrance of Edinburgh is not prepossessing but the New Town is very fine.' The Palmerstons installed themselves at Drumbrecks Hotel in St Andrew Square where they would stay for a month to see Harry safely launched on his new career.[16]

The Palmerstons' first week in Edinburgh was spent largely in sightseeing. Harry took a keen interest in visits to Holyrood House where he was enthralled by accounts of the murder of David Riccio in 1566 and was shown 'some marks on the floor said to be his blood'. His attempts to master the history of the 'hundred and eleven kings of Scotland' were hampered by the portraits in the palace which 'seem all done by the same artist, who was but a bungling blockhead, as he has made half of them so alike that one can hardly tell one from the other'. Nevertheless, Edinburgh quickly grew on Harry. He told his sister Elizabeth, a week after arriving, that the town 'is really *unique*' and enthused about the architecture of the recently built and, he thought, surprisingly very clean New Town, which he compared favourably to Bath, although the Old Town he found a little less charming and thought some of the houses 'to be sure look beastly enough'. He was also struck by the 'violent winds' which blew through the town, and although they made carriage travel potentially dangerous, Harry thought that they did at least 'keep the town healthy', ventilating the Old Town's narrow and dirty streets. Meanwhile Harry had started to get to know Dugald Stewart himself who, although 'he does not prepossess one much in his favour at first sight . . . improves amazingly, on acquaintance'. Stewart's wife, Helen, Harry judged 'a very pleasant agreeable woman' and on the whole the Stewarts to be 'excessively good natured'. He was pleased, too, with the arrangements at the Stewarts' home, Lothian House, a 'perfectly quiet and pleasant' place and in which his own room afforded a fine view of Arthur's Seat. One of Stewart's other lodgers, Lord Ashburton, had still not returned when Harry arrived, and he was warned that Ashburton was 'an odd fish'. But Harry took consolation from the presence of Stewart's twenty-year-old nephew, Peter, and sixteen-year-old son, Matthew, who also lived at Lothian House and who, Harry expected, would 'be a great comfort to me, when his *Lordship* is seized with one of his odd humours'.[17]

A month after arriving in Edinburgh Harry's parents bid him adieu. His mother felt 'wretched' at leaving behind 'so amiable a being' as her 'dear Harry' but it was no doubt some comfort that Harry was now safely lodged with the Stewarts, as his father observed, 'much to our satisfaction'.[18] Harry soon found himself at home. 'I like Mr and Mrs Stewart amazingly, it is impossible for any body to be kinder than they both are,' he told his father in late November. Even the young Lord Ashburton was said to improve upon acquaintance, although Harry found his eccentricities 'surprising'. Ashburton's 'dread of squinting' had already caused him to spend a day holed up at home in order to miss Stewart's lecture on the anatomy of the eye for fear that this would bring the condition on.[19] It was at about this time that Maria Edgeworth first published her *Moral Tales* in which the story of 'Forester' presented 'the picture of an eccentric character – a young man who scorns the common forms and dependencies of civilized society; and who, full of visionary schemes of benevolence and happiness, might, by improper management, or unlucky circumstances, have become a fanatic and a criminal'.[20] Harry reported to his father that it was Ashburton 'exactly, only he is much more eccentric, and differs in many respects from *Ash.* especially in his contempt for gentlemen, as Ashburton has very high notions of rank, and old families, but I am persuaded that he furnished a great many hints for it'.[21] Nonetheless, Harry and 'Ash' appear to have got on well, and Harry took a polite interest in Ashburton's collection of animals kept in the Stewarts' attic and accompanied Ashburton in his regular ascents of Arthur's Seat.[22]

Stewart's house was a lively and stimulating place. According to Stewart's son, Matthew, writing some years later:

> Justly conceiving that the formation of manners, and of taste in conversation, constituted a no less important part in the education of men destined to mix so largely in the world, than their graver pursuits, he [Stewart] rendered his house at this time the resort of all who were the most distinguished for genius, acquirements, or elegance in Edinburgh, and of all the foreigners who were led to visit the capital of Scotland.[23]

At the end of his first full week with the Stewarts, Harry had already dined with Mungo Park, the celebrated African explorer, who had recently published his account of *Travels in the Interior Districts of Africa*, detailing life in west Africa and around the Niger. Harry was 'very much pleased with him, his manners are very pleasant and agreeable, without the least affectation. "His airs sat round him easy, genteel but unaffected", as the ballad says. His countenance is very good natured, but one should not think by his appearance that he was at all calculated to undergo the hardships he suffered.'[24] These regular weekly dinners and meetings, 'which happily blended the aristocracies of rank and letters, bringing together the peer and the unfriended scholar', did much to place Stewart's household at the very centre of Edinburgh society.[25] A few months later, Harry was disappointed not to have seen a black woman visiting Edinburgh from Sierra Leone. The woman, as Harry informed his mother, was said to be

> remarkably clever and well-informed and she is at present come over with some Negro children from Sierra Leone, which they have brought to England to be educated with a view of civilizing the natives. She came to see them safely disposed of, and is going to return immediately. She has a great facility of expressing herself, and is very eloquent. She also preaches very well. Mr Stewart, Sir James Hall and some more, breakfasted with her one morning, and were very well satisfied with her talents. Mr Stewart was the more interested about her, as he is very desirous of establishing a favourite doctrine of his, that the Negroes and blacks, are not deficient in their intellectual powers naturally, and that the difference between them and the Europeeaner [sic] is owing chiefly to education.[26]

That European education, for Harry, proceeded apace under Stewart's guidance. Classes started on 11 November and Harry's time was occupied principally in attending lectures on algebra given by John Playfair, on moral philosophy by Stewart and by Alexander Fraser Tytler on history which filled the hours respectively between 9 and 10, 12 and 1 and 2 and 3 each day, although Harry soon found the arrangement 'rather awkward as no two lectures come together'. There was no time to return to Lothian House between lectures to any useful effect and recurrent headaches militated against using the spare hour before Tytler's history lecture for horse-riding. Stewart suggested a drawing class with John Walker, on Tuesdays and Thursdays, an idea which Harry adopted, if, as it turned out, with more enthusiasm than ability. He found Playfair's algebra class 'goes on too slow', and even though his lack of knowledge of arithmetic was 'rather inconvenient', still 'as algebra is another sort of arithmetic learning that teaches me the other two', but he liked Stewart's and Tytler's classes 'very much'. Later in the year a series of 'excessively entertaining' botanical lectures with Dr Rutherford was added to the timetable.[27] To keep up his study of the classics, Harry attended classes three times a week with a Mr Williamson and read with Stewart at home. He continued to make good progress in Latin and Greek, although he did not feel especially challenged by the reading, tackling in his first term Sallust's *War with Catiline*, part of which, he noted, he had 'read for my own amusement at

Harrow, indeed it is as easy as an English book', in order to 'qualify' him to take on Cicero's *Orations against Catiline* later in the year, and Xenophon's *Anabasis*, 'which is I believe the easiest Greek book there is', although he subsequently admitted that although it was 'very easy I am by no means thoroughly master of it, for I often meet with some long verb the exact meaning of which I do not know though by the sense I can generally give a good guess at it, but after I have read a little of it I suppose I shall take a harder one'. Meanwhile, with Stewart he worked through the first and second books of Euclid.[28] Modern languages continued to be one of Harry's strengths. For pleasure he read the 'very clever though in some things excessively extravagant' Bernadin de Saint-Pierre's *Etudes de la Nature* which he found excellent on botany but in its discussion of the theory of tides 'rather wild and absurd'.[29] He also took up German, finding it, he claimed, even easier than French. He had found a master, most likely the Benedictine James Robertson,[30] whom he liked,[31] and by March 1801 reported confidently to his mother that he was 'going on famously' with the language which was, he said, 'incomparably easier than I expected; I am sure French is a hundred times harder and I begin to have my doubts whether it is not to the full as easy as Italian. I am reading a novel Ashburton lent me, called the *Todtenritter*, or Knights of Death. I already begin to understand a good deal of it as I read it'.[32] Harry's application to his work was noticed favourably by Stewart. He judged Harry 'uncommonly' talented and an 'assiduous' student, all combined with an evenness of temper that made him one of the most 'faultless' and 'amiable' characters of his age.[33]

Stewart staged periodic debates in the evenings at his home for the entertainment and edification of his lodgers. In an early such debate, Ashburton, 'as senior member', presented an essay on 'the inutility of classical learning' in which he became 'carried away by his enthusiasm against Latin and Greek, he preferred German to the latter, Pope to Milton, whose Paradise Lost he abused as dull and immoral, denied the revival of learning was in the least owing to the Classics, and wished that Latin and Greek as they were *dead* were also *buried*, for having translations of all the Classics surely the originals were of no use'. Harry judged that in countering Ashburton he and Matthew had enjoyed the upper hand in a debate raging from eight until almost half past nine in the evening. Inspired by the experience Harry looked forward to a further battle the following week over a paper from Matthew, and to his own debut a week after that in which he was to present a defence of Mary Queen of Scots, 'which as both Ashburton and Matthew are outrageous against will produce a good sharp debate'.[34] In a book of 'Essays on various subjects Historical and Political', Harry copied some of the papers he delivered at this time which 'were written to set off to the best advantage a given argument or a particular side of a debateable question', and which were 'therefore to be considered as exercises in composition and not as records of decided opinion'. While at Edinburgh, he is known to have spoken on 'A vindication of Mary Queen of Scotland' in

December 1800, 'On the comparative advantages and happiness of a savage and civilized life' and 'On public and private education' the following January, and in March 1801 he presented papers 'On Gowry's conspiracy' and 'On the advantages derived from the invention of printing'.[35] The debates were evidently highly charged. Recounting another, a 'tough debate' on the union between England and Scotland, Harry had argued strongly against Ashburton's proposition that the Scots had been 'completely humbugged', insisting instead that 'Scotland was very much benefited by it', rejecting notions of representative imbalances at Westminster in favour of a cold assessment of 'the advantages their trade obtained'. The following week, Matthew was to take as his subject 'that the intellectual powers of women are naturally equal to those of men' and only education rendered them unequal; Ashburton was expected to oppose the notion vigorously.[36] Harry had soon found that Ashburton was 'amazingly fond of a good tough argument' and would indulge him during their hill-walking. 'We generally have some dispute as we go up Arthur's Seat upon some subject or another,' Harry reported in a letter to his mother. 'He is a staunch Jacobite, and I am on the other side, so that that has frequently furnished us with a good conversation. Though he maintains a great many curious and ridiculous opinions, yet I must do him the justice to say that he has a most sovereign contempt and hatred of all Republicans and Jacobins. He does not even spare the Republics of Greece, which some admire so much.'[37]

There was a lighter side to Edinburgh academic life at this time too. In the autumn of 1800 it was all the rage among the professors of the University to get high on nitrous oxide.[38] The results were entertaining, as Mrs Stewart recounted to Harry after one such evening, and as Harry communicated to his mother:

Mr Stewart Lord Webbe Seymour and Mr Sidney Smith went to Doctor Cannaby's to breathe the nitrous oxide, or exhilaratory gas. Mr Stewart sat still in his chair, and only felt perfectly happy but without any disposition to gesticulate, but a dimness in his sight. Mrs Stewart and Mr Playfair were there for spectators. Lord Webbe started up with his eyes fixed, and danced and capered about the room like a madman, crying out that he was in heaven, in about five or six minutes the effects went off and he said he never was so happy (except when he had breathed this gas, for he had taken it several times before). Mr Sidney Smith jumped up and dancing up to Mr Playfair, collared him, and said 'why do not you dance *old square roots*, come *old Problem*, dance thus'. . . . Mr Stewart said that he felt no depression of spirits after wards but on the contrary he was rather in higher spirits than usual, for the rest of the day. As Mr Playfair is writing a book on something or other, he said, he should decline making the experiment till he had finished it.[39]

Harry himself, meanwhile, displayed outwardly a serious demeanour. He was 'charming', thought Lady Minto, and without 'fault or failing', except for his 'want of the spirits belonging to his age'. Yet this belied his more athletic side. On one occasion, at a party in the Stewarts' drawing room, to relieve the ennui of the event, Harry had vaulted over the Gothic couch, spraining his ankle in the process.[40] On another occasion, it is said, Lord Buchan remembered having been taken to Lothian House, where Harry had 'beat[en] them all at jumping on the lawn after dinner'. High jump may or may not have been his forte, then, but Harry was certainly disappointed to find that his Harrovian cricketing exploits were not to be repeated north of the border, where the game was unknown and he was obliged to take up golf, a pursuit, he found, which consisted of striking a ball with a 'kind of bat' into a certain number of holes successively. It was 'a poor game compared to cricket', he thought, 'but better than nothing'.[41] He was, at least, able to divert himself with other types of entertainment, taking up Scottish dancing during his first year in Edinburgh, and he continued to be a keen player of chess. He found the newly opened Edinburgh Playhouse offered a promising theatrical programme, but the quality of the performances left him disappointed: *Macbeth*, for example, he had seen 'murdered in every sense'.[42]

During his first year at Edinburgh, Harry discovered that he was, as he put it, 'a Paddy'. Invited to celebrate St Patrick's Day by a neighbour, Harry had displayed his ignorance of his Irishness by failing to wear a shamrock for the occasion. He did not hide his prejudice against the Irish when he recounted the story to his father. 'An Irishman here is a different animal from what he is in England for, as they say of the Scotch that they let no fools go beyond Berwick Bridge, it might with more propriety be said of the Irish that they let none but blackguards come over here. They are to be sure the vilest set that can be conceived, if any row or disturbance is made in the town every body naturally says, O I suppose it was some *Irish Students*, which is a synonymous word for blackguards.'[43] His father agreed that such events were 'very disagreeable', but encouraged Harry to familiarise himself a little with Ireland by reading a copy of *Castle Rackrent* in which Maria Edgeworth had, he suggested, produced 'an excellent picture of the way of life and manners of the Irish country gentleman', which, although he hoped they were dying out, continued to be a feature of society there.[44]

Harry and his father remained close and as well as personal letters increasingly began to exchange political correspondence, notably concerning foreign policy and the course of events in the wars with France.[45] Palmerston derived the 'greatest satisfaction' from his son's 'improvement' at Edinburgh and wrote in April 1801 to encourage him 'to persevere in the good course you are pursuing and to use every effort to maintain thro your life the good character with which you have begun it and the esteem and approbation of the world and of your own mind which are the sure consequences and reward of good conduct'.[46] Harry apparently impressed all around him in these years. A family friend, the antiquarian Sir Henry Englefield, wrote to Lady Palmerston in January 1802 reporting that his nephew, Francis Cholmeley, who knew Harry, had found in him 'proof that it is possible to unite the manners of a perfect gentleman, with the utmost attention to science', while Minto, whose own son Gilbert Elliot had by now joined Harry at the Stewarts' house, wrote that Harry was 'as charming and as perfect as he ought to be', a judgement, he noted, that was universally shared of a young man in whom it was thought, echoing his wife's earlier observation, that it was 'impossible to find any fault'. 'Diligence, capacity, total freedom from vice of every sort, gentle and kind disposition, cheerfulness, pleasantness, and perfect sweetness, are in the catalogue of properties by which we may advertise him if he should be lost', he concluded.[47] In January 1802, Palmerston wrote to his son: 'as to what remains before you, your love of knowledge, a just disdain for being insignificant, and an honest pride not to disappoint the general good opinion and expectation of the world will I trust induce you never to relax in your efforts to secure those attainments of which you will feel the advantage to the latest period of your life'.[48]

Only a couple of months later, Palmerston would be dead. The blow to Harry was a severe one, and the manner of its delivery only added to the shock. Palmerston's health declined rapidly during the spring of 1802. In mid-March he was struck down with 'a severe cold' and by the end of the month was increasingly ill, suffering from what was described at the time as 'ossification of the throat'. Though he remained in obstinate good spirits, joking with friends and reading from morning till night, it was clear that he would not survive long and on 14 April it was decided that Harry should be sent for from Edinburgh. Palmerston died, however, on the 16th, before Harry could reach Hanover Square, the Palmerstons' London home. Lady Palmerston asked Lord Minto, as a long-standing close friend of the family, to meet Harry and break the news to him before he arrived in town.[49] Fifty-seven years later, Harry was still haunted by the memory of that encounter and finding himself in Barnet, for the first time since Minto had journeyed there to meet him, he was reminded of the episode. Harry had travelled through the night from Edinburgh with his friend Gilbert Elliot and the two weary students had arrived in Barnet at breakfast time. Minto's servant, Hunter, had been instructed to show Harry straight to Minto's rooms, where Minto intended to break the news. Hunter, however, not recognising either Harry or Gilbert by sight, mistakenly took Minto's own son upstairs, introducing him to Minto as 'Mr Temple'. Returning downstairs, Hunter set about preparing the breakfast table and, turning to the young man he took to be Elliot, as Harry later remembered, 'barbarously and coolly told me "Lord Palmerston is no more" '. The news hit Harry, who knew of his father's illness but had no notion of its severity, 'like a thunderbolt'.[50] Minto was 'provoked' at the episode, but as he told Lady Palmerston, there would have been no easy way to tell Harry the news.[51]

To Lady Palmerston the bereavement was no less cruel and she retreated to Lavender House, near Henley-on-Thames, the home of her sister and brother-in-law, Sarah and William Culverden.[52] Her thoughts soon turned, however difficult it was to face, to Harry, now third Viscount Palmerston. Before his death the second viscount had made provision for his son's future by turning to friends to act as his guardian. Minto, with whom Harry was 'a real and great favourite',[53] would stand as a constant and close source of support and counsel while two of Palmerston's other friends, Lords Chichester and Malmesbury, were appointed officially as guardians to Harry,[54] and it was to the latter that Lady Palmerston addressed herself once she had begun to come to terms with her own grief. She explained that she wished Harry to return to Edinburgh with Minto and in due course, as she knew her husband would have wished, to resume his studies with Stewart at the University. She then sketched out the next few years of Harry's life. Once his time at Edinburgh was over, he was to be 'entered at Cambridge', where he should be 'placed under the care of the most eminent man as tutor'. With an eye to the changing economic as much as to the physical landscape of the country, his mother also directed that Harry should undertake a tour of England 'with some intelligent clever man' who would, while improving Harry's knowledge, 'open his mind to the advantages his country possesses and give him an insight into the manufactory and various excellence of England'. Ireland was also to be made the object of exploration before Harry spent two years with 'some amiable friend', such as Malmesbury's own son, James Harris, or Minto's son Gilbert, on a European tour, which would, she hoped, serve to broaden her son's horizons. She hoped that he would learn to 'see with the eyes of a traveller who wishes to improve by viewing other nations and other countries and not living with his own countrymen, despising those who are the object for which he travels'. Then would Harry be well placed to become his father's inheritor, through a distinguished parliamentary career.[55]

Palmerston, as Harry now was, compliantly returned to Scotland, but the Mintos found him disconcertingly subdued for some time afterwards. As the summer approached, Minto opined that Harry remained 'entirely silent' and 'dejected'. He had 'too little spring for his age'; Minto wrote to his wife, 'but his heart and disposition, and indeed capacity are good'.[56] The latter half of the young Palmerston's academic year 1801–2 was therefore severely disrupted but in the autumn of 1802 he was back at Lothian House and, during what was to be his final year at Edinburgh, threw himself back into his studies, much to the satisfaction of Lord Malmesbury. He filled his weekly timetable with a mixture of forty hours' worth of academic and leisure activities. A full seven hours were devoted to drawing lessons with Alexander Nasmyth, a more agreeable art tutor than Harry's first instructor, Walker, who had turned out to be, apparently, 'a bad master and a rogue'.[57] Four of these hours spent drawing, however, were the occupation of a Saturday afternoon. He took lessons in Scottish dancing three times a week and fenced and rode a further four. Meanwhile, his academic studies now included bookkeeping with Paton, five hours of fluxions under Playfair, supplemented by two further hours of mathematics with Jardine, six hours of chemistry with Hope, five of natural philosophy with Robison and two hours' reading Latin and Greek with Christison. The most important, however, were the three hours each week he spent listening to Stewart's lectures on political economy.[58] Malmesbury particularly welcomed Palmerston's taking Stewart's course on political economy which 'is a very important and interesting subject' and which, Malmesbury told his charge, he was confident would be taught 'on its right principles and in the way which can the best tend to qualify you to act as becomes you in the rank you hold in life and in the part you will probably be called upon to act'.[59]

Thomas Chalmers, who attended Stewart's lectures in 1801, professed disappointment in them. 'I never heard a single discussion of Stewart's which made up one masterly and comprehensive whole,' he complained. 'His lectures seem to me to be made up of detached hints and incomplete outlines, and he almost uniformly avoids every subject which involves any difficult discussion.'[60] While there was agreement among many students that Stewart's lectures lacked 'a stronger infusion of dry matter', this was not always something to denigrate. Walter Scott, who had studied under Stewart in the late 1780s, observed that 'Stewart was most impressive and eloquent',[61] and while later commentators would agree that Stewart's philosophy was cautiously expressed and paled when compared to the works of, for example, Locke, Leibniz, Kant, Adam Smith or Ferguson, nonetheless, he should not be thought 'devoid of originality, independence, or profundity'.[62]

Dugald Stewart was first and foremost an educationalist, however; indeed, it has been said that 'his disciples were among his best works'.[63] In turning 'common sense' philosophy into a 'pedagogically viable system', principally through his most important works, *Elements of the Philosophy of the Human Mind* (1792) and *Outlines of Moral Philosophy* (1793), he became 'the most influential philosophy teacher in the West outside Germany'.[64] Thus, although he has not been remembered as one of the Enlightenment's most innovative thinkers, he stands as one of its towering luminaries.[65] Stewart was a rigorously practical philosopher, less interested in abstract theorising than in the functional application of ideas.[66] Yet if Stewart's philosophical theory was in some respects unfinished, it was not insubstantial. He consolidated the practice of treating political economy as a reputable academic subject in its own right, teaching it as separate from moral philosophy, although in devoting so much time to its study Stewart has been seen as a innovator,[67] and in this way did much to fashion important tenets of the Victorian Whig mindset, not least as an inspiration to those who went on to write the *Edinburgh Review*.[68]

In 1800–1, just as Harry was embarking upon his Edinburgh career, Stewart delivered his first series of lectures on political economy, having initially given them as a private undertaking for select students and local worthies, but in a very short time establishing the course as a popular and important feature of the Edinburgh curriculum. These lectures, as Henry Cockburn remembered, 'made a great sensation'. Some hoped that in lecturing on systems of government, Stewart, with his known sympathies for the French Revolution, might be caught in 'dangerous propositions', but, in fact, these lectures represent arguably Stewart's most enduring legacy, leaving his students, as well as assorted listeners from outwith the academy, with a 'permanent taste' for this 'new' philosophy.[69]

If Edinburgh did have a marked impact on Harry's intellectual development, then it was primarily in his exposure to Stewart's analyses of the 'science of the legislator'. These disquisitions on the function of government and society were to frame Harry's subsequent conception of the role, duties and purpose of governors and governed, and to lay the foundations of his political conscience. The subsequent rhetorical overlap between Stewart's teaching and Harry's political speeches and essays highlights the importance of what was being taught at Edinburgh in 1800–3 to the development of the third Viscount Palmerston's world view.

Dugald Stewart did much to fashion the 'system of the north' which distinguished the Scottish intelligentsia from that south of the border, yet he was himself building on the earlier work of those such as Thomas Reid and Adam Smith by whom he had been influenced. Within this system, politics formed a central element in the study of moral philosophy. If 'understanding' and 'will' framed the examination of man's intellectual and moral powers, they were necessarily complemented by an investigation of duties, or of the political responsibilities, by which happiness could best be promoted and/or guaranteed. Thus, metaphysical and ethical considerations were to be studied in the context of the political communities within which they operated in practice. As Stewart explained, only by examining the principles of human nature invoked by political community was it possible to form 'a just idea of our situation in the world, and of the most important duties we owe our fellow creatures'.[70]

Stewart first began to work out his views on politics in his *Elements of the Philosophy of the Human Mind* (1792). His discussion therein of the 'use and abuse of general principles in politics' served to establish the parameters within which his political philosophy and teachings would evolve. Stewart evinced a belief in an irresistible progress towards modernity. Even allowing for the vested self-interest of governing elites, Stewart professed an unequivocal faith in an almost divine advance towards improvement.[71] 'In every society ... which, in consequence of the general spirit of its government, enjoys the blessings of tranquillity and liberty, a great part of the political order which we are apt to ascribe to legislative sagacity, is the natural result of the selfish pursuits of individuals; nay, in every such society ... the natural tendency to improvement is so strong, as to overcome many powerful obstacles which the imperfection of human institutions opposes to its progress.'[72] Stewart was interested, therefore, less in specific or precise models of legislative ideals than in the general principles that would defend society against the limitations of mortal government.[73] Indeed, imperfect systems of government that were at least known were preferable to unknown models or theoretical ideals. Thus, while 'Wherever a government has existed for ages, and men have enjoyed tranquillity under it, it is a proof that its principles are not essentially at variance with each other', even 'in the most imperfect governments of modern Europe, we have an experimental proof that they secure, to a very great degree, the principal objects of the social union. Why hazard these certain advantages for the uncertain effects of changes, suggested by mere theory, and not rest satisfied with a measure of political happiness, which appears, from the history of the world, to be greater than has commonly fallen to the lot of nations?'[74]

Crucially, however, for the principles of government not to be at variance with each other, it was necessary to accord appropriate weight to the views and interests of the governed as well as the governors. The 'stability and the influence of established authority must depend on the coincidence between its measures and the tide of public opinion', insisted Stewart, and crises in government and society derived largely from a 'bigoted attachment to antiquated forms, and to principles borrowed from less enlightened ages'. In an age that had recently witnessed bloody revolution, which until it turned violent in France, he had observed first hand with approval,[75] Stewart was convinced that it was 'this reverence for abuses which have been sanctioned by time, accompanied with an inattention to the progress of public opinion, which has, in most instances, blinded the rulers of mankind, till government has lost all its efficiency, and till the rage of innovation has become too general and too violent to be satisfied with changes, which, if proposed at an earlier period, would have united in the support of established institutions, every friend to order and to the prosperity of his country'.[76] 'The general conclusion to which these observations lead,' Stewart judged, 'is sufficiently obvious; that the perfection of political wisdom does not consist in an indiscriminate zeal against reformers, but in a gradual and prudent accommodation of established institutions to the varying opinions, manners, and circumstances of mankind.'[77]

The watchwords of Stewart's teachings were prudence and gradualness. Though public opinion was now to be counted as a vital element in the body politic, this was to be no unmediated role. Herein, then, lay one of the key elements of Stewart's philosophy: the rise of an enlightened opinion, which was dependent on 'rapid communication' in which 'the universal diffusion of knowledge by means of the press, renders the situation of political societies essentially different from what it ever was formerly, and secure infallibly,

against every accident, the progress of human reason'. This press had 'emancipated human reason from the tyranny of ancient prejudices' and demagogic
influences were held in abeyance: 'now when the effusions of the orator are, by
means of the press, subjected to the immediate tribunal of an inquisitive age,
the eloquence of legislative assemblies is forced to borrow its tone from the
spirit of the times; and if it retain its ascendant in human affairs, it can only be
by lending its aid to the prevailing cause, and to the permanent interests of
truth and of freedom'. Harnessing and understanding public opinion would
underpin the stability of government and the relevance of politicians: 'we may
venture to predict, that they are to be the most successful statesmen who,
paying all due regard to past experience, search for the rules of their conduct
chiefly in the peculiar circumstances of their own times, and in an enlightened
anticipation of the future history of mankind'.[78]

The future, then, was not only brighter, but to be seen as unencumbered by
the past. In attending Stewart's lectures in December 1802, Harry dutifully
noted down, as the first principles of political economy, that 'In prosecuting
the study of political economy the histories of the ancient nation will be of
very little use to us, as the systems of politics pursued by Greece and Rome
were so different from those of modern states, as to render them completely
inapplicable to the governments of modern Europe'.[79] Stewart's lectures on
political economy, it is said were subsequently corrected from, among other
sources, Harry's notes, when they were edited in 1855 by Sir William
Hamilton.[80] It is instructive to pay attention to what Harry was taught in this
series of lectures since it helps explain his subsequent emergence as a
Whiggish statesman.

In defining his objectives in studying political economy, Stewart identified
the most important as being 'the solution of that problem which Mr Burke has
pronounced to be one of the finest in legislation: – "*to ascertain what the State
ought to take upon itself to direct by the public wisdom, and what it ought to
leave, with as little interference as possible, to individual discretion.*" ' Thus, its
'general aim is to enlighten those who are destined for the functions of government, and to enlighten public opinion with respect to their conduct; but unless
it be previously ascertained how far the legitimate province of the Statesman
extends, it is impossible to draw the line distinctly between those subjects
which belong properly to the science of legislation, and those of which the
regulation ought to be entrusted to the selfish passions and motives insepa-
rable from human nature'.[81] This role was not to be, as he explained elsewhere,
that of 'mere *spectators* of the progress and decline of society'; instead the state
should engage in what was essentially a patriotic duty to shape legislation to
the demands of enlightened political wisdom.[82]

Stewart insisted on the importance of studying political economy before
forms of government, an inversion of the usual system of the study of politics.
Political economy, he said, determined 'the happiness of the people' and he

described it as but a 'remote tendency that wise forms of Government have to produce wise systems of Political Economy'. It was 'extremely possible that inexpedient laws may, in consequence of ignorance and prejudice, be sanctioned for ages by a Government excellent in its constitution, and just in its administration; while the evils threatened by a Government fundamentally bad, may, to a great degree, be corrected by an enlightened system of internal policy'.[83] The legitimacy of government, therefore, depended explicitly on its ability to underwrite the happiness of the population. This was, he said, 'the only object of legislation which is of *intrinsic* value', and was to be achieved through political liberty. The emphasis, however, was properly on liberty and not power. 'With the advantage of good laws, a people, although not possessed of political power, may yet enjoy a great degree of happiness; and, on the contrary, where laws are unjust and inexpedient, the political power of the people, so far from furnishing any compensation for their misery, is likely to oppose an insurmountable obstacle to improvement, by employing the despotism of numbers in support of principles of which the multitude are incompetent to judge.' The value of popular political privileges, then, was 'determined, not by the degree in which every individual consents, directly or indirectly, to the laws by which he is governed; but by the share of power which it is necessary for the people to possess, in order to place their civil rights beyond danger of violation'.[84]

Indeed, Stewart was adamant that in ascribing to public opinion a role in politics, he was not prescribing democracy as a means of securing liberty and happiness. As he pointed out, 'the most wealthy states are those where the people are the most industrious, humane, and enlightened, and where the liberty they enjoy, by entering as an elementary principle into the very existence of the political order, rests on the most solid and durable basis'.[85] That robust foundation must accommodate but not bow down to the wider populace; 'the most perfect Democracy that can be realized', noted Stewart, 'must admit of certain delegations of power to select councils, or to individual magistrates'.[86] Thus, for example, where a suffrage was granted, this ought to be given in public. Quoting Montesquieu, Stewart observed that ' "The body of the people ... ought to be directed by those of better education, and to be restrained within bounds by a respect for the opinion of their superiors." '[87] If the press had contributed to 'the diffusion of knowledge among the lower orders in every part of the island',[88] this was primarily to secure a check and balance to legislators, not to direct them. 'The people are incapable of making the distinction between reality and the shew of virtue', he lectured his students, 'and those are commonly the loudest in their professions, and the best acquainted with the various arts of popularity, who are at bottom the most deficient in principle'.[89] The past may have had no role in shaping the future in a positive sense, but there were nevertheless lessons to be drawn from history. ' "It was one great fault," says Montesquieu, "in most of the ancient Republics, that the people had a right to influence immediately the public resolutions; – a thing of which they are absolutely incapable. *They ought to have no hand in the government but for the choosing of representatives.*" If this principle of Montesquieu be admitted, that "an indirect share in the legislation, by means of delegates or representatives, is the utmost length of political freedom that is consistent with the ends of government," *some* of the inconveniences now stated as incident to democratical constitutions, may undoubtedly be obviated."[90] Thus, 'the happiness of mankind depends *immediately*, not on the *form of government*, but on the particular system of *law and policy* which that form introduces', and democracy was not to be seen as necessarily superior to any other system of government:

> Under every form of government, (whatever it may be,) provided its general spirit be favourable to liberty, and allows an unrestricted freedom of discussion, these enlightened views of Political Economy will gradually and slowly prevail in proportion to the progress of reason and the diffusion of knowledge. And they will command the general assent of mankind soonest in those countries where a strong executive power and a vigilant police allow men to prosecute calmly and dispassionately those important but difficult studies, which lead to the melioration of the human race.[91]

As the general populace gradually became better informed, so would it become safe to move towards a more democratic system in which hereditary wealth and power were undermined, but in the meantime, a benevolent, paternalistic compact between the educated, governing elite and the uninformed general populace was a necessary precondition of society's improvement.

In England, as Stewart pointed out, such a compact was already secured in the ascendancy of parliamentary government. The House of Commons comprised a blend of men, 'some of whom, from their situation, may be presumed to lean to the regal part of a government, others to the aristocratical; while, on important questions, the majority may be expected to maintain the interests of the community at large'.[92] Concluding his series of lectures, Stewart underlined the importance of a sense of *noblesse oblige* in his students, the legislators of tomorrow: 'As the leading object of these discussions has been to illustrate and enforce the great duties of life, so the duty of *Patriotism*, which, among those we owe our fellow-creatures, certainly holds the most distinguished rank, is that which I was more particularly anxious at this moment to impress on your minds'.[93]

When Stewart published his *Philosophy of the Active and Moral Powers of Man*, shortly before he died in 1828, a copy was sent to Palmerston.[94] Of all the congratulatory letters Stewart received, so his daughter reported, it was that from Palmerston 'that gave most pleasure. It was read repeatedly over & talked of with the greatest delight'.[95] It is no fancy to suggest that the lectures he had attended in 1802–3 had marked the young Palmerston deeply. Following Stewart's death in August 1828, his widow, Helen, wrote to Palmerston to explain how much the former student's approbation and public conduct had meant to his erstwhile teacher: 'when your conduct & your speech came to shew your character more fully than ever there had before been any opportunity,' she wrote, 'what added rapture there was.'[96] Palmerston had made several contributions to debates during February and March on the justice of Catholic claims for an end to discrimination on religious grounds,[97] and in reply to Helen Stewart's letter he wrote that he derived 'great pride & gratification from knowing that the line of public conduct which I pursued this spring met with the full approbation of one whose sanction was to me of so high a value.'[98]

Palmerston rounded off his life in Scotland with a tour of the Highlands. During May and June 1803 he passed a month and a half touring the country, making visits to St Andrews, Dundee, Montrose, Aberdeen, Inverness, Culloden, Elgin, Fort William, Oban and Inverary.[99] By this point, it had already been decided that Palmerston would go up to St John's College, Cambridge, in the autumn of 1803. His guardian, Malmesbury, doubted that this would represent much in the way of an educational opportunity, however: the 'useful and amusing information' which Palmerston had acquired at Edinburgh, he feared, would leave him 'nothing to learn' at Cambridge; at least, he would be able to study nothing with which he would 'not be previously acquainted'. The chief attraction of St John's, it seemed, was that it offered 'a quiet & comfortable residence for a year or two which you may dedicate to reading', which, if it did that, Malmesbury judged, 'it will answer the going there perfectly'.[100] Such modest anticipations were, it seemed, well founded. As Palmerston himself remembered in later life, although he was obliged 'to learn more accurately at Cambridge what one had learned generally at Edinburgh', this cramming of information was not really something that advanced his understanding. 'The knowledge thus acquired of details at Cambridge was worth nothing,' he concluded, 'because it evaporated soon after the examinations were over.'[101] Indeed, it is claimed that he said in later years, and perhaps he only half joked, that in East Anglia he had spent much of his time forgetting what he had learned north of the border.[102] The apparent insularity of the English universities was something on which Malmesbury and Palmerston were agreed. 'It is the leading fault in both our universities,' Malmesbury wrote in response to one of Palmerston's early letters from Cambridge, 'that they concentrate themselves too much on themselves, get too *commonroomish* and do [not] allow their talents & science space to spread & thrive. Not so the Scotch professors, they have more activity of mind, more *growing* power in them, they are young plants, which ever extend & Cambridge scholars are old trees & sometimes even pollards.'[103] Another St John's alumnus of about this period, Edward Law, later Lord Ellenborough, likewise 'used to say that the Fellows of St John's only realised the evil of the Walcheren expedition [a failed attempt in 1809 to broaden the allied front against Napoleon] when some one calculated the amount of its cost in bottles of port wine.'[104]

The curriculum at Cambridge, then, in so far as it offered an academic challenge, represented something of a revision exercise for Palmerston. In a letter to the Stewarts written once he was settled in St John's he described a course of study similar in content to that which he had followed while a lodger at Lothian House. During that first term he was again reading the first and third books of Euclid and Xenophon's *Anabasis* in preparation for examinations at Christmas. To this was added 'between two & three hundred octavo pages on Jewish antiquities, and the evidences of the Christianity the latter part is the most difficult as I must commit the substance of them to memory' but Palmerston's timetable was not a crowded one. Each morning at eight he attended lectures alternately dealing with Euclid and Xenophon, and then studied with his private tutor, Edmund Outram, between ten and eleven. He filled the hours between this class and dinner (at two o'clock) with riding, after which the time until he retired to bed, with the exception of attendance at chapel four times a week, was his own.[105] It was the examinations, however, that distinguished Cambridge from Edinburgh. In Edinburgh Palmerston had been accustomed to attending courses of lectures with no prospect of an examination; at Cambridge he found a system of half-yearly exams. Although, as a nobleman, he was not obliged to sit examinations and would have been quite entitled to graduate an MA of the University purely by virtue of his birth and short residence in college, Palmerston was keen to measure his mental faculties. Though he denigrated the fact-rather-than-theory approach of Cambridge, he was later drawn to concede that the 'habit of mind acquired by preparing for these examinations is highly useful'.[106] Palmerston remained a conscientious student. His mastery of languages and his ease with the classics stood him in good stead and he set himself to remedying his deficiencies in mathematics, notably in algebra, which he had become aware of in Edinburgh with Playfair. In private classes with Dr Outram he 'made *considerable progress*' in arithmetic,[107] yet this continued to be his weakness. At the end of his first year at Cambridge it was a slip in the algebra paper that kept Palmerston in second place in the College's first class list behind a student named Cook. Outram was encouraging, however. 'It is easy to see where you will in all probability be at the next examination,' he wrote to Palmerston when the lists were produced, attributing his absence from the first place to an 'unlucky mistake'. At least Palmerston was being spoken of widely as a first-class scholar, Outram noted with some evident pride.[108] Palmerston maintained his place in the first class throughout his three years at Cambridge, although he never exceeded second place in the list and even getting into the first class required 'some very hard work', as he observed after the summer examinations of 1805.[109]

It is clear that Palmerston was gaining something different at Cambridge from that which he had acquired at Edinburgh. In a letter to his sister Frances in February 1804, for example, Palmerston detailed a day of hunting, dining and socialising with fifteen or sixteen 'illustrious' friends.[110] Life there was 'remarkably pleasant' and he found many old friends in the University.[111] As well as hunting and entertaining, Palmerston also found a career in the University Rangers an opportune and advantageous way to fill his time: 'a little military knowledge is indispensable; it may be your lot to pass many years of your life in *wars & tumults* and as it is becoming to be prepared for every thing, the *drill* makes a very essential part of education,' noted Malmesbury.[112] Palmerston progressed through the ranks of the Rangers rapidly and by November 1803 had 'gone through the intermediate steps from the awkward squad to the front rank of the Grenadiers' and was already a sergeant in a company of approximately 140 men.[113] Within a matter of weeks he had been made permanent captain of the fourth, or light, company of the University Rangers, a 'remarkably fine' and 'efficient' troop of sharpshooters, according to one army colonel who had recently reviewed them.[114]

Cambridge also gave Palmerston an opportunity to exercise his debating skills and he picked up where he had left off from the evening encounters at Stewart's house with Matthew Stewart and Ashburton. In February 1804 he reported to his sister that he had read an essay proving that 'Europe never will relapse into barbarism' to a '*select party of literati*' and that it had produced 'an animated discussion'.[115] He retrieved his Edinburgh essay book and over the next two years added five more essays, now dealing with notably more political than philosophical themes. In addition to his defence of European civilisation, he spoke on 'the policy of opening the East Indian trade' (in October 1804), on 'the policy of transferring the Portuguese government to the Brazils' (May 1805), on 'the political character of Cardinal Henry' (October 1805)[116] and 'Upon the disadvantages arising to Great Britain from the loss of her American colonies' (March 1806).[117]

On the occasion of the British victory at Trafalgar, Palmerston wrote jubilantly to his sister Frances, celebrating with a particular kind of patriotism the honour and heroism of the event. It was a sign of his developing English sensibilities. 'Well I wish you joy of this most splendid victory, undoubtedly the most brilliant achievement in the naval annals of Europe,' he wrote to his sister:

As far as regards ourselves our joy must be much dampened by the loss of Nelson. We shall not easily find a commander so brave so zealous and so active, or who will so thoroughly gain our affections as well as excite our admiration; for *him* we should rather rejoice, it was a glorious termination of an honourable life, 'Telle vie telle mort'. Had he escaped in this action he might probably, before an other opportunity presented itself of so nobly ending his career, have been put hors de combat by blindness, or have sunk unhonourably into the grave a victim to diseases that were silently preying upon a constitution and frame worn and shattered in the service of his country. One cannot help regretting that [Robert] Calder was not

able to take a share in the action, he might perhaps have retrieved his reputation.[118] What a contrast between the English and Austrians on the same
day. The army of the one executing a disgraceful capitulation. The navy of
the other almost annihilating a superior force. It was rather unfortunate
for Buonaparte that he chose on that day to tell the world he wanted *ships*,
colonies and commerce; I was glad to hear the majority of captures were
French. Villeneuve [the French naval commander] considered himself
sure of victory, and his rage was equal to his disappointment.[119]

From Cambridge Palmerston also began to take an ever closer interest in the
day-to-day business of politics. His own sympathies, thanks no doubt to the
influence of Malmesbury, were Pittite, and anti-Addingtonian,[120] and with
friends such as Edward Clive Palmerston made trips to London to listen to
debates in Parliament where he paid particular attention to the quality of the
speeches. In May 1805, for example, he observed that 'Ld Hawkesbury's speech
was the best he ever made, it certainly reads very well and seems to have
had more animation than his proses commonly possess. The Duke of
Cumberlands I think was rather a good one. Ld Grenvilles lasted upwards of
two hour and was very sophistical and very eloquent.'[121]

In contrast to the glamour of London politics, Cambridge by 1805 was
starting to lose its appeal. His close friends, Laurence Sulivan, Lord Percy and
George Shee had left by the summer of that year and in their absence
Palmerston found life at the University becoming more 'melancholy'.[122] With
only Thomas Knox, another old Harrovian, and Clive still at Cambridge in the
autumn of 1805 Palmerston's 'set' had been 'completely knocked up' and he
lamented that student life was such a transitory one: 'I wish people would not
grow so old and so wise as to be obliged to leave college in such a hurry,' he
complained to Frances.[123]

Yet Palmerston's Cambridge career was not to end when he left St John's in
March 1806. As he later explained: 'Dr Outram, my private tutor at
Cambridge, more than once observed to me that, as I had always been in the
first class at college examinations, and had been commended for the general
regularity of my conduct, it would not be amiss to turn my thoughts to
standing for the University whenever a vacancy might happen.'[124] Lady Minto
had once observed that 'A boy of nineteen may be seduced by a fair face, or led
into gaming, or drinking, or racing, but nobody at that age cares about politics
that is worth a farthing. It is, like the love of money, belonging to those who
have exhausted or left behind them the light and cheerful pleasures of life.'[125]
Now a man in his early twenties, Palmerston was not quite ready to leave
behind cheerful pleasures, but his thoughts were, like those of his tutor,
turning towards a more formal involvement in political life.

WAR AND PEACE, 1806–1828

Harry is doing very well – with a clear head and a good understanding. He will never be a great man because he has no great views; but he is painstaking and gentlemanlike to the highest degree, and will always swim where greater talents might sink. Nothing can be more answerable, and I have always regretted that he should have set out in life on the shabby side, which he must now stick to.

Lady Minto to Lord Minto, 1812[1]

THE YEAR 1805 closed amid disturbing portents for Europe. News of the allied victory at Trafalgar in October was tempered by the almost simultaneous surrender of the Austrian army to French forces at Ulm in Bavaria. Napoleon Bonaparte's victory over the armies of Austria and Russia in the 'Battle of the Three Emperors' at Austerlitz (Slavkov) in Moravia at the beginning of December therefore marked a worrying turn of events from the point of view of British influence and the coherence and unity of the allied powers. As Palmerston himself later described it: 'Europe saw with astonishment the ancient and powerful empire of Austria laid in the dust in the course of three months. The battle of Ulm, the consequent surrender of the Austrian army, and the battle of Austerlitz, reduced the Emperor to the abject conditions of the treaty of Pressburg.'[2] At the time Palmerston was shaken by the 'dreadful news from the continent' and predicted that 'Europe will now be placed at Buonaparte's feet, and he will in truth be chief of the western family'. Nelson's victory had offered some limited succour, but while he hoped that Napoleon's ambitions for an invasion of Britain might have been checked, Palmerston recognised also that there was little Britain seemed able to do to overturn the setbacks of recent allied defeats. 'These reverses are unfortunate for Pitt,' he told his sister Frances.

People in general are too apt to consider success as the only criterion of merit, and to infer incapacity from failure; so that this confederacy from which six weeks ago, every body seemed justly to augur the most happy consequences, will doubtless by many be called one of Pitt's capital blunders. However if we have but a strong administration, Buonaparte will find the high road to London even more *detestable* than that to Vienna, and his brother Fred [Frederick William III, King of Prussia] to whom he said he would teach better manners at Berlin, more docile than brother George [III, King of Great Britain and Ireland].[3]

Like his father before him, Palmerston looked to Pittite resoluteness as the best defence against French aggrandisement. It was a setback, then, when William Pitt, aged only forty-six, died in January 1806. It was said that he had never fully recovered from the shock of the 'heavy news' from Ulm and Austerlitz.[4] Yet Pitt's unexpected death also presented an opportunity for Palmerston. As Pitt had, since 1784, sat in Parliament for the University of Cambridge there was to be an election to select his successor. The idea that Palmerston might stand for the University had, of course, already been suggested,[5] and Palmerston's first thought on learning of Pitt's death was to offer himself as a candidate. It was certainly a more attractive prospect than the one that had, apparently, been mooted in October 1805 that he follow in his father's foot-steps and stand for Southampton: the constituency and its constituents were, no doubt, too close for comfort to Palmerston's family home at Broadlands; it was also an expensive, unpredictable and not particularly attractive seat. Cambridge University, by contrast, was not only prestigious but also, once won, a much more agreeable seat. The electors were notably loyal to their members and, often valuing college affiliations as highly as party political ones, were more easily won over by an alumnus.[6] At the time Pitt died, at half-past four in the morning on 23 January, Palmerston had only just returned home from a ball, but later on that same morning he started out from London for Cambridge. He knew that Lord Henry Petty and Lord Althorp would stand and he suspected that Lord Royston might also be tempted to come forward, so Palmerston's expectations of success were limited. He went, he told his sister, 'not with any view to present success so much as by way of future intro-duction in case of the Duke of Grafton's death', which would have elevated the University's other MP, Lord Euston, to the Lords and created a new vacancy for Cambridge. Indeed, Palmerston swore his family to secrecy, insisting that 'it is just possible I may not stand', preferring to assess the field when he got there.[7]

On arriving back at St John's Palmerston was encouraged to discover that no other member of his college had yet presented himself for the contest and, having hastily made arrangements to graduate a Master of Arts by the end of the week in order to be entitled to vote and stand for the University, and having secured the backing of his 'friends at St John's', Palmerston proceeded to solicit support among the University's voters in the Tory interest.[8] John Ward, later the first earl of Dudley, who had been a lodger at the Stewarts' house in Edinburgh shortly before Palmerston arrived there, reported to the Stewarts that he thought Palmerston, standing in the 'Court interest', had 'every chance of beating both Petty and Althorp, unless one gives way and unites his strength to the other'.[9] Palmerston came forward as a moderate designed to appeal to the establishment tastes of the institution. He assured voters that it would be his 'anxious study to promote the interest and honour of the University and to support that constitution which has so long secured the welfare and independence of this country'.[10] Palmerston's friend George Shee sought to promote Palmerston's cause and found some support in Cambridge over the weekend of 25–26 January. Yet, although he had commenced his canvass early, Palmerston had been too slow to declare his hand. Some voters were already promised to the other candidates, while the geographically disparate nature of the University electorate, comprising all 600 or so MAs who had kept their names on the college registers and were willing to travel to Cambridge in order to vote, left Palmerston, who was still focusing primarily on those voters still resident in the town, somewhat behind in the race.[11] 'I have been *canvassing* like Apelles all day,' he punned, but acknowledging his situation urged his sister, who was keen to do everything she could to secure influential support for her brother, to make his candidature 'as public as you can'. Shee had said to Palmerston that even if he were not successful, he would 'bet 1000 to one on you next time', and Palmerston consoled himself with the thought that he had 'some chance if not of success at least of a respectable minority'.[12]

However, while he was supported by a good number of Johnians (though not all) and was expected to take his own college, more especially once two leading Pittite Johnians, Royston and Charles Yorke, had declined to stand,[13] Palmerston found that Pittite sympathies were not enough to underwrite success generally and he immediately urged his friend Laurence Sulivan to pick up any votes he could among the Cambridge MAs at the Inns of Court in London.[14] He had discovered very early on that 'the Pitt party in the University was broken up', and hopes for government preferment now rested with the new 'Ministry of All the Talents', the Whig-based coalition assembled in the aftermath of Pitt's death under the premiership of Lord Grenville, which Cambridge men apparently thought 'would for many years have the disposal of patronage as well as the command of the power of the country'.[15] This was to prove crucial to the course of the election as both of Palmerston's rivals for the seat, Petty and Althorp, were closely connected with the government.

Henry Petty, the future third marquess of Lansdowne (and a future government colleague of the later Palmerston), was the son of the former Prime Minister Shelburne (now the first marquess of Lansdowne). He had preceded Palmerston at Dugald Stewart's home in Edinburgh and had subsequently graduated from that other Cambridge powerhouse, Trinity, in 1801. In 1802 Petty had been returned as MP for Calne in Wiltshire and quickly rose to prominence in Whig circles. Pitt himself had acknowledged Petty's promise by courting him with an offer of ministerial office in 1804, but Petty remained loyal to the Whigs and had long entertained hopes of standing in that interest for the Cambridge University seat, an ambition for which he had the backing of Charles James Fox himself. Petty had already been offered the seals of the Exchequer when he stood for Cambridge, which, as the constitution required newly appointed ministers to stand for re-election to Parliament, justified his resignation of Calne and so Petty came forward as the government candidate for the University of Cambridge.[16]

Lord Althorp was another Trinity man, but was better known to Palmerston than Petty, having been a friend of Harry's at Harrow. Althorp had been returned for Okehampton in 1804 but continued to be more a devotee of field sports than of parliamentarianism. His father, Lord Spencer, however, was a key member of the new Whig ministry and in January 1806 had just been made Home Secretary. By convention, the Home Secretary was entitled to appoint his son a Junior Lord of the Treasury, and Spencer duly promoted Althorp to that office. The government was thus fielding two of its own candidates against each other, but Althorp, who had been assured by Lord Ellenborough, the Lord Chief Justice, that his appointment to the Treasury would be worth a hundred votes at the University, was unwilling to concede to his more ambitious and better placed colleague Petty.[17]

While Petty and Althorp might have been considered front-runners in that they both, variously, offered the prospect of favours, the fact that the Whig government was fielding two candidates threatened to split Whig (and Trinity College) support to the benefit of Palmerston and the Tories. Such a likelihood indeed would explain Palmerston's initial optimism. By 24 January he believed that he had already secured the backing of a number of voters having 'met with only two refusals to day in eight colleges', although he admitted that this support fell short of definite promises and he had studiously avoided setting foot in Trinity, bastion of Whig support, from which 'little is to be hoped'.[18] He wrote enthusiastically to his friend Laurence Sulivan at the end of January:

> Things go on very well, thanks to you, Shee, and the Malmesburys. This morning's accounts from town were excellent; here we advance too, I think. Mansel [Trinity] has promised not to oppose me. Pearce [Jesus], Sumner [King's], Milner [Queen's], Turner [Pembroke] are for me, and, I hope, the masters of Emmanuel and Catherine Hall. I am very glad to hear Lord Spencer declares Althorp shall not yield to Petty. *'Divide et imperia'* is true and applicable. . . .
>
> I am glad to know Petty and Althorp, as, since we run foul of each other perpetually, it would otherwise be awkward. I took my degree yesterday, and got a very short buttering. Outram was taken quite unawares, and did not expect to be called upon until today or tomorrow, as the Vice-Chancellor thought no other business could be done the day the king's answer was read. I heard that Percy was expected this week; I hope he may come, if he intends to be of use to me, of which I have no doubt, if the old boy will let him.

... The election will probably come on this day week. I own I *entertain strong hopes of success*, if my two rivals do not coalesce, and even then do not despair. At any rate, whatever be the event, I shall consider my having stood as one of the most fortunate circumstances of my life, it having procured me such gratifying proofs of the warmth of my friends' attachment to me.[19]

This confidence belied Palmerston's doubts about the real strength of his position. As soon as he had arrived in Cambridge Palmerston had urged Sulivan to canvass London-based voters; within a couple of days he was to be found sending a '*long* list' of the non-resident voters who he now realised would be essential to his success.[20] However, the London voters never rallied to Palmerston's cause and if Sulivan could report on 28 January that he had secured eight or nine supporters in the Inns of Court, he had also to concede that a 'host' were aligned against him.[21] Politically, the tide was against Palmerston in Cambridge too, and his supposed unsoundness on the question of suppression of the slave trade was to prove in large part his undoing. In fact Palmerston was the victim of unfounded supposition and rumour on this subject, yet he failed ever to convince electors that he had been misrepresented. Henry Brougham had written to Zachary Macaulay, the editor of the *Christian Observer*, at the time of the 1806 election describing Palmerston as 'a young man who only left college a month ago and is devoid of all qualifications for the place. I remember him well at Edinburgh, where he was at college for several years, and what I know of his family and himself increases a hundredfold my wish for Petty's success. The family are enemies to Abolition in a degree that scarcely ever was exceeded. I presume that he is so himself. His maxim is that of all the objects of ambition in the world the life of a courtier is the most brilliant. Don't you think that the friends of the cause have the more reason to support Petty the more strenuously?'[22] Brougham's presumption stuck and Palmerston was widely associated with his father's erstwhile, and genuine, scepticism on the question of immediate abolition,[23] even though Palmerston himself had made no public declarations on the question and anyone who bothered to take the time to discuss the matter with him privately found him, if not advanced, at least progressive in his thinking and, if not determined, at least steady in his support of gradual abolition. Isaac Milner, Dean of Carlisle, for example, wrote to Palmerston on the morning of 7 February to explain that Palmerston's 'very candid explanations' on the question of slave trade abolition had persuaded him to support Palmerston's candidature (on this occasion though with no definite promises for future contests), 'in full confidence that that same ingenuousness of mind, which has determined you to think & speak *so far* in favour of the Abolition as you do at present, cannot fail, *on such a subject*, to terminate in your being a warm & active abolitionist'.[24] The same day Milner wrote to William Wilberforce explaining that during an hour's conversation with Palmerston on the subject of the slave trade, he 'could not discover the most latent hostility, or ground for suspecting hostility [to aboli-tion of the trade], and he must be a deceiver, indeed, of a very deep cast, if he deceives at all in this instance'. On this basis Milner had declared for Palmerston. Despite this, as Milner conceded, whatever benefits his late declaration may have brought for his candidate, and reports of an additional thirty-four votes were circulating, they remained, nonetheless, 'in a woful [sic] minority'.[25] As Francis Horner observed, it was widely assumed that Milner 'must have made the Viscount swallow the Abolition', for the belief persisted that the cause was 'supposed to be much against his stomach'. Horner also suspected that Milner was drawn to Palmerston in large part because of fears that Petty 'would emancipate the Catholics'.[26]

There was a certain naïvety in Palmerston's failure to recognise the impor-tance of moral and religious concerns in this election. He accepted uncritically the hint from Lord Headley, who had declined to run against his fellow Trinity candidates, 'that all *his* friends were *mine* also', from which Palmerston inferred that Headley meant the 'Wilberforcians'. He declared that he 'had no qualms about the religious tenets of my voters' and so long as they supported him, Palmerston did not mind whether they were 'Simeonites or Atheists, or, what may happen, both'.[27] Yet only a day after this optimistic assessment he was obliged to concede that in fact the 'Saints and Sinners' were united behind Petty who had also the full backing of Wilberforce. It might have been 'unfor-tunate' but it was perhaps a sign of Palmerston's political inexperience that he also thought it 'unexpected'. Palmerston relied instead on the fears of some of the smaller colleges that 'it would [be] dangerous to the balance of power in the University if both members were returned by Trinity'.[28]

Petty remained the man to beat. He enjoyed the backing of the largest number of declared voters and his Foxite credentials and avowed soundness on the slave trade injured Palmerston's prospects.[29] Palmerston hoped to coun-terbalance Petty's ascendancy by soliciting support among the London-based voters and paid for the horses that would bring them up to Cambridge. He also began to hope that Althorp might choose not to contest the seat and on 29 January had asked Sulivan to canvass the 'Althorpites' for their second votes against Petty.[30] By early February voters were 'dropping in from all quarters', indeed the 'out-voting Johnians' were 'dropping in incessantly', and the town was as 'full as it can hold'. Palmerston believed he had also won the valuable backing of leading figures in the University such as Samuel Blackall of Emmanuel, while the prize catch of Isaac Milner had belatedly come over to his side.[31] Yet the result was a disappointment for Palmerston. In the event he registered less than half as many votes as Petty and came a clear third in the poll, securing only 128 votes to Petty's 331 and Althorp's 145. As he later observed, 'I stood at the poll where a young man circumstanced as I was could alone expect to stand; that is to say, last, and by a large interval the last of the three. It was an honour, however, to have been supported at all, and I was well satisfied with my fight.'[32]

The defeat was a comprehensive one and although Palmerston clung to hopes that Petty's appointment as Chancellor of the Exchequer might, technically, have been judged to have been made after his return for Cambridge, and that the contest would have to be re-run as anyone taking up an office of profit under the crown was obliged to seek re-election (and furthermore, a contest this time without Althorp who would shortly take a Spencer family controlled pocket borough in Northamptonshire), he had been advised by Malmesbury against investing any further hopes in the University in the event of a defeat.[33] Indeed, Malmesbury urged Palmerston to concede graciously. 'You have a very great consolation in the number & description of your friends who gave you their votes, & considering against *whom* you stood, and, that it is your first *flush* in life, it does you infinite honour & credit, while it holds out to you a very reasonable prospect of carrying your point either at the next general election or at a vacancy,' he wrote on 8 February. Any attempt to perpetuate a contest, said Malmesbury, would smack of 'peevishness towards Petty', and he counselled that a 'moderation of temper' on the part of his supporters and 'a manly concession' from Palmerston himself would be the best means by which 'to conciliate & increase the number of yr friends.'[34]

Palmerston's failure at Cambridge in 1806 has usually been explained as a product of the combined forces of Petty's superior college and government associations and his more effective campaigning. An Edinburgh friend consoled Palmerston afterwards by saying that as soon as the change of government gave Petty the advantage of crown support, he had 'despaired' of Palmerston's cause and in such circumstances 'it never can be a subject of regret to you that you muster'd a respectable number of adherents, when power, interest & a very high reputation were all on your adversary's side.'[35] Certainly Petty was the more convincing candidate. Philip Guedalla described the by-election as merely 'a pleasant flutter',[36] while Herbert Bell ascribed Palmerston's defeat to the common perception that he was opposed to abolition of the slave trade, a view echoed by Jasper Ridley.[37] Muriel Chamberlain simply dismissed the contest as having been, from the outset, nothing more than a 'forlorn hope.'[38] However, Palmerston lost the election just as surely as Petty won it. As Wilberforce noted, believing the slave trade question to have been central to the result, while Petty had gained much 'owing to his known zeal' for abolition, Palmerston, by contrast, 'lost much, owing to his being supposed, mistakenly I believe, to be our enemy; and numbers declared they would not, though satisfied in all other points, vote for an anti-abolitionist.'[39] Palmerston had entered the contest with a lack of conviction; determined only, it would seem, to secure an agreeable seat in Parliament. As Lady Amherst observed, not only had Palmerston failed to refute criticisms of his position, but he had also failed to capitalise on the tangible strengths he did bring to the campaign. 'Ld P's failure seems entirely owing to a mistaken or rather *misrepresented* idea that was not sufficiently contradicted that he was not Mr Pitt's friend,' she wrote to Lady Malmesbury. 'I make an extract out of a letter [from the brother of Samuel Blackall of Emmanuel College] of the 4th Feby from Cambridge, "I find that a large body of the University & amongst the rest most of the resident members of this (Eman. Coll.) College give their votes to Ld Althorpe [*sic*] upon the *principle* that in so doing they are acting in the manner most respectful to the memory of Mr Pitt. Lord P's chance is considerably diminish'd since this strange idea has taken possession of people's minds".'[40]

There was an absence of ideological drive behind Palmerston's campaign and his ambitions seem to have been parliamentary rather than political. His Pittite sympathies were adopted by default rather than conviction and it is important to underline that at this point Palmerston was not a dyed in the wool Tory. He had left the Whiggish household of Dugald Stewart less than three years earlier and there was nothing in his political outlook in 1806 that separated him fundamentally from the Whigs with whom he would later work. Yet he proved unable, despite the best efforts of family and friends, to challenge the notion that he was opposed to abolition of the slave trade and in coming forward as a Pittite candidate supposedly sympathetic to the established Church, he made no mention of his developing concerns about religious exclusion, even if they were in origin a pragmatic response to the need for stability and not strictly ideological. This is, as more than one biographer has observed, ironic given that these were two causes on which Palmerston's later claims to a moral political conscience would, to a large extent, rest. There was, then, at least in early 1806, perhaps some truth in Brougham's jibe that Palmerston thought a courtier's life the 'most brilliant'. In contesting the Cambridge University by-election, Palmerston appeared more interested in securing a prestigious seat that would underwrite a comfortable parliamentary career befitting a man of his social standing, than in pursuing an overtly political vocation. He had, after all, made little enough effort to counter misunderstandings of his position. He had also, shortly beforehand, rejected the notion of representing Southampton, however unrealistic that might have been, on the grounds that it would have entailed too much constituency work.

None of this is to suggest that Palmerston had no political views. Jasper Ridley described Palmerston as having 'remained a Tory in a Radical atmosphere' at Edinburgh,[41] but this fails to appreciate the impact of Stewart's teaching on Palmerston. The Whig orthodoxies preached by Stewart had yet to find overt expression in Palmerston's political make-up, but his moderate Pittite inclinations do not preclude judgements that Palmerston would adhere to broadly Whiggish notions in his political maturity.

In July 1806 he wrote a letter to his friend George Shee in which, prompted by the ill health of Fox, he was induced to reflect on his political leanings and affiliations. Harbouring no personal animosity towards Fox, Palmerston could not, however, help feeling that his removal from public life would be for the public good. He feared Fox's continuation in office would mean nothing other than the conclusion of a 'bad peace' (an 'advantageous peace' Palmerston took to be 'a contradiction in terms') and indeed Fox, he perceived, 'seems now very much in the situation of Sampson tugging at the pillars'. But Palmerston bristled at the accusation that Shee had levelled at him of political inconsistency in his avowed wariness of Foxite politics. Claiming that he had been willing to give the Foxites a fair hearing, Palmerston maintained that only recent policies, such as Petty's iron and beer taxes, had undermined his confidence in the government; although entertaining no great faith in 'Fox and his gang' (the 'quondam friends of the people'), Palmerston had looked to Grenville to exercise a controlling and guiding influence. The apparent marginalising of Grenville and a Foxite ascendancy boded ill, but even so, Palmerston insisted, he had never resolved to go into 'systematic opposition'. His opposition to the Foxites, he said, was born of experience: 'in their financial exertions' they had 'stumbled out of the path chalked for them by their predecessors', imposing, for example, ill-conceived new taxes; in military matters they had sown confusion in the army and militia; and in foreign policy, a 'spirited interference about Hanover' notwithstanding, they had undermined Britain's interests 'by involving us in a peace with Buonaparte'. So a change of ministry was to be welcomed in which, Palmerston believed, it would be possible to unite the Grenville party with the present opposition to form a government 'possessed of such talents, principles and vigour, as would engage the confidence of this country and command the respect of Europe'.[42] This, replied Shee, was disingenuous. Palmerston, he insisted, had not been so opposed to the Foxites as his letter suggested, and he practically ascribed Palmerston's apparent inconsistency to his 'fertile imagination'.[43] Thus, one of Palmerston's closest friends, political allies, and one of his electoral agents, remained unconvinced of Palmerston's ideological opposition to Fox, and, by extension, his general party political consistency. In this he was not altogether wide of the mark. As Palmerston later confided (on the occasion of Fox's death), it was only the peculiar circumstances of tumult and war that underpinned the essential separation of the Foxites and Pittites. 'Had Fox lived in times less troublesome than those in which he was thrown – or had he not been opposed to such a rival as Pitt – he would, undoubtedly, have ranked not only among those statesmen the brilliancy of whose genius has reflected honour upon the country that produced them, but among those illustrious patriots whose names, consecrated by the applause of a grateful people, are held up to the admiration of posterity as fathers of their country and benefactors of the human race', he wrote. Fox was set on a divergent course from Pitt, and his advocacy of the 'rights of the popular part of our constitution' and adherence to a 'frantic' reform agenda, Palmerston suggested, had been exaggerated largely by a lack of prudence, driven by the pressures of the 'violence of debate' and inflamed by an impetuosity of temper; but Palmerston stopped short of outright censure of Fox.[44]

Palmerston's politics as he sought to enter Parliament, therefore, were moderate, lacked the tinge of overt political coloration, and so far as there was a centralising focus, it was to be found in his patriotic conservatism, motivated by the experience of war and a trait shared, it might be said, with numerous erstwhile Whigs, such as Palmerston's own father, who had 'defected' to Pittite Toryism at the close of the eighteenth century. In 1806-7, for one of the very few times in his life, Palmerston kept a political journal. Its entries are sporadic, but in so far as they disclose their author's political opinions, they reveal a man preoccupied with European events, with war and peace. Napoleon's 'pacific professions', as documented in his recently published correspondence, Palmerston felt, could not be trusted and he quoted approvingly the definition accorded to Napoleonic notions of peace by Friedrich von Gentz in his 1806 study of the balance of power in Europe: 'What, in his vocabulary, is meant by *peace* – the liberty of doing whatever is suggested to him by the feelings of unbounded power or momentary desire, and the unconditional subjection of his neighbours to every form of his increased and insupportable domination.' What other interpretation, after all, could be placed on Napoleon's plans for a 'Rhenish Confederacy' led by France and including, *inter alia*, Bavaria, Württemberg and Baden, by which he would form 'an alliance offensive and defensive'?[45]

Meanwhile, in June 1806, Palmerston, in company with the Malmesburys, returned to Cambridge for Commencement week where Palmerston was grati-fied to act as steward to a ball at the end of the month. There was no mistaking the fact that this was a political as much as a social visit. Palmerston felt that Petty was beginning to lose ground in the University, largely as a result of his decisions to increase taxes on pig iron and brewing and this combined with, as Palmerston believed, the dissolution of the government that was possible when, as seemed likely, Fox died, made Petty 'very insecure in his seat'. With Fox's health declining, Palmerston saw the initiative passing to the Pittites at Westminster, now 'undoubtedly the strongest party of the two', and he derided Grenville's ability to negotiate a peace as fanciful.[46] The fact that Petty came down to Cambridge at the same time Palmerston took 'as a great compliment' and an implied acknowledgement of his strengthening political position in the University.[47] Palmerston's having taken a leading role at the ball annoyed Petty 'a good deal' and even if a couple of weeks later Palmerston thought his chances of unseating Petty were not so good as he had initially hoped, his assessment of his prospects in a future contest remained upbeat. Political affairs in Cambridge, he reported to Sulivan, 'remain nearly *in statu quo*, though I fancy Petty has certainly lost ground since he has been in office'. Palmerston refrained from overt canvassing during his June visit, though he did call on his resident supporters and allowed himself to court two or three MAs thought to be favourable to him, while Baines, of Christ's College, had spontaneously announced his conversion to Palmerston during the ball. His de facto agents in

Cambridge, Wood and Outram, considered 'things as going on well, but as probably no dissolution will take place this year nothing further can be done', for the moment at least.[48] Palmerston's informal Cambridge canvass, then, yielded mixed results. He remained hopeful that he might topple Petty but at the same time fully acquiesced in Malmesbury's attempts to procure a fall-back option. The problem, as he discovered, was that this was both difficult and expensive. The going rate for a borough seat was at that time about £4,000 but could cost as much as £5,000 and the proprietors of these corrupt seats were loath to enter into any bargain before a dissolution was actually announced so as to maximise their negotiating power in selling the seat to a prospective candidate. The only way to moderate the expense was to try to organise payment by annuity, but such spreading of payments was a rare arrangement. Palmerston admitted his ignorance in such matters and had charged Malmesbury, who 'understands that sort of thing very well', with managing the task of finding him a safe seat in the event of a second disappointment at Cambridge. 'These are certainly transactions in which one can be neither too cautious or too explicit with the other party', he observed, 'as the whole affair is strictly speaking illegal and one rests entirely upon his honour.'[49] Malmesbury had identified seats in Horsham, Sussex, for both Palmerston and his own son, James Fitzharris, and in late September he wrote to ask Palmerston whether he would be willing to pay £4,000, for which sum he thought he could ensure the seat.[50]

When Parliament dissolved again in October 1806, however, Palmerston had not given up on Cambridge. With Horsham apparently in his pocket, should he need it, he returned to the University in mid-October 'to see how the land lies'. He suspected that the best course of action would still be to wait for the death of the Duke of Grafton and Euston's elevation to the Lords, rather than attack Petty, but he resolved to 'be guided by the opinion of my friends at Cambridge'.[51] Within a couple of days Palmerston's reservations about standing were affirmed by enquiries around the University. Petty, 'though sunk in the opinion of some individuals' since his election, was 'still too strong to be assailable'. Petty now commanded the '*undivided*' and '*energetic*' strength of the government while Euston remained, effectively, beyond challenge. 'There appears therefore a very bare chance of success', Palmerston concluded, 'for the accession of strength I may have made since last winter though something is not to be reckoned upon.' A second defeat would do no good, and 'by making a merit of not disturbing at present the tranquillity of the University I may claim their support at the Duke of Grafton's death with a better prospect of success'. With Horsham certain, and with no other candidate thought likely to usurp his position as pretender to Euston's seat, Palmerston withdrew from the Cambridge University contest before it had begun.[52] 'Actuated by motives of delicacy, and respect to the University, I have at the present general election, declined offering myself as a candidate for the high honour of becoming one of your representatives in Parliament', Palmerston wrote in an open letter to the Vice-Chancellor and the rest of the senate of the University. 'But since the assurances of support which I have received have been too flattering in their nature not to encourage the most sanguine hopes, it is my determination to embrace the first opportunity that shall occur, again to solicit that distinguishing mark of your favour, which it is the object of my most ardent ambition to obtain.'[53] More than just a marker for the future, this was also Palmerston's way of warning off, in a public way, the perceived threat posed by Lord Percy, a fellow Johnian, who had arrived in Cambridge a week before the end of October; Palmerston remained unconvinced that Percy really would defer to Palmerston's superior claims on the seat in the event of Euston's elevation to the Upper House.[54] Seeking to deter Percy, and encourage him to take one of the seats under the control of his father the Duke of Northumberland, Palmerston asked Percy, 'Might not the world if they saw you attack a friend with whom you are known to have lived at College in the habits of the closest intimacy, and who had by priority of occupancy established a sort of claim upon the University, might they not I say indulge their propensity to view men's actions in their worst light and attribute to you motives and sentiments which I am persuaded it is the furthest from your nature and character to entertain.'[55]

Lady Malmesbury reassured Palmerston that he had made the right decision in walking away from Cambridge on this occasion. 'I entirely approve of your decision,' she wrote. It is a very *wise* one & I hope will be rewarded by *future success* in *better* times. Cambridge is no better than any other borough & will always go with the loaves & fishes. I hope Lord Malmesbury will succeed about Horsham though we must *all live upon bread & water* in consequence it appears to me to be so very much au *poids de l'or*. But I *suppose* it is *right*. At all events it is better to pay *any thing*, if you are to be in Parlt. than to court & canvass people for 7 years together.'[56] Confidently expecting to be returned Member of Parliament for Horsham, Palmerston went to Sussex in November where he would stay with Lady Irwin, from whom he would buy the seat, for the duration of the poll only, respecting the usual borough-mongers' desire to keep candidates out of constituency affairs as much as possible.[57] The seats had been bought, after all, with guarantees of a return to parliament at this general election and at all subsequent re-elections (gratis) during Lady Irwin's life, for £4,000 each for Fitzharris, and Palmerston.[58] However, the claim of Lady Irwin to control the seat was not as secure as Malmesbury and Palmerston had been led to believe. Instead of enjoying an unopposed return, Palmerston found that he and Fitzharris faced a genuine contest for Horsham from two candidates put up by the Duke of Norfolk who also laid claim to influence in the constituency. As Lord of the Manor, Norfolk had attempted back in 1790 to get his candidates elected, largely by the device of selecting the returning officers himself. However, although the returning officers duly declared the Duke's candidates elected, the result did not withstand the scrutiny of Parliament when it was challenged by petition and in 1792 they were unseated. The outcome had confirmed Lady Irwin in her belief that she really controlled the constituency, but by 1806 Norfolk was keen to test his influence again. By dividing his supporters' land-holdings, he acquired influence over more voters, albeit ones with ever smaller burgages, or land-ownership. Whatever the legality of the practice, this meant that there was a real and immediate challenge to Lady Irwin's control of the seat and to Palmerston's and Fitzharris's automatic return, in the form of Norfolk's new candidates, Love Parry Jones and Francis John Wilder. At the conclusion of the poll, Jones and Wilder had a declared margin of victory of 44 to 29. The reliability or legitimacy of the result was, inevitably, immediately brought into question.[59] When the returning officers declared all four candidates elected in order to avoid a repeat of the debacle of the early 1790s, responsibility for determining the victors passed to Parliament. Palmerston remained sanguine, telling Sulivan, 'Our double return will be productive I fancy of no other bad consequence than putting several guineas into the pockets of some of your brother lawyers, a misfortune to which, as they will not come out of my pocket, I submit with Christian fortitude.' He was confident that the House of Commons committee would find in his favour and in that of Fitzharris, but he was to be disappointed. When the committee met on 8 January it displayed a marked bias towards Norfolk's men and Jones and Wilder were declared the winners on 20 January.[60] Palmerston had been wrong to assume that the appeal would cost him nothing, although the financial impli-cations could have been worse. The full £4,000 was only to have been paid once the candidates were 'securely seated' but he was still charged heavily in legal fees by Gordon and Troward, Horsham's returning officers, for the expense of conducting the Commons committee. In the event, as Palmerston remem-bered: 'Fitzharris and I paid about £1,500 each for the pleasure of sitting under the gallery for a week in our capacity of petitioners. We thought ourselves unlucky in being unseated; but in a short time came the change of Government, and the dissolution in May, 1807, and we rejoiced in our good fortune in not having paid £5,000 for a three-months' seat.'[61]

In the meantime, the question now was where, or how, would Palmerston fulfil his parliamentary ambitions? Malmesbury urged Palmerston to take his time having, in the space of one year, failed at Cambridge (once at election, once not even judging it worthwhile to throw his hat into the ring), and at the supposedly secure Horsham. 'Our object now is to look out for other seats & on that point we had better take time & consent to lose perhaps one session,' he told Palmerston, 'as besides the difficulty of finding them now, the price will sink.'[62] Minto hoped that Palmerston would soon 'take your place & act your part in the world' and that he would 'not be discouraged by the few untoward events you have experienced in that pursuit, from persisting in the same views'.[63] Indeed, Palmerston was not discouraged, but nor was he inclined to delay as Malmesbury suggested. He began immediately to look for a new seat and his attention turned to Great Yarmouth where the election of Edward

Harbord and Stephen Lushington was being challenged on the grounds of corruption. Even though they had been returned unopposed, there was a suspicion that they were being manipulated to cede one seat which, if they refused to do and were unsuccessful in confirming their return, would run the risk of their being barred from standing again. Thus they were thought 'likely to be ejected by the treating acts', in which case, it was apparently agreed they were to be replaced by Lushington's elder brother, Sir Henry, and Palmerston. The seat would cost Palmerston 3,000 guineas, less than Horsham which would itself have been a 'very good bargain'. If Harbord was turned out, which was by no means certain, Palmerston was confident of getting his 800 (out of 1,100) votes, Harbord's supporters having apparently greeted Palmerston's proposed candidature with approval. The deal was to be kept 'as secret as possible' but in reporting the negotiation to his sister Frances, Palmerston spoke with guarded optimism of this new opportunity. The canvass he had conducted alongside Harbord had yielded encouraging results: on one day 'trotting about Thames Street and the Minories' meeting the Yarmouth dock workers employed there at the time, Palmerston secured about forty votes and soon secured a further 119 promises in the event of a contest.[64] The question, however, was to prove an academic one: on 11 March the Commons committee ruled in favour of Harbord and Lushington and so, whatever machinations really were at work in this case, Yarmouth was to be yet another disappointment for Palmerston.

On 25 April Palmerston learned that the government was to resign and his thoughts turned instantly to Cambridge, once again, and to unseating Petty. He was one of the first to hear of the decision, as 'an independent friend of the government' having just accepted office in the recently formed ministry of the Duke of Portland.[65] Portland was an 'old and intimate friend of Lord Malmesbury' and Malmesbury had used his influence with the Duke to secure a public office for Palmerston, who was duly appointed one of the six Junior Lords of the Admiralty in April 1807, a post once held by Palmerston's father under the ministry of the Duke of Grafton in 1766; indeed Lord Mulgrave, then First Lord of the Admiralty, had apparently suggested the idea to Malmesbury on the grounds that Palmerston had 'a sort of hereditary claim to a seat there' and would, no doubt, 'bring to it all the advantages of hereditary abilities'.[66] Portland had been appointed to form a government at the very end of March; Palmerston, who was spending Easter at Broadlands, received a letter from Malmesbury desiring him to come to town to accept the offer in person, on 1 April.[67] He lost no time in writing to Mulgrave to accept the offer: 'I am just arrived in London in consequence of a letter I this morning received from Lord Malmesbury,' he wrote, '& I hasten to seize the first opportunity of expressing to your Lordship my grateful sense of the very flattering communication it contains. The situation which your Ldship has thought proper to offer me at the board of admiralty is on many accounts particularly gratifying to my feelings, and the circumstance of its having been held by my father together with the very flattering manner in which you have been pleased to notice me are not among the least inducements which I feel to accept it.'[68] This, said one early biographer, was a recognition of Palmerston's 'well known' interest in foreign affairs.[69] Although the work consisted, Palmerston said, of little more than simply signing his name,[70] he was, apparently, 'very pedantic and very pompous' in its execution.[71]

Whether or not Palmerston had now found his vocation, the fact that he occupied a public office at the Admiralty made it all the more desirable, if not essential, that he also find a seat in Parliament. Palmerston lost no time in commencing a new canvass at the University. He had already been assured that Spencer Perceval, another Trinity man, would not stand against him, thereby removing at least one perceived potential obstacle, but the proposed candidature of Sir Vicary Gibbs, the new Attorney-General, was a more serious considera-tion. Palmerston asked Sulivan to form an election committee as soon as possible and begin the London canvass without delay.[72] From Cambridge Palmerston reported a favourable start to his campaign. By 28 April he had secured the support of the masters of at least eight colleges and pledges from a number of heavyweight fellows. His programme, such as it was, however, was again a modest if not anodyne appeal to the supporters of 'Church and State'. 'I purposely avoided in my circular letter any unnecessary allusion to recent events,' he told Sulivan, 'conscious that to those who were likely to concur with me a slight hint would be sufficient while to others a more explicit allusion would only afford an opportunity of abuse.' Gibbs, meanwhile, remained an unknown factor in the equation. He had been sent down by the government to strengthen Palmerston's position,[73] and Palmerston tended to believe that he would help 'neutralize some of Petty's votes & thus deduct from Euston', since Palmerston's voters would now have a second Pittite candidate to support if they wished to cast a double vote.[74] Gibbs, however, was not the most attractive of running mates. Although a prominent and successful lawyer, and since 1794 a King's Counsel, his professional accomplishments were not matched by social grace. He was thought by contemporaries to be physically unprepossessing and was said to speak with a 'shrill, sharp and unmusical' voice while his brusque and sarcastic manner attracted the epithet 'Vinegar Gibbs'.[75] Perhaps this was why, only two days after talking of the need to unite with Gibbs, Palmerston sought to steer clear of any formal avowal of an alliance, judging that a joint canvass and union between the two would have cost him a good many second votes. With between seventy and eighty resident voters apparently committed to Palmerston, he was reluctant to dilute his support within the University by standing on a joint platform with Gibbs, although he conceded that a joint canvass in London might still be advantageous.[76]

Despite Palmerston's sanguinity, the result was never a foregone conclusion. Palmerston had sent to Malmesbury an encouraging list of likely supporters but had to acknowledge that the members of King's College, Gibbs's alma mater, were almost all for Petty and Euston. In such a state of uncertainty Palmerston was 'cautious of making actual promises to Gibbs', hoping not to weaken the mainstays of his own support, at St John's in particular (where the members were, as one Trinity fellow observed, 'exerting themselves to the utmost in grunting out the praises of their brother Palmerston'),[77] with a split Pittite vote.[78] Although Gibbs's candidature was supposed to have augmented Palmerston's strength, as Palmerston later remembered, 'my colleague was almost as dangerous as my opponents' and he found that wherever government supporters had only one vote to cast, they were being urged to use it in Gibbs's interest.[79]

Malmesbury worried that any perceived divisions among the two Pittite candidates would be damaging to them both. They must, Malmesbury told Palmerston, 'act or at least appear to act on the most perfect unison & concert', particularly as their opponents were looking to exploit perceived differences. Palmerston had little to fear from Gibbs at the poll and could only gain by having Gibbs 'fling all his might into yr scale', he concluded.[80] With Cambridge 'all in a flame for Church and King' (as Milner put it), supporters of the constitution were drawn to Palmerston and Gibbs and there seemed to be electoral capital to be made from 'Protestantism and loyalty', which one later Victorian account pointed out 'were roused to passionate enthusiasm in the country and in the University'.[81] Palmerston had already decided that a 'cordial cooperation' would be a wise course, and though he remained sceptical of the real benefits that would accrue, judged that if there was an advantage to be had, it was all on his side, and by a 'strongly *co-operative*' approach he might 'be a considerable gainer by the junction'.[82] It was agreed that Gibbs and Palmerston would 'give to the other the second votes of all his disposable plumpers',[83] that is, share the support of those voters who had declared (or plumped) for one candidate only in the first instance.

It was perhaps not surprising that an agreement of such a nature yielded to confusion. As the poll closed on 8 May, Gibbs complained to Palmerston that the agreement was not being honoured and Palmerston's supporters, rather than giving a second vote to Gibbs, were tending to 'plump', that is, cast one vote only, for Palmerston. Palmerston went immediately to Senate House where he found his former tutor Outram dead against any attempt to help Gibbs who was, he said, running Palmerston hard for second place behind Euston. Euston had a clear lead for the first of the two seats and the other sitting member, Petty, damaged by his recent budget, was trailing in fourth place; the contest for the remaining second seat, therefore, was very much one between Palmerston and Gibbs. Palmerston, however, dismissed fears that he was throwing away victory and, claiming to be 'bound in honour' if nothing else, appealed to his voters to give their support to Gibbs as well, which they did 'with much ill humour and grumbling'. Hoist with his own petard, Palmerston lost the election by the very narrow margin of three votes, and discovered that the plumping, such as it was, had been very much in Gibbs's favour, as he had received twelve to Palmerston's seven; a margin that would have been more than enough to explain the defeat.[84] It was 'provoking', Palmerston said, that he had personally directed four plumpers to give their second votes to Gibbs which had, effectively, swung the result.[85]

On reflection Palmerston felt that Gibbs had not behaved dishonourably, but he 'was very much mortified & disappointed' to fail for a second time at the University where he had been sure, at the beginning, that his prospects were good. Whatever bitterness he may have reserved for Petty who, he claimed, had surreptitiously aided Euston's campaign to the detriment of his and Gibbs's, the fact was that Cambridge University was not a seat through which Palmerston would be able to make his debut in Parliament.[86] However, Malmesbury's efforts to devise a fall-back plan this time bore fruit. For £4,000 he had bought for Palmerston the seat of Newport, Isle of Wight. The owner of this pocket borough, Sir Leonard Holmes, had imposed one condition only on Palmerston's tenure of the seat: that he 'should never, even for the election, set foot in the place; so jealous was the patron lest any attempt should be made to get a new interest in the borough'.[87] Perhaps this was why neither Malmesbury nor Palmerston could quite get the name of the place right: Malmesbury could not decide whether it was 'Winton' or 'Newton' while Palmerston, in later years, remembered his first parliamentary seat as having been Newtown.[88]

The new Junior Lord of the Admiralty had barely entered Parliament when his political mentor and erstwhile guardian, Malmesbury, suggested a move to a more prestigious situation. Malmesbury's son, James Fitzharris, planned to resign his post as Under-Secretary at the Foreign Office and Malmesbury wrote in August 1807 to enquire whether Palmerston should like to succeed him. The proposal was to be treated as '*quite & most strictly* for your private ear', and not even mentioned to Fitzharris himself. If Palmerston was tempted, Malmesbury offered to mention his name to the Foreign Secretary, George Canning. The work, Malmesbury warned, was 'very laborious' and therefore 'not fit for a married young man', not, apparently, a problem for the bachelor Palmerston, but he promised that it was 'very interesting'.[89] Palmerston responded quickly in the affirmative, but it emerged that the scheme might yet prove stillborn: Canning, it seemed, had already made a commitment to Charles Bagot and Palmerston's appointment was not certain.[90] Bagot was, it transpired, disposed to accept the post at the Foreign Office and pressed his claims based on an apparently long-standing promise from Canning and he refused Canning's (half-hearted) suggestion that he exchange offices with Palmerston at the Admiralty. Palmerston would remain where he was, but Malmesbury harboured hopes that 'some *other* means may be yet found' to satisfy his wishes in this direction.[91]

Meanwhile Palmerston had little by way of official business to occupy him by day other than to 'sign his name' on Admiralty papers. So he took the opportunity to prepare his parliamentary speaking debut in early 1808. As a Pittite minister he no doubt felt obliged to support government policy while as a lay Lord of the Admiralty he had time and opportunity to deliberate on that policy and in February 1808 came forward to make his maiden speech, in which he defended the navy's attack on the Danish fleet at Copenhagen the previous September. Since Denmark was still neutral, the attack had been the subject of parliamentary censure, but the government insisted, with some justification, that it had reason to believe that the Danish navy had been about to fall under French influence. It was a good subject for a member of the Admiralty and it played well to the patriotic sensibilities of much of the British population at the time. Palmerston's intervention was a considered and carefully prepared one. He had profited from the 'leisure' afforded by his undemanding work at the Admiralty to study the papers relating to the Copenhagen expedition and rose to speak on the second night of the debate, following Robert Milnes who made a second speech having, the night before, made a 'splendid' first speech on the opening of the debate. Palmerston remembered receiving 'many compliments' on his first appearance on his feet, benefiting from a favourable comparison with Milnes's 'bad' second contribution.[92] It is worth noting the grounds on which Palmerston denied the wisdom of producing the papers outlining the terms of the expedition. He objected, he told the House, 'to making public the working of diplomacy, because it is the tendency of disclosures in that department to shut up future sources of information'. With regard to the specific case of the Danish expedition, Palmerston argued that rather than revealing a violation of the rights of nations, this was a matter of self-preservation and in such cases the laws of nature superseded those of nations: the ascendancy of French influence in Denmark was, he argued, tantamount to French coercion and the rise of an implicit Danish antagonism towards Britain. 'England, according to that law of self-preservation which is a fundamental principle of the law of nations, is justified in securing, and therefore enforcing, from Denmark a neutrality which France would by compulsion have converted into an active hostility,' he concluded.[93]

To his sister Elizabeth, Palmerston joked the next day that he had been 'tempted by some evil spirit to make a fool of myself for the entertainment of the House', but it had, he felt, been a 'good opportunity of breaking the ice, although one should flounder a little in doing so, as it was impossible to talk any very egregious nonsense upon so good a cause'.[94] In the event, it had not been quite so alarming an experience as he had anticipated. 'I certainly felt glad when the thing was over,' he said, 'though I began to fear I had exposed myself, but my friends were so obliging as to say I had not talked much nonsense & I began in a few hours afterwards to be reconciled to my fate.' He even expressed some disappointment that the newspapers had 'not been very liberal in their allowance of report' of his speech.[95]

The effect, however, was uncertain. If the vote on Ponsonby's motion demanding the production of papers were used as a measure of success,

Palmerston did well, participating in a government victory by a margin of 145 (smaller than Palmerston had anticipated but respectable enough),[96] and his prepared speech, which lasted around half an hour, was generally well delivered. Yet Palmerston also displayed his lack of experience, and was reported to have been not quite a natural parliamentarian. When he endeavoured to speak spontaneously, as Bulwer noted, 'there was that hesitation and superabundance of gesture with the hands, which were perceptible to the last when Lord Palmerston spoke unprepared, and was seeking for words; for though he always used the right word, it often cost him pains to find it.'[97]

The speech was a rare highlight in Palmerston's year. He complained of the ennui of London life where stasis seemed to be the order of the day: 'The town looks as dull as fogs and east winds can make it. Every other person one knows has measles or ophthalmia. The Chancellor is going to shut up the Opera. Scarcely one party is given in a week. Even at that nothing is to be seen but women yawning at each other. The only two things anybody says are "Do you belong to the Argyle,[98] and have you read 'Marmion'?"[99] And before you have pronounced the first to be bad, and the second inferior to the "Lay,"[100] you are called upon to answer the same interrogatories to a dozen other people.'[101] It was a good time, then, for Palmerston to pay his first visit to Ireland, which he did in September 1808, and he took the opportunity to survey his estates there and consider plans for their improvement. However, by the end of the year he was back at his desk at the Admiralty and made little effort to consolidate what parliamentary reputation he had so far established, choosing, it would seem, to make only one contribution throughout the session of 1809, in order to ask a question about the scandal surrounding the alleged sale of army commissions by Mary Anne Clarke, the mistress of the commander-in-chief, the Duke of York.[102] It was, unconsciously, an apposite line of enquiry for a man whose own career would soon be tied to that of the British army.

In the spring of 1809 the Austrians had launched renewed attacks on French forces, this time in Bavaria, the Tyrol, Venetia and the Adriatic. Napoleon's response was swift and effective, culminating in a comprehensive defeat of the Austrian army at the Battle of Wagram on 5 July 1809.[103] A British expedition designed to effect a diversionary attack on the River Scheldt, which left England on 28 July, was too little, too late. News of the Austrian defeat had reached Britain on 21 July but the expedition, which was to occupy the island of Walcheren, and attack arsenals, dockyards and enemy shipping around the Scheldt, was dispatched anyway. The mission was a disaster. Walcheren was occupied, but at a great cost while other targets, notably Antwerp, were never reached; disease and the French army proved to be more than a match for the British forces. The Foreign Secretary, Canning, had long nurtured a desire to see the back of the Secretary for War, Lord Castlereagh, and when news of the failure of the Walcheren expedition became known this change seemed all the more pressing. As the Cabinet discussion gave way to recriminations, Castlereagh learned that Canning was demanding his resignation and he in turn demanded 'satisfaction' for the perceived insult to his honour and reputation. So it was that at six o'clock on the morning of 21 September 1809 two government ministers were to be found twelve paces apart on Putney Heath aiming pistols at each other. Canning, who had never fired a gun before, missed with both of his shots; Castlereagh's second tore through his opponent's left thigh. Although wounded, Canning demanded of Castlereagh 'Are you sure we have done?', before being led to the nearby home of Lord Yarmouth where a surgeon was waiting.[104] Canning survived relatively unharmed – 'you can hardly conceive how slight a matter it is,' he wrote later the same day – but the reverberations of Castlereagh's shot were felt around Westminster for some time afterwards.

Palmerston was taken by surprise by the news when finally he learned of the recent events in south London. 'I knew nothing to write and was as much surprised at hearing of the duel as the man at John of Groats house,' he told his sister Frances. He continued: 'Now I am in town I can give you another reason for saying nothing which is that I *won't* tell you anything and I leave it to you to chuse between my ignorance & discretion.'[105] It is perfectly possible that Palmerston was unaware of events, but his reluctance to speculate was perhaps a sign that he recognised that this affair portended important changes in government.

Portland's administration was profoundly weakened by the duel, and the associated crisis and Portland's death at the beginning of October made the anticipated collapse of the administration inevitable. In early October the King accepted the demands of what remained of the Cabinet that Spencer Perceval be called to form a new government. There would have to be changes at the War Office, but more problematically for Perceval, although he sought to build a government from broadly the same Pittite stock as Portland had worked with, such was the damaged nature of the erstwhile ministerial body that he was obliged to look to the second rank of politicians to fill many of the posts in his administration. Thus was Palmerston thought of for promotion. Perceval summoned Palmerston up to town from Broadlands on 16 October and offered him the Chancellorship of the Exchequer, an office thought suitable for a promising junior. If Palmerston chose not to take a post at the Treasury, Perceval told him, he might be able to offer him something at the War Office, specifically the post of Secretary at War. 'I was a good deal surprised at so unexpected an offer,' recalled Palmerston, 'and begged a little time to think of it, and to consult my friends.'[106]

His first instinct was to prefer the possibility of an appointment as Secretary at War but Palmerston wanted the advice of his brother William and particularly also that of Melbourne before he committed himself.[107] (The Secretary *for* War was the senior of the two War Office ministers, usually sitting in the Cabinet and taking charge of the Colonial brief as well; the Secretary *at* War was a more junior, almost bureaucratic office.) Perceval's plan had been to divide the labours of the Treasury and to relieve his own burden as First Lord of the Treasury by appointing a new Chancellor who would have a seat in the Cabinet. In his reply Palmerston was cautious, fearing, as he told the new Prime Minister, that he would find himself 'wholly incompetent for the situation both from my inexperience in the details of matters of finance and my want of practice in public speaking'. As he explained further to Malmesbury, the offer placed him in an embarrassing position: 'one's vanity & ambition would lead [one] to accept the brilliant offer first proposed; but it is throwing for a *great stake* & where much may be gained, *very much* also is to be lost. I have always thought it unfortunate for anyone, & particularly a young man to be placed above his proper level, as he only rises to fall the farther.' And with the economy in an apparently parlous state Palmerston risked, he thought, appearing foolish before the House, '& I should be apprehensive that instead of materially assisting Perceval, I should only bring disgrace & ridicule upon him & myself'. Perceval had suggested a more junior Lordship at the Treasury by way of a short-term stepping stone to the Chancellorship but this seemed only to be postponing problems. The post of Secretary at War Palmerston thought 'better suited to a beginner' and one in which failure was less likely, or at least short-comings were likely to be less conspicuous. 'One consideration not to be over-looked,' thought Palmerston, 'is, that we may probably not remain in long enough to enable one to retrieve one's blunders made at the outset, & the ground of Secretary at War is I think quite high enough to leave off upon.' He hoped that Perceval might find a better 'second rate' member of the party for the Exchequer and that the War Office post, the offer of which was not yet certain, might prove possible.[108]

Malmesbury fully endorsed Palmerston's view of the situation. The government, he felt, was likely to be widely attacked in Parliament and Palmerston would do well to avoid being so exposed politically. The Secretary at War, however, with a seat in the Cabinet, Malmesbury thought 'very respectable' without bringing Palmerston 'too forward *at once*': from it much could be gained and relatively little lost.[109] Palmerston's brother William also urged the same course, fearing that the offer of the Exchequer, though flattering, was really a sign of 'the weakness of the present administration'. The Chancellorship would also involve too much parliamentary labour and, in addition to future dangers, brought with it the risks of 'comparisons with Pitt & with Petty the former can never be advantageous to any one, and the latter is likely to bring an additional share of persecution from the opposition & his friends who would be very unwilling to let the world imagine any young man could succeed in the situation where he in some measure failed'.[110]

On 18 September Palmerston informed Perceval that he would prefer the post of Secretary at War, but recognising that this was conditional on Robert Milnes agreeing to take the Exchequer (if he did not, Milnes would be offered the Secretaryship at War), Palmerston promised, if necessary, to go to the Treasury 'willingly'. 'Whatever may be the result of this business,' he told Malmesbury, 'it must always be a source of great pride & gratification to me to have been thought worthy of so splendid an offer, & I am persuaded that no after thoughts will diminish the satisfaction I feel that I acted right in declining it.'[111] Milnes refused the offer of a ministerial appointment on 23 September which meant that Palmerston could become Secretary at War, but still the offer was conditional on satisfactory arrangements being made at the Exchequer and for the head of the War Office; Perceval hoped Sir David Dundas would become Secretary for War. Palmerston remained reluctant to join the Cabinet when the offer was repeated. Although it might have been necessary to join had he become Chancellor, it was unusual for the Secretary at War to be there and as well as inviting suspicious enquiries as to why so young and inexperienced a figure was so placed, Palmerston felt there would be more than enough to occupy him at the War Office. 'It would undoubtedly have been highly interesting,' he thought, 'but for all purposes of business of debate Perceval will of course keep one sufficiently informed to answer all one's wishes; at first at least.'[112] Perceval's attempt to assemble a new government was not an easy one and Lord Melville raised objections to Dundas going to the War Office while George Rose vacillated over whether or not to go to the Treasury. At the end of October Perceval suggested that he might yet offer Palmerston the post of Treasurer of the Navy and the vice-presidency of the Board of Trade rather than the War Office, which Palmerston undertook to accept if that proved more convenient.[113] Matters were finally resolved, at least so far as Palmerston was concerned, on 26 October when, despite the refusals of two more candidates for the Exchequer, Perceval determined to prevaricate over the War Office no longer and Palmerston was confirmed as the new Secretary at War. Huskisson judged it 'a very bad appointment', but Perceval insisted that he had 'brought forward into a more prominent and useful situation a young man of considerable parliamentary promise', a view echoed by William Wellesley Pole who knew Palmerston from the Admiralty and who professed 'a very high opinion of his sense and judgement'.[114] On the morning of 27 October, therefore, Palmerston swapped the Admiralty for the War Office, where he found he would have 'full employment' but which he thought would not be overwhelming and, all in all, that he would like his new post 'very much'.[115] He had already written to Frances to explain what he could expect as Secretary at War:

> The War Office will be a very great confinement & fag, in fact perhaps barring the House of Commons in which of course I shall not be called upon to take so prominent a part, not much less laborious than the Exchequer would have been *when learnt*, but requires less preliminary preparation. The business is, to superintend all the accounts of the army militia & volunteers, together with other subordinate duties connected with the army, & from the great increase of our military establishments of late years, unaccompanied

by a corresponding augmentation of our official means, there is an immense arrear of accounts unsettled, & daily accumulating – during the session of Parliament it will be a very fatiguing situation, and I fancy admits of scarce any holydays during the course of the year. However one must do something, and if one can make oneself useful one must submit to a certain degree of inconvenience & labour.[116]

Malmesbury, who felt 'a parental anxiety & solicitude' about Palmerston, revelled in his protégé's advance and, as he told Palmerston, entertained 'the vision of your being the leading man in the country'.[117] A little over a week later Palmerston reported to Malmesbury that he continued to 'like this office very much', and it was, he judged, 'some satisfaction to have some real business to do', but, by the same token, he hoped that the government would survive long enough for him to remedy the defects in the internal organisation he had found at the War Office. 'Its inadequacy to get through the current business that comes before it is really a disgrace to the country; and the arrear of Regimental Accounts unsettled is of a magnitude not to be conceived,' he observed.[118] In fact it was not until 1826 that Palmerston felt that the War Office had really made meaningful progress in the settlement of arrear accounts.[119]

During these years Palmerston displayed a marked aptitude for bureaucracy. While Britain remained at war, making the case for carrying the annual army estimates through Parliament was not an arduous one, little more than 'arid exercises', as Philip Guedalla put it.[120] The impositions and demands of wartime management extended beyond the military front line and Palmerston was energetic in his attempts to maintain a sizeable local militia. As he explained in 1812:

Now, though at present there is no great prospect of invasion, yet it is by no means improbable that whatever may be the issue of the Russia war it may be followed by menacing movements upon the enemy's coast, calculated to embarrass, & prevent us from sending troops to Spain; the interior of the country is at present quiet, but there is no saying what might next summer be the effect of the continued pressure of the war with America, or the prospect of a bad harvest; in any or all of these contingent cases, it would be of the utmost importance to have the whole loc[al]. mil[itia]. in a state of tolerable efficiency & preparation; & as each corps when called out either for riots or invasion cannot be kept together longer than one month of 28 days, it would be very awkward to have to spend half that time in fitting jackets & breeches and teaching men to march & go through the manual & platoon exercises.[121]

Palmerston found his initial assessments of the want of resources of his department validated by experience. While making plans for supplying the army and expanding the local militia, the Secretary at War was simultaneously managing an office barely fit for purpose. Once peace was concluded in 1815, the pressure for retrenchment in the military departments grew and six years after the Treaty of Vienna had been signed, Palmerston's department was still struggling to get the accounts for the war in order.

Part of the problem for Palmerston, for the army, and for the government, was the arcane institutional structure of early nineteenth-century military administration and the fierce guardianship of petty fiefdoms and privileges that prevailed within it. The gentlemen of the War Office led 'an administrative life of exquisite confusion', said Guedalla, inhabiting a world of 'splendid anarchy', at a great remove from the 'towering hierarchy' of the Napoleonic empire and military against which it had been pitted.[122] Palmerston's role was, superficially, reasonably easily defined. The Secretary at War, as J.C. Hobhouse, a later incumbent of that office, explained in 1833, 'is the proper channel of reference on all questions between the civil and military part of the community, and is the constitutional check interposed for regulating their intercourse and he is especially charged with the protection of the civil subject from all improper interference on the part of the military'.[123] Yet, as Palmerston and Hobhouse both discovered, serving as a link between the civil and military branches of public life was far more easily said than done. As an early historian of the War Office, Charles Clode, put it in 1869:

There was perhaps no office ever created the powers of which were, at its establishment, so undefined, as that of Secretary at War. In the course of time, and in the progress of events, certain duties became definitely assigned to the office; but even in the discharge of these the Secretary at War held an ambiguous place of responsibility: neither a Military Officer – though the Commander-in-Chief claimed his allegiance as such, nor a responsible Minister – though the House of Commons strove to fix upon him that character.[124]

Although the title implied a military and a ministerial position, the Secretary at War was, in origin, merely a financial and ministerial agent, that is to say, a subordinate, if not primarily bureaucratic, appointment. The Secretary at War's principal duties included the presentation of army estimates in Parliament. As a Treasury agent, in matters of finance the Secretary at War claimed precedence over the commander-in-chief in so far as those matters concerned numbers, pay and allowances, as settled by the government (on behalf of the crown). Yet the War Office, of which he was the head, was not an exclusively civil administrative body. Within military circles, the Secretary at War had also, since 1702, claimed the right to direct the affairs of the Ordnance Offices (which the latter had, for their part, always denied). More importantly, since the late eighteenth century, the War Office had assumed direct ministerial responsibility for the army, thereby encroaching on the traditional domain of the commander-in-chief. In response to calls by General John Burgoyne for the commander-in-chief to be 'considered the Military Minister', the then Secretary at War, Sir George Yonge had asserted in the Commons in 1789 that 'he did not hesitate to stand up in his official situation, and say that he conceived it was the notion of our Government that he was in some sort officially responsible for every measure taken in the military Department'. In 1793, a separate Horse Guards establishment emerged through which the commander-in-chief could more readily impress his authority. There were therefore two heads of army business – the commander-in-chief at the Horse Guards and the Secretary at War at the War Office – claiming superiority in military business. As the Treasury's representative the Secretary at War claimed independence and ministerial authority in the discharge of his duties. The commander-in-chief, however, tended to regard the Secretary at War as holding a military commission, subject therefore to military discipline and the authority of the commander-in-chief himself.[125] Such blurring of official remits could only ever have led to obfuscation and conflict.

If the two military offices had worked in tandem, however uncomfortably, for a century, that situation was not to survive the reformist zeal of Palmerston and the counterbalancing conservatism of successive commanders-in-chief, Sir David Dundas, Frederick, Duke of York, and the Duke of Wellington. Palmerston had not been at the War Office a year when the first major disagreement with Dundas broke into the open. The grounds of the altercation were apparently trivial – and, as has been noted, were a source of irritation to those who at the time (and subsequently) saw more important matters of life and death at stake in the Peninsula[126] – but in the end even the Prime Minister and the Prince Regent were dragged into the dispute. Seeking to make arrangements for various payments to the army, Palmerston had, in the autumn of 1810, circulated certain officers requesting information on particular subjects. Firstly, he asked the commanding officers of all regiments to supply the War Office with duplicates of bread and forage returns which the Office had requested but not received. He also asked all colonels for details of their expenditure on clothing for their regiments in order to verify that these off-reckonings were being appropriately spent. Finally Palmerston wanted to check a suspected abuse of payments to aides-de-camp; generals on the home staff of the army were entitled to a certain number of such aides, paid for out of the public purse, but it was widely known that many posts remained vacant while the generals continued to claim and receive payment for them.[127] Palmerston's requests were essentially for the purposes of financial audit and well within the legitimate bounds of his official duties. However, Dundas, sensitive to the least slight, complained to Perceval, the Prime Minister, in late September 1810 that in the manner of their execution these requests served as 'fresh proofs of a disposition in Mr [William] Merry [the War Office's Chief Examiner] to exalt the War Office to the degradation of the Comr in Chief'. Palmerston, just as prickly as Dundas, responding to the attack on Merry and the Office as one on himself, insisted that while never intentionally wishing to give offence, he would not accept the commander-in-chief's chastisements: 'I certainly have always considered myself when communicating with him to have stood upon a footing at least of independence, & to be placed at the head of an office (of what relative importance in the state is immaterial) but exercising a free & separate jurisdiction,' he told Perceval. If he was not to be allowed to 'call for a return to enable him to discharge his duty, or issue a circular to the Army upon matters within his province, without injury to the discipline of the Service or shewing disrespect to the Comr in Chief, the Office had really better be abolished altogether & the Department placed under the superintendence of the Horse Guards', he said. Drawing a sharp distinction between the financial and disciplinary functions of the two offices, Palmerston claimed to have observed the convention 'that on questions in which the two are blended, previous mutual communication should take place'. Launching an offensive of his own, or rather a tit-for-tat, Palmerston contended that the Horse Guards had been guilty of similarly denigrating the standing of the War Office in issuing orders relating to army finance. It was a something-and-nothing case, but the something was a clear revelation that Palmerston and Dundas were unable to work together. Dundas, said Palmerston, 'though at the bottom possessed of much good nature, is a little irritable & hasty in transacting business, & apt to take up matters somewhat warmly before he is quite in possession of the circumstances of the case'. He urged the Prime Minister to take soundings and 'to decide between me and Sir David'.[128] In one respect at least Palmerston was quite right: Dundas had been somewhat precipitate. Palmerston's request for information about bread and forage returns Dundas had mistakenly believed to be a request for copies of the monthly returns of the effective strength of the army. Yet the disagreement had rapidly turned into a stand-off and a broader 'principle' was thought to be at stake, that of whether the Secretary at War was entitled to make any circular instructions to the army, something which Palmerston thought Dundas was determined to prohibit. Yet, citing regulations issued by the commander-in-chief, Palmerston argued that 'officers are directed to correspond with the Secy at War on all matters relative to finance, & if the Secy at War is recognized to have the power of writing a letter or giving directions on these subjects to *one colonel* of a regiment, of necessity he must be competent to give the same directions to the colonel *of every regiment*, which in fact is issuing a circular to the Army'. This had been established practice for a number of years and thus, said Palmerston, 'in calling for the returns in question I did not depart from what has been the accustomed & recognized practice of office'.[129]

As the dispute rumbled on into December, Dundas conceded that Palmerston's conduct had not been innovatory, but, Palmerston feared, Dundas was using the matter to undermine his position and place the Secretary at War 'on a level with the appointments of Adjutant & Quarter Master General'. 'It is perhaps not wholly unnatural that a person who has commanded an Army abroad should entertain ideas of the dignity & power of a Comr in Chief different from those which have been applied to that situation in this country,' said Palmerston, 'but it is quite certain that in this case it is Sir D. Dundas who is desirous of innovating & of entirely altering the system which has been acted upon for years as the established arrangement of office.' Opening a new line of attack, Palmerston also underlined the political dimension of his office, claiming that Dundas 'entirely overlooks the parliamentary responsibility of the Secy at War' and pointing out that not only was he a member of the government but he served as a confidential adviser to, and agent of, the King on matters military.[130]

Perceval obviously did not care for the character of the disagreement and pleaded an inability to arbitrate between the two parties. Dundas therefore turned in February 1811 to the Prince Regent, hoping that George's sympathies would be with military rather than political officers.[131] Palmerston presented the Prince with a robust and lengthy justification of his conduct, reiterating his earlier insistence that all financial matters as well as civil–military questions such as quartering, billeting and the marching of troops required 'the sanction and authority of the Secy at War'. As Palmerston stressed, this matter went beyond the ambit of a parochial difference of opinion between himself and Dundas. In his memorandum, Palmerston argued that, 'according to the principles which regulate the British constitution, power cannot be vested where there is no responsibility, or responsibility be imposed where authority does not exist'. If the Secretary at War was not permitted to discharge his duties independently, Palmerston continued, then his position became 'perfectly anomalous, & unknown to any one office in the constitution'. A civil officer could not be subject to military hierarchies if he was to remain effective from a political point of view.[132] A year after the dispute had begun with Dundas, the Duke of York, who in May 1811 had returned to the office of commander-in-chief following his ignominious resignation over a selling-of-offices scandal, took up the argument and produced a detailed rebuttal of Palmerston's carefully argued memo-randum.[133] The matter was finally resolved, or fudged, at the end of 1811 when Perceval, in consultation with Lords Eldon and Liverpool and Charles Yorke (who had been Secretary at War in 1801–3), concluded that Palmerston had been correct in his 'legal construction of the letter of the laws as they stood' and they had amended those laws in order to prevent future confusion over the sepa-ration of responsibilities. However, Palmerston was criticised for his lamentable failure to communicate openly with the commander-in-chief.[134] In future, insisted the Prince Regent, in a memorandum drafted by Perceval and officially settling the dispute, the Secretary at War and the commander-in-chief should respect the separation of financial and military discipline, but any circular orders issued by the Secretary at War to the army ought properly to be announced to the commander-in-chief beforehand.[135] A further two years later, in February 1814, Palmerston reported to Liverpool, now Prime Minister, that the differ-ences between the War Office and Horse Guards were 'drawing to a close'.[136]

If the differences were drawing to a close, however, they were not yet ended. In 1816 Palmerston complained that a proposal to place the Board of General Officers entirely under the authority of the commander-in-chief was 'so material an innovation upon the constitution' of the War Office as to make the execution of its duties 'impossible', placing as it would the Secretary at War in the invidious position of commissioning such a board while having no right to require reports from it.[137] Similar complaints recurred frequently and in 1820 Palmerston once again turned to Liverpool for support. The Duke of York felt that the Secretary at War was an unnecessary and unwelcome check on the military authorities of the army, 'and this feeling', said Palmerston, 'is perpetually breaking out in objections & discussions upon the petty details of our respective departments'. On the whole Palmerston and Major General Sir Henry Torrens, adjutant general of the forces, were able to get over such obstacles 'by personal intercourse & amicable explanations', but the more the Duke ratcheted up tensions in public, the harder it was for Palmerston to maintain cordial relations between them.[138] At the beginning of 1823 relations between the Secretary at War and the commander-in-chief had again broken down in a manner strikingly reminiscent of 1810–12 and exposing the ineffectiveness of the 1812 'solution'.

Ostensibly the dispute centred on staffing questions; in reality it was the boundaries of departmental authority that were again at issue. During the winter of 1822–23 a restructuring of the military led to the transfer of barrack and ordnance duties from the Quartermaster-General's department to the Ordnance department. Palmerston consequently issued a circular letter to all commanding officers instructing them to identify those clerks who were made redundant and to make any case as appropriate for keeping on those clerks still judged necessary to the service. The measure was in itself uncontroversial but Palmerston had, as in 1810, taken it upon himself to introduce a 'new' measure without prior communication with Horse Guards. In response the commander-in-chief drafted an instruction to those commanding officers addressed by Palmerston that they would 'not upon this occasion, nor upon any future occasion of a similar nature, (namely on questions of changes or of reductions, affecting in any shape the military departments under your command) comply with the instructions of the Secretary at War, unless conveyed to you by His Royal Highness at the request of the Secretary at War'.[139] Were this order to be formally issued (in the event the Duke's instruction was not sent), what was a commanding officer to do? Damned if he did and damned if he did not: the impracticability of dual headship of the military was exposed in a manner inconvenient and 'equally derogatory to both the Departments concerned'.[140] The Duke of York was clear that this was a response to an 'indirect attack' by the War Office on his power and authority,[141] and it was obvious that the anticipated 'war' between the departments would not be, as both parties professed to hope, 'carried on with as much courtesy as a state of contest in its nature admits'.[142] The commander-in-chief's issuing of travelling allowances, a 'matter of finance', without prior reference to the Secretary at War was served up as evidence that the bad faith cut both ways.[143] By the time the matter was put before Lord Liverpool a third head of complaint, Palmerston's refusal to appoint a Captain Ford as Paymaster of the 16th Foot Regiment, except under certain conditions (which the commander-in-chief denied that Palmerston was entitled to impose), had been added to the grounds of dispute. Yet the disagreement remained above all a territorial one. According to Palmerston:

> The principles which I understand H.R.H. to maintain in argument, & which H.R.H. has only suspended His order to execute in practice is, that when the Secy at War shall do an official act which in H.R.H.'s own opinion shall be a departure from the line of separation between the duties of the C. in C. & Secy at War, & shall in H.R.H.'s opinion trench [?] upon the province assigned to the authority of the C. in C. the proper course for the C. in C. to pursue is, not to state his objections to the Secy at War, & by remonstrance to invite explanation; not to call for the interposition of the confidential advisor of the crown that they may enforce obedience to the King's orders, if those orders have been violated, but at once to dispatch his own orders to the officers of the army, commanding them to disobey the orders which they have received or may hereafter receive in the King's name from the Secy at War.[144]

Neither side appeared willing to compromise. The Duke of York claimed that Palmerston 'wished me to acknowledge myself guilty of an unjustifiable act, and having obtained such admission, he would then agree to discuss with me whether it could or could not be justified'. Palmerston simply retorted that the Duke's claims to have discussed the questions 'amply' with him had 'not by any means' been the case. Neither side could agree whether the subject was military or financial and whether it was with or without precedent.[145] There is more than a hint of exasperation in Liverpool's ruling. Two public departments, he said, should only contradict each other overtly as a 'matter of *dernier resort*'. However, he also noted that the Duke's countermanding order had only been prepared and not actually issued. Yet Liverpool's summation was little more than an evasion: Palmerston should not, he said, have transmitted the communication without previous consultation, but the matter was indeed one of finance and account and therefore fell properly within his sphere of responsibility; Palmerston was therefore entitled to issue the order without prior consultation, unless the commander-in-chief objected to it (or unless it had come directly from the King).[146] The matter reared its head again in May 1823 when the two offices disagreed over the superintendence of paymasters, but such questions notwithstanding, they appear to have reached something approaching a working relationship by this point.[147] The differences were not merely personal, however, and the demarcation of civil and military roles remained ill-defined for some time to come.[148] More than a decade later, Palmerston was to be found encouraging ministerial attempts to 'build up' the Secretary at War's office and 'restore to it some of its antient functions and importance'. 'By adding to the powers & duties of the Secretary at War,' he wrote to Howick in 1836, 'and by rendering it necessary that he should always be a Cabinet minister you establish a more efficient check upon the Commander in Chief, and diminish to a certain degree the inconveniencies arising from that officer being separate from & practically independent of the government.'[149]

Palmerston's difficulties with the commander-in-chief were illustrative of the frustrated bureaucratic reformer he had become. The civil and military management of the army was muddled at the time when Palmerston entered the War Office. He had objected from the outset, for example, to the expensive and inefficient means employed to clothe soldiers, but as he explained in 1826, after a decade and a half in post, his fractious relations with the military establishment had frustrated even his attempts to reform such provisioning. Since the commander-in-chief was opposed to any change that would take provisioning out of the hands of military offices, whatever economies that might generate, Palmerston conceded that, 'not wishing to multiply points of difference', he had 'always abstained from pressing any alteration in the existing arrangement'.[150]

When Palmerston had first entered the War Office in 1809, he was confronted with an estimated 40,000 regimental accounts that were in arrears, some older than the new Secretary at War himself, dating back to 1783.[151] One of his first tasks, therefore, was to master the enormous backlog while simultaneously carrying on the business of the Office during wartime. Palmerston reorganised the internal structure of the Military Accounts department and recruited additional clerks as necessary in order to transact the business: past and current accounts were now managed under separate heads (arrears to 1798, from 1798 to 1803 and from 1804 to 1810 in three divisions, while current and outstanding accounts were supervised by another). Clearing the arrears was no easy task – though he received the support of commissaries-in-chief such as J.C. Herries in this[152] – and it is testament to the application to the task on the part of the clerks and of Palmerston that this work was actually completed by 1826.[153] As Palmerston himself had observed in 1822, 'in no office is the public business more efficiently discharged than in my own, and with no set of men work harder than the clerks connected with it. I will state one proof, and a melancholy proof of this fact; namely that since the year 1810, no fewer than twenty-six clerks, all of them in the prime of life, have died of pulmonary and other complaints, arising from sedentary habits.'[154]

During the war years military expenditure was relatively uncontroversial. Palmerston was first called upon to present the estimates in Parliament in February 1810 and if it was a dry subject that did not lend itself to high-flown rhetoric, nonetheless his performance was generally thought to have been conscientious and thorough. Malmesbury, who feared the Perceval government was too weak to thrive ('it is brandy against milk – gunpowder against flour,' he said) believed his protégé had done enough to safeguard his own political survival. 'I hear from so many correspondents of all colours & all descriptions that you acquitted yourself in the most masterly manner,' he wrote shortly afterwards, 'you have insur'd your political consequence throughout *life* & as the period of your existence in this globe will be a very eventful and very important one, the being of consequence is every thing. It is better to resist the torrent as a good swimmer than to be carried down it like a logg [*sic*].'[155] Malmesbury's wife, though no less certain of Palmerston's accomplishment, shared the reservations of others that, though he might have secured his longevity, his eminence was less certain. 'Harry spoke extremely well on the Army Estimates,' she noted in her journal. 'On such subjects where clearness & perspicacity are the requisites & time is given for preparation, he will always succeed, but where *opinions* are to be given & *effect to be produced* by *spontaneous* eloquence I doubt it. He is *reserved* & so *singularly* so for a young man, so afraid of *committing himself* even in common life & conversation with his most intimate friends, that it will throw a *coldness* & want of effect on such speeches of his. Il ne se levera jamais *afin* to carry people's feelings along with him.'[156] This did not signify much at constituency level, however, at least not at the University of Cambridge, and Palmerston's seat was, for the moment, even strengthened (if only by dint of donnish apathy) by ' "the ability displayed by Lord Palmerston in the administration of the country," ' and at the election of 1811 the contest 'excited comparatively little interest beyond the walls of Palmerston's own College'.[157]

Once peace had been established in late 1815, Palmerston's ability to carry measures for the financing of a large standing army became more taxing. In the first post-war estimates, presented in February 1816, Palmerston sought to exploit a lingering patriotic sentiment in arguing for the maintenance of military forces that could effectively guarantee Britain's defence. 'I am firmly persuaded that among nations, weakness will never be a foundation for security,' he told the Commons.[158] He rejected suggestions that a peacetime military establishment represented a threat to the internal stability of the country: the liberal traditions of England stood as an effective safeguard against military despotism. 'Before the civil constitution of any country can be overturned by a standing army, the people of that country must be lamentably degenerate; they must be debased and enervated by all the worst excesses of an arbitrary and despotic government; their martial spirit must be extinguished; they must be brought to a state of political degradation, I may almost say of political emasculation, such as few countries experience that have once known the blessings of liberty.' After all, the leaders of that army were all, by virtue of property and general interests, committed to the welfare and 'civil prosperity' of the country.[159] It was a false economy, he said, to maintain only a small peacetime establishment, and previous 'financial embarrassments' were attributable to the failure to sustain a viable military force that could be called upon when needed.[160]

After the war there was mounting pressure for retrenchment and economy, both within and outside government.[161] By 1821, for example, it had become a source of concern that six years after the conclusion of peace, the size of the army continued to increase year on year – the rank and file could safely be reduced by at least 13,000 men simply by suspending recruitment of new soldiers, suggested one *Times* reader – and with an estimated establishment of regular and irregular soldiers numbering almost 200,000 *The Times* was inclined to agree.[162] 'Indeed,' observed the 'Thunderer', 'if any independent man had been previously of opinion that the estimates were proper and reasonable, he would surely begin to suspect the justness of that opinion, when he discovered that they could only be carried by a phalanx of placemen.'[163] A large army in peacetime, insisted *The Times* was a threat to liberty, and at £10 million a year, an exorbitant levy 'on so impoverished a people'.[164] Palmerston, pupil of Dugald Stewart that he was, shared the desire to reduce the financial burden of the military departments and by 1826 he had lost his erstwhile enthusiasm for peacetime standing armies completely, although he couched his argument in the language of economics rather than political philosophy. It was 'absurd', 'ill-judged' and 'inconvenient' to maintain a large peacetime establishment, he said: 'It is not only bad economy as regards the public treasure, but it answers no purpose of political strength and security; and, in a military sense, for the preservation and maintenance of an effective service and sound discipline, it is notoriously defective. I am no advocate for large military establishments in time of peace.'[165]

It was not just the ranks of the army that were to succumb to this economising zeal. Palmerston, noted *The Times* in December 1821, was one of the 'most strenuous supporters' of Treasury plans for retrenchment in subordinate offices of public departments and appeared, 'notwithstanding the general hostility manifested to the measure, in no way to relax in his exertions to carry the system into operation throughout the offices under his immediate control'.[166] In fact a month earlier Palmerston had proposed significant savings that could be made in his department: by the abolition of ten posts paid at between £300 and £1,200 each per annum, he anticipated a total saving of £6,800. He did, however, argue for a more numerous staff in order to cope with the volume of business (almost 100,000 more circulars were sent in 1820 than in 1797, for example),[167] albeit one with fewer high-paid posts. While the business of the Office had 'very greatly increased' since 1797, the numbers working there had 'not been augmented by any means or in the same proportion'. Not only was the Office having to deal with accounts in arrears (and doing so with ever greater efficiency) but, as a sign of the times, 'the progressive diffusion of education among the lower classes enables a much greater number of persons to address to the War Office written commns upon points & claims interesting to the individuals & fully intitled to the attention of the military departs, but upon which at former periods the parties would probably not have had the means, or would not have thought it worth while to make a written application, & this source of corre-spondce is still extremely abundant'.[168] Reflecting on his enthusiasm for the work of this Treasury 'self denying committee', some time later Palmerston began to regret his having 'laid about me with a vigorous & unsparing pruning knife' when it transpired that heads of other small departments had been 'less stoical' and the reductions, which had been adopted in 1822, placed the War Office at a comparative disadvantage. Among the clerks at the Office this had been the 'subject of dissatisfaction & remonstrance', but although Palmerston was deaf to their complaints, he was sensible of their grievances and in the summer of 1826 admitted that he 'should not be doing justice to them; nor should I be making due provision for the dispatch of the public business, if I omitted now to recom-mend to you some little modification of my establishment'. Since the financial and accounting responsibilities of Irish regiments were now more fully within the purview of the War Office, along with enlarged responsibilities occasioned by changes in the local militia and army reorganisation, Palmerston argued for modest increases in the staff of the Office to bring it into line, proportionately, with other comparable departments such as the Admiralty, the Navy Office, the Navy Pay Office, and the Victualling Office. This would achieve two things: it would make the work of the Office more efficient; and it would provide fair prospects of promotion and advance for deserving clerks.[169]

Over the course of his tenure of the office, however, Palmerston successfully reduced the overall cost of his department from a high of £72,412 in 1814 (the last full year of war) to £57,938 in 1827 (though there remained extra economies to be made and further abuses to arrest).[170] Yet, although he had sought to protect salaries (except in the cases of plural office holders whom he went after with a vengeance) and increase meritocratic promotion, Palmerston was, within the War Office, an unpopular Secretary. It was said, at least by Harriet Arbuthnot, that when he left the Office in May 1828 the clerks would have liked to burn candles in the windows to celebrate the departure of a 'detested' master, although such claims are perhaps exaggerated.[171] Nonetheless, he had acquired a well-merited reputation for pedantry and abrasiveness. The Office, wrote one former clerk, 'was not itself exempt at times from little wars within its own walls', and Palmerston was reported on one occasion to have locked the Chief Examiner of Accounts, Edward Marshall, in his office, without lunch, to prevent his being 'interrupted' while preparing an urgent dispatch. Marshall, for his part, was incensed at being treated like a 'schoolboy'.[172] Many letters and memoranda were returned by Palmerston to be rewritten because of a lack of clarity in the handwriting of a clerk or orthographic errors, while in Parliament Bourne later perceived the strain to be showing in Palmerston's 'petulant and apparently disdainful treatment of Hume' in debates over the estimates in 1821.[173] Ridley suggested that by 1820 a decade at the War Office had made 'Lord Pumicestone', 'disliked because of his high-handed behaviour, his quarrelsomeness, and his lack of consideration for others'.[174] Even his official biographer was obliged to concede that in debate Palmerston could be 'flippant and overbearing'.[175]

Two senior members of the War Office staff, Michael Foveaux and William Merry, felt particularly aggrieved by Palmerston's management of the Office. Foveaux, as Senior Superintendent, resented what he perceived to be the under-mining of his position as reform of the Office diluted his personal authority over the accounts. When he was finally pensioned off in 1821 the full extent of his bitterness was revealed. Foveaux insisted that he had finally been pushed into retirement to make way for the less experienced Laurence Sulivan whom Palmerston had appointed in 1811, Foveaux said, purely on the grounds of their personal connection as friends and, from December 1811, as brothers-in-law. Foveaux pointed to the recent history of retrenchment in the Office during which time Palmerston had consistently ensured that there was a place for Sulivan. A bitter correspondence of claim and counter-claim between Palmerston and Foveaux and his wife followed, during which Foveaux also gave vent to his resentment of colleagues in a series of disparaging remarks, but what-ever merits the attack on Sulivan's appointment may have had, it became rather lost in a bitter wrangle over Foveaux's departure.[176] It is certainly plausible, there-fore, that Foveaux was the 'blackguard' (as Palmerston put it) who had encour-aged the *Morning Chronicle* in 1817 to criticise Sulivan's initial appointment.[177]

Sulivan's rapid advancement within the Office and Foveaux's opposition to it captured the tensions at the heart of Palmerston's establishment: just as he sought to modernise the Office and introduce some measure of nineteenth-century effi-ciency through a spread of meritocracy, here was a shining example of eigh-teenth-century nepotistic patronage suggesting that little had in fact changed. Palmerston had, indeed, promised to share the bounty of his appointment to the War Office with his friend Sulivan as soon as he had arrived there in the autumn of 1809. The Secretary at War was entitled to appoint a private secretary as confi-dential adviser and assistant and Palmerston urged Sulivan to 'come and at least *try it*' and not to worry about the feelings of clerks towards a new person unfamiliar with the business of the Office.[178] Sulivan served as Palmerston's private secretary until January 1811, at which point he was formally appointed to the Office itself, when he took up a vacant position as Superintendent of Military Accounts. Under Palmerston's tenure, Sulivan subsequently went on to become Chief Examiner in 1824 and Deputy Secretary in 1826. Kenneth Bourne has pointed out that Sulivan 'must have been reasonably competent', if only on the grounds that his career survived Palmerston's departure in May 1828 and lasted, under twelve different ministers, until 1851, while Hardinge, who succeeded Palmerston as Secretary commented on Sulivan's 'very able superintendence' when he himself retired in 1830.[179] Yet the suspicion remained among the staff of the Office that Palmerston was not above favouritism.

Sulivan's elevation to replace the retiring William Merry as Deputy Secretary in 1826 elicited just the same suspicions as Foveaux had expressed a few years earlier. *The Times*, ever vigilant in its monitoring of government retrenchment, had picked up on the suggestion that Merry was pushed out of the Office and published a number of articles furnishing 'topics of suspicion against the integrity' of Palmerston.[180] Palmerston grew increasingly weary of these attacks, and in early 1828 prevailed upon Merry to correct the falsehoods. Although his 'general principle is to treat newspaper attacks with silent contempt', Palmerston was unwilling to ignore 'a false statement when it relates to a simple fact'. As he insisted, he had never '*forced*' retirement on Merry, but rather had proposed it to the Treasury on the dual grounds that it 'would be a well deserved reward for your long & meritorious services' which also 'would enable me to make an arrangement . . . wh wd be conducive to the efficiency of my Office & advantageous to the public service' in promoting Sulivan. Thus did Palmerston 'suggest' for Merry's 'consideration whether it is not due both to me & to yourself that . . . you should call upon the editor of the Times in your own name to contradict a statement which you know to be untrue'.[181] A letter from Merry duly appeared in *The Times* on 17 March in which he pointed out that the resignation from the Office had been his own decision, without any coercion from Palmerston to make room for Sulivan.[182] As Bourne observed, the 'grievances of clerks are boundless',[183] yet it was not only the illiberal exercise of patronage within the Office of which Palmerston was accused. Only Lieutenant David Davies took his complaints so far as an attempted assassination, however.

Davies was a half-pay lieutenant of the 62nd Regiment of Foot and had returned from duty in Canada shortly after the conclusion of the war in Europe. The next few years were evidently not easy ones for Davies. Some time during 1816 he had been confined in York Hospital 'in a state of mental derangement' and there, as Palmerston later noted, 'in a fit of delirium he cut off his penis'. The story had come to Palmerston's attention and he had written to Davies's friends, who duly took him into their care in south Wales. From Wales Davies 'made his escape or was liberated' and journeyed to London where he began a fruitless campaign to persuade Palmerston to award him a military pension on account of his self-inflicted injury. Palmerston of course could not make this the grounds of a military pension, but he had resolved, he said, to make some augmentation of Davies's half-pay.[184] Life had evidently become increasingly difficult for Davies. In March and April 1818 he twice applied, unsuccessfully, for a personal interview with Palmerston and on 8 April he was due in court to face charges of assault having clubbed with a poker a man who had accused him of making improper passes at the man's daughter. Davies did not keep his court appointment. Instead he went to Chelsea, redeemed a pair of pistols which he had earlier pawned, and proceeded to the War Office where he secreted himself in a dark staircase to wait for Palmerston. Returning to the Office at lunchtime, Palmerston, as was his custom, raced for the staircase, past Davies who was hidden against the bottom steps. Davies fired at Palmerston and hit him in the back, causing the Secretary at War to let out a heavy groan which alerted

William Owen, a messenger in the Office, who was close by and who appre-hended Davies. Dropping his gun, Davies exclaimed: 'You know me, and you know my wrongs; I have killed him.'[185]

Palmerston meanwhile continued to his own room where, realising he was injured, he directed that a surgeon be sent for. Paston Astley Cooper arrived within a quarter of an hour of the assault and, according to contemporary reports, found Palmerston writing a letter at his desk. The latter invited Cooper to take a chair while he finished his letter, whereupon he turned to Cooper and said, 'Now, sir, you shall examine.'[186] As Palmerston reported to his brother, the escape had been a lucky one: 'The muzzle of the pistol must have been almost touching my back as it burnt my coat to a great extent. The bullet penetrated my waistcoat, braces & shirt & grazed the skin of my back making a violent contusion just close to the back bone. A quarter of an inch would have made the whole difference.' Palmerston attributed his good fortune to 'the habit of ascending & descending stairs with rapidity' but it was still, he felt, 'a most narrow & providential escape.'[187] He took a wry comfort in joining such 'illustrious company' as the Duke of Wellington and the Prince Regent in having survived an assassination attempt, claiming an advantage over the Prince in that 'my bullet *has* been found, though luckily *not in me*.'[188] After two days spent 'confined at home' Palmerston resumed his normal duties and pastimes with no apparent after-effects.[189] He well knew that Davies was a 'reasoning madman' subject to 'occasional attacks of absolute insanity',[190] but he displayed a marked sympathy for Davies and in May 1818 sent £20 to the Chaplain of Newgate to 'defray the expense of Davis's defence [as] he would otherwise have had no counsel as he had no means of his own to procure any'. At the end of the trial Davies was found guilty and, on the grounds of insanity, committed to 'Bedlam for life'.[191] Three years later Davies wrote to Palmerston from Bethlehem Hospital to express his 'admiration for the truly dignified, and magnanimous generosity I experienced at your hands, after mine had been so sacrilegiously raised for your destruction', and imploring Palmerston to 'afford me an opportunity to make some reparation for the parricidal outrage I have unfortunately been tempted to commit in an unhappy moment' by awarding him a full-pay pension. Palmerston's magnanimity did not stretch quite this far; he endorsed the letter: 'Lieut Davies who shot at me asking to be set out & put on full pay!!!'[192]

Davies's claim for support might have been fantastical but Palmerston was not unmoved by the hardships of servicemen. Clerks in the War Office might have complained of his cutbacks and abuse of patronage, but in questions of military discipline and pensions, he revealed a more humane side. As soon as war was over in 1815 he had lobbied successfully for an increase in the mili-tary pensions paid to the veterans of Waterloo.[193] At the same time he pressed for improved medical care for soldiers. There were sound economic grounds for providing better treatment, as Palmerston argued, but there was also a hint of moral responsibility in his injunctions to Colonel Torrens, for example, regarding the treatment of ophthalmia.[194]

Palmerston felt that the army suffered at the hands of a society disposed to regard military service as a hardship to be endured, or inflicted, on the less fortunate and he supported moves to prevent military service being passed as a criminal sentence.[195] A similar spirit influenced his efforts to ameliorate the conditions of serving soldiers. His attempts to reduce the use of flogging in court-martial punishments (influenced perhaps by the campaigns against such punishments led by Henry Grey Bennet and Sir Francis Burdett) in the army met with comparatively little success, but they underline a desire to moderate excess brutality.[196]

In general, the relatively gentle pastures of the War Office suited the self-indulgent temperament of man-about-town Harry Temple, for whom a nightlife of soirées, clubs, parties and balls was the reward for days spent in public service in government and the costs of which could, to a large extent, be set against the anticipated revenues from his 'improved' estates in Ireland. Lady Lyttelton had expressed a hope on Palmerston's initial appointment to the War Office that 'it may divert his Lordship from flirting, in the same way people rejoiced at his predecessor's appointment because it was to cure him from gambling'.[197] It was to prove a disappointed hope.

CHAPTER 4

THE MAKING OF PALMERSTON I:
LORD CUPID, IRISH LANDLORD

His light and jaunty manner did him great disservice in his earlier years; and I recollect perfectly well that, on our first acquaintance, I could see nothing in him of the statesman, but a good deal of the dandy.
Lord Shaftesbury to Evelyn Ashley, 6 January 1876[1]

ON 28 MAY 1829, Palmerston enjoyed a '*fine day*' with '*La K*' which included a visit to a 'Spanish bazaar' and, later on, it may be assumed, much more besides. 'K', however, was not Palmerston's only, or most frequent, lover that year. Inside the back cover of his diary for 1829, Palmerston noted the number and frequency of his liaisons:

E.   40 to 26 Aug
K.   1 to 28 May[2]

'E', or Emily Cowper, had been Palmerston's mistress for some time by this point. So had, at different times, 'K', 'Whalley', a 'Mrs Brown' and potentially many other unidentified women (there are a number of allusions to '—'). Palmerston recorded his conquests in surprising detail, barely troubling about subtleties or discretion. It was Kenneth Bourne who first pointed out that the meteorological references in Palmerston's diaries had nothing to do with the weather, but so far as his journals were encoded, they are not difficult to decipher, despite a partial smattering of idiosyncratic Italian phrases. To look at two early years for which Palmerston's diary survives, several entries in the 1818 diary, for example, record a '*Fine day*', or '*Fine evening*' while Sunday 16 July was a '*Fine day (*)*'. There were a number of 'failed mornings' too.[3] In 1819 he was a little more expansive. The year began with a '*Fine night*' 'in the garden' until 2a.m. and a 'fine' morning at half-past five, but that was followed two days later on 3 January by a 'failed' night, even though he had 'waited from 2 to 5 in morning'. Mid-February brought more fine mornings and a couple of '*fine nights*' on the 16th and 18th. There were numerous other fine nights and several records of a 'visit in morning', or 'at 3' or 'at 5', but the 'garden' continued to be a scene of failure as well as success. Thursday 4 March 1819, however, was a '*Fine night (2) restato. From 1 to 5*'. September 1819 was a relatively prolific month with '*sera' entered for the 13th, 14th, 16th, 18th, 21st, 22nd and 25th. In October and November he again saw '* *La Whaley*', perhaps in part because 'E not well pains cd not venture to see. Bella.'[4]

Early biographers drew a discreet veil over these affairs (assuming they were aware of them) but Palmerston was just as much, and just as importantly, 'Lord Cupid' as he was 'Lord Pumicestone' and a sense of his *vie amoureuse* goes some (though of course not all) of the way to an understanding of both his financial difficulties in early life and his widespread popular, plebeian appeal in later years. Susceptible to blackmail by former lovers and illegitimate offspring and loathed by some (notably Victoria and Albert) as a sexual pred-ator, Palmerston's known womanising, whatever else it did, also endeared him to a certain section of the wider population.[5]

Jasper Ridley, in his chapter on 'Lord Cupid', almost lamented that 'Palmerston and his contemporaries conducted their affairs discreetly, and care-fully burned any love letters which they found; if any still exist, they are prob-ably hidden among the archives of those families which today . . . hide their family secrets and scandals from the eyes of prying historians.'[6] He confined himself to speculative asides about a possible liaison with Princess Lieven, wife of the Russian ambassador and known mistress of many European statesmen of the time, and the more familiar attachments to Emily Cowper and Lady Jersey, both also known to have had many lovers.[7] Yet, through Palmerston's diary, his account books and miscellaneous correspondence it is possible to discover a little more about Cupid's life. Bourne re-created in laborious detail an elaborate virtual genealogical tree which linked, one way or another, a good number of the branches of society through a series of clandestine and open relationships, flirtations and affairs.[8] Palmerston certainly played his part in this very Regency prelude to apparent Victorian stuffiness, but it is clear that he was neither unique (though he may have been more energetic than others) nor that such behaviour was confined to the excesses of the pre-Victorian period. Palmerston did not want for admirers at the time and he evidently felt no need to hurry a decision about marriage. In 1825, for example, he was courted by, or courting, at least three women: Lady Georgina Fane and Lady Jersey both flirted with him with a view to a possible union; Lady Georgina, according to Harriet Arbuthnot, had come to regret turning Palmerston down a couple of years earlier, particularly now that Lady Jersey was doing 'every thing she can to get him away'. Palmerston, for his part, preferred to pursue Emily Cowper.[9]

Palmerston's affairs are important not just for a sense of the libidinous para-mour that he evidently was. There is, of course, a superficial tension in the pre-eminence of this louche adventurer at the forefront of apparently strait-laced Victorian society; yet he was, perhaps, not so very much out of line with the standards of a good number of his contemporaries, the Queen and Prince excepted. Culturally, Palmerston's jaunty bonhomie and perceived man-of-the-people accessibility were not undermined by such associations. Politically, his links with the leading patronesses of the age were crucial to his making good his early promise and turning that into actual eminence. And economically his liking for a good time not only affected his financial affairs, but made all the more urgent his development as an effective landlord, reliant as he was on income from Hampshire, and later Wales, and especially Ireland, for his precarious state of solvency.

Palmerston had inherited from his father an extensive though heavily indebted estate. From his landed property Palmerston estimated that he would receive an annual income of almost £8,000, made up of rents from Ireland, Hampshire, Yorkshire and London. In 1805 he calculated his position as follows:[10]

Feb. 20 1805

Landed Property

	Gross Rents	Net Rev.
Dublin County	4589	3302
Sligo	3222	2800
Broadlands (lands let to Bourne round the House nt. included)	1615	——
Sheen {House included}	450	350
Yorkshire Estate	450	400
House in Hanover Square To be let furnished	650*	550
Timber, annual average (about)	300	300
Gross Total.	11,276 Net Total	7702

The property tax as calculated after the addition in Feby 1805 is deducted in this statement

* Let for 900 which deducting Taxes leaves about 750 net.

	Net Income
From Land	7902.0.0

Yet if income tells only half of the accountant's story, particular attention should be paid to Palmerston's debts and liabilities. When his father's executors wound up the second Viscount's estate in 1811 (once Elizabeth had come of age) they estimated that Palmerston faced a 'probable deficiency' of £28,000, his father's extensive stock holding of a little over £43,000 notwithstanding. Palmerston's own stock holdings of around £18,000 were inadequate to cover the shortfall. He was fortunate, however, that each of his three siblings who were entitled to a legacy of £20,000 a piece from their father's estate, instead mortgaged more than half of that capital (£10,200) back to Palmerston, thereby alleviating one of his heavier obligations.[11] Yet even this arrangement, though it allowed mortgages on the Broadlands estate to be paid off, in turn further encumbered the Irish estates – which already, as Palmerston's own 1805 estimate showed, provided the greater part of his income – with a debt of a further £30,000 accumulating interest, at 5 per cent, amounting to £1,500 per annum.[12]

Palmerston's own accounts are incomplete, though a reasonably extensive run of material exists, largely in Palmerston's own hand, for the years between *c*. 1815 and the early 1830s, and though Palmerston's occasionally erratic arithmetic did not always help, there is, throughout the years into his middle age a recurrent concern, if not obsession, with the precarious condition of his personal finances.[13] If contemporaries and historians have wondered why, for example, he spent so many years in the humble office of Secretary at War, they might have found a partial answer in his various scribbled estimates and calculations in which the salary he received from the War Office was a vital subvention and worries that it might cease stimulated attempts to make further economies in household expenditure. Quarterly payments for annuities to his sisters Elizabeth and Fanny and his brother William of £127 1s. each and further payments to Emma Godfrey of £75 and £50 each to Gaetano Ravizzotti's widow,[14] and Mrs Murray Mills, when set against his quarterly War Office salary of £620, left a surplus of only a little over £62 (per quarter). This was in itself hardly enough to cover his other expenses. Between 1815 and 1828 his other main sources of income, based as they were on land revenues, fluctuated wildly, and his disposable income per year varied from a high of almost £10,000 to a low barely one fifth of that figure:[15]

Gross Income (in £s) including War Office Salary

Year	Income	Fixed payments	Disposable
1815	10,569		
1816	11,530		
1817	11,632		
1818	11,381		
1819	14,244	4,614	9,630
1820	8,382	4,808	3,574
1821	12,539	5,142	7,397
1822	9,925	5,672	4,253
1823	9,106	7,278	1,828
1824	12,106	4,664	7,341
1825	11,822	6,248	5,573
1826	8,375	5,442	2,933
1827	8,885	3,888	4,997
1828	8,702	5,279	3,423

Against this, Palmerston's own analyses of expenditure for each year between 1818 and 1830 revealed that the costs of maintaining his households, lifestyle, family, mistresses and other dependants amounted to around £7,000 to £11,000 per annum. The most expensive single year for which Palmerston's records survive, 1828, cost him an estimated £10,813, in expenditure on servants (£1,501 2s. 7d.); horses (£1,538 18s. 11d.); rent and taxes (£370 13s. 2d.), household expenses (£972 1s. 9d.); pocket money and travel (£500); subscriptions and gifts (£249 2s.); general bills (£243 0s. 7d.); books and subscriptions to clubs (£389 17s.); interest payments on debts (£2,817 9s.) and 'miscellaneous' expenses (£2,231 3s.). Palmerston's records were occasionally vague, but while he might have carefully elided payments under broad general categories, it is clear from his own more detailed breakdowns that he stinted neither himself nor his mistresses in these lean years. At no time (except in 1826 when he paid subs to only three) did he subscribe to fewer than four clubs in any one year and often five (a permutation of the Alfred, Arthur's, the Athenaeum, the Travellers, University, White's, and Watier's). A number of women appear as recipients of payments, including Mrs Fletcher, E[mily Cowper], Miss C., Ms M[ills]., Mrs Graham, Mrs Roe, Whaley, Miss C. Yatman, Mrs Brown and in 1829 almost £94 was paid for 'Nicholas Schooling'. Though these sums varied enormously, from the £827 paid to Whaley in 1819 to a more modest £3 to Mrs Graham in 1818, the majority of the payments ran to three figures and are indicative of ongoing responsibilities to lovers and former lovers. It is perhaps not surprising that many invoices were not paid. An abstract of such bills for the early 1820s suggests that £6,781 in bills for the years 1820–23 remained unsettled.

While he remained at the War Office, Palmerston could just about keep his head above water, but in the early 1820s he calculated that if he lost that post, and the annual salary of £2,480 that went with it, he would be faced with a need to make about £1,500 in savings and in his own rough calculations he could only find a potential £1,400 of that amount. By 1824 the 'State of Affairs' looked tight. Palmerston estimated his expenditure for that year at £7,080 but his total disposable income at only £6,934.

It was at about this time, therefore, that Palmerston increased his speculative investments, though with mixed results. In 1825 he bought into the Welsh Slate Company yet it would be twenty-two years before he saw any profit from that investment and even though dividends began to be paid in the later 1840s, the history of the stock during Palmerston's life was one of 'frequent falls'.[16] Only in the 1850s and 1860s does this investment appear to have made a meaningful contribution to Palmerston's funds.[17]

At the same time as he first bought into the Welsh Slate Company, in the mid-1820s, Palmerston became embroiled in the scandal surrounding the corrupt and fraudulent dealings of the Cornwall and Devon Mining Company. John Wilks, MP for Sudbury, had led a delegation of six speculators in April 1825 to Cornwall to inspect mines there in which they subsequently invested. However, there was a discrepancy of £41,000 between the sum charged to the Company by Wilks for the purchase of the mines and the £79,500 he had actually paid out for them. On the launch of the Company's shares in mid-April Wilks further increased his profiteering by dishonest dealing in shares – that were not, it was alleged, yet his to sell – the price of which had been artificially increased by making sure that demand significantly outstripped supply. The matter came to light in the summer of 1826, at which point Palmerston, who had invested along with Laurence Sulivan, declared himself 'astonished' by the revelations and it was generally accepted at public meetings of shareholders that Palmerston was 'wholly blameless' by virtue of being 'wholly ignorant' of the ways in which his name had been used to reassure other investors. However, there remained a lingering suspicion that Palmerston's connection with the Company had been used to add a lustre of credibility to the venture of which he ought not to have been unaware and many investors felt 'deceived' by him. Although later reports were misleading, suggestions that Palmerston had subsequently tried to exclude the press from scrutiny of the fraud hardly absolved him from the mistrust of the shareholders. He was at least to be censured, they claimed, along with other company directors, for exhibiting a 'want of due caution and circumspection' and it was a source of disappointment to many that Palmerston had not more actively sought to prevent or mitigate the effects of the corruption. When the affair reached the House of Commons in the spring of 1827 Palmerston affected indifference to the matter, but there is evidence that he had entertained misgivings about Wilks and other individuals connected with the Company such as a Peter Moore before the matter broke into the open, and the affair cost him at least £800 in reparations.[18] It was a salutary lesson in the midst of the industrial revolution that though there was certainly muck, there was not always brass to be found there.

Throughout the 1830s, however, Palmerston's records suggest an improvement in his fortunes and he recorded an annual 'excess of income over expenditure', for his English estates at least, of between £1,164 and £2,851 per annum.[19] Significantly, though, it was to his Irish estates, which already contributed about £8,000 of his gross fixed annual income (out of a total of £12,630) in 1830, that he looked for further revenue. Short-term gains were to be had from selling off property in Hampshire and Yorkshire, but sustainable increases in receipts were to be found, he judged, particularly in estate 'improvements and termination of leases' in Sligo and Dublin.[20] Indeed, by 1830, Palmerston was even forecasting an annual 'excess of income' of £44 with an optimistic assessment of a further £200–£300 to be saved by the reduction of certain variable expenses.[21]

Despite, or perhaps because of, the comparatively modest income he received from his Hampshire estates, Palmerston did not undertake any major works around Broadlands until the mid-1850s, preferring instead to repair rather than to replace.[22] It had been mooted, briefly, in 1803 that Broadlands might be sold in order to pay off the Palmerstons' debts but the idea was soon scrapped (largely it seems by Lady Palmerston's desire),[23] and so with the estate Palmerston became a Hampshire landlord and thus, by definition, a figure of some local importance. The county assumed an important role in both his social and political life. He certainly appears to have played the part of local squire with aplomb: he was said to provide very fine roast beef and plum pudding dinners to his farm workers every year and generally is usually reported to have taken a sincere interest in the welfare of his tenants and servants; he encouraged agricultural excellence among the labourers on his farms while in Romsey itself he seems to have made regular financial donations to the people of the town;[24] he paid for various improvements such as a local school for poor children and improvements to the Abbey at Romsey; and acted as patron of a variety of local charities and societies.[25] It was also in Hampshire that Palmerston could indulge his interest in the turf. This was undertaken more for pleasure than profit, but as he reported on one occasion, in 1826, to his brother, his eye for a racehorse was a good one:

> I have started most prosperously with my racing concerns. I have 4 horses this year Luzborough, Grey Leg, and a mare new 4 yr old which I got last year & call Conquest, as she is by Waterloo out of a mare by Rubens and my fourth is a 3 yr colt I call Foxbury bred by myself got by Whalebone out of Mignonet the large Sorcerer mare which you must remember & which I bred also & have had some time. Last year my horses were ill a great part of the season & though I won several races I had to pay forfeits for many which were the best worth winning because my horses were ill & could not start.
>
> I ran for the first time this year the other day at Bath, Luzborough won the Bath Stakes, a very good stake, beating several good horses. Conquest won a race also, worth 110£ beating likewise some tolerable nags, & Foxbury won one race, & lost a second only because he swerved from the course the boy probably not knowing just how to manage him. I thus won three out of four. Foxbury is to run today at Wells & I think may win, & Luzborough is to run at Cheltenham next week for a race which will be worth 700£ probably & is favourite for it among the betters, his most formidable rival being Shakespear who was second for the Derby, but with respect to whom, age considered, Luzborough has the advantage. I shall let you know how I go on, but I hope to make a brilliant campaign of it.[26]

Palmerston had employed local trainer John Day to look after his racing stock since about 1817. Day was a well-known and respected trainer and counted a number of peers and politicians among his clients. When in residence at Broadlands Palmerston would 'ride over to Danebury [Day's stables nearby] to see his horses, mounted on a thoroughbred hack, and his groom on another; and starting from his own front-door, gallop all the way until he reached his destination. Indeed, on arriving at Danebury he would go round the yard once or twice, gradually reducing the pace, until he could pull up.' He would race across the Hampshire countryside with his dress coat unbuttoned and 'flying open, [so that it] gave him a strange appearance in riding so fast'. Not bothering to 'partake of any repast' and not entering the Days' house when he reached Danebury, Palmerston would simply discuss matters equine with John Day before heading back to his estate 'just as fast as he came'. Riding so 'furiously', Palmerston insisted, was 'capital exercise'. It was probably interest rather than a desire to interfere that animated Palmerston: he left all management decisions in Day's hands, charging him to 'Run them where you like and when you think best. Only let me know when they are worth backing, or that you have backed them for me.' He rarely troubled to watch a horse actually being put through its paces in training and only occasionally watched them race, usually when he could tie this in with a constituency visit to Tiverton or at local meetings within striking distance of Broadlands. Palmerston's horses included 'several good ones' and in addition to those of which he wrote to his brother in 1826, he owned other notable rides, including: Enchantress, Ranvilles, Biondetta, Black and All Black, Toothill, Zeila, Romsey, Dactyl, Buckthorn and Iliona. It was Iliona that brought Palmerston most success and fame at the racecourse, though John Day's son, William, who had experience as a jockey, thought Buckthorn probably a better quality horse and, as Palmerston later admitted, Iliona, though she was a good prospect for profit-making – in 1841 'she won me about 1700£ in one stake at Newmarket' which even after Day's fees represented a healthy return – was not the best horse of the day.[27] As in so many other matters, however, Palmerston trusted his own judgement before that of others. As William Day remembered:

> In these days, Lord Palmerston was in the habit, when in town, of going every Sunday afternoon to 'the Corner' to see the horses that were up for sale the next day. Here it was he caught sight of a filly by *Priam* out of *Gallopade*'s dam, and bought her for 'a song'. He sent her to my father, saying, 'I hope you will like the little filly when you have seen her' – not knowing that she was one of Lord George Bentinck's cast-offs, to which *Crucifix* as a yearling could give over two stone, and no doubt could have done so afterwards – a filly, in fact, that was not thought to be good enough to win a large stake. And this was *Iliona*, who proved herself able to win for his lordship the Cesarewitch, besides other good races. Truly a proof that 'ignorance is' sometimes 'bliss'; for had the facts been known, it is certain she would not have been bought.

When Iliona won the Cesarewitch it was thought the prize money was as welcome to Palmerston as the glory.[28]

With influence and standing in the county, of course, came also the tribulations of being a landlord and the following dated 1834 was no doubt a typical report from Hampshire:

I was a week at Broadlands, entirely by myself, working all day, and almost every day, at F.O. boxes, and Holmes' accounts for the last three years [Henry Holmes a local lawyer and Palmerston's agent in Romsey], which I had not been able to look at; they were all right, however. I must part with Thresher, who spends his nights at the alehouse, in order that the poachers may spend theirs in my covers. Conceive five guns killing sixteen pheasants in Yew Tree, and beating the whole wood thoroughly![29]

Palmerston's early life in Hampshire furnishes many examples to support the impression that he was essentially a conservative figure, or as John Vincent judged of later years, whatever his foreign policy might have suggested, Palmerston's parliamentary and political methods were at least based on 'class fear at home'.[30] While a debatable view, it does seem, to some extent, to hold for the pre-Victorian Palmerston-in-Hampshire. If not driven by 'class fear' per se, then Palmerston was at least committed to upholding traditional interests and the preservation of the status quo. Thus, following the 'massacre of Peterloo' in 1819, Palmerston's signature (along with Wellington's and those of other Hampshire landlords) was appended to the counter-requisition sent to the High Sheriff of Hampshire seeking to prohibit Radical meetings in the county designed to criticise government suppression of the demonstration in Manchester. When called to account about this and government measures designed to restrict any further public meetings and protest, Palmerston made clear his determination to bolster the existing social order and limit the actions of those who were 'endeavouring to overthrow our institutions'.[31] Indeed, it was at just about this time, according to Kenneth Bourne, that Palmerston may well have been associated with attempts to establish a Tory-leaning newspaper, the *Hampshire Advertiser*, to further consolidate what he described as 'patriotic' interests in the county.[32]

It should perhaps come as no surprise that there was little sympathy for a local poacher, Charles Smith, caught hunting hares in Palmerston's woods in 1821. Smith and an accomplice were disturbed in the woods by one of Palmerston's assistant gamekeepers and on being cornered, Smith shot the gamekeeper and effected an escape. He was soon identified as the culprit and Palmerston took a close interest in the case, even offering a reward of 30 guineas for information leading to Smith's arrest. Smith was eventually caught, tried (in 1822) and found guilty of unlawful wounding, a crime that still carried the death penalty. Palmerston's interventions on Smith's behalf were half-hearted. Indeed, despite considerable local pressure, Palmerston refused to support an official petition for leniency, regarding Smith's death as an important, if unfortunate, defence of cherished liberties, even going to far as to suggest that any punishment other than Smith's execution would be an abrogation of the rights and freedoms embodied in the principles of 1688.[33]

While these episodes offer telling insights into Palmerston's political outlook, his Hampshire life was also much more obviously politically significant in terms of his involvement in local political affairs. Palmerston, whose early career was characterised by Tory patronage, was keen to use such influence as he had in Hampshire to consolidate this attachment to the Tories. In 1806, for example, he gladly cast his support behind the two Conservative candidates for the county seats, instructing their agent to canvass 'all those voters over whom I may be supposed to have any influence and inform me of the result. If there are any freeholders in the neighbourhood to whom it would be of any use for me to write let me know their names.'[34] Although in order to get into Parliament in 1807 Palmerston might have been willing to sacrifice a personal interest in the Isle of Wight as an MP, he was not prepared to surrender claims to influence in the rest of the county as a landlord. After 1811, now installed as the representative for Cambridge University he continued to offer what support he could to those whom he saw as 'men of good family and good property, of sound political principles and of an independence of character' in Hampshire.[35] What he meant, as one of his correspondents noted, was that he was keen to use such influence as he had in the county in the Tory interest and to help secure the return of a candidate who would be a 'stedfast [sic] supporter of the established authorities of the country, and well disposed towards the present ministry'.[36] Palmerston's patronage was not always decisive in these contests, but it is significant that he sought to use it at all and was a sign that he saw local politics as subservient to the broader demands of the national interest.

Palmerston played the role of landlord in Hampshire fully, but it was on his other estates that his developing sense of the relationship between landlord and the local community, or more widely of the interaction between the governing and governed classes, was played out on a more significant plane. In Ireland in particular his evolving political and social conscience can be seen.

Palmerston's title was an Irish one and from an economic point of view he was heavily dependent on his estates in Ireland, notably in Sligo, and yet Ireland rarely features prominently in studies of Palmerston's life. In his official biography Henry Bulwer noted that the improvements Palmerston made to his Sligo estates demonstrated 'in the most agreeable manner' his 'business-like habits and generous and liberal views', but there was an absence of any meaningful analysis of the broader ramifications or import of that generosity and liberalism.[37] More recently, Kenneth Bourne omitted discussion of Palmerston's estate business in Ireland (it would, apparently, have figured in the projected but unwritten second volume), referring to Ireland's place in Palmerston's 'early years' briefly, and only with regard to his personal finances and as a feature of debates about Catholic emancipation, notably in the later 1820s.[38] Apart from a need to acknowledge the fact that Palmerston's was an Irish peerage, and that he was the proprietor of estates in Dublin and Sligo, biographers and historians have been content to marginalise discussion of his interests in Ireland in favour of attention to his work as Foreign Secretary and Prime Minister in the hey-day of the Pax Britannica. Perhaps for the more sympathetic of biographers (if not hagiographers) this was a reflection of the fact that Palmerston frequently emerged from the histories of Ireland, and particularly of the famine of the later 1840s and the tenant evictions that followed, with a tarnished reputation.[39] As an absentee landlord who assisted the emigration of his tenants aboard the so-called 'coffin ships' which carried undernourished, impoverished and often diseased tenants from western Ireland to the frequently empty promises of the New World, Palmerston has traditionally been castigated as one of the worst perpetrators of this offence against the Irish population of the mid-nineteenth century. Recently, attempts have been made to reassess this episode in Palmerston's and Ireland's shared history. Tyler Anbinder has argued that the 'shovelling-out' of Palmerston's tenants during the later 1840s was not always detrimental to those tenants' interests, while Desmond Norton, in a series of studies based on the archive of Stewart and Kincaid, Palmerston's principal agents in Ireland, has echoed this appeal to revise the received opinion of Palmerston as a malign absentee landlord.[40] Yet if Anbinder and Norton have to some extent reinvigorated interest in Palmerston's Irish career, though they disagree over some details, both have simultaneously perpetuated the historiographical problem of reading that career primarily within the narrow parameters of the 1840s (in Anbinder's case largely of 1847 only), and specifically of the response to the famine which dominated that decade. Anbinder noted that Palmerston 'was reputed in the pre-famine years to be a relatively fair and generous landlord', yet proceeded in what little space was given to discussion of those years simply to relate accounts of the 'truly miserable' conditions endured by Palmerston's tenants.[41] Norton, meanwhile, though acknowledging that Palmerston undertook numerous improvements to his estates in the 1820s and 1830s, devoted little discussion to such reforms, preferring to focus on the issues of estate management and post-famine emigration programmes in the 1840s.[42] This serves to distort the picture of Palmerston in Ireland (or at least to paint in only part of that tableau) and although his response to the famine of the 1840s rightly suffers in comparison to that of, say, his Sligo neighbour Sir Robert Gore-Booth,[43] Palmerston's interest and activities in Ireland deserve to be considered in a wider perspective.

When Palmerston inherited his title and estates in Ireland on the death of his father in 1802, those estates formed part of a heavily indebted legacy and in Sligo at least, that part of his Irish interest to which Palmerston would most consistently direct his energies, the prospects at first seemed doubtful. As Archdeacon O'Rorke would later put it in his history of Sligo:

When the traveller, on the way from Sligo, reaches Cooldruman rising ground, and looks northward, he is chilled by the change of scene, finding before him a bleak, bare, cheerless country, instead of the rich smiling landscape through which he has been passing; so that it was not altogether the spleen that occasioned Carlyle's exclamation at Cooldruman, 'Lord

Palmerston's country – a dingy, desolate looking country. Would we were well out of it!'

As O'Rorke continued, 'When it came into the hands of Lord Palmerston it was very much in the state in which Nature formed it: without houses worthy of the name, without cultivated land to speak of – a mere patch here and there, for potatoes, barley or oats – and with two thousand Irish acres of bog, abandoned, in the less sunken spots, to ground game, and, in the swamps, to the snipe, the curlew, and the long-legged crane.'[44] The estate was, further-more, where habitable, densely populated and obstacles to improvement existed at every turn in the form of land leased to middlemen under the rundale land system (a structure of land-holding whereby individual plots of disconnected land were rented as single leases and under which, therefore, tenants were unable to consolidate holdings and achieve potential economies of scale).[45]

Palmerston's first visit to the island was not made until 1808. Up until this point his knowledge of Ireland drew on little more than the popular prejudices he had encountered in Edinburgh and novels such as *Castle Rackrent*. By the later 1820s, however, Palmerston had acquired a better understanding of the country not just from reading fictionalised accounts but from personal expe-rience. Visiting Ireland in the early nineteenth century Palmerston found it little surprising that the 'imperious' English approach to its government had generated ill will and tension, rendering a harmonious state of affairs there unattainable. He likened the situation to the ruthless suppression of Anglo-Saxon England by Norman invaders generations earlier.[46] His response was to engage in a series of progressive measures to assist the physical and moral improvement of the people living on his estates. More than this, in exercising a direct and day-to-day influence over the lives of his Irish tenantry, Palmerston was able to work out his own notion of societal relations and bring to bear on real life the abstract Whiggish paternalist liberalism learned as a student at the University of Edinburgh.

The estates in Sligo which Palmerston first encountered showed a high dependency culture in the relationship between tenant and landlord. In September 1808, having recently met and spoken with Palmerston during his recent visit, Hannah Corkran, a descendant of Palmerston's grandfather's agents in Ireland, wrote to Palmerston in order to share with him papers recently discovered relating to the estate's history. Corkran was evidently still looked to as a medium for communication between the tenantry of Sligo and their new landlord and many whose leases were about to expire had appealed to Palmerston, through Corkran, for renewals. Corkran herself, significantly, wrote to Palmerston as 'the worthy representative of yr father, as my *first best friend*', and pointed out that one tenant's appeal demonstrated a 'belief that you will be our protector against farther injury'.[47] A year and a half later, another letter from Corkran was unequivocal in its pleading. She had received, she told Palmerston, 'many *petitions & visits*' from tenants asking for assistance which were not untypical since, as she pointed out, '*yr poor are oppressed*'. As an example, Corkran extended an appeal for help from a Pat Devins, '*a dependant* poor relation, without *house or home*', but who was 'willing to earn a subsistence if he has but means'. Palmerston's agent, Chambers, had apparently refused to lease land without Palmerston's authorisation, and so Devins, like other petitioners, looked to Palmerston to intervene directly that he might, with a modest award, live out his days with his family. It was the unscrupulous practices of Palmerston's agents, notably Robert Lyons (deemed 'to be capable of every villainy'), that so provoked the tenants who 'eagerly looked for' Palmerston's presence in Sligo as a remedy for alleged abuses and mistreatment.[48] Complaints against Palmerston's agents were not infrequent and reflected both the difficulties of raising revenue from unproductive land and agents' desire to fulfil the demands made by an absentee landlord for regular income yield. Lyons explained to Palmerston some time after his work there, but in response to complaints made against him that

> when I commenced I found the parish of Ahamlish in a state of barbarism & insubordination. I spared neither time nor pains until with the strictest & most firm perseverance I brought them to some degree of order & amenable to the laws which they antecedently almost set at defiance. Your father (whose memory & kindnesses to me I shall ever remember with a grateful heart) well knew this. I sometimes was obliged to assume an appearance of severity which I never feel & which with the active duty of a magistrate for Sligo & Leitrim that had been forced on me in the troublesome times by the then Lord Chancellor must have made me many enemys [*sic*] among persons of the description of the Ahamlish inhabitants but their good or bad view being of equal indifference to me I never studied [*sic*] either the one or the other. To oppress any poor man never formed any part of my character.[49]

Palmerston displayed no marked enthusiasm for retrospective redress of alleged grievances,[50] yet nor was he inured to the sufferings of his tenants. Early on he gave directions that his agents in Sligo afford relief to impoverished tenants where necessary, and those agents in turn extended Palmerston's 'bounty', mainly in the form of remittance of rents.[51] Unstructured and essentially arbitrary relief measures, however, could only ever be a temporary remedy. By 1813 Palmerston was investigating ways to restructure the manner by which land was leased, receiving in that year recommendations from one of his agents, Graves Swan,[52] that in order to achieve the required improvements in Sligo, and for Palmerston to maximise his revenue from the estate, perpetual leases ('leases for lives renewable upon payment of half a year's rent as a fine') were necessary.[53] The inducement was not simply a pecuniary one; just as Europe appeared at last at peace in 1814, Palmerston was warned by Swan that Ireland was becoming more not less 'disturbed' and, 'Whether the happy changes on the continent will or will not be the means of restoring quiet to us, seems doubtful, but of *this* I have no doubt, that without those changes, we should have to take up arms again to put down rebellion in this country.'[54] Amid reports of bankruptcy and civil disorder on estates where tenants had been evicted, Palmerston was informed that the 'fair side of the picture is to be seen in Dublin & its immediate vicinity, where the might of the civil & military power, aided by the exertions & influence of the gentry, keeps down the turbulent spirit of the lower classes'. The manufacturing base of Palmerston's estates, notably mills at Chapelizod and Palmerstown, would help protect Palmerston from shortfalls ('there is no proprietor of an estate equal to yours in extent of income & number of tenants who will suffer less loss'), but the lesson was clear: Ireland stood in need of a firm hand and prompt reform.

Although Palmerston remained a benevolent landlord, subscribing regularly to relief committees and agreeing to adjustments to rentals where necessary, he was also mindful of the pressing need to make his estates pay. Thus, while examining proposals for reform of land-holding on the estate, Palmerston was determined to collect his 'due'. In the spring of 1826, for example, he received a petition from the tenants of a Captain Jones in Ahamlish, asking Palmerston not to enforce his demand for tithe payments. Palmerston was unmoved:

I demand the tythes from you because they belong to me by right; and because they are justly due to me, as the rent which you pay is due to your landlord; and there is no reason why I should forego my rights, and make you a present of that which lawfully belongs to me.

If in consequence of neglect on my part to enforce my just rights, you have hitherto escaped from the payment of these tythes, you ought to be thankful for having so long enjoyed an exemption to which you were not intitled, instead of complaining of being required now to pay what is legally due by you.

You say that my demand if it is enforced by me, may produce riot and disorders; of this I have no fears at all; In the first place I am quite sure that you have all of you too much good sense and understanding to expect to derive any advantage from resisting by riot or disorder a claim which is founded upon law and that you will therefore pay your tythes directly and peaceably and in the next place even if you were so foolish as to attempt to resist by force you would find that the arm of the law is much stronger than you are, and the only consequence of such an attempt on your parts would be that you would have to pay your tythes all the same and would be punished for your riot into the bargain.[55]

Palmerston in his early encounters with Ireland demonstrated little interest in political life there, his influence in Sligo in the early years of the century being, he was informed, 'small' ('but will be of more consequence in future'),[56] and where Palmerston did intervene, he declared his 'interest must of course be at [the] disposal of [the] Irish Govt'.[57] In the later 1820s Palmerston would become a more active 'Catholic' politician in Ireland, but in the early years his interests there were primarily economic, and occasionally humanitarian.

Palmerston used the occasion of William IV's death in 1837 to accelerate reforms to the system of land-holding on his estates. Many of the middlemen holding leases on Palmerston's land held those leases for the life of the King and Palmerston was urged by his agent Joseph Kincaid to use this as the grounds on which to press ahead with plans for 'squaring' the land, to amalgamate many small (subsistence) holdings into larger, more efficient, farms.[58] This was apparently advice given to all clients of Stewart and Kincaid, but Palmerston was resistant to Kincaid's plans 'to *thin* those parts of the Estate of a portion of the population and to divide the land into farms of a proper & moderate size'. Palmerston insisted that, 'I have long ago made up my mind not to do so unjustifiable an act. I never yet have acted on so cruel a system & shall certainly not begin now. There is no extent of pecuniary gain that could in the slightest degree make amends for the painful reflections which such proceedings would give rise to. If any can be persuaded to emigrate voluntarily well & good; but not a single creature shall be expelled against its will.'[59] Although initially wary of the human cost of such reforms, Palmerston's estate was largely 'squared' by late 1846,[60] but his concern not to impose a 'cruel' system on his tenantry should not be dismissed as hyperbole. Whereas the history of the late 1840s suggests that Palmerston was ready, if not eager, to see his tenants depart, that should not be allowed to colour understanding of his approach in earlier periods.

In fact Palmerston's estate management in the first four decades of the century demonstrates a sincere commitment to what he saw as the moral and physical improvement of that land and its tenants. Although the death of the monarch provided the occasion for a revision of tenant leases, Palmerston had been actively pursuing measures to improve his estates since almost his first acquaintance with them. In part driven by the economic imperative to make his estates not just viable but profitable in order to offset debts and expenses inherited and incurred in England, Palmerston also sought to alleviate, to some extent, poverty on his estates by means of reforms and improvements designed to make those estates self-sufficient and productive. As Palmerston had reported to his sister on his first visit to Ireland in 1808, 'there is a great deal, I may almost say, everything, to be done', and though the land was 'wholly unimproved', Palmerston was confident that 'almost all the waste ground or bog is capable of being brought into cultivation, and all the arable may be rendered worth three times its present value'. Palmerston listed his priorities for estates as firstly to address deficiencies: to repair the parish church and build or establish schools and roads; get rid of middlemen wherever possible. Secondly, he proposed to set about improving his estates and their management: 'I mean to introduce a Scotch farmer, to teach the people how to improve their land; to establish a little manufacturing village in a central part of the estate, where there are great advantages of water and stone; and to build a pier and make a little port near a village . . . called Mullaghmore.' Schools and roads Palmerston identified as the 'most important points at present', addressing fervent demands from his new tenants. He believed over-population and profiteering by 'petty landlords' would be ameliorated as he gradually got rid of the middlemen: as Palmerston recorded, 'In my last ride . . . the whole tenantry came out to meet me, to the number, in different places, of at least 200 or 300. The universal cry was, "Give us roads, and no petty landlords!"' [61]

Palmerstonian reforms of the physical landscape took three general forms: innovation, in terms of completely new development, notably the building of a harbour at Mullaghmore and laying the foundations of a more secure fishing industry; improvements to existing towns and associated facilities; and the reclamation of erstwhile uncultivable land. He concerned himself, too, with the general moral, spiritual and educational welfare of his tenants. Taken together these improvements and reforms developed in Palmerston a more rounded appreciation of the relationship between governors and governed in society.

The harbour at Mullaghmore stands as one of the most significant and tangible examples of Palmerston's approach to reform of his Sligo estates. In October 1820 Palmerston was advised that the well-known civil engineer Alexander Nimmo had just completed a survey of the west coast of Ireland and had identified Mullaghmore as 'an improvable and useful harbour', and recommended that Palmerston 'should without delay address the Commissioners [for the Improvement and Encouragement of the Fisheries of Ireland] by a short memorial expressive of your wishes to improve the harbour of Mullaghmore, and praying the aid of the government in the undertaking'. The funds, Nimmo was reported as suggesting, 'would be immediately afforded'.[62] Palmerston endorsed the plan enthusiastically and when it became clear that the Commissioners would not be able to finance it due to a serious miscalculation of their disposable funds, he undertook to pay for the works himself, and seek reimbursement in the future, even though the prospect of such reimbursement seemed hopeless.[63] The work proceeded not without difficulty due to adverse weather conditions and the 'dilatory, negligent & drunken' character of certain supervisors of works,[64] but the first stage of building was finally approaching completion by late 1826. At this point Palmerston wrote to the Fisheries Board explaining that he did not intend to apply to the Board for any part of the money allocated to aid in its building ('I mean myself to bear the whole charge of the expenditure which I have incurred in its formation'). Having assumed sole responsibility for financing the scheme, Palmerston proceeded to discuss the importance of developing the fishing industry on the west coast of Ireland, 'because a great part of that coast is thickly peopled, much too thickly for the purposes of agriculture, and in the absence of manufactures the abundant fishing grounds which are to be found along the shores afford the readiest means of calling into activity the industry of the sea coast population'. Recognising, however, that the best fishing grounds were 'some distance from the shore' and beyond the reach and capacity of the rowing boats currently in use, Palmerston proposed that the Board provide two 20-ton vessels, the people of Mullaghmore being too poor to provide such boats for themselves.[65] The Fisheries Board was receptive to the proposal, but it is not clear whether it furnished the population with the boats, although a cutter, the *Benbulben* was in operation by the summer of 1829.[66] The harbour was in a state of readiness by spring 1828 and Palmerston himself drafted an advertisement for the Sligo and Fermanagh newspapers, leaving his agents in Ireland only to fill in statistical details:

Mullaghmore Harbour

This well sheltered Harbour which is now fit for the reception of trading vessels contains an area equal to an Irish acre and has alongside the Quay — feet water at high spring tides, and —feet water at high neap tides.

It is so situated on the southern side of Donegal Bay, that vessels of suitable draught can get in and out at every tide, and with almost every wind and there is good anchorage on a clean sand off the mouth of the Harbour.

It is connected by good roads with Sligo —miles distant, with Ballyshannon —miles distant; and with Belleek —miles distant. Its local & natural advantages adapt it to serve as the port of communication for the County of Fermanagh for all articles of export and import and especially for the trade in timber.

Several lots of ground well calculated for sites of warehouses or other buildings have been marked out contiguous to the Harbour, and any applications respecting them will be duly attended to if addressed to James Walker Esq. Rathcarrick Sligo.[67]

Early reports of the expansion of the fisheries off Mullaghmore were encouraging, as were reports that the harbour was regularly receiving significant cargoes.[68] It seemed that in addition to boosting local fishing and supplementing local agriculture, the harbour was also well placed to provide fresh stimulus to the local economy. John Lynch, a Palmerston agent, reported in December 1831, for example,

that the *Brig Britannia* of Sligo sailed in to Mullaghmore Harbour on the morning of the 1st of December I may say on an ebb tide *from Quebec* laden with timber and consigned to Mr Kernighan of Enniskillen, burthen registered *135 tons* and carrying *180 tons* drawing 11 feet of water. . . . I have also to let you know about a *month ago* the schooner *Henrietta* from Danzieth laden with timber and bound for Ballyshannon anchored off the Harbour and unloaded the greater part of her cargo and got it carted to Ballyshannon.[69]

Yet despite an auspicious beginning, the harbour's capacity was soon found wanting. 'It was only last week that a Mr Kelly of Sligo ship[pe]d the last of £1,300 worth of corn bought in at Mullaghmore last winter & spring,' reported an agent, James Walker, in August 1835. 'He says he could not get a vessel to venture in, when his speculation might have been more beneficial than it is likely now to be from corn having fallen in price. And unless yr Lord[shi]p will extend the pier, I am afraid our corn trade will not succeed.'[70] This time Palmerston sought financial aid from the Board of Works, but again invested heavily in the building works himself, adding another £1,000 to the account.[71] The resulting, extended, harbour was judged a great improvement.[72]

If the harbour was a success, it was not enough to alleviate poverty on Palmerston's estates. Palmerston diverged from the Committee of Relief for the Town of Sligo and the Union of St John in his approach to reforms. The committee, Palmerston was told in 1822, had 'adopted as the rule of their conduct a principle recommended by the Relief Committee in Dublin, viz that it is expedient in providing labour for the poor from the funds of charity, not to employ them in public or other works which must, or probably will be done, at a future time with government, county, or other monies, but the labour of a future day should be anticipated, and the poor be deprived of subsistence then, to supply their present exigencies.'[73] This was not the principle that had informed Palmerston's harbour building and it was not to guide his work in other directions either; he drafted, but did not send, an outraged response to the committee, criticising it for its 'shortsighted policy' and 'ignorance'. The committee's plan was, he wrote, 'simply that the funds so munificently subscribed throughout the Empire for the relief of the Irish should be purposely devoted to works of *absolute inutility* when they might be applied to works which would afford equal relief & employment to the people, which they contributed by their general or local utility to the advancement of the commerce, the wealth and the prosperity of Ireland'. Any improvement to roads, canals, harbours, public buildings, bridges and land would invariably alleviate hardship by underpinning economic growth and increasing employment. Investment now, argued Palmerston, promised to 'confer great & lasting benefits upon Ireland', yet the committee seemed 'determined wilfully to throw away the means thus placed in their hands, and not to allow their country to reap the full advantage which might arise from a wise application of these resources'. There was, he said, no merit in delay; it was incumbent on those with the means to do so to 'accelerate' society's 'march in internal improvement' and the committee's plan would only act to 'diminish the number of public improvements, to retard the development of the national resources, and thereby to prevent the increase which might otherwise take place in the permanent demand for labour and in the means of employment'.[74] Palmerston had recognised the need for improved road and rail links to and across his Sligo estate, and his tenants, too, were clearly anxious for better roads. Throughout the 1820s, partly at his own expense and partly with public subsidy, the towns and farms on his estates were linked with each other, with the coast, and with markets in the rest of Ireland.[75] Yet while the infrastructure was developed, there remained the problem of the land itself.

As Archdeacon O'Rorke had observed in his history of Sligo, Palmerston's estates there were dominated by bog. Palmerston's own calculations, based on figures produced some time between 1818 and 1821, estimated the area of uncultivated bog at almost 2,200 acres.[76] Palmerston set about draining and reclaiming these lands, turning again to Alexander Nimmo to prepare schemes that would allow him to extend the cultivable land on his estates that it might then be let to tenants. 'The greater part of the bogs either are or in a few years will be in my own hands; and the occupying tenantry upon the estate are much too poor, & too incapable of any systematic efforts of their own upon a great scale, to be made use of as anything but the operating labourers in these improvements,' Palmerston observed, but he envisaged a dramatically changed landscape in coming years: 'My view would be to divide such reclaimed bog into sections of about *ten* acres each, & to settle upon each section a family to be moved up from the coast, & whose present holding would be applied to enlarge that of some of their present neighbours. Each of these sections therefore would require to have a house built upon it, & might if possible be surrounded by a skreen of plantation to consist of ash, larch & fir, oak would probably not thrive in so exposed a situation'.[77] Not content simply with draining and populating the land, Palmerston demonstrated that he was alert to new methods of stabilising agricultural land. Many letters between Palmerston and his agents discuss the sowing of bent, a type of grass, that would help prevent loose and fragile land being blown away.[78] Yet Palmerston also exploited his Foreign Office contacts to investigate other methods. In 1835 he had the British government's consul in Bordeaux send over, at Palmerston's expense, twelve bags of the seed of the *Pinus maritima* which had apparently served well on the sandhills of Bordeaux.[79] What is striking is that in doing so Palmerston evidently, and to some extent self-consciously, positioned himself as a progressive and innovative landlord; and as one commentator noted (in 1854), 'this has been by far the most extensive . . . experiment of the kind yet undertaken'.[80] Within a month, Palmerston was approached by Robert Stevenson of Edinburgh who wanted to know more of Palmerston's attempts to use 'sea fir to stop blowing sand',[81] and in the spring of 1836 Palmerston wrote to Daniel O'Connell, who had also enquired after the experiment, urging him to try the Bordeaux pine as well: 'I should have great pleasure in directing my agent in Dublin, to send a portion of it, to any person who may be authorized to take charge of it for you. I should indeed be glad if you would do so as we should be giving the seed a fairer trial, if part of it were sown in a spot more to the south, than my Sligo sea coast. I would take care that the seed should be accompanied by the proper directions for sowing it.'[82] In addition, Palmerston used his estates as a nursery: in 1832 an advertisement for a sale of 'Forest trees to be sold on Lord Palmerston's Nursery' listed 182,000 trees for sale, one the following year about 300,000.[83]

It would be misleading to represent Palmerston as a model landlord, yet his programme of improvements during the 1820s, '30s and '40s did effect signif- icant changes to his Sligo estates. In late 1827, for example, in Palmerston's own estimation, his estates had undergone varied and significant change. 'I returned about a fortnight ago from a three weeks trip to Sligo where I found my improvements going on well, & I hope to find my people in a few years somewhat resembling a civilized race,' he reported to his brother. 'My harbour is just finished & will be very useful for the fishery, and in the end will be a little commercial port.'[84]

In 1835 one of Palmerston's agents, a William Bowles, conducted a tour of the estates and reported on the universally improved circumstances prevailing there. Mullaghmore, he observed, was 'wonderfully altered for the better since I saw it last', thanks to the new pier which was almost finished, a 'very good corn store full of fine oats', as well as 'a small neat inn, and several cottages of better description, besides the coast guard buildings which are very comfort- able'. Elsewhere the picture was equally pleasing: the bent planting had succeeded and with new grass and clover growth would soon create fine pasture for sheep; former bog was now the site of 'a very fine crop of oats growing where neither man [n]or beast could set foot two years ago'; the town of Cliffony and its school, he reported, were thriving, as was a nearby nursery garden which supplied the neighbourhood with trees. 'Indeed I never was more struck than with the great change for the better which I observed in and around Sligo, and in the great number of neat villas and comfortable houses which are gradually rising up on all sides of the town, as well as in it,' Bowles enthused. He was dismissive of reports of hardships as having been 'exaggerated by the priests and others whose purposes it suited to magnify the distress, that they might have the whole credit of relieving it'.[85] By 1848, even in the wake of the disastrous effects of the famine, Palmerston's estate seemed to stand out as a model for others to emulate. A lengthy letter from a J.R. Bertolacci to Sir Charles Trevelyan in that year surveyed the condition of various English landlords' Irish estates and singled out Palmerston's lands for especial praise: 'there is a farm on the property of Lord Palmerston', he wrote, which 'is like a star on the face of the country compared to the land I have before described and shows what *could* be done'.[86] Palmerston's tenants, too, seem to have regarded his exertions as having produced beneficial results. In 1840, on the occasion of a visit from their landlord, Palmerston's Castlegarron tenants presented an address observing that in the previous twelve years Palmerston had reinvested in the region almost all of the rental income he had derived from the estate: 'We most certainly attribute such unexampled liberality to benevolence alone, as no adequate remuneration can probably be derived from such an expenditure'. In return they hoped that 'by our peaceable, industrious, sober, and temperate habits to give your Lordship the most decided proof that your munificence and liberality have not been thrown away upon us, and in acting thus we feel certain we best meet your Lordship's wishes'.[87]

The last point was well made since Palmerston, as well as wanting to make the estate pay, was also, as Archdeacon O'Rorke would later put it, 'zealous in promoting their mental and moral improvement'.[88] As Palmerston recorded in a private notebook in November 1829, in a short entry on the 'Internal State of Ireland',

> Gentlemen may reside on their estates & yet be absentees from the hearts & affections of their people; they may hold themselves sternly & haughtily aloof from all intercourse with their peasantry like feudal barons in their fortified castles; they may treat the rural population as if they were the unsubdued guerrillas of a half conquered country. If such a state of things should exist any where, could we wonder at finding the people surly, turbulent & even ferocious. But instead of having recourse to violent & coercive measures, to change this character we should rather look to the healing effect of milder measures and a more genial temper in the higher classes of society.[89]

In part this was a pragmatic response to the perceived volatile nature of Irish society. As Palmerston had told his sister Frances in 1808, the country was in dire need of agrarian improvement but he saw at that time limited means for its accomplishment: 'the farmers have neither capital to enable them to improve their ground, nor a ready market for their produce were it more abundant,' he wrote. Yet though the country was then at peace, Palmerston did not think that would necessarily last and this inhibited external investment: 'The people in fact are at all times ready for a rising'; and he repeated how he had heard that the 'lower orders' in the south of the country celebrated past rebellion as 'a lawless time when they indulged without restraint their innate propensity for plunder & rapine'.[90] If in 1808 he spoke of the value of securing the 'tranquillity of the people' in Ireland at 'the point of a bayonet', he came to modify that position over time. Twenty years later he observed, 'it is quite impossible I should hope, that Parliament can determine that it is fitting to go on permanently governing a country as we now do this, by sword & bayonet; at least if that is the right way, we have all been in a great mistake about the British constitution'.[91] Palmerston, if not an altruistic landlord, did come to demonstrate a sincere and benevolent concern for the moral and spiritual welfare, and religious independence, of his tenants.

Another eulogy to Palmerston, delivered in 1827 by Dr Burke, the Catholic Bishop of Elphin, praised the 'extensive improvements' Palmerston had made to his estates and his 'humane and good' disposition, but singled out his commitment to the establishment of a school at Cliffony as deserving of special mention. As Dr Burke told the seventy or so 40-shilling freeholders who attended a dinner to John Lawless in November 1827:

> I am under the strongest conviction that he is steadfastly attached to the religion of the state, and to the Church by law established, and would be as anxious as others to increase the number of its members by an acces-sion of Catholic conformists, did he see a fair chance of success; but he had the candour to admit that such an expectation was chimerical and delusive. As he cannot make them good Protestants, he is willing to make them good Catholics, good subjects, and good members of society.[92]

To that end, Palmerston had undertaken to establish schools for boys and girls on his estates by which to diffuse religious tensions. All books used in those schools were to be 'signed in the inner cover, as approved by Lord Palmerston', though Palmerston agreed not to approve any book to which local priests objected on religious grounds. Catholic children were to be instructed in the catechism and no distinction was to be drawn, or preference to be shown, to either the Protestant or the Catholic faith. Palmerston set out explicitly that: 'No attempt shall be made directly or indirectly to influence the religious opin-ions and feelings of the children, either Catholic or Protestant, with the view of changing their religion; and Lord Palmerston will immediately take such steps as the occasion may require, if any attempts should be made, and reported to him.'[93]

The provision of school education had been a concern of Palmerston's for some years already. The winter of 1819–20 witnessed the first concerted attempts to address the issue of schooling on Palmerston's estates. An unsuccessful application was made on Palmerston's behalf to the Hibernian Society in late 1819 for finan-cial assistance in establishing schools,[94] while at the beginning of the following year local appeals from a Mrs Isabella Soden for assistance in her projected girls' school were favourably received by Palmerston.[95] In the summer of 1823 the Reverend Charles Hamilton wrote to offer his support to the 'benevolent designs of Lord Palmerston in the establishing of schools upon his estates in this neigh-bourhood'.[96] Palmerston had by this point granted Lucinda Faniset land on which to build a new girls' school,[97] but as Hamilton was quick to point out, the projected schools brought with them likely religious conflict. He asked Palmerston 'whether it might not be expedient, with the view of upholding the interests of the estab-lished Church here, & to enable its clergy to resist successfully any attempts (should such be made) by sectarians, to render this school an engine for estranging the children of Protestants from the Church to the conventicle, that *the rector of Sligo & his successors* should be *conjoined as trustees* with those other persons to whom his Lordship has promised the grant of the site whereupon to build the said female school house'. The proposal, noted Palmerston, was 'quite proper' and 'Sh[oul]d be attended to', and he added that he was 'disposed to require also that children should attend parish church on Sundays'.[98] The Reverend Hamilton wrote again on the same theme in October 1823, fearing that among the teachers at the new school, 'Some of those ladies are members of an independent chapel' and that there was a disposition 'to proselytize thereunto from the established Church some of the Protestant children attending their school'. Palmerston agreed that it was 'expedient that [the] rector sh[oul]d be [a] visitor of [the] new female school to prevent proselytism to sectarians', and '[I] have desired that his suggestion may be adopted'.[99] Any attempts to reform the schooling provision on the estate automatically brought Palmerston face to face with the religious tensions there. The Society for Promoting the Education of the Poor of Ireland, and the Catholic clergy, Palmerston was informed in a report from Swan, 'hate each other' and, 'In short, Protestant interference, in the present temper of the friends of the Catholics, will not be tolerated, where it can be resisted'. Palmerston was clearly becoming exasperated by this impasse and noted that 'This report decided me to go immediately over to Ireland by shewing that nothing out of the ordinary routine of collecting rents & making out accounts can be expected even from a very good agent'.[100] By the spring of 1825 Palmerston had already spent £626 on schoolrooms for Cliffony, Castlegall and Mount Temple,[101] and was evidently determined not to see his investment squandered in religious disputes.

When it became clear that the Catholic clergy were endeavouring to intervene and prevent the reading of the scriptures in schools, fearing that this would weaken their own and the Church's standing in society, Palmerston saw this as an unwarrantable intrusion. On learning that the clergy were forbidding people to send their children there, Palmerston declared 'war' on the priests.[102] He wrote to the master of Cliffony school, Felix Conolly, to steel Conolly's resolve:

I know very well that there are some people who ought from their education & station in life to know better, who nevertheless are so narrowminded & illiberal that they would wish to deprive the peasantry of all instruction literary &, or moral, & would if they could do so, keep them in that state of brutish ignorance and moral abasement in which so many of them are now lying; what the true motives of such persons can be God only knows, but they must not be surprized if the world at large impute their conduct to the most selfish & interested considerations, & conclude that they fancy that their own temporal interests & advantage are promoted by perpetuating the degradation of the people. Far different are their duties & ought to be their conduct. But I am firmly resolved that such attempts come they from whom they may shall not prevent me from extending to my tenantry the blessings of instruction. I know that the people wish for knowledge & their wishes *shall* be gratified oppose me who will & thwart me who may.

Palmerston regretted that the Irish Catholic priesthood should thus 'injure' the interests of the Catholic population by actions 'calculated to disgust the friends of the Catholics & alienate them from their political cause' in the rest of the United Kingdom. With the movement for emancipation of Catholics in public life gaining ground in Britain, Palmerston saw the priests' conduct as a relic of a past 'age of darkness', but he trusted that they would 'find that their arm is powerless to arrest the advancement of knowledge & that by vain endeavours to stay the progress of instruction they will only lose their own authority by accustoming the people to disobey & disregard their injunctions'. Palmerston insisted that requiring the scriptures to be read in his schools was not 'in the slightest degree incompatible with the Roman Catholic religion' and remained determined to weaken the priesthood's hold over the population.[103]

The priest of Drumcliffe, Roger Burne, complained to Palmerston that the new schools were 'viewed amongst us as a crude and mischievous scheme conceived and matured for the covert purposes of proselytism', but Palmerston refused to enter into further discussion of the subject.[104] The issue turned on the question of 'the practice of putting the sacred volume into the hands of schoolboys'; the clergy would not stand for young children reading the Bible for themselves and the dispute threatened the prospects of addressing what all agreed was 'the neglected state of education' in the region.[105] Palmerston, however, was resolute. 'I can only say that I will be dictated to by no man as to the manner in which I may think fit to conduct my school & that the objection made to reading the Testament in the school upon the ground that it is improper to make the sacred writings a school book appears to me to be perfectly childish,' he wrote. The Bible was not to be used simply as a means 'of teaching the children the mechanical act of reading'. What Palmerston intended, he said, was that literate children should read a portion of the Testament each day in order to 'acquire that moral instruction which that volume is so well calculated to convey'. If the Church had no objection to children reading the book at home, Palmerston asked, 'Can there be such a difference between a slated roof & a thatch, between your presence & that of their illiterate parents, that the very act which is permissible in the one case, should be forbidden in the other?' The conclusion, he thought, was clear: 'This is all miserable nonsense, and it is not to be supposed that I or any other rational man should not see through the flimsy pretence which is meant to conceal a deeply rooted determination to prevent the peasantry of Ireland from emerging from their barbarous ignorance.'[106]

Even though the number of children attending Cliffony school had reached more than one hundred by the end of 1827, still they were 'so very ignorant' and still the tension between Protestant and Catholic remained. The schools were withdrawn from the 'Kildare Street Society', otherwise known as the Society for Promoting the Education of the Poor of Ireland that had formerly so antagonised the Catholic clergy and in November Palmerston decided that 'Saturday [was] to be declared no school day, & Catholics to come at one time to be instructed in their catechism & Protestants at another to read scriptures & their own catechism'.[107] This compromise appears to have satisfied all parties and it was in the same month that Bishop Burke paid tribute to Palmerston's 'liberality'.

The establishment of schools on the estate is important. His support for local schools was extensive,[108] and the number of letters and reports Palmerston read and wrote on this subject shows that he took a keen personal interest in the question. Once it became clear that subscriptions and grants of land were inadequate to achieve the desired improvements, Palmerston frequently assumed personal responsibility for directing school policy, corresponding with local schoolmasters and monitoring which books were issued to children on his estates. This was no passing fancy; he insisted on receiving monthly accounts of attendance at the schools, directly from the schoolmasters and mistresses themselves,[109] and at least two records survive indicating that he would comb through the class lists he received to identify pupils who ought to be rewarded for good attendance with a shilling (which was duly paid from Palmerston's own account).[110] When in mid-1830 it appeared that the school at Cliffony was being ill managed, Palmerston again monitored the situation personally. Isabella Soden first alerted Palmerston to the problems at Cliffony. The teacher, Anne Jordan, it was alleged, rarely turned up at the school before noon, was in the habit of submitting false reports of attendance and devoted little attention either to the children's education or to maintenance of the building and school materials.[111] Jordan claimed ill health,[112] but soon rumours began to circulate suggesting she was of dubious moral character ('there were strong suspicions of her having had connexion with the master [of the school] before they were publicly married,' according to one report sent to Palmerston).[113] Despite a rebuttal of the charges by both Anne Jordan and her husband William Jordan, the master of the school, Isabella Soden's repeated allegations persuaded Palmerston of the poor management of the establishment and in October 1830 he endorsed the appointment of a Matthew Leonard, as proposed by Bishop Burke, as a new master for the school.[114] For Palmerston, occupied at Westminster with political manoeuvring that in November 1830 would see him appointed to the Foreign Office, this micro-management of the affairs of Cliffony school, its broken window panes and lack of writing materials, is remarkable.

According to Kenneth Bourne, it would appear that the only point at which 'Ireland' became significant to an understanding of Palmerston's more familiar public career was with regard to his increasingly 'advanced' views on the Catholic question, which 'probably' had something to do with his experiences in Sligo.[115] Bourne is undoubtedly correct, but his biography provides no real material to substantiate the claim. This is unfortunate as in the late 1820s, and especially 1829, Palmerston's career came to be defined in large part by his 'Catholicism' and in working out his attitude to religious policy Palmerston drew heavily on his experiences as a landlord in Ireland. In his 'education policy' of the 1820s he had already demonstrated that he was no theological dogmatist. He regarded sectarian divisions as a hindrance to good government and a stable society. It may have been, as Bourne suggests, that Palmerston recognised that his 'progressive' views on Catholic emancipation made his proposed appointment as Chief Secretary of Ireland unworkable in 1812,[116] but it did not betoken antipathy to the issue of religious diversity and tension. Palmerston's adherence to the cause of Catholic emancipation cost him dearly in political terms; certainly it was one of the factors that would weaken his hold on his seat for Cambridge University in May 1831.[117] Yet it was a consistent principle and one that facilitated or obliged his move to the Whigs and away from his Tory 'roots' in the later 1820s. As Palmerston shifted from 'liberal Tory' to Whig he saw the move in terms of Anglo-Irish political expediency and religious liberalism.

In 1826 Palmerston made a small number of revealing entries in his diary on the subject of 'Ireland' and the 'Catholic Question'. At first he noted that he would be 'disposed to vote for any securities which did not require from Cathcs sacrifices incompatible with the principles of their faith and which would reconcile the Protestant to the proposed concessions'. He wrote that the 'best security to make people peaceable & loyal is to make them contented & happy, & the true security this measure would carry with it would be that attachment to the constitution which would be created by a full participation in its blessings. Take away from men the sense of real injury & give to them real & substantial justice & there needs no state machinery to make them orderly & well affected. Leave them degraded & deprived & though you may force your oath of allegiance from their lips, *their* vows of abjuration will be found recorded in their hearts'. But in subsequent entries he made the connection with his experience in Ireland explicit. It was, he wrote, with 'a sense of deep humiliation' that one should see that 'in this enlightened country it should still be a matter of debate whether it is wise to convert 5m of our fellow subjects into friends'. Only by according to Catholics the same rights as Protestants in public life could the country be at peace and would it be possible to 'quell the swelling of unsatisfied but legitimate ambition' of the majority of the Irish population. Talking of the 'undeserved injustice' and 'unmerited degradation' suffered by Catholics in Ireland, Palmerston maintained that 'Every man who knows anything of the state of Ireland must be convinced of this truth' and, he asked rhetorically, 'Can any but the enemies of England survey with pleasure the flames of civil discord raging throughout Ireland?'[118]

In June 1828 Palmerston said that he 'must go' to Ireland,[119] though it was the end of the year before he made the trip. Writing to his brother on 9 December, having just returned, he observed:

> I left Ireland in a dreadful state for a civilized country a free govt and an enlightened age. The whole of the people without any exception are now divided into two parties, the agitators & the irritators, the Catholic & the anti-Catholic, neutrality has disappeared & with it temper and moderation & common sense; the two parties are only kept from flying at each other by the interposition of the army & the other armed bodies, & the tranquillity of the country is preserved only by the sword & musket; & yet this is a practical application of the principles *which seated the family of Brunswick upon the throne*, and this is the state of things which the lovers & patrons of the British *constitution* are afraid of endangering by admitting Catholics into Parliament.

Although Palmerston suspected Wellington's government would be forced into some measure of reform, he doubted the Tories' willingness to grant full emancipation. Yet he was equally convinced that only full equality would do.[120]

There is no doubt that Palmerston's experiences in Ireland had affected his views of society and of religious toleration. It is a nice point to debate whether he would have been so persuaded of the need for reforms, and especially Catholic emancipation, had he been a landowner in Hampshire exclusively, where sectarianism, poverty and political strife intruded upon his bucolic idyll but rarely. Yet as Palmerston returned to the bustle of Westminster in the late 1820s to define his political position, he was very much under the influence of what he had witnessed in Ireland. This coincided with the culmination, in London, of his separation from Tory patrons and accommodation, however awkwardly, with liberal Conservatism and, indeed, Whiggery.

CHAPTER 5

THE MAKING OF PALMERSTON II: THE POLITICIAN

Do you still direct the military body, or are you become civil? Provided you are well, happy, contented, & thought of as you deserve to be, I care little where you are, as far as you individually are concerned – for the sake of the public I wish to see liberal-minded unprejudiced men in prominent situations. Give us honesty, talent, zeal, & liberality & 'Trop sérieuse' say I. . . .

Edward Berens Blackburn (Harrow school-friend)
to Palmerston, 15 Nov. 1823[1]

A WEEK AFTER Napoleon's final defeat at Waterloo in June 1815, Palmerston wrote to his friend, Lord Fitzharris, son of Lord Malmesbury, to express his hope that 'the Allies will not be duped by this second rehearsal of the farce of abdication, but will move on straight to Paris and put *le Désiré* to bed in the Tuileries and hang Buonaparte on one of his own triumphal arches'.[2] Swept up, like so many of his contemporaries, in the patriotic fervour of allied victory, Palmerston took an early opportunity to visit France in the late summer of 1815 where he had ample opportunity to see at first hand the army which he had been so preoccupied with provisioning from London. The travel journal which Palmerston kept during his visit is revealing in that the trip evidently reinforced his uncritical sense of an easy English (perhaps rather than British) politico-cultural superiority and a Pittite Toryism which basked in the glow of Wellington's apparent humbling of Bonaparte.

Landing in France at the end of August, Palmerston made initially for Rouen but as he travelled through Normandy took time to converse with the people he met there. All of them, he noted, 'beadles, barmaids, postillions, hairdressers, boatmen, carters and national guards appeared fully to expect that they should be annexed to England', a fate, he believed, they welcomed 'from fear & servility of character'. It was this air of defeat and of crushed spirit that most resonated with the British Secretary at War. 'It is indeed quite striking to observe how totally every thing like manly feeling and independent spirit has been crushed by the successive tyrannies under which the people have suffered since the beginning of the revolution,' he wrote at Rouen on 1 September, 'and it is hardly possible to extract from any man a political opinion; they all say the same thing that it is indifferent to them who governs provided they are allowed to enjoy la tranquillité. But they all said also Ce sont des tem[p]s bien malheureux pour la France. La France est bien malade monsieur.'[3] As he travelled on towards the French capital Palmerston continued to record his impressions of a country run by a 'despotic monarchy'. Passing through the Bois de Boulogne and along the Champs-Elysées, Palmerston noted that 'Everything is upon a great scale and is evidently the result of a well directed but over whelming authority'. But such grandeur, he thought, came at a cost: the 'public enjoy everything individuals nothing; The strong arm of power has made the will of the few bend to the convenience of the many'. All around him Palmerston saw evidence of the popular will being made to bow to the demands of the imperial capital.[4] Much of the visit to France, however, was occupied in watching the reviews of the allied armies of occupation, often in company with figures such as the Emperor of Russia, the King of Prussia and the Duke of Wellington.

In 1813, a young Lord Aberdeen had been appointed to the Vienna embassy and so found himself in Austria and Prussia at the height of the fighting. Travelling between Prague and Teplitz, Aberdeen had been overwhelmed by the impact of war: 'Novice as I am in the scenes of destruction the continual sight of the poor wounded wretches of all nations is quite horrible and haunts me day and night,' he had written to his friend Harrowby. In the aftermath of the allied victory at the Battle of Leipzig in October 1813, Aberdeen visited the battlefield and reeled in horror at what he saw: 'For three or four miles the ground is covered with bodies of men and horses, many not dead. Wretches wounded unable to crawl, crying for water amidst heaps of putrefying bodies. Their screams are heard at an immense distance, and still ring in my ears. The living as well as the dead are stripped by the barbarous peasantry, who have not sufficient charity to put the miserable wretches out of their pain. Our victory is most complete. It must be owned that a victory is a fine thing, but one should be at a distance.'[5]

Palmerston viewed victory at a distance measured both geographically and temporally. Whereas Aberdeen, Palmerston's erstwhile school-friend and subsequent political rival and colleague, had witnessed the full horror of conflict, Palmerston's experience of the recent wars was altogether more triumphalist. A review of 20,000 Prussian infantry, cavalry and artillery on 3 September 1815 was followed the next day by the dramatic reconstruction of the successful Prussian attack on Paris of 1814. Subsequent battlefield tourism took in sites in and around Paris and north western France. There was none of the revulsion at the human cost of war displayed by Aberdeen, only vicarious enjoyment through the sanitised theatrical battlefield reconstructions of allied victories. Aberdeen had noticed the dead soldiers; Palmerston saw only the living, and whereas Aberdeen had witnessed the levelling and humbling aspect of war, Palmerston saw only the glory of (a primarily British) victory. On 5 September, for example, Palmerston

Rode out at eight to the Bois de Boulogne to see some of the English troops out in the open fields next to their encampment; our men certainly do not look so smart & uniform in a body as the Russians & Prussians but still they have a more soldierlike air, they look more like business, & fighting. The foreign troops look like figures cut out of card ours like a collection of living men, The former move like a machine, ours without any irregularity or break yet bear the appearance of individual ease & vigour; their men seem to depend entirely on each other, ours look as if they moved independently & yet with equal uniformity as a mass. There is a character of individual energy about our people which one does not see in theirs.[6]

Palmerston revelled in the 'mortification' of the French population, humbled by the presence of an occupying and controlling allied force.[7]

All of which tended to confirm Palmerston's sense of English superiority. In 1816, when he set off for the continent again, this time in hotfoot (and hot-blooded) pursuit of Emily Cowper,[8] Palmerston travelled once more through France and Italy before arriving in Switzerland. In Basle, Palmerston found himself in need of cash and went to exchange a letter of credit with a French banker. The banker, Palmerston remembered, 'made as usual some little diffi-culties about not knowing me, as an excuse for taking a half per cent too much by exchange', but then complimented Palmerston on his proficiency in French, suggesting that Palmerston spoke the language so well that one would never know he was English. Palmerston answered that he hoped at least that he would not be taken for a *Frenchman*. 'This seemed however at least to satisfy him as to my country,' he noted.[9] When he returned to France again, in 1818, to conduct a final review of the armies of occupation, Palmerston struck a similar tone. His assessment of the British army echoed that of 1815, but he had not even got ashore before his latent prejudices came to the fore. His party had arrived at Calais at seven o'clock in the morning on 13 October 1818, but the tide being then out, he had disembarked, he remembered, 'as an Englishman ought to land on the French coast, riding on the necks of Frenchmen'.[10]

There was an innate conservatism about Palmerston's faith in the superi-ority of English or British government over that of other countries. The army had not only defeated Napoleon, but, as Palmerston had learned at the War Office, the propertied interests of its officer class had safeguarded the consti-tution of Britain at home.[11] 'No man can mix much in public life in this country;' Palmerston told the House in 1820, 'no man who has the slightest opportunity of witnessing daily and hourly, in private life, the blessings derived from the constitution under which we live, can entertain any other feeling but the determination, if necessary, to sacrifice his life in its defence.'[12] When agricultural distress and poor harvests threatened social order in the months following victory over France, Palmerston believed that transportation and execution of some of the ringleaders would serve as useful 'examples of the severest nature' which he judged 'absolutely necessary in the present state of the country'.[13] Along with Hampshire neighbours such as the Duke of Wellington and Lord Malmesbury, Palmerston was nervous in 1819 lest support for the protesters massacred at 'Peterloo' 'disturb the tranquillity of this loyal and peaceable country', and in a letter to Fitzharris, he explained how the survival of the government at this point depended on the 'cold support of the friends of social order'; indeed, Palmerston thought the preservation of that order sufficient ground, on its own, to rally support to a government which had struggled since the peace to find or maintain any sort of momentum.[14]

If Palmerston derived a vicarious satisfaction from Britain's military achievements in Europe, closer to home, and with regard to his own career, Palmerston's story was a less confident one. He emerged from the war years a respected and conscientious departmental administrator, but, along with Peel, one of the government's avowedly 'promising young men', he was still unproven in Parliament, at least in general debate.[15] By the early 1820s, judged his official biographer, 'although Lord Palmerston's ability was fully acknowledged, and his public position a good one, it was an isolated one'. Fifteen years in Parliament, the vast majority of them in ministerial office, had left Palmerston, remarkably, politically marginal and somewhat anonymous. He had no intimate friends, said Bulwer, and he did not sit comfortably with any particular wing of the Tory government within which he served. As the Tories splintered into 'ultra' and liberal factions, Palmerston did not appear to ally himself with any one of them. 'He was not then an adherent of Canning, never having followed that statesman out of office; nor was he an adherent of Lord Eldon, nor even of Lord Liverpool, for he had voted since 1812 in favour of concessions to the Catholics. He certainly was not a Whig, and yet he lived chiefly with Whig society, which since the time of Mr Fox, was the society most in fashion. George IV always disliked him. No one, therefore, had a very lively interest in him, or felt a strong desire to make his parliamentary position more important.'[16] Perhaps this was all that was to be expected of a man who had declared himself 'sick' of politics as early as 1809 (when Parliament debated the importance of the Scheldt expedition).[17]

Bourne, however, dismissed the future Lady Byron's cutting aside of 1812 that Palmerston was 'devoid of party spirit, of public spirit, or of spirit of any kind' and similar assessments of Palmerston's political non-partisanship as 'implausible', and suggested that the 'essential dilemma' about Palmerston is not how he 'failed to be promoted, but how he managed to survive so long in minor office'.[18] For Bourne the answer lay in Palmerston's pre-eminently social rather than political approach to public life. His 'conversion' from 'Protestant' to 'Catholic', some time between 1806 and 1812, insisted Bourne, owed

nothing to notions of either constitutional or religious freedom, but was probably 'in large part a matter of expediency' and circumstance. Membership of
clubs such as the Alfred (from 1808), argued Bourne, did more to shape
Palmerston politically through their complex webs of social patronage than
any political convictions he may have held. Thus Palmerston, like his father,
seemed to be following a literary, if not dilettante, and certainly a society, route
to public position, whether among the 'most distinguished literary & scientific
characters of the day' at the Alfred, or alongside the (Whiggish) society
hostesses, notably Emily Cowper, who congregated at Almack's to decide
the fate of aspiring (and established) politicians with invitations that were
just as much tickets of admission to the rarefied milieu and political society
of the *ton* as invitations to Wednesday soirées. Bourne was undoubtedly
correct in his view that Palmerston was influenced as much by individuals as
by badges of political allegiance during his War Office years: he was an
adherent of Spencer Perceval more than he was a Tory; and he was certainly
never a Canningite during the 1810s and earlier 1820s, said Bourne. Indeed,
Palmerston seemed to lack any sort of political rudder in these years. He 'alienated' ultra, 'Protestant' feeling within the government by his support of greater
freedoms for Catholics in 1812–13 but failed, at the same time, to endear
himself to the more liberal, Canningite, wing among whom such views would
have found a more receptive audience.[19]

Palmerston appeared to admire efficiency and competence above other qualities. When faced with Castlereagh's imminent departure from the War Office
in the autumn of 1809 (largely at Canning's instigation), Palmerston thought it
'rather hard' on Castlereagh and lamented that he knew 'no one whose loss
would perhaps be less felt than poor Cas[tlereagh], since whatever his talents
for business may be, & I confess I rather think highly of them, he is dreadfully
unpopular & is somewhat of a millstone about the necks of his friends'.[20] There
was little to suggest in his observations on the Malmesburys, through whom he
had entered political life, that he shared any great ideological concerns or
indeed any particular ambition with them beyond a desire simply to maintain
the status quo. 'The Cattery [his name for Lady Malmesbury and her daughters]
goes on very well,' wrote Palmerston in the summer of 1810, 'but I begin already
to feel a disposition to purr & mew, & an amazing inclination to go rat-catching.
This will however wear off again probably before the next session of Parliament
as an aversion so decided to that species of animal might be inconvenient in
St Stephen's.'[21]

Palmerston was astute enough to recognise the importance of patronage
and social connection to his early political advancement. Even though he had
been, since 1807, a Member of Parliament, Palmerston continued to harbour
ambitions to win one of the prestigious seats for the University of Cambridge.
In the first week of 1810 he went up to Cambridge and spent two and a half
days 'in paying visits and playing whist & drinking punch with the fellows; I

found every thing looking very well although a number of new candidates
have been shewing themselves, but I am not much apprehensive of their
doing me great harm'. His only perceived rival, Edward Law, son of Lord
Ellenborough and a fellow Johnian, had been making a canvass riding on the
back of Petty's interest, but his progress with the electorate was modest and at
just nineteen years old he was not only inexperienced, but a good year and a
half off being able to stand at all.[22] When Palmerston finally won a seat for the
University in 1811, the event occasioned little excitement; in his own later
account, Palmerston remembered, matter-of-factly: 'In 1811, upon the death
of the late Duke of Grafton, Lord Euston made a vacancy at Cambridge, and I
stood against Smyth, his nephew, and was elected.'[23] The election had indeed
lacked the ferocity of Palmerston's earlier contests there. John Henry Smyth
was the only other candidate for the seat and despite his formidable academic
and political connections (he was a Trinity man and through his family
enjoyed considerable Whig backing) Smyth proved no match for Palmerston,
who this time enjoyed unencumbered ministerial support. The latter sailed to
an easy victory of 451 to 345 votes; almost a little too easily perhaps as some of
his supporters had had to be actively chased (through the pages of the *Courier*)
to bother to vote at all, many apparently believing the victory a foregone
conclusion.[24] Smyth won the University's other seat in 1812 in succession to Sir
Vicary Gibbs, who had been appointed to the Court of Common Pleas but
whose resignation was also ascribed to declining health, and in the following
elections Smyth and Palmerston enjoyed unopposed returns from the
loyal University electorate.[25] Palmerston's 'usual excursion' to Cambridge
at Christmas, though political in intent, was very convivial in character: in
December 1817 the visit, made in the company of Laurence Sulivan, had them
looking forward 'with great delight to the whist the punch and the turkey pie
of the Combination Room'.[26] Palmerston repaid his constituents with the sorts
of favours they expected from an alumnus now in government office. In
November 1820, for instance, Palmerston prevailed upon Lord Liverpool to
appoint James Wood, Palmerston's former tutor, to the about-to-be-vacant
deanship of Ely.

> This deanery would I know be more acceptable and gratifying to Doctor
> Wood on account of its local proximity to Cambridge than any other
> could be, and I am very confident that such an appointment would be
> particularly agreeable to the friends of good principles religious & polit-
> ical in the University of Cambridge. Dr Wood has long been looked up to
> as the leading head of that party in the University who have supported
> sound principles in church and state, and though I know that my opinion
> on such a point may be thought to be biased by my personal and local
> interests, yet I have no hesitation in saying, setting those considerations
> out of the question, that the preferment of Ely could not be disposed of in

a manner more advantageous to the cause of good government, or more creditable to the advisers of the Crown than by conferring it upon Doctor Wood.[27]

Liverpool obliged and four days later Palmerston thanked him for a promotion that would 'give the greatest satisfaction to a large proportion of the University of Cambridge, and will be both advantageous and creditable to the government'.[28]

If Palmerston's success at Cambridge had been dependent on old-fashioned patronage and collegiate ties, his representation of the University in the years after 1812 acquired an increasingly political character, one shaped largely by the dominant issue of the day. As Palmerston himself put it in his autobiographical sketch: 'From 1812 downwards I constantly voted for Catholic Emancipation, and was re-elected in 1812, 1818, and 1820, at the general elections in those years, with the full knowledge on the part of the University as to what my opinions on that subject were.'[29] Bourne, as noted, observed no discernible moment of 'conversion' and certainly Palmerston's first public statement on the subject spoke of a pragmatic concession more than an open embrace of the principle of religious equality; this was the politics of toleration rather than a recognition of parity. 'Although I wish the Catholic claims to be considered,' Palmerston told the House of Commons in March 1813, 'I never will admit those claims to stand upon the ground of right.' He insisted that it was a basis of 'civilized government' that the legislature should reserve 'the right to impose such political disabilities upon any class of the community, as it may deem necessary for the safety and welfare of the whole'. But as Palmerston also pointed out, such disabilities were not to be regarded as fixed and unalterable: 'Putting this question, however, entirely on the ground of expediency, I cannot concur with those who think that they have proved the expediency of continuing the Catholic disabilities now, by showing that they were necessary in the times when they were originally imposed. These disabilities are not the rule of the constitution, but an exception from that rule; their necessity in one century is no evidence of their expediency in another; and it is [as] much incumbent on those who now contend for their continuance, to show that they are required for the present security of the state, as it was upon those who first framed them to prove the necessity of their original enactment.' Rejecting fears that the 'Protestant establishments of the Empire' would be overrun by 'Catholic' votes in Parliament, Palmerston remained sanguine that 'whatever may be the error of individuals, I never can bring myself to believe that there would at any time be found in this House a sufficiently powerful and numerous Protestant party, so profligate in principle, and so dead in everything which would be due to themselves and to their country, as to barter away the religious establishment of any part of the Empire, for the gratification of political ambition'. It was unjust, not to say counter-productive to the national good, he maintained, to disbar a section of the population from public service and reward on these grounds. Warming to his theme, Palmerston asked:

> If it had unfortunately happened that by the circumstance of birth and education, a Nelson, a Wellington, a Burke, a Fox, or a Pitt, had belonged to this class of the community, of what honour and of what glory might not the page of British history have been deprived! To what perils and calamities might not this country have been exposed! The question is not whether we would have so large a portion of the population Catholic, or not. There they are, and we must deal with them as we can. It is vain to think that by any human pressure we can stop the spring which gushes from the earth. But it is for us to consider whether we will force it to spend its strength in secret and hidden courses, undermining our fences and corrupting our soil, or whether we shall, at once, turn the current into the open and spacious channel of honourable and constitutional ambition, converting it into the means of national prosperity and public wealth.[30]

Whether the University fully appreciated Palmerston's Catholic sympathies, or whether Palmerston was not the vehement pro-emancipationist that he later liked to suggest, the University's electors were not fully apprised of Palmerston's views, at least not as early as 1812. Although Palmerston stood as a 'Catholic' MP, the question of emancipation remained an open one within the government. While this was really just about papering over the cracks on a highly divisive issue rather than tackling it head-on, Palmerston's pro-Catholic sympathies made his position increasingly difficult within Liverpool's ministry where a sizeable number of its senior members was by inclination more or less hostile to the measure. Palmerston was neither wholly with the government nor wholly against it, but, crucially, within an increasingly divided ministry, he was not readily to be identified with any particular faction or grouping. This was potentially damaging to Palmerston's grip on office.

In November 1821 Liverpool asked Palmerston to answer a question 'quite fairly, explicitly, and without embarrassment' concerning proposed new arrangements of the government. Palmerston was offered an English peerage and a move from the War Office to that of Woods and Forests 'with the expectation of being appointed to the Post Office, or to some other more agreeable situation, when the opportunity may offer'.[31] Palmerston claimed to be flattered by the proposal, but, although he declared himself 'not insensible to the value of a seat in the House of Lords', there is no evidence that he harboured any desire to take an English title and there was no mistaking the real intention and ramifications of Liverpool's approach. As he told the Prime Minister: 'it is now twelve years since I was selected to hold an important and I can assure you a very laborious office; in point of rank, one among the highest of those which are out of the Cabinet; I have discharged its duties faithfully, and I trust not without credit both to myself and to the government; and taking into view the relative nature & extent of the duties and responsibility of the two offices which are now proposed to be exchanged, I cannot but feel that under all circumstances the arrangement in question would be liable to misconstruction'.[32]

This episode served to underline the essential fragility of Palmerston's parliamentary position. At Westminster his star, if not on the wane, certainly was not in the ascendant, while in Cambridge Palmerston's growing identification with the Catholic interest threatened to cost him his treasured University seat. At a by-election in November 1822 prompted by the death of the University's other MP, John Smyth, the 'Protestant' Tory William John Bankes won a resounding victory, a result which demonstrated, as Palmerston told Sulivan, 'that Protestantism is very rife at Cambridge'. Palmerston insisted that he felt secure in his own seat and did not see 'with what face people who have year after year promised me support knowing my sentiments on the Catholic question can all of a sudden turn round & leave me because a Protestant enters the field agst me; but however one must take one's chance and let things come as they will'.[33] According to Lord Colchester, the 'common talk of London since the election is that Lord P. must look out for some other seat in one of the two Houses of Parliament at the period of the next general election'.[34] Palmerston remained determinedly sanguine, telling Canning, for example, that although Bankes had stirred up a good deal of Protestant feeling among his constituents, this would soon dissipate and Palmerston would remain safe in his seat.[35] It did not help, however, that Palmerston's ability to call on government support and patronage seemed weaker than ever. 'I grow less of a Tory every time I see Shee whose head makes me wish for the *Wigs*,' observed Palmerston in 1823, 'though unlike Burke I should appeal from the old to the new Wigs'.[36] It is debatable how far Palmerston ever was a Tory in anything more than name. In the mid-1820s he began to outgrow his Tory connections and the Whiggish stamp left on him by Dugald Stewart and Edinburgh can be more clearly seen.

In January 1825 Palmerston reported that the new year had begun amid 'very pleasant parties' at Cambridge where he found 'things looking very prosperous'.[37] A few months later affairs would prove to be much less satisfactory. At the beginning of December Palmerston greeted the approaching general election, scheduled for the summer of 1826, with a sort of weariness bordering on complacency. 'It is rather a bore to have to go through the labour of a canvass so long before the time,' he wrote to his brother William, 'but this is just a time of year when I have more leisure to attend to it, and I shall not be sorry to get the matter over. I do not feel much apprehension as to the result, because I think I am sure of a great many Protestants, from a coincidence of opinion on other questions; and of many Whigs, from an agreement on the

Catholic question. Indeed if there is no Whig candidate, I should expect to have all the Whig interest at Cambridge.'[38] The early results of the canvass were promising and Palmerston appeared to be winning considerable backing from members of both Trinity and St John's where he was apparently embraced by Tories as a Protestant and by Whigs as a Catholic. However, very few fellows were willing to give a definite promise and Palmerston's optimism rested to no small degree simply on 'expressions of personal goodwill'.[39] Palmerston's pledges to continue to guard his constituents' interests and 'promote the welfare of the Empire, and to maintain and strengthen our constitution in church and state',[40] were perhaps sufficiently vague and all-embracing to permit potential supporters of differing hues to indicate general support, but one of his committee members admitted on 8 January that 'Lord Palmerston's chance is good yet his seat is by no means secure without the greatest exertions by those who support him. In the next place if he go out it will be entirely in consequence of his vote on the Catholic question. A defeat will be a complete triumph for the *no popery* faction, it will consolidate their interests, & the noise of it will ring thro' every corner of the kingdom. If the Catholic question be an important question it is important for us to defeat the country parsons & the bigots who at this moment are dishonouring the land we live in.'[41]

Meanwhile, Palmerston continued to entertain hopes of victory, but as he admitted to George Canning on 22 December, although his canvassing of voters in Cambridge and London had been very successful, still the intentions of the far greater numbers of 'outvoters' remained unknown and Palmerston felt some anxiety given that the majority of these non-resident voters were country clergymen among whom anti-Catholic feeling might yet prove a deciding factor.[42] Indeed, the 'Catholic question', Palmerston observed the following day, was making 'a great schism' within the University, but with Johnian college support and Whig political support, Palmerston told his brother, he expected still to 'do well'.[43]

Palmerston's growing reliance on Whig support is telling, as both his political sympathies and his interests became more explicitly aligned with that party. Whereas Palmerston had won the University seat in 1811 in part because he enjoyed official connections, in 1826 he would be obliged to do so from the anomalous, though not unfamiliar, position of minister without government backing. Lord Eldon, the Lord Chancellor, claimed in response to a request from Palmerston for an explicit demonstration of support that 'Report was so current that we were to have you in the House of Lords that your letter rather surprised me.' Though he promised to do nothing adverse to Palmerston's interests at Cambridge, Eldon, noting a divergence of opinion over the Catholic question, also observed that in the light of Bankes's and Goulburn's candidatures, both with ministerial endorsement, he felt he 'must be passive' in the campaign.[44] If Liverpool had attempted to move Palmerston discreetly in 1821, in late 1825 the lack of warmth for the Secretary at War

among his own colleagues was more abundantly clear. When he arrived in
Cambridge to canvass voters, Palmerston had been dismayed to find that the
unofficial balance maintained between Protestant and Catholic representatives
was no longer respected and while it was no surprise to find Bankes there,
defending his seat, it was disappointing to say the least to find that for the other
seat, Palmerston's, two other candidates were about, and both, remarkably,
were government colleagues: Henry Goulburn, the Irish Secretary, and John
Copley, the Attorney-General. Both of Palmerston's rivals, furthermore, were
'Protestants'. Palmerston expressed astonishment 'that an official man should
find himself endangered in a seat which he has held for fourteen years, by
the undisguised competition of two of his colleagues in office'.[45] Despite the
protestations of Lord Bathurst, the Secretary for War and Colonies, for
example, that in supporting Goulburn he was not opposing Palmerston,
Palmerston could not help but notice that he was being left in the cold, and
assurances of support from Robert Peel were not sufficient to alleviate his
anxieties.[46] Only 'the cordial & active assistance of the Whigs can effectually
aid me', thought Palmerston, hoping to create a Whiggish committee to revive
his flagging campaign in the face of 'an underhand Protestant cabal'.[47] A
number of Whig supporters had begun to recognise a growing accord between
liberal Tories and liberal Whigs,[48] and there is some evidence that erstwhile
opponents of Palmerston were, sometimes more reluctantly than enthusiastically, willing to endorse the Secretary at War. Adam Sedgwick, for example, a
Trinity fellow and a Whig, was one who found himself 'in the Committee
room of a Johnian, a Tory, and a King's Minister; and I am going to give him a
plumper'. As he explained in an (unsuccessful) attempt to convince a fellow
elector to plump for Palmerston:

> My motives are that he is our old member, and a distinguished member,
> and that I hate the other candidates – I mean with public and political
> hate, without private malice. Bankes is a fool, and was brought in last time
> by a set of old women, and whenever he rises makes the body he repre-
> sents truly ridiculous. Copley is a clever fellow, but is not sincere, at least
> when I pass him I am sure I smell a rat. Goulburn is the idol of the Saints,
> a prime favourite of Simeon's, and a subscriber to missionary societies.
> Moreover he squints. Now, my good fellow, though I believe you have the
> liberality of a great inquisitor, yet I think you will hardly vote against your
> own college, your own friends, and the cause of common sense.[49]

Palmerston took his concerns to the Prime Minister, whose 'shabbiness' for
'not stir[ring] or do[ing] anything' he had already criticised in a letter to
Sulivan,[50] outlining the 'extreme embarrassment of the situation in which I am
placed by the contest now carrying on for the University of Cambridge; a situation so extraordinary that I can scarcely imagine that any official man could

ever before have stood in similar circumstances'. For members of the same
political party, let alone of the same administration, to act with such mutual
hostility as Palmerston perceived at work in Cambridge struck at the heart of
stable government, he said. Maintaining that the Catholic question had, from
the outset, been an open one within Liverpool's government, Palmerston
protested against his pro-Catholic sympathies being used explicitly in this
election with the aim of dispossessing him of his seat. Liverpool, Palmerston
said, had been remiss in not giving a firm enough lead on this subject, allowing
colleagues such as Eldon and Bathurst, from whom Palmerston had solicited
support, to withhold it. By default the election had become one which turned
on the Catholic question and among both supporters and opponents in
conducting his canvass, Palmerston claimed, he had 'met with a general
expression of a feeling to which I purposely abstain from applying a stronger
expression than surprize'.[51] Liverpool refuted suggestions that he had acted, or
had encouraged anyone else to act, improperly, pointing to the fact that Bankes
and Goulburn were both relations and friends and it was unreasonable to
expect that Liverpool would do any more than not actively court votes in their
interest. 'I admit that there is a great difference between electing a Member for
the first time & declining to re-elect him,' wrote the Prime Minister, 'but for
this you must blame the principle upon which the University of Cambridge
think proper to act, which I have always considered as rendering a seat for that
University one of the least desirable seats in the Kingdom.'[52]

This was in January and the canvassing and electioneering still had some
weeks to run, but, by the end of May, as the poll approached and acknowledging the possibility of defeat, Palmerston informed Liverpool that in the
event of his losing at Cambridge he would sever his connection with the
government; to which Liverpool simply responded that he hoped that in such
a case they might have some prior conversation.[53] If the election campaign had
been a trying one, however, Palmerston had at least acquired a better understanding of where he stood with his colleagues. The canvass had 'hung upon
me like a nightmare', he admitted in a letter to his brother in early June, a week
before polling began, but, he continued, 'I think I shall succeed if I can prevail
upon people to come up which I hope to do. My own opinion is that Copley
will be first I next, Bankes third & Goulburn fourth. . . . The Whigs have
behaved most handsomely to me, they have given me cordial & hearty support,
and in fact bring me in; Liverpool has behaved as he always does to a friend in
personal questions shabbily, timidly & ill. If I am beat I have told him he must
find another Secy at War for I certainly will not continue in office.'[54] At the
poll, Palmerston's expectations were confirmed as he took second place with
631 votes to Copley's 776. Bankes polled 509 and Goulburn only 439.[55]
Palmerston's success owed a good deal to the support of the largest colleges,
St John's and Trinity, where he topped the college voting, but it was also,
perhaps more significantly, as he noted himself, a victory won with Whig

votes.[56] Palmerston was in no doubt that the outcome had been determined by the Catholic question and that 'we may now appeal to the experience of facts to shew that there does *not* exist among the people of England that bigotted prejudice on this point which the anti-Catholics accused them of entertaining'. He was also quick to link this result to recent events in Ireland and he hoped that the 'breaking loose' of the Irish tenantry from their landlords would add decisive weight to the balance '*for* the question' and lead the landlords 'to adopt a system of management more advantageous to themselves & to the progress of society in Ireland'. Palmerston sensed a much broader shift in the political sands:

> as to the common place balance opposition & government the election will have little effect upon it, the govt are as strong as any govt can wish to be as far as regards those who sit facing them, but in truth the real opposition of the present day sit behind the Treasury bench & it is by the stupid old Tory party, by those ignorant country gentlemen who drown in port the little senses which nature bestowed upon them & bawl out the memory & praises of Pitt, while they are opposing all the measures & principles which he held most important it is by these that the progress of the government in every improvement which they are attempting is thwarted & impeded. On the Catholic question on the principles of commerce, on the corn laws, on the settlement of the currency, on the laws regulating the trade in money & colonial slavery, on the game laws which are intimately connected with the moral habits of the people on all these questions & every thing like them the govt find support from the Whigs & resistance from their self determined friends; however the young squires are more liberal than the old ones, & we must hope that Heaven will protect us from our friends as it has done from our enemies.[57]

Palmerston later wrote that this contest 'was the first decided step towards a breach between me and the Tories, and they were the aggressors'.[58] While this might have been the first sign of an overt divergence, the erstwhile bond between Palmerston and the Tories should not be overstated. Until this point, Palmerston, in his public career had not, on the whole, displayed any overwhelming ideological political commitment. He had served in Tory ministries, but that was due largely to the connections of his early patrons, especially Malmesbury, and was not an accurate guide to Palmerston's own beliefs and inclinations. His entry into politics, at Newport, had not been an ideological one and his victory at Cambridge in 1811 had occasioned no particular test of loyalties while his subsequent returns in 1812, 1818 and 1820 were all uncontested. At the general election in June 1826, following a lengthy canvass of more than six months, Palmerston had been, for the first time, really tested on a political issue, obliged to take a stand, and to take stock of his political position and affil-iations. As he had explained to his brother, his concurrence in Whig policies was reasonably broad-based, and in focusing on questions of trade, commerce and slavery, as well as religious toleration, Palmerston was simply reverting to the ideas and principles he had absorbed from Dugald Stewart at Edinburgh. This is perhaps more evident to historians than it was to Palmerston himself, for it took another couple of years for him to make a clean break with the Tories, but that should not inhibit the judgement that Palmerston was, and had always been, at heart and by temperament, more a Whig than a Tory. This might explain why he was seemingly reluctant to exercise what influence he might lay claim to in Cambridge in the following months.[59]

Less than a year after the general election, in February 1827, Lord Liverpool suffered a massive cerebral haemorrhage at home and the following month the King began his search for a new Prime Minister. George Canning was not his first choice, but he was commissioned to form an administration on 12 April. To some of Palmerston's biographers this represented a genuine turning point for Palmerston as Canning built a 'Catholic' ministry having seen the ultra, Protestant, Tories secede with Liverpool's demise. Palmerston himself, though a 'Catholic', did not care for suggestions that Canning's ministry was only defined by its attitude to religious freedom (he baulked at the implication that if the 'Protestants' refused to serve now with Canning then the 'Catholics' had displayed a want of conviction in participating in Liverpool's administration), but as he acknowledged, if Canning did not succeed, the country risked 'an *anti everything* government'.[60] 'Palmerston's time, it seemed, had come at last', concluded Herbert Bell: of the middle-ranking Tories (the 'sergeants and corporals' according to Lord Londonderry) who stuck to Canning, Palmerston was judged by many as the most capable and important.[61] Bourne was not surprised to find Palmerston among those whom Canning turned to first, but there is some truth in Donald Southgate's observation that this was an 'accidental by-product' of the departure of the ultras; despite this, he saw Palmerston's Canningite association as a natural one.[62] Certainly relations between Palmerston and Canning had grown closer during the 1820s, although to a large extent this had been because Palmerston had sought to exploit a rela-tionship with the Foreign Secretary in order to advance his brother William's diplomatic career, soliciting on his behalf an appointment to the Frankfurt mission in 1822 before, in July 1823, successfully securing for William an offer of the Secretaryship of Legation at Berlin.[63]

Nonetheless, two days after kissing hands, Canning met Palmerston and discussed Palmerston's taking the Home Office or the Chancellorship of the Exchequer. The King had made it clear to Canning that he wanted 'an anti-Catholic' at the Home Office but if that were to prove impossible, Canning hoped Palmerston would accept the promotion himself. In the event, William Sturges Bourne took the position and Palmerston, it was agreed, was to have the Exchequer. Given that this would mean Palmerston facing re-election (in accepting a new office of profit), and given that one of the Cambridge University seats was already being contested (again) by Bankes and Goulburn in the aftermath of Copley's elevation, as Lord Lyndhurst, to the Lord Chancellorship, it was agreed that Palmerston's appointment would be delayed to allow him to seek, as was conventional at Cambridge in such circumstances, an unopposed return rather than risk becoming embroiled in the Bankes–Goulburn contest which threatened a repeat of the previous year's general election. However, if this decision saved Palmerston his seat, it lost him the Exchequer. Sir William Knighton and the King, it was supposed by Palmerston, used the interval to persuade Canning not to appoint Palmerston to the Treasury and instead to keep that department exclusively in Canning's own hands and make John Charles Herries a royal placeman there. As Palmerston later remembered events: 'The fact was as I believe that Knighton & others thought that while Canning was Chan of Exr being also Leader of the Hs of Cns & head of the govt Herries as Secy of Treasy would of necessity be virtually Chanr of Exr in consequence of the multiplicity of Canning's other occupations, but that if I were appointed, having nothing else to do, I should be effective in the office & Herries would sink into a mere instrument.'[64] Herries, then Secretary to the Treasury, himself denied this although it was said that when Canning had asked him whether he would be prepared to continue in that office and work under Palmerston Herries had refused, prompting Canning to declare, 'Then let us say no more about it.'[65] Whether it was because, as Palmerston had it, 'George IV, who personally hated me, did not fancy me as Chancellor of the Exchequer',[66] preferring Herries, out of deference to whom Canning may have dropped the notion anyway, what is clear is that some time after his interview with Palmerston on 14 April, Canning decided not to move Palmerston to the Treasury and met him some little time later to propose an appointment which the King claimed would much gratify Palmerston's ambitions: the Governorship of Jamaica. Canning for his part was not sure that Palmerston did fancy such a posting, but was nevertheless 'disconcerted' when Palmerston burst out laughing at the suggestion. An offer was also made shortly afterwards for Palmerston to become Governor-General of India but this he rejected, with a little more composure (as indeed he had when the same offer had been made earlier, in 1826), as 'an appointment which from climate & distance had to me objections that outweighed the very splendid inducements which it held out'. He was not willing to oblige the King who, he believed, 'would be glad to get me civilly out of the way'.[67]

Even if he was to remain at the War Office – and there is no sign that Palmerston was unhappy to do so – he did, finally, accept a seat in the Cabinet. From there he spoke more authoritatively of the government's position and early on described for William the changing political climate:

Canning has all along received from the Whigs assurances of their support in the event of his forming a govt of which he should be the head even though he made no stipulation on the Catholic question, because they are wise enough to know that in the present state of the King's opinion no govt can be formed upon the principle of carrying that question as a Cabinet measure, and the next best thing is to secure the influence of govt in the hands of men favourable to the question. My own opinion however is that some of them ought to be brought into office Lansdowne & Holland perhaps, & Abercromby & Tierney in the Commons, and I should not be surprized if this were to happen. The govt wd then be very strong & without some such arrangt its chief reliance must be upon a party upon whom we shall have no hold and who may throw us over at any moment of caprice or cabal. For as to the Tories who would hardly vote for our measures before we must not look for any cordial support from them now. Not but that by degrees & one by one they will all by instincts come round to the oat sieve, but I know that Canning means to deal out that sieve very sparingly & to found his govt upon public opinion rather than borough interest, in which I think he is as right as possible.[68]

Palmerston saw that there had been an irreparable breach with the Tories. The Whigs had 'joined us manfully & in earnest' and though Palmerston regretted the loss of Peel personally, he welcomed the clear divergence within Tory ranks.[69] Had Canning lived, his government might well have inaugurated a new era in the party political history of the period; as it was, and aged only fifty-seven, Canning died on 8 August, following a short though painful illness, leaving his government less than four months old and headless.[70] 'What a loss!' wrote Palmerston, 'not merely to parties but to nations, not to his friends only but to mankind.'[71] When, in a debate the following year on the provision to be made for Canning's family, Palmerston told the House, 'I believe . . . that his principles and his policy were most excellently adapted for the benefit of this country; and that as the principles which emanated from him are followed, just in that proportion will those who adopt them conduce to its interest and advantage, and obtain for their Government the confidence and approbation of the people',[72] it seemed only to confirm for many the extent to which the Tory breach had been an irreparable one and Palmerston was now firmly on the liberal side. As he said to his brother at this time, a ministry including the Tories would be at best unstable; one comprising only Tory members 'would be most unfortunate in every possible way & would produce the worst consequences on our foreign relations & domestic policy including commerce & Ireland'.[73] The ideological cross-currents within the Tory party had certainly been more clearly mapped out than previously and it was necessary for a politician such as Palmerston to pay more attention, henceforth, to their navigation. But although it was becoming clear that Palmerston was growing uncomfortable with the strictures of 'Protestant' Toryism and, via liberal Canningism, was moving closer to an overt Whiggish position, it is important to bear in mind that this was a relatively slow process and, in the absence of sharply defined party lines, it was possible for Palmerston to remain within what were essentially Tory governments while adhering to broadly Whiggish nostrums. The Whig Brougham was at this time counselling patience: within a year, he told Palmerston, his power would be 'incalculably greater' and this was, he said, 'a prodigious motive to bearing & forbearing'.[74] Perhaps the ties of party were indeed becoming more fluid. In October 1827, with the Whigs 'getting into good humour again', Palmerston suggested that 'Whig and Tory will soon be erased from our vocabulary'.[75]

Lord Goderich, who already regarded 'the odious distinctions of Whig and Tory' as redundant, had been the leader of the government in the House of Lords and, in effect, Canning's deputy. It was not surprising that the King turned to him immediately to form a moderate coalition of Whigs and Tories along the lines of Canning's and at the end of August he took office as the third Prime Minister of 1827. Goderich had initially, and perhaps superficially, seemed a natural choice to succeed Canning. He was an independent and liberal Tory, but was able to deal with his own party's ultras as well as with Whigs from across the floor. He was, furthermore and not insignificantly, widely regarded as a personable man.[76] His government, however, did not survive long enough even to meet Parliament and in January 1828 finally collapsed amid bitter in-fighting.

Goderich had approached Palmerston to become Chancellor of the Exchequer as soon as he had taken up the seals from Canning, and Palmerston had accepted. But in a whispered conversation a few days later at Canning's funeral, Goderich told Palmerston that the King had again raised objections and insisted that the place go to Herries. Herries himself pleaded a lack of ambition in that direction and '*jouait la victime*' as Palmerston put it, but in a series of interviews with the King and Goderich, Herries was finally prevailed upon to accept the post. The task was not straightforward: on 17 August, Palmerston reported to Princess Lieven that meetings to arrange the Privy Council had lasted four hours and achieved little beyond demonstrating the absence of unity and clear purpose among the Tories.[77] During the August deliberations, observed Palmerston, Herries emerged 'Chancellor of the Exchequer – but the King's Chancellor of the Exchequer and not Goderich's'. Palmerston accepted this royal rebuff with outward good grace but he later claimed he had been chastised by Huskisson for not holding Goderich to his promise to give Palmerston the Exchequer that could not have been denied had it been insisted upon. Now, however, complained Huskisson, Herries had 'been thrown in like a live shell into the Cabinet to explode and blow us all up'.[78] It is true that Palmerston had hoped that William Sturges Bourne, who was also acceptable to the King, would take the office, 'as one of Canning's most attached, most esteemed and valued friends' and protect Canning's political legacy,[79] but Sturges Bourne was 'in despair and miserable' at the prospect of moving to the Treasury and having initially accepted, 'took fright' later the same day and left 'the whole thing . . . at sea again'.[80] Goderich might have felt that 'Any settlement would be preferable to this uncertainty & agitation',[81] but it is not at all clear from Herries's own account that his appointment was quite so controversial. Huskisson, indeed, was reported to have been 'a warm friend' to Herries and had himself urged Herries's appointment on the King in the face of primarily Whig opposition.[82] However, the prevailing sense was that Goderich's task was not an easy one. As Herries's record of events confirms, Whig–Tory–Canningite tensions delayed even the first appointments being made to the new Cabinet throughout August 1827. Goderich's attempts to construct and maintain a durable ministry were plagued by such in-fighting throughout the autumn and early winter that by December it was obvious that the game was all but up. Palmerston regretted Goderich's failure,[83] but when George Shee received Palmerston's account of recent events in December he could find in it only further proofs of his earlier conviction that 'Goderich is really *not* up to the work' and that 'a nervous fidget about him . . . peculiarly incapacitated him for trying situations', such as the clique-ridden atmosphere of Westminster. Shee thought either Peel or Lansdowne would have to form a new government; at any event it was abundantly clear that Goderich could not continue much longer.[84]

By early January those who identified themselves with the late George Canning felt increasingly torn. As Huskisson, the leading light in that group, explained to Lord Granville: 'I see that attempts are making in various quarters, & from different motives, to identify me with the Whigs. I believe that there is no Whig in office that will not admit that I have stood fairly by them, & done everything in my power to keep things as they were. But if in the present crisis they withdraw, or refuse to continue, & if the violent ones determine to run at the K[ing] for insincerity (as it is said they do) I do not see that it is necessary for me to adopt the same line. I am determined not to do it; and I hope you will think me right. At the same time I think it *ten* to one that, on other grounds, I may find it necessary to retire.'[85] But if Huskisson decided to go, then Palmerston, too, would be in an insecure, not to say unknown, position.[86] His friend George Shee counselled Palmerston to stand above petty party intrigue. 'If you *should* chance to be left out in the new arrangements do not suffer any feelings of personal annoyance to identify you with the *Whigs*,' he urged. 'Rather adopt the line that Peel chalked out for himself & stand *aloof* from the *party* discussions in the House of Commons as much as you can do in fairness by your late colleagues. Take part as much as you like in *new* & *general* questions but do so in your *individual* capacity not as a member of a party.'[87]

When a disagreement between Huskisson and Herries occurred Goderich told the King he did not know what to do; the King did, however, and 'he bid Goderich go home and take care of himself, and keep himself quiet; and he immediately sent for the Duke of Wellington to form a government'.[88] Some time before, Lord Anglesey had warned ministers that a Wellington premiership would 'trip up all your heels' and Palmerston conceded that in January 1828 'our heels were up'. Wellington held out a helping hand to the Canning party and invited Huskisson, as head of that group, to a meeting at Apsley House to discuss arrangements for a new government.[89] Palmerston met the Duke on the 13th, during which interview Wellington asked Palmerston to remain a member of the government, forgetting past differences and looking only to the future. Palmerston, for his part, laid down certain stipulations that must be met for him to agree; above all, he said, the Empire must be 'pacified' as a first priority and this and domestic peace demanded a settlement of the Catholic question, a question which, Palmerston indicated, he regarded 'as the most important which would probably occur during the rest of my life'.[90]

The formation of the new government under Wellington had forced Palmerston to confront a clear turning point in his own political career. As he explained to Emily, he must, henceforth, follow Huskisson in office as the best guarantee of 'those liberal principles which we both profess', trusting to Huskisson as a guardian of liberal (Whig) as against 'pig tail' (Tory) interests.[91] For many years it had been possible for Palmerston to fudge any discussion of his political position and instincts so long as the charms of society outweighed the dubious attractions of departmental drudgery and so long as political partisanship had, to some extent, been subsumed in a general patriotic consensus during war. However, since the conclusion of peace in 1815 and the gradual fragmentation of Tory unity under the broad umbrella of Liverpool's 'liberal Toryism' in the later 1810s and 1820s, crucial political questions, both domestic and foreign, had begun to underscore political tensions. Palmerston had come up against this at Cambridge in the early 1820s, but the rarefied and peculiar nature of Cambridge University and college politics had, to some extent, insulated him from the blunt realities of ideological disagreement – unlike Peel who lost his seat at Oxford University in 1827 over his 'Protestantism' – and allowed Palmerston to continue the comfortable life of a well-connected bachelor about town. To adapt a phrase later used by the Marquis of Salisbury in speaking of British foreign policy, there was something of the floating 'lazily downstream, occasionally putting out a diplomatic boathook to avoid collisions',[92] about Palmerston's early parliamentary career. This is not to suggest a want of spirits or conviction in Palmerston; rather it is to underline the ambiguous or ill-defined nature of political identity and the absence, at least for a junior minister representing a relatively loyal university seat, of the need to bother too much about such alignments and antagonisms. However, by the late 1820s, in no

small measure due to the incapacity of the heretofore conciliatory (if ineffectual) Liverpool, politics was thrown into a state of flux in which Canningites sat
somewhere, not altogether comfortably, between ultra Tories and Whigs.
Canning's partial success and Goderich's abysmal failure to construct viable
governments had, at least, caused a Canningite, liberal, group to act rather more
coherently. In the wake of Canning's death Huskisson had stood as de facto
leader of this group in which, in particular, Huskisson, Palmerston, Lord
Dudley and Charles Grant were emerging as a connected, if not united, party
consciously working together.[93] As Palmerston explained to his brother, it was
important that Canning's principles be preserved as 'a great tribute of homage
to his memory': 'Dudley will carry them on in our foreign relations, Huskisson
& Grant in our colonial & commercial. Peel will probably return to his Home
Office where he will prosecute his system of reform – all this, instead of a pig
tail Tory govt shews the great strides which public opinion has made in the last
few years.' The Whigs, Palmerston judged, would be 'furious', and he regretted
this as he 'like[d] them much better than the Tories, & agree with them much
more, but still we the Canningites, if we may be so termed, did not join their
government, but they came and joined ours, & whatever regard we may feel for
them we have not inlisted with them so as to be bound to follow their fate &
fortunes or to make their retention a condition of our remaining; & indeed if
we had all gone out I should certainly not have sat with them in the Hs of Cns
but should have taken an independent & separate position.'[94]

Having satisfied themselves that they could accede to office alongside Herries
with 'a proper regard' to Huskisson's honour following their disagreement over
the chairmanship of a finance committee under Goderich, Palmerston, Dudley,
Grant and Huskisson looked to possible reconciliation with the Tories.[95]
However, differences over the Catholic question remained an obstacle, not least
because, as Grant pointed out, the Treasury, the Home Office and the premiership itself were all to be in the hands of 'decidedly anti Catholics' who would
'dispose of the whole of the domestic patronage of the country'.[96] On 18 January
Palmerston met Wellington again to discuss terms on behalf of the Canningites.
The Catholic question, he insisted, was to remain, as under Liverpool, an 'open
question' (though what confidence Palmerston placed in such precedents must
be doubtful), government patronage was to be administered 'in a spirit of strict
neutrality' with regard to that question, and most especially appointments to
Irish offices, notably the Lord-Lieutenancy and Chief Secretaryship, were not to
be filled by anyone hostile to the Catholic claims.[97] Wellington, Palmerston
afterwards noted, 'seemed to receive these propositions like a person who was
more accustomed to prescribe to others than to have conditions suggested to
him, but took the line of treating them lightly & laughing them off, saying that
the first was asking him if he was honest the second whether he was a madman.'
During the course of the interview, Wellington, according to Palmerston's
account, treated the issue casually, saying he was not mad enough to send a 'fire

brand' to Ireland and that he would keep the Catholic question 'out of sight by moderation'. Palmerston remained unconvinced and uneasy after this 'desultory conversation' and though Wellington thought an agreement had been reached about joining together in government, Palmerston entertained lingering doubts on these important points.[98] Huskisson sought to reassure himself that 'in a Cabinet of 14 to have 8 Catholicks to 6 Protestants is a sacrifice of the principle upon which Mr C wished to form his administration in respect to that question',[99] but though a verbal agreement had been reached at the Apsley House meeting on 18 January between Huskisson, Palmerston, Dudley, Grant and Wellington that the Catholic question should remain one of conscience,[100] the sense persisted that this was a cobbled-together and not a unified new ministry.

The Whigs, favourable to the Catholic claims, resented Huskisson leading the Canningite element into union with the Tories, but Palmerston defended their conduct on the grounds that it was the Whigs who had joined the Canningites, and therefore they who had also left them, and concluded that 'hypocrisy may go any length in words but soon betrays itself when it is put to the test of deeds, and they cannot deny that he [Huskisson] took great pains to prevent them from retiring when they wanted to do so, & why therefore should he scheme to make them go when they did not wish it.'[101] Huskisson for his part insisted that, contrary to the imputations of Canning's widow, he had taken the best course to defend Canning's memory and uphold his policies by refusing to become a mere 'appendage' of the Whigs who, most of them, 'care but little for his public character'.[102]

The new government was barely two months old, however, when Palmerston wrote to William to say that 'affairs are becoming embroiled at home & abroad; our government consists of some discordant elements', and while Peel, he thought, 'is so right headed & liberal & so up to the opinions & feelings of the time', that the difficulties might be overcome, the picture painted was not one of stable government.[103] In foreign affairs, the Canningites took up a determined position over Greece in April, worried that a proposal to allow the Ottoman Porte a veto over the Greek choice of a president put the prospect of a workable Greek government in jeopardy. Palmerston could see only one potential candidate for the presidency, Capo d'Istria, the former Russian representative at the Congress of Vienna, and feared that a Turkish veto would disrupt Greek government and not convey any advantage to Turkey. 'The great object for which this country embarked in this understanding was *peace*', insisted Palmerston, 'and it would therefore seem that our purposes will best be accomplished in proportion as we exclude from our settlement the elements of future discord.'[104] In May any semblance of Cabinet unity over foreign affairs began to evaporate as the Canningites accused the Tories of trying to pick a quarrel with Russia. While Wellington, Ellenborough, Bathurst and Aberdeen worked to provoke a dispute, Palmerston claimed, Peel and the Canningite elements of the Cabinet sought to pour oil on troubled waters. 'It is however heavy work dragging on in a govt that differ upon almost every point that comes under discussion & that involves any general principle & our meetings are always debates instead of deliberations,' Palmerston complained. 'There are a set of violent Tories who beset the Duke in private & sway him powerfully. Still however we have public opinion & the House of Commons to fight with & these are powerful weapons. The result has not yet been to lead us to *do* anything we disapproved of, but only to make us leave *undone* things we should have wished to have done; & this conflict of opinion leaves the government in a state of inaction at a moment when it ought to be taking a lead in the affairs of Europe.' The difficulties were not confined to the East: over Portuguese policy, Palmerston tried to preserve some semblance of a Canningite line, arguing that 'as we did not *go* to interfere [in internal affairs] so we could not *stay* to do so'.[105] Nor, indeed, were the differences limited to foreign policy. Over religious policy, Palmerston also expressed some unease, explaining in a letter to William that

> This party however is going down fast, and the reign of Toryism is drawing to a close. Peel is perfectly liberal in every thing, and the old hens who see this duckling taking so stoutly to the water are in perfect dismay. The line which Peel & the Duke have taken about the Test & Corporation acts has made a considerable impression, but especially in Ireland. The Orangemen there say that it is a virtual abandonment of the Catholic question, and to be sure the Duke's language in the House was such as to lay the ground for his taking any course he likes upon the Catholic question. He supported the Test repeal, for the sake of obtaining *religious peace* in the country, and because the House of Commons had passed it; whenever therefore we send up to the peers a Catholic bill, the same arguments will serve for it; the bishops too are beginning to take their cue, & facing outwards to prepare to wheel quite about; In short I begin to think this great measure fully as near as it was last year under Canning.[106]

Palmerston meanwhile was acquiring a reputation for awkwardness among the government's ultra Tory members. When, in May 1828, during a debate on the provision to be made for Canning's family, Palmerston paid warm tribute to Canning and Canningite principles, he caused 'great offence' and Wellington began to speak of '*a mutiny*'; Palmerston's days in the government, thought Ellenborough, were numbered.[107] A few days later, Ellenborough began to look and hope for the departure of both Huskisson and Palmerston,[108] and by the end of May the union of liberal and ultra within Wellington's administration was effectively over. Palmerston had met Wellington on 20 May and repeated three times that he was prepared to resign; Wellington, however, did not deign to flatter Palmerston's sense of importance: as the Duke told Ellenborough, 'Palmerston must follow Huskisson, and he [Wellington] did *not choose to fire great guns at sparrows*'. The world, as Ellenborough put it, was growing weary of the tribulations of the government and 'begins to be very impatient for a *dénouement*. The inconvenience to the public service has been great already'.[109]

By the end of May Huskisson, Palmerston and the other 'Canningites' had resigned from the government.[110] Wellington maintained afterwards that the departure of Huskisson, which he regretted, and of Palmerston which followed and which he did not, was Palmerston's fault. Palmerston could have averted the break-up, Wellington claimed, but, attributing Palmerston's truculence to War Office spats between Palmerston as Secretary at War when Wellington had been commander-in-chief, the Duke said Palmerston 'was by no means an agreeable colleague' and he believed it was Palmerston who had 'put Huskisson up to the move which led to the tender of his resignation'.[111] However, as Palmerston remembered, 'the friends of Mr Canning' had 'joined as a party; and as a party we retired'. Dudley hesitated, not because he liked Wellington, but because he loved the Foreign Office, but once Huskisson had tendered his resignation, the rest, Palmerston, Grant, Dudley and William Lamb, all followed.[112]

By the summer of 1828 Palmerston had been in office, continuously, for over two decades and he found it 'quite comical to have no tie & to be able to dispose of my day as I like'. However, politics ran too deep to be immediately forgotten. His resignation speech, delivered on 2 June, had been generally well received, although he was amused to have been assailed afterwards by Lord Cumberland who claimed Palmerston had 'grown quite a democrat'. His 'democratic' credentials were perhaps questionable, but there was no doubting that Palmerston saw recent events as a signal of a wider liberal ascendancy. He hoped the government might incline to be more liberal ('*now that they themselves have the credit of whatever they may do in that line*') but be that as it may, Palmerston was confident that the 'ejected Liberals' were 'for a nascent party in Parliament' and he counted a number of 'respectable men and many men of talent' in both Houses ready to nail their colours to that mast.[113] As he enthused to Emily Cowper, a purely Tory ministry could not now survive without some sign of deference to public demands for more liberal government and it would be enough of a result to have turned Wellington's administration some way in that direction by the recent resignations.[114]

On foreign affairs Palmerston claimed something of an accord with Wellington, or at least that Wellington had, since their departure, adopted all of the policies of the Canningite faction which he had so opposed when they shared places in the Cabinet. 'There is now no one thing which we urged upon the Duke & which he peremptorily & obstinately refused to do, which he has not been brought to adopt,' he claimed. Conference diplomacy had been resumed, Russian and British fleets were cooperating in the Mediterranean, a liberal settlement of the Greek question, establishing a 'substantial if not complete independence from Turkey' had been agreed; all points which had been subjects of 'angry disputes' in Cabinet and which were now 'settled exactly in conformity with *our* opinions'. Palmerston's eulogy to Canning might have been taken as a 'slur' in the past, but the government's Eastern policy, judged Palmerston, was now decidedly Canningite.[115] However, Palmerston increasingly focused on a settlement of the Catholic question as the overriding political priority of the moment. The state of Ireland was 'coming to a crisis' he said, and a clash between the Orangemen and the Catholic Association was far from impossible. Failure to do anything in the coming session of Parliament would lead to the frustration of Catholic expectations 'burst[ing] like a thunder cloud' and he doubted the government could weather such a storm. 'My own opinion is that things are come to that pass that no man who is *for* the question should take office without stipulating for its being carried, & though there is little chance of the option being put to me, I have pretty well made up my own mind so to act upon that principle'.[116]

The year 1829 was a crucial one for Palmerston and represented the point at which he reached political maturity.[117] In parliamentary debates, notably speaking to great effect on foreign policy in June, Palmerston finally staked out something approaching a political platform and, superficially at least, laid claim to the mantle of Canning's legacy. But Palmerston was also becoming a serious 'domestic' politician and in a series of revealing entries in a political journal penned in that year (significantly one of the very few times when there is evidence that Palmerston consciously reflected on political theory), he sketched out ideas on a range of questions which borrowed, strikingly and explicitly, from the teachings of Dugald Stewart and the ideas of Whiggish Enlightenment thought.

The core themes of Palmerston's Edinburgh years – especially Stewart's lectures on political economy – recur in Palmerston's notes from this period and his notebook even includes some direct references to, and quotations from, Stewart's work. Free trade, commerce, religion and politics, liberty, freedom and constitutional government, alongside pieces on Ireland and on slavery, all figured in Palmerston's 'memoranda'. It is no coincidence that these (Whiggish) themes appear at the moment when Palmerston – separated from his erstwhile political bases and floating uneasily between the major parties in the company of Canningite–Huskissonite–liberal Tories – was called upon to define his political identity and philosophy.

On economic policy, he turned his attention, first, to the protectionist levies imposed by the Corn Laws. He rejected arguments that it was 'not politically safe' to become dependent on foreign countries for the subsistence of a large proportion of the population, arguing that for a manufactures and exports based economy, such as Britain's, this was an inevitable state of affairs and, after all, he said it 'is the same thing to a man whether the corn he eats comes from abroad, or whether the means by which he buys his food come from thence.' Free trade in a basic foodstuff such as corn, Palmerston maintained, was essential when it was traded for manufactured (or less essential) goods since it 'is easier to forbid people to buy articles produced by others, than to forbid them to sell articles produced by themselves. It is easier for a foreign government to prevent its subjects from buying our cotton, than to prevent them from selling their own corn. The one would deprive them of a luxury the other would deprive them of the means of existence.' Only if the British population and economy were to cease to grow, Palmerston argued, would the domestic corn grower risk losses, and he dismissed agrarian claims that protectionist duties were the only means by which to safeguard the position of the British producer. He denied that additional food supplies would undermine domestic supply – more food, he argued, would support population growth and therefore more consumers, ensuring that 'the demand for British corn, would be undiminished'; manufacturing industry too, he believed, would benefit from access to larger markets. Indeed, argued Palmerston, expansion of markets and output, and a larger population, were interrelated and essential: 'The burthens of a country remaining the same the share of each individual must diminish as the number of those who contribute increases; and thus if the burthens increase, an increase in the number of contributors may save each of the former contributors from any additional contribution.' The national debt, reasoned Palmerston, did not militate against free trade in corn; on the contrary, by facilitating a more rapid accumulation of capital, unfettered trade would actually reduce the burden on the agriculturalist. After all, Britain was in a healthy economic condition in which, he calculated, '22 millions of people, active industrious, & intelligent; possessing the advantages of a temperate climate, a fruitful soil and an insular position, must every year, make a large addition to their national capital. That this is really so, the slightest observation will shew; traverse the country in every direction, see the houses that are building, the roads, the canals, the railways, the inclosures, the docks, the harbours, that people are every where making; all these investments of capital are calculated to afford an increase in the future annual produce of the national industry.' There was no escaping the conclusion, he felt, that 'Protecting duties are taxes laid upon the bulk of the community, & expended in paying a few individuals for the loss they sustain in carrying on an unprofitable trade.' Indeed, 'the interest of the debt is paid by the industry of the country. That part of the national industry which is employed on the land, cannot alone pay it. If the burthen were thrown upon the land, the land would be overwhelmed. A portion & a large one of the burthen must be thrown upon commerce & manufactures; but then to enable them to support the burthen & contribute to the utmost of their power, their industry must have free scope given to it; what is commonly called the system of free trade, then, has for its object to relieve the land from the pressure of the debt, by calling up to its aid the elastic resources of manufactures & commerce.'

The prescriptions of Whig (and Smithian) political economy were also brought to bear on Palmerston's view of the state's responsibility to the poor. Free trade extended to a free market for labour and Palmerston was critical of the over-provision of state-supported relief:

> Our poor laws profess to find employment for all those who cannot find it for themselves; that is, to accomplish an impossibility. If the employment which they find is unproductive, it is obviously useless; if it is productive it clearly must supersede an equal amount of employment which would otherwise have been given spontaneously.
>
> Suppose for instance 100£ a year taken from any man for poor rates; he becomes 100£ a year poorer, & must spend 100£ a year less; that is, he must give 100£ a year less employment to the industry of the country, in some way or other; and thus poor laws are not a creation of capital but a mere forcible transfer of capital from one hand to another. But the labour performed for an individual who watches over his workman, & sees that he earns his wages, & who applies the mans labour in the way he thinks most profitable to himself, must be more productive than that of the man who works for the parish, & therefore it is more conducive to the progressive wealth of the community. Besides the idle are employed in easy labour by means of that money which would give harder work to the industrious. Then comes the effect upon the moral habits of the community. The chilling of spontaneous charity in the upper classes towards those whom they are forcibly compelled to relieve; the damping of industry among the lower classes by the certainty of having relief found for them; if they cannot or do not find it for themselves by their own exertions. The extinction of the honest pride of independence and the total annihilation of those little good offices of reciprocal benevolence which cast a cheering and redeeming beam even over the local barbarism, & occasional ferocity of the lower classes in Ireland.

Here then, in a desire for progress and improvement in society, there are clear echoes of Dugald Stewart in Palmerston's later rhetoric. Religion and politics were also to be separated not on theological but on societal grounds:

> If there was any sense in imposing tests as qualifications for civil & political office, the tests should have relation to the duties & powers of the office, & should be declarations of political & not religious opinions. There is nothing to prevent civil & political power from being placed in the hands of a man who would wish to overthrow the constitution either for

tyranny or republicanism, but the laws which have been lauded as the bulwarks of the constitution prohibit such power from being placed in the hands of a man who believes in transubstantiation or who will not take the sacrament in the form prescribed by the ritual of the Church of England. Would the most ignorant electors in England act upon so absurd a principle in chusing their representative. Do they ever inquire whether the candidate is an Anabaptist or a Socinian or Presbyterian or an Episcopalian, is not the question always whether he is a Whig or a Tory, an advocate for free trade or a friend to agricultural monopoly.

This speaks of conviction based on experience and was therefore cumulative as Palmerston was exposed to the realities of life on his Irish estates and the inhibiting effects of partisan divisions at Westminster. Yet there was also an ideological, humanitarian tone to Palmerston's theorising. Along with Catholic emancipation, the other issue of conscience which had touched his career up to this point was that of slavery and the slave trade. He had been thought insufficiently sincere in 1806 at Cambridge, but there is evidence that by 1829 his opposition to slavery, though he did not at this point trouble to draw any conclusions about means for its abolition, was important. In his notebook he observed:

The slave owners & their supporters allege the vices of the slaves as proof of their unfitness for liberty. But these very vices are the effects of their slavery. This is therefore as much as to say, that as long as the inevitable effect of an ever working cause shall continue to exist, you will not remove that cause. It is to give it perpetuity. But to tell the negroes that you will not relieve them from their abject condition, till they cease to have the degraded qualities which that abject condition necessarily & invariably produces, is to add to injury, mockery & insult. It is no less illogical than unjust. It is as repugnant to the common sense as to the common feelings of mankind, & those who thus argue, must either be insincere, or else their minds must be incapable of appreciating the tone & value of the simplest conclusion.

And this served to inform his perspective on foreign affairs and especially the Eastern question:

To hear masters of slaves talk of slavery one should suppose mankind in a universal error about it, & that it is the most delightful condition in which a human being can be placed. If you believe the West Indian, none are so happy & so well off as the negroes of a sugar plantation; listen to Mehmet Ali Pasha of Egypt in his interview with Sir E. Codrington at Alexandria on 6th August 1828 about the evacuation of Greece by his son

Ibrahim, and the opinion of Europe as to the condition & treatment of the Greek slaves (who were dying by 5 & 6 every day from fatigue privation & disease) was quite erroneous. So well according to him were the slaves of the Egyptians treated, that Turks often called themselves Mamedukes in order that they might become slaves.

At the same time, Palmerston's notes also reveal his deep prejudices against Islam which would, to some extent, underpin the tensions of his later foreign policies:

The Mahometan religion seems like a parody upon Christianity by the evil spirit. Like an expiring effort of renewed malice against the human race, to counteract the last & greatest act of benevolence on the part of the deity. The deity sends to man a revealed religion which teaches him to practice charity towards others & controul over himself; & which holds out virtuous happiness hereafter, as the consequence of good conduct here. The Mahometan faith tells him to commit criminal violence in this life, & promises a reward, the enjoyment of vicious indulgence in a life to come. But it assumes as a cloak some of the precepts of Christianity, for the purpose of disguising its fundamental & inherent deformity.

Palmerston drew a similarly crude parallel in terms of liberal, constitutional government and more despotic varieties, echoing Stewart's essays on such questions:

There are some govts who seem to treat constitutional freedom as they would the plague, & who cannot sleep easy in their beds unless they shut off its approach by a precautionary chain, from the countries whose welfare they are charged to protect. Thus Austria trembles at the idea of independent Greece coming in contact with her Adriatic provinces; and thus the govt of England think they have a mighty advantage, when they have interposed a stripe of non-conducting Turkish despotism between the Ionian islands & emancipated Greece. Gracious heaven, what a miserable policy! Are these the feelings by which mighty nations ought to be governed! Are these the principles to which the destinies of mankind are doomed to be sacrificed. Patience indeed while such maxims actuate govts whose vital principle is arbitrary power & who live only by the suppression of thought & the extinction of independent mind, patience indeed while such motives actuate statesmen who find that the frozen & slippery surface on which their artificial fabric is reared would break up on every side if the warm tide of human improvement were permitted to rise around them; but that ministers of England who owe their every power, & their political being to constitutional freedom; who as ministers of a free state are enabled to hold a language to the rest of the world, which as servants of a despot they would not venture to use; that they should deal with liberty as if it were a pestilence, is indeed matter for astonishment. But let them not be deceived; if there *is* infection in a free state, it is not by the intervention of a few Turkish guard posts, that that infection can be cut off. The contagion of ideas is of a far subtler & more diffusive nature, it requires not like the plague the actual contact of bodies; but like the pretended magnetism of the enthusiast it is transmitted by indescribable & mysterious sympathies. Neither mountains nor seas can obstruct its passage nor the scymitar nor the bayonet arrest its progress.

There were, for Palmerston, in this preference for constitutional government, clear ramifications for the construction of foreign policy: 'one should have thought that there was something in the spectacle of a nation struggling against tyranny, for independence, which would have worked upon the feelings & have commanded the sympathy of every man; but most of all of men administering the affairs of a free & independent state. That it would have tempted them almost to break through treaties, & even made them long to violate obligations; but would surely make them rejoice to find their obligations point the same way as their feelings & to find that a regard to the good faith of treaties coincident with the dictates of generosity.' And he felt, like a good Whig, that though the monarchy had a role to play in constitutional government, it was a limited (not to say, in advance of the notion, Bagehotian) one: 'The kingly office is to a constitution what the fly wheel is to the steam engine; it regulates & equalizes the motions of the whole.' None of these aims and objectives, however, was to be realised so long as Wellington remained in office. The system of that government, Palmerston said, 'has been bad faith towards the strong, and violence towards the weak; the Duke's maxim at the head of his army was parcere subjectis et deballare superbos; the reverse has been his practice at the head of his Cabinet.'[118]

So when in October 1829 Sir Richard Vivian had made overtures to Palmerston to rejoin the government, in the light of apparent growing Tory uneasiness with the 'tyrant' Wellington, Palmerston insisted that he 'should not of course like to join a government who had in contemplation to propose measures at variance with the opinions which I held', and those differences, Palmerston pointed out, had been 'upon almost all points foreign and domestic'.[119] Palmerston's notebooks reveal a man working out his political priorities in private and drawing on his early influences, but in public he had already forced a breach with Wellington's government, choosing in June 1829 to deliver an attack on the ministry's foreign policy that was more wide-ranging and intellectually robust than his previous Westminster performances. For many later commentators, this was the first parliamentary glimpse of the later Palmerston;[120] it was, in fact, more accurately the flourishing of the early Palmerston.

In May Palmerston had begun to express alarm at the state of international affairs. He had visited Paris earlier in the year 'to get acquainted with some people there whose names one hears much & often',[121] and he now saw France as a weak power, something which threatened to pave the way for the ascendancy of the conservative policies of Wellington's Britain and Metternich's Austria. Greece and Portugal would, from the perspective of liberal politics, suffer as a result, he told his brother.[122] These were the grounds, then, on which he addressed the House of Commons on 1 June.

The question in Portugal, for Palmerston, was simply whether one supported constitutional or despotic government. The issue had been thrown into sharp focus on the death of King John VI in 1826, but even before this point it was obvious that the liberal constitution of 1821, which John had upheld since his return from Brazil, was threatened by conservative aristocratic and clerical intrigues that looked to John's younger son, Dom Miguel, for leadership. Miguel indeed had led an abortive military rebellion in 1823, but since then had been living in exile in Vienna. Following John's death, however, there was an inevitable struggle for the succession between Miguel and his elder brother, Dom Pedro (since 1822, Emperor of Brazil), although Pedro preferred to stay in Brazil and abdicated his claim in favour of his daughter Donna Maria. Miguelites claimed that Dom Pedro's decision applied to his descendants too and refused to recognise Maria's position, insisting instead that Miguel should be the new King. George Canning, as Prime Minister, had sent British troops to defend Maria and subsequently, in October, a compromise was brokered by Britain, France, Austria, Portugal and Brazil in which Miguel would marry his niece and govern as regent until she came of age. On the basis of this arrangement, Britain was to withdraw its forces. Just as Wellington's government came to power, however, it was becoming clear that Miguel had no intention of respecting the agreement; but as Miguel rolled back the liberal constitutionalist reforms of the 1820s and proclaimed himself King in 1828, Wellington chose not to protest. The British army continued to withdraw from the peninsula and Wellington acknowledged the claims of Miguel. This, for Palmerston, represented a betrayal of Canningite promises to the Portuguese people. He determined, therefore, to call the British government to account over a foreign policy different from that which people had been 'authorized to expect' and which had 'inspired every Englishman, who values the good name of his country, with deep mortification'.

Palmerston opened his case with an unambiguous assault on Miguel and on Wellington's government. 'The civilised world rings with execrations upon Miguel,' he said, 'and yet this destroyer of constitutional freedom, this breaker of solemn oaths, this faithless usurper, this enslaver of his country, this trampler upon public law, this violator of private rights, this attempter on the life of a helpless and defenceless woman, is in the opinion of Europe mainly indebted to the success which has hitherto attended him, to a belief industriously propagated by his partisans, and not sufficiently refuted by any acts of the British government, that the Cabinet of England look upon his usurpation with no unfriendly eye.' Thus warmed up, he proceeded to question the principle of non-interference by which the government had, he said, given implicit approval to Miguelite intrigues. Interference, 'by force of arms', agreed Palmerston, could never be justified; however 'intermeddling, and intermeddling in every way, and to every extent, short of actual military force', was not only legitimate but the basis upon which Britain's relations with Portugal in recent times had been founded, if only as a means of preventing Portugal, and thus the entire peninsula, from falling under Spanish control. There was therefore a natural alliance underpinned by 'mutual usefulness' in which British self-interest served as a guarantee of Portuguese independence, dating back to the seventeenth century, but exampled within living memory notably in 1807 and 1824 when Britain had been instrumental in safeguarding the Portuguese government and the interests of its people. More than this, diplomatic agreements reached in October 1827 which were supposed to have secured the peaceful succession of legitimate government from Pedro to Maria – and to which Miguel had apparently acceded under the watchful eye of the British ambassador – gave Britain now 'an absolute right' to interfere. It was a betrayal of Portugal, and its legitimate constitutionalist inheritors and supporters, to do nothing when 'the wolf cast off his borrowed clothing, and appeared in his own natural garb'. Indeed, worse than this, the British forces stationed in Portugal as guarantors of the constitution had, in remaining to oversee the transfer of power, allowed themselves to become not even bystanders but active defenders of Miguel's 'usurpation'. Britain's honour was impugned: 'Was it fitting that the king of England, should be the stalking-horse under whose cover this royal poacher should creep upon his unsuspecting prey? Was it becoming that the king of England, should be made use of, as the attesting witness, to engagements never meant to be fulfilled, and to oaths forsworn by the heart, ere yet they had found utterance from the lips?'

There was an unsatisfactory logic about the government's refusal to interfere: not interfering to prevent Miguel from conquering Madeira (Palmerston, in denying the legitimacy of Miguel's claims to the Portuguese throne, argued that, by extension, he had similarly no rights over Portugal's dependency, Madeira) was in fact a betrayal of the principle that no country had the right to impose upon any other a particular ruler or form of government; in other words, interference was justified if its aim was to correct a perceived infringement of another's sovereignty. Two wrongs did not make a right, said Palmerston, and 'Those who deny premises cannot accede to conclusions.' The British government ought not to stand 'the most irregular frolics of a spoiled and favourite child', said Palmerston, but should treat Miguel as the malefactor he so patently was. War to defend the interests of the Portuguese people would have been justified but unnecessary had the British government but resisted Miguel's claims; yet Palmerston found evidence of the weakness or incompetence of the British government elsewhere, notably in Greece where failure to execute in timely fashion the Treaty of London of 1827 had led to the very outcome it was designed to avert: war in the east of Europe. Worse still, it would appear to public opinion, he claimed, that it was France that had demonstrated an 'enlightened liberality' in its attitude to events in the Morea while 'England will bear the odium, of having vainly attempted to clog the progress of France'. Turkey was the aggressive party in Greece and in the interests of avoiding a wider European conflagration, as well as of minimising the damage to Turkish interests, Turkey ought, Palmerston said, to have been induced to come to terms with Russia and recompense Russia in pecuniary (rather than territorial) fashion; and Palmerston doubted, therefore, whether the British government had 'laboured, *bona fide*, and in good earnest, to bring about peace, in the only way in which peace can be accomplished'. These questions, then, for Palmerston, were vital ones of war and peace; but the responses to them were, no less significantly, ones reflecting an ideological division. 'There are two great parties in Europe;' he said, 'one which endeavours to bear sway by the force of public opinion; another which endeavours to bear sway by the force of physical control', and while the Wellington government was unequivocally to be grouped with the latter, Palmerston was equally sure justice rested with the former.[123]

Palmerston's speech has conventionally been portrayed as both staking a claim to Canning's intellectual legacy and as a bid for the Foreign Office itself. It was, said Donald Southgate, and with a reference to Palmerston's sporting tastes, 'like the innings which gets a man chosen for a test match'.[124] It is certainly not insignificant that Palmerston published this speech as a pamphlet straight afterwards.[125] Henry Gally Knight wrote from Paris to congratulate Palmerston on a speech that would do much to advance Canningite policy and British interests and arrest the decline in Britain's standing under the 'dictator' Wellington.[126] Certainly there are signs that Palmerston's thoughts were turning more systematically to foreign affairs. In the same month that he publicly attacked Wellington's foreign policy in Parliament, Palmerston also sketched out a list of ten 'points to be inquired into in the session of 1830', ranging over British policy in Portugal, Spain, Russia, Turkey and Greece.[127] But as Southgate also pointed out, while the appeal to public opinion echoed Canningite rhetoric, in attacking the government's policy on Portugal, he was attacking those who also thought themselves to be following Canning's policy. Canning, it was true, had 'flown to the aid of Portugal' in 1823 and 1826, but Palmerston (and others) had 'misinterpreted' Canning's commitment to principled foreign policy if they thought that this was a signal of a commitment to constitutional government there. As Southgate noted, Canning had emphasised the power of

British opinion, but had also insisted that Britain adopt a position of neutrality not only between conflicting nations but between conflicting principles. Canning had gone to Portugal's aid in 1823 not to defend constitutional government but to maintain the balance of power and protect a border; Palmerston, argued Southgate, 'wrongly assumed' that to Canning this constitutionalism 'was a virtue'. It was not to support any particular party that troops had again been sent to Portugal in 1826, on Canning's authority, as Peel reminded Palmerston in the June 1829 debate, but to maintain 'a strict and undeviating neutrality' and simply to underwrite, so far as possible, stability in that country. It is idle and misleading to speculate what Canning might have done had he still been in office in 1829 and whether, indeed, Palmerston was adopting his erstwhile leader's mantle. Southgate is quite right to stress that Palmerston had, on some levels, misunderstood Canning; had he confined himself to the 'special case' of Portugal, which 'always must be English', perhaps Palmerston might have been opening a valid debate on the best interpretation of what Canning would have done; but Palmerston's inclusion of Greece in his assault on the government and his reflections on liberal and despotic government make quite clear that this speech had somewhat broader intentions.[128] Or, at least, it had wider connotations.

By the summer of 1829 Palmerston was ready, if not impatient, to reveal himself as a thinking politician. Historians have tended to confuse this period in Palmerston's life by adopting a too-narrow perspective. It is true that Palmerston was grouped with Canning's friends and called himself in the later 1820s a 'Canningite',[129] but politically he was closer to, and more influenced by, Huskisson and the Whigs. It was not altogether disingenuous on Palmerston's part to deny, in later life, that he had ever been a Canningite.[130] For Southgate the difference between Palmerston and Canning was that, ultimately, Canning spoke of the power of opinion and of the importance of constitutional government, but Palmerston really meant it: 'Palmerston . . . was deceived by Canning's propaganda into believing that Canning had been a Palmerstonian. The orthodox Canningites knew better.'[131]

Palmerston was a Canningite in the sense that he was a liberal- rather than an ultra-Tory; but he was, in fact, not much of a Tory at all. The real purpose of the June speech had been for Palmerston, as he wrote to William, 'first, to put on record my own opinions, both now and when I was in the Cabinet; secondly, to excite public attention to these matters a little; and, thirdly, to let the government see that they were not to suppose that they could have their own way entirely in foreign affairs.' Recognising that his preferred option, a reconstruction of 'the Government of Goderich', though now to be led by Huskisson and Lansdowne, was 'mere moonshine', Palmerston argued that public opinion, which would be applied to foreign affairs in the coming session, should at least regulate Wellington's conduct.[132] This was not Palmerston's first parliamentary speech, but it was his first, or to date most revealing, political one. In April 1823, while still a member of the Tory government, Palmerston had criticised the opposition for indulging in elaborate dissertations and had asked 'of what use is it to dwell upon abstract principles with those who are accused of measuring right by power and of ruling their conduct by expediency and not by justice? – If one wishes to convince men one must apply one's arguments to the principles which they recognize'.[133] In his speech of June 1829, Palmerston did not entirely subvert this maxim, but he did allow himself a more theoretical reflection on politics, albeit one grounded in an appreciation of the potential of the power of opinion. In approaching the end of his speech, and setting forth an important political axiom, Palmerston had asserted:

> There is in nature no power but mind, all else is passive and inert; in human affairs this power is opinion; in political affairs it is public opinion; and he who can grasp this power, with it will subdue the fleshly arm of physical strength, and compel it to work out his purpose. Look at one of those floating fortresses, which bear to the farthest regions of the globe, the prowess and the glory of England; see a puny insect at the helm, commanding the winds of heaven, and the waves of the ocean, and enslaving even the laws of nature, as if instead of being ordained to hold the universe together, they had only been established for his particular occasion. And yet the merest breath of those winds which he has yoked to his service, the merest drop of that fathomless abyss which he has made his footstool, would, if ignorantly encountered, be more than enough for his destruction; but the powers of his mind have triumphed over the forces of things, and the subjugated elements are become his obedient vassals. And so also is it, with the political affairs of empires; and those statesmen who know how to avail themselves of the passions, and the interests, and the opinions of mankind, are able to give an ascendancy, and to exercise a sway over human affairs, far out of all proportion greater than belong to the power and resources of the state over which they preside; while those, on the other hand, who seek to check improvement, to cherish abuses, to crush opinions, and to prohibit the human race from thinking, whatever may be the apparent power which they wield, will find their weapon snap short in their hand, when most they need its protection.[134]

The echoes of Dugald Stewart could not have been stronger. Going further, Britain, insisted Palmerston, should be seen as 'the model of constitutional freedom, as the refuge from persecution, and the shield against oppression', and he looked forward to a time when, as before, 'England was regarded by Europe, as the friend of liberty and civilization, and therefore of happiness and prosperity, in every land; because it was thought that her rulers had the wisdom to discover, that the selfish interests and political influence of England, were best promoted, by the extension of liberty and civilization.'

It is not certain that this was an overt strike for the Foreign Office by Palmerston. His name, it is true, had already been connected with that office in certain sketches of possible Cabinets (such as that sent to Palmerston by George Shee in January 1828),[135] but Palmerston's conduct in 1829 is more a sincere commitment to principles – such as honour, liberty, constitutionalism and progress – than a cynical bid for personal promotion. Apparently, the speech had been well delivered: Bulwer, who was in the chamber to hear it, later recollected that Palmerston had 'never stood so high as an orator'.[136] Subsequent assessments, however, have been equally disposed to conclude that Palmerston's speech did not make any special impact at the time.[137] Yet Palmerston's Ciceronian credentials are not the most important aspect of the performance; its significance lies in what it reveals about his emergence as a front-rank liberal politician. Whereas Bulwer had chosen to interpret a comment Palmerston had once made to him that 'England is strong enough to brave consequences', as signifying that he 'had not any system of policy relative to foreign states', this was not to imply, as Bulwer suggested, that Palmerston's 'theory' of foreign policy was simply to react to events.[138] On the contrary, it was merely a statement of fact, as Palmerston saw it, concerning British power and authority. What was revealed in June 1829 was that Palmerston, drawing on his experiences in Ireland as well as England and using the language he had learned in Scotland, was committed to pursuing politics in the interest of the many, on the basis of a perception of liberal, civilised progress and the validation of popular approval (or endorsement).

In November Palmerston went to Brocket Hall and during the course of a 'very agreeable visit' he and the three Lamb brothers spent much time talking politics and with Frederick and Lord Melbourne in particular he had some '*serious* discourse'. All three agreed on the need to oppose Wellington steadfastly; they also agreed that they should do so while maintaining a position of political independence, siding with neither Whig nor Tory factions exclusively. Only Melbourne, thought Palmerston, stood as a viable leader of liberal interests – Lansdowne lacked experience, Grey had 'bolted out of the course and never can win the race', Holland was too 'old & infirm', while Goderich's copybook was well and truly blotted by late events. Melbourne, by contrast, offered a fair prospect of rising above partisan divisions. In discussions ranging over the Eastern question and the economy and free trade, an attempt was being made to establish a rallying point for liberals that would sidestep the personal shortcomings of the current Whig leadership and not alienate too many Tories.[139] (Palmerston regretted that the government had not sought to mediate between Russia and Turkey and urge Turkey to come to terms with Russia. Britain had missed an opportunity to place itself at the head of Europe, he said – a policy he thought Canning would have advocated.)

One should not take Palmerston at his word uncritically, least of all a parliamentary word, but it is worth noting the terms on which he returned to the theme of foreign policy, and specifically the settlement of affairs in Greece, in the new session of Parliament in early 1830. Challenged by Robert Peel to explain who and what he spoke for, Palmerston replied: 'I stand here, humble as I am, as one of the Representatives of the People of England; and next, as the Representative of my own opinions', and those opinions, he claimed, he would not bend to the prevailing winds of others' views. 'I also stand here, I trust, as one of that body which represents, or which at least ought to be the maintainers of the honour and interests of England'. He cared little whom he pleased or displeased so long as he could satisfy himself that he had done 'what I most firmly believe to be my duty'.[140] There are, arguably, Burkean overtones to this conception of the role of the parliamentarian.[141] Palmerston was not chasing office for its own sake but instead sought to map out an alternative to the 'inept and contradictory' policies of the Wellington government, revealed most notably in their handling of the Eastern question.[142]

Ellenborough was mistaken, therefore, in early July 1830 when he thought that though Huskisson remained 'sulky and sour', Palmerston might be welcomed back into the Tory fold where even Wellington was disposed to be warm and it was thought Palmerston might be offered, again, the Chancellorship of the Exchequer.[143] In a memorandum written in response to a suggestion from Wellington that he rejoin the government in June, Palmerston noted that nothing had changed since 1828 to justify a change of heart on either his own part or that of Huskisson, Grant, Melbourne or Dudley. Though office was creditable, attractive and useful, Palmerston insisted that they must stand by their convictions or else face the censure of parliamentary allies who 'would empty upon us their full quivers of shafts dipped in the bitterest venom of disappointment'.[144] The impasse was later attributed to a disagreement over the question of parliamentary reform,[145] but Palmerston insisted that nothing – not even a substantial concession to the Canningite group – could induce him to return to office under Wellington.[146] Now more than ever was the moment to hold one's nerve. Palmerston observed the growing power of public opinion and judged that it would be all that could be done to regulate and direct that opinion without further exciting it. Conjuring images of a rampant force in political life, Palmerston assured Huskisson that the current government was not competent to control popular feeling and he foresaw its imminent collapse.[147] In the autumn the Whig Brougham brought forward proposals for a measure of parliamentary reform which the Duke of Wellington said he would not support. When Brougham subsequently published a pamphlet asking, *What has the Duke of Wellington gained by the dissolution?*,[148] Palmerston regretted that, though it was a 'clever' work, Brougham should have resorted to bitter and personal attacks. Thus, though some of the Whigs had been making explicit overtures to, for want of a better word, the Canningites, Palmerston argued that they must 'maintain the *dignified & imposing attitude* of independence which we have hitherto preserved and that however we may admire the faculties of Brougham & court his cooperation whenever we agree with him it would do us no good to merge ourselves among the followers of his erratic standard'.[149] Palmerston then resisted overtures from all sides, and they were renewed by Wellington again in October, and openly allied himself only with Charles Grant and Lord Melbourne though in any accession to office they would hope to include 'auxiliaries of the liberal persuasion'.[150]

The death on 15 September of William Huskisson beneath the wheels of the *Rocket* on the Manchester to Liverpool railway had left the embryonic liberal-Tory/liberal-Whig fusion without its acknowledged leader and moves were made from both sides at Westminster to effect a union with this influential 'third party'. Palmerston became de facto leader of the group – Ellenborough had begun to talk of a 'Palmerston party'[151] – and though the offer of the Colonial Office was made to him personally, insisted that not only did he act in concert with Grant and Melbourne, but that they could not consider entering the government unless it was reconstructed to include the Whigs, especially Lansdowne, Grey, Holland and Carlisle.[152] Barely a fortnight before his death, Huskisson had urged on Palmerston the need both for a new government and to look to a more sensitive administration. 'In every part of it public opinion is making rapid advances,' he had told Palmerston, 'and I am much mistaken if one of the most difficult duties of those who have the means of influencing that opinion will not be, not to excite, but to regulate and direct its march.' The Cabinet, he said, was 'not competent to such a task' and whatever short-term support the ministry derived from the King and aristocracy, the advent of a new administration was not far in the future, and that must mean a completely new reconstruction of the government.[153]

If Wellington had been put clearly in the picture, some of his closest allies remained ignorantly or stubbornly wedded to the notion that Palmerston would return to the Tories. Ellenborough was alarmed lest 'we shall have all the Huskissonians, Whigs and Ultra-Tories (the last are insane), united against us', but it was already far too late to expect a reunion.[154] A few days after his meeting with Wellington, Palmerston was visited by John Wilson Croker who wished to urge him to reconsider his parting from the Tories. 'Well, I will bring the question to a point,' said Croker at last. 'Are you resolved or are you not to vote for Parliamentary Reform?' Palmerston said that he was resolved to support Whig proposals for change. 'Well, then,' replied Croker, 'there is no use in talking to you any more on this subject. You and I, I am grieved to see, will never sit again on the same bench together.'[155]

That parliamentary reform should have been the ostensible reason for separation was not in itself surprising. Palmerston had for some time been well disposed to plans for some rearrangement of the electoral system, though on limited and pragmatic grounds. When in 1828, for example, plans for the disfranchisement of the corrupt seats of East Retford and Penryn had been debated, Palmerston's support for a reallocation of these seats was based on the desire to stave off more far-reaching change. In endorsing plans to give the East Retford seat to Birmingham, Palmerston had told the House that 'extend[ing] the franchise to large towns, on such occasions as the one in question, was the only mode by which the House could avoid the adoption, at some time or other, of a general plan of reform'.[156]

This was not radicalism, but it was enough of a moderate Whiggism to facilitate Palmerston's (and Canningite) accession to office when Lord Grey formed his administration in November 1830. Palmerston exaggerated when he said that Grey had 'immediately' sent for him on being commissioned to form a government,[157] but the door to the Foreign Office, which many commentators have been keen to argue Palmerston had been pushing at for some months, was now open to him. Herbert Bell expressed some doubts as to whether Palmerston really knew his own mind. In quitting the scene to spend October in Paris, he was, said Bell, 'playing for time', holding out for (and against) offers from Tories and Whigs alike.[158] Princess Lieven famously claimed the credit for Palmerston's appointment for herself, and though many historians have mocked her for her conceit, there are some grounds for thinking that her influence over her then lover, and new Prime Minister, Earl Grey might have worked to Palmerston's advantage. Ridley for one repeated the Lieven version in his biography, recounting that the Princess had pressed Palmerston's case in order to 'keep down English Jacobinism' (and because she believed him to be 'Russian' in his international outlook) and was delighted with an appointment that was 'perfect in every way' when Palmerston entered the Foreign Office on 22 November.[159] Bourne judged that though not a definitive influence, Lieven's encouragement to choose Palmerston would have created in Grey a sense that Palmerston was, at least, a possible choice.[160] This makes it easier to understand how, according to some other accounts, such as that of Charles Webster, Palmerston came to be appointed, though a second choice, once both Lords Holland and Lansdowne had turned it down and recommended Palmerston instead.[161] There was certainly no inevitability about Grey's decision. Southgate argued that since his speech of 1 June 1829, Palmerston had been 'a candidate' but not the 'principal' candidate for the Foreign Secretaryship, but that speech had at least oiled the wheels of such a promotion.[162] When Lytton Bulwer, recently returned from the Netherlands, met Palmerston at one of Lady Cowper's parties in November 1830, he thought the new Foreign Secretary's 'air was more that of a man of the drawing-room than of the senate', but, Bulwer also observed, Palmerston was no mere dilettante: he asked acute questions about public affairs, 'and one could see that he was gathering information for the purpose of fortifying opinions'.[163]

Whether or not Palmerston was an automatic choice for the Foreign Office is immaterial. That the Canningites must be accommodated within any viable Whig ministry was beyond doubt, which is why they secured all three secretaryships and control of the India Office, much to the chagrin of certain Whig grandees. There are no reliable accounts of the discussions that gave rise to this arrangement and biographers have been obliged to conclude that Palmerston must have negotiated hard for these prize offices for his allies, but the documentary evidence remains scarce. In Palmerston's own subsequent comment to his sister Elizabeth there is a sense of personal victory in the Canningites' accession to government: 'The Whigs wish Althorp to lead as likely to keep their Party from straying,' he wrote. 'Perhaps this may be well; as I have the Foreign Office I do not care.'[164] A month into his new occupation, Palmerston was striking a more sober tone: 'I have been ever since my appointment like a man who has plumped into a mill-race, scarcely able by all his kicking and plunging to keep his head above water,' he admitted to Sulivan.[165]

CHAPTER 6

THE WHIG FOREIGN SECRETARY, 1830–1834

England, then, never had a clearer course before her, and never held a more digni-
fied, or more honourable station. She stands umpire between hostile and excited
parties; she holds the balance between extreme and opposing principles; her task is
'Pacis imponere morem;' and this task she may continue to perform no less to her
own advantage, than for the benefit of the rest of the civilized world.
from Palmerston's contribution to *The Reform Ministry* (1833)[1]

IN THE CLOSING months of Wellington's government Palmerston and his political allies had become increasingly troubled about the course of foreign affairs.
Revolution, radicalism and the threat of renewed European conflict haunted
Europe and Palmerston was not sanguine about the outlook for Britain. Crisis
in Belgium, he told his brother in October, had brought matters to a head: 'I
believe the fact to be that Russia, Austria and Prussia want England to join in
a new alliance to put down revolutions & curb France, that France on the other
hand wants England to come to a fair understanding with her upon terms
mutually advantageous to both parties, or rather, consistent with a due regard
to their mutual interests.' Wellington, however, Palmerston thought lacked
sufficient parliamentary means to take up the first option since this would
inevitably lead to 'a second edition of the French war'.[2] Yet, for Palmerston, this
was not simply a balance of power, *realpolitik* consideration: the choices facing
Britain in 1830 were not strictly ones of alliances, he felt, but of ideological
alignments and accommodations. The July revolution in France had ushered
in not only a new dynasty, but new opportunities. Palmerston, who had spent
much of the previous couple of years attacking conservative systems of government at home and abroad, had greeted the advent of a more constitutional
regime across the Channel with marked enthusiasm. 'We shall drink to the
cause of Liberalism all over the world,' he enthused. 'Let Spain & Austria look
to themselves; this reaction cannot end where it began, & Spain & Italy &
Portugal & parts of Germany will sooner or later be affected. This event is
decisive of the ascendancy of Liberal principles throughout Europe; the evil
spirit has been put down and will be trodden underfoot. The reign of
Metternich is over & the days of the Duke's policy might be measured by

algebra, if not by arithmetic.'[3] Palmerston applauded the political changes in
France, and when Charles X was forced to abdicate following public insurrection in Paris during 'Les Trois Glorieuses' of 27–29 July, it seemed only to
confirm the ascendancy of more liberal principles. 'Well, what a glorious event
this is in France!' he wrote shortly afterwards. 'How admirably the French have
done it! What energy & courage in the day of trial; & what wisdom & moderation in the hour of victory! Who, that remembers the excesses, & outrages, &
horrors, & insanity of 1792 & 93, could have expected to see in so short a time,
a nation of maniacs & assassins converted into heroes and philosophers.' It was
a 'miraculous change', he insisted and, significantly and however imperfect and
short-lived it might yet have been, one attributable solely to the 'enjoyment of
a free press and a free constitution'. Those 'three days in July', he concluded,
'have brought about the complete & permanent triumph of the liberal &
constitutional principle, over the arbitrary & despotic', and he anticipated
similar developments in Spain, Portugal and Italy and the discomposition of
Tory strength at home.[4] After all, as he put it in language redolent with the
spirit of Enlightenment progress, Palmerston saw in events in France the
harbinger of profound change. 'Is not this the most triumphant demonstration
of the advantages arising from free discussion, from the liberty of the press,
from the diffusion of knowledge, & from familiarizing even the lowest classes
with the daily examination of political questions;' he asked Graham, 'for to
what else can be ascribed the honourable contrast which the proceedings of
last week exhibit with those of the beginning of the last revolution.'[5] Bulwer
described a turning point in European affairs:

> There are certain epochs in which the atmosphere of Europe, if I may so
> speak, seems to change – in a manner similar to that in which by modern
> contrivances the atmosphere is refreshed and renewed in our apartments.
> The old air, long pent up within narrow limits, and which has lost its life
> and vivacity, passes out on one side, and is replaced from another by fresh
> air, which the lungs receive and breathe out more freely than that from
> which they are delivered.[6]

At home this new atmosphere had about it the scent of imminent parliamentary reform and Palmerston's tenure of the Foreign Office under the Whig
premierships of the 1830s was dominated by questions, domestic and foreign,
of representation, constitutionalism, freedom and reform. First, however,
Palmerston had to master the day-to-day practicalities of a new domain. The
work of the Foreign Office multiplied the demands that had previously been
made on his administrative abilities. Though widely regarded at the time as an
efficient department, the Foreign Office employed a staff of only about thirty
when Palmerston arrived there, less than one-third of the number he had
had at his disposal at the War Office. Though he failed to tempt Lord Ashley

(son-in-law of Lady Cowper and in due course of Palmerston himself) with an offer of appointment as Under-Secretary of State for Foreign Affairs,[7] Palmerston was assisted in his new situation by generally capable under-secretaries, Henry Addington, George Shee and, from 1834 in place of Shee, William Fox-Strangways. As he had at the War Office, Palmerston was keen to attack an office culture of nepotism, jobbery, and, as he once put it when he discovered that office-keepers habitually received Christmas boxes from foreign missions, 'brigandage'.[8] The staff at the Foreign Office, he was to complain a few years later, had come to expect promotion by virtue simply of length of service, and in place of a system whereby the clerks expected by 'the prescriptive right of idleness and dullness to succeed hackney coachlike from bottom to top of an office by dint of mere living', Palmerston hoped to intro-duce a more meritocratic approach; 'it may sometimes be much for the public interest,' he observed, 'that an able man should be promoted over his seniors.'[9] The ideal was perhaps more easily expressed than executed and Palmerston was not above using the varied patronage opportunities available to him to advance the careers of those who enjoyed the right connections. Nonetheless, if he demanded high standards and hard work of his clerical staff (and his chastisement of poor handwriting was just as insistent as it had been at the War Office),[10] Palmerston led by example. 'Palmerston never can last at the rate he is now going,' wrote one clerk, Frederick ('Poodle') Byng, in January 1832, observing how his chief never left the office before 2 a.m. and often was at his desk until five o'clock in the morning. 'He deserves that his labours should be crowned with success,' Byng concluded.[11] It was, therefore, if not necessarily a typical day then at least not an unusual one that Palmerston described to Emily at the end of December 1831:

> We did a great deal of business here in town yesterday and I hope with future good results. My day was not an idle one; for having left the office only at 3 in the morning the night before, I had before the Cabinet at one, to write an important despatch to Vienna, to hear Czartorisky's account of the whole Polish war, and to discuss with Ompteda [the Hanoverian minister] all the squabbles of the German Diet. At our Cabinet my despatches to Berlin & Vienna were approved & amended. I had then to see Van de Weyer, Lieven, Bulow, Esterhazy & Wessenberg, upon various different subjects, and afterwards to send off messengers with despatches & private letters to Vienna, Berlin, Paris & Brussells. However I continued to get it all done by about two this morning; and now for my consolation I have staring me in the face 13 boxes full of papers, which ought all to be read forthwith, and which have come to me since yesterday morning.[12]

Much of this intense labour derived from Palmerston's baptism of fire in diplo-macy: chairing a concert of the great powers to determine the fate of Belgium.

The July revolution in France had served as a tangible example of possible change within a western Europe increasingly straining at the strictures and boundaries of the 1815 post-war peace settlement. The agreement reached at Vienna had been one forged by the great powers and one concerning their interests; the redrafting of Europe that contorted smaller nationalities into new or reformed states would ultimately prove its undoing and the strain told noticeably in the Netherlands.

In 1815 Belgium and Holland had been united under the House of Orange not only as a more stable and secure barrier against any future French aggression, but on the grounds that their economies were naturally complementary – an industrialised Belgium coupled with the trading empire of the Dutch. It was thought in 1814 and 1815, as Palmerston later explained, 'that notwithstanding the differences of language, religion, & habits, between Holland & Belgium, there were nevertheless points of contact enough, common to both, to justify the expectation, that in process of time, their political union might be followed by a real amalgamation of the two nations: and such a result would have been most advantageous to the general interests of Europe'.[13] The union, however, was never a particularly stable or durable one and although linguistic and religious differences between Belgium and Holland can be exaggerated, the 'maladroit' policies of the Dutch monarch, William, consistently undermined the union and alienated its Belgian subjects.[14]

Alongside the revolution in Paris the revolution which broke out in Belgium towards the end of August 1830 marked a critical moment in post-war European diplomatic history. Initially, Wellington's government had hoped for some sort of compromise, perhaps home rule for Belgium under the House of Orange, representing only a very minor revision of the Vienna settlement and upholding the primary aim of that treaty, namely containment of France. However, once the Belgians had risen up the Dutch had immediately appealed to Prussia for assistance, which duly garrisoned the fortresses of Luxembourg, a duchy in the possession of Orange. There was now a real danger of a French invasion in support of the Belgians, whose cause was being openly espoused in France. If the French were to enter Belgium the concern in Britain, of course, was how they would subsequently be removed. All five great powers were interested in any threat to the 'settlement' of Europe, but all were uncertain how far the terms of 1815 sanctioned direct involvement; and if any outside power did intervene, how would the rest be reassured that it would be an impartial part that would be played? As Charles Webster observed: 'The confusion of that time has been expressed by the famous "mot", attributed to Talleyrand by Lord Alvanley, that non-intervention was a metaphysical and political phrase meaning almost the same thing as intervention. Some strange things were indeed done in its name. But they all sprang ultimately from the fact that states are not isolated bodies but part of an international community and that the events which take place in each of them must be of interest and concern to all the rest.'[15] The King of the Netherlands had appealed to the great powers for help in dealing with the unfolding Belgian crisis and by the time Palmerston entered the Foreign Office it had previously been decided that a robust settlement would only be achieved by renewing the conference diplomacy of the 1810s and early 1820s, and, significantly, in spite of Metternich's concerns, it had been agreed that this conference would be held in London. Palmerston was in a prominent and privileged position, by accident rather than design, but by virtue of his chairing of the London Conference he led and oversaw the first major territorial revision of Vienna. It was a position of dubious attractiveness. Palmerston certainly enjoyed some authority, but to what extent, and indeed over what, was less clear. He was the most senior delegate as the only Foreign Minister, as opposed to ambassador, attending and as well as chairing the conference also enjoyed the benefits of doing so 'at home', with much readier access to information and immediate advice. Having behind him 'the weight of a government on the spot', Palmerston said some time later, he had enjoyed 'double authority' as Britain's plenipotentiary.[16] However, though they occupied many days' and weeks' labour, the function of the meetings was frequently ambiguous; as Metternich later admitted, he had never really known whether this conference was 'intervenante, mediatrice ou arbitre'.[17]

Palmerston had made it quite clear to the British diplomatic corps that preserving peace was the new government's 'first object'. In preserving the peace of Europe, Palmerston saw Russia as a natural ally: the interests of both and of Europe would be served, he argued, by these two powers 'availing themselves of every occasion of cultivating that friendship, & of cementing the union between the two countries', and 'as neither country has any selfish interests to pursue, the motives of their union cannot be misunderstood'. Britain, he said, was committed to 'the general principles of non-intervention in the affairs of other countries' and so long as the other powers did the same (and he believed, for example, that France would act on these lines), then there seemed 'no reason why local commotions which may unfortunately arise any where, should disturb the general peace'. Thus, the London Conference on Belgium was conceived as a disinterested great power response to a 'scheme' that had 'failed'; Belgium and Holland must of necessity be separated and unless Belgium were simply to fall under the ambit of France, 'the only way of avoiding evils of greater magnitude, was promptly to acknowledge the independence of Belgium'. Just as Palmerston in late 1830 looked uneasily at the threat posed to Russia and European stability by growing unrest in Poland, this was a question of maintaining the balance of power and safeguarding European peace.[18]

Palmerston's objective in late 1830 was not to remodel European politics, attacking autocratic rule and championing liberal constitutionalism; yet he was acutely aware of the shifting ideological tenor of the times, which chimed with his own Whiggish Enlightenment sensibilities of advance, movement and progress, and to which the European order must of necessity adjust. Peace was to be preserved, but it could only be so if that peace accommodated the forces of change and reform which Palmerston himself had been schooled to anticipate, if not necessarily to welcome. Lord Clancarty, who had spent considerable time on the continent as a British minister and had served as one of the British plenipotentiaries at Vienna in 1814 and 1815,[19] was alarmed by this new atmosphere:

> Diplomacy has now become a new science, governed by, I cannot guess what principles. The leading one seems to be a total disregard to all treaties, prior to the promotion of those men. The great first cause after the hunt for popularity, by an attempt to force a liberal constitution down the throats of the poor Portuguese, was the Greek treaty; here we see a forced mediation, unknown before in politics, & decision [sic] made before either of the parties were heard, and this in favor of rebellion & against legitimate govt to the encouragement of treason throughout the world. Why, for the further encouragement of treason was the King of the French to be so speedily acknowledged? Why in the face of solemn deputations are conferences in Downing Street under the name of non-intervention, to force what they call a mediation upon the parties and to interfere in every thing? I am quite lost in all this. Wise indeed would be the man, that could see his way out of it.[20]

For Palmerston the rationale was perfectly simple. The shortcomings of the Vienna arrangements had been exposed and in order to preserve a balance of power it was necessary for the powers to acknowledge the strength of liberalising forces. Yet, if the union of Holland and Belgium was bankrupt, Belgian independence was necessary not because it would satisfy Belgian nationalist aspirations, or because it would set a marker for future constitutional reform, but because an independent Belgium would be a more stable bulwark and in turn this would underpin the primary objectives of 1830, just as much as those of 1815, to contain France and avert a collision between the great powers. As Palmerston explained in the House of Commons in February 1831, 'When he [Bonaparte] was conquered by the Allied Powers ... the Powers of Europe disposed of Belgium by uniting it to Holland, not for any purpose of advantage to Holland, not as an act of grace and favour to the Netherlands, but for the purpose of making appropriation of Belgium contribute to the peace and security of Europe. The other powers of Europe, and England among them ... had a right to say to Belgium: "You, never having been an independent state, have no right to despoil Holland of its ancient and historical boundaries. Holland is a state whose independence concerns the security of the other countries of Europe; you are but a power of yesterday, and have no right to convert yourselves into aggressors and to claim as yours that which belongs of right to another".'[21]

A spirit of moderation and a search for stability underpinned Palmerston's approach to the question. 'Pray explain,' he urged Ponsonby in April 1831, 'that we, the Conference, have no right to make an arbitrary distribution of Europe upon the principles of the Holy Alliance or the Congress of Vienna. That we are not conquerors disposing of subjugated Kingdoms, but Powers looking after our security and mediating between contending parties.'[22] Thus in turn had Metternich welcomed the renewal of conference diplomacy, even if that did mean the axis of power turned at London and not Vienna, because it offered the best prospect of upholding the largely anti-French alignments established in 1815. 'Nothing could be more desirable than the most perfect harmony among the *four ancient allies*. Let it be our endeavour to establish it, and to give it as much weight as possible,' Metternich told his ambassador in Paris in the summer of 1831. Yet, significantly, while recognising that Britain must share the desire of the other three great powers, Austria, Russia and Prussia, to contain France, Metternich also made it clear that Britain's position was different and secondary within the four-power alliance. As he continued, 'we must never forget that the position of the British Cabinet differs, in very many respects, from that of the *three* allies, and that the latter cannot subordinate all the requirements of their policy to objections which may appear insurmountable to the *fourth* member of the alliance.'[23]

Given that the Dutch–Belgian union had been drawn up with an eye to international power balances, the unravelling of that union inevitably attracted the attention of all the major European powers. There were, at the heart of an exceedingly complicated series of negotiations, certain key areas of debate and contention. The powers had first of all to determine whether Belgium was to become an independent state. If so, the frontiers of this new Belgium had to be negotiated. Belgium's future neutrality had to be agreed, and consequent on this, the barrier fortresses, which had been built to mark and protect the original borders, became a further source of dispute. An independent Belgium would also need an independent sovereign.[24] Ostensibly these questions were all settled by the end of 1831, as had been the tricky problem of the reallocation of the original debts of the united Netherlands and Belgium, yet it would be the end of the decade before the powers and Holland had come to anything approaching an accord. It was, said Sir Robert Adair in October 1831, 'the most difficult negotiation ever known in our history.'[25]

On 20 December 1830 the conference had agreed on the need for the 'future independence' of Belgium and in January 1831 it drew up the *bases de séparation* and associated promises of Belgian sovereignty. Yet in pursuing conditions 'raisonnables' and 'équitables', the powers in fact proposed concessions and frontiers that were soon seen to be too favourable to Holland, leaving the conference members uneasy about the durability of the proposed arrangement.[26] Too much of the proposed settlement relied on Dutch acquiescence and great power concord. Holland was to be what it had been in 1790 while Belgium was to occupy the remainder of the Netherlands, minus Luxembourg (which would remain part of the German Confederation). But the powers were to supervise the re-division of territory and guarantee the navigation of rivers and Belgian independence.[27] Each power, however, envisaged the role of the new Belgian state, and specifically its relationship with themselves (and its position relative to France) differently, and the devil had done his work in the detail. The powers' inability to reach agreement about a Belgian sovereign further undermined the prospect of a settlement. There were initially two principal candidates: the duc de Nemours, second son of Louis-Philippe, and the duc de Leuchtenberg, an adopted Bonaparte. The French would not have Leuchtenberg; the other powers would not countenance Nemours who was seen as little more than a French placeman. Two further possibilities were considered: Leopold of Saxe-Coburg, the 'British' candidate, and Prince William of Orange. Leopold lacked admirers among the Eastern courts, while William's candidature, which was mooted alongside a union of Belgium and Luxembourg, soothed east European concerns about undue French influence in the settlement, but likewise antagonised the French, who saw the move as a direct challenge, as Talleyrand put it, to France's weakest border.[28]

The conference meetings dragged on throughout 1831. The frequent gatherings were time consuming and though Palmerston was able on occasion to sketch a pen portrait of bonhomie and camaraderie – describing a meeting in late 1831, for example, he observed: 'I am writing in the Conference, Matucewitz copying out a note for our signature, old Talley jazzing and telling stories to Lieven and Esterhazy and Wessenberg, the latter laughing high Latin, while Bulow is writing a confidential note in a corner, and the patient Van de Weyer in the adjoining room waiting to know his fate and scratching out and altering just as we tell him to do'[29] – there was no escaping the fact that the work was arduous. The meetings were long and frequently dry; as Palmerston noted following a series of discussions in January 1831, Talleyrand had been 'brought to terms' over proposed territorial distributions of the Netherlands only 'by the same means by which juries become unanimous – by starving.'[30] The Belgian question occupied leisure time just as much as business hours, and Emily Cowper was drawn to complain in January 1831 that Palmerston's work had begun to impinge disagreeably on her soirées. 'Leopold was here last week & Lord Grey, but the Ambassadors and Secretary for foreign affairs made our party so political that there was no going into any room without disturbing a conference. . . . Our friends will I hope do themselves great credit & save the country if it is to be saved, but their society is certainly the worse for their exertions.'[31] A year after he had first entered the Foreign Office and assumed the direction of the conference, however, Palmerston wrote to Sir Charles Bagot, Britain's ambassador to the Netherlands, expressing his hopes that the labour might finally be bearing fruit. 'Conferences and elephants,' he wrote, 'have the same period of gestation, twelve months, with a fortnight occasionally over their time; in sagacity we know the resemblance holds good. On the 4th Novr 1830 this Belgian Conference was impregnated by the King of the Netherlands, and on the 15th Novr 1831 it brings forth a treaty which the unnatural father absolutely disdains. I trust however that a little more reflection will induce him to adopt it; and that we shall then have bon ménage again in Europe.'[32] The omelette, however, to borrow Sir Charles Webster's analogy, had not yet been unscrambled.[33]

If Palmerston had displayed his bureaucratic skills at the War Office, then in the London Conference he played to those abilities and 'Lord Cupid' began, to some extent, to be eclipsed by 'Protocol Palmerston'. On 15 November the plenipotentiaries signed a treaty by which Belgium and Holland were separated, the former to be independent and neutral. Rivers were to remain freely navigable, as under the terms of the treaty of 1815, and provision was made for the division of the debts of the former united kingdom of the Netherlands and Belgium.[34] Palmerston described the signing of the agreement as 'an immense thing done', but the treaty of November still had to be ratified by the parliaments of each power and, as Palmerston was to discover, this would take some months to achieve.[35] Though the discussions about Belgium had formally been about borders, fortresses and loans in the Low Countries, the real issue at stake was the balance of power among the great powers, and specifically the role and place of France.

From the very beginning of the conference negotiations, Palmerston had entertained doubts about the good faith of Britain's neighbour. In early January he reported to the British ambassador in Paris, Lord Granville, his suspicion that France was intriguing to make territorial gains from the instability in Belgium, expressing his fear that France was juggling proposed deals with Prussia over Saxony, and Britain over Philippeville and Marienburg, in order to secure a surer foothold on its northern borders. 'I do not like all this;' he wrote on 7 January, 'it looks as if France was unchanged in her system of encroachment, and it diminishes the confidence in her sincerity and good faith which her conduct up to this time had inspired.' He urged Granville to 'hint' to the French government that Britain would not look favourably on 'a new chapter of encroachment and conquest'.[36] Real and not nominal independence for Belgium was non-negotiable, and Palmerston was not averse to stoking fears in France of a naval war with Britain if that induced the French government 'to make the efforts necessary for the preservation of peace'.[37] Yet as chair of the conference, he perceived Britain's role to be that of 'impartial mediator' between, on the one hand France, on the other Russia, Austria and Prussia and, in that role 'as long as both parties remain quiet we shall be friends with both; but . . . whichever side breaks the peace, that side will find us against them'. If there were to be a threat to peace, he observed, 'it is more likely to come from than against France', and though desirous of a cordial cross-Channel understanding, Palmerston could not help but notice the bellicose and quarrelsome disposition of the French government and the 'underhand proceedings' it was carrying on with regard to Belgium.[38] Within a month of the treaty's signing, the sincerity of the powers' agreement reached on 20 January 1831 to pursue and maintain Belgian independence seemed doubtful. Talleyrand had even encouraged Palmerston in his diplomatic correspondence with Granville 'not to treat the Belgian affair *comme une grande chose*' and suggested that it could 'be soon and easily settled'.[39] Palmerston remained unconvinced, and though he was sympathetic to certain French qualms over the fortresses and acknowledged that the 'most menacing' ones near France's border might safely be dismantled, he was wary of French acquisitiveness and, as he told Granville in late March, it would be fatal to the hopes of peace and stability to grant France even 'a cabbage garden or a vineyard'.[40]

Though relations between Britain and France warmed a little in the early summer of 1831 and Palmerston began to speak of a 'close friendship' that would 'secure the peace of the world' and 'confirm the liberties and promote the happiness of nations', he warned at the same time that 'underhand intrigues' and 'double diplomacy' would immediately threaten such aspirations. Britain had, Palmerston said, been moving towards closer association with the Eastern courts and he only hoped the installation of Casimir Périer as prime minister of France would lead to amelioration in cross-Channel relations between Paris and London.[41] As he told Lord Holland, Périer's 'language & conduct certainly inspire great hopes that peace will be preserved; the fact is that nobody wants war but a small Buonaparte faction in Paris, and if the French Govt are only willing to controul that faction, they will also be able; and in that case we shall have no war'. Yet the political weakness of both Louis-Philippe and Sebastiani in France, thought Palmerston, meant that peace rested principally in the unity of Britain and the other three, Eastern, powers and in the hope that French military ambitions would remain muted.[42] Thus, when French troops invaded Belgium in August, Palmerston feared 'a general war' and stressed that they must quit immediately lest France's demands for Marienburg and Philippeville be granted and Prussia gain Luxembourg in return. It was essential that the avarice of no one power should compromise the fragile unity of the conference: 'let us stave off all these nibblings: if once these great Powers begin to taste blood, they will never be satisfied with one bite, but will speedily devour their victim,' he warned.[43] It was a matter of 'great importance' to get France out of Belgium, therefore,[44] and when by the end of August that retreat began, Palmerston applauded the unity of the Four powers and, interestingly, the sway of British public opinion, for having achieved the result. 'We must now make peace between Holland & Belgium as fast as we can and in adjusting the terms, we must discard all personal considerations, & look only to justice & the general interests of Europe,' he told Heytesbury.[45]

So, despite Palmerston's initial enthusiasm for constitutional advances in France in the summer of 1830, this had not translated into an immediate and unequivocal west European liberal alliance. There is no mystery in this. Palmerston's political and philosophical instincts had encouraged him to welcome the move towards a more constitutional form of government in France as evidence of the rise of liberalising forces and the ability of enlightened states to accommodate these changes. It was the inevitable consequence of 'progress' and without necessarily making a judgement about the desirability of such advances, Palmerston saw future stability not in resisting such movements but in adapting to them. Yet, when Dugald Stewart had taught that good government must mould itself to the demands of informed opinion, he had not counselled a reckless abdication of responsibility by the ruling elite. The maintenance of the great powers' strategic and commercial interests continued to underpin notions of international stability and when Palmerston detected a 'Bonapartist' tone in French foreign policy in 1831, he was quick to distance himself from an unduly close 'friendship' with France. If the early 1830s were to witness the rise of a western liberal, constitutional, alliance, it was not an inexorable development. Less a coalition of the willing, west European unity was more a partnership of the threatened. Yet, that this union was shrouded in the rhetoric of constitutionalism, freedom and liberty is not incidental: France, Britain, Spain and Portugal might ultimately have been drawn together by a perceived common menace but that association was sustained by a belief in, and a commitment to, a more modern, inclusive and tolerant system of governance. Such a marriage of pragmatism and idealism would become a byword of Palmerstonian politics.

Belgium was not the only scene of nationalist uprising at this time and Palmerston's concern to drive the conference towards a pragmatic settlement of the future of the Netherlands should be set against the backdrop of a widespread reaction among the smaller European states to the strictures of the Vienna settlements. In Poland and in the Italian Papal States in particular, local grievances against great power rule threatened the stability of central and eastern Europe just as Belgium posed a risk in the west. In Poland nationalist uprisings against abuses of power by Russia and in Italy challenges to papal authority, and by extension to the interests of neighbouring Austria and France, revealed how widespread was European radical discontent. In each case, though sympathetic to the demands for independence and for the advance of constitutional government, Palmerston remained above all concerned to uphold the balance of power among the great powers as established under the terms of 1815 at Vienna. 'Our chief reason for taking an interest in ... [the "Italian affair"],' admitted Palmerston, 'is that unless the Pope puts his house in order, his domestic squabbles will bring on a quarrel between Austria & France. Unless he removes the cause of discontent among his subjects, he will have periodical insurrections; these risings he cannot repress without Austrian aid; and Austrian interference cannot be repeated without exciting jealousy in France, & indeed in other powers. This then is what we wish to avert; the existence of a state of things which exposes Austria at any moment to a discussion & quarrel with France.'[46] The 'father' of Belgian independence was a supporter of international stability before he was a friend to freedom and a champion of self-determination. In this he was not so far removed from Metternich himself.[47]

So, as Palmerston argued in March 1831:

> The fact is that though the Treaty of Vienna left to the Emperor to grant the Poles what constitution he pleased, yet the fair spirit of that Treaty seems to require that when the Emperor had upon deliberation granted them a constitution, that constitution should have been observed. That it was violated is notorious; that the Poles have been subject to much tyranny & oppression from Constantine is admitted even by the Russians themselves; whether their grievances were of sufficient magnitude to justify the desperate step they have taken was perhaps a question as much of discretion & prudence as of right, but that they had not well founded complaints cannot truly be asserted.

It would be 'greatly for the honor of the Emperor' to respect that constitution, and it would relieve the other 'representative governments who were parties to the Treaty of Vienna' from 'embarrassments' to witness the abnegation of supposed guarantees of constitutional freedoms.[48] Yet the spread of constitutional government was a secondary object to that of maintaining the balance of power and peace. In 'my heart and as an individual,' Palmerston confided, 'I would rather see an independent state erected in Italy by a successful revolt against the Pope or the Austrians, than the restoration of precisely the old order of things by German bayonets'; he preferred to talk of 'moral influence' than physical force in promoting political change.[49] Though he welcomed events that were 'sowing the seed of liberal institutions in the Papal States' and though he 'should like' to see Poland 'restored to independence', he told Holland, 'one scarcely sees how that can be accomplished without breaking the Treaty of Vienna which however objectionable in some of the details of its arrangements, is yet with its accessories of Paris & Aix La Chapelle, the great security of Europe against the inveterately encroaching spirit of France'.[50] Later in 1831 Palmerston was to describe the Poles as having displayed 'qualities of both intellect and courage', but though he thought this showed they could be 'useful', he also said that it could make them 'dangerous subjects'. Concessions to radical demands were all very well, but in urging a conciliatory attitude on the Russian government, Palmerston's principal concern was international stability. 'Is it on the very frontier of an empire & in contact with military neighbours, that a wise govt would wish to place such elements of danger?' he mused. 'Is it in the very outworks of defence that a prudent administration would incur the risk of having a population disaffected to its government, & ready to join any invader, who might promise them a milder rule & a better fate?'[51]

Lord Holland, meanwhile, carried the banner of Foxite Whiggery in the Cabinet and urged Palmerston to treat France as a natural partner for Britain. He agreed that the Russian threat to Britain (and France) in the spring and early summer of 1831 could be exaggerated, yet counselled against relying on an unwarranted sense of security. The Russian government, he believed, 'have many designs in their own neighbourhood which nothing but a cordial understanding between France & England is certain of preventing, & they consequently direct all their endeavour to keep up suspicion & ill will between us, possibly to embroil us in war but at all events to keep us in a state of estrangement.'[52] Indeed, it was perhaps the Francophile 'inner Cabinet' on foreign affairs that Grey had assembled that prevented a more severe Franco-British divergence during Palmerston's first year at the Foreign Office. The two ministers who had initially turned down the Foreign Office when Grey consulted them in the autumn of 1830, Lansdowne and Holland, now, along-side Grey and Palmerston, constituted something of a subcommittee on foreign affairs. Lansdowne had served in, and Holland had supported, Canning's brief ministry in 1827, yet in the more distinctly Whiggish govern-ment of Grey, both had come to see themselves as guardians of the Foxite legacy and a counterbalance to Palmerston's perceived Canningite tenden-cies.[53] Palmerston sought to downplay the bearing of the inner Cabinet, in particular the influence of Lord Holland of whom he wrote in later years that he had 'carried into government all the factious and wrong headed feelings & opinions which he had taken up in opposition.'[54] The existence of an inner Cabinet was not unprecedented; the history of such a body could be traced back at least to the administration of Pitt in the late eighteenth century,[55] and despite Palmerston's claims it was certainly a body looked to by the Prime Minister as a means of monitoring an area of business in which he took a profound, though often inadequately fulfilled, interest. It did not help Palmerston's quest for departmental autonomy, furthermore, that certain plenipotentiaries were known to be consorting with the government's avowed parliamentary opponents: Heinrich, Baron von Bülow, of Prussia, for example, had taken the first opportunity in January 1832 at the suspension of the conference 'to revel among the Tories at Hatfield', while Austria's Philipp, Baron von Neumann was 'known to be in Tory councils'.[56] Though the Hollands' close connections with French political society occasionally yielded benefits to Palmerston in terms of access to Parisian gossip and intelligence, more often than not he tended to find this frequently impulsive Francophile element within the Cabinet more a hindrance than an aid to his conduct of policy. In January 1832, for example, Palmerston complained that Talleyrand was causing him 'bother' and 'trouble' by 'worrying us all' in the Belgian conference by his continued 'intrigues' over the fortresses question. It was, said Palmerston, a nuisance attributable to Lord and Lady Holland who 'are quite in his pocket, and they always make him think by agreeing with him that he is making an impression on the Cabinet, & then he goes down to Grey & then he writes to Paris to tell them to talk big, and in short I meet his intrigues at every turn & corner'. The only way Palmerston believed he could bring Talleyrand to heel and induce France to ratify the Belgian treaty was to threaten him with expulsion from Britain (something that 'would by no means be convenient or agreeable to him [but] I think it will have some effect').[57]

The drawn-out ratification process that followed the signing of the Treaty of London of November 1831 underlined a divergence among the European powers that gave the lie to Metternich's hopes that 'if differences of judgment may exist among the Powers on questions of form, none exist or ever will exist on the real questions at stake', in Belgium or elsewhere.[58] Palmerston grew frustrated, not just by the manoeuvrings of Talleyrand (he and Sebastiani, he complained, 'must learn that they are no longer the instruments of the imperious wishes of a Napoleon'),[59] but by the apparent infidelity of the Eastern courts to the negotiated settlement. He urged Frederick Lamb to impress upon Metternich the importance of acquiescing in the conference decisions, warning against unilateralism and pointing out 'that if the cabinets of Vienna, Petersburgh, Berlin, Paris, London, Hague, & Brussells are all to be discussing & planning & contriving, & proposing & rejecting & negotiating about this matter, the Tower of Babel itself would, in comparison, be a model of order & good understanding'. The separation of Belgium and Holland, he insisted, could be achieved by the conference or by war, 'but there is no third way'.[60] What the conference had not mitigated, and could not mitigate, was the fact that, as Metternich had it, 'however the truth may be disguised, it starts with countenancing a rebellion', and the best that could be hoped for was 'the least unfavourable conclusion possible'. By 'upholding *non-ratification*', Metternich hoped the three courts might facilitate a reconciliation in spite of Britain's 'mistaken policy'.[61]

Significantly, the demise of the apparent great power accord revealed an ideological as well as geographical split in the continent. France and Britain did ratify the treaty, but they were seen to do so independently, implicitly devaluing the agreement. Palmerston blamed Metternich for not using his influence with Russia and Prussia to urge a settlement but discerned an ulterior purpose: the validation of autocratic principles of government across Europe. 'Metternich is glad, from motives of personal vanity', he told Lamb,

> that England & France have ratified separately, & that the Conference is, by that step, virtually broken up. He has long been vexed at being one of the mute characters in the piece; at being obliged not only to follow the impulse of the two Jacobin cabinets of England & France, but even to register the edicts of his own plenipotentiaries, Esterhazy whom he looks down upon, & Wessenberg whom he hates. He thinks that now, the negotiation has got out of the hands of the Conference, and that he has again

become the arbiter of European affairs. That he will be able to direct the march of Russia & Prussia, when the three courts are acting separately though he was borne along by the Five when London was the scene of negotiation. . . . The only way then of preventing collision between the 3 Powers & the 2, is for the Three to ratify also. Now, his be the glory of bringing about that ratification; let him get the proxies of the Two, or else let him decide their course by setting them an example.[62]

With disturbances in Germany and Italy at hand, Palmerston felt it imperative that the Belgian question, and hence French disarmament, be settled immediately. 'I do not know that any security can arise from having three fires burning at once instead of two,' avowed Palmerston and hoped at least to squeeze this final result out of the crumbling unity of the powers.[63] If not, he lamented that a settlement that might have been 'accomplished by moral power' would instead have to be achieved by the military force of a Franco-British-Belgian alliance.[64]

Russia, just as much, if not more so than Austria, Palmerston believed, was intent on destabilising Europe, using the Belgian affair, a question in which neither had any direct or material interest, to assert that theirs 'ought . . . to be the law for Europe.'[65] When in April it became clear that Metternich had 'humbugged' the powers and 'made April fools of us,' with a 'pretended ratification' ('pretended' in the sense that it was ultimately dependent on the concurrence of both Russia and Holland, yet in the full knowledge that the King of the Netherlands would not comply), Palmerston did not hide his feeling that this could be perceived as an incitement to wider conflict.[66] By the first week of April, therefore, Palmerston was becoming impatient for a conclusion to the matter.[67] He was also starting to refer to the question in an altered tone, adopting a distinctly more ideological cadence and speaking of something approaching a Conservative conspiracy.

I have long had an instinctive contempt of these arbitrary cabinets, but it is only of late that I have learnt how just the sentiment has been. Pray make Metternich understand that we are all furious, and that if he wants to quarrel with us, this is the right way to set about it, but if he wishes to be friends he has chosen an unfortunate manner of accomplishing his object. The fact is, it is all a miserable intrigue between the D of Wellington & Metternich, & the D of Cumberland & the Prussian princes. Wellington & Cumberland persuade their correspondents that we are going out; that by ratifying now, they would give us strength & help us to stand; that by waiting for a new govt they would have friends to deal with, & would have an opportunity of paying them a compliment on their accession, & enabling the new govt to say that they had accomplished, what we had been unable to effect.[68]

For Metternich, the British–French partnership trumpeted by Palmerston was an artificial one. 'From the time Liberalism gained the upper hand in France and England, this kind of [conference] meeting began to degenerate,'[69] he said in January 1832 and though Britain seemed more reliable than France,[70] nonetheless, the 'English and French Cabinets, after making parliamentary capital out of the Belgian affair, and the unfortunate proceedings connected with it, have latterly permitted themselves to extend the political significance to that fact'.[71] By April Metternich was complaining that this 'asserted friendship' was no more than 'an empty phrase', and rather than 'alliance' he suggested Franco-British relations might better be described as 'complicity'.[72] However, Metternich did acknowledge that there was a perceived ideological divergence between Britain and Austria. In a dispatch to be communicated to Palmerston in the autumn of 1832, the Austrian minister pointed out that the 'principle of Conservation forms the basis of the internal and external policy of Austria', though he denied that this policy (which he also labelled 'preventive') was pursued to an extreme and he suggested, furthermore, that in fact the rhetorical garb of Palmerstonian policy, which he characterised as 'concessionary', was used merely to disguise the relative decline of British power. The apparent differences between East and West were therefore exaggerated: both systems – preventive and concessionary – were, ultimately, Metternich said, obliged to 'fall back' on some measure of 'repression' if they were to preserve stability.[73]

However, the points of friction between the powers were numerous. As well as difficulties in Belgium, Italy, Germany and Poland, the Iberian Peninsula was the scene of a yet more explicit contest between constitutional and autocratic government and by extension a test of power for what seemed to be two emerging power blocs. Conservative government had been in the ascendant in both Spain and Portugal since the late 1820s as King Ferdinand VII of Spain and Dom Miguel in Portugal consolidated their position and by the early 1830s both were looking to Russia, Austria and Prussia as potential allies in the face of west European liberalism, which the July revolution in France and the accession of the Whigs in Britain seemed to indicate was really gaining ground. In 1832 Dom Pedro landed in Portugal and, supported by the British military, finally installed his daughter Maria as Queen. The following year, in Spain, Ferdinand's death opened up a direct contest between his daughter Isabella – whose claim was supported by her mother, Maria Christina, who acted as her regent – and Ferdinand's brother, Don Carlos, who claimed the throne in the conservative interest. As these succession contests raged in the Iberian Peninsula in the early 1830s, the issue seemed as much about east European conservative monarchism and west European constitutionalism as it was about dynastic struggles in Spain and Portugal.

As with Belgium, Palmerston's first concern was to avoid independent French action: it was the threat of French intervention that prompted him to anticipate that 'we might find ourselves compelled very unwillingly to interfere & to assist the Portuguese,[74] more than any sentimental (pseudo-Canningite) attachment to the Portuguese cause per se. It was a relief when that French threat dissipated,[75] but the potential remained for Spain and Portugal to disturb the fragile European peace. So in parallel with the Franco-British rapprochement over Belgium Palmerston began to look to similar concerted action between the two Western powers in a matter of mutual historical and strategic interest. In October 1831 he asked: 'Are we all to stand by & see Pedro make his attack on Portugal from Ferreira, & have civil war in Portugal[?] *Would* Spain be passive, & *could* we permit her to be active[?] Is it not better for England & France at once & openly to take up Donna Maria, & by throwing their weight into the scale make it preponderate immediately, & without a civil struggle, & might they not then have a right to require from Pedro, as the price of assistance, such securities, as the tranquillity of Spain might stand in need of [?]'[76]

On the same day that the conference on Belgium signed the draft treaty, 15 November 1831, Palmerston wrote to Emily revealing how far he really remained from uniting both his ministerial colleagues and the great powers. The Cabinet, Palmerston complained, were 'afraid of taking up Pedro', fearing overseas entanglements and were 'in short very mealy mouthed', but Palmerston saw the constitutional struggle in Portugal as something more than an isolated Iberian affair. He advocated interference in Portugal to serve wider European interests: 'if we do not resolve to do it, I think events will compel us. The Russians thirst for vengeance on the Poles, and Mad. Lieven not the least.'[77]

By February 1832, Palmerston was beginning to despair of a satisfactory result. 'Recognition of Miguel is out of the question;' he wrote to Henry Addington, 'a marriage between him & Maria is equally impossible. What then remains to be proposed except an arrangement by which Miguel should enter upon a suitable provision and make way for Maria, without civil war. Spain perhaps will not lend herself to such a plan; Miguel possibly would reject it; Pedro in the mean time will land, Miguel's troops will go over to the elder brother and Miguel in the end will have to retire across the frontier without his provision, and become a charge upon the hospitality of Spain.'[78] The truth was, as Palmerston explained in a letter to Fred Lamb, real balance of power questions had become lost in the rhetoric of ideological conflict:

If you give people without fighting, that which by fighting first they may either win or lose, you have a right to expect them to abstain from some things which if they won it, by their arms, they would unquestioningly do; and though we must utterly & absolutely deny the doctrine which asserts the rights of Spain to march into Portugal to put down free institutions, because the example of such an improvement, would be irresistible in Spain, yet it would be quite a different thing to persuade Pedro to moderate his notions of the changes which might be suitable to the present state of Portugal, and to prevail upon him to postpone & to qualify, in such a manner, as to tranquillize the alarms of all but the thoroughbred apostolicals in Spain. But there is not much time for such a negotiation and therefore to do any good, it should be begun forth with; but without Spain it could not be undertaken.[79]

Palmerston had tried, in vain, in the spring of 1832 to avert an overt ideological division of the continent, appealing to Austria to resist action in Spain that would inevitably bring France into the fray on the side of constitutionalism. In a conversation with Neumann, Palmerston 'begged him to look at the present state of public feeling, for it is more than opinion, in Bavaria, in Baden, in Hesse, and in many other parts of Germany & then tell me what would be the consequence of a war waged and begun against France, by what would be called the arbitrary governments of Europe, in order to prevent France from interfering to assist the Constitutional party in Portugal when in danger of being crushed by the absolutists of Spain. Austria would in that case deliberately and of her own malice prepense, be beginning a war of principle in Europe, and I should like to see the man, who would venture to predict how it would end, and who would be the greatest sufferers by it. But be that as it may, such a proceeding at all events would not be the way to *prevent* or put down *revolutions*.'[80] Likewise, in Italy, Palmerston advocated support for reform not on the grounds that it would be just, but as a means of averting perpetual Austrian intervention there, which would only provoke conflict among the powers: 'War so excited must be necessarily a war of principles & opinions,' cautioned Palmerston, 'and that cannot be for the interest of Austria whose maxim is quieta non movere. In such a war too, she must not expect to have England on her side.'[81]

   However, it was apparent that the Five powers could not work in harmony. By October 1832 Metternich was complaining that France and Britain appeared determined to work together and the only response for the three Eastern powers was to do the same: 'we have deemed it incumbent upon us to lay down the following proposition: *That the carrying out of any decision adopted by the two Cabinets exclusively ought to impel the three courts to adopt a uniform course, and induce them henceforward to form but a single, compact and indissoluble whole*'. The notion of a concert of great powers was at an end. Within the Belgian conference Metternich observed the separation of the powers and read into this a broader lesson for strategic alignments. '*The principle of the union of the three courts is now de facto established. Allies find themselves confronted by accomplices*; the former have right on their side, and reason must pronounce in their favour as well. . . . A demonstration that any moral disunion, and not less any material disunion, which might arise at any time among the five courts, in reference to this affair, would be the work of the minority; A firm determination on the part of the three monarchs not to give their assent to any enterprise undertaken by the two maritime Powers for purely fanciful considerations or for the sake of effect.'[82]

Whereas in October 1830 Metternich had admitted that London was one of only two places where a conference to settle Belgium could legitimately be held (the other was The Hague), by the end of 1832 he judged London to be an 'eccentric point' for such a conference, giving undue and unhelpful weight to the opinion of the British government.[83] Palmerston rejected out of hand Metternich's proposal to move the conference to Aix-la-Chapelle, but felt backed into a French corner by Austrian conduct: it was a reaction to the Three powers, Palmerston suggested, that drove Britain closer to France: 'Every month that he has passed since the arbitrary powers have forced England & France to cooperate, has strengthened the union between those two govts, and the course which Austria is apparently determined to pursue & which is founded upon nothing but prejudice & vanity will only drive us further on in the same course.'[84]

The division had by now an identifiably ideological quality. Palmerston in a letter to Emily in September 1832 had noted:

The folly & blindness of these despotic governments, and their incapacity of seeing inevitable consequences, would make one laugh at them, if the interests of millions were not at stake & constantly liable to be sacrificed by their prejudices. They fancy all mankind born & treated only for the advantage & use of a few very ordinary gentlemen, decorated with stars & crosses & titles; and deeply convinced themselves, that this is the inten- tion of Providence they conceive in their silliness that the rest of mankind are penetrated by the same conviction.[85]

Metternich meanwhile judged the British Foreign Secretary as little more than a naïve dupe of the French. Palmerston was also, Metternich thought, trying to make domestic political capital out of perceived differences of opinion between Britain and Austria and was not to be relied upon. Metternich could not resist noting that 'it concerns me to know whether, when others besides myself say *good-morning* to Lord Palmerston, he replies with a justification implying that he has understood them to say *good-night* to him'.[86]

Metternich was quite right that Palmerston was using current events in Europe to serve wider interests. Palmerston insisted that the division of European powers was not of his making and that his policy was directed in all cases simply to the protection of national interests, but he well understood the value of political rhetoric which he would employ to good effect.[87] He would turn to his advantage what he described as the 'bad faith, and duplicity, and trickery, & treachery, of these three good allies of ours, in this Belgian affair'.[88] 'The triumph of Maria, & the accession of Isabella,' he enthused in a letter to his brother William in 1833, 'will be important events in Europe, and will give great strength to the Liberal party. England, France, Belgium, Portugal & Spain looked upon merely as a mass of opinion, form a powerful body in Europe; and Greece further on is rising into a state upon similar principles.'[89]

It was above all, so said Palmerston, the actions of Britain's partners in the Belgian negotiations that had driven Britain and France together, and he was resentful of the manipulation that this implied.[90] By January 1833 there was a hint of exasperation in Palmerston's correspondence – 'in public affairs it never rains but it pours', he told Graham – but there appeared no way now to dam the waters that had been unleashed in France in July 1830. The Three powers, Palmerston suspected, had been hoping that this torrent would wash away the liberal movements of western Europe and their prevarication over the November 1831 Treaty of London was a ruse only to draw Britain and Belgium into 'a scrape'. Belgian independence had become, therefore, effectively a test of British stamina: 'I am convinced,' wrote Palmerston, 'that the timely employment of a firm and steady but temperate language, and a fixed refusal to give way without reason upon small points which are put forward as skirmishes & feelers to try the mettle of parties concerned, have a more powerful effect in preventing serious differences between governments, than many people imagine.'[91] Frustration more than disagreement pushed East and West apart and if there was a west European unity, it was one forged to a large extent in adversity. As Austria, Russia and Prussia indulged the 'chicanery' of the King of the Netherlands in his resistance to Dutch separation from Belgium, Palmerston wondered that 'the three courts have not had the wit to see how the prolongation of this discussion prejudices their own interests; how it irritates us against them, how it unites us with France, how it shews their impotence to make head against England & France united; since in spite of their resistance & obstacles, settled it *must & will* be'.[92] Palmerston was to be disappointed, however, in his hopes that in the absence of significant advances for conservatism across Europe (and there was 'no chance' of the British government 'being *Tory*fied') Austria and Russia would concede defeat and desist from stirring up a conservative reaction, such as he suspected they were trying to do by funding the Tories in Britain.[93]

The divergence among the Powers, such as it was, was not necessarily founded on irreconcilable ideological differences. By the time he quit the Foreign Office in 1834, Palmerston had staked a clear claim to the leadership of the 'Liberal Movement' in western Europe, but to read this as the realisation of a determined ambition is a distortion just as much as it is to suggest that Palmerston opportunistically seized the mantle of Canningite liberal constitutionalism for personal and party political gain. By happenstance events saw Palmerston enter the Foreign Office at the moment that liberal political movements began to sweep Europe. Palmerston neither stoked these fires, nor did he seek to extinguish them. He believed in stability and, where this meant maintaining the status quo, he advocated conservation (or 'non-interference'); where matters were already unsettled he argued for constructive reform. Dugald Stewart had persuaded Palmerston that durable and effective government depended on popular acquiescence in its authority, and a modern government would ignore that maxim at its peril. Thus, as the 'autocratic' governments clung to power to serve vested interests in the wake of what was, essentially, popular rejection of the Vienna settlements in the early 1830s, they proved themselves, in the Palmerstonian view, selfish, inflexible, unenlightened and, as a result, ineffective and unstable. To align Britain with those powers that spoke the language of political inclusion, therefore, was to reconcile Palmerston's political and philosophical instincts.

Thus, Palmerston's predilection for constitutional government was tempered by a spirit of moderation and compromise. In Portugal, for example, his support for Maria was designed to advance the cause of constitutionalism without needlessly alienating the absolutist forces supporting Miguel. As he explained to Lamb in early 1833, it was a practical response. Miguel could not succeed, he thought, and a regency for Maria would be welcomed by both Miguelites and Constitutionalists if that led to stability.[94] There was, then, nothing evangelical about Palmerston's 'liberal' foreign policy. 'Not that we want all other countries to adopt our constitution of King, Lords & Commons, or fancy that because such institutions are good here, they must necessarily answer *at once* everywhere else;' he wrote in June 1833, 'and least of all do we want, as the absolutists *affect* to think we do, to see *revolution* spread everywhere. But we do think that the maintenance of good order no less than the happiness of mankind is promoted by redressing admitted grievances, & remedying acknowledged evils, and we think that policy, which consists in prescribing the bayonet as the sole cure for all political disorders, to be founded in ignorance of human nature, and to be pregnant with the most disastrous consequences.'[95] He had already admitted that he did not particularly care what form of government existed in the Netherlands since (and presumably so long as), 'Republican Holland would be just as good an ally & customer of England as monarchical Holland.'[96]

This was the politics of prudence. Whereas the pressure for change in Italy might have stimulated Palmerston's 'natural disposition to reform glaring abuses,'[97] Poland and Germany revealed the limit of the so-called Liberal Movement's reach. This is not to say that such a 'movement' was unimportant: in terms of rhetoric Palmerston was beginning to come into his own and to make a meaningful connection with his parliamentary oratory of 1829 and 1830. The first twelve months of his tenure of the Foreign Office had been 'no time to preach a Liberal crusade', with settlement of the Netherlands pressing and an precarious domestic situation – as Whigs, Tories and Radicals argued over parliamentary reform – always in the background, but, by 1832, it has been argued, those restraints were loosening and shifting power balances were demanding a more overt stand.[98] Testing the pen against the sword, Palmerston, much to the chagrin of Lamb, the British ambassador in Vienna, lectured Metternich indirectly by conducting a protracted discussion with

Lamb on the merits of constitutional and monarchical government via the medium of the ordinary post, fully aware that these letters would be intercepted by the Austrian Post Office. Thus Metternich was left in no doubt that Palmerston saw it as a central British concern to preserve the 'general condition of Europe', by 'moral influence' in the first instance, and by 'armed interference' only if necessary. Palmerston thought Metternich needed 'to have some good genius at his ear to whisper to him sounder & sager principles'.[99] As radical and nationalist, or at least reforming, movements gained ground in the dependent or neighbouring states of Austria and Russia, notably in Poland, Germany and Italy, Palmerston intensified his 'moral' challenge to the autocratic powers. In August 1832 he told the House of Commons that 'the independence of constitutional states, whether they are powerful, like France or the United States, or of less relative political importance, such as the minor states of Germany, never can be a matter of indifference to the British Parliament, or, I should hope, to the British public. Constitutional states I consider to be the natural allies of this country; and . . . no English ministry will perform its duty if it be inattentive to the interests of such states'. This speech had been delivered in a near empty House of Commons (only eleven members were present).[100] He was under no obligation to make it and it was clearly a statement of principle that Palmerston had wanted made public. He would not have been dismayed by Metternich's annoyance that 200,000 copies of the speech had apparently been ordered for circulation by liberals in Germany.[101] The significance of this should not be underestimated. Palmerston reassured Neumann that the 'constitutional states' speech must be taken in its 'parliamentary' sense and was not a call to immediate action,[102] but it was, nonetheless, a 'dramatic departure from the norms of British diplomacy' for the Foreign Secretary explicitly to tie policy to ideology in this manner. Canning's appeals to popular 'applause' had been mere flirtations by comparison.[103] British public opinion in the early 1830s was, certainly, thought to be particularly pro-Polish, and there may well have been a degree of popularity-hunting in Palmerston's conduct, but though he spoke in Britain he wanted above all to be heard in central and eastern Europe. As he underlined in another letter to Lamb, 'to wrest free institutions from 10 to 12 millions of Germans, swarming with professors and newspaper editors and in actual contact with France, is a quixotic enterprise. It would be about as easy to persuade these worthy people to quit their cities and go back and live like the aboriginal ancestors in the mountain caves and in the recesses of the forest as to induce them to submit to arbitrary government.'[104]

In fact, there was little Palmerston could do beyond issue warnings and veiled threats. He, had, for example, conceded as early as September 1831 that though 'heartily sorry' for the 'poor Poles', 'their case had become for some time hopeless'.[105] And likewise, in neither Italy nor Germany did his supposed efforts to advance constitutional government meet with tangible success. About Germany, judged Bourne, what Palmerston said 'was even more ineffectual in improving the lot of its [Germany's compared to Italy's] inhabitants, but even more effective in promoting differences with Austria and extending them to Prussia'.[106] What all of Palmerston's constitutionalist bombast did do, then, was to convince Metternich *et al.* that Palmerston had consciously positioned himself as the 'principal supporter' of the Liberal Movement and that in doing so he had effectively drawn a line between the two European 'blocs'.[107]

Influenced though it no doubt was by a sense of frustration, notably with Metternich, Palmerston's growing preoccupation with theories of government was nevertheless sincere enough. Although he might have been willing to work for peace in collaboration with the autocratic powers over Belgium and would again be happy to bind France by alliance with Russia in the future, his commitment to liberal constitutional government should not be dismissed. In April 1833 Palmerston wrote a letter from his sickbed to Fred Lamb which might credibly have issued from the pen of Dugald Stewart himself:

I am sorry we differ so much in our principles of govt, and that I have not leizure to convert you from your absolute doctrines, as I think I could, if I had time. But *all* countries, not Germany only, are and always have been in a state of transition and it is the character and purpose of human nature that all societies should be constantly altering. Were this not so we might still have painted [ourselves] blue like the Britons. The province of a wise govt is to keep pace with the improved notions of the people; not to insist upon knowing better than those they govern, what those they govern wish; neither to chain down society to a point, nor to hurry it along too fast, to be ever and anon modifying institutions to suit them to attend habits, and new wants thus to render safe and tranquil those changes which if made violently might be dangerous, to lead & direct; and not to hold back till a superior force drags them along.

Now Metternich et id genus omne just invest all these maxims, and the consequence is, that these grand conservatives are in their own persons the immediate causes of all the revolutions that happen from time to time. Philip of Spain, Charles & James of England, Constantine in Poland, Polignac, Wellington, all thought themselves Conservatives while they were busily employed in pulling down the fabric. For after all, power is with numbers, & the King, the Minister or the General as a unit against a nation must give way.[108]

And in November he adapted this specifically to events with which he was dealing, claiming:

We shall soon be able to add Spain & Portugal to the Anglo French alliance. It will be western against eastern Europe; the liberal & constitutional

against the despotic states. The contest will be a moral one only, because
the West will not wish for war, and the East will not dare to make it. But
the West will gain upon the East; and the East will be obliged to be
more moderate in their tone & their measures. The Western union
will have a natural attraction for other associates; the Eastern a natural
repulsion. The Spanish Peninsula well organized will resume its proper
place among the states of Europe; and many results favourable to the
civilization and happiness of mankind may be looked for in due course
of time.[109]

Metternich judged the Franco–British western connection disingenuous and
rejected the notion that there were any political differences between the
powers, only moral ones, hinting that it was Palmerstonian exaggeration that
presented the Three powers as repressive and reactionary ones in conflict with
a liberal West.[110] Palmerston, however, as Herbert Bell pointed out, hoped to
achieve many things at once when he claimed a natural alliance between
Britain and other constitutional states.[111] The European crises of the early
1830s were also being played out against the background of Reform debates
and riots in Britain. There were many potential domestic advantages to the
Whig government in presenting Britain as the international champion of
constitutional government abroad. Yet, it would be unjust to read Palmerston's
stance on constitutional government as merely oratorical garnish conjured up
for popular appetites in the country at large. In a private letter to Lord
Heytesbury, the British ambassador in St Petersburg in late 1831, and himself
a person of conservative tastes, Palmerston had insisted that, with regard
to Poland:

> It is said that the word constitution is a vague expression & means
> anything or nothing. I cannot subscribe to that opinion; common use &
> general consent have invested the word constitution with a meaning suffi-
> ciently distinct & precise. There are few people in Europe who if they
> were told that a nation was to have a constitution granted to it, would not
> understand that that nation was thenceforward to have a government
> consisting of a sovereign and one or more assemblies, one of which at
> least, was to be elected by the people, and to represent the nation at large.
> There is a difference etymological as well as political between constitu-
> tion and institution, between the Polish Diet, and the provincial states of
> Prussia; the Treaty marks this distinction, and to obliterate it by substi-
> tuting in Poland local institutions for a general constitution would clearly
> be a breach of engagement. . . .
> This question of preserving or not, the constitution, is not one of mere
> form; it is true that the Diet need only assemble once in two years, & can
> sit for but 30 days, but its existence would afford a security for those

personal rights which the constitution grants to the Poles, and which are essential to their happiness & well being. I mean their freedom from arbitrary arrests, from banishment out of Poland, from confiscation of property, and from many other of those abuses of power, which form the daily grievances of the Russian subjects. There can be no security for the enjoyment of these privileges, which I presume even the Russian plan does not contemplate the depriving them of, unless there remains a popular assembly, whose consent is necessary for the alteration of laws, and to whom appeal may be made against their violation. . . .[112]

Palmerston was confronted by questions of constitutional reform not only in the dispatches that crossed his desk at the Foreign Office. Britain, too, was being jolted by unrest over the iniquities of the corrupt and outdated (un-)representative system at home. The parallels were not lost on Palmerston. Writing to Lamb in January 1832 about Hungary he observed: 'The crown and the people are to execute a reform for the purpose of depriving the aristocracy of powers & privileges adverse to the commonweal; some of the most enlightened nobles are in favor of the measure, but it is opposed by the rest from interested motives, and by the great mass of the gentry from want of sufficiently enlightened views. Are you sure you were not copying a letter of last year about the Reform Bill?' Britain, he felt, stood as a model of timely compromise and wise concession. The measures championed by the Whig government in 1831 and 1832, he argued, had effectively addressed the needs of modern society. 'I am confident that the institutions of the monarchy have gained a solidity of which many people have no adequate idea by incorporating with the governing portion of the community a vast body of the middle classes who have hitherto been excluded,' he said in January 1832. Radicals 'may perhaps wish to clip some few of the Corinthian capitals, but they will not allow anybody to undermine the column itself'.[113]

The Prime Minister, Lord Grey, had entered Downing Street in November 1830 at a time of life 'when retirement and repose are more to be desired than that active and anxious exertion to which I shall be subjected,'[114] and though he had a genuine interest in foreign affairs, and closely monitored Palmerston's conduct, he was obliged to devote more of his time to questions of parliamentary reform at home than to diplomacy. Pressure for Reform in Britain was becoming acute. Palmerston admitted that his own task would have been much more complicated had public opinion not been preoccupied with domestic change, observing in August 1831, for example, that popular support for Polish constitutional reforms would have been much more vocal if 'every body had not been so entirely engrossed' with domestic reform questions.[115] Having been elected on a programme of Reform, it was essential that the government saw through this commitment. For Prime Minister Grey, there was no mistaking the duty of modern government to respond to such demands; as he warned Princess Lieven in September 1830, he had 'never yet known a popular revolution that might not be ascribed to provocation on the part of the government', thereby drawing an implicit parallel between Russian problems in Poland and the remedies the Whigs were soon to apply in Britain.[116] Whatever enthusiasm there was for European radicalism and liberalism, the future and reputation of Grey's government rested on its ability to deliver meaningful change at home first. As Palmerston admitted to Emily in October 1831, although measures had yet to be resolved upon, all members of the government knew that it was their 'imperative duty to stay in' and satisfy the demands of the country for change which they had done so much themselves to excite.[117]

In May 1831 Palmerston had lost his seat for the University of Cambridge. His support for Catholic emancipation in 1829 had already tarnished his image at the University and when he came forward soliciting support to be returned again as one of the University's MPs, his membership of Lord Grey's ministry and support for reform is said to have further undermined his position. One Trinity voter wrote to deny Palmerston his vote on the grounds that he feared it would be to support measures of reform which tended 'inevitably to the subversion of the constitution both in Church and State'.[118] The defeat, when it came, Palmerston described as 'a terrible bore', after a twenty-year tenure during which he had 'weathered even the Catholic question', but he viewed it as a political and not a personal rebuff. The voters, he told Lady Holland, 'were frightened at parts of our Bill, & the stupid phrase which has been invented against us by our opponents, "The Bill the whole Bill & nothing but the Bill". The laity of whom there are great numbers, among the Masters of Arts were nearly as bad as the clergy;[119] But it must not be supposed that all who voted against us are adverse to Reform; for a great number declared to me that they were for an efficient & substantial Reform, though they could not approve of our arrangements for carrying it into execution.' Though he found the University's rejection disagreeable, Palmerston declared himself confident that he would regain his seat 'at the next election when the Bill & the panic shall have passed'.[120] Palmerston had, however, lost convincingly, coming last in the poll, and he could not avoid the conclusion that 'all the anti-Reformers in England are concentrated in Cambridge; there is no end of them here'.[121] Instead of Cambridge, Palmerston was found a seat for Bletchingley, in Surrey, a rotten borough for which he paid well above the going rate and which was to be disfranchised anyway under the terms of the 1832 Reform Bill.[122] At the election of June 1832, therefore, the Foreign Secretary had neither a seat, nor the obvious prospect of one. Taking the first opportunity he could, Palmerston expressed his desire to resume the representation of Cambridge (the University, not the Town seat for which he had lately received an offer),[123] but he was again to be disappointed, learning from friends within the University that his chances were poor. The Master of Corpus Christi, John Lamb, for example, feared leading Palmerston 'into a scrape by being too sanguine respecting your success'. Grey's government had demonstrated its conservative credentials, Lamb observed, but not sufficiently to unite old Tory support with Palmerston's liberal backers and it was no doubt in the light of such intelligence that in August Palmerston finally gave up hopes of regaining the University seat.[124] It was, said his old tutor James Wood, a regrettable yet unavoidable breach, though he consoled Palmerston with a hint that the University might not be irretrievably lost to him.[125]

With his current seat at Bletchingley abolished, and his old favourite not disposed to readopt him as its candidate, Palmerston was obliged to look else-where. He soon received offers from Lambeth, Tower Hamlets, Falmouth and Penryn, and South Hampshire, though he declined to launch into an immediate canvass in any of them.[126] The Hampshire seat at first seemed to him the least desirable: he doubted his prospects in such a wide-ranging constituency and thought the seat did not necessarily merit the exertions that would be required. After all, in supporting his neighbour John Fleming in the county contest there in 1820, Palmerston had observed that the 'honor of representing a county is one which I think one rather covets for one's friends than for oneself'.[127] Having had his fingers burned in Bletchingley where his seat had cost him dear, Palmerston was somewhat more cautious in his approaches in the autumn of 1832. It is thought that while Lambeth and Tower Hamlets would not have incurred great expense, Palmerston was wary of new metropolitan seats and preferred the West Country offer from Falmouth and Penryn, a constituency at such a distance from London, moreover, that he perceived the additional benefit that he would not be expected to turn up there very often.[128]

Letters from Palmerston's brother William and a William Lake, who were canvassing on his behalf in Penryn and Falmouth in June and July 1832, suggested that all was well there and 'numerous promises' had been secured during a first day's canvass.[129] As many as nine-tenths of the electorate were likely to vote for Palmerston in Falmouth, thought William, so only a 'respectable minority' of the Penryn votes would be necessary to secure victory.[130] In late September, however, Lake sounded a note of caution. 'I am of opinion,' he wrote in a letter designed to be seen by Palmerston, 'if acts of bribery are not resorted to at Penryn, that Lord Palmerston will stand a very fair chance of being returned, but if on the contrary recourse is had to any extent to such means by the other candidates, he will not succeed.'[131] This news confirmed other reports that victory in Penryn and Falmouth would prove costly (it was recorded by Lady Cowper that each vote might cost as much as £5) and Palmerston saw fit to investigate other offers more fully.[132]

In Lambeth Palmerston's prospects seemed promising and he appears to have given his supporters reason to believe that he would stand there, though Lord Holland, who offered to lend his weight to Palmerston's campaign, continued to press for a definite decision.[133] Palmerston, however, continued to vacillate. On

13 September William Jones wrote to Palmerston from Portsea in Hampshire informing him of a meeting that had taken place to select Reform candidates for the county election. 'Upon your name being mentioned, there was a strong expression of approbation,' he reported, 'and no doubt is entertained of your triumphant return without trouble or expense.' Jones accordingly enquired if Palmerston was willing to stand for South Hampshire against his old friend John Fleming, and alongside Sir George Staunton.[134] The next day, Palmerston wrote to Richard Cannon, one of his supporters in Lambeth and apparently something of an agent for him, asking whether his inclination to rebuff Hampshire in favour of Lambeth was 'prudent' in light of his prospects there.[135] Cannon's assessment was evidently favourable, for on 15 September Palmerston politely turned down the Hampshire approach and apparently committed himself to Lambeth.[136] 'I am likely to suffer under the embarrass des richesses as to seats,' joked Palmerston at the end of the month, as he eyed the various offers from around the country, perhaps indicating that his pledge to his supporters in Lambeth had not been final.[137]

Hopes of securing Palmerston's candidature for South Hampshire indeed were undimmed and at the end of September John Bonham-Carter approached Palmerston to appeal to him to reconsider. Bonham-Carter, whose family's influence was considerable in the county, had been the MP for Portsmouth since 1816 and was a pillar of Liberal strength in the region.[138] Liberals in the county were concerned about their chances against Fleming – 'the difficulty in the South seems almost insuperable,' admitted Bonham-Carter[139] – and they were keen to secure Palmerston's candidature as an effective counterpoise to the Tories. Bonham-Carter promised Palmerston that as he was a member of the government the voters of South Hampshire would not expect 'the same explicit avowal of opinions' as they might demand of a non-ministerial candidate and hoped further to reassure Palmerston that the contest would be an undemanding one by stressing that this call 'from your own county' was '*the act of the people*'.[140]

Yet if the call from Hampshire was popular, it was also discordant. Alongside the appeals from Bonham-Carter, Palmerston was also being urged by the Conservatives to join Fleming and 'drive Staunton out of the field'. The Tories were at least in agreement with the Liberals that Palmerston's vital influence could be exercised without any great 'personal exertions' in the county.[141] Sir James Graham, then at the Admiralty, counselled Palmerston to go with the Reformers whose political strength he thought superior to the Tories', or to give up on Hampshire altogether: an independent stand, he warned, would be expensive and probably not successful. While Palmerston toyed with multiple offers, Graham argued that his position was not in fact such a rich one. Neither Lambeth nor Falmouth seemed a sure bet and only Hampshire, 'where you are most desired, and where you may best command your own terms', seemed to offer a reasonable prospect of a satisfactory return.[142]

Graham's advice weighed heavily with Palmerston, who duly wrote to Bonham-Carter to ask for assurances of success by a canvass and guarantees about the extent of the expenses (Palmerston was prepared to put up no more than £500) before he would consider the proposal further.[143] Within a week he had assurances from William Nightingale (father of Florence), the chairman of the committee established to secure the election of Reform candidates, that a three-day canvass had shown a distinct advantage to Palmerston and Staunton, though this intelligence was to some extent confused by a letter from Henry Holmes, a local lawyer and Palmerston's (not altogether reliable) agent in Romsey, written at the same time as Nightingale's to say that Fleming's supporters would still give their second votes to Palmerston.[144] Palmerston told Nightingale that the assurances he had received were inadequate,[145] especially since the pressures of public office meant that he would be unable to conduct much of a personal campaign and was therefore heavily reliant on the actions of his supporters in Hampshire.[146] Bonham-Carter continued to press Palmerston to declare unequivocally for Hampshire 'because you are sure of your seat',[147] while Lord Holland expressed his view that Hampshire was 'the natural & permanent seat' for Palmerston and hoped that though Palmerston might prefer 'a metropolitan or even an academical seat', he would settle on a sure thing in Hampshire.[148]

Palmerston infuriated his supporters by his failure to commit to what they perceived to be a safe seat. Bonham-Carter complained to local Liberal supporters that a clear advantage was being squandered in a seat that was, he said, 'perfectly safe' by a margin of 'several hundreds'.[149] Palmerston finally gave an unequivocal promise to the South Hampshire Reformers in late November and wrote to Nightingale that he looked forward to 'the certainty of triumph'.[150] Sir George Staunton was in many ways the natural partner for Palmerston. Having returned from a diplomatic career in China at the beginning of the century, Staunton had sat as a 'liberal tory' for Mitchell in Cornwall from 1818 to 1826 and more recently for Heytesbury in Wiltshire from 1830 to 1831.[151] By his own estimation, Staunton identified himself with Canningite liberal Toryism and, after 1830, the Whigs.[152]

Before the election could be held, there was the task of registration to be undertaken. For the first time, every voter was required, under the terms of the Reform Act, to have his name placed on an electoral register. With a new franchise the matter was further complicated and in each district barristers were charged with establishing the legitimacy of voters' claims, and candidates, or their representatives, had an opportunity to oppose any such claims. Since a name, once placed on the register, could only be removed by being challenged, there were great incentives 'for the parties to flood the lists with names of their own supporters and file claims against persons registered by their opponents'.[153] A letter from Bonham-Carter to Baring of 4 November gives an illustration of this process:

I came yesterday just in time to have my fingers in the first county pie – the whole lot of objections is 88 & I very soon began with Baring Wells notices – having first by way of a good beginning got rid of one of the Montague tenants at Beaulieu without any notice of objection on our part at all. We had a very stout argument about the notices & to my surprize my friend Gambier has raised a crotchet in their favour and the barristers have taken time to consider & will give their judgement tomorrow morning.

The notices of Sharp the attorney our friend have hitherto been right and we have knocked off some 5 or 6 of the enemy & I had besides the great satisfaction of protecting the vote of the dissenting ministers at Botley against the *personal* objection of Mr Barker the Tory Clergyman.

I believe the work will occupy all Monday & Tuesday & then I must go to Lymington to throw my broad shield over a radical dissenting minister there a great friend of Villiers.[154]

Both sides declared themselves confident of victory, though the contest was much closer than any of the candidates would have liked to admit. The election turned on a number of issues of both national and local bearing. In the wake of the Reform Act, it was perhaps inevitable that the legitimacy of this restructuring of the franchise would be taken as a central issue in the contest. But as this involved the Foreign Secretary as well as local worthies, the debates were bound to be wide-ranging.

While there was particularly lively discussion on the subject of the Corn Laws and tariff protection for agricultural produce, not unexpected in a largely rural constituency, the election debates were concerned above all with national questions such as parliamentary reform but, as the *Hampshire Advertiser* argued, the distinctions drawn between the Reformers and Fleming on this issue were exaggerated. Palmerston, the *Advertiser* claimed, was well known not as a reformer, but as 'having previously supported those constitutional principles which are so ably defined in the manly address of Mr Fleming',[155] and the election increasingly came to turn on personality as much as it did on issues, with Palmerston, as a prominent national minister, an obvious focus.

The Tory-leaning *Advertiser* attacked Palmerston vigorously. His conduct, claimed the paper, had been at all times opportunistic (there was no other example of a minister whose career represented such constant 'desertion of principle for the emoluments of office') and, it charged, he had contrived to be a placeman in every government since Lord Liverpool's.[156] He was also widely criticised – in both the local press and on election posters – for failing to intervene more decisively to protect the Low Countries from French incursions.[157] This was so much knockabout electioneering. On one issue, however, there was a general accord among the candidates: that slavery should be abolished; and on this Palmerston was pushed to stake out his political position. It represented an important and meaningful test of his commitment to liberal reforms. Anti-slavery campaigners by the early 1830s sprang from two distinct camps. While the abolition of slavery was undoubtedly a common goal, the means by which this end would be realised were not unanimously agreed. The Agency Committee, established in 1831 as an offshoot of the Anti-Slavery Committee, pushed for immediate abolition in contrast to the gradualist approach – which argued for apprenticeships to 'ease' the transition from slavery to freedom and also a system of compensation for dispossessed slave-owners – advocated by the Anti-Slavery Society. The tensions between these different approaches were highlighted by the effects of Reform in 1832, not least because campaigners now sought to secure additional support from newly enfranchised electors. This, according to one historian of the movement, was not inconsequential: 'Sympathizers were further urged to obtain pledges of support from candidates, and when candidates disagreed with one another, to concentrate on "the two or three respectable voters who could, often, decide a candidate's fate." '[158] There had been an active Anti-Slavery Society in Southampton since 1825, despite (or perhaps rather because of) the town's close connections with the West Indies and thus colonial slavery, and by 1830 the issue was starting to 'feature prominently in local parliamentary elections'.[159] There was little doubt in South Hampshire that Palmerston was the candidate most likely to give a meaningful pledge, though it is perhaps also significant that the majority of the Southampton aboli-tionists were Liberal in their politics and drawn primarily from the upper middle-class, Nonconformist, urban milieu;[160] in many ways Palmerston's natural constituency.

But Palmerston was also being pushed towards support for immediatism. More than simply being expected to endorse abolition of slavery, he was being forced to make a choice about method. In November 1832, a petition, signed by twenty local electors and abolitionists, was sent to Palmerston requesting that he support in Parliament moves towards the immediate abolition of slavery, in return for which they would increase their efforts on his behalf at the election.[161] Palmerston, however, seemed anxious to avoid a hasty promise and replied to a letter from Dr Robert Lindoe (chair of the Southampton Anti-Slavery Society) in December that while no one could hold slavery 'in greater detestation than I do', he was reluctant to apply his name to an unspecified measure which, he feared, might create a new evil to replace the old. His promise, however, that he would 'feel it my duty to give to this important matter all that deliberate attention which it deserves and the spirit of my senti-ments is such as I have stated to you above',[162] seems to have satisfied the local abolitionists.[163]

Yet despite the groundswell of opinion that apparently favoured Palmerston and Staunton, it seemed even on the day of nomination that Fleming would win. The official nomination was held at Southampton on Saturday 15 December and according to the *Hampshire Advertiser*, 'Upon the names of the candidates

being put to a show of hands, there appeared a very large majority for
Mr Fleming over the other two candidates, and a slight one for Lord Palmerston
over Sir George Staunton. The under-sheriff declared the election to have fallen
on Mr Fleming and Lord Palmerston, and a poll was then demanded for
Sir George Staunton.'[164] The poll, held on the following Tuesday and Wednesday,
turned the *Advertiser*'s estimates upside down, though the result was still a close
one: Palmerston and Staunton were returned as MPs with 1,628 and 1,532 votes
respectively to Fleming's 1,279.[165]

Palmerston gave a full account of the contest, which had been 'highly gratifying to me personally because I was brought in by a large majority, without
having canvassed a single vote', in a letter written the day after the election. He
had, he said, been returned not simply by the votes of many of his 'personal
friends', but also by the 'wealthy farmers, men engaged in business, chiefly
above the class of shopkeepers; and two or three attornies, who gave their
services gratuitously'. It had been a lively campaign, with a high rate of voter
participation and Palmerston took some satisfaction from what he perceived to
be an implicit vindication of Whig measures of Reform. 'The Tories said that
when the Reform Bill was carried we should elect riff raff to represent us, and
now we answer them by presenting to them Ld Palmerston and Sir George
Staunton: – we are neither radicals, they said, nor republicans, but good and
loyal subjects of the King, attached to the constitution and devoted to the
person of our Sovereign, and as you from your official situation must have
frequent occasion to see the King, we beg you to tell him so, and to make a true
report of our sentiments. This was said to me by many'. Significantly,
Palmerston observed that at no point had he been asked for 'a pledge of any sort
or kind', but he also noted that two issues in particular had occupied voters'
attention: the Corn Laws and colonial slavery ('The people wishing the first to
remain unchanged, & the second to be immediately abolished'). On agricultural affairs, Palmerston was satisfied that he had carried the electorate with
him in regarding the corn question as 'rather a landlords' than a tenants' question, that rents must rise & fall with the price of corn, while the farmers profits
cannot on the long run differ much from those of other trades; & that the
manufacturers have as good a right to ask for cheap corn, as the farmer has to
wish for dear corn'. On colonial slavery Palmerston's account suggests a
groundswell of opinion in favour of gradual abolition. He recollected that there
had been support for his argument that 'we are bound when we do justice to the
slave, not to do injustice to the planter'. Explicitly endorsing gradualism,
Palmerston argued: 'although there must be much abuse where arbitrary power
is vested, yet the planters do not always eat the young negroes or salt the old
ones for winter provision, but that the infants & the infirm, & the aged are
supported by the master, and that to manipulate 800,000 negroes by the stroke
of a wand, without many accompanying provisions would be to deprive
all but the able bodied of their present means of existence'.[166] This echoed the

information Palmerston was receiving privately on the question of slavery: Foreign Office correspondents such as a recently returned diplomat from Buenos Aires assured him that in the West Indies, for example, slaves were generally well treated, often preferred to remain subject to a master and that in 'promoting therefore on *principle* the extinction of slavery, it was not necessary to *practice* [*sic*] to enforce it to the detriment of existing rights'.[167]

The commitment to abolish slavery was, however, duly honoured in 1833. Lord Howick had introduced plans for the emancipation of slaves which in March the Cabinet had decided would be unacceptable to the slave-owners and so pressed instead for a measure which would 'be a very delicate compromise between the maximum concessions of the colonial proprietors and the minimum demands of the abolitionists'. This prompted abolitionists to mount a public campaign with the intention of forcing the government's arm, and within a short time of the campaign being launched on 27 March petitions were flooding into Parliament from all over the country, reaching a daily average by mid-April of seventy-five. The Slavery Abolition Bill finally received the royal assent in August 1833 (with effect from 1 August 1834).[168]

With parliamentary reform and the abolition of slavery enacted, the government had sated some of the more prominent of the radical demands, for the moment at least. Palmerston's attention was already far from his new constituents. Although he offered judicious support of, and donations to, prominent and worthy causes in Hampshire following his election, and was applauded for his 'liberality' as a landlord in Romsey, there was limited political capital to be made from such works.[169] Palmerston had wanted a trouble-free seat (or one that would be as trouble-free as possible) that would represent a minimal diversion from his work at the Foreign Office and in Parliament. 'Everything went on smoothly during the sessions of 1833 and 1834,' observed Palmerston's Hampshire colleague George Staunton,[170] and Palmerston could, once again, turn his thoughts back to foreign affairs.

Palmerston's attention on entering the Foreign Office in 1830 had been occupied principally by affairs in western Europe and, having made this 'choice', it took him, said Webster, 'a little time' to appreciate the intricacies of Eastern affairs.[171] One contemporary commentator, David Urquhart, thought this emphasis on the West misguided, observing some little time later: 'A distinguished diplomatist, in the late apprehensions occasioned by the complication of the Belgian affairs, and the representative of one of the great powers, observed, "Why all these alarms? No gun will ever be fired in Europe for Belgian independence. It is in the East, that the arena will be opened for the European struggle." '[172]

Initially Palmerston had been content to witness liberal, nationalist, constitutionalist challenges to Ottoman control of its empire and, as commentators have since observed, he took a traditional 'Canningite' view of the Eastern question, that perennial problem for the great powers of responding to, or managing, the decline of one of their own, Turkey. He had welcomed moves towards Greek independence in the late 1820s, and in early 1831 was keen to afford protection to Greece against Egyptian threats in the interests of general peace.[173] Almost four years later, he still clung to the notion of independent, constitutional, government for Greece as the only safeguard against instability. 'There are no doubt many opinions, prejudices and interests adverse to such a proceeding and many men who will say that Greece is not ripe for a representative assembly,' he wrote to Britain's representative in Athens. 'But this is more easily said than proved; all nations are ripe for a representative assembly who have interests with respect to which it is necessary to make laws.' As he pointed out somewhat more stridently in September 1835: 'No set of men are too ignorant to understand their own interests and to manage their own affairs; besides the knowledge requisite for political affairs is speedily acquired by the very act of taking a part in them.'[174]

Championing independence for Greece struck two Canningite chords: it weakened a rival (Turkey) and advanced constitutional government at the expense of absolutism. 'The fact is that Turkey is falling rapidly to pieces. Greece must necessarily profit by its dissolution; and we want a government there, capable of taking advantage of circumstances which a short period of time may give rise to,' Palmerston had written to Granville in the summer of 1831.[175] Though Palmerston adhered to this platform with regard to Greece throughout his first term at the Foreign Office, a more profound strike at the heart of the Ottoman Empire caused some modification of the broader strategy. In 1833 a potentially more destabilising challenge to the integrity of the Ottoman Empire refocused the great powers' attention.

In October 1831 Mehemet Ali, the pasha of Egypt, had dispatched his army, under the command of his son Ibrahim, into Syria with the objective of securing Egyptian control over areas traditionally dependent on (but not formally subservient to) Egypt. As Ibrahim advanced on Acre, Damascus and Aleppo, the Ottoman Empire, which ruled over this area and Mehemet Ali himself, was demonstrably losing its grip on power within its territory. By the end of 1832 Ibrahim had gone much further and inflicted numerous defeats as his forces reached Anatolia, thereby bringing Egyptian forces alarmingly close to the Ottoman capital Constantinople. Russia and Austria were the only great powers seemingly alert to the implications of these developments – the potential collapse of Ottoman rule and the creation of a scramble for power and influence – and in early 1833, preferring to maintain the status quo than risk a destabilising power vacuum, Russia sent a naval force to the Bosphorus in an attempt to shore up the Sultan's position. The Sultan, however, was already buckling in the face of Egyptian power and in the spring granted Mehemet Ali formal control of the Syrian pashaliks that his forces had conquered, as well as further concessions in Adana that effectively made Mehemet Ali an autonomous leader within the Ottoman Empire and, by extension, a rival to the Sultan for pre-eminence in the region. In late 1832 Ottoman emissaries who had visited London in search of support had received no offer of help from Palmerston, who was well disposed but unable to secure Cabinet approval (Palmerston later described this as a 'tremendous blunder');[176] the Russians, however, had demonstrated their willingness to back the Sultan's position and in the summer of 1833 it was Russia that was able to secure, by the Treaty of Unkiar Skelessi, an important influence in Ottoman affairs. The treaty was ostensibly a defensive one – a commitment on both sides to support the other in the event of attack – but in effect what it meant was that Russia had gained an advantage over European rivals in dealing with the future of Ottoman territory by securing control over access to the Straits. It was obvious in London that this represented a threat to British influence in the area and to Britain's access to its own empire.[177]

During the course of this crisis, Palmerston's attitude to the Ottoman Empire apparently underwent a fundamental change as he shifted from an anticipation of the collapse of Turkish power to a determination to uphold that power. Palmerston outlined his position in January 1833:

> I own I attach no weight to all that we hear about the benefits which civilization would derive from an augmentation of dominion by the Pasha. If he could be made Sultan at once instead of Mahmoud, perhaps he would make a more vigorous administrator, though that is doubtful. . . . But it is impossible for Mehemet to become Caliph and Sultan, and therefore he cannot succeed to the unbroken empire of Mahmoud, and can only dismember it, by severing the Asiatic provinces wholly or in part. And surely the injury which would thus be done to the great interest of Europe, by placing the ruler of European Turkey completely in the hands of Russia, would far more than counterbalance the advantages which we should derive from the establishment of ecoles primaires and anatomical dissection in Syria and Mesopotmia.[178]

Palmerston came to the view, therefore, that the maintenance of the Sultan's control over his empire was vital. Considerable attention has been devoted to this ostensible volte-face and it is now broadly agreed that it was, in some way and at some point during 1832, the influence of Stratford Canning, Britain's sometime representative in Constantinople, that proved crucial in shaping Palmerston's opinion on this issue.[179] Conventional wisdom has it that by 1833 exposure to the *realpolitik* machinations of Vienna, St Petersburg and Berlin, not least with regard to Belgium, combined with Stratford Canning's political intelligence from Turkey, had shaken Palmerston's faith in indigenous reform of the Ottoman Empire as a bulwark against Russian encroachment into Turkish-controlled territory. Yet though this is superficially a break with Palmerston's supposed Canningite preferences, it is worth bearing in mind that, as Charles Webster pointed out, George Canning's policy towards the

Ottoman Empire in the late 1820s had been worked out very cursorily; indeed, in so far as that policy had a goal, it was simply to kindle tensions between Austria and Russia and above all prevent Russia from acquiring a strong hand in its dealings with the Porte.[180]

For Palmerston in 1833 the paramount concern was to prevent, firstly, Russian ascendancy at Constantinople and, secondly, any augmentation of French influence in Egypt. He took a very pragmatic view of Mehemet Ali's position. 'Where Mehemet Ali is, there the negotiation will be & I should have more apprehension of Mehemet being unreasonable than of [Sultan] Mahmoud's being so,' he wrote in April. 'Besides after all Mehemet is only a rebel who has no *right* to any terms but such as force may give him and if force turns against him, the right disappears.' Stability, then, was to take precedence over idealised notions of respect for the Egyptian right to self-determination. 'I am convinced,' he continued, 'that it is for the general interest of Europe that Mehemet should derive as little benefit as possible from his conquest and the less he gets in Syria, the better – & for this reason, because if he gets much then the Sultan is thrown permanently into the hands of Russia'; and not only this, but Palmerston was, he said, 'convinced that there has been a deep & long standing intrigue between the French govt as a corporation & the Pasha of Egypt & therefore all the people connected with the French govt wish the Pasha to get a large allotment of Syria.'[181]

The real sources of danger, therefore, were the Sultan's connections with Russia and Mehemet Ali's with France. But though Palmerston clung briefly to the hope that this might prove sufficient ground for an Austro–British mediation between the two European powers – 'especially as we & Austria are connecting links to hold them together', in both east and west, he argued[182] – it soon became clear in London that Britain (and France) were being outmanoeuvred by Austria, Russia and, partly at their bidding, Prussia. 'Eastern affairs seem to grow more & more complicated,' Palmerston complained to Lamb in May. 'I confess I have the greatest suspicions of Metternich's good faith; the language he holds to you, and through Neumann is that of a man who is cheating those he speaks to; and I cannot help suspecting that he is far advanced in a secret understanding with Russia for a partition of Turkey in certain contingent cases. A regular Polandizing of Turkey. When predictions are made by those who have the means of realizing them one cannot but suspect that they mean to make good what they foretold, & Metternich's gloomy language about the destruction of the Turkish Empire savours much more of intention than of mere foresight. However, this must not be, and cannot be.'[183] Had Russia not broken up the concert of the Five powers over Belgium, insisted Palmerston, Metternich would not have enjoyed such influence in the East.[184] Indeed, there was a note of exasperation in Palmerston's language about Austria at this time as he argued that but for the divergence over Belgium, common interests in Turkey should have been drawing Britain and Austria closer together, not further apart. 'On what Neumann founds his opinion as to our *hostility* to Austria I know not but I know very well what I have more than once said to him on Turkish affairs, & which certainly is of no hostile character,' he told Lamb. 'I told him that if we attach a great importance to the maintenance of the Ottoman Empire in its integrity and independence, it is not so much on account of the direct interest which England has therein, as because any great change in those quarters would materially affect Austria whom we look upon not merely as an antient friend and ally, but as a most important element in the balance of power in Europe; and consequently Turkish affairs become an English interest, mainly because they are an Austrian interest.'[185] Yet Palmerston knew that this was untenable. Only the day before he had written that 'we think we begin to perceive that the views, I speak not of the real interests, of England & Austria on this question are not so identically the same as we had hoped & imagined'. Whereas Britain hoped to see 'a strong and independent' Turkish empire, Austria wanted a 'weak' and 'dependent' one, even if that meant the Sultan became a virtual Russian vassal. Palmerston suspected that Metternich had already entered into an understanding ('tacit perhaps, but very decided') with Russia for the partition of the Ottoman Empire. It was, if so, an unjustifiable agreement, one that 'set all principles of international & public law more completely at defiance', but it would, said Palmerston, only serve to draw Britain and France together. They 'would in such case take Mehemet by the hand, and with the whole Mahometan population on our side it is far from clear that we should not be the strongest party'.[186]

If Palmerston was unsure what drove policy in the Eastern courts, he did not have long to wait for enlightenment. At the beginning of August he had learned the terms of the treaty agreed between the Tsar and Sultan at Unkiar Skelessi. It was, he said, 'a regular E[ast] I[ndia] Company, or Governor General's treaty'.[187] Under its terms, which stressed the importance of mutual aid, an appended article relieved the Ottoman government of any obligation to provide material or direct military aid to Russia in the event of need, but simply directed that it would act in the interests of Russia by closing the strait of the Dardanelles to foreign warships.[188] Though this did not hand the Tsar control of the Dardanelles, it did give Russia significant influence over the region and this caused much consternation in Britain.

If there remained any doubt about the fissuring of Europe, such were eliminated in the autumn when Austria, Russia and finally Prussia reaffirmed their common commitment to opposing revolution. The agreements reached and finalised at Münchengrätz in October 1833 re-established the Holy Alliance. Palmerston was in no doubt that the Russo-Turkish Treaty of 1833 and now the union of the three Eastern powers augured ill for the Ottoman Empire and he began to talk more frequently of Austro-Russian schemes for the partition of the European parts of that empire (Palmerston denied that Metternich did not know precisely what the Tsar and Sultan had agreed: he 'lied like a toothdrawer' in claiming so, said Palmerston). Palmerston's thoughts turned now not to opposing Mehemet Ali, therefore, but to backing him; to supporting him, indeed, as Turkey's potential saviour. Britain and France, he said, could back 'a national resistance' in Turkey to Russian aggression, and 'in such a case, Mehemet Ali would come well into play'. With Franco-British support, Mehemet Ali might advance against Russia and, he concluded, 'It is not then quite so chimerical as may at first appear, to suppose that England, France, & Mehemet would be a match for Austria & Russia in preventing those two powers from Polandizing Turkey'. Turkey would be saved, the British government would gain kudos at home, and Russia would be taught a lesson: 'A war with Russia would be extremely popular in England, from the King to the cotton spinner; and we should have many means of making Russia smart for all her insolence and encroachment,' he told Lamb. He only regretted that such a determined course had not been adopted sooner, at reduced political and diplomatic cost.[189]

By the end of 1833 Palmerston had become convinced that Russia's government was intent on 'pursuing steadily & perseveringly an undeviating system of encroachment upon neighbouring nations on all sides, instead of labouring to civilize the barbarous millions over whom they already rule, & to fertilise and cultivate the boundless wastes which lie within the extensive frontier of the empire'.[190] In such circumstances, support for Mehemet Ali was part of a policy of securing the position of the Sultan from the much greater external threats than those posed within the empire. Indeed, in the spring of 1834 he tried to argue that 'rotten as the Turkish Empire may be, it will hold together many a long day, if other powers will only leave it alone; and in all probability it has much greater internal resources than people in general imagine; if there was only a head to plan, good hands to execute. A great fertile country with an active & hardy people, facilities for commerce, unrivalled in any other quarter of the globe; all this ought to give revenue & an army'.[191] However, as Mehemet Ali's ambitions grew, and he launched an attack on Acre, a part of the Ottoman Empire still tranquil and loyal to the Sultan,[192] the logic of Palmerston's policy began to unravel. Palmerston long afterwards blamed himself for his failure to provide a convincing answer to the Eastern question in 1833. His equivocal policy towards Mehemet Ali, his ambiguous *idealpolitik* versus *realpolitik* perspective on Greece, Egypt and Syria combined, and his inability to impress a clear policy, either way, on the British Cabinet, helped ensure that the future of the Ottoman Empire would continue to bedevil European great power relations. Metternich, Palmerston was sure, was intent on partition of the Ottoman territories rather than reform and he bemoaned the spirit of '*fatalism*' that appeared to be in the ascendant at Vienna.[193]

Palmerston's position at the end of 1833 was a tricky one. The west and east European powers seemed, on all diplomatic questions, to be diverging and though this might have been squared in terms of philosophical commitments to differing systems of government, cold balance of power considerations nonetheless played a major part in any decisions made in the Foreign Office. At the beginning of his term of office, Palmerston had entertained notions that Britain and Austria might form some sort of axis on which great power relations would turn: both seemed politically and materially strong enough to bear such a role and both occupied geographic and political positions that would enable them to mediate between the other powers. In retrospect the idea might seem fanciful, but Palmerston, though he drank to liberalism in the summer of 1830, was quite willing to act alongside more autocratic partners where necessary. Belgium, Italy, Germany, Poland, Spain, Portugal, Syria, Turkey and the Levant, however, all provided ample illustrations of the fact that whatever great power accord had been established in 1815 (and let it not be forgotten that that accord had rested to a large extent on a mutual suspicion of France among the other four) had broken down by the early 1830s. Britain stood potentially friendless on the edge of Europe. Palmerston recognised that British foreign policy relied heavily on an ability to exert leverage over neighbours and rivals alike, but with Austria an unlikely partner it was to western Europe that Palmerston must look to establish a platform from which to exercise British power.

Portugal remained an unresolved problem for the powers. If a durable settlement of the absolutist–constitutionalist struggle there could be effected in favour of the constitutionalists, Palmerston saw that he could satisfy two key objectives: harmonising western Europe and asserting British leadership in the west by cloaking it in the language of liberalism. His perceived triumph he described to his brother William in April 1834:

I have been very busy ever since I returned from Broadlands on the 4th of this month working out my Quadruple Alliance between England France Spain & Portugal for the expulsion of Carlos & Miguel from the Portugueze dominions. . . . I carried it through the Cabinet by a coup de main, taking them by surprize, & not leaving them time to make objections. I was not equally successful with old Talley[rand] & the French govt, for they have made objections in plenty. But they were all as to the form in which I had proposed to make them parties to the transaction, and not to the thing itself; I have however at last satisfied their vanity by giving them a proper place among us. My first plan was, a treaty between the other three to which they should be acceding parties. I reckon this a great stroke; In the first place it will settle Portugal, and go some way to settle Spain also. But what is of more permanent & extensive importance it establishes a Quadruple Alliance among the constitutional states of the west, which will serve as a powerful counterpoise to the holy alliance of the East. I have, ever since Ferdinand's death, felt that morally this alliance must exist, but it was not till a fortnight ago that I saw the opportunity of giving it a substantive & practical form.[194]

Furthermore, this union, he claimed, would have a not inconsiderable moral effect in Europe and he amused himself by imagining Metternich's shocked reaction to it.[195] The treaty uniting the Four powers was, he said, 'a capital hit, and all my own doing'.[196] Though the three Eastern courts were unhappy, Palmerston feared the only threat to the alliance in the West was Pedro's reluctance to acquiesce: he and his ministers, suggested Palmerston, 'know that when the waters grow calm, they must sink to the bottom, & they wish to prolong the agitation'.[197] It is significant that the formal expression of this liberal union, the Quadruple Alliance of Britain, France, Spain and Portugal in 1834 to settle Portugal and the Iberian Peninsula, originally relegated France to little more than being an 'acceding power'. This was scarcely the expression of a deep-rooted Western accord. As Bell has argued, Palmerston's commitment to liberal foreign policy objectives elsewhere in the world was ambivalent and the Quadruple Alliance itself very quickly needed bolstering by Talleyrand and Palmerston to make it in any sense effective. However, what Palmerston had achieved, in the longer term, was to place Britain metaphorically at the forefront of European liberalism. This was in itself a considerable achievement. Though the Quadruple Alliance may have lacked teeth and proved in real terms short-lived, Palmerston was sincere when he maintained that he had finally achieved the diplomatic expression of his firmly held Whiggish-liberal faith.

This result was almost in question before it had even been gained. The Prime Minister, Grey, was growing weary and his thoughts were turning to retirement: in September 1833 he had admitted to Edward Ellice, the Secretary at War, that he thought 'it will be impossible for me to go through the work of another session'.[198] In January 1834 Grey made clear that he intended to resign, not least because he was unhappy about British commitments in Portugal. The Cabinet, fearing instability, tried to dissuade him but in the event only the King succeeded in convincing him to remain, which Grey pointed out that he did 'knowing himself to be unable to regulate his foreign policy according to his own views of what was safe and expedient'.[199] It was an indication of Palmerston's ascendancy in foreign affairs, but it was not one that boded well for the longevity of the government. Yet at the end of May, Palmerston sounded an optimistic note suggesting that 'Grey has not thoughts of going out', but as he reflected on continued ministerial divisions, the situation remained uncertain.[200]

Palmerston saw that the position of the Whigs under Grey was a fragile one and he worried that the Prime Minister's ongoing weakness and the coalescing of opposition forces around Peel (even though he insisted that 'a *Tory* govt indeed will never be formed again') jeopardised the Whig reforms and, in the summer, that 'all the requisite reforms' should be carried through before any ministerial change.[201] Palmerston's mood had swung wholly to pessimism by July, however. If the Whigs were replaced by a Wellington and Peel government the political world would erupt in a way that would 'be attended with fatal consequences': an agitated press, revived political unions, politicised trade unions and

Whigs and Radicals seeking to outbid each other on the hustings would produce an unstable and stormy Parliament in which the Tories would soon succumb to more extreme Radical demands. 'Even the most moderate men who could be placed at the helm under such circumstances, would soon find themselves & the Hs of Cns, in collision with the Hs of Lds, and I do not wish to carry my anticipations further,' Palmerston said. Various mooted permutations of Whigs, Tories and Peelites Palmerston thought all unworkable; neither Whigs nor Tories, he maintained, could now offer a convincing prospect of stable government.[202] This was not, for Palmerston, merely a question of party interest. He perceived ominous challenges to the established political order and counselled Melbourne against allowing in-fighting to lead to a full-blown constitutional crisis. The apparent paralysis within government was, he feared, manifesting itself in growing hostility to the peers in the House of Lords: 'The press, The Hs of Cns, the Whigs, the Radicals, the manufacturing, the commercial interest, the dissenters of England, the Catholics of Ireland, are all from various motives arrayed in hostility against the upper House, as the great obstacle to the several improvements which each of those parties desire.' This 'progressive alienation of the respect & attachment of the nation from one of the three branches of the legislature' threatened the fabric of the constitution, the monarchy included, and he called for 'some alteration in the temper of that body, brought about by the judicious & timely exercise of the prerogative of the Crown'. Thus, he argued for the introduction of between twenty and twenty-five new peers who could 'break down at once the D[uke] of W[ellingto]n's ascendancy in the House', and reaffirm the Whig ascendancy and reforming agenda.[203]

The general election of 1834 followed a remarkable demonstration of monarchical authority, and not the sort of royal intervention of which Palmerston had written to Melbourne. Grey's government had been divided over lay appropriation of surplus revenues of the Established Church in Ireland and although Grey had been replaced by Melbourne in July 1834, William IV still took it upon himself to dismiss the ministry in November by objecting to the appointment of Lord John Russell (a prominent advocate of lay appropriation) as leader of the House of Commons and thus effectively forcing Melbourne into offering his resignation. Sir Robert Peel formed a minority government in Melbourne's place and was immediately granted a dissolution of Parliament and thus a new general election.

The Tory *Hampshire Advertiser* greeted the dissolution with some relish, sensing an opportunity to overturn the Whig victory of 1832 and demonstrate the popular dissatisfaction with 'the imbecile measures' pursued by the late government. The paper had no doubt that 'reasonable men expect far more real and substantial amelioration of the burdens affecting trade and agriculture'.[204] Only a couple of years after first taking the South Hampshire seat, Palmerston was again facing a serious fight at an election. His Tory opponents, John Fleming and Henry Compton, positioned themselves as the best guarantors of 'the happiness and prosperity of all classes of the people' and the prospects for what the *Advertiser* quickly labelled the 'constitutional candidates' even at this early stage seemed promising.[205] Fleming and Compton's friends hoped that the duplicity of their rivals, especially Palmerston, had been sufficiently exposed in the preceding two years to guarantee their success. Palmerston was again portrayed by his opponents as an opportunistic place-seeker and since the 'county now knows the delusion that has been practised on it', voters were called on 'to prevent its repetition under the disguise of Reform'.[206] Palmerston, meanwhile, welcomed an opportunity to re-establish his acquaintance with the local electors and declared himself confident that the government's record would suffice to justify his claims to be returned once again for the county.[207] He did not expect the Peel government to last long – no more than forty-eight hours, he suggested in a letter to his sister Elizabeth – though did recognise in Compton a 'formidable opponent'.[208]

The agenda in the election seems to have been set to a large extent by the Conservatives. However much Palmerston and Staunton believed that success would surely follow a fair estimation of the achievements of the previous two years, the Conservatives successfully whipped up concern about the danger to the constitution posed by their continuation in office: one polemicist in the county even spoke of the danger of a 'fierce revolution' if Reformers carried out what it seemed was their clear intention of annihilating the House of Lords,[209] and saw the appeal made by the Reformers for a stand to be made 'in the House of Commons for the liberties of the people' as yet further evidence of their disregard for the proper governing trinity of King, Lords and Commons.[210] Despite Palmerston's own concerns on this front, his pledges were inadequate to convince many of his constituents.

Throughout December both sides remained confident of victory. Fleming and Compton, the *Advertiser* reported, were successful in the canvass throughout the county,[211] while Palmerston, making 'masterly and eloquent' and 'clear, manly' speeches gave confidence to the Reformers.[212] Palmerston himself was a little more candid in a letter to his sister on 28 December. 'The ultra Tory composition of the govt and our agitating speeches at eight places, have done us a great deal of good, and I hear that the opinion of the county is becoming more favourable to us every day. Fleming is, as you say, very unpopular individually, and it is quite wonderful how many people he has contrived to make his enemies. He is besides a bad canvasser, stiff and unconciliatory.' Yet he also sounded a cautionary note: many voters had admitted that they felt obliged to vote according to their landlord's wishes, that is, for Fleming and Compton, even though they themselves supported the Reformers' cause. 'I am very nearly a convert to ballot,' mused Palmerston.[213]

The election was held in mid-January 1835 and at the close of the poll Fleming and Compton had registered 1,764 and 1,689 votes respectively while Palmerston won 1,509 and Staunton 1,469.[214] Staunton saw defeat as exclusively a political one, rather than a personal rejection, and in a commiserative letter Palmerston reasoned that 'the distress of the farmers and their inability to pay rent and tithes, may be classed amongst the main causes of our defeat'.[215] To his sister Elizabeth, however, Palmerston admitted that he 'never was more annoyed & disappointed in my life'; he attributed his defeat to a 'want of activity on the part of our friends', but more especially to the dishonourable conduct on the part of his opponents' supporters (he acquitted Fleming and Compton personally) who, he alleged, had used threats and intimidation to force certain voters to break their promises to Palmerston and Staunton: 'it was unlucky for us that the price of corn is very low & the farmers much distressed. They are looking for abatements in their rent, & more than usually dependent on their landlords.'[216]

Among other things, the newspaper press had played an important role in both chronicling and guiding the election campaigns in Hampshire in 1832 and 1834. After the latter result in particular Palmerston appears to have recognised the value of a sympathetic journalistic voice in the county. Although he had helped to set up one county paper, the *Hampshire Advertiser*, in 1823, by the early 1830s this paper, with its Tory leanings, had become 'a personal and political embarrassment', something that had grown abundantly clear in the recent elections. Having failed in his bid for re-election for South Hampshire in January 1835, it was suggested to Palmerston that he subscribe to a new 'liberal' paper, the *Hampshire Independent*, to be run by a one-time *Morning Chronicle* parliamentary reporter. It was rumoured that Palmerston contributed £1,000 to the venture – James Grant, a leading figure in the newspaper world, insisted that he 'was privately assured at the time' of this contribution[217] – although Palmerston's own note on the original invitation reads simply: 'agreed provided I have no connection with the paper as proprietor, & my £50 is taken as a gift'. Bourne says the evidence is inconclusive, and certainly the connection, whatever its nature, never amounted to much.[218] The paper did, however, produce a number of highly favourable reports on Palmerston's conduct of foreign policy once he returned to the Foreign Office in Melbourne's second government of 1835–41. It was no doubt significant that when the editorship of the *Independent* subsequently changed, it passed into the hands of a Mr Behan who had previously held the sinecure office of editor of the *London Gazette*, a post given to him by Palmerston.[219]

Whatever influence Palmerston did exert on Hampshire newspapers, it was indisputable that the press was by now widely acknowledged to occupy an important place in the political culture of the period, and especially so once the changes wrought by the Reform Act of 1832 had begun to shift the balance of power, albeit very slowly and for the moment very subtly, towards the population at large. Even before the reforms of the 1830s had taken effect, the Duke of Wellington, as Prime Minister in the late 1820s, had observed that 'I hate the whole tribe of news-writers and I prefer to suffer from their falsehoods to dirtying my fingers by communication with them,[220] but though he and fellow arch-sceptics, such as Robert Peel, 'despis[ed] the press on the one hand', they nonetheless spent 'hours poring over it on the other'. On the whole, though, the Tories were not so successful as their rivals in the arts of media management; it was the Whigs who seemed alert to its possibilities and, significantly, adept in its execution.[221] Henry Brougham, for example, who helped found the *Edinburgh Review* and orchestrated effective press campaigns (by writing for several papers) in the early years of the nineteenth century, sought in 1830 to counter the influence of *The Times* (which he described as a 'vile' newspaper) by exploiting his legal connections (he was soon to be Lord Chancellor in Grey's ministry) to establish a secure footing in the newspaper world for the Whigs by placing the editor of the expanding *Morning Herald*, a junior barrister 'who therefore is *under my eye*', in direct contact with a leading Whig salon of the time.[222] Similarly, a number of leading Whig ministers established close relations with, in particular, the *Morning Chronicle* as well as the *Morning Herald* in the 1820s and 1830s, supplying articles and information to those papers. Though not 'a systematic press campaign', it was often effective enough.[223] Like many of his Whig colleagues, Palmerston, erstwhile supporter of Canning that he was, recognised the value of this and joined in such enterprises early. It was grist to his foreign policy mill that he could champion the cause of a dynamic newspaper press at home (though often 'spinning' himself, this was only because it was necessary to counter articles in hostile journals) and he did not hesitate to highlight the importance of a 'free press' as a contributory factor in the rise of liberalism, such as he had applauded in France in July 1830. It was also another ideological link back to Dugald Stewart's theories of political economy by which Palmerston had been taught that a free newspaper press provided a direct connection between legislators and the governed population. It was a further reminder of Palmerston's separation from the Toryism of his early patrons; for example, back in 1810 Malmesbury had complained of the 'liberty of the press, which is now carried to the most dangerous degree of licentiousness, & has done, & does, & will do the greatest mischief'.[224] Palmerston no doubt also remembered how disaffected clerks at the War Office, such as Foveaux, had been able to exploit connections with journalists to smear his name as Secretary at War a few years earlier.

Though it would be some time before Palmerston fully realised the benefits, both at home and abroad, of good relations with journalists, it is no surprise to find him starting to cultivate certain newspapers and journalists once he entered the Foreign Office in 1830. In a much-quoted letter to Emily Cowper of September 1831, Palmerston explained, in response to a disagreeable article in one paper, how such connections worked:

I was furious & disgusted with the article in the *Courier* which you mention, and I desired the editor to be well rowed for it; but the fact is, that the only influence which my office possesses over the *Courier* or any other paper, is *positive* & not *negative*. I could get him to insert any article I wished today, but I have no means or power of preventing him from inserting any other of quite a different kind tomorrow. I can impel but I cannot control.

The only communication which takes place is, that every now & then when we have any particular piece of news, it is given to the editor, & he thereby gets a start of his competitors, and on the condition of receiving these occasional intimations he gives his support to the government; but no editor would bring his daily articles to a public office to be looked over before they are printed, and no public officer who had any sense in his brains would undertake the responsibility of such inspections. I have three or four times desired the *Courier* to be told that he was doing the Govt a great deal of harm by attacking Russia, besides doing Russia great injustice; but among a number of people who take a part in the management of a paper, the blame is always shifted off from one partner to another; and like an accident among your best china, *nobody* has done it. Though they look to government for news, they look to their readers for money, and they never can resist flying out upon popular topics when they think that by a flourish they shall gain a little éclat among club & coffee house politicians, and have their paper talked of for four & twenty hours. . . .[225]

Palmerston had still to master the arts of media management – bribery, flattery and patronage – that in later years would secure him a more dependable set of allies, but he was evidently well aware of the need to counterbalance hostile factions.[226] The deliberations of the Belgian conference, for example, were not conducted exclusively in the closeted atmosphere that Palmerston's private letters might occasionally have suggested. The negotiations furnished the fourth estate with considerable opportunities to scrutinise, represent and misrepresent proceedings, the impact of which might extend beyond the narrow confines of its domestic readership. As Palmerston learned from Robert Adair in Brussels in the summer of 1832, as the treaty ratification debates continued: 'The press governs every thing – King, ministers & chambers and the scurrilous abuse of the conference in the Times & other papers is echoed every where in this town, & represented, in the true spirit of the "mouvement" faction, as the voice of the people of England against their government.'[227]

For a Foreign Secretary who by this point was beginning to stake a claim to the moral leadership of liberalism in western Europe, a movement which, by his own estimate, depended in no small part on a free and widely circulated press, it was useful to open channels of communication between journalists and the diplomatic corps. In July 1834, for instance, John Maberley, MP for Abingdon, a friend of John Easthope who had recently bought the *Morning Chronicle* wrote to Palmerston seeking an introduction at Madrid for a Mr Irving whom Easthope proposed to send to Spain to report for his paper. Maberley was glad to be able to offer Palmerston 'a good channel of counteracting the unfair attacks of the Times on your government and of opposing the Tory party statements in the Herald'.[228] Palmerston grabbed the opportunity to secure the support of the *Chronicle* and at just the same time as Irving was being recommended for Madrid, Palmerston was also encouraging his own brother William to afford 'all the assistance in your power' to a 'respectable barrister' named Quin, who was going to Naples 'to make arrangements for an extensive system of foreign correspondence' for the *Chronicle*.[229] Debates about the morality of such information management could be left, for the moment, to others.

CHAPTER 7

PALMERSTON, *REX* AND AUTOCRAT, 1835–1841

Foreign Pol[itic]s are coming into fashion.
Benjamin Disraeli to Sarah Disraeli, 22[?] June 1838[1]

IF PALMERSTON HAD entered the Foreign Office in 1830 with high hopes of working towards, and quickly celebrating, a rapid change in international politics with the rise of liberalism, his second term, beginning in April 1835, seemed to offer altogether more prosaic duties. As Herbert Bell observed, beyond western Europe there seemed little prospect of achieving any meaningful advance for liberalism (at least not that would justify the effort) and so Palmerston was left simply to tie up the loose ends of earlier projects: to ensure that Holland would finally accept the settlement of November 1831, to see that the promise of a new constitution for Greece was honoured, and to ensure that in the Iberian Peninsula Portugal was settled peaceably and Carlos was expelled from Spain. Britain was still to be a champion of European liberalism but this was tempered to some extent by the reality of Britain's circumscribed world position and influence, however much Palmerston might like to argue in private that that power was undiminished.[2]

Palmerston had been reappointed to the Foreign Office in April 1835 when Melbourne returned to power and formed a new government. It was said that Melbourne had been reluctant to return Palmerston to his post, and Earl Grey apparently thought he ought not to have waived his doubts about Palmerston so readily, but these claims were made many years later by Grey's son, then Lord Howick, who had his own reasons for wanting to besmirch Palmerston's reputation.[3] Charles Wood recorded in his journal that Russell had been lined up to take the Foreign Office but that Palmerston had been adamant that he would 'have that or nothing' for himself and had also strenuously resisted proposals that he be elevated to the House of Lords, which he evidently took to signal political marginalisation.[4] Whatever doubts these Whig grandees entertained about Palmerston at the time, though he had no parliamentary seat for the moment, Palmerston was unequivocally a major figure in political life. He was not necessarily a universally popular one, however. 'Lord Palmerston's return to office,' observed Princess Lieven, 'will certainly give an unpleasant shock of surprise to the whole of Europe. Everybody had thought he had made himself sufficiently unpopular in political circles for foreign Governments to be spared the infliction of having again to do business with him.'[5] Bell described Palmerston at this time as out of tune with the public; neglectful, furthermore of both Parliament and the Cabinet, and somewhat haughty in his manner. It was perhaps no coincidence that Palmerston was the only member of the former Whig administration to have lost his seat at the election in January 1835.[6] When Melbourne came to reconstruct his government in the spring of 1835, however, it was obvious that Palmerston could not be ignored.

Peel and the Conservatives had won approximately one hundred new seats at the general election in January 1835 and it seemed that there was a definable and successful Conservative agenda emerging. Once again, the non-Conservatives had a common antagonist, a renewed sense of something against which to act in concerted opposition. And beyond the shared antipathy to a Peelite government, there was in addition the renewed threat of unchecked monarchical authority to draw the Reformers together: William IV's arbitrary dismissal of the government in 1834 might have been constitutionally justifiable from a technical point of view, but it seemed only to underline just how far the existing system of government had to go if traditional Whig concerns about royal power were to be allayed. Early 1835 witnessed renewed Whig efforts to establish a meaningful platform on which to base non-Tory government. In February and March Whig, Radical and Irish repeal MPs met at Lichfield House in order to look for ways to defeat Peel's new administration. This was a tactical alliance more than an ideological one. Although there was concurrence that they would oppose Peel's nominee for the post of Speaker of the House for the coming session and a broad consensus on Irish appropriation (albeit no formal pledges on behalf of a future Whig government were made), beyond agreeing that a Whig government was more desirable than Peel's little else of substance was established during these meetings. Nonetheless, this was recognisably party behaviour and as a number of differences were to a large extent set aside, there were some general hints at a liberal tone and careful discussion of how to turn out the government. On these grounds 1835 has been seen by some as the date at which a Liberal party emerged.[7] Even if, as Jonathan Parry has suggested, this 'was not a professionally managed party, nor were its principles embodied in regular policy packages', the 'Liberal party was a liberal party' and 'it was effective enough'.[8] Certainly contemporaries, both within Parliament and in the newspapers, were starting to define or describe these groups as 'liberal' instead of 'reformer' or 'radical' or 'Whig' and in linguistic terms at least there seems to have been a developing sense of party. Yet however much the events of late 1834 and early 1835 can be seen to have reinvigorated reformist and liberal spirits, still the 'party' was a thinly conceived one. Despite appearances at Lichfield House, divisions continued to plague the 'liberals'.

Although Peel's government was quickly overturned, the Whigs' readiness to accommodate their Radical and Irish associates was limited: Lord John Russell, by now a leading voice in Whig politics, was quick to declare that Melbourne's second government, which replaced Peel's in 1835, would comprise the 'Whiggest part of the Whigs' and would be able to 'hold our own Whig course'.[9] Such a determination may have been a natural reaction to Russell's own fear, as he would later put it to Melbourne in 1837, that it was the 'very old difficulty of Whig administrations, that their friends expect them to do more than is possible; so that if they attempt little, their friends grow slacker, and if they attempt much, their enemies grow strong'.[10] Yet this commitment to Whiggery sat ill with supposed attempts to broaden the base of liberal politics. Arguably the rhetorical and unifying value of Palmerstonian liberal foreign policies was thus thrown into even sharper relief.

Following his exertions in Hampshire, Palmerston had been keen to enjoy a period of relaxation at Broadlands, hunting and shooting, but although his anticipated electoral success in January did not materialise, he demonstrated no immediate desire to return to the maelstrom of parliamentary labour.[11] According to his diary, at least, Palmerston did not overwork himself in seeking to resurrect Whig-Liberal fortunes. The days of January, February and March 1835 were once again 'fine' ones, filled with 'visits' to and from 'E' and 'L'; in April he roused himself to political action, but not ostensibly to recover for himself his position at the Foreign Office. On 9 April Grey had informed the King that he could not undertake to replace Peel and advised him to turn, again, to Melbourne. Palmerston, along with Melbourne, Holland and Thomas Spring Rice appealed to Grey a couple of days later to reconsider, or at least to take either the Foreign Office or Treasury, but Grey again refused and on 12 April Melbourne was formally commissioned by the King to form a new administration. On 13 April, Palmerston seemed more interested in taking advantage of an adjournment of the House to enjoy another 'Fine day L'.[12]

In reality, of course, Palmerston was not so cavalier in his approach to politics as his diary suggests. On 12 April he had told Melbourne in an interview that he thought Grey should go to the Foreign Office and with Melbourne at its head he foresaw a viable government. Melbourne, however, was less certain and spoke of giving up the commission, to which Palmerston responded that 'no man is justified in pronouncing difficulties to be insurmountable till he has tried to overcome them'. If the task of forming a new government was a great one, it was not, thought Palmerston, an impossible one: 'It is wonderful moreover how difficulties sink before us when we set to work in good earnest to scale them. But I do not see (probably from want of full information on the matter) any difficulties *so great* as to inspire one with despair.'[13]

Palmerston, meanwhile, had lost none of his interest in earlier European projects and continued to monitor foreign affairs closely. He wrote in evident alarm to the Portuguese Minister Plenipotentiary to London, Chevalier de Moraes Sarmento in early April, for example, to declare 'the affliction which I feel at the calamitous event' of the death of the Duke of Leuchtenberg, consort to Queen Maria, which he worried about on a personal level for the Queen and politically as 'a loss' to both Portugal and Europe.[14] With memories still fresh of the struggles in the Iberian Peninsula, any threat to order there alarmed the erstwhile Foreign Secretary. His 'fine day' with L on the 13 April, therefore, was perhaps a welcome distraction from the 'hurt' he had felt the day before when Melbourne had intimated that Palmerston's claims on the Foreign Office were not indisputable and that the confidence that it was in some way his to dispose of, implied perhaps in Palmerston's willingness to bandy the offer of it to Grey, was misplaced. Palmerston had evidently taken the suggestion that he must sacrifice his old post, even for one of an equal standing, badly (it is unlikely that he saw any other office as equally desirable) and Grey sympathised with Melbourne's embarrassment over a 'very painful subject'.[15] It was said, at least by Palmerston, that Grey and Melbourne were reluctant to place Palmerston in his old employment because of the efforts of 'a knot of intriguers headed by Ed[war]d Ellice', and indeed it seemed, somewhat curiously, that the King was one of the few declared allies that Palmerston had at this time.[16] Yet Palmerston refused to succumb to the perceived plotting of others. In a strident defence of his previous record, he pointed out to Melbourne that though the Tories had long criticised his conduct of foreign policy, even they had 'upon almost all the great questions followed the track which I had marked out'. And although he had run up against the 'ill will' of Russia, Austria, Prussia and the Netherlands, Palmerston's most important policy actions in the early 1830s – those relating to Belgium, France, Spain and Portugal – had all been approved, he reminded Melbourne, by his colleagues and the Whigs' supporters as being 'in all respects consistent with the true interests of Great Britain'. 'It is always disagreeable to speak of oneself,' he continued, 'but upon this occasion I must be permitted to say, that I consider myself to have conducted our foreign relations with great success, during four years of excessive labour, and through extreme difficulties arising not only from the complicated nature of the questions to be dealt with, but also from the resistance opposed to me by a combination of domestic with foreign opponents. All the important questions connected with Greece, Belgium, Portugal, & Spain which essentially affected the interests of England, I left either virtually settled or in a satisfactory train of adjustment.' In the Near East Palmerston conceded that his record was less positive, but with regard to his handling of Turkey and Russia, he said, 'the blame does not lie at my door; for if my advice had been taken by the Cabinet in the autumn of 1832, and if we had then given to the Sultan our moral support against Mehemet Ali, the subsequent treaty of Constantinople would never have been signed'.[17]

Melbourne mollified Palmerston with a placatory letter, in reply to which Palmerston intimated that he would not stand on his pride and would accept the Foreign Office seals if they were offered.[18] By April, therefore, Palmerston was back at the Foreign Office, but he was still without a parliamentary seat. If he had failed to build a winning reputation and body of reliable allies at Westminster, however, his supposed unpopularity was not to be exposed at an election. As soon as he had lost in Hampshire Palmerston had received an offer of another seat from an erstwhile supporter, Joseph Croucher, who claimed to have acted successfully as an agent in various London contests, but even if Palmerston had been willing to fork out the £3,500 Croucher indicated would be necessary, Palmerston's solicitors were unable to track Croucher down when they paid a visit to his address in the City.[19] Instead, a seat was available in Tiverton and Palmerston took it, or rather (despite recent reform) bought it, without any real contest;[20] the election, it was said, was a 'very quiet affair'.[21]

Palmerston regarded the approach from Tiverton as a recognition of, or tribute to, the reformist tendencies of the Grey administration and he accepted the invitation, he told electors, 'as an acknowledgement of Reforms that have been effected; and as an earnest of Reforms to come'. Of those future reforms, Palmerston enumerated four broad areas of concern. Catholic emancipation and the repeal of the Test and Corporation Acts, he said, had done much to advance the cause of civil and religious liberty, but, 'the Dissenters have still some well-founded causes of complaint'. He hoped for a resolution of the question of a commutation of tithes that 'may on the one hand respect the rights of property, and secure a due maintenance for the ministers of religion, while on the other hand it may give a freer scope to agriculture, and relieve that most important branch of national industry from a vexatious burthen'. Church reform in England and Ireland, he said, was necessary, though he hesitated to give any promise beyond that, being 'by education and conviction a sincere member of the Established Church', he would 'endeavour in helping to reform that Church to strengthen and secure it, and to promote those interests of religion which constitute its legitimate purpose'. Corporation reform, he suggested, was also required, but he trusted to a 'satisfactory' measure being proposed in Parliament.[22] It was not an especially radical, nor even a far-reaching programme; it was, however, a statement of general intent suited to the moderate demands of an uncontested liberal seat.

According to one witness who remembered Palmerston's first appearance in Tiverton, he had scored a distinct hit with the people of the town. 'I can well recall the jaunty peer as he shook hands with me,' a John Sharland noted some years later. 'Conspicuous in his white trousers, blue frock coat with gilt buttons, and white hat, his personal appearance created a most favourable impression. It may seem strange that men of Radical proclivities should receive with open arms a candidate who, if in any sense a Reformer, was only so as a Whig. The Chartists called him a time-serving Tory; but in the almost evenly-balanced state of parties in Tiverton, the local Reform Club adopted him as the only possible candidate. The truth is he had a happy knack of referring to the Tory party as if their opinions and his were wide as the poles asunder.'[23] There may have been some embellishment of the story over the years, but Palmerston left Devon with a similar sense of general popular support. He had been returned unopposed, and reflected with satisfaction that the electors had proven themselves 'so determined to have me' that Tory attempts to put up alternative candidates had been fruitless. 'There are about 420 electors, perfectly independent all liberal in their opinions and I think the probability is that with a very little management I shall be able to keep my seat here as long as I like, at least that is what they all told me,' he reported to his brother once his return was confirmed. The Tiverton electors, he said, 'were delighted to have me for as you well know, in this country, even the veriest Radicals love rank & station, and had ten times rather be represented by a gentleman than by a person of their own class. The chairing was a procession like a triumph.'[24] It had been, all in all, a very satisfactory result, thought Palmerston, and confounded the schemes of his parliamentary opponents. Writing again to William, a few weeks after his return, he noted:

> I have been most singularly fortunate in lighting upon Tiverton. It is a quiet borough which gives me very little trouble, & which by all I can learn, I am very likely to keep. I gave my predecessor two thousand pounds to go out; with a distinct understanding that that made us quits; and the election cost me about 300£. My Hampshire contest cost me only 1,390£, which was cheap enough for a county contest. On the whole our ousting of last November has been rather an expensive thing to me as these elections have come to about 3,700£. But thanks to your assistance & to other means I had, I have cleared it all off, and if we stay in as I think we shall, my salary will soon cover this expense. Some of our party wanted me much to go to the Hs of Lds when the govt was formed; but I saw at once their object, it was to shelf me, & get rid of me; and though the Hs of Lds is more convenient for a man in a laborious office, and much less expensive, as it saves one these election charges, yet the Hs of Cns is the place where a man *out* of office can make himself of consequence.[25]

It was a great advantage to Palmerston that the Tories in Tiverton were in such an apparently weakened state. Even when his commitment to his new constituents was questioned, less than six months after taking up his new seat, Palmerston's agent in Tiverton, George Coles, advised Palmerston that this would be easily rebutted if he contributed £100 to the relief of the poor in the town who were suffering under the harsh weather conditions of the winter of 1835–36 and if he allowed Coles to make similar donations whenever the need arose: 'we should at once silence our adversaries', promised Coles, and the 'very generous contribution' that Palmerston made accordingly left Coles in 'no doubt it will experience a most grateful reception'.[26] Meanwhile, Palmerston was assured, the reforms undertaken by Melbourne's government, such as of municipal corporations, were securing the liberal position in Tiverton.[27] In the autumn of 1836 Palmerston was instrumental in arranging with the Postmaster-General to establish a mail coach service that would pass through Tiverton on its way to Exeter,[28] but although Palmerston was regarded by his Tiverton constituents as a useful ministerial 'insider', they looked first to John Heathcoat, the town's other MP (and consistently also its first choice in a two-seat constituency) as their real local advocate. Thus while Palmerston was urged to support a petition from Tiverton for the abolition of church rates in April 1837, for example, he was to take advice and a lead from Heathcoat in presenting it to Parliament.[29] His Tiverton constituents regarded Palmerston as a representative of the Whig-Liberal government; his endorsement and patronage were to be called upon and exploited when and where necessary but on the whole Palmerston was left free to concentrate on his official business at the Foreign Office.

King William appeared to tolerate rather than welcome the reconstituted Melbourne ministry and Palmerston believed that it was only the lack of an opportunity that prevented the King from again trying to turn them out. Though the Whigs generally were disagreeable to the King, Palmerston at least enjoyed a reasonably good personal relationship with him. William had already indicated his support for Palmerston's return to the Foreign Office in April and in a conversation in the autumn of 1835 the King told Palmerston that the two of them, in conjunction with Melbourne, could 'settle all matters that may arise, and as to the other members of the Cabinet being away why my Lord there is no great harm in that, for as you know "too many cooks spoil the broth" '.[30] Indeed, as relations between the government and the Palace soured over the course of the ministry's first year, Palmerston remained one of the King's few trusted ministers. The King and the court, Palmerston observed in July 1836, 'wish[ed] us at the devil', but, he continued, 'I believe I am the only one of the ministers whom the King likes personally. He was fond of Melbourne too, but has not yet forgiven him for cramming Dr Hampden down his throat the other day for an Oxford professorship. He likes Lansdowne & Minto also. The rest he dislikes.'[31] Although the King had been a regular critic of Palmerston's 'liberal' policies in the early 1830s, Palmerston's ability to maintain harmonious relations with the monarch had been an important pillar supporting his political position. By virtue of his age and experience William was a significant influence in British politics, yet the constitutional position and authority of the monarch were subject to challenge, and even if that was implicit more than it was explicit, and despite William's success in turning out Melbourne in 1834, the spirit of Reform had already made some inroads into the authority of the aristocracy and the monarchy. Even though, as Palmerston acknowledged in August 1835, the 'King hates & detests us politically', and felt the ministry had been *'forced* upon' him, Palmerston was nonetheless 'inclined to think . . . that we shall last till next session; & then I see no reason why we should not go on longer. If we do, it will be a proof of the strength of the Hs of Cns & majority of the nation, against King, Court, Lords, and aristocracy'.[32]

The King's death in the summer of 1837, therefore, was, from a political point of view, both advantageous and disadvantageous to Palmerston. It removed a critic of the government and in his place installed an inexperienced (and potentially malleable) young queen; it also, however, deprived Palmerston of a heavyweight figure who was appreciative of his talents at a time when many of his colleagues continued to entertain misgivings about the Foreign Secretary's abrasiveness. In a letter to his friend George Shee, written as the King's illness entered its final stages, Palmerston chose to emphasise the positive aspects of the forthcoming change:

> The young princess will have an arduous task. She succeeds at 18 to the throne of a king of 72. She brings total inexperience of the world to the government of a great empire. She has much natural talent good sense, & firmness of character, and all the good feelings & perception of right & wrong which belong to artless youth, and to a mind endowed by nature with the best disposition. But it is scarcely in the nature of things that at first at least the nation will look with the same deference to the will of a person of 18, as to that of one of mature age. Her sex will be in her favour, & the generosity of John Bull will lead him to support a young queen, even more than a young king of the same age.[33]

Victoria's greatest attribute, however, was that her accession promised to free the British monarchy from unwelcome continental influences. Though her youth meant that 'some of the ballast which keeps a monarchy on its keel will for a while be wanting', and Britain would therefore have to 'make a step in approach to a republic', nonetheless, 'the Hanoverian dynasty, and the German prejudices which belonged to it, and which for a century have embarrassed & impeded our march both at home & abroad will cease'. The new Queen's apparent willingness to stick with her Whig ministers would also, Palmerston hoped, stabilise parliamentary government and check the 'factious mutiny' of the House of Lords. 'I am inclined to think she will turn out to be a remarkable person, & gifted with a great deal of strength of character', he concluded.[34]

It soon became apparent that the government was in a privileged position with regard to the Queen, who looked to her new ministers, and particularly to Melbourne, as well as to her uncle, Leopold of the Belgians (whom Palmerston, for the moment, had good reason to regard favourably) for guidance.[35] 'The Queen goes on as well as she began; is quite with us, and will give us a vigorous support,' Palmerston enthused to Shee,[36] and if she was showing signs of firmness of character, her openness to argument and desire to be well informed offered the Whigs a significant opening to fashion the embryonic Victorian monarchy. 'She continues to do all the things which she ought to do, & to do nothing that she ought not to do, and the opening of the reign is most auspicious,' Palmerston told Lamb; little wonder, then, that after spending a month at Windsor in the autumn of 1837, Palmerston 'could not find a point in her character which one would wish to alter if one could'.[37] He no doubt meant it as a compliment when he told his brother that Victoria 'is more like a sensible man of 30 than a girl of 18'.[38]

Victoria's early letters to Palmerston reflect her inexperience in the arts of government and diplomacy. During the first few months of her reign, Victoria was motivated more by the need to master diplomatic protocol than the desire to offer a commentary on politics. She asked Palmerston for advice primarily on issues such as how to compose official correspondence, the suitability of gifts for different sovereigns, and invitations to functions at Windsor (whom she should invite, where they should sit at dinner, whether or not they should be invited to spend the night at the Castle). Where she did write about policy, it was simply to acknowledge and approve suggestions made by the Foreign Secretary.[39] It was perhaps no disappointment to Palmerston to receive a request from the Queen in August 1837 'not to send any more [dispatches] until she has done with those which she already has with her'.[40] However, though the days of conflict with the Palace lay yet some time in the future, Palmerston gradually found the Queen's maturing interest in politics troublesome. In November 1838 Palmerston was chastised by Melbourne for failing to send private letters and foreign dispatches to the Queen often enough (especially when Melbourne himself was out of town) and in fact Palmerston was starting to develop the habit of sending off dispatches prior to their receiving royal approval, something that was to cause particular friction with Lord John Russell in the later 1840s.[41] In part such 'disregard' for constitutional niceties was an inevitable consequence of an ever-expanding portfolio of work. As Palmerston complained on one occasion when visiting the Queen at Windsor:

I am over whelmed with business, for being here is a continuation of the session as far as business is concerned because after four o'clock when the Queen starts for her ride there is little business to be done; as the ride lasts till past six, & then we dine at 1/2 past 7, & then the evening is unavailable. This is rather a serious inconvenience to me, especially as I have a great many private matters to look to which have gone into neglect since Feby last when the session began. But each successive day brings with it more business than can be despatched in the day, & I can make no progress whatever with arrears.[42]

It was impossible for the Whigs to educate Victoria to her new role and not expect her to fulfil it. And before the end of Melbourne's ministry there was another element that tended to increase royal scrutiny of public business. In April 1838 Palmerston had dismissed talk of Victoria's desire to marry, and noted that though her coronation might be likely to bring forth suitors, 'after being used to agreeable & well informed Englishmen, I fear she will not easily find a foreign prince to her liking'.[43] When Victoria did marry Prince Albert in February 1840 Palmerston celebrated with a grand dinner at home for thirty-six guests following an 'excellent' day during which the royal couple's conduct had been 'perfect'.[44] Albert, indeed, Palmerston observed, was 'much liked' in London political and society circles.[45] The political ramifications of the Queen's marriage may not have been understood straight away and Palmerston, at least, did not immediately realise the consequences of Albert's keen attention to public affairs, but the royal marriage represented something of a turning point in British politics. Albert's position may have been constitutionally uncertain – it was 1857 before he received the title of 'Prince Consort' and even then his status remained ambiguous – but his marriage to the Queen did force a breach between Victoria and her beloved and devoted Melbourne and, more broadly, it undermined the cosy accommodation with the Whigs which had prevailed since her accession. Charles Greville, on learning that the Queen had planned her wedding without reference to Melbourne presciently saw in this cause for concern about the future: 'If she has already shaken off her dependence on Melbourne, and begins to fly with her own wings,' he asked, 'what will she not do when she is older, and has to deal with ministers whom she does not care for, or whom she dislikes?'[46] Albert, in contrast to Victoria, had been formally prepared for public life. Educated as a student of the 'Historical Law School', an increasingly fashionable branch of scholarship which concerned itself with the origins of representative institutions, Albert had emerged with a commitment, encouraged by his advisers, to assert the proper prerogative rights of monarchy. Not long after the wedding, King Leopold had urged that Albert 'ought in business as in everything to be necessary to the Queen', and that there 'should be no concealment from him on any subject',[47] envisaging for the Prince the role of personal secretary and counsellor. The Prince was not quite so 'disinterested an advisor' as Lord Aberdeen would later claim him to be, however,[48] and Albert was soon alarmed by the extent to which the monarchy in Britain had become a party politicised and, under Melbourne's influence, decidedly Whiggish, institution. He thought it a priority that the Queen 'should by degrees regain possession of the privileges which through youth and inexperience she had been induced to yield up. . . . The Prince said he could never feel satisfied till he saw her in the same position as when she ascended the throne.'[49]

From Leopold, Victoria regularly received intelligence of affairs in Europe, but though these letters underlined the continuing instability in Spain and Portugal in particular, they did not lay down a course of action.[50] The initiative for policy still lay largely in Palmerstonian and governmental hands. And, significantly, members of the Cabinet were also now much more satisfied with Palmerston's sense of collegiality, which helped secure his position within the government and smooth his conduct of the Foreign Office.[51]

Melbourne expressed his reservations about acting precipitately in foreign affairs at the beginning of 1836. He feared that Palmerston's disposition to work with France, and by implication to work without (or even perhaps against) Austria and Prussia, would be liable to be construed as 'having acted with unnecessary haste & unjustifiable jealousy' by the Eastern powers at a time when they appeared willing to act in concert with Britain.[52] Melbourne had one eye on 'the recent temper of the House of Commons' and urged on Palmerston that the government 'must be very careful what we do in foreign affairs'. The recent naval estimates might have been passed but if the government appeared overly bellicose MPs would, he said, 'leave us in the lurch' and this would undoubtedly be 'encouraging' to Russia.[53] Palmerston, however, insisted that Britain must have a strong naval presence in the Mediterranean, citing the earlier crisis in Egypt as evidence of the need not to be placed in the position again of saying, as the Cabinet had then, 'we must not hold strong language without the means of enforcing it "*& we have no fleet in the Mediterranean*" '.[54] Thus he argued for 'making a clatter' against Russia in the east ('expose her plans & you half defeat them') but also for a firm military stand to demonstrate earnestness.[55] Thus Palmerston adhered to the general principles of foreign policy which he had observed during the Grey years given that the world was, he said, basically unchanged. In March 1836 he spelled out this essential continuity in a letter to Melbourne:

> The division of Europe into two camps . . . to which you so much object, is the result of events beyond our control, and is the consequence of the French Revolution of July [1830]. The three powers fancy their interests lie in a direction opposite to that in which we and France conceive ours to be placed. The separation is not one of words, but of things; not the effect of caprice or will, but produced by the force of occurrences. The three and the two think differently, and therefore they act differently, whether it be as to Belgium or Portugal or Spain.
>
> This separation cannot really cease till all the questions to which it applies are decided – just as it is impossible to make a coalition ministry while there are questions pending in which public men disagree.[56]

The unity of the Eastern powers was indeed unmistakable, the agreement made at Münchengrätz having been reaffirmed in September 1835 at Teplitz.

Palmerston spoke of a 'complete union of the 3 Powers on every question of European policy'. Europe was, he said, divided into two camps, and what bothered Austria and Prussia, he said, was 'not the existence of two camps, but the equality of the two camps. The plain English of it all is, that they want to have England on their side against France, that they may dictate to France as they did in 1814, & 1815; and they are provoked beyond measure at the steady protection which France has derived from us.' Yet without that protection, he said, 'there would long ago have been a general war'.[57]

Whether the Quadruple Alliance partners were as united as the Eastern powers was uncertain.[58] At the heart of west European stability, in the Palmerstonian model, had been the maintenance of stability and harmony in Franco-British relations. Palmerston, who continued his sporadic debate by correspondence with Frederick Lamb about the virtues of constitutionalism, admitted in April 1837, 'You amuse me with your despotic zeal against representative government; but I am so intirely convinced of the contrary doctrine, that to argue seriously the superior advantages of a representative government for a nation would seem to me like setting to work, in these days, to demonstrate the Copernican system, or the circulation of the blood.'[59] However, it was still the imperative of diplomacy that frequently held sway over the appeal of rhetoric and ideology. One of the dominant motifs of the early years of the Melbourne government was a dramatic cooling in Franco-British relations and the rupture of the supposed good understanding. In large part this might well have been attributable to Talleyrand's personal antipathy and Palmerston's arrogance, but, as Bulwer noted, these differences were exposed in the Iberian Peninsula – 'precisely on the spot where it was most for the public interests that they should not appear'.[60]

By the end of 1836 the apparent capriciousness of the French government seemed to make preservation of the entente an impossible goal. 'As to France she is useful to us as an ally, & it is our interest not to break with her;' Palmerston wrote to Hobhouse, 'and it is not wise to abuse an ally whom one intends to go on acting with; but I am afraid that free institutions and public discussion have not yet existed long enough in France to have produced that honesty in public men which even our own constitution took some time to establish generally in England, and as to Louis Philippe if he had been a straight forward singleminded man, and no intriguer would he now have been on the throne of France? I doubt it. We may then blame & regret but ought not too much to wonder at his eel-like march in Spanish affairs.'[61] By November 1836 when Palmerston made this complaint, the continuing civil war in Spain had revealed the distance separating the so-called Western allies. For much of 1836 Palmerston's policy objectives, centred for the time being on Europe, were to stabilise the Iberian Peninsula and to frustrate Russian, Austrian and Prussian attempts to exploit constitutional instability in Spain and Portugal to further the interests of autocratic government. With France proving, as time passed, to be an awkward partner, however, British policy had also to negate, or moderate, French influence in the question.

In 1836 the new French minister, Thiers, had begun a re-evaluation of French external policy. Unhappy about working within the constraints of the Quadruple ('liberal') Alliance, he began to explore, through overtures to Russia and Austria, possible new alignments in Europe that would disrupt the two power bloc model that had emerged in the early 1830s, and also reassert France's great power status. He also planned to increase France's influence in Spain by augmenting French military forces there. It was an untidy policy in its execution and achieved little beyond demonstrating a growing divergence between Paris and London and the weakening of the supposed entente. There existed significant commercial rivalries between Britain and France at this time, but, more than this, what was underlined during 1836 was the extent to which the Quadruple Alliance had failed to reconcile political differences between the two powers. Louis Philippe saw the Alliance less as a vindication of constitutional government and rather more as a device by which Britain could harness France in order to constrain French power and influence. Palmerston's keen support for an entente was of comparatively recent vintage, after all, and arose in large part from the reluctance of the three Eastern powers (and notably Austria) to concert with Britain in the early 1830s. The fact that post-April 1834 French diplomatic power had been effectively tied to Britain's lead was not lost on Louis Philippe and when in May 1835 the two Spanish queens, Christina and Isabella, appealed to their Quadruple Alliance partners for assistance in the Carlist wars, their application received a luke-warm reception in Paris. The joint Franco-British efforts that were made to pacify Spain were not, therefore, wholehearted and this French and British military intervention did not prove decisive.

Meanwhile, the suspension of the Foreign Enlistment Act that had been necessary to facilitate the raising of a mercenary British foreign legion was not uncontroversial. By the beginning of 1836 the British government was in danger of fracturing over the issue. Palmerston remained committed to the Franco-British entente as a prominent vindication of his earlier European policies, but he faced increasingly stern Cabinet and royal opposition. In March 1836 Melbourne warned Palmerston that though he 'leaned to the opinion' that French military intervention in Spain was necessary to bring the war to a conclusion, he worried that Louis Philippe's government seemed reluctant to undertake the task. The King, it was reported, believed Louis Philippe had 'acted falsely' all along and feared too that any French intervention would drag Austria and Prussia into the fray on the side of the Carlists. The matter threatened to destabilise the government at home, too, the Prime Minister feared, amid growing parliamentary concerns about Britain's financial exposure in the peninsula.[62] Palmerston, in a letter to his brother the day after he had received Melbourne's warning, insisted that there would 'be no change in our policy in

France' and ascribed the supposed disruption of the entente to (failed) Parisian intrigues. 'Louis Philippe is really minister, & Thiers is all for English alliance, & Mad. Lieven & Talleyrand will be disappointed,' he wrote. 'They tried to rout out Broglie as they tried to get rid of me in hopes by that means of breaking off the alliance between England & France.'[63] The alliance, he assured Shee, was still 'intimate', founded as it was on the 'personal opinions & feelings of Louis Philippe' and was 'confirmed by the mutual interests of the two nations.'[64] Indeed, Palmerston argued that the Spanish affair was no longer even between constitutional and arbitrary government – Carlos, he said in March 1836 was 'out of the question' – but between moderate and extreme varieties of constitutional rule. He rejected out of hand the notion that French military intervention would draw in Russia, Austria and Prussia ('I am perfectly convinced they would not stir a man') and the only thing to fear was French failure.[65]

Palmerston was correct at least in his perception of rapidly shifting alignments in French policy. By late 1834 Talleyrand had already begun arguing that the entente with Britain had run its course and though this position found favour in Russian diplomatic circles, at least with Princess Lieven, Louis Philippe remained hesitant about forcing a breach with Britain if that was only to exchange one form of subservience for another. He tried, therefore, to reassure Britain of French commitment to the entente, while simultaneously establishing a working relationship with the Eastern powers in the event of a rupture. Broglie and his successor Thiers at the French foreign ministry both vacillated in their attempts to steer the ambiguous course mapped out by Louis Philippe, but when, in September, Thiers was replaced by the 'Russian' Molé (and when Thiers's arguments in favour of French military intervention in Spain were overridden) the direction of French policy became clear: 'We might nearly as well have had Nesselrode at Paris,' Palmerston would observe later.[66]

French plans for Isabella to marry a son of the French King caused further consternation in London and although in the summer Palmerston still insisted that Louis Philippe was 'on the whole ... not a bad ally', he expressed some concern about the French King's tone in recent conversations with Frederick Lamb which had been, he said, 'curious' and suspicious. Palmerston clung to hopes that Thiers would be able to steer French policy along a Western course in Spain, but the posting of Baron Boise le Comte, a known ally of Broglie, threatened to undermine Franco-British unity. 'He is a superficial coxcombical, intriguing anti-English subaltern,' Palmerston wrote. 'He picks up hastily any gossip which is brought him by the French clique in the place he goes to & retails it with pompous pedantry as indisputable truth; he builds systems upon the narrowest foundations and defends his airy castles as if they were so many Gibraltars. I fear his mission is not likely to do much good. I hope it may do no harm.' But, Palmerston insisted, ambiguities in the French position must not be permitted to distract the Western powers from the broader and more sinister intrigues afoot. The Holy Alliance powers, he maintained, continued to regard Spain as an arena in which to test Holy against Quadruple Alliance strength and, in promoting a Carlist victory, to assert the dominance of arbitrary government in Europe.[67]

Palmerston's inability to impose a decisive common policy on the Quadruple Alliance powers worried a number of ministers at home. Melbourne complained that 'anarchy & military rule' had been endured too long in Spain and he disliked the uncertainty that hung over that country.[68] Above all, Melbourne told Palmerston, he must act resolutely: 'It would be as well to look back to the course which was taken by the government of that day from the year 1788 when the violence & bloodshed of the French revolution began until the autumn of 1792 when our ambassador quitted Paris. Remember it was Mr Fox's opinion, that Pitt had held aloof too compleatly & too long, & that he ought to have interfered sooner by remonstrance & expression of opinion.'[69]

The perhaps inevitable breach with France came in the early autumn. Palmerston was horrified by the 'outbreaks of democracy' in the peninsula which were the direct result, he said, of the 'injudicious means adopted to keep democracy down'. However, while the Holy Alliance had made 'a mess' of Spain and Portugal, Palmerston reserved his especial censure for the French King who, he claimed, had failed to fulfil his treaty obligations. 'Louis Philippe has quite thrown us over as far as Spain is concerned & is determined to do nothing to help the Queen, how fortunate that we threw our lasso round him in time, & bound him by the treaty, or he would by this time have been openly instead of secretly assisting Carlos.' Even so, he continued, 'the cause of all the bad events' that had hindered resolution of the Spanish question was 'French intrigue'. 'LP', Palmerston told Shee, 'is actually a tricky fellow' and he doubted the success of the French King's plans to augment French power and influence by marrying his children into the smaller states of Belgium, Portugal and Greece.[70] As Melbourne pointed out in October, the only reason Britain had left for supporting the French government was 'the general interest in there being something like a stable government in France'.[71] It was a far remove from the high-flown rhetoric of two years earlier infused as it had been with the promise of a western European liberal ascendancy and unity. At the end of 1836 Palmerston lamented that Spanish radicals had lacked resolution and courage but hoped that liberal forces there might still be able to 'patch up a tolerable sort of constitution'.[72] It was not a resounding liberal, constitutional victory, but there was one consolation: 'the success of the good cause in Spain' would at least have been achieved '*without French aid*' and the 'biter will be bit, & Louis Philippe by our finessing will lose all his influence in Spain'.[73] As Palmerston put it later, 'we wish to see neither an Austrian-Spain nor a French-Spain, but a Spain which shall be essentially Spanish'. If that 'Spanishness' manifested itself, as Palmerston hoped it would, in the form of 'free and constitutional

Government', then Spain would be a good strategic, political and commercial neighbour to Britain.[74]

In the spring of 1837 Palmerston came before the House to defend his Iberian policy. Looking forward to future Spanish and Portuguese prosperity and power, and insisting, in the face of allegations to the contrary, that Britain and France remained as close as ever (perhaps significantly he said that he 'look[ed] upon their present relations as a stable alliance between the two nations, not merely between their respective governments'), Palmerston continued to promulgate the image of Britain, or at least England, as a liberal force for good in the world. English influence, he told the House, 'means that respect which is felt in foreign countries for the English nation – for the English character – that promptitude to give redress for injuries, however involuntarily inflicted, and that friendly disposition which manifests itself in continued acts of kindness to others, and acknowledgements of kindnesses received from others'; and that influence, he insisted, 'we do possess'. Parliamentary opponents of his policy in Spain, Palmerston said, were just sympathisers with 'arbitrary and despotic government' and he proceeded to deliver a eulogy on the achievements of recent Whig-Liberal foreign policy. The 'principles of national liberty have made greater progress in Europe than they have ever before made, within the same time, at any period of our history', he told the House. While British contributions to this 'progress' were not limited to the efforts of Whig governments, Palmerston conceded, he did draw attention to the advances they had been responsible for, highlighting that 'the people in Belgium have been free, happy, powerful and tranquil; that Portugal, which had been worse governed than Spain, and of which the natural resources had been, so to speak, crushed and exhausted, and rendered unavailing by a long course of misgovernment – Portugal has established free institutions, is prepared to profit by them, and is on the high road to that prosperity which, in my opinion, free institutions can alone open to a country. Spain, . . . I may be allowed to hope . . . may yet follow the example which has been set to her by Belgium and by Portugal. She may yet become . . . what she was in former times, a great and powerful member of the European community.' All of this, Palmerston claimed, would be attributable to Britain's benevolent inspiration.[75]

Palmerston's speeches on Spain were widely circulated and discussed and it became clear that although some people had been disposed to swallow the rhetoric,[76] the widely assumed popularity of Palmerston with the British public was yet open to question. If Palmerstonian policy was meant to underline the British commitment to freedom and liberty, certain sections of the British public were beginning to doubt its sincerity. Following the debate of 10 March, for example, one pamphleteer was prompted into print by the 'erroneous and dangerous' view Palmerston took of Spanish affairs. Far from championing liberties, it was asserted, Palmerston wilfully neglected the ancient constitutional claims of Basque liberals in the north of the country and appealed to the base interests of domestic party politics. Shame, then, on the forces that attacked 'those gallant Basques, who breathe that free air in which the "harlot's petticoat," the tawdry red and yellow rag of Christina, had so often been shivered into shreds'.[77] Three years later, Palmerston said that 'Queen Christina must learn that she can only govern a nation so long as that nation chuses she shall govern it; and that they will chuse this no longer if she attempts to deprive them of their liberties and privileges'.[78] In 1837, however, Palmerston stood accused of a simplistic and naïve faith in the viability of an imposed liberal system of government in Spain: constitutional government, he was reminded, could not be imposed but must be allowed to develop organically over time. His blind faith in the potential of the Quadruple Alliance had led Palmerston to invest it with a relevance it had lost the moment Carlos and Miguel quitted the peninsula. By clinging to a treaty which, it was suggested, had 'died a natural death' because Spain and Portugal could not, and France would not, honour its terms, Palmerston caused the denigration of British prestige: French newspapers, it was reported, 'gloated' over the inability of the British military forces in Spain to achieve a victory.[79]

Palmerston had expressed confidence at the end of 1836 that Tory attacks would not diminish Radical support and a raft of 'good measures' about to be brought forward would make the government 'popular'.[80] That was not what critics of his foreign policy thought. James Harris, the future third earl of Malmesbury, accused Palmerston of wilfully entangling Britain in Spain without fully appreciating the broader ramifications and alleged that the much-vaunted Quadruple Alliance had cost Britain dear and yielded little tangible return. Palmerston, he suggested, was motivated by a 'thirst for excitement' and, fearing that the 'government to which he belongs would have been too *uninteresting* to the country, if unaccompanied with the clashing of arms, and the sound of trumpets', the Foreign Secretary had, trusting to 'the apathy with which his department is usually considered "faute de mieux," dashed into the confusion of a civil war'. Palmerston, Harris argued, was more a 'zealot' than a statesman, and though 'doubtless conscientious' in his desire to extend 'the blessings of liberty', he had forgotten 'that pure liberty has never yet sprung from such a fratricidal field, as Spain is now displaying to Europe'.[81]

In private Palmerston admitted that affairs were not in quite the good state he had claimed publicly. In a letter to Shee he lamented that Britain had lost ground to Russia, Austria and France over Greece, and the good understanding with France which he had been at pains to commend to his audience at Westminster was not evident in his opinion that 'France plays a miserable part in this as well as in most other European affairs. It is very extraordinary that there should always be such a want of dignity, honesty, and good faith in French policy. But so it has been in all periods of history; and the present reign does not seem destined to form an exception to the general rule.' He could only claim that in Spain 'the results are not the less sure for being slow in their approach'; he could not yet, apparently, prove it.[82] Later in the year, in September, he would attribute feelings of jealousy towards Britain to the French government, but, contradicting his earlier insistence that political differences would always be countered by a genuine commonality of interests between the two nations, Palmerston told Fred Lamb that on all counts, Britain and France were growing far apart and throughout Europe – in Greece, in Spain, in Portugal – French policy was driven by a determination to do 'what they fancy the reverse of us'. This French 'jealousy', he concluded, was the result of past military defeats at the hands of British forces and the fact that 'since the war has been over, we have surpassed them as much in the arts of peace as we had done in the conflict of war. In industry, commerce, wealth, legislative improvements, internal tranquillity, we leave them far behind; and the contrast must necessarily wound the self love of a peculiarly vain race of men.'[83]

Despite claiming that the 'emancipation of Spain & Portugal, will lay a solid foundation for a future confederacy to check Russian aggression', Palmerston appeared, by the summer of 1837, far from convinced that there existed any real western unity. The Quadruple Alliance had clearly failed and, as his private correspondence reveals, he had accepted that notions of a liberal alliance did not really exist beyond the rhetorical embellishments of diplomatic correspondence. And yet, it was just at this time that eastern Europe and the Near East seemed most unstable and potentially hostile to British interests. 'I believe indeed that the true danger to Europe, is not from the strength of Russia, but from the crouching baseness of Austria & Prussia towards her,' Palmerston told Lamb in June 1837. 'Those two powers might if united without any other help, dismember Russia, and separate from her empire the Polish & German Provinces, & some of her Turkish acquisitions; but from the mean spirit of their political rulers, they lick the dust from the Emperor's shoes, instead of letting him know that they are able to dust his jacket. You will say this is very fine vapouring from us, who have just been making a so so settlement of the Vixen affair. It is however not the less true.'[84] The *Vixen* was a British merchant ship carrying salt from Constantinople to Circassia which the Russians seized when it reached its destination. The apparent attack on British maritime trade stirred up considerable anti-Russian feeling in Britain and Palmerston made a demand for compensation, but no one was quite sure who had the stronger case. In the event an *ex gratia* payment was offered and accepted and Palmerston tried to play down the incident.[85]

It was against this diplomatic backdrop that Palmerston had to face his constituents in the election of July 1837. Early reports from Devon suggested that the contest would be a rough one,[86] but the promised test of Palmerston's popularity did not materialise. The Tories had continued throughout 1836 to perform badly in Tiverton and local party activity amounted to little more than a series of dinners and soirées, which while lavish were frequently derided (at least by their opponents) as politically irrelevant. The Reformers, meanwhile, had established a more ascetic association ('no eating or drinking allowed' in committee), but also a more effective one, to support the Melbourne government and keep a weather eye on their opponents. As the Tories fell 'an immense distance behind' Palmerston, the new Reform Association looked forward to enrolling 200 subscribers in early 1836.[87] When a 'Tory squire' began canvassing in the spring of 1836, five years before an election was due, Palmerston thought it worthwhile to head down to Devon for the purpose of 'nailing votes' and he spent the second week of April 'working like a two penny postman from morning till night, & reading like a newspaper writer from night till morning'. By such means he 'made all safe', he told Shee.[88] Whatever strength the Tories might have acquired in the spring, George Coles thought it all spent by the summer.[89] In 1837, therefore, Tiverton seemed a safe seat and Palmerston was not at all tempted by an approach to stand for South Lancashire.[90] In July, when the death of the King necessitated a general election, Palmerston was called to Tiverton by his agents to meet a new Tory challenge in the shape of Benjamin Bowden Dickinson. Francis Hole, the mayor, stage-managed a hustings appearance to demonstrate to the 'trades people' that Palmerston 'had the support of the neighbouring gentry'.[91] It was perhaps unnecessary; despite an active campaign by his supporters, Dickinson evinced no real interest in a public career and was greatly reduced in popular estimation by revelations that his parsimoniousness extended to an unfortunate member of his own family said to be incarcerated and ignored in a local workhouse.[92] It was alleged in some quarters that Dickinson, by common consent an unfit and unwilling candidate, had only been put up for the sake of making a contest, of any sort, in order to assuage the disappointment of electors, agents and lawyers who had missed out on fees and dinners at the uncontested election of 1835.[93] Palmerston at least did not stint this time, laying out almost £200 for dinners and a further £400 in payments to lawyers and agents.[94]

The result of the election was no great surprise. Heathcoat and Palmerston topped the poll with 323 and 246 votes respectively, comfortably ahead of Dickinson who finished on 180. Only 'bribery and intimidation' on the part of the Tories had deprived Palmerston of a full demonstration of support, he claimed.[95] Palmerston had stood on a platform of continued reform, citing in particular past successes such as the restructuring of municipal corporations, extension of the parliamentary franchise, advances in religious liberty in England and Ireland, improvements to poor relief provision, and the promotion of civil liberty and maintenance of peace in Europe as evidence of his and the government's good claims to continued support in accordance with what he called the 'improving Spirit of the Age'.[96] The majority return of the Whigs nationwide confirmed, in Palmerston's view, the advance of moderate politics and the decline of extremes.[97] Only in Ireland, he argued in his victory address in Tiverton, did 'the greatest abuses' persist, and the return of Whigs there showed that they were the ones trusted to apply the necessary remedies.[98] Palmerston had not been taken to task on his policies by Dickinson and the contest had turned on electioneering devices more than principles. What is interesting, however, is to reflect on the apparent sources of Palmerston's support. According to one witness, the polling on election day had started badly for the Liberals and it was only in the middle of the afternoon that the outlook improved as a procession of thirty or forty voters, led by the local Congregationalist and Baptist ministers, came down to vote for Palmerston. 'This demonstration was conceived and acted on by Mr Heudebourck [the Congregationalist minister, "a zealous Radical and an advocate for disestablishment"], who took this method of showing Lord Palmerston that his election or rejection was virtually in the power of the Nonconformist voters.' It was said, at least in Tiverton, that Palmerston never forgot this lesson and paid careful attention to courting Nonconformist votes there in the future.[99]

The rapidly expanding and increasingly influential extra-parliamentary scrutiny of policy in the 1830s was not lost on Palmerston. It has already been noted how, along with other Whigs, he had begun to experiment with techniques of press management and manipulation earlier in the decade; by the mid- and later 1830s Palmerston was increasingly alert to the potential gains to be had from newspaper allies. 'Popular' election successes in South Hampshire and Tiverton, as well as a defeat in the former, had indicated the greater level of popular engagement in public affairs (or at least the more powerful electoral impact of that engagement) and, more importantly, the ways in which popular endorsement, or otherwise, of policies exerted an ever more perceptible influence at Westminster. Furthermore, after years of conducting foreign policy in the face of (and ostensibly in support of) the advance of Liberalism, it was necessary to master public as well as private debates in the diplomatic arena. The press offered an increasingly attractive medium through which to guide, mediate and form these discussions. It was said of Palmerston about this time that he was 'a strange mixture of caution and imprudence; that as long as he did not commit himself *on paper* he thought himself safe; that he would see any Newspaper Editor who called on him, and often communicate to him matters of great delicacy'.[100]

Most newspapers had identifiable political leanings. The *Chronicle*, 'a much better paper' than *The Times*, Palmerston said, for example,[101] enjoyed significant Whig support and patronage at this time. However, though he was keen to court press support, Palmerston was always careful to conceal this so far as possible. When, in the summer of 1836, a prospectus for a new bi-weekly paper, *The Englishman*, was sent to Palmerston it was no doubt hoped he would prove receptive to calls for support of a paper born from 'an anxious desire . . . to frustrate the designs of the Ultra Tories'. Perhaps it was the fact that though it was to be a 'liberally conducted paper', it was also to be 'unencumbered by the trammels of party', that concerned Palmerston, for he responded with a polite refusal: 'considering the official situation which I hold, I do not think that I could with propriety connect myself in this manner with a publication over the management of which I could of course exercise no controul,' he noted.[102] However, where control might be possible, Palmerston was not averse to more clandestine links with major journals (*The Englishman* was also probably too obscure and uncertain a venture for Palmerston to bother with). Although he again repeated his insistence that governments and politicians 'have no power of *preventing* articles from appearing which we should not have approved of', and that any paper that did 'put itself into such complete trammels under the govt . . . would soon lose its circulation in consequence of its tameness; and we should have no means of repaying it for its loss', this protestation was written in an attempt to persuade the Austrian government that a recent article in the *Globe*, which had given offence at Vienna, was not something to be treated officially.[103] Palmerston well knew that, as he had intimated to Lady Cowper some time earlier, persuasion could be just as effective as direct control, and this impellent could take a variety of forms. Journalists and correspondents connected with favoured newspapers were often granted privileged entrée to European political society through the exertions of the British diplomatic service.[104] The arrangements were mutually beneficial: as well as introductions, journalists might receive preferential treatment from the Foreign Secretary. The editor of the *Morning Post*, for example, was placed in Palmerston's debt when the Foreign Secretary acted to rescue two of the *Post's* writers from being shot by Christinos in Spain; in return the *Post* alerted Palmerston to news from the peninsula which it had gained before the government's official sources.[105] That was one aspect of the quid pro quo arrangement by which such relationships thrived. Indeed, the imperfect state of the government's intelligence machinery meant that minsters were often reliant on the press for diplomatic news. Opportunistic journalists would try to inveigle Palmerston with promises of useful but surreptitiously obtained information which Palmerston would accept or reject according to the perceived political bias of the writer.[106] News was always to be treated as susceptible to partiality and the press was clearly an agency of political 'spin'. Pecuniary devices were often just as effective as non-pecuniary ones and Palmerston was perfectly willing to sanction the use of secret service funds to bribe newspapers and journalists, both at home and abroad, if that would secure allegiance and support.[107] Not all secret service expenditure went on bribing newspapers, of course, but Palmerston averaged a monthly expenditure of around £2,500 from such accounts.[108] Had he had access to more, he said, he would have felt no compunction in using it wherever he thought he might be able to 'purchase peace', even if that meant bribing foreign soldiers and politicians.[109]

The press also offered a means for foreign policy to be tested at a comparatively safe distance. Diplomatic relations could be conducted via the pages of the *Globe* and the *Augsburg Gazette*, for example, sometimes more easily than in dispatches between London and Germany.[110] When Palmerston received a letter from Munich informing him that the editors of the *Augsburg Gazette* were 'desirous to open their columns to the advocacy of British policy; and . . . are willing to insert papers written in favour of Great Britain, in every political question in which Her Majesty's government may be interested, including those in which Austria and Greece may be involved, if a certain forbearance be exercised by the writer, in order to elude the attention of the Censorship, to which they are, in a degree, subjected in their communications bearing reference to these two countries', Palmerston minuted on the letter: 'Might not some use be made of this man's pen? Who is he?'[111]

The press could be a powerful agency, then, in diplomatic circles. When, in the autumn of 1836, the *Morning Chronicle* among other papers published articles abusing Louis Philippe, it was argued that this could play a vital role in affecting the cooling Franco-British relations. Melbourne worried that 'Louis Philippe is very susceptible with respect to the tone of the English newspapers, & with good reason, for they may do him a great deal of harm'.[112] Though Palmerston was keen to encourage this effect in France, Melbourne feared 'that we should contribute to drive Louis Philippe into a decided course of anti-liberal policy, which may or rather must lead to a crisis in Europe – either he will succeed & establish an absolute monarchy in France or he will fail & the Revolutionists & Republicans will get ahead'.[113] The newspapers may not quite have held the balance between war and peace in Europe, but Melbourne's cautionary tone underlined how important the print media could be in influencing public affairs across the continent.

If ministers, and particularly Palmerston, had needed any demonstration of the potential of the press in diplomatic questions, they were to find it in the pages of the *Portfolio* and the activities of David Urquhart and his supporters. Urquhartism would become one of the longest standing and bitterest campaigns against Palmerston (Southgate called it Urquhart's 'hymn of hate'),[114] even if Urquhart and his acolytes rarely succeeded in making a telling attack. David Urquhart had served at the Constantinople embassy in the early 1830s and had won the support and even admiration of the Foreign Secretary while he served there. Since the end of 1835, however, Urquhart had been intimately connected with a new polemical periodical, the *Portfolio*, in which he published and discussed documents relating to foreign policy. Lord Holland judged it a 'strange publication' and though he discerned a desire for war with Russia within the editorial 'clique', he could not 'divine what is the exact mischief they mean to prevent or the precise benefit they hope to obtain', by such a conflict.[115] The early numbers of the *Portfolio* were, if not officially endorsed, at least well supported from within the Foreign Office. Palmerston's Under-Secretary, Strangways, conducted a cordial correspondence with Urquhart discussing which extracts from dispatches should be included in the paper and advising on helpful editorial excisions.[116] Indeed, the *Portfolio* was welcomed as a valuable medium for educating the public about diplomatic affairs. Yet while Palmerston and his Foreign Office staff appeared to have been content to stand before the bar of public opinion, some ministerial colleagues were more wary. Within the Cabinet there was evidence, in early 1836, of growing unease as perceived bids for popular support seemed to smack of underhandedness. As the *Portfolio* acquired an increasingly distinct, and Russophobic, character, concern grew and it was questioned whether open discussion, which, it turned out, often meant public criticism, really served the government's interests. Urquhart's known connection with the Foreign Office and his widely assumed authorship of the *Portfolio* was, said Melbourne, 'very awkward' and he grew impatient to see Urquhart sent off to a diplomatic posting in the Levant (admitting, however, that he doubted 'whether he will do you most harm here or there, but I rather think the former'), particularly when he read articles arguing, in contradiction of British commercial policy, for increased duties on imported Russian tallow.[117] Palmerston's apparent inability to control Urquhart risked a serious breach with his Cabinet colleagues.[118]

Palmerston was coming to understand the damage the *Portfolio* could do to his foreign policy, not least since disaffected diplomats such as Lord Ponsonby were increasingly trying to use it as a means of undermining Palmerstonian strategy. When Palmerston severed the Foreign Office's semi-official link with the paper in late 1837 and expelled Urquhart from the diplomatic service, he only stoked Urquhartite opposition. From this point, Urquhart's attacks on Palmerston spoke of treason and sought to portray him as a Russian agent. Only such an explanation could account for Palmerston's failure to help Turkey in 1833, or his refraining from challenging Russia over the Treaty of Unkiar Skelessi, or, for that matter, his decision to recall Urquhart himself.[119] Such, then, was the basis on which Urquhart sought to expose the Foreign Secretary in the autumn of 1840. Urquhart had, by this point, consolidated support for his view of foreign policy in the East, and especially among working-class groups in northern England, and in September 1840 the Urquhartite 'Committees for the Examination of Diplomatic Documents' published a protest against recent Palmerstonian activity which, they alleged, demonstrated 'a long course of treasonable collusion between . . . [Palmerston] and the cabinet of St Petersburgh'.[120]

It was known, or at least believed, within the Foreign Office that Urquhart was by this time 'in intimate relations' with the *Morning Herald* which had recently published a series of articles of an Urquhartite tone and hostile to Palmerston.[121] So alarmed was Palmerston about what he called the 'Urquhart Conspiracy, 1840', that he took legal advice from the Attorney-General on the recent attacks made by Urquhart who, he said, in attacking him personally, was, 'there is no doubt, at the head of an organized Society here having that object, & which is in connection with a party in Paris'. This Society, inspired by

David Urquhart, along with Charles Attwood, William Cargill and William Cardo (all of Birmingham), Robert Monteith (Glasgow),[122] and Thomas Doubleday (Newcastle) was, Palmerston feared, thriving across the country. 'The Society have endeavoured for some time past by meetings called at Glasgow, Newcastle on Tyne and Birmingham to induce the lower classes of those places to take an active part with them but without much success, though the speeches and resolutions being afterwards printed and circulated gratis are made to serve the object of the parties by spreading the most atrocious calumnies against Lord Palmerston under the pretence of merely examining and canvassing his public conduct as Foreign Minister, to which, if they confined themselves, he would have no objection.' Palmerston was advised that there was insufficient evidence against Urquhart and Attwood and the only course left open, of prosecuting the booksellers and publishers, would not be becoming, though it might afford 'a legitimate opportunity of denying personal corruption.' Though the attacks were 'scurrilous', the advice from the Attorney-General was that 'a Minister should not prosecute the press except upon a distinct charge of personal corruption, and as before stated we cannot discover any such direct charge to that effect as properly to challenge denial on his Lordship's part'.[123] Even if the allegations of treason were patently ridiculous and widely mocked at the time, it was evident from his reaction that Palmerston's confidence in his easy rapport with the 'people' had been shaken by the accusations.

Urquhart insisted that to allow the Ottoman Empire to collapse and to count on a series of independent successor states to act as a barrier to Russia – as was advocated in certain sections of the British press at this time – would be an 'uncertain', 'suspicious', 'perplexing' and 'mistrustful' line of policy. What was required, he said, was 'vigorous action': 'If England anticipates Russia, she has with her France, Prussia is left aside, Austria enters to hasten the termination of the struggle, if necessary, the whole Ottoman empire is called to arms, the troops and fleet of Mehemet Ali united to them, and the only result that will then be worth accepting, will be the retreat of Russia behind the Dnieper, which moderate prudence and sequence in the policy of the cabinets of France and England would never have permitted her to traverse.'[124]

Britain's failure to adopt such a vigorous line of policy, therefore, was grounds for Palmerston's impeachment and Urquhart set out his case in a series of articles written in the autumn of 1839 and published in the *Glasgow Herald* between December 1839 and April 1840, subsequently republished as *Diplomatic Transactions in Central Asia*.[125] Close examination of the fluctuating Franco-British relations of the 1830s, Urquhart insisted in a preface to the book, simply revealed the deviousness of Russian diplomacy. The foundation of the Urquhartite critique, therefore, was to see the inevitable temporal shifts in international alignments not as the adjustment and readjustment of tactical *realpolitik* calculations, but as the product of a malign scheme, orchestrated from St Petersburg and observed obediently in Paris and, especially, London. If that conspiracy was, on Palmerston's part, one of omission more than commission, it was no less worthy of condemnation. Although these criticisms singled out Palmerston as the sole architect of Britain's supposedly Russophile policies, in reality much of the antagonism towards Urquhart and his clique in ministerial circles was shared, or even originated, elsewhere. Melbourne, Stanley and Holland, among others, had been alarmed by Urquhart's connections with the *Portfolio* while Palmerston himself had only come to acknowledge the risk somewhat later. Similarly, although it was Palmerston who was blamed for the government's failure to back Urquhart's negotiations for a commercial treaty with the Porte in 1836, it was in fact Poulett Thomson, the President of the Board of Trade, who had formally rejected proposals for the reduction of duties on Turkish goods for fear of offending the Russian government.[126] Indeed, in 1838 Palmerston positively welcomed a commercial treaty with Turkey in which the Sultan abolished 'the system of monopolies in his dominions which greatly hamper our commerce, & strike at the root of the prosperity of his own subjects'.[127] Yet it remains to be considered why Palmerston appeared to vacillate in the East, or whether there was a logic to his and Britain's policy. There is no need to be distracted by allegations of his having acted as a paid Russian agent – even many of those sympathetic to Urquhart's broader concerns about Russian gains at Britain's expense mocked such suggestions – but there was evidently a body of popular opinion (albeit a minority) alarmed by Britain's apparent loss of standing and influence under Palmerston.

Palmerston, it is true, had not demonstrated a high regard for Turkish culture in the past, casting the Ottoman peoples as an inferior counterweight to Western civilisation and progress. 'I should not be sorry some day or other to see the Turk kicked out of Europe, & compelled to go and sit cross-legged, smoke his pipe, chew his opium, & cut off heads on the Asiatic side of the Bosphorus;' he had written to his friend Edward Littleton in September 1829: 'we want civilization, activity, trade & business in Europe, & your Mustaphas have no idea of any traffic beyond rhubarb, figs and red slippers.' In later years, when Palmerston was thought to be less keen to see Turkey 'kicked out of Europe', he had been offered and accepted the chance to amend the word 'sorry' to 'surprised'.[128] However, this private letter had been written at a time when attention in Britain was focused on Ottoman suppression of Greek nationalism and when philo-Hellenic sentiment held considerable sway in high political debate just as Russian influence at Constantinople seemed acceptable, if not indeed irresistible. Palmerston had also written it while in opposition. As he had found in his first term at the Foreign Office, practical diplomacy often demanded a degree of 'flexibility' not allowed for in the passionate rhetoric of opposition politicians. So it was in the later 1830s when the Eastern question was again inflamed and, as Urquhart *et al.* argued, Britain's material interest and asserted influence were brought under scrutiny that Palmerston's policy was tested.

William IV, a patron, admirer and careful reader of Urquhart, was a thorn in the ministerial side over Eastern policy: 'for God's sake try to get his Syrian policy out of his head,' pleaded Melbourne in a letter to Palmerston in February 1836.[129] Just as the King was absorbing an Urquhartite view via pamphlets and the *Portfolio*, ministers wished to play down the Russian threat; so far at least did Urquhart have a point. Palmerston, however, criticised the timidity of some of his colleagues, notably Lord Grey, on this question and advocated in many respects the sort of policy Urquhart was calling for. When a mooted Franco-British coalition against Russia was opposed in Cabinet by Grey in early 1836, Palmerston remonstrated that if Britain did not take 'advantage of the existing weakness of Russia & good will of France in order to raise up a barrier of treaty against Russia', the government risked ridicule if, while using menacing language about Russia, it continued 'to wait in this state of indecision & irresolution till Russia is grown strong enough to brave us, or till she has succeeded in detaching us from France, & in leaving us either to resist her singly or to submit to her encroachments'. Mere 'language' was no deterrent said Palmerston and facing a Russian danger 'more imminent' than Grey and others appreciated; only an explicit Franco-British determination, embodied in a formal treaty, to resist Russian aggrandisement – by war if necessary – would suffice.[130] Melbourne replied simply that one argument against a treaty was 'getting embroiled in these Eastern affairs earlier and deeper, than there is any necessity to warrant'; but he worried, after all, that debates about the East 'inflame imaginations wonderfully'.[131] Two Prime Ministers – one current and one former – more than the Foreign Secretary, were holding back an overt British challenge to Russia.

Palmerston did not deny that the Russian threat, though he believed it real enough, was easily exaggerated and, despite what he had said in answer to Grey, he conceded to Holland that 'Russia has no immediate intentions of attacking Turkey'. Yet, he maintained, that was only because other powers appeared willing to back the Sultan if called upon. Though he had doubted the long-term viability of the Ottoman Empire when he first came to the Foreign Office, Palmerston had now adopted, by default if not conviction, a firm commitment to preserving the position of the Sultan and the existence of the empire as essential counterweights in the balance of power. Thus, as well as keeping Russia out of Ottoman territory, the internal stability of that empire must be maintained, and here were grounds for a divergence from France since the close ties between Mehemet Ali and Paris were not compatible with Palmerston's view that it was necessary, if possible, to prevent 'a rupture between Mehemet Ali & the Sultan & I hope we may be able to do so. But the Sultan *is* the sovereign & Mehemet Ali *is* the subject; and it is impossible to deny the *right* of the Sultan to appoint another man to govern his province of Syria, or his province of Egypt if he chuses to do so'. Anything else simply undermined the principle of the rule of law.[132]

Palmerston was reluctant to undermine Turkey as an independent power by agreeing with France (and possibly Austria as well) a treaty of protection; it would, he said, place the Ottoman Empire under their guardianship and would lead to constant demands for advice and require 'incessant interference in her internal affairs; & conferences of ministers either at Constantinople or elsewhere, & hence differences between the parties; and England & France in a minority'. A Franco-British and, if possible, also Austrian demonstration of support for Turkey would be helpful, he said, but at any event Britain ought to 'endeavour to assist Turkey in developing her own resources & let her look to alliances according to circumstances, when danger may arise. Every step Turkey makes towards regeneration, weakens the strain of Orloff's Treaty upon her.'[133]

It had become clear in the fracturing of the proclaimed unity of the Quadruple Alliance over the Iberian Peninsula in 1836–37 that France and Britain in particular were far from reconciled to an untroubled entente. The divergence was further emphasised by the Eastern question, and in terms yet more ominous (from Britain's point of view) given the extent to which British policy towards Turkey henceforth pushed Britain, and Palmerston, into increasing diplomatic isolation.

In his Eastern policy, Palmerston rejected the oft-repeated belief that the Ottoman Empire 'must fall' as a 'mistaken assumption'. 'Turkey cannot fall except by a war;' he wrote to George Hodges, Britain's Consul-General in Serbia, at the beginning of 1838, 'and a war is at present not likely. Turkey is not going down; on the contrary she is rallying; slowly if you will, and to superficial observers imperceptibly. But light from without has been let in upon the interior of Turkey; communication has been established between Turkey & the rest of Europe. The attention of Europe has been directed to Turkish affairs & if we have ten years more of peace which, as far as any man can predict of the future, I think we have a fair chance of seeing, we shall find Turkey becoming at the end of that time far more capable of maintaining her independence than she has been for a long time past.' Even if war did break out, Palmerston argued, Russia would not pose a menace to Ottoman rule: the majority of the European powers would find it in their own interests to defend Turkey against Russia while Russia, meanwhile, 'would have plenty on her hands if war were to break out' given that all 'her frontier provinces are discontented & ripe for revolt. Her Mahometan, German, & Polish subjects are all dissatisfied with her rule, and she would have enough to do to keep what she has without aspiring to acquire more.'[134]

Russia remained a pre-eminent threat to Britain, however. In the spring of 1838 Persia seemed bent on conquest of Afghanistan. This caused consternation in Britain and provoked debate about whether Britain could, and should, still rely on Persian treaty promises (dating from 1814) to prevent any other European power gaining access to India via Persian territory. Palmerston did not want to exaggerate Persia's hold over Britain by raising an alarm about this issue.[135] But it was not exclusively an imperial defence question: Palmerston saw also that 'Russia and Persia are playing tricks in Affghanistan', and was obviously alarmed that Russia was testing a perceived British weak spot; this must, he said, 'be put an end to'.[136] By June matters looked 'ill' according to Palmerston. Russia appeared determined to underwrite a proposed Persian–Afghan settlement 'defensive against England' and this, said Palmerston, 'is coming a little too near to our door in India'. It was no coincidence, he argued, that Tsar Nicholas was at the same time meeting the King of Sweden and the visit, which implied a recasting or reaffirmation of diplomatic alignments, betokened, unequivocally, 'a rupture' between Britain and Russia.[137] Persia had reneged on earlier agreements 'to be our friend' and 'to promote our interest' and had deliberately, in consorting with Russia in Afghanistan, removed the protective barrier between India and Europe and was 'laying the road open for invasion up to our very gate'.[138] Palmerston claimed a similar freedom from treaty obligations for Britain in its relations with Persia.[139] It was as much a statement of the mixture of suspicion and fear that now existed between Britain and Russia as it was about British–Persian relations.

When in September proposals were put forward for a British invasion of Persia to reassert Britain's position there, Palmerston's objections were founded on his view of Russian policy objectives. Destabilising the Shah, even causing his dethronement by stirring up indigenous resentment, would be a likely and highly undesirable outcome, he argued. In such a case, the Shah would simply turn to Russia for military aid which, though not certain, might be granted, risking a British defeat and (worse still) humiliation which would, if that Russian support were given – as it most likely would be – in clandestine fashion, be disavowed and could not become a formal ground of complaint on Britain's part. The only way for Britain to check Persia militarily, Palmerston maintained, was to do so in Afghanistan, 'because the Russians would be too far off to come to their aid' and because Russia would find it more difficult to justify action in Afghanistan whereas intervening to bolster a neighbour, in the case of a direct attack on Persia, would be comparatively straightforward.[140] British military intervention in Afghanistan, when it came, encapsulated Britain's diplomatic fears and aspirations in microcosm. As Palmerston wrote to Hobhouse at the end of October 1838, so long as Britain successfully established control over all parts of Afghanistan simultaneously:

This vigorous decision of Auckland's will do us the utmost service, in India in Europe and at home. We shall utterly defeat the Russian schemes in the East; That will tell upon Persia, & probably reestablish our-influence there. That again will tell in Turkey, and give us a good footing there. That will tell again upon all other European questions now pending, and upon American ones too. The world had begun to think that England had really become what the Russian scribe in the Augsbourg Gazette called her, 'a power known only by tradition'. But all this vigour will have to be followed up in the spring, by some little naval reinforcement at home; for it will not do to be strong at the extremities and defenceless at the heart of the Empire.[141]

In early 1838, Palmerston had explained to Fred Lamb wherein lay the greatest threats to European peace. A union of France and Russia, he said, was a 'great danger which hangs over Europe' but he also believed that there were 'two obstacles to that union': the personal animosity between Nicholas and Louis Philippe and, in France, the decisive influence, or even perhaps control, of public opinion and the parlement over the government. Death, of course, would remove the first obstacle and, though he doubted the depth of French popular and parliamentary appetites for aggrandisement, there was always the risk that 'the allurement of territorial acquisition' might yet seduce the French people and overcome the latter. That, Palmerston said, was the danger, 'and a union of Austria, Prussia & England would be the defence against such danger'. This, however, was always an improbable alliance. Though Britain and Russia might 'continue to be on good terms . . . as far as outward civility goes', the fact remained that the two countries' political systems were 'like two entirely different orbits, with nothing in common' and his policy projections were based on the assumption that 'the next war that breaks out in Europe will be one in which Russia and England will be on opposite sides'.[142] If Russia orbited an autocratic system, then Britain's compass, Palmerston continued to argue, was still the liberal sphere. In that, Britain was comparatively isolated: his 'doctrine', he told Lamb in March, 'is that we should reckon *upon ourselves*',

pursue a policy of our own; aim at objects of our own; and act upon principles of our own; use other govts as we can; when we want them, & find them willing to serve us; but never place ourselves in the wake of any of them. Lead when & where we can, but follow, never.

The system of England ought to be to maintain the liberties & independence of all other nations; out of the conflicting interests of other countries to secure her own independence; to throw her moral weight into the scale of any people who are spontaneously striving for freedom, by which I mean rational government; and to extend as far, and as fast as possible civilization all over the world. I am sure this is our interest; I am certain it must redound to our honor; I am convinced we have within ourselves the strength to pursue this course, if we have only the will to do so; and in your humble servant that will is strong & persevering. We have already done much in Belgium, Portugal & Spain, & I trust we may yet see our good work in those countries secured.[143]

Palmerston's ministerial colleagues endorsed this policy, as Melbourne put it, 'to have our hands free' in dealings with the Eastern question.[144] By the same token, though he wanted to maintain a free hand, Palmerston recognised that the threat of recurrent instability within Ottoman territory required, if possible, some outward display of great power solidarity. In Egypt Mehemet Ali was reviving his challenge to Turkish rule and Palmerston believed that the Pasha's hopes of success were founded 'upon expected jealousies & divisions between the powers of Europe'.[145] Despite his wariness of European powers, and especially Russia, Palmerston saw benefits in a concerted negotiation of the problem. The Turkish Empire, he insisted, 'will last our time if we try to prop it up, and not pull it down'; adding that, 'an empire which has endured for centuries is likely to outlive the creation of yesterday, such as Mehemet Ali's authority'.[146]

Mehemet Ali's determination to declare his independence of the Ottoman Empire had not diminished in the years since the 'first crisis' of 1833. He had only desisted from pressing his claims in the autumn of 1834 on the urging of his son Ibrahim, who believed the time was less not more propitious than it had been when such plans had failed in 1833. By 1838, however, Mehemet Ali's thoughts had again turned seriously to the issue and in late May he announced his decision to proclaim himself leader of an independent Egypt. This was not unexpected: only the day before Palmerston had proposed a great power agreement for cooperation in the event of just such a reassertion of the Pasha's claims and although Mehemet Ali was induced to withdraw his declaration under great power pressure in mid-July, he made it clear that this was a postponement and not an abandonment of his demands. It was even maintained in certain circles that Mehemet Ali's drive for independence was divinely ordained: the Book of Daniel, said a Reverend Fysh, prophesied 'that at the final break-up of the Ottoman Empire, Egypt would declare its independency in Turkey, and seek to establish itself as a separate kingdom'. The omens were clear: 'war is foretold between "*the king of the north*" ie the Emperor of Russia, and "*the king of the south*" ie the king of Egypt', and: 'The subversion of all the kingdoms of the world is to prepare the way for the setting up of the kingdom of the Messiah, and the strife and conflict of Armageddon are to herald the millennial reign of the Prince of Peace'.[147]

The Eastern question was as far from resolution as ever and possessed the power still, in the tense political atmosphere of the late 1830s, to do considerable diplomatic damage in Europe. Palmerston persisted through the summer in his attempts to draw the European powers into a concert, determined above all, as he explained to Clanricarde in October, to avoid a unilateral resolution of the problem by any one great power.[148] Palmerston feared the potentially destabilising effects of European in-fighting: 'we ought to support the Sultan heartily and vigorously; with France if France will act with us; without her if she should decline,' he had written to Granville in June, adding shortly afterwards, '*It must not be forgotten that one great danger to Europe is the possibility of a combination between France and Russia.*[149] The impending crisis also offered an opportunity to revise the long-resented Treaty of Unkiar Skelessi and exploit a developing Russian diplomatic isolation to limit the advantages in the Straits won by St Petersburg in 1833.

In a letter to Lamb that was shown to Metternich and Nesselrode, Palmerston outlined his favoured course: 'Unkhiar Skelessi should merge in an agreement between the Five Powers & Turkey. Our Treaty of 1809 with Turkey acknowledges the right of the Porte to keep the Dardanelles (& Bosphorus of course also) closed, while Turkey is at peace; when she is at war, she of course will open the channels to her friends, & shut them to her foes.'[150] Mehemet Ali had good reason to suspect that he could play upon the tensions between the European powers to his own ends. In London, Palmerston had been told in May that 'an understanding does exist between the cabinets of Vienna and St Petersburgh as regards the European provinces of the Turkish Empire', which Palmerson noted was a 'long established belief',[151] and which added urgency to the search for, or gave the lie to the possibility of, great power cooperation on this issue. It only confirmed Palmerston's own sceptical assessment of Metternich's character and sincerity and affirmed his suspicion of a secret understanding between the two major east European courts – even if that was a misreading of an arrangement simply to cooperate in the event of, not to provoke, the dissolution of the Ottoman Empire in Europe[152] – which he had outlined in a private letter in April:

With respect to Egypt the thing to be tried for in the event of Mehemet Ali's falling, is that the authority of the Sultan should be re-established there and in Syria. Such an addition to his resources, & such a diminution of his cares & dangers would enable him to make head again against Russia; and yet even that would not make him strong enough to give just cause of alarm to Austria. But is Austria, that is to say Metternich honest about Turkey? I never have believed it and cannot bring myself to believe it. Assume that he is, and his conduct is inexplicable except on the supposition of weakness, cowardice, & short sightedness inconsistent with his general character. Assume that he has all along been playing the rogue, and that while professing to us a desire to uphold Turkey, he has a tacit understanding with Russia, or without any understanding has made up his mind to unite with Russia, for a division of the spoils of Turkey; and then his whole conduct from 1828 downwards becomes clear & intelligible. He is still a dupe even in that case; but a dupe of his own covetousness, instead of the dupe of his fears. It has always seemed to me that he preferred considering the case of Turkey hopeless, rather than endeavouring to keep her alive; and that he thought it better for Austria to get her share, be it what it might of the inheritance of Turkey, than to spend any money or exertion in helping Turkey to continue to enjoy that inheritance herself.[153]

The Sultan, Mahmud II, meanwhile, aware of the acute external interest in his empire's fortunes, was steeling himself for a final showdown with an insubordinate Pasha. Palmerston's position was unequivocal and he hoped that British support for a (concerted European) defence of the Sultan would achieve many things at once: British routes to the east would be safeguarded by a fortified and stabilised Ottoman Empire; Russian power and territorial aggrandisement would be checked in the Near East; and a concert of the great powers would help mask Britain's inability to live up to the rhetoric of hegemonic power that characterised so many foreign policy declarations. More than this, opposing Mehemet Ali meshed well with the supposed liberal civilising mission of which Palmerston made so much play. As he put it in June 1839: 'For my own part, I hate Mehemet Ali, whom I consider as nothing but an arrogant barbarian, who by cunning and boldness and mother-wit has been successful by rebellion; . . . I look upon his boasted civilization of Egypt as the arrantest humbug; and I believe that he is as great a tyrant and oppressor as ever made a people wretched.'[154] Bulwer had written to Palmerston from Constantinople in the summer of 1838 that a sober and fair exercise of 'power and justice' was the route to influence in Turkey.[155] Palmerston could not, on principle, use the Ottoman Empire to further strategic aims without at the same time trying to improve it; in this he still adhered to the pursuit of the policy objectives, or 'great landmarks', which he had put to Ponsonby in 1833: 'Our great aim should be to place the Porte in a state of internal organization compatible with independence, and to urge the Govt to recruit their army and their finances, and to put their navy into some order.'[156] Internal reform of the Ottoman Empire satisfied a *realpolitik* and, to some extent *idealpolitik* agenda and represented for Palmerston both a bulwark to Russian advance and a testament (if successful) to Western superiority. As he wrote in the autumn of 1838, 'for some years past, the foundations at least of improvement have been laid; and it is certain that the daily increasing intercourse between Turkey and the other countries of Europe must in a few years, if peace can be preserved, throw much light upon the defects and weaknesses of the Turkish system, and lead to various improvements therein.'[157]

Though he spoke for a large number of Britons, however, Palmerston did not speak for them all in this. John Kinnear, for example, a traveller who had spent some time in the Levant on commercial business, published a series of letters in which, *inter alia*, he argued (conscious that he was out of step with majority opinion in Britain) that though imperfect, Mehemet Ali's 'government in Syria has not been productive of such unmitigated evil as has been represented – that it is, on the whole, better than that of the Turkish pachas who formerly ruled in that country, and that Mehemet Ali himself is by no means so universally hated as is imagined'. In a letter originally written to his family on 15 September 1839, he pointed to the extension (though not universalism) of religious tolerance, improvements in medical provision, the introduction of printing, and advances in education (especially where that had been along European lines) as evidence that Mehemet Ali 'has done something to advance the country in the scale of civilisation'. Although he acknowledged that many abuses still existed in Syria, Kinnear maintained that many had existed before Mehemet Ali arrived in that country and critics of Mehemet Ali's government simply displayed their own misunderstanding of Muslim society. 'In order to form a fair estimate of the good or evil of Mehemet Ali's government in this country [Syria],' he argued, 'you must not try it by the standards of enlightened and civilised government in Europe, but by a comparison with that which it superseded. It is not a good government, but what is bad in it belongs to the Turkish government also, and what is comparatively good is Mehemet Ali's.' When considered in context – as the government of a Muslim society and by comparison with the policies of the Ottoman Porte – Mehemet Ali's reforms, said Kinnear, 'give evidence of great energy, and of very considerable political sagacity'. Yet Kinnear himself was too steeped in European traditions to apply his own objective test: when discussing the extension of 'European education' in Syria (primarily through the spread of missionary schools) and the teaching of European languages (French and English), and a knowledge of European history and institutions, for example, he wrote that this would 'awaken the people from that self-satisfied ignorance which characterises all Oriental nations'. Thus was Mehemet Ali's encourage-ment of these 'advances' welcomed: 'Under the Turks, not only will many of his [Mehemet Ali's] reforms be overturned, but this source of knowledge and civil-isation be stopped, and the country recede into the state of barbarism which characterised the reign of the Turkish pachas'.[158]

Whether the Sultan or Mehemet Ali was the more efficacious reformer, however, in diplomatic terms, the irony of the developing crisis was that it might just as well, ultimately, serve to bring Britain and Russia closer together as push them further apart since neither could hope to outmanoeuvre the other at Constantinople.[159] Palmerston, therefore, was unwilling to commit Britain, or encourage other European powers to launch into an agreement with the Sultan *unless* Mehemet Ali's threatened declaration of independence was made good. This was explained to Reschid Pasha, the Turkish Minister for Foreign Affairs when he visited Vienna, Berlin, Paris and London on a special mission at the end of 1838. For Palmerston, an open-ended promise to Turkey risked entangling Britain in near-future Turkish attempts to reconquer Syria, which, in its offensive aspect went beyond the defensive aims of British policy towards the Ottoman Empire. The terms of Palmerston's limited alliance, therefore, fell short of what the Sultan hoped for and were rejected in April 1839 as a Turkish army crossed into Egyptian-controlled territory. Militarily the move was disastrous for Turkey and by the end of June Ibrahim had comprehensively defeated the Turkish army in northern Syria, the Sultan's army having put up scant resistance during a conflict lasting only a couple of hours, while two Turkish regiments were reported to have deserted to the Egyptians.[160] There followed a disastrous week for Turkey: on 30 June Mahmud II died and was succeeded as Sultan by sixteen-year-old Abdul Medjid, described in one later account as 'weak and stupid'. In the first week of July the Turkish navy defected to Mehemet Ali. Recognising Turkey's fragile position, on 5 July the Sultan offered Mehemet Ali terms that would have granted him hereditary possession of Egypt; recognising that Constantinople was in a poor negotiating position, however, Mehemet Ali responded by demanding the same rights in Syria and Adana. This, as everyone knew at the time, would have sounded the death knell for the Ottoman Empire; without external intervention, however, there appeared little the Sultan could do to maintain his rule and this effectively forced the hands of the great powers into making this conflict a question of European diplomacy.

Considering how to expel Mehemet Ali from Syria, Palmerston observed that he would not be removed 'by his own goodwill'. A coordinated European manoeuvre might succeed, he told Lamb, now Lord Beauvale: 'if the Five Powers, or if the 3 Powers Engd, France, Austria, or if the Two, Engd & France were to tell him that he *must* go; go he would; for go he *must*. But will the Five or the Three or the Two make their minds up to tell him this nakedly & simply, & to force him to do it? I think not. He has no right on his side; nothing but successful wrong; but even wrongful possession, if upon a great scale, does in the present imperfect state of mankind as to moral feelings inspire the vulgar with some notion of concomitant right; & nations are swayed by the vulgar & governments by nations.' Palmerston was willing to countenance a hereditary title to Egypt for Mehemet Ali by way of compromise, but on condition that all other claims were renounced. If Palmerston entertained doubts about the ability of the powers to work in tandem, however, he was no less determined that this should be pressed for; he was even willing to cede diplomatic precedence to Vienna if necessary: 'This is a most favourable moment for making such an arrangement,' he continued in his letter to Beauvale. Russia, he said, had been 'foiled and exposed in the East' and was losing influence in western Europe while the country's resources were inadequate for a major conflict. France, meanwhile, might never again be 'in better trim for acting fairly on this question' and Palmerston was convinced that the French government was 'very sincerely desirous of acting cordially with England'. Even Metternich, he thought, could be worked up 'to concert pitch'. If the Austrian minister 'could be brought to take in hand such an arrangement as I have chalked out,' argued Palmerston, 'he would do more to consolidate the peace of Europe than any man has done since the evening of the 18 of June 1815. It would indeed be a great settlement and why should not Austria have the merit of carrying it?'[161] Metternich, Palmerston maintained, deserved 'the highest praise' for his 'bold and statesmanlike' approach and he had high hopes of Austrian success as the foundation of an Austro-Franco-British alliance to counter Russian influence. Yet with the Ottoman Empire in a perpetual state of apparent near-collapse, Palmerston continued to argue for a meaningful five-power accord: one power gaining an ascendancy at Constantinople would be dangerous and, as he pointed out to Beauvale, Palmerston thought the 'peculiar emergency might give facilities for such an arrangement [of the Five powers], by bringing more openly to the eyes of all, the extent of the dangers which such an arrangement would prevent'.[162]

On 27 July 1839 the Five powers, Britain, Russia, Austria, France and Prussia, presented a note at Constantinople promising their collective support of the Sultan (and thereby narrowly averting Turkish concession to Mehemet Ali's demands). Writing optimistically at the beginning of August of this new situation, Palmerston declared that 'nothing can be more complete than the concurrence of the 5 Powers in all their opinions upon the present state of things in the Levant', and that now was 'the time to complete our work and shelve this important matter for some years to come'. There was even a hint of a diminution of his earlier fear of Russian influence, an influence which he thought now might be mitigated, indeed 'might be rendered comparatively harmless if the Five Powers were to take advantage of the unanimity and apparent confidence in each other which have been produced by the greatness & imminence of the danger, to conclude with the Sultan a treaty, by which they should for a limited time, say ten years, bind themselves to protect him in common'. Turkey might never again be a 'formidable' power, but by these means, argued Palmerston, might at least become 'a very respectable defensive power', and although he did not promise that the Ottoman Empire would survive intact for ever, he did at least believe that they could 'postpone till after the end of our own lives the great evils which a falling to pieces of Turkey would bring upon the other Powers of Europe'.[163] Thus the outlook from London at the beginning of August seemed promising: the Five were agreed, Mehemet Ali would be brought to heel (diplomatically if possible, militarily if necessary) and though he suspected France might have 'a sneaking kindness for Mehemet Ali', still with Soult in charge France seemed again a power Palmerston could work with.[164]

Yet within weeks, such optimism was shown to be misplaced. On 22 August, stipulating only that it would not cede Syria to Mehemet Ali, the Porte effectively handed over responsibility for negotiations to the Five, thereby Europeanising a war which exhaustion was stalemating anyway. Placing the emphasis on great power diplomacy, however, only served to underline how brittle was their avowed accord. British–Russian relations had always been sensitive in the Near East, while a breach was simultaneously developing between Britain and France. Though France did not declare openly for Mehemet Ali, neither would the French government adopt an anti-Egyptian line: important commercial interests in Egypt and a desire to construct a viable counterpoise to British influence in the Mediterranean area weighed heavily in Paris. Indeed, the French government began to suggest that Mehemet Ali's victories did entitle him to some gains, such as Syria; to Palmerston this was alarming: as he argued, control of Syria brought Mehemet Ali (and, if matters went badly any power that allied with him) dangerously close to routes to India and the Persian Gulf, striking at the heart of British imperial interests. Here then were possible grounds for rapprochement between Britain and Russia where British Francophobia combined with a Russian desire to take advantage of an opportunity to conciliate a Near Eastern rival and upset whatever remained of a Franco-British entente.[165] The only certainty, however, was that nothing was certain. As Russian State Counsellor P.G. Divov had noted at the end of 1838: 'The passing year witnessed an amazing series of events which did not shake the desire of the European cabinets to guarantee peace, although they held all the while the potential to ignite war in Europe, Asia and America.'[166]

On the morning of 2 September Esterhazy sent Palmerston what he called 'not . . . a very diplomatic note', but one which went 'to the point'. 'This is Sunday,' he wrote, '& good folks eat their plum pudding. Now *before* this is brought into any proper shape or form it is required that the cooks should have agreed completely about all the materials it is to consist of, from the oatmeal to the currants. *I have reason* to recommend you particularly not to lose sight of this culinary principle. We have many cooks, and if you begin the next discussion about the *form*, *before* all the materials are agreed upon I am afraid we shall have no pudding at all.'[167] Palmerston, for his part, was determined to uphold the integrity of the Ottoman Empire and resist the secession of Egypt (with Syria): 'confederation', he said, should be considered only 'when unity shall have been proved to be impossible'.[168] On 19 September Palmerston drafted a memorandum on how Mehemet Ali might be compelled to evacuate Syria in which he set out terms granting hereditary tenure of Egypt to Mehemet Ali and specified the tribute payable to the Sultan as well as Egyptian military obligations to the Ottoman Empire, all of which was to be put into effect, if necessary, by force of arms of the Five powers combined. However, as Palmerston acknowledged at the end of this document, French participation was not certain.[169] Palmerston had told Beauvale a few days earlier that success was still possible without France, but it was important to keep Britain aligned with Russia and Austria whose cooperation was much more valuable. Brunnow had arrived in London from St Petersburg in mid-September to open discussions about the East, which Palmerston believed was a sign that Russia 'will do anything we like, & either with or without France', although Brunnow hoped to keep France on side if possible. France, he said, had been 'behaving very shabbily' but with Russia and Britain acting together, 'we shall compel her to be honest in spite of herself'.[170] Palmerston began to lay aside his earlier misgivings about Russia and even to speak of military and naval cooperation between the two countries.[171]

This warming in Russo-British relations did not go unnoticed in Paris and in October France rejected Palmerston's proposed compromise solution to the impasse over Syria, of granting Mehemet Ali Acre as well as Egypt.[172] Britain's points of difference with Russia were now 'less than with France', Palmerston told Hobhouse, 'and it is more likely we should come to an understanding with the autocrat than with Louis Philippe'.[173] The ideological division of the continent was no less apparent but where and how Palmerston aligned Britain amid that fissuring remained fluid and negotiable. Brunnow was emphatic, however: 'The Anglo-French alliance is already dead', he wrote late in November 1839. 'England is still not with us [Russia]; but neither is she with France.... England is a widow. To marry her much skill and patience are needed, for she is a handsome and capricious woman'.[174]

The rapprochement with Russia could not have been more productive of friendly relations. Palmerston had been encouraged by Brunnow's mission (as well as finding Brunnow himself agreeable – a mutual personal regard)[175] and by early November Palmerston was professing his confidence in Russian good faith. It helped, no doubt, that before he arrived in London Brunnow had consulted Shee in Stuttgart 'as to his own bearing in London' and Shee had duly advised him to avoid not only the government's parliamentary opponents, but also certain members of the Cabinet known to be hostile to Palmerston.[176] Palmerston in turn urged Shee to cooperate with Russia '*with discretion*', in order 'to encourage this humour of hers while it lasts especially as we do not for the moment hit matters off clearly with France'.[177] When Algeria declared war against France at the end of the year, Palmerston could not have been more satisfied: with a demonstrable unity between Britain, Russia and, by extension, also Austria and Prussia over Turkey, and now a crisis within its own empire (the 'French certainly have not the knack of managing their affairs successfully', said Palmerston), France might soon be expected to fall into line over Egypt, he thought.[178]

Yet Palmerston remained wary of placing too much trust in potential allies. His confidence in Russia was only ever expressed in conditional terms and though he thought Britain and France were drifting apart, never did he imply that this was irreversible. In the meantime, he made it clear that he was willing to commit Britain alone to the defence of the Sultan if necessary, and when this raised alarm among certain members of the government, Palmerston defended his course robustly. 'This Turkish question is one of more extensive interest & importance to England than any other European question in which we have been engaged of late years', he explained to Melbourne, 'and no administration could well stand the blame which would be thrown upon it, if by its neglect or indifference the projects of aggrandisement in the Levant either of Russia or of France were to be carried into accomplishment to the manifest detriment of England'.[179]

In January 1840 Britain and Russia reached an understanding that any settlement of the Eastern question required that Mehemet Ali be confined to

Egypt; to this they secured the assent of Austria and Prussia. If France was initially unhappy about these terms, the change in the French government in March made agreement between the Five powers even less likely. Thiers, who replaced Soult at the head of this administration, proved less willing than his predecessor to compromise on Mehemet Ali's claims to Syria.[180] Palmerston's belief that France would soon come to terms with the other four powers over the crisis and that France was 'extremely anxious to get out of her isolated position and to have a decent excuse for putting an end to the wasteful and ruinous expense which her armaments occasion', was shown to be so much wishful thinking.[181] Palmerston was forced to concede that in fact little progress was being made in solving the Mehemet Ali crisis largely because France's intentions were unknown,[182] and by the end of March he had come to the conclusion that France, or at least Thiers, could not be relied upon. 'Thiers professes much attachment to the alliance with England;' Palmerston wrote to Beauvale, 'but he is a slippery fellow, & not to be depended upon for anything, nor can any body safely reckon upon what he will do under any given circumstances.' It was clear, he argued,

> that France has vast schemes of ambition along the whole of the southern coast of the Mediterranean, and that the separation of Egypt & Syria from the Ottoman Empire is part of her plan. That done she would convert them into protected dependencies, and as England would cling to the Sultan, while France would take part with his rival, she would always be able to outbid us in Egypt, and would be paramount in influence over the separate state. This is a matter of great moment to us, but if possible of still greater moment to Austria. But such being the schemes of France she will pursue them as far as she can and dares, whoever may be her ministers and she will stop only when stoutly and firmly opposed.[183]

France was, or rather 'a few intriguers at Paris' were, Palmerston feared, seeking to 'controul the other Four Powers, and dictate to Europe, and lay the foundations for future war'; thus, he argued, negotiations among the Four must succeed, preferably with the addition of France, but without if necessary.[184]

In support of this objective, Palmerston had adopted a secondary, parallel, course of action, designed to swing the popular mood in favour of concerted great power action and against support of Mehemet Ali – not just in Britain but particularly in central Europe where he felt Prussian and Austrian backing might prove useful. Knowing that the *Morning Chronicle* was widely regarded as a ministerial organ Palmerston was alarmed to see that its Constantinople correspondent had 'become intirely Mehemet Aliish'. He asked George Hodges, who was on the spot, to 'endeavour to inspire him with sounder views'.[185] There were plentiful means by which a resourceful (Palmerstonian) diplomat could effect such a change of mind. Averting a misconstruction of the British government's position was one thing, but Palmerston also saw scope to influence diplomacy if he could manipulate domestic opinion abroad. His press contacts in the German states, for example, extended now beyond the offices of the *Augsburg Gazette* and in March he asked Shee to look into the possibility of getting some articles favourable to the Sultan and hostile to Mehemet Ali into the *Allgemeine Zeitung*. Invoking again the language of civilisation and progress, Palmerston sketched out a series of subjects that might sway readers in Germany. The topics, he said might be:

> The right of the Sultan, and the injustice & treachery of Mehemet & his baseness in turning against the Sultan means entrusted to him by the Sultan for very different purposes. The tyrannical system of the Pasha's govt which has ground the Egyptians down to the dust, and impoverished the whole people, leaving none rich but himself; while the only use to which he applies his ill gotten gains, is to create armies & fleets for the purpose of carrying on still further aggressions against his sovereign. He has been represented by some as a promoter of civilization, but it ought not to be forgotten that during the Greek Revolution he had conceived the scheme of carrying off the whole population of the Morea to be slaves in Egypt, and of repeopling the Morea with Arabs & Egyptians; and he was only prevented from doing this by the interference of the Three Powers. The peace of Europe & the maintenance of the balance of power require that the Ottoman Empire should be maintained in its independence & integrity. But what becomes of either if Mehemet is allowed to lever Egypt Syria & Arabia & Bagdad from the Empire under the pretence of an hereditary government, which next year he would convert into an independent dominion. The interests of Germany France & England require that this should be prevented.

Contemporaneous reports in the French press suggested that the French government hoped for a protective alliance with an independent Mehemet Ali in Egypt and Syria that would 'make the Mediterranean a French lake' and Palmerston hoped to demonstrate that this could only be achieved at the cost of a war that France might well lose.[186] Palmerston's suggestions were incorporated in an article which appeared in the *Allgemeine Zeitung* shortly afterwards.[187] It would be an exaggeration to suggest that this article did much to alter the course of great power diplomacy. What it does point to, however, is Palmerston's continued, and developing, faith in the power of public opinion to influence political decisions and his consequent exertions to master techniques by which to guide that opinion. It is significant, too, that his popular arguments against Mehemet Ali emphasised the moral dimension to any judgement on his rule; expansion of Egyptian influence was not only a threat to the balance of power but was also, he insisted, a menace to popular liberties.

The Ottoman government, meanwhile, stepped up its calls for the great power protection that had been promised in July 1839, making direct appeals in April and May for a mediated solution. Negotiations centred, as before, on Mehemet Ali's claims to Syria and although proposals were put forward granting Mehemet Ali much of southern Syria, or even lifetime possession of the country, the French government dug in its heels and insisted that it would endorse nothing less than hereditary possession of the whole of Syria for Mehemet Ali. By the end of June it was apparent that an attempted concert solution was not going to be possible.[188] In London, Palmerston insisted that Britain could not allow the Porte to make damaging concessions to Egypt, but he faced growing Cabinet unease about sticking to a strident policy that offended the Francophile sensibilities of a number of Whig ministers and threatened to embroil Britain in extended military engagements. While the prospect of a genuine five-power accord held, ministers in Britain reluctantly sanctioned Palmerston's policy,[189] but once France had made clear its separation from the rest, their doubts multiplied. Shortly after the French had drawn a line in the Syrian sand, Melbourne warned Palmerston that he was not optimistic that his policy would continue to enjoy the backing of his colleagues. 'Some are, as you know, entirely for Mehemet Ali,' he wrote on 4 July, 'others will be apprehensive of the House of Commons & the country, upon neither of whom can any reliance be placed for support & depend upon it that intelligence from Alexandria & the disposition shewn by Mehemet with respect to the Turkish fleet will, whether it ought or not, have a great effect upon their minds.'[190] Lords Clarendon and Holland were both firmly opposed to Palmerston's policy and among other members of the Cabinet Palmerston found 'such lukewarmness' that he decided on a threat of resignation to force the issue.[191] He wrote to Melbourne on 5 July tendering his resignation, telling him that he was tired of being undermined by colleagues (particularly when recent history bore out his view rather than that of his opponents, of the dangers posed by Mehemet Ali),[192] but the Prime Minister, who saw as a result of this move the inevitable and speedy destruction of his government, told Palmerston he was being 'premature' and suggested his perceived isolation in Cabinet was not yet certain; Howick, for example, was reported to have said that many members of the government remained undecided and looked for an opportunity to discuss the matter carefully. Besides, Melbourne continued, defeat loomed elsewhere, over Canadian policy, for example, and it would be better, he thought, to fall over that than over differences 'upon these Oriental affairs'.[193] Wishing to avert a ministerial crisis, Melbourne again pressed Palmerston to reflect on the ramifications of his resignation a couple of days later, and urged him to reconsider his determination in the light of growing

Whig disquiet.[194] Palmerston, however, viewed anything less than determined support for the Sultan as 'injurious to the interests of my country, & full of danger to the peace of Europe'.[195] More than this, as he told Beauvale, Britain's prestige and authority were at stake: 'for if we had shrunk from pursuing a course separate from that of France and if we had truckled to the French Govt upon this occasion, we should henceforward justly have been considered as merely a second rate power in Europe, held in leading strings by France, and incapable of any manly and independent course of action'.[196] Not for the last time, Palmerston found that by these means he could bring his colleagues to heel: in the face of his threatened resignation, the 'dissidents', he said, 'withdrew their opposition, and the waverers came round to my views'.[197]

The entente with France apparently abandoned and his colleagues, however reluctantly, in agreement, Palmerston proceeded to negotiate with Russia, Austria, Prussia and Turkey a convention which was signed in London on 15 July 1840. This was intended to underwrite a final settlement of the Mehemet Ali question. The Four committed themselves to protect the Sultan and granted Mehemet Ali Egypt on hereditary terms and Syria for his lifetime, albeit subject to Ottoman suzerainty, providing he accepted these terms within a specified number of days. Egyptian military forces were also to be placed under Turkish control. No less significantly, the Straits, through which Russia had enjoyed privileged access since 1833, were now to be closed to all foreign warships in peacetime. The powers insisted that the terms of the agreement were not disclosed to France. Neither the French government nor the French newspapers welcomed these developments.[198] Palmerston, however, was not concerned about French discontent; France, he said, had neither the means nor the will to go to war with the Four powers in support of Egypt. And if France did decide to test its naval strength against Britain, Britain's first act would be to cut off communication between France and Algiers and 'fever and the Moors would soon dispose of the French troops in Africa'. As well as Algeria, Palmerston also threatened, in the event of continued French non-cooperation, an attack on France's colonial possessions in the West Indies: 'and we should take them both without trouble;' he said, 'the Arabs would help us expel the French from Africa, the blacks whom we should emancipate, would help us to drive them out of the West Indies'.[199] Mehemet Ali himself was to be told 'that we are not guided by any ill-will to him in the course which we are pursuing but solely by paramount considerations of European policy, and indeed the terms we offer him are the best proof that we do not wish to destroy him, or to press upon him more heavily than necessary but he should clearly comprehend that these offers are like the Sibylline Books and that the longer he holds off the less he will ultimately get'.[200] Palmerston was confident of success. 'Mehemet Ali though he is merciless enough to the weak, has a thoroughly Mussulman respect for the strong;' he wrote to Holland, 'and I should be very much surprized indeed if at 72 he were to change his natural character & run a muck.

His successes through life have been the result of a prudent comparison of means with ends, and of a cautious calculation of risks & consequences.'[201] At the end of July Guizot told Melbourne that though events might prompt France to take action, so far as the Mehemet Ali question in Syria was concerned, 'if you end it quick, you will have judged right. If it drags into length, you will have made a mistake. I only come to advertise you that under all circumstances you can rely upon the quiescence of France.'[202] Palmerston was delighted. France had apparently been checkmated and Britain, Russia, Austria and Prussia had agreed a mutually satisfactory settlement of a perpetual source of diplomatic friction.[203]

Again the optimism was premature. Tensions between Britain and France continued and were magnified by being translated into domestic Cabinet squabbles in London which revealed, as Melbourne was to put it, how 'a great measure' in the Convention of July had been 'undertaken upon a basis of support so slender and so uncertain.'[204]

Lord Spencer, who, as Lord Althorp, had played a leading role in Grey's government of 1830–34, expressed the dismay of several Whigs at seeing the fissuring of Britain's relations with France. 'I have as you know always thought that the only means there were of preserving the peace of Europe was a cordial feeling between France & this country,' he wrote to Melbourne in early August. This was, furthermore, a view Palmerston had himself endorsed, he continued, and the current alignment of Britain with Russia, Austria and Prussia against France was 'so total a breaking up of the whole system on which Grey's government as well as yours has been acting' as to threaten a continental war 'in a very short space of time.'[205] Palmerston well knew that colleagues were whispering such criticisms of his policy, but he dismissed talk of a dangerous breach developing with France. War between the two countries, he maintained, was 'extremely improbable' and while French newspapers had been 'blowing their hurricane', the French government's communications, he said, had been 'invariably pacific'. Guizot had told Palmerston that France would 'remain quiet' and watch events, but since Britain had no intention of dismembering Turkey Palmerston did not believe events would lead to conflict.[206] Not only did France have no legitimate grounds of complaint against Britain, but the very excitability of French public opinion was, said Palmerston, reason enough to trust to the country's aversion to war: the 'violence of the French newspapers still further confirmed me in my conviction that France would be peaceable', he told Shee, 'because they who mean to strike do not often prelude their blows by a volley of scolding'. Meanwhile, the Treaty of July, which Palmerston now described as 'our Quintuple Treaty', he judged 'as good a job as our Quadruple one was and I trust we shall one of these days be able to say in a Queen's speech the same thing of the one which we said three days ago of the other namely that *"its objects have been accomplished"*'.[207] The course he had pursued, he was confident, was the only one 'which could prevent the affairs of the Levant from creating serious disturbance to the peace of Europe' and driving Mehemet Ali out of Syria would not be 'so difficult as some imagine'.[208] Palmerston attributed the recent tensions between Britain and France to petty jealousies: 'I never placed the slightest trust in Thiers professed attachment to English alliance,' he said, suggesting that the 'only meaning of it was that he meant to make us his dupes & employ us as his instruments for serving French purposes', and adding that it was exacerbated by the malign patronage of the French minister by Palmerston's long-term rival, Edward Ellice.[209] When Thiers was dismissed and replaced by Guizot in late 1840, the latter's professions of peaceful intent carried more weight.

Colleagues saw this as so much Palmerstonian bravado. Russell worried that Palmerston and Thiers had both been engaged in a test of nerve, neither willing 'to lower the dignity of their respective nations by using the first word of concil-iation', long after real points of difference had been resolved. Indeed, he feared this antagonism played into the hands of Russia who, though for the moment working alongside Britain, 'would be glad to have us engaged more deeply, & desperately against France'.[210] By the late summer there was 'great uneasiness upon these Eastern affairs' within the Cabinet and Russell led the Whig attempts to press a more conciliatory line on France.[211] Melbourne issued a blunt warning to Palmerston in mid-September: 'The present state of things, unless you can find a way out of it or something that will open a prospect of a speedy termination to it, will lead to a dissolution of the government. This will be an evil for the country because it will appear & it will be, that the English government will have been changed by the outcry of the press & populace of Paris, & by the mere apprehension of a serious difference with France. What a prospect for the country & [?government] who are hereafter to administer its affairs.'[212] Russell was 'in a very uneasy state' as Palmerston continued to ignore his proposals ('rather peremptorily & without much reason being given');[213] so too, by this point, was the Queen, who, with Melbourne's backing, Palmerston was told, 'urges strongly fresh overtures to France'.[214] Victoria, it was reported by Beauvale, was being worked on by Leopold 'with his intriguing disposition' to get Palmerston replaced with Clarendon, who, it was felt, would steer a course closer to France. Beauvale urged his sister (and now also Palmerston's wife), Emily (who did not at this point entertain a very high opinion of Victoria),[215] to show the Queen in turn how she was in danger of being led into an 'unEnglish course': Leopold was too dependent on France, he said, and 'Louis Philippe thinks it his interest to get rid of Palmerston and he is far too *retors* to be moved by any motive but his interest, but the Queen should be taught that its being Louis Philippe's interest to be rid of him sufficiently proves it to be hers to keep him.'[216] It was this tension that had prompted Lord Ashley to seek a meeting with Palmerston to outline his plan, as Emily explained at the beginning of September, of 'writing constantly in the Times against Mehemet Ali to unmask his bad proceedings & take away all sympathy from his atrocious character'; 'would not this do good[?]' she asked.[217] It was better, said Ashley, that this was not done in Palmerston's own name, indeed his participation 'must not even be suspected', and Ashley himself offered to write the necessary articles in order to '*impress the* public mind more deeply with the atrocious character & conduct of Mehemet Ali' by 'repeated statements' in the larger newspapers two or three times a week.[218]

Palmerston, meanwhile, conceded that ministerial 'boxing matches' ought, so far as possible, to be kept within the confines of the Cabinet, but he could not resist laying before Holland, one of his critics in Cabinet, what he took to be the true state of parliamentary opinion on Eastern affairs. An 'intelligent' back-bench MP and 'staunch Whig' had spoken to Palmerston on 17 September, suggesting that Palmerston's policy in the East enjoyed widespread support on both sides of the House and 'that the only danger we have to fear springs from among ourselves; that there are persons belonging to the government itself, who hold language upon these matters, more resembling that which men in opposition would hold with respect to the measures of a government which they wanted to drive out, than like that which members of a government hold with respect to the measures of the government to which they belong; he said that this was doing much harm; that it was damaging the government by creating a division among those who support it, and was adding to the danger of war, by encouraging the French govt in the line they are pursuing'.[219]

By the end of September, the Cabinet was seriously divided. Melbourne was growing weary of the 'talking at Holland House' and though that salon was a useful 'point of union for the party', he began to question its long-term value.[220] Russell continued to lead pleas for negotiation with France on the basis of France's '*good faith* at Alexandria' that would lead to the acceptance of Mehemet Ali's calls for hereditary claims to Egypt and lifetime possession of Syria. Lords Holland, Clarendon and Lansdowne all backed Russell, as did Prince Albert, who hoped to prove to Palmerston that negotiation with France would not be 'construed into a demonstration of fear'. Palmerston disliked negotiating the compromise of a treaty which had not yet been put into effect and insisted that 'if we give way now it will be to the menaces of France, & that if we so yield when backed by all Europe, all Europe will treat us henceforward like a nation afraid to fight; France will take Morocco & Tunis in spite of our teeth & will settle every other matter her own way, Russia will do what she likes in Asia, and the disputed territory will be laid hold of by the United States'. Melbourne, Minto, Labouchere, Sir Francis Baring, Normanby and John Hobhouse tended to back Palmerston (though, it should be acknowledged, Baring 'hesitate[d] from the natural dread a Chancellor of the Exchequer has of war estimates' and Normanby's opposition was described by Palmerston as being 'not for' Russell).[221]

In a letter to Charles Napier in early October, Palmerston reiterated his distinction between the 'swaggering and threatening' tone of French newspapers and the moderation of the French government in its disavowal of calls for armed support for Mehemet Ali. However, he also argued for a 'speedy termination' of the question for fear that delay until the spring might 'lead to embarrassing dissensions between us and the French' (which by that time the French might be better placed to do something about from a military point of view).[222] Although good Whig ministers such as Lansdowne, who felt that care was needed 'when there is so much irritable amour propre to be dealt with', urged that Britain at least 'keep the door open for future good understanding' with France,[223] Palmerston's friends saw only evidence of intrigues against the Foreign Secretary within Westminster circles. Charles Greville, for example, was known to be in correspondence with Guizot to whom he communicated news of the ministerial divisions, describing in one such letter the 'factious and profligate opposition which would thwart your exertions to maintain the world in peace' and the 'pernicious influence which has been so unaccountably permitted to predominate in our councils'.[224] Greville also provided Guizot with access to certain British newspapers, acting as a link between the French minister and Thomas Barnes of *The Times*, allowing Guizot to remedy items published in London 'calculated to produce a very mischievous effect here' (in this particular case a letter to *The Times* from Constantinople which 'I do not believe to be true').[225] Palmerston was alerted to this connection in October 1840 by Ashley who told him in '*strictest confidence*' that 'The Times paper has exhibited lately a leaning to Mehmet Ali; this is caused, I am told, by the influence of Guizot who has communicated with one of its editors thro' the intervention of a man who, *tho not a Cabinet minister*, is *necessarily* cognizant of many *secrets of council*. You had better be on your guard; this same person is reported to be intriguing generally; & I can well believe it.' Palmerston had no difficulty identifying the schemer as Greville.[226] When French dispatches appeared in the newspapers, Guizot, for his part, sought to reassure Palmerston that leaks in the press from the French government did not come from him, but from a subordinate intent on stirring up intrigue.[227] Palmerston complained sardonically that he might as well withdraw his ambassador in Paris and the two countries could conduct their relations through the pages of *The Times*, the *Morning Chronicle*, the *Journal des Débats* and *Le Capital*.[228] Guizot and Palmerston both knew what could be achieved by these means. Palmerston certainly was in the habit of sending material to trusted newspaper allies, such as John Easthope at the *Chronicle* (with whom he discussed foreign policy openly and sometimes unguardedly), to whom he sent '*confidential* communications', 'solely', he said, 'that you may know what has really happened'.[229]

While the different parties in the Cabinet and at Westminster debated how best to deal with France and settle the affairs in Syria and Egypt, the great powers hovered uneasily on the brink of war throughout September and October 1840. Only the defeat of Mehemet Ali's forces in Syria in October reduced this risk and Palmerston was evidently relieved to report to Hobhouse that he had learned from Guizot that France would be satisfied if Mehemet Ali was left in possession of Egypt. These 'things have shewn that we were in earnest; that the intrigues put into play had not stopped the execution of the treaty, and that our means of execution are fully adequate for our object', he concluded.[230]

The tensions within the British government, however, remained as divisive as ever. Palmerston complained in October that he was still struggling in the Cabinet against colleagues who wanted Mehemet Ali to be given possession of Acre, and who seemed intent on handing an advantage to France. He was, he said, 'surprized and much grieved at the want of courage & national feeling' among some colleagues and told Hobhouse that if 'we had not had among us some people who are *men* such as yourself & Minto, the government would have gone to pieces or have been disgraced'.[231] Melbourne, however, continued to press Palmerston to adopt a more conciliatory line towards France but, as Palmerston minuted on one such appeal from the Prime Minister, this was tantamount to asking him 'to yield to French threats and intrigues, which I was fully resolved never should be done by *me*'.[232] Though he doubted its authenticity, Palmerston had in mind a report recently received from a source in Paris which stated that the French government was plotting revenge on Britain for having formed an alliance with Russia and Austria by releasing 30,000 Carlists with a view to reviving the civil war in Spain, with France siding with either party to secure an ascendancy in the peninsula while the other powers were preoccupied elsewhere. At the very least, the Spanish government should, he thought, 'be on its guard, & should take all measures of precaution within its reach'.[233]

Crucially, during this period Russell shifted his position. In late September Russell had been insistent that the government 'demonstrate our willingness to settle the question by negotiation',[234] and when, at the end of the month, it seemed Palmerston had finally established his ascendancy over the Cabinet, Russell informed Palmerston he was disposed to resign, 'leaving to you the whole credit of the success of your policy', which, he said, it 'seems to me that I have no right to share in any claim to foresight, when my predictions are anything but sanguine'.[235] Yet, however much traditional Whig sympathies for a French alliance persisted, it was patently clear that Russia, Austria and Prussia all stood alongside Britain against France and French support for Mehemet Ali, and such odds were too steep to overcome. In early November, therefore, Russell wrote to Palmerston to propose draft instructions to Ponsonby, whom he had until recently been insisting must be removed from Constantinople, hoping thereby still to contribute to the deliberations on British policy.[236] Palmerston was evidently in no mood to proffer olive branches. He endorsed Russell's letter simply to note that these proposals were 'Not adopted by me'.[237] Palmerston had told Hobhouse in October that Russell's change of heart surprised him: Russell was, he had thought, 'stouter of heart and firmer in mind, but he has been worked upon by private influences'.[238] He later identified these influences as the duc de Broglie, acting on behalf of Thiers, as well as 'other influences at home', no doubt the familiar collection of Whig and Radical discontents. Hence Palmerston's reluctance to weigh Russell's views too seriously: 'He is discontented with himself and with others,' wrote Palmerston, 'he wants to *do something* and as all that is good & useful in this matter is doing without him he is casting about to see what mischief he can do in order to be able to say that he has controuled & thwarted us in something.' It did not speak of reconciliation that Palmerston expected Russell to 'start some new crotchet upon us' within a matter of days.[239] The friction between Palmerston and his colleagues did not go unnoticed: as the King of the Belgians observed in a letter to Prince Albert, 'Palmerston, *rex* and autocrat' was becoming 'far *too irritable and violent*'.[240]

Lansdowne continued to sound the Whig call for resurrection of an entente with France, arguing that political instability in Paris, notably the fall of Thiers, was a sign of Louis Philippe's determination to 'recover if he can the English alliance'. It would be 'madness', said Lansdowne, not to favour Louis Philippe's 'attempt by every means that does not compromise our honor & our engagements', not least because this was the best way to stave off war or revolution across the Channel. Moreover, he argued, the French people would welcome a renewal of cross-Channel friendship and it would serve Palmerston's other goal of keeping close with Austria since Metternich had been no admirer of Thiers.[241] Palmerston was unconvinced. Having carried his points in Cabinet he was not willing to make concessions to France now. He believed the powers would soon succeed in removing Mehemet Ali from Syria and he dismissed talk of needing to support Guizot and Louis Philippe. Palmerston thought Guizot just as likely as Thiers to argue for Mehemet Ali and said that as for Louis Philippe, 'He & Thiers have been playing off a grand piece of acting; they understand each other tolerably well and Thiers will probably wish to enjoy the money he has made in the funds, & will not for the present endanger it by getting up a revolution.' Talk of war, he said, was exaggerated.[242]

Guizot saw Palmerston in London at the end of October and left the Foreign Secretary certain that he did not mean to lead France on a collision course with Britain.[243] It was Britain (and Austria), said Palmerston, that had made an 'immense concession' in the affair by allowing Mehemet Ali even to retain an hereditary claim to Egypt ('I would pledge my existence that if we were to go on with hostilities we would drive Mehemet clean out of Egypt before the end of July') and he was not yet willing to relent in his suspicions of France: 'It has been manifest for four or five years that a desire for war with somebody has been growing up among a certain portion of the French people;' he wrote in a letter to Beauvale, 'and though there have grown up also counteracting interests to which war would be highly injurious yet incidents might at any time happen that might bring on a quarrel upon some point of honor.'[244] Palmerston's position, then, was still a fraught one. Ashley tried to help: 'I have sent you a dozen of strong beer, brewed at St Giles', for your own especial drinking. It is too good for any strangers who may dine at your house,' he wrote on 9 November. 'Taken in moderation, it will give you enormous pluck, & enable you to stand firm against Mehmet Ali, & every Frenchman, whether they be found in Paris or in the Cabinet.'[245]

By the second half of November Palmerston thought his policy vindicated. France, it seemed, would advise Mehemet Ali finally to give up all claims to Syria and though Palmerston believed the powers could demand more, a settlement that saw Mehemet Ali keep Egypt was better than a prolongation of the crisis. And anyway, there were still tricky battles to win at home: the 'cabals in the Cabinet and out of it by those in connections with some persons in it still go on,' he wrote to Hobhouse and, though 'very reluctant' to believe his colleagues guilty of 'unfair play', he could not deny that *The Times* seemed to have access to a member of the Cabinet.[246] Lord Clarendon was certainly believed to be using the *Morning Herald* (which was already exploiting foreign sources to undermine Palmerston's diplomacy)[247] to publish Cabinet discussions and further damage Palmerston.[248] Thus Palmerston advised his friend at the *Morning Chronicle*, John Easthope, to be wary of ongoing intrigues at home and, especially, those emanating from Paris.[249]

Though 'a mean jealousy' had driven France to try to undermine Britain, Palmerston rejoiced that France's 'dishonest course' had ultimately redounded to Britain's advantage: it had served only to strengthen Britain's ties with other European powers (including erstwhile rivals such as Russia), and given Britain a platform on which to demonstrate military and naval superiority. Thus, 'we have been greatly raised by the very efforts made to pull us down'.[250] Surveying the country's diplomatic position towards the end of the year, Palmerston presented an upbeat assessment of Britain's standing: 'We grappled with Russia last year in Asia, & having beaten her we have got her for a civil & for the present well conducted friend, we have now grappled with France, and have beaten her, and she will be likewise well behaved for some little time to come.'[251] He looked forward to 'the permanent establishment of an intimate good understanding between England & Austria' on the back of recent cooperation between the two countries against Mehemet Ali and France;[252] indeed, such an alignment was essential to peace and Palmerston thought the Austrian fear of French 'principles' and the British fear of France's 'political ambition' would hold them together and perhaps induce Spain to join them as well.[253] Elsewhere he saw only good news, from Europe to the Far East: 'We shall have a capital story to tell about external affairs when Parliament meets,' he wrote to Hobhouse. 'But our colleagues ought to be greatly obliged to you Minto and me, for we have furnished them with a good catalogue of deeds and yet I do not think that all of them are as much pleased as they ought to be. However as the French say there is nothing succeeds like success, and all past differences will now be merged in our common triumphs.' With Ibrahim's forces in Syria 'melt[ing] away like snow before the sun',[254] Palmerston's only regret, as he told Beauvale, was that he had not insisted on more severe terms against Mehemet Ali: granting him an hereditary pashalik in Egypt was, Palmerston felt, an unnecessary concession that would make him more difficult to control in the future.[255]

Given the difficult nature of the negotiations over the Mehemet Ali question both at home and abroad, it is perhaps not surprising that Palmerston tried to use the press to justify his recent actions in public estimation. The *Examiner* began to 'come round' from its 'shabby and absurd line', said Lady Palmerston at the beginning of December and she found it 'a great pleasure to see all our enemies floundering in the mud, and not knowing how to get on their legs again'.[256] The *Chronicle*'s treatment of the recent debates, she continued, revealed Thiers as 'wretched' and even 'a disreputable villain', Guizot as standing 'a little awkwardly on two or three points' and Holland and Clarendon's cabal ruined. Such an account 'only places you on a higher pinnacle of glory', she told her husband. Even the Tories were apparently 'loud' in their praises.[257] Ashley assured Palmerston that the same article 'will prove to you that we have begun to prevail in our turn'.[258] Palmerston, meanwhile, coached John Scanlan, editor of the *Observer*, on how to present recent events, not least 'that all the boastings of the French about their projected alliance with Russia against England are mere childish ebullitions of pique, and silly attempts to sow distrust & disunion among the allies'; attempts that would not, he said, succeed.[259]

Palmerston's faith in a liberal foreign policy had been publicly tested over the Eastern question and certainly he was not willing to be hamstrung by a rigid ideological commitment when *realpolitik* considerations demanded an accommodation with 'autocratic' governments. Yet, there remained an important undercurrent of liberalism that continued to infuse Palmerston's broader policy objectives. Palmerston carried on working, for example, for an end to the slave trade. Though this issue did not attract, and has not attracted,[260] the same level of attention as more high-profile subjects such as the Eastern question – which raised the spectre of war and was, therefore, to Victorian minds, of more fundamental significance – Palmerston continued to use his and Britain's position to agitate for 'improvement'. In May 1841 he told the House of Commons that

As long as England remains pre-eminent on the ocean of human affairs, there are none, be they ever so unfortunate, none, be their condition ever so desperate or forlorn, who do not turn with a look of hope to the light that beams from here. They may be beyond the reach of our power, still our moral sympathy and our influence can support them under their reverses, and hold out to them, in the midst of their difficulties, the hope of better days. But if by the assaults of her enemies, or the errors of her sons, England should fall, or her star lose its lustre, with her would fall the hopes of the Africans, whether on their own continent or on the vast regions of America; and they would for a time at least be buried in despair. (Loud cheers.) I know no nation that is now ready to supply our place.[261]

Of course, it was not Palmerston's exclusive right to claim this moral high ground for Britain's opposition to slavery and the slave trade. Considerable British opposition to the trade pre-dated his arrival at front-line politics. Of the slave-trading nations, Portugal remained one of the most active, at least in Europe, and Britain's relations with Portugal had, since 1808, been influenced by a British insistence that any proposed alliance between the two must include provision for the 'gradual disuse and ultimate and not distant abolition of the [slave] trade'. This, indeed, had been enshrined in a treaty of alliance and friendship signed in 1810 and more generally forced on Portugal as part of the negotiations at Vienna in 1815. Further agreements in 1817 and 1819 saw mutual rights of search, and two courts of mixed commission further attack the trading system. It was attacked, but not defeated, however, and reductions in slave traffic in the early 1830s had almost as much to do with a temporary saturation of the Brazilian market as any acts of British or Portuguese suppression. Evasion of the various treaty regulations was notorious and, especially with confusion over the extent of British rights of search in the southern hemisphere, the trade often continued there under Portuguese flags of convenience. Palmerston had entered office in 1830 keen to close such loopholes and hopeful of pressing Portugal to adopt stricter rules against slave trading in Portugal and in Portuguese territory in Africa. Only when civil war abated in the peninsula in 1834 did an opportunity present itself, however, and negotiations proved slow. Even when the trade was declared illegal by Portugal in December 1836, the legislation to back that up was too weak to be effective. Lord Howard de Walden, Britain's representative in Lisbon, had taken a new draft treaty with him in the autumn of 1834 but it was more than a year before any progress was made with negotiations and even then they were long-drawn-out, lasting until the early part of 1838.[262]

Palmerston was frustrated that large sums of money, including remitted loans, had been spent on this issue and pressed de Walden to hold a firm line in Lisbon. 'The unrestricted permission to transfer domestic slaves from the continent to the islands would open a door to abuses which we should have no means afterwards to prevent, and the intire prohibition of such transfers would be the best security against such an abuse,' he wrote in July 1836. 'But we are willing to agree to such a modification of the prohibition as shall give scope to the bona fide transfers; without permitting any extensive abuse. We are not dictating to Portugal, we are only asking her to fulfil contracted engagements.'[263] Palmerston made the same point to the Portuguese government directly, telling Viscount Torre de Moncorvo: 'if an unlimited exportation of slaves from your possessions on the coast of Africa to your islands, is to be permitted, there will be no limit to the slave trade which will thus be sanctioned, except the capacity of your islands to receive and employ fresh slaves. No consideration shall induce me to agree to a treaty by which England would thus deliberately sanction, not merely a continuance, but a renewal of the slave trade; and upon your government must rest the responsibility of any measures we may be compelled to resort to.'[264] Aware that parliamentary champions of abolition were watching events carefully, Palmerston was keen to be seen to be doing something and took an increasingly tough line, insisting that he was prepared to go to war with Portugal over the issue if necessary.[265] Commercial negotiations between the two countries, Palmerston complained, were becoming 'a farce',[266] but as he told Howard de Walden, an agreement to suppress the slave trade was 'absolutely necessary' and must not be delayed by commercial negotiations. If a treaty could not be agreed, Britain would 'really be obliged at last to seize her slave ships & treat them as pirates; set the crews on shore on the African coast to be dealt with by the negroes on shore; land the slaves at Sierra Leone; & scuttle the ships', he said. 'The Portugueze would not find such a course of proceeding redound much to their honor & dignity as a nation.'[267]

In the summer of 1837 Thomas Fowell Buxton brought a motion before the House attacking Portugal for violation of slave trade treaties (which were anyway, he said, inadequate) and, as he forewarned Palmerston, he meant to 'shew that all treaties must be nugatory till by a combination of the civilised nations it is declared piracy & I shall labour to convince you & the House that the accomplishment of such a measure is not hopeless'. As Buxton argued, 'the slave trade cuts off the commercial nations of Europe & America from commerce with one quarter of the globe'. He urged Palmerston 'not to give me a peremptory negative' on the question of piracy.[268] He was pushing at an open door; Palmerston had no reason not to agree with Buxton on this point and Palmerston subsequently assured the House that the government 'fully shared those sentiments of indignation . . . at the extent to which the traffic in slaves still continued under the flag of Portugal', and that no effort had been spared to bring this 'disgraceful trade' to an end.[269]

The discussions between Palmerston and the representatives of other European powers used just this language. Palmerston spoke of the need for 'a league against the slave trade' of 'all the powers of Europe', which he hoped to see begun by the end of 1838.[270] Franco–British relations may have been tense elsewhere, but the two countries were drawn together in their common opposition to the slave trade and over which issue they led Russia, Austria and Prussia. A memorandum signed by the representatives of these four powers and Palmerston at the Foreign Office in late 1838 stated that it was their combined objective to suppress 'this infamous commerce', conducted by 'pirates' who 'pursue[d] their criminal enterprizes with impunity'.[271] As this attempt to prevent the trade under adopted flags of convenience dragged on into 1839 Palmerston began to talk of war and conquest (at Portuguese colonial expense). In January 1839 he wrote to Howard de Walden that until Portugal put an end to the trade and 'to her commercial hostility to England', no friendly relations could subsist between the two countries. 'We consider Portugal as morally at war with us and if she does not take good care & look well ahead, she will be physically at war with us also,' he concluded.[272] In July 1839 the Slave Trade (Portugal) Bill was introduced in Parliament but it was August before a much watered down version (thanks in large part to Tory opposition in the House of Lords) was finally passed into law.[273] It had, like previous pieces of legislation, many shortcomings and was not easily enforceable. As contests between Britain and Portugal continued over the finer points, Palmerston insisted that 'I will not give way the hundredth thousandth part of an inch. Our bill is permanent, and the treaty which is to stand in lieu of the bill must be permanent also'.[274]

The limitations of slave trade abolition policy are attributable to commercial, strategic and even domestic party political conflicts. Yet if Palmerston was unable to translate his vehement opposition to slavery and the slave trade into sufficiently robust legislation and treaties to eradicate both, he was not the less sincere and focused in his resolve. When Spain threatened Portugal in late 1840, Palmerston was sanguine about the danger and hoped to turn it to his advantage: 'it is not amiss that the Portugueze should be a little frightened and should be brought to remember their political connexion with England,' he observed, evidently hoping to use this remembrance as leverage in suppression of the slave trade.[275] In October 1842, in answer to an address of the Anti-Slavery Society, Palmerston insisted that he remained committed to the cause and that it had been a priority while he was at the Foreign Office, though he acknowledged that abolishing the trade while the institution survived, if not indeed thrived, was difficult. Significantly, however, he said that there remained a great opportunity for the governments of Christendom to reduce dramatically the trade and continue pressure for abolition.[276] Yet it was Lord Aberdeen who would have to deal with the ongoing question of slave trade abolition in 1842; by then the apparently invincible Whig ascendancy had faltered.

In March 1840 Palmerston had reported confidently to his brother that 'public affairs are going on well', and he wondered at the 'foolishness' of the Tory opposition which had allowed the government to win a 'good majority' on a recent vote of confidence that had 'fixed us for the rest of the session, & has enabled us to survive defeats on smaller matters'.[277] By the summer the situation looked even more propitious: having 'quarrelled' over the Canada Union bill, Palmerston observed that Peel and Wellington were 'not upon speaking terms'.[278] A year later, however, Melbourne's government was out and Peel was once again Prime Minister.

Melbourne, like Grey before him, had grown tired of office long before leaving it. He had devoted considerable time during the late 1830s to the young Queen Victoria, but when she married Albert in early 1840 Melbourne found he had much less of a role at the Palace. However, as an alternative occupation, parliamentary and Cabinet politics held comparatively little attraction. He tended simply to acquiesce in the majority view of the Cabinet and offered no meaningful leadership. It is said, for example, that following a discussion in March 1841 as to whether or not the government should reduce the Corn Law duty in the forthcoming budget he asked ministers to agree whether they would decrease the duty or leave it alone: 'I don't care which,' he told them, 'but we had better all be in the same story.'[279] In the face of such apathy, the government could not expect to last much longer. In May Palmerston's was the clearest ministerial voice calling for a dissolution: as Greville noted, he 'has never any doubts or fears, and is for fighting everybody.'[280] In mid-July 1841, anticipating the coming ministerial changes, Palmerston admitted to Shee that 'it would be silly affectation to say that I do not on many accounts quit my office with great regret, but luckily I have held it long enough to bring to a successful issue most of the great questions which I have had to deal with and so far I go out with credit to our party'. He looked forward, moreover, to a little more leisure time: 'I shall certainly not be sorry to have some relief from the galley slave labour which I am at present performing;' he wrote, 'and I cannot help chuckling into my sleeve to think how Aberdeen will be worried with work just double in amount, as compared with that which he had to do in 1828, & 1829.'[281] The number of dispatches received and sent by the Foreign Office had increased dramatically, but although he could not resist the jibe that Aberdeen 'will probably have less to do, because he will do less', it was nonetheless true that, as Palmerston conceded, much of the increase in the volume of paperwork arose 'from an extension of our relations in every part of the globe, and cannot be avoided by the will of the Secy of State'.[282]

Palmerston did not anticipate a lengthy absence from office. Though it would 'take some time to eat down their majority of between 70 & 80', he thought election petitions and 'their own daily increasing unpopularity' would soon see the Tories ousted. Palmerston even ventured a prediction that by 'about May 1843 we shall be pressing them very hard'. It was not necessary for the Whigs to do much other than wait: Peel, he thought, would find his party divided over protection and free trade as well as over Ireland and a burgeoning military expenditure. 'There never was a man who came into office with more difficulties to encounter or apparently with less chance of surmounting them,' he wrote. 'And then when these Tories have been in office a little time the country will see what a narrow minded & prejudiced set of people they are, and how unfit to govern a great country.'[283] In a letter to Shee he repeated how internal division would soon break up the Tories and their policies would soon lose them support. 'As a party they are narrow minded ignorant, behind hand with the rest of the world in the progress of knowledge, full of prejudices which they mistake for principles. In opposition these defects are not much observed, in office they will become more striking.'[284] Detested though he was said to have been at the Foreign Office (where he was regarded, said Greville, as 'a Bully, a blackguard and a Coward'), even Palmerston's critics had to admit that his 'indefatigable industry' made him essential to any durable new ministry.[285] Meanwhile, Palmerston looked forward to shooting some partridges at Broadlands and planned an autumn visit to his estates in Sligo, which he had not seen since 1829.[286] Though he anticipated only a brief respite from parliamentary labours, in fact he and the Whigs were to be out of office until the summer of 1846. It was, said Herbert Bell, to be Palmerston's 'longest holiday'.[287]

CHAPTER 8

THE ABSENTEE, 1841–1846

'I trust I shall find myself none the poorer for being out of office; and certainly as yet I have been much the better for it in health, and much the freer & more amused in mind. I suppose that like a horse about his stable, though now glad to have got out, I shall soon wish to get back again to my office; but that wish has not yet arisen; and I should as far as regards myself very much regret any change which should bring me back to my former labours for a year and a half to come.'
Palmerston to William Temple, 26 November 1841[1]

IT WAS NOT only Palmerston who felt he had been working like a galley slave throughout the 1830s. Stories circulated in society that Palmerston should never be expected to quit his desk in time for the soup course at dinner and he was said to keep guests waiting at home while he got through business (and that included his evening constitutional horse ride after work).[2] His brother-in-law, Beauvale, and his wife, Emily, worried about the 'life of a galley slave' that he led (the phrase crops up frequently), but as Beauvale observed, 'He don't like help so he must work.'[3] Yet it was not mere habit that kept Palmerston's shoulder to the wheel; there was an element of genuine political alarm in his correspondence as Peel's ministry settled into office in the autumn of 1841. 'Depend upon it no nation will prosper to the full extent of its natural capacity till it blots the word "protection" from its commercial vocabulary,' he wrote to Beauvale. 'Let men sell where they can get the best price, & buy what they want, & where they can get it cheapest. That is the only sound principle. Taxes on property are objectionable; they are arbitrary & vexatious, & as is seen in France easily resisted. I am all for indirect taxation; but I would have all duties laid on for revenue; and not for what is miscalled protection.' It would take a couple of years, he still thought, to turn Peel's government out, but operating on the principle of 'find[ing] fault with every thing his govt does which shall savour of ignorance, prejudice, bigotry, folly; and composed as that govt is, we shall be at no loss for opportunities for opposition'. In the Tory ministers he perceived only weaknesses:

when I see such men as Buckingham, Knatchbull, Ripon, Goulburn, Hardinge, appointed to govern the world, I well know that they can do no such thing; and I do not think that the decrepitude of the D. of Wellington, or the submissive habits of mind of Aberdeen, will add much to the stability of the govt. Peel as Wakley says has fine organs in his skull, and would have been a very great man indeed, if the organ of caution had not been so excessively developed. But he, & Stanley & Lyndhurst & Ellenborough are men fit to conduct human affairs, & Graham though like Peel, too timid has also the mind of a statesman. But these men will never be able to drag their jolter headed colleagues along; it will be like police men taking culprits to the station house; there will be scuffling, and lying down & clinging to every post, animate & inanimate; and then their friends in the crowd will interfere to help them, & the police will be beat in the end. I fear these Tories will do much mischief in the mean while, but we must try to make it as little as possible.[4]

Yet if politics continued to command his attention, it was perhaps no bad thing that Palmerston now had a little more time for his private interests as well. The 1830s, particularly the second half of that decade, had been an eventful period, and not always an easy one personally. Though he had married Emily, he had lost two sisters and his brother's indifferent health had been a regular source of concern. The rate of improvements to his Irish estates had slowed down and his pecuniary state, though perhaps a little more stable, was not much better overall than it had been in the 1820s (he was obliged to turn to William in 1839 for a loan of £1,000, for example).[5]

Palmerston's sister Elizabeth died in 1837; his sister Frances in 1838. The bereavements left Palmerston 'sick in spirit'. He wrote to George Shee in a disconsolate tone:

To have sustained two such calamities in the course of one short year is indeed an infliction; I had leant too upon Fanny for comfort & consolation for the loss of Elizabeth and in losing the former I feel that I have lost the latter a second time. It is as if half myself had ceased to exist; It is the cutting off of all the dearest & tenderest recollections of ones past life, & earliest years. I trust however, as you say, that these misfortunes may tend to improve the temper of my mind, & lead my thoughts & feelings more towards things of a more lasting nature than the joys & sorrows of this life.

In the meanwhile the impossibility of casting intirely aside even for a day the business of my office has been inexpressibly irksome & painful, & to be forced to go through the drudgery of business even though it be alone & in ones own room is revolting to every feeling of ones nature.

It was a melancholy prospect, then, to gather 'the remnants of our family', as Palmerston put it, under one roof at Broadlands as Christmas approached at the end of 1838.[6] Palmerston remained close to the Sulivans and the Bowles, but his friends recognised that 'poor Palmerston is . . . much cut up by his sister's death', and his outlook would not have been brightened by the news that his brother William's 'life is far from a good one'.[7] In the autumn of 1839, Palmerston and William spent some time together in Hampshire, but it was a bitter-sweet experience. 'I could not be alone with you at Broadlands,' he wrote afterwards, 'without calling up to my memory in vivid remembrance the recollection of all those so near and so dear to us, who formed that family circle, in the midst of which we began our lives; and of whom none now remain but you and me. Harrassing [sic] business and urgent & unceasing occupation, keep down these thoughts, but do not extinguish them; and the feelings which are thus by necessity repressed, become more keen when moments of comparative leizure allow them to take their sway.' Not willing to see the house empty, Palmerston impressed on his brother that he was to 'make what use you like of Broadlands & its shooting. . . . If you meet with any friends whom you would like to have over with you at Broadlands ask them; & remember that my house is your house & my servants are yours.'[8]

The house was unlikely to lie dormant by this point, however. Palmerston had, a few months earlier, finally married his long-term lover Emily Cowper, who had been widowed in 1837. A seemly period of time had now elapsed since Earl Cowper's death. Cowper, in declining health since the spring of 1837, had finally died in the summer of that year and Emily's family had immediately urged her to look forward rather than back. Her brother, Frederick, counselled her to 'dwell as little as may be on what is irreparable, for it saps health and life, and rather turn yr thoughts as far as depends upon you on the other objects which are left to you, who love you beyond any thing, and to whom you are so necessary'.[9] Emily, for her own part, had been deeply affected by the loss of 'the best of friends and the kindest of husbands', but in the midst of her grief she, too, had recognised the need to 'Gaze on to the light & glory of a renewed & progressive existence'.[10]

Perhaps Palmerston wondered whether or where he figured in this 'renewed and progressive existence': it would at least help explain his apparent jealousy and insecurity. Neither he nor Emily had been exclusively faithful, and they both knew this. Emily was regarded as a beautiful and desirable woman; Queen Victoria, for example, told Melbourne that she thought Emily more attractive than younger women, with which Melbourne agreed, observing that his sister 'was always like a pale rose'.[11] Yet Emily maintained that Palmerston was her only true love – 'there is not another person *in the world* of whom I should ever think of, for one moment in that light,' she pleaded in response to Palmerston's doubts – and she insisted that 'there exists *no other person* with whom I could ever have the least prospect of happiness'; '*pray pray* do me justice,' she entreated. 'Look into my heart, and cease your suspicions.'[12]

It was, according to the Countess of Airlie, the late summer of 1839 before the two decided to marry. It was said that Palmerston did most of the running and Emily was apparently concerned not to displease her children, while her brothers were decidedly equivocal on the subject. 'Sir Fred advises her if she likes to to do it, not to potter about it,' Melbourne reportedly told the Queen in October. 'I wrote to her she must do what she liked, I couldn't advise her. The thing is, what his (Palmerston's) circumstances are; some say he is very much indebted, and then they might both be poor together were he to be out of office. . . . He (Palmerston) presses her very much, she says, . . . it would be a great change for him, accustomed to run about everywhere: she says her own family like it. I said to her, you mustn't deceive yourself about it – if you do you must take the consequences.'[13]

At first Palmerston told only his closest family of his engagement; indeed, his brother William and brothers-in-law Laurence Sulivan and William Bowles were sworn to secrecy about it;[14] it was in December, only a week or so before the wedding, that he wrote to his friend George Shee with news of 'an event that will contribute so much to my future happiness'.[15] The wedding, Palmerston told William, was to be 'as simple & unostentatious as possible, & will be unattended with the numerous presents & other things which do very well for two young persons but are unsuitable for people of a certain time of life. I am quite satisfied that I could not have made any other choice that would have contributed so much to my future comfort & happiness; and I am sure it will make my house an agreable home for all who belong to us.'[16] As he had a good deal of government business to attend to, the marriage was scheduled for 16 December, once the Cabinet had separated for Christmas: 'People in public life have no command of their time for any purpose of private arrangement,' Palmerston remarked.[17]

The wedding took place on a 'beautiful day' which Emily took as a 'good omen', and she wrote in her diary of her hopes for their future 'mutual happiness'; but she had spent the previous day feeling 'low' thinking about her first marriage and rereading old letters. Her children, Emily (Minny) and Frances (Fanny), it was said, were unhappy about the alliance and Lady Granville thought it took 'courage' for Lady Cowper to 'face her angry children'. Her brother Fred had been less than encouraging, as Melbourne had reported to the Queen. The best he could say to his sister was that he had no opinion on the match and offered in lieu of congratulations the comment that 'I don't think women do very well alone myself, and so if she determines against remaining so I can only say God bless her be it happy to her.' He subsequently disavowed any hostility to the marriage, and said he hoped their combined resources would see them well settled, but he also urged Emily to 'secure her own property to herself', as 'there is no such source of good intelligence as mutual independence'. As late as December Fred sensed that Emily entertained doubts and counselled her 'in dubio abstine', but there is evidence that, unlike his brother Melbourne, he thought the marriage might alleviate Emily's financial worries. The Queen, however, approved of two lonely hearts coming together and Princess Lieven wrote of her 'spontaneous' joy on hearing the news and her hopes for a renewal of her friendship with Palmerston.[18]

The newly-weds spent that Christmas at Broadlands and Palmerston invited the Sulivans to pay a visit over New Year as he wanted them 'to be well acquainted with my partner'; Emily, for her part, found the holiday 'very comfortable and cheerful'.[19] For all the doubts expressed by Emily's family, the union was to be a particularly happy and close one. In their first year of marriage, during a period of separation, Emily wrote to reassure Palmerston that 'I *did* lock every door and I always *do* all you tell me', and sought to cheer her husband, who did not enjoy being apart ('What is the use of people being married if they are to pass their lives away from each other?'),[20] with the thought that 'I believe it is a good thing to be sometimes away, to feel the very *great pleasure* of returning to one's love and companion and husband & friend – in short *all*, and everything – and I assure you I feel it so.'[21] As evidence of her contentment, Emily thought Palmerston would 'be glad to hear that I weigh heavier than I have ever done in any part of my life (see what it is to be happy, formerly I used to vibrate between 8 stone, & 8 stone 7 now I weigh *9 stone 10*!!'.[22] She said she loved Palmerston 'for being the cause of all my comfort'.[23] Palmerston's brusque public demeanour was at odds with the softer private side now evident in his life with Emily. On the occasion of their tenth wedding anniversary he was moved to compose a few lines:

To Emily Sunday morning
16 December 1849

Ten quick revolving years have past
Since hand in hand securely claspt
Before the altar bending low
We pledged the heartfelt marriage vow
The sun shone bright upon that day
And chased December clouds away
But brighter on that day so blest
Shone forth the sunshine of the breast
And that bright light by love assured
No darkening clouds have since obscured
Then let us to the shrine repair
And humbly breathe the thankful prayer
For bliss which the decrees of Heaven
To few in equal lot have given
          Palmerston.[24]

A love story though the Palmerstons' was, it was yet much more than this. Abraham Hayward, a journalist for the *Morning Chronicle* and a personal

friend of Emily's wrote later that her marriage in 1839 had marked the beginning of her 'public life'. Motivated by her love for Palmerston, said Hayward,
Lady Palmerston had become herself a politician: 'To place him and keep him
in what she thought his proper position, to make people see him as she saw
him, to bring lukewarm friends, carping rivals, or exasperated adversaries
within the genial atmosphere of his conversation, to tone down opposition and
conciliate support – this was thenceforth the fixed purpose and master passion
of her life.'[25] She thought she could moderate Palmerston's frequently terse
manner and open doors to a wider spectrum of political (she was a Lamb),
social and literary circles. Indeed, she once said that advancing Palmerston's
career was 'the consolation which Heaven has vouchsafed to me since my
sorrow, and for which I am duly thankful'.[26] When she accompanied
Palmerston to Tiverton for the election in July 1841, the first time she had
visited the constituency since their marriage, it was said that 'her soothing
influence and sunny smiles delighted the electors'.[27]

For many contemporary commentators as well as later hagiographers, it was
enough to dismiss Lady Palmerston as little more than a palliative to
Palmerstonian abrasiveness. Yet though her soirées and her management of
access to Palmerston did much to influence his public career, it would be unfair
to present Emily as simply her husband's secretary and political assistant. K.D.
Reynolds has pointed out that the influence of aristocratic women was both
subtle and profound in this period and, for this element of high society at least,
transcended the bounds of 'separate spheres' in Victorian society which had
women confined to the private domain and men inhabiting the public. 'It is at
this interface between the social and the political that the aristocratic woman
found a role which, while having a limited impact on the content of political
discourse, was of immense importance in defining its context,' argues
Reynolds.[28] An invitation to a Palmerston gathering was an entrée to metropolitan high society without distinctions of political party.[29] The guests were not
chosen indiscriminately, however, and the character of the event was often as
much a reflection of current political concerns as any judgement of a guest's
social charm.[30] Whatever Emily may have said in later years to Lady Salisbury
about the importance of never mixing social and political parties, she knew that
the distinction between them was often a very fine one.[31] On hosting twice
weekly 'at homes', Lady Palmerston commented that 'my house is a very
convenient meeting place for these gentlemen, and, moreover, helpful also to
Lord Palmerston, because very often a little word on the quiet is more
successful than a long interview'.[32] If Emily was descended from unimpeachable
Whig stock, this represented no bar to her soliciting the support of figures of
varied shades of political opinion when this was thought beneficial to
Palmerston's position or interests. Like her husband, Emily was also alert to the
growing scope, role and potential of the newspaper press. Newspaper editors
and writers were among the guests invited to the Palmerstons' London parties

(and weekend retreats in the country) and it is argued in some quarters that it was Lady Palmerston's courting through such social events of the previously hostile John Thaddeus Delane that turned *The Times* into a Palmerstonian paper in the 1850s. With her keen eye for media manipulation, there is evidence that Lady Palmerston also advised Palmerston on his use of particular newspapers for news 'leaks' in order to ensure maximum impact.[33]

For the moment, however, the Palmerstons were 'enjoying the fun of opposition',[34] and though Palmerston had, at the fall of Melbourne's government, expected to be returned to office within a couple of years, he was soon wishing Peel's ministry would last a little longer. 'Opposition gives one quite interest enough in public affairs,' he told William in March 1842, '& I should much like to have two good years holyday, if holyday it is for those who have to attend Parliament regularly. But indeed that is an amusement & not a labour for those who are out of office.'[35] As well as finding politics more entertaining, Palmerston was profiting from a reduced political workload to take a keener interest in his Hampshire estates. Hunting provided a regular diversion and exercise, but Palmerston also found that following 'an absence of ten or eleven years' there was a good deal to attend to in and around Broadlands. Managing the thinning of trees on his plantations and similar duties filled much of his time, and he found that the accounts kept by his Hampshire agent, Henry Holmes, had fallen considerably into arrears. Holmes had allowed tenants 'to fall with their farms into confusion', and had himself embezzled £2,000 of Palmerston's own money (Palmerston had sureties for Holmes, but he found it, nonetheless, 'very annoying to find that a man whom one has known all one's life, & trusted implicitly, turns out to be a rogue'). While the landlord was occupied in London, estate business had been allowed to slide. The Broadlands gardener, Stewart, had to be dismissed swiftly – he was 'a regular do nothing' complained Palmerston – and there was work enough for his successor, Watson, to do: the kitchen garden, for example, had become 'almost a wilderness, and we could not get even a carrot out of it the other day, to make soup of'.[36] Palmerston's guiding hand had seemingly put matters in better order by spring 1843:

I have been busy reading books on agriculture & horticulture & trying to acquire some knowledge on those matters which are now become sciences. If one does not know something of them oneself one can never hope to get one's estate or garden well managed. I have let all my farms at Broadlands that were out of lease, & tolerably well in spite of the badness of the times. I had a shocking set of bad tenants, but have got rid of most of them, & have brought in people with skill & capital. Our new gardener does pretty well & understands the theory of his department, but he is a Methodist & goes preaching about the country every Sunday, & I fear he thinks too much of his sermons to be very successful in his garden. I must try to put a stop to his preaching.

At least Palmerston had something to do since 'London has been thin & dull this year'.[37] With affairs in Hampshire in hand, Palmerston was interested to monitor progress on his lands and investments elsewhere. In January 1841 the Palmerstons' Sligo neighbour, Sir Robert Gore-Booth, had asked them to stay with him at his estate at Lissadell whenever they next visited Sligo, an invitation that Palmerston was pleased to accept.[38] 'I should like it so much,' said Lady Palmerston, anticipating an opportunity to celebrate the improvements to the Palmerston estates. Accounts from Ireland were 'full of your praises', she wrote to Palmerston: one, from a Mr Cooper, 'says there never was such a landlord as you are – that your works are stupendous, he only fears the people have not spirit enough to profit by your harbour, and that it can never pay but he says the money you have laid out is enormous – and a great advantage to all that part of the country. He says also that your bent sowing has had the best result, & reclaimed a great deal of land, that he was afraid it would not succeed, but now he is going to follow your example'.[39] The Palmerstons' son-in-law Lord Jocelyn, however, sent word in the summer that he had found 'Ireland is quite in a state of revolution';[40] it underlined at least the need for the Palmerstons to reacquaint themselves personally with the country. They eventually went to Ireland at the end of the year, spending October, November and December 1841 on a tour that had also taken in north Wales *en route* (where Palmerston was able, *inter alia*, to check his investment in the slate quarries and found every reason to anticipate their becoming 'a very profitable concern').[41] From Ireland Palmerston wrote an account to his brother which seemed fully to confirm Cooper's reports:

> I found everything belonging to me in Ireland going on satisfactorily. My estate much improved, and the people better clad, and living in better houses than when I last saw them 12 years ago. My harbour, which I have been obliged to enlarge lately, is nearly finished; and though it has cost more than I reckoned upon, it will now fully answer all purposes. It will be about eight hundred feet long by three hundred wide, and will have 13 or 14 feet water at high spring tides. The income of the estate has also increased a good deal by the falling in of old leases; and by some new houses built in Dublin & Sligo; but the latter source of increase goes to a very small extent. I can also justly count upon further increases, by the falling in of some other leases, and by the progress of building in the neighbourhood of Dublin, where I have land which must sooner or later let at foot rents for building.[42]

Within a short compass of time, however, the accounts from Ireland were far less positive. In September 1843 Kincaid sent Palmerston a copy of a letter published that month in a newspaper by 'One who has whistled at the plough' (in fact, according to Kincaid, a writer for the *Morning Chronicle*). It was, said

Palmerston's agent, a 'mischievous publication' and contained an 'artifice of falsehoods' and 'gross distortions and misrepresentations of facts', but it was evidence of growing public criticism of and discontent with landlord activity in Ireland. The letter described 'a series of petty aggressions on the tenant' such as eviction on the grounds of religion or arbitrary rent hikes followed by seizures of land and goods. There were, said the writer, who had travelled extensively in the south of the country gathering reports, a variety of illegal means, as 'common as the clouds of night', used to force tenants into default. Citing the landlord's desire to appropriate the benefits of improved lands, or evict tenants perceived to be unwilling to reform in favour of those who would, as well as motivations of straightforward religious bigotry, the writer constructed a damning critique of absentee landlordism (such landlords were chastised, additionally, for their cowardice in using paid agents 'to do the thing . . . and to bear the blame'). It was true, admitted Kincaid, that 'acts of oppression & injustice by individual landlords' were known about, but though 'there are bad landlords as well as bad tenants', the allegations made in the article were, he said, 'utterly false'.[43]

Nonetheless, Palmerston cannot have been unimpressed by the hostility demonstrated towards his class. A short while later, in the winter and spring of 1847, Alexander Somerville, a reporter for the *Manchester Examiner,* toured Ireland 'as a self appointed missionary for free trade in both food and land',[44] and his letters back home fuelled criticism of absenteeism. The leases used in Ireland, Somerville observed, adopted English legal forms and, making specific (though not exclusive) reference to the leases granted on Palmerston's estates in Sligo, he said 'read like a sarcastic chapter from *Punch,* the only thing about them to make you feel that they are not from *Punch* is their great length and absolute want of meaning. The law-jargon of those leases is hopelessly unintelligible'.[45] Between the autumn of 1843, when the *Morning Chronicle* letter appeared, and Somerville's 1847 commentary, conditions in Ireland had deteriorated markedly for the vast majority of tenants. Landlords were not responsible, from a strictly environmental point of view, for the spread of the fungus *Phytophthora infestans* that arrived in Ireland and ravaged the potato crop in the second half of the 1840s, and it was not the first time the Irish potato crop had been thus damaged. However, they had created a structure of land management and tenant–agent–landlord relations that did little to ameliorate the devastation wrought by the potato blight. All parts of Ireland were severely affected by the blight but few more so than Sligo. In 1845, 49,906 acres of the county had been under potatoes; in 1847 this figure fell to 3,352 (a decrease of 93.3 per cent) and only increased in 1848 to 13,262 acres, meaning that averaged over the period 1845–48 the drop in potato acreage was 73.4 per cent (the averages for all Ireland were falls of 87.5 per cent (1845–47) and 63.2 per cent (1845–48)).[46]

On 13 November 1845 Joseph Kincaid wrote to inform Palmerston that they were receiving in Dublin 'unfavourable' reports from around the country indicting a failure of the potato crop. There was, he said, 'great reason to fear that the poor will suffer materially by the destruction of that their principal article of food. There is not a part of Ireland free from the disease.'[47] Yet such a harvest failure was not unprecedented and in the past all that Palmerston had been called upon by his agents in Ireland to do was pay a subscription to aid relief measures in the short term.[48] According to Desmond Norton, the 'earliest indication by any of Palmerston's agents that a major famine was at hand' was contained in a letter received by Stewart and Kincaid from John Lynch, their agent in Ahamlish, dated 12 November 1846.[49] The question presumably turns on definition: if the prospect of an imminent 'major famine' was not realised, there was, nonetheless, no doubt that Palmerston's representatives knew long before Lynch's letter reached them in Dublin that matters looked grim. In February Kincaid had reported to Palmerston that although the picture across Ireland was mixed, they had investigated every estate managed by Stewart and Kincaid and found disturbing portents of widespread hardship on Palmerston's land. 'In some of these places we regret to say that the potatoes are almost entirely gone,' wrote Kincaid. 'In others they are daily getting worse, and in others a very large proportion of the crop is safe & the disease does not appear to be on the increase. In parts of Roscommon & in the south west of Sligo they are very bad. On the Ahamlish estate the disease was late in appearing but in some parts of the parish it has committed dreadful ravages. There is however a very large supply of corn in the country chiefly in the hands of the farmers and we hope there will not be any scarcity of food tho' no doubt the labouring class will be very badly off from the failure of their ordinary supply.'[50] As late as May 1846, Palmerston appears to have largely set aside such reports as evidence of the sort of 'distress . . . that is almost always the case at this time of year'.[51] Lynch wrote directly to Palmerston in June from Ahamlish advising him that reports of hardship were exaggerated: there was, he said, 'no distress here yet except among a few of the very poor who had no land', and though some preparations had been made for a scheme of public works to provide employment (principally road-building, on which subject an engineer had been consulted), Lynch told Palmerston this was not pressing and he would write again if anything was actually required. In the meantime, he said, 'there never was a finer appearance of the potatoe [sic] crop than there is at present in this neighbourhood, indeed all the crops are looking well'.[52]

The reports reaching Palmerston, therefore, presented an ambiguous picture. On 6 August Kincaid again drew Palmerston's attention to an anticipated 'general failure' of the potato crop in County Sligo, for which the people were inadequately prepared; and the people themselves were already in a distressed condition. Palmerston was advised to expect demands for relief and employment.[53] The following day Lynch wrote to say that the supply of edible potatoes was in fact all but exhausted.[54] It might, as Kincaid politely intimated, have been an oversight on Palmerston's part that, amid parliamentary tumult, he had overlooked the need to contribute to relief measures in Sligo, but there was growing bad feeling on Palmerston's estates at his tardiness and perceived neglect.[55] At meetings of the Sligo Relief Committee in September, agents for Palmerston argued that he had 'expended several thousands of pounds in the vicinity', instituting numerous programmes to provide employment. The problem was that, even if this was the case, much of the money had been ill directed: a great deal had been spent on further developing the local fishing industry, for example, but though the infrastructure may have been improved, fish remained 'scarce' and catches were poor.[56] Doubts were being raised about the usefulness of Mullaghmore, to which access in high winds was difficult, as a viable fishing harbour anyway.[57] A letter from Kincaid written in late September outlined a number of relief measures then in hand or in preparation, but significantly he admitted that it was Sligo tenants rather than landlords or their agents who were applying pressure for assistance: Kincaid said that though the company had long intended to write to Palmerston about tenants' distress, they had desisted from doing so because they did not see what practical measures they should recommend and 'would not now trouble your Lordship on the subject but that it has been forced upon us by repeated & pressing representations from the country'.[58]

Public relief measures, at the hands of local relief committees and the Board of Works, Kincaid reported in October, were proving far too slow to be effective. He was unequivocal now about the pressing responsibilities of landlords, writing to Palmerston: 'I have no doubt that . . . the principal landed proprietors must endeavour to provide more profitable employment for their tenants on their own farms and in their own localities and I hope & trust that by this means the national calamity may prove in its results & consequences a national blessing.'[59] Meanwhile, with less than three months' worth of grain in reserve for a population of between five and a half and six thousand, temporary sales depots for Indian corn meal were set up in Cliffony, which were but poorly supplied, and arrangements were hastily made for additional grain to be imported from America. All this meant in the short term was a lengthy journey for hungry tenants to stores in larger towns like Sligo where limited purchasing power and scarce supplies meant they could at best only buy two or three days' worth of food at a time.[60] The Reverend Malachi Brennan put the case starkly and appealed to Palmerston's benevolence. 'I beg leave to tell your Lordship that your Lordship's tenants in Ahamlish are in a very deplorable state at present,' he wrote on 24 October:

> It is my Lord a well known fact that nearly all the good lands of this parish
> have been planted under potatoes, these all gone now the people there
> have nothing to live on but the small quantities of grain they sewed. This
> stock will not last long. In the village of Mullaghmore they have only six
> acres of grain and in this town land there is a population of 720 souls even

the fishes of the sea have deserted us. Many of your Lordship's tenants are at present in a state of starvation having nothing to eat but *boiled* cabbage and a little salt this vegetable has now nearly disappeared and to their praise be it told they are in this state of destitution perfectly *quiet* and *peaceable*. The population of Ahamlish exceeds ten thousand souls and with this great stock of people we have only 248 employed in the public works. All the land lords here are up and stirring buying Indian meal and selling it to their poor tenants in small quantities. You will not my Lord look on me as an alarmist or as giving you an exaggerated account of the state of yr tenants. No my Lord I tell you the plain truth and if required am ready to declare it on oath. Nothing short of general employment can save the bulk of your tenants from death occasioned from want of food. You my Lord in particular were an example to other land lords you gave employment to your tenants when others did not, you my Lord seemed to love your tenants as a father would love his child you will not then forget (I trust) your people in the *hour* of their misery and destitution. I have been frequently pressed not only to write but even to wait on your Lordship on the subject of their destitution this I declined thinking that matters would not be so bad I could no longer shut my ears against their cries. . . .[61]

Brennan also forwarded reports to Palmerston's agents and Kincaid duly passed these on too. The 'destitution' therein described, Kincaid admitted, was 'not much overdrawn'. In Mullaghmore, for example, 129 families, comprising 728 people, were dependent on just six acres of corn in the wake of the potato failure. All along the Sligo coast, from Drumcliffe to Mullaghmore, Palmerston's tenants were reported to be in dire straits. The majority, said one newspaper in early November, had been 'subsisting for six weeks principally on cabbage and pernicious offal'. Palmerston certainly read these reports.[62]

On 10 November the Ahamlish and Rossinver Relief Committee addressed a memorial to Palmerston pointing out, again, that in a county of almost 10,000 individuals (more than half of whom lived on Palmerston's land) most had no means of support: of 1,500 families, the Relief Committee had been able to provide work for only one member in each of 600 of them. If life was hard for those 600 families, for the remaining 900 'unhelped' and 'really distressed families' it had become unsustainable. With government assistance unforthcoming the committee appealed directly to private landlords. The committee urged three lines of action: that landlords such as Palmerston 'afford help towards emigration'; that they press for drainage of land as a means of both improving farmland and creating employment; and that they contribute to a relief fund to provide cheap, or even free, food.[63] A letter from Stewart and Kincaid on 21 November effectively endorsed the committee's position. Palmerston's tenants, they said, were 'in great distress and suffering great privations' and what food was available would not suffice for more than 'a very few months, or weeks'. Public works schemes were providing some work as well as draining land and constructing roads and Palmerston was urged to take advantage of preferential government loan rates under the Million Act (6.5 per cent over 22 years), but whatever might have been hoped for from such schemes, they were unlikely to find work for the 4,000 people reported by Kincaid to be in need of employment and support.[64]

In light of the finite potential of the land to support the population, there remained the first of the Relief Committee's recommendations. This was not the first time that Palmerston had been urged to think about assisted emigration, yet he had previously been reluctant to resort to such measures (unlike his neighbour Gore-Booth).[65] Kincaid, giving evidence to the Devon Commission in 1843–44, had insisted that 'Palmerston's distinct orders were, that no man should be dispossessed, unless he chose to go, and then he was to have assistance to enable him to go to America or elsewhere'. However, Palmerston had, it was said and admitted, increased rents in the process of squaring his lands and, much as had been alleged in the *Morning Chronicle* earlier, made life for his tenants more difficult.[66] Many now had little or no land on which to subsist, even discounting the effects of the potato blight.

Although measures were reportedly in hand in early 1847 to carry the Relief Committee's proposals for land reclamation and soup kitchens into effect (it took some time to acquire the necessary 'boilers for soup'),[67] the actions, such as they were, were too little, too late. In March, 150 families, or about 900 people, from Palmerston's estates expressed their desire to emigrate to Quebec. Though they knew not what they would face there, many tenants preferred to take their chances in Canada than face 'misery and starvation' if they remained. There were apparently, from Palmerston's perspective, compelling medium-term economic arguments in favour of acquiescing. Despite public relief measures, warned Kincaid, the greater part of the cost of supporting distressed tenants would fall on private landlords and he estimated that it would cost Palmerston £10,000 to feed those living on his lands for the next seven months alone. Yet Palmerston could reduce this bill by assisting the emigration of the 900 who had expressed a wish to leave at a cost of about £2,500. Kincaid urged Palmerston to finance the emigrations 'on the principle of profit and economy'. 'Your estate,' he said, 'will be of more value in the course of a year or two with the population reduced by 1,000, than if they remained. The cost of supporting these 150 families for the next 7 months would be at least £1,500, and at the end of that time they are still upon the property as dead weights.'[68]

Conditions on his own estates, he thought, were not as bad as those elsewhere in Ireland; in March Palmerston noted that distress in the country was 'fearful' and that the 'extent of suffering still exceeds the extent of our expense in endeavouring to relieve it'.[69] The 'consequences of the distress of this last winter will be felt for a long time to come,' Palmerston concluded in April 1847.[70] He saw little alternative for many of his tenants but to start again in the

New World and that month the first of the ships carrying Palmerston tenants sailed for Quebec. The *Carrick* took 173, the *Springhill* 229, and the *Transit* a further 156 at a total cost to Palmerston (not including provisions) of £1,339 17s. 6d.[71] By the summer a total of 894 people from 136 families had left Palmerston's Sligo estates.[72] Almost 900 left, but not all arrived. The *Transit* and the *Springhill* reached port safely, but the *Carrick* was wrecked on 18 May, four miles from shore, and only forty-eight survived (this figure included all members of the crew, except one boy). Those Palmerston tenants who did land were received at the Government Emigration Office in Quebec where they were found to be 'in good health', according to local officials. A.C. Buchanan, the chief agent in the office, wrote privately to London to say that the passengers' condition owed much 'to the good food provided for them' on the crossing.[73] Indeed, Buchanan observed, Palmerston's tenants arrived in Quebec in larger numbers and better health than other Irish emigrants, 'in marked contrast with several of the other vessels from the same port', and he lamented that Palmerston's example was not more widely followed.[74]

The good reports did not last long, however. In July 1847 the *Eliza Liddell*, carrying 165 emigrants, including 77 from Palmerston property, arrived in New Brunswick to be met by a barrage of local protest insisting that these 'destitute' arrivals would spread disease.[75] In November 1847 another ship containing 428 displaced Palmerston tenants, the *Æolus*, arrived at St John in New Brunswick. When the ship docked, it was found that eight passengers and one member of the crew had died while at sea while a further twenty-two people (sixteen passengers, six crew) 'lay ill with fever'. Many more passengers were found to be suffering from fever when they came on deck (among those that were actually able to come up from below). What really shocked the emigration officers, however, was the material and moral wants of those on the ship. 'There are many aged persons of both sexes on board, and a large proportion of women and children, the whole in the most abject state of poverty and destitution, with barely sufficient rags upon their persons to cover their nakedness;' wrote one, 'none of the younger portion of the inhabitants have either shoes or stockings; there is a great deficiency both of petticoats and trowsers, and one boy about ten years of age was actually brought on deck stark naked.' The arrival, in winter, of 'destitute and naked emigrants is deeply to be regretted', continued the report and while the ship lay in quarantine the passengers were obliged to look to Canadian sources for clothing, work and, in some cases, most probably it was thought, permanent public support.[76]

Palmerston, facing demands for explanations, turned to his agents.[77] Stewart Maxwell, an agent of Stewart and Kincaid at Sligo, produced a description of provisions aboard the *Eliza Liddell*. The weekly ration for each 'full passenger' was as follows:

1 Pound Beef or Pork
1 Pound Sugar
2 oz. Tea
4 oz. Coffee
½ lb Treacle
1 lb Rice
6 lb Biscuit
3 ½ lb Flour
Vinegar   }
Soap   }   at the discretion of
Candles   }   the Capt. of the Ship
Herrings   }

Enough of all essentials, he said, had been laid in for an eight-week voyage.[78]
Certainly such rations were superior to those provided by Palmerston's ministerial colleague Lord Lansdowne to emigrants from his estates in the south-
west of Ireland travelling to New York in 1851,[79] though that is not to say that
they were therefore generous measures. Stewart and Kincaid produced two
lengthy justificatory letters to Palmerston at the end of 1847 defending their
emigration policy. On 3 December they wrote arguing that the adverse reports
submitted by emigration authorities concerning the conditions aboard two of
Palmerston's ships, the *Eliza Liddell* and the *Lady Sale*, were often inaccurate
and sometimes simply untrue.[80] Noting that more than 2,000 people had been
'sent out last season', Stewart and Kincaid insisted that they had been well
provided for in terms of food and clothing, and had some funds for onward
travel. Conditions on the estates in Sligo had left these emigrants, they said,
'very little better than paupers' and their departure had been voluntary and at
their own 'urgent' entreaties. Local brokers in Sligo might have profited
from the commissions to oversee the emigrants' departure, it was conceded,
but though it was 'certainly much to be regretted that the passengers were not
in better circumstances, that they suffered so much from disease and poverty,
that they were for a short time a burden to the inhabitants of New Brunswick',
it was also 'gratifying to find that so very few died, and that thro' the benevolence and attention of some of the inhabitants of the colony, their distress and
misery were relieved and they were restored to health'. No blame for any of the
emigrants' misfortunes, they concluded, attached either to Palmerston or his
agents, and they argued that all parties – tenants, landlord, and those receiving
them in Canada – would benefit from continued emigration 'upon a scale
equally large' in the following year.[81] A second letter from Stewart and Kincaid,
a fortnight later, made similar rebuttals of allegations from Canada about the
poor conditions on board the *Æolus*. Though the emigrants on this ship were
admitted to be 'very poor', they were not, insisted Stewart and Kincaid, 'helpless, or infirm, or destitute'. They could have remained on the estates in Sligo,

but 'their entreaties to be sent to America were so urgent that we have seen some of them on their knees on the roads praying to be sent and it was impossible to resist the earnestness of their entreaties'. Pre-voyage medical care, clothing and generous food rations had been provided and, Palmerston's agents said, the deaths of eight passengers among more than 400 on board 'will be found to be much below the usual average'. If the *Æolus* had been dispatched at an unpropitious time of year, that was due, it was said, to factors outwith their control, such as delays in the vessel's being sent from Scotland, and to the impatience of tenants themselves to leave Ireland. Private landlords, said Stewart and Kincaid, were caught between disquiet and hardship on both sides of the Atlantic:

> The landed proprietors of Ireland are placed in an unpleasant dilemma. If they keep the surplus population of their estates at home, the property will not be sufficient to maintain them, and they are exposed to the charge of either neglecting them, or obtaining support for them out of the public funds. If they make extraordinary exertions in the hopes of benefiting the people and relieving their properties by providing free passages for them to the British Colonies in North America, they are abused by the colonists for sending out paupers to them, altho' every account that we receive from the emigrants themselves proves that their condition is much improved by the change, and that there is ample demand for their labour at remunerative wages.[82]

As Desmond Norton pointed out, these two letters were written with a view to public exculpation.[83] Yet if Stewart and Kincaid, and by extension Palmerston, were poorly briefed in forming their policy – a Stewart and Kincaid memorandum admitted that in sending out the *Æolus* 'We did not inform ourselves enough of the circumstances of the place they were sent to & the suitable seasons' – there is evidence that they had planned according to what they did know: Norton documents grocery and clothing bills showing significant amounts spent on the *Æolus* and its passengers. He suggests that Stewart and Kincaid could and should have better understood the 'circumstances of the place' but though they were culpable for their 'ignorance', the agents, and Palmerston, he argues, did at least have 'good intentions towards the emigrants'.[84] Further evidence of the supposed benignity of the emigration policy is found in an account written by a Sligo merchant, William Kernaghan, more than thirty years later. Kernaghan had been contracted by Stewart and Kincaid to manage the emigrations and in a 'reminiscence of Lord Palmerston', wrote that

> In 1847 when Messrs Stewart & Kincaid contracted with me for the voluntary emigration from his estates in the County of Sligo, Lord

Palmerston wrote 'that if the terms were not sufficient to treat *his people well*, to rescind them & to put in a higher tender to enable them to get the best entertainment on board the ships'. I replied that the bargain was my own & sufficient to enable them to be well used when he wrote 'As you state the contract is all right, let every man & woman have a hot tumbler of the best Jamaica rum-punch after dinner on Sundays &c'. Ten puncheons[85] of the best Jamaica were purchased in bond @ 4s/9 a gallon (Leeward Island & Demerara being only then 2/9 to 3s/–) a cask of lump sugar & some lemons were put on board each ship to make the famous 'Glasgow punch'. Three ships sailed with the rum on board when I had another letter 'The clergy write to me that I am doing away the good effected by Father [Theobold] Matthew [a famous temperance reformer] among the people, you will therefore sell the rum shipped in the other ships on arrival at Quebec & if any loss debit me with the amount & let every man, woman & child have a cup of hot coffee with a biscuit every day after dinner in lieu' half a ton of coffee was shipped in each vessel in bond with coffee mills &c.

Mr Maxwell from the Dublin Office superintended the emigration giving at the request of Lord Palmerston £10 to each captain to induce them to be kind to 'his people on board' & some brandy & port wine in bond as well for the use of the passengers if sick as for the enjoyment of the skippers. Mr Maxwell also bought clothing for such poor passengers as required them. (During the famine year the Marquis of Westmeath only gave half a crown to the poor leaving his estates while Lord Palmerston's emigration cost £11/–[?] a head).[86]

In a letter to the Colonial Secretary, Earl Grey, in March 1848 Kincaid repeated his insistence that every effort had been made to 'procure the very best quality of food' for emigrating tenants and pointed to the fact that 'considerable sums of money' had already been sent home by the previous year's emigrants along with 'several most pleasing letters' in which the tenants remaining on Palmerston's estates were encouraged by their erstwhile neighbours 'to proceed without delay' in emigrating to Canada and America, 'and assuring them of success and prosperity on their arrival'.[87]

In the summer of 1849 conditions on Palmerston's estates were little better, especially for the smaller tenants, cottiers and labourers, that is those with little or no land from which to provide for themselves, many of whom were 'almost in a starving condition'. With rent revenue diminished Palmerston had already issued instructions to reduce 'ornamental' or inessential works on his estates (such as new planting and development of the nursery) while his agents pressed him to secure loans to finance land improvement works to create new employment.[88] Even though the population on Palmerston's estates had been reduced during the 1840s, both by famine and emigration – in Ahamlish, for example, the population fell between 1841 and 1851 by approximately 25 per cent[89] – the potential of the land was inadequate for the support of the inhabitants. Based, no doubt, on the reports he had received from his agents in Dublin about assisted emigration, Palmerston continued to regard this policy as a viable means of alleviating economic and social pressures.

Assisted emigration passed into folk memory as a bleak episode in history, says Patrick Duffy, largely because of attention to 'well-publicised shipping disasters, such as Lord Palmerston's, which have been used to illustrate the callous disregard of the landlord and his alliance with reckless coffin-shipowners'.[90] Certainly Palmerston's name is linked to examples of ill-fated Atlantic crossings and it is clear, for all the buck-passing of Stewart and Kincaid, that many Palmerston tenants were sold a hollow promise of prosperity and contentment across the ocean. Yet, Palmerston's assisted emigration programme was not evidence of a disregard for his tenants' interests per se. Palmerston's continuing concern, post-famine, to establish a model of sustainable emigration of benefit to both tenant and landlord spoke of a more sincere regard for his tenants' interests than did the conduct of many fellow absentee landlords (and political friends) such as Lord Lansdowne. When Lansdowne began shipping tenants from his estates to America in the early 1850s, he provided no more than an uncomfortable sea passage. The majority of these Lansdowne tenants ended up in Manhattan's notorious Five Points slum and although a number did eventually escape the poverty, vice and violence of that New York neighbourhood, it was by dint of their own efforts and from a low starting point.[91] Imperfect though they might have been, Palmerston's measures in a similar direction at the same time were indicative of a more constructive approach, even if that was in real or absolute terms still of a modest nature.[92]

In May 1851 Palmerston wrote to Kincaid outlining a plan for establishing a connection with a landed proprietor outside New York. James S. Wadsworth had come to Palmerston's notice through diplomatic channels: Charles Murray, Britain's Consul-General in Egypt, had recently married Wadsworth's sister and Murray had approached Palmerston on his brother-in-law's behalf. Wadsworth was reported to be keen to bring under cultivation a large property for which he proposed hiring English (Murray's term) agricultural emigrants. Palmerston saw an opportunity to forge a connection between his own and Wadsworth's estates that 'would be advantageous to him, to me, and to my tenants'. Wadsworth's plan, Palmerston understood, was to provide each new tenant with land and support to develop it, in return for which he would recoup his outlays in rent. Palmerston looked to his agents to identify ten or fifteen suitable men from his estate at Ahamlish and Palmerston would then pay their passage to New York and a further £1 to pay for them to reach Wadsworth's estate.[93] By the end of July Kincaid had found twenty men aged between eighteen and twenty-eight whom he put forward for the scheme.[94] These were to be the first cohort and both Wadsworth and Palmerston intended these twenty men to establish a durable connection between New York and Sligo. As Murray had written to Palmerston in April, when first raising the proposal: 'the success of the operation on an extended scale depends mainly upon its commencement; for if these first emigrants are industrious & steady they will inevitably prosper, & when they write for their families to follow, others, hearing of their success will assuredly follow; whereas if the first lot sent out are idlers or men given to drink & brawling, such men will not of course prosper any where & the consequence would be that the operation would prove a failure.'[95] Despite the high hopes, however, the scheme appears to have led only to confusion and disappointment. Wadsworth reported in the autumn of 1853 that of twenty men recently sent out, only two had actually made it to his property. Even had they all made it, they would not have found what they had expected: whereas Palmerston had taken the plan to be to offer the emigrants land and facilities, Wadsworth claimed he had only ever promised 'to get work for them on a rail road in a healthy district' and had given no undertakings to employ them on his own property. The eighteen who never made it to Wadsworth were reported to have found work themselves on a railroad near Albany ('at good wages'); Wadsworth said the majority of emigrants preferred to take their own chances in New York 'where they found work at high wages'. This 'line of experiment in emigration', concluded Wadsworth, had been taken 'as far as it is in his Lordship's interests to go'. Palmerston evidently agreed and thought that in future any emigrants from his property should 'merely be sent to New York with free passage'.[96] The venture was poorly planned and easily derailed, but while it might have been naïve for Palmerston to expect a lasting solution to hardships on his estates from an idea mooted by a friend-of-a-friend, his willingness to pursue the scheme suggests that within his own conception of responsibility to his tenants there was a modicum of liberal intent. At least it might be argued so when his conduct is contrasted with the expulsions from other absentee landlords' Irish property.

The system of absentee landlordism permitted numerous abuses against tenants during the nineteenth century. The English absentees were not altruistic benefactors but inheritors of (frequently aristocratic) legacies that could, and often did, yield substantial incomes which subsidised English high society. This was part of a wider English governing *mentalité* which disregarded Irish culture and fostered a sense, among many, that the famine was a necessary, even providentially ordained, liberation of Ireland from the antiquated forces holding back 'progress'.[97] Palmerston was not totally innocent of such charges: he benefited economically from his estates (those in the west of Ireland in particular; his lands near Dublin were less extensive and less remunerative) and even used building works in County Sligo to create a market for other of his commercial interests such as Welsh slate which was used extensively in house-building in towns such as Mullaghmore.[98] In this Palmerston stands as a visible symbol of an exploitative system. Yet this is not the same as judging him as unconcerned with the well-being of those living on his estates. In his civil engineering projects, his interventions in education and religious life, and in his commitment to environmental development, he was not motivated by profit exclusively. In Ireland he could test the Whiggish principles studied in his early life and when he learned of the destructiveness of the famine, his response, while tardy, was intended (at least as he saw it) to be constructive.

Absentee landlords such as Palmerston were excessively reliant on agents who were, as in the case of Stewart and Kincaid, insufficiently sensitive to rapidly changing circumstances and inadequately prepared to respond to them. Palmerston was guity of exploiting his Irish estates at a distance – hence he emerges from the 1840s with a reputation more tainted by the famine experience than that of his neighbour, and resident landlord, Sir Robert Gore-Booth – but he was also reliant on imperfect managerial support. Palmerston was, therefore, properly to be accused of some neglect of his tenants' interests when famine struck in the mid-1840s. Criticism of Palmerston personally, however, should be qualified by an acknowledgement of the deficiencies in the information on which his conduct was based. Absentee landlordism created the framework within which abuses and tragedies could and did occur; the operation of the system of devolved management and the actions of agents frequently exacerbated their effects.

In fact Palmerston was later commended by Archdeacon O'Rorke for his efforts to reduce the influence on estates of middlemen (whom O'Rorke described as 'bloodsuckers'), and though O'Rorke was critical of Palmerston's plans to develop Mullaghmore as 'a watering place . . . or sea-side resort' for the wealthy, he absolved him at the same time of any lack of consideration for his tenants' interests.[99] Tyler Anbinder judges Palmerston to have been a more generous, or less cruel, landlord than many of his contemporaries and chooses to lay emphasis on the relative preference of many tenants for the hardships of America over the destitution in Ireland.[100] Desmond Norton points out that early twentieth-century assessments suggesting that absentee landlords 'had little interest either in the welfare of the peasants or in improvement of their property' do not hold up for the 'notably benevolent' clients of Stewart and Kincaid. These agents, he argues, found emigration 'distasteful' but 'necessary', and 'they attempted to facilitate such departures with humanity and even with compassion'.[101] Palmerston's emigration programme had thus 'acted as a safety valve' and by the end of the 1840s his estates were apparently more efficient and productive (though there had most likely been forcible evictions once the majority of assisted emigrants had left that contributed to this); Palmerston was, according to Norton, a 'humane landlord' who 'does not fit the caricature in popular belief of lazy, uncaring and inhumane owners of Irish estates during the famine decade'.[102] Almost a decade after the first emigrants had been sent to Canada, Lady Palmerston observed in May 1856 that her husband 'has an overflowing, poor and wretched population on his Sligo estate and he has done much good there by enabling them to emigrate – and in all cases it has answered well'. The majority of these emigrants had gone to North America but there was also a number to be found in Australia,[103] and there is evidence that Palmerston-assisted emigration continued until the early 1860s.[104] In country-wide assessments of the early nineteenth century, Palmerston is often identified as one of the 'notable improvers' of his estates.[105] In the pre-famine years it has been estimated that Palmerston spent in excess of 20 per cent of the gross rental receipts from his Sligo estate which 'was exceptionally high among progressive landlords in Ireland', a figure of only 4 or 5 per cent thought to be the average among 'conscientious' landlords. In the early 1850s Palmerston's harbour at Mullaghmore was described as the 'finest port' in the north-west of Ireland, although the absence of a railway link and the infeasibility of developing an integrated fishing station inhibited its subsequent development.[106] (Palmerston claimed that though he personally favoured a railway line between Dublin and the west coast, he had no influence in such matters.)[107]

Palmerston was not overtly interested in electoral politics on his estates, underlining his primarily socio-economic view of his role in Sligo. The years after the worst effects of the famine had passed were, in Ireland, comparatively stable ones. Most landlords and remaining tenants, as Theodore Hoppen pointed out, enjoyed a period of relative prosperity and though in the 1850s and 1860s some landlords tried to reassert themselves locally through electoral politics, the period was dominated, essentially, by 'practical politics' of 'an essentially non-ideological flavour'. Often this boiled down to attempts to augment landed proprietors' reputations with a view to political promotion or further advancement in the peerage (either in Ireland or Britain).[108] For Palmerston, these were not attractions. Although Palmerston's experiences in Ireland did much to fashion or consolidate his political character, there was no evidence of a desire to turn this to effect in politics in a specifically Irish context. Palmerston was a Westminster politician and though he would import into his political life in Britain lessons from Ireland, he had no need to use Sligo as a platform for political advancement. In so far as he did wield influence in the county at elections, he displayed a marked ambivalence about exploiting it, and though he corresponded with Gore-Booth about support for potential candidates, it is evident that the two rarely agreed and Palmerston was not too worried about it.[109]

Yet the 1840s were not without political occupation and interest for Palmerston. At the same time as famine hit his estates in Ireland, Palmerston was again in ministerial harness at Westminster having been returned to the Foreign Office under Lord John Russell in the summer of 1846. While this had undoubtedly meant that more responsibility for handling the effects of famine fell on Stewart and Kincaid in Sligo and Dublin, it also points to the importance of recognising that while Palmerston spoke warmly of a 'holiday' from politics in the early 1840s, he was too steeped in parliamentary life to take more than a brief half-step back and that his return to office in 1846 was not out of the blue.

Writing to his brother in the spring of 1844, Palmerston said that he had 'been busy with the affairs of the session, for though opposition is less laborious than office, yet still those who sit on the front benches of opposition have a good deal to do, and must be constant in their attendance. I have moreover been chairman of a committee to inquire into the laws about gaming which sits two days a week and is not yet over.'[110] Palmerston had been overly optimistic in anticipating a swift return to office within a couple of years of the fall of Melbourne's government; as Beauvale had pointed out at the time, the ejected ministers would have to wait a while for the country to grow tired of Peel and, indeed, he suggested this was no bad thing: in an increasingly hostile international climate, Palmerston had been 'most fortunate to get out now'.[111] Lady Palmerston had encouraged her husband to look upon the enforced sabbatical as a necessary one: 'The fact is,' she wrote, 'our party in Govert & in the Country were grown supine and tired, but I think this change will now alter the whole character of the party and that we shall before long prove stronger than ever. It is a bore to have to *passer par là*, but it could not be helped – and it will be pleasant to start up like a Giant refreshed.'[112]

Although Palmerston had quitted the Foreign Office in 1841 confident that he left behind a record of success and the country in a strong international position, the opinion was not universally shared. While Lord Aberdeen had applauded Palmerston's handling of the Eastern question (Aberdeen, as Palmerston reported it, conceded that Palmerston's conduct in this matter had 'made him forgive me many things of former years, which he had thought he never should have forgiven'),[113] some Peelite figures were beginning to speak of Palmerston's policy towards France and Egypt as the herald of inevitable European war and, as Richard Monckton Milnes put it in January 1841, 'Thiers publicly says that he will make Lord Palmerston cost more to England than did ever before the support of a Minister to a nation.'[114] Greville recorded numerous examples of ministers, officials, newspaper writers (especially for *The Times*) and European statesmen attributing Britain's friendless position in the early 1840s variously to Palmerston's 'insolence', 'violence', 'impertinence' and a 'tenacity of purpose that was like insanity'. Even Melbourne had apparently been drawn to concede that Palmerston had inspired 'aversion' in France and also Germany by his 'notion . . . that everything was to be done by violence; that by never giving way or making any concession, and an obstinate insistence, every point was sure to be gained'.[115] This merely served to confirm, to those of a Palmerstonian frame of mind, that the Peelites were excessively malleable to the French will. It was only to be expected that what had come to be, in many respects, Palmerston's personal fiefdom during the past decade, foreign policy, would, under the direction now of Aberdeen as Foreign Secretary and Robert Peel as Prime Minister, become an area of political debate and conflict. And as Donald Southgate suggested, 'Palmerston had every incentive for activity, for it could make him – especially if foreign affairs could be kept to the fore –

indubitably the second man among the Whigs in the House of Commons, and who knew what might happen to Russell, younger but far less robust?' Such indeed was Palmerston's enthusiasm for attacking ministers that it seemed the 'strong wine of opposition . . . had gone to his head'.[116]

In foreign affairs, Aberdeen appeared to be everything that Palmerston was not. While Palmerston was thought ready to bloody noses abroad, Aberdeen was judged to be more interested in preserving goodwill and peace and he stood accused of being too pro-Austrian and too willing to conciliate France. The two foreign secretaries seemed to share little beyond their alma mater, Harrow. Although Aberdeen's receptiveness to French overtures was born of pragmatism rather than sentiment, Palmerston worried that this would be exploited by Paris. In October 1841 he said he had reason to suspect that France, smarting from 'defeat' by Palmerston over Syria, was hoping to regain influence in Spain as a means to exert 'revenge'. When he heard that the French government had attempted to establish a direct, clandestine link between Paris and Queen Isabella – bypassing ministers and the Queen's regent guardian – even though the scheme ultimately failed, it implied a determination, Palmerston said, on the part of Guizot and Louis Philippe, to pave the way to a marriage between the Spanish Queen and one of Louis Philippe's sons. Despite Guizot's 'professions of a desire to be on the best terms with England', therefore, Palmerston believed the French minster 'would not be able to resist the offer of a scheme which was calculated to obtain for France a diplomatic triumph over England'.[117] This information Palmerston had shared with John Easthope of the *Morning Chronicle* who was taking a right view of the matter. Returning from his trip to Ireland in December 1841, Palmerston again confided in his newspaper ally. Evidence of French 'intriguing' in Greece served only to underline the divergence between French and British policy: since the previous year, Palmerston said, the French government had been 'actively engaged in exciting the Greeks to create insurrections in the Turkish territory', while at the same time they 'were always profuse in their assurances that nothing of the sort was authorized or done'. Destabilising Turkey Palmerston took as a direct, almost personal, attack on his policy. Although he saw with some approval that the government in London was expending some effort to counter French activity in Spain, he worried that 'Aberdeen & some of his colleagues are greatly afraid of France, and I should be inclined to doubt their firmness on trying occasions'.[118] Palmerston was 'delighted' therefore when revolution in Greece in October 1843 showed that country 'perfectly fit for popular institutions'; it was a sign of liberalism resurgent in Europe.[119]

It is significant that Palmerston wrote extensive critiques of British policy in letters to John Easthope at this time; the editor of the *Chronicle* could be counted on to make 'very good use' of the material Palmerston sent him and while urging him to write 'delicately', he encouraged Easthope to maintain a sceptical position with regard to France.[120] Moreover, with Aberdeen in the

House of Lords and the urbane Peel handling foreign affairs in the lower chamber (Peel's 'calm, analytical manner was the perfect foil for Palmerston's exuberant invective', said Southgate),[121] Palmerston could exploit his newspaper connections to drive his message home to better effect than he could achieve by parliamentary speeches alone. With the *Chronicle* 'devoted exclusively to him', as was remarked on some time later, this was a powerful device.[122] Indeed, the government seemed to some extent to be taking the fight to Palmerston on his own terms; at least Palmerston thought ministers were using the press to dangerous ends which must be challenged. 'I hope you will give the Times a good dressing for its coarse, vulgar & unjust attack yesterday upon the kings of Prussia,' he wrote to Easthope in January 1842. 'It is a strange greeting for a government paper to give to a friendly sovereign who has been specially invited by the queen to come over upon an occasion of the greatest interest to this nation, and that sovereign too a most distinguished man, and sure to play an important part in the affairs of Europe, is this the system of conciliation towards foreign powers which Peel has always talked so much about, but which he seems disposed to practise only by submission to France?'[123] During 1842 Palmerston grew worried about French attempts to stir up antagonism between Britain and Germany; this he argued would give France greater freedom of manoeuvre between the two powers and uncouple Britain from Germany (a negative connection between the two based on a shared suspicion of France) and facilitate, under Aberdeen and Peel's uncritical watch, an ascendancy for French influence in Europe. It was through the press that Palmerston thought best to counter such movements: Easthope, he said, had 'dealt with the matter in the right way by exposing the manoeuvre and letting the French govt see on the one hand that they fail in their attempt to make us angry with the Germans; & by letting the Germans understand on the other hand that these attacks upon us spring from the westward of the Rhine, and are not of German origin'.[124] Indeed, though he felt the government had 'got themselves into a nice hobble' about it, the only issue for which Palmerston was willing to give Aberdeen and Peel credit was in their handling of ratification of slave trade treaties in early 1842. With pressure apparently being exerted by America to effect some form of understanding between Paris and Washington to subvert the right of search of ships, Palmerston was gratified to see that 'our govt have shewn more firmness & vigour in this matter than I gave them credit for', in 'throwing down the gauntlet of defiance to the French government'.[125]

Despite this praise, in the context of European unease, Palmerston was all the more concerned about Aberdeen's politically anaemic approach to American policy. In 1842 Palmerston complained loudly and bitterly about Aberdeen's handling of negotiations with the United States over the Maine boundary, the one point, indeed, on which all accounts of Palmerston's career agree that he was still publicly active. During insurrections in upper Canada in 1837, an American steamboat, the *Caroline*, had been torched and sent over the Niagara Falls by Canadians, killing one American on board. Britain had ignored American protests over the incident, which dragged on into 1840 (when Alexander McLeod was eventually cleared of the killing), but Britain did finally admit its responsibility for having ordered the attack on the ship. There were further tensions between the countries over the rights to search ships in order to suppress the slave trade and in 1841 Palmerston had inflamed American feeling by insisting on this prerogative. This was the context, then, in which the American overture to Peel's new government in 1841 to open discussions over disputed territory between America and Canada was made. Peel's government dispatched Lord Ashburton to negotiate with the American Secretary of State, Daniel Webster. What Webster described as the 'battle of the maps' was in fact settled relatively smoothly, the American government securing approximately seven-twelfths of the disputed lands along the Maine boundary, while Oregon remained under joint occupation. Provisions were also made for joint American–British patrols off the African coast to tackle the slave trade.[126]

In the late 1830s, when Palmerston had interested himself only sporadically in American affairs, Melbourne had encouraged him to 'have great regard & make great allowance for the situation of the American government', and in particular show due respect for north American territorial boundaries.[127] Yet when Lord Ashburton was sent to negotiate with the government in Washington, Palmerston did not hide his reservations. Though he welcomed any prospect of a settlement of Britain's disputes with the United States, this should only be, he said, 'provided they were settled without disadvantageous concession on our part, but the Times of yesterday rather seems to wish to prepare the public mind for concession on our part; & I fear Ld Ashburton is not an unlikely man to make it'. After years of careful control of diplomatic negotiations, it was perhaps only to be expected when Palmerston argued that 'it is far better to keep important negotiations in the hands of the govt at home than to send a special envoy abroad to settle them' and he denied that communications between London and Washington were not now 'rapid enough for direct negotiation'. Envoys, he suggested, were liable to make any arrangement and if they could not make a good one would settle for a bad one; Ashburton, he clearly felt, would return with a bad one. A negotiator should understand the subject, know his own mind (and hold 'fixed opinions') and, unequivocally, he should be someone of 'only one country and whose whole heart & soul & interests of all kinds are bound up with that country'. Ashburton, Palmerston told Easthope, did not satisfy these criteria and he 'rather distrust[ed] this mission; and shall be agreeably surprized if its result shall prove satisfactory to our national interests'. Ashburton, he said, did not rate Britain's possession of Canada highly enough, but more seriously Palmerston worried that he was weak on suppression of the slave trade and he saw in this boundary dispute the potential undermining of much higher objectives. Although historical attention to this question has highlighted he worries over British prestige, his private correspondence shows that he drew a clear link between firmness in the handling of the boundary question and Britain's ability to check the growing assertiveness of the American government in denying rights of search (for slave traders) of merchant vessels. Treaty agreements made to outlaw the trade were meaningless if patrolling ships were obliged to limit their inspections of merchant vessels simply to observations of their flags. And just at the same time that Ashburton was heading to negotiate about Maine, the American government was questioning the right of the British navy to search American ships in peacetime. Palmerston insisted that a boarding party should always be permitted to inspect papers carried by ships for evidence of nationality, aware that slave traders were apt to fly the flags of those nations they perceived more likely to avoid such policing. Palmerston obviously feared Ashburton's 'bad' arrangement would make concessions on this point.

> Nationality is proved by a ship's papers, & not by the piece of bunting she may chuse to hoist for the moment at her mast head; and if the United States pretension were admitted and a vessel were to be respected as American merely because she has flying at her mast head a piece of bunting with seventeen stars on a blue background; every pirate in the world, every slave trader, even though she were English, would obtain impunity, & might traverse the seas unmolested with her cargo of half smothered Negroes on board. All our laws & all our treaties with foreign powers against slave trade would become waste paper & the United States would not only exercise the right which they possess of refusing to make a treaty for the suppression of the slave trade; but they would exercise the power of annulling de facto all the treaties which the other governments of Christendom have made for that purpose. If the United States are prepared to enforce such a pretension by war; even by war it ought to be resisted; but the American govt & people will never be so foolish as to go to war upon so unjust a ground, if we are not soft enough to give way to Stevenson's menacing notes.[128]

Thus, in September 1842 when he read details of Ashburton's dealings in America, Palmerston declared the results 'disgraceful' and 'disadvantageous', yet, predictable enough given that they had sent a 'half Yankee' who had 'if possible greater interests in America than in England' to do Britain's bidding, and who valued peace above all else and did not esteem British possession of Canada.[129] Palmerston and Ashburton's reciprocal disregard was not diminished by time.[130] However, even though he thought the Tories were becoming 'indignant with Peel', they still rallied to the government in preference to a return of the Whigs. For Palmerston, in just a little over two years, the Peelites had undone all of his earlier efforts. 'Our foreign affairs are getting into the most miserable state & the country is fast falling from the position in which we had placed it,' he told William. The treaty with the United States was, he said, 'the most disgraceful surrender to American bully; for I cannot even give Ashburton & the govt the credit of having been outwitted'. The concessions which Ashburton had made were both expensive and unnecessary and, Palmerston feared, 'instead of finally closing our account with the United States, will only be looked upon by them as a first instalment'.[131]

Russell was wary of pressing for a motion against the treaty in Parliament which would 'rip open these sores again' and he preferred a settlement to a non-settlement, however unfavourable. Palmerston agreed that the opposition could not 'prove' that a better settlement was possible, but he insisted that Ashburton's was demonstrably a 'very bad one' (the published correspondence, he said, showed this) and he disagreed with Russell that they should simply acquiesce in a *fait accompli*. The treaty was an established fact – Russell he said misapprehended the situation if he thought the question was simply one of ratification – but Palmerston wished to take the matter to the public. The government had concluded 'an excessively bad bargain' and the opposition should 'shew them up, and expose their folly & weakness' and not allow them 'plenary indulgence upon this matter'. It is significant that Palmerston looked to an extra-parliamentary jury and he argued in a letter to Melbourne that the 'public at large' were 'much more impressed, than some of our party think them to be with the demerits of that treaty'.[132] It did Palmerston no harm in wider Whig circles to be seen to be willing to press an opposition line; Whigs were said to be 'delighted' by his efforts in contrast to Russell's hesitancy.[133] However, Palmerston's claims to carry the public feeling with him on this question are debatable. The *Morning Chronicle* dutifully printed articles attacking the Ashburton–Webster treaty in September which were, according to Greville, *totidem verbis* versions of Palmerston's own comments on the agreement. Yet several papers, including *The Times*, the *Examiner*, the *Standard* and the *Spectator*, defended the treaty, and letters in the *Chronicle* and the *Globe* suggested that even among the Whigs there was more support for the settlement than Palmerston admitted.[134]

By October 1843 Palmerston felt Peel's government must soon fall and looked forward with relish to coming parliamentary battles. He doubted that Peel would actually resign and foretold that with regard to Ireland and commercial policy the government might well introduce measures with which the Whigs and Liberals would agree, but this would be, Palmerston thought, at the expense of Tory unity. 'All this will tend to prepare the ground for us at the next general election by weakening the bond of union among our opponents, & by cutting from under their feet some of their strongest grounds of attack against us,' he wrote to Hobhouse.[135] Palmerston's private commentaries on politics from this point forward made frequent reference to an impending collapse of Peel's government. Yet, Palmerston reserved for Peel personally some measure of praise; it was the rump of the Tory party that he looked

forward to seeing expelled from office. Peel meanwhile, Palmerston acknowledged, would attempt some good: he welcomed Peel's initiatives in Ireland, for
example, where he expected, in late 1844, that the Prime Minister 'means
certainly to do a good deal for the Catholics' by increasing the government's
financial support of Maynooth College and the University of Dublin. This,
said Palmerston, would be as much as his Tory colleagues would permit, but
nonetheless 'will be a good step of progress for one year' (one which, he
claimed, the reforming ministries of Grey and Melbourne had done much to
foreground). It would, however, also weaken Peel's grip on power: the House of
Commons would, on the whole, be against it, he thought, and would thereafter
be much less loyal to Peel.[136] Yet Palmerston recognised that much would
depend on registration (and management) of electors and in this Peel might
hang on for a little while longer.[137] Thus while the government continued to
'lose credit daily', even by the summer of 1845 Palmerston perceived that their
majority in the House remained undiminished. A general election would return
them, he thought, albeit with a reduced majority. 'Elections turn more upon
local feeling & local bribery than upon great public questions,' Palmerston
wrote, 'except in moments of extraordinary crisis.'[138] This may well have been a
reflection of a sense of the continuing lack of effective non-Tory constituency
and electoral administration and hints at Palmerston's own ideas about the
popular political imagination – that it was the intensity of a national emergency
that would attract widespread engagement in politics not the quotidian banali-
ties of executive administration. It is noticeable that Palmerston's popular
'triumphs' were based on responses to perceived threats to national honour and
interest. Thus he wondered at Peel's inattention to popular feeling on foreign
affairs. In January 1845 he had noted that 'the high tone taken by the English
newspapers' had been the determining force in inducing France to make
concessions to Britain over Tahiti, and, he mused, whatever this might imply
about Guizot's failure to appreciate the power of (British) public opinion, 'It is
also curious that the government who evidently owe to the newspapers the very
little which they obtained, did their utmost at the time to silence those who it
now appears were their most useful & powerful allies.' Tahiti had been the scene
of clashes between French Catholic and British Protestant missionaries for
some time and when, in 1843, France encountered resistance to its establishment of a protectorate over the island, the French blamed British missionaries
and the British Consul, Pritchard, for encouraging Tahitian opposition.
Pritchard was arrested and deported by the French, and Aberdeen demanded
an apology from Guizot and sent a British warship to Tahiti; but the British
government's approach was widely derided as unduly conciliatory. Thus, Peel's
failure to press France for immediate reparation for the 'gross outrage' and
'great indignity' committed against Britain over Tahiti was 'disgraceful &
contemptible'; the affair, Palmerston said, was 'absurd' and 'humiliating'.[139]
Peel's supporters thought Palmerston was exploiting 'strong feeling' in the

House of Commons against 'French aggression' among dissenters with little else in view save to undermine the government.[140]

Yet the summer of 1845 was not perhaps an auspicious moment for launching a parliamentary attack. Greville painted a picture of political apathy:

> The world is absorbed by its material interests, railroads, and speculation in its multiform aspect, and it is in vain that John Russell reviews the Session and delivers philippics against Peel; still more in vain that Palmerston harangues upon the Right of Search, Texas, Greece, or Spain, and endeavours to rouse the public indignation or contempt against Aberdeen and his foreign policy. It all falls dead and flat, and nobody takes the slightest interest in orations, though they are prepared with indefatigable industry and delivered with extraordinary skill.[141]

Palmerston did not have to wait long for an 'extraordinary crisis'. It had been clear to him for some months that Peel was directing a ministry increasingly out of tune with the views of its Tory supporters and in the face of agrarian and consequently working-class distress it was inevitable that some measure of commercial reform be introduced to ease the pressure. Palmerston did not envy Peel his task of convincing a protectionist party to adopt free trade; indeed, he doubted whether a Whig or Liberal Prime Minister would find the job any easier. Repeal of the Corn Laws was to shatter the Tory party for a generation. Palmerston was equivocal about removing the duty on corn completely and acquiesced on the basis that it was the least bad option; even so, and assuming Peel could carry the measure, he expected 'a terrible rumpus'.[142] Greville suspected that Palmerston would be willing to compromise a good deal in domestic affairs now that he scented a possible return to the Foreign Office: 'I don't imagine he cares about corn, fixed duty, sliding scales, or anything else except so far as they may bear upon his return to that abode of his bliss,' he wrote in December.[143] Peel had been forced to resign that month having failed to push through repeal in the face of resistance from his own party. Though the Whigs, when Victoria turned to Russell, were able to agree on a policy regarding corn – of complete repeal combined with financial relief offered to landowners – they were themselves almost as internally divided as Peel's party. Russell had won unanimity for complete repeal on the grounds that this was the most pressing question of the moment; he had consciously tried to paper over divisions on other issues – such as sugar (what to do about a commodity produced with slave labour) and Ireland (principally religious freedoms) – stating that 'he thought it wiser not to complicate . . . [discussion of Corn Law repeal] by other declarations which would produce a good deal of animosity', and that other matters 'might be discussed in Cabinet when circumstances required it'.[144]

There was, however, a split within the party ranks that could not be dismissed so lightly. Howick, now the third Earl Grey, Edward Ellice, Henry

Labouchere, George Grey and T.B. Macaulay formed an awkward squad within the proposed ministry, said to be trying to engineer a Conservative–Liberal coalition (a scheme argued in some quarters to have been in Grey's mind ever since Melbourne fell in 1841). But with internecine warfare bedevilling both sides of the House, there were few enough grounds to forge an intellectual accommodation. Instead their hostility to a Russellite–Whig government manifested itself in opposition to Palmerston's return to the Foreign Office.[145] A pamphlet published at the time pseudonymously by a 'Free Trader' described the apparent danger presented by Palmerston:

> You may think to control tendencies – but not intentions. . . . You may expect new things from caprice, but not from determined will. . . . You may check what you know, but you may be fatally committed by acts concealed and purposes unavowed. Such *has* been before, the case between us and this colleague – between him and Parliament. . . . [He] is not to be trusted. Be it from arrogance – be it from inveterate, unacknowledged, yet not deliberately culpable predilections if you will: – still, the fact remains, he has undershafts and galleries in which he labours at his solitary tasks . . . which are only disclosed to us when some mine is to be sprung, when the match is already lighted, and we have nothing to do but retire behind the screens he provides. . . . [He] *cannot* be controlled, and . . . we have oft-times been puppets in his hands. . . . Lord Palmerston cannot act secretly, and at the same time enjoy the benefits of frankness and candour.[146]

According to Lord Ashley's account, Grey had intimated to Russell that 'he objected to other members of the Cabinet, & should say so by and by', but it was Palmerston to whom ostensibly they were opposed. Grey tried to hold Russell to ransom, saying his compliance could only be bought on certain conditions. Ashley thought this 'arrogance, ill-temper, and selfishness!', but though Russell was prepared to face them down, he was advised by Lansdowne and Clarendon 'that they could not encounter his temper in the H. of Lords, (being weak there) in addition to the whole force of the opposition!'[147] There was evidence of earlier 'misunderstanding' between Howick (Grey) and Palmerston, although Howick had gone out of his way to deny any intended criticism of Palmerston in a speech made in 1843, which Palmerston had accepted ('no objection could be taken even if I were as touchy as Stratford Canning,' Palmerston noted wryly).[148] Yet Howick does appear to have been receptive to suggestions of Palmerston's dangerousness and in his correspondence with his brother, Frederick Grey, a naval officer who had been stationed in South America and in Spain and was 'a decided anti-Palmerstonian', he had been fed accounts of how Palmerston 'encouraged those miserable feuds [between Britain and France], or at any rate did not discourage them'.[149] In December 1845 Palmerston ascribed the problem

1 This portrait was drawn by a Miss Mary Tate a fortnight before Harry's seventeenth birthday while he was still a student at Edinburgh. Six months later Harry would succeed his father to the Palmerston title.

2 Dugald Stewart was Professor of Moral Philosophy at the University of Edinburgh. Palmerston lodged with Stewart and his family at Lothian House while in that city. The professor's influence on the future Prime Minister's political outlook was profound; and his lectures on political economy, in particular, did much to frame Palmerston's subsequent conception of the role of government.

3 Palmerston enjoyed a number of affairs but his love for Emily was deep and abiding. After years as lovers they finally married in December 1839.

MULLAGHMORE

BR 1547 3

A

Strand to be clear'd

Sand

To be Quarried to Low Water

Neaps

300 feet

Low Water

C. BREAK WATER

70 Ft

B

To be cut away

Low Water Spring Tides

A. Pier and pavement in part executed
B. Part of Pier not commenced
C. Breakwater not commenced

4 Watercolour plan of Mullaghmore Harbour showing the building work in progress, 1825. The harbour was built at Palmerston's expense and did much to help develop the local economy in and around his estates in Sligo.

Palmerston's relationships with prime ministers were frequently difficult. He quit Wellington's government in 1828, was dismissed from Russell's in 1851 but survived to the end in those of Grey (1830–34) and Melbourne (1835–41). Melbourne was the brother of Emily, Palmerston's wife after 1839.

5 The Duke of Wellington

6 Earl Grey

7 Lord Melbourne

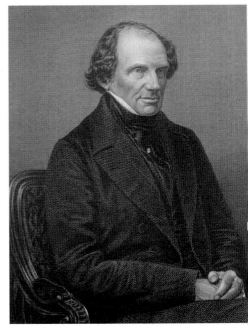

8 Lord John Russell

9 By the mid-1840s Palmerston had been in Parliament for almost four decades, and for most of that time in government. Arguably, his most testing and important years were still ahead of him.

ELECTORS

OF THE BOROUGH OF

TIVERTON.

4, *Carlton Gardens,*
23rd July, 1847.

Gentlemen,

PARLIAMENT having been dissolved, and fresh Elections being about immediately to take place, I venture again to offer myself to you as a Candidate for the high honor of representing you in the House of Commons. Having now for a period of Twelve Years enjoyed your confidence, I trust that I may refer to the past as an earnest for the future; and that I may indulge the hope, that those Political Principles which first made me the fortunate object of your choice, and which have since enabled me to retain your good opinion, will justify me in now soliciting the high distinction of a continuance of your confidence and favor.

I shall take an early opportunity of presenting myself to you in person, and in the mean while I have the honor to remain,

Gentlemen,

Your most obliged and devoted Servant,

Palmerston.

10 An appeal to the electors of Palmerston's constituency, Tiverton, which he represented from 1835 until his death in 1865. Contrary to his initial expectations, the election of 1847 proved to be one of the sterner contests Palmerston faced there.

11 Palmerston inherited his estate, Broadlands in Hampshire, in 1802. The house was a valued retreat from London as well as a place to conduct diplomacy.

12 Cambridge House, the Palmerstons' home in Piccadilly (from 1855), was ideally placed for access to Parliament and to local parks for horse riding; it was also the setting for many of Lady Palmerston's celebrated soirées.

13 Although serving at the Home Office in the government of Lord Aberdeen (1852–55) Palmerston continued to take a close interest in foreign policy. He advocated a tough line against Russia in the Crimean War, and it is significant that he is depicted here in Sir John Gilbert's painting *The Coalition Ministry, 1854* (see below, p.371) as taking the lead in discussions of the conflict.

NOW FOR IT!

A Set-to between "Pam, the Downing Street Pet," and "The Russian Spider."

14 Public opinion relished the prospect of an assertive policy in the Crimea when Palmerston became Prime Minister in February 1855. The portrayal of Palmerston as the one minister capable of taking on the might of the Russian Tsar played on the popular identification of the Prime Minister as a masculine and patriotic hero and on his known enthusiasm for boxing. With the people at his back it was thought that the end of the war would be swift and decisive. This was, arguably, a disappointed hope. *Punch*, 17 February 1855.

15 Palmerston's reception at Romsey, October 1855. Although the war against Russia ended without a decisive British victory, Palmerston continued to play on the image of himself as a patriotic hero and guardian of popular liberties. The people of Romsey, at least, endorsed the idea.

16 Shaftesbury married Emily Cowper's daughter Minny in 1830 which brought him ultimately into the Palmerston family circle. Shaftesbury was an important advisor to Palmerston on religious policy and ecclesiastical appointments in the 1850s and 1860s.

17 Lady Palmerston (*centre*) with her daughters Emily (Minny, *left*) and Frances (*right*). Minny, who married Lord Ashley, later Earl of Shaftesbury, was a particular favourite of Palmerston's. Both daughters are widely thought to have been Palmerston's natural children.

18 and 19 Palmerston was both an inspiration to, and opponent of, Disraeli (*top*) and Gladstone (*bottom*) as they emerged to the front rank of politics.

Text on background (labels): INDIAN DIFFICULTY, CHINESE DIFFICULTY, ITALIAN DIFFICULTY, AMERICAN DIFFICULTY, REFORM DIFFICULTY

Text on tightrope: ...RSTONIAN POLIT...

BLONDIN OUTDONE.

20 Palmerston's second government had to perform a delicate balancing act as it negotiated various international difficulties in India, China, Italy and North America, as well as dealing with demands for political reform at home. Although an ageing Prime Minister, it was Palmerston, apparently never more politically sure-footed, who carried his Foreign Secretary, Lord John Russell, through diplomatic crises. 'Blondin' (Jean François Gravelet (1824–97)) was a celebrated French tightrope walker who had successfully crossed the gorge below Niagara Falls in June 1859 (a feat he would repeat on sixteen occasions and each time more elaborately, variously blindfolded, carrying a man on his back, stopping to cook and eat an omelette mid-way, and, as referred to here, pushing a wheelbarrow). He appeared in London for the first time in 1861. *Punch*, 8 October 1859.

21 Though increasingly frail and never an especially assured parliamentary performer, Palmerston continued to command the attention of the House of Commons up until the end of his life.

DRAWING THE STUMPS.

COBDEN TO DIZZY. "CARRIES OUT HIS BAT? OF COURSE HE DOES! YOUR UNDERHAND BOWLING 'LL
NEVER GET HIM OUT! I'LL SHOW YOU HOW TO DO IT NEXT INNINGS."

22 Political opponents disagreed over how to get Palmerston out. The cricketing metaphor may or may not have been a conscious reference to one of Palmerston's favourite sports, but it is significant that none of his rivals, either in the direct (fast bowling) attacks of a Richard Cobden, or the more subtle (underarm, or perhaps spin) approaches of opponents such as Disraeli, could find the ball to dismiss a political master. Although leading the Opposition in the House of Commons, Disraeli's effectiveness as an opponent was undermined by a certain sympathy on his part for Palmerstonian politics. Palmerston was never one to accept the role of a night watchman. *Punch*, 16 August 1862.

23 Pictured here in the final year of his life, Palmerston rode regularly and prided himself on his physical fitness into old age.

to Ellice's 'long cherished malice against me' and his 'general love of doing mischief' and said he had used Grey as 'his tool' (Grey himself complained that though Labouchere, George Grey and Macaulay all shared his objection to Palmerston, 'the whole odium of making the object[io]n will . . . be left to me').[150] There was also, he believed, the likelihood of French intrigue: he thought it quite possible the Grey–Ellice faction had received 'liberal grants of secret service money from Louis Philippe who hates the notion of a Whig government', and this had been used to keep Aberdeen in place as *'Under Secretary of State* to Guizot'. Observing the approaching separation, Guizot lamented the parting of two kindred spirits, but this was not necessarily an indication of Aberdeen's erstwhile subservience.[151]

It was certainly the case that Aberdeen and Guizot had established a good understanding: Guizot spoke in 1845 of how together for the past three years they had pursued 'de la bonne, honnête, et grande politique', founded on a cordial friendship.[152] He described this as a 'nouvelle et solide intimité' between the two countries, but he underscored his judgement with the sort of rhetoric Palmerston had himself been disposed to use. Writing to Aberdeen in June 1845, for example, Guizot had spoken of the importance of their common political outlook to the maintenance of peace and to moral progress and justice in the world.[153] If imitation is the sincerest form of flattery, it can also be a source of jealousy. There is reason to suppose that Palmerston's irritation with Aberdeen's foreign policy stemmed in part from a gnawing sense that it was his rival who was harvesting the fruits of Palmerston's own (liberal) projects. Greville had remarked on this frustration as early as 1842:

> The Palmerstonians are still screaming themselves hoarse in their endeavours to get the credit of the success. Lady Palmerston writes to Madame de Lieven (dear friends, who hate one another cordially) in a rage, because the latter said to her that She was sure, setting all party feeling aside, as a good Englishwoman, she must rejoice at the successes in the East. The other Lady replied, that She did not know what she meant, and that all the merit of the success was due to Palmerston and the late Government. To this Madame de Lieven responded as follows: 'Je vous demande bien pardon de ma légèreté, mais je vous assure que moi et toutes les personnes que je vois, ont été assez niais pour croire que les grands succès de l'Orient étaient dus à Sir R. Peel et à son gouvernement. Apparemment nous nous sommes trompés, et je vous demande mille excuses de notre légèreté.'[154]

Such mockery no doubt exacerbated the Palmerstons' 'bitterness and disappointment at their exclusion from office'.[155] In December 1845, therefore, Palmerston was drawn to detail a record of success throughout the 1830s, in Portugal, Spain, Belgium, Syria, China and 'elsewhere', in a letter to Melbourne and argued that it was only a perceived '*tendency*' of his policies to produce war that had been used by political opponents, including 'a little cabal in our own ranks', to undermine him.[156] In fact, Palmerston considered the failure to form a new Whig government in the winter of 1845–46 to be a lucky escape: he doubted such a ministry's long-term prospects and he preferred to see the Tories carry measures that would prove unpopular, not least augmenting military spending and granting 'more summary powers for the govt of Ireland'. Beauvale believed 'this whole affair seems . . . to have turned out a triumph for P. instead of a check'.[157] Indeed, the supposition that Palmerston had been the obstacle to a new government elicited testaments to the value of his previous foreign policy from both Peelites and Liberals, and in the press (predictably the *Chronicle* defended Palmerston's record) while Grey and Ellice, Palmerston thought, had been exposed as cynical opportunists, the object of the 'Grey cabal' as he discovered having been, among other things, to secure the Foreign Office for Ellice himself.

> Grey & Ellice thus finding themselves disavowed by everybody have quarrelled together, [Palmerston wrote to his brother] each throwing upon the other the chief blame of the transaction and each giving me to understand Ellice in person & Grey by message that they regretted what had happened. As to Grey he is only an ill tempered, crotchety, over-bearing, conceited, spoilt child; who never has had the wholesome buffet-ting of a public school, and has been inspired by the too great affection of his father with an exaggerated opinion of his own ability & importance; & this failure will do him good & render him more practicable in future; though John Russell is so disgusted with his whole proceeding, that if he was to come into power now, he would not I am sure, offer Grey a seat in his Cabinet. As to Ellice he is essentially, radically, thoroughly, & incorri-gibly dishonest; no rebuffs will ever alter his bad nature, and I am delighted that now it is known that he is my enemy, & that he can no longer do me the injury which he has hitherto frequently done me, in the character of a supposed friend, but spiteful backbiter.[158]

Ultimately, therefore, Russell was obliged to concede that he could not 'form a government which can have a chance of success, even in the first measure they would have to propose'.[159] Peel described Russell's failure to honour his promise to form a government as 'unconstitutional',[160] but both he and Russell knew that whichever of them took the reins of government and repealed the Corn Laws faced a difficult task. It was further consolation to know that the Queen approved of Russell's conduct, and was even 'convinced' that he was 'right in wishing to retain Palmerston at the Foreign Office' (though this was only once the Queen – who was reportedly alarmed at the prospect of Palmerston's return to the Foreign Office and preferred offering him the

Colonial Office – had been persuaded that this was unworkable; she relented but insisted that Palmerston understand the Foreign Office 'is to be a Department of the Government' and not to be 'dealt with according to his good will and pleasure').[161] When Peel's restored government enacted repeal in the spring of 1846, therefore, Russell's position was strengthened. As Palmerston pointed out in April, since Peel had come round to free trade he was 'placed . . . almost on the same ground on which we stand', and, he thought, if electors were to be obliged to choose among 'rival men' rather than 'between conflicting principles', they might as well elect Whig ministers to execute Whig measures. While Peel hoped for a couple of years 'on the shady side of the House' in order to regroup his forces, Palmerston talked about 'a five year spell of it' for the Whigs.[162] Shortly after the Whigs had been ejected in 1841, Charles Greville had written that he saw Russell as the only possible future Whig premier and Palmerston, he reckoned, would 'agree to anything which took him back to the Foreign Office'. But he also doubted the viability of such a government: Palmerston's 'vindictive nature' would never allow him to forgive Russell's dissent over the Eastern question while Russell 'has a very bad opinion of and no confidence' in Palmerston. 'I don't see how they could possibly go on,' he had concluded.[163] Yet in the summer of 1846 just such an arrangement was made. Radicals such as Richard Cobden and the Peelites had proven unreceptive to Russell's overtures and Russell himself was not prepared to countenance an accommodation with the Protectionist rump of the Tory party.[164] This of course left Lord John only Whig material from which to cut his government and this raised again the question as to whether he would be able this time to surmount the Grey–Palmerston hurdle.

Matters now stood a little differently. Humbled by the experience of December, Grey and Ellice proved less willing to isolate themselves and, according to Grey's own (much later) justification, circumstances had changed enough to warrant a different attitude. Writing nearly forty years later, Grey claimed that his principal concern about Palmerston's return to the Foreign Office in December 1845 had been inspired by events in America where he felt a serious 'rupture' was imminent over boundary disputes. However devious the American government's conduct (subsequent revelations, he wrote, showed that it had acted 'very ill' and 'very dishonestly'), a war at the time, Grey said, would have been 'calamitous (even if we proved successful)' and, given Palmerston's past record in dealing with the United States (in which 'he had shown a temper which was the reverse of conciliatory to the Americans') and his known links with the *Morning Chronicle* which was loudly critical of the US government, such a conflict would have been even more likely had Palmerston returned to the Foreign Office. The subsequent conclusion of a treaty resolving the boundary disputes by Ashburton and Webster, under Aberdeen's direction, Grey continued, removed this fear and so he waived his objection to Palmerston's return in July 1846, though he still considered it 'a bad appointment' and felt Palmerston's subsequent criticism of the 'Ashburton capitulation' only bore out his earlier misgivings.[165]

Meanwhile Palmerston had taken upon himself (with the friendly assistance of Easthope) to repair his reputation at home and abroad. In December 1845 a chief cause of opposition to Palmerston had been his supposed hostility to France. Peel, on retiring (temporarily), had intimated to Guizot that he regarded it as a significant achievement of his government to 'have established foundations of concord between England and France strong enough to bear the shock of all ordinary casualties, and of personal changes in the administration of this country at least'. When he observed that his administration and Guizot's had 'succeeded in elevating the tone and spirit of the two nations, have taught them to regard something higher than paltry jealousies and hostile rivalries, and to estimate the full value of that moral and social influence, which cordial relations between England and France give to each for every good and beneficent purpose', it was not difficult to discern a criticism of Palmerstonian diplomacy which would, no doubt, have been the cause of 'many miserable squabbles' and 'terrible national controversies' that had been avoided since 1841.[166]

Palmerston had visited the continent in 1844,[167] and toured extensively there; he now looked to France with more overtly political objectives in view. Easthope had intervened to put Palmerston and Thiers back in contact and they exchanged a series of letters in the winter of 1844–45: Greville thought this 'flirtation' between 'the quondam rival Statesmen' curious and speculated that it was based on little more than hopes on both sides that they could help each other back into office; Greville's editor ascribed it merely to a mutual loathing of Guizot.[168] Palmerston and Thiers (his supposed 'antagonist' of 1840) were, said Palmerston in December 1845, on 'very good terms', however, and he claimed Thiers had 'promised to introduce me to all his friends whenever I should go to Paris',[169] though Thiers's respect for Palmerston was perhaps grudging rather than effusive.[170] Palmerston visited Paris in April 1846, from where he wrote to his brother:

I have for some time been desirous of coming here, first because I had not seen this town since Oct. 1830, and secondly because I wished to convince the French by ocular demonstration that I have not cloven feet & a tail as many of them really believe that I have. Political opponents at home & political opponents abroad have so industriously spread about the notion that I hate France & love war, that this is become the fixed opinion of every man who troubles his head at all about me from Calais to Marseilles; quite forgetting that I maintained peace through ten years of unexampled difficulty, and that the constant accusation made against me by the Tories when I was in, & they were out, was that I was far too partial to France, and that I leant unduly to an alliance with her, & neglected too much the other three powers. However nothing can be kinder than our reception has been. Men of all parties have met us with the greatest cordiality, and I really think that my visit will be useful to the common interests of the two countries by removing an unfounded and hurtful prejudice. Whether I am in office or in opposition it is important that the French should not attribute to me sentiments which I do not entertain, and their belief in which must tend to impair that cordiality which ought to exist between the two countries.[171]

The visit seemed to have served its purpose, even if only temporarily: Greville noted that the visit to France, where Palmerston's 'name has been held in terror and execration for some years', had been 'triumphantly successful'. He had dined with Louis Philippe, Guizot, Thiers, Broglie and Molé and been greeted everywhere with 'smiles, *prévenance* and *empressement*'.[172] Guizot described how Palmerston had done much to heal old wounds and circulated widely in French society in an attempt to convince French politicians (and the wider population) of his genuine desire for peaceful relations. The French people, Guizot said, had responded by treating Palmerston with a mixture of curiosity and courtesy rather than animosity. So far, at least, feelings had warmed. Guizot had impressed on Palmerston in a personal interview how close and how mutually beneficial had been his relationship with Aberdeen, but Palmerston had insisted that he had no wish for anything different. Yet, Guizot could not help sounding a warning note: perhaps they had all been carried away in April, he suggested in a letter to Aberdeen, and Palmerston had not really changed but had simply taken people in with promises of peace; at heart, he wondered, was Palmerston still just the same as ever?[173] Guizot had warned that any shift in British perceptions of Palmerston based on this Paris visit would be 'très exagéré' but Palmerston himself was quick to point to his warm welcome in France as evidence of repaired relations. 'All the Liberal party, who as you know, attach great importance to a good understanding between England & France are delighted at our good reception,' he wrote again to William in the middle of May, 'because it removes an unfounded apprehension which Ellice and some other low intriguers had contrived industriously to spread, that if I returned to the Foreign Office there would be an immediate quarrel with France.'[174] Grey capitulated: in January he had claimed, implausibly, that had he known his opposition to Palmerston would scupper Russell's attempts to form a government he would have yielded then;[175] now, in June, as Russell put together his government, the erstwhile wrecker said that he 'was quite prepared to waive any objection on the score of Palmerston . . . and that he felt the necessity of making the machine work easily if he came in. He felt the separation from all his friends very much if he was not included.'[176] Palmerston had been discussing possible grounds for coalition (primarily forging some sort of compromise over protection) with Disraeli and Lord George Bentinck in May, but if his aim had been to provoke a crisis within

Whig ranks (and thereby unsettle Russell) he failed, and succeeded only in encouraging Russell to commit even more forcibly to free trade and the Whigs came forward in the wake of Peel's decision to repeal the Corn Laws united against fixed duties even if that was, said the Whig Thomas Frankland Lewis, a 'measure (which as Lord Palmerston told a friend of mine) they almost unanimously disapproved'.[177]

In July 1846 Palmerston re-entered the Foreign Office for the third and, as it transpired, final time. Aberdeen apparently handed over to his successor with marked good grace. 'When I came into office five years ago,' he is reported to have said to Palmerston, 'you wanted to come back again and turn me out, and you accordingly attacked me in every way you could, as you had a perfect right to do. Circumstances are very different now. I do not want to turn you out, and I never mean to come into office again, and I am therefore come to tell you that I am ready to give you every information that may be of use to you, and every assistance I can. I have been so long in office that there are many matters of interest, on which it may be of great use to you to receive information from me; and if you will ask me any questions, I will tell you all I can that you may desire to know, and everything that occurs to me as desirable you should know.'[178]

CHAPTER 9

THE GUNPOWDER MINISTER, 1846–1851

Lord Palmerston is either a most incautious or unlucky minister – for his advent to power has been the coincident circumstance with a general feeling of uneasiness every where – It is no use to conceal it from ourselves that he has a character abroad for a brusque manner of treating national relationships which is very prejudicial to those ideas of friendly intercourse which are beginning to spread amongst every civilized people.

Richard Cobden to John Bright, 18 January 1847[1]

ON 6 JULY 1846 Russell had finally formed his government and on that day Palmerston went, with the other new ministers, to Osborne where he was once again entrusted by the Queen with the seals of the Foreign Office. There were many who looked on this administration as condemned to a brief and fractious life. Only a week after formally inaugurating her new government, the Queen wrote to her uncle, King Leopold, that the 'present government is weak, and I think Lord J. does not possess the talent of keeping his people together'.[2] Prince Albert, who had been closer to Peel than he would be to any of the new Whig ministers, noted on the day the Russell government was formed that the Whigs remained at sixes and sevens: 'There is the *Grey Party*, consisting of Lord Grey, Lord Clarendon, Sir George Grey, and Mr Wood; they are against Lord Lansdowne, Lord Minto, Lord Auckland, and Sir John Hobhouse, stigmatising them as old women,' he wrote. 'Lord John leans entirely to the last-named gentlemen. There is no cordiality between Lord John and Lord Palmerston, who, if he had to make a choice, would even forget what passed in December last, and join the Grey Party in preference to Lord John personally. The curious part of all this is that they cannot keep a secret, and speak of all their differences.'[3] Russell had toyed with the idea of sending Palmerston to the House of Lords with an English peerage, in part to strengthen an acknowledged parliamentary weakness, in part to counterbalance Grey (should he come in), but Palmerston was 'very unwilling', believing himself, as his wife reported it, 'necessary in the House of Commons'.[4]

In September the new Foreign Secretary was among the ministers attending the Queen and Prince Albert aboard the royal yacht in the Channel Islands.

Although Palmerston had been Foreign Secretary when the royal couple married in February 1840, that alliance and its political impact had been but slightly realised before the fall of Melbourne's ministry in 1841. Now, however, the Prince had had a little more than six years in which to master British politics and had become, as Palmerston found, a far more interested and involved political figure. As he had explained to Palmerston in August: 'our chief wish and aim is, by hearing all parties, to arrive at a just, dispassionate, and correct opinion upon the various political questions. This, however, entails a strict scrutiny of what is brought before us.'[5] While Victoria remained in Jersey isolated from politicians and passed her time principally in the company of her ladies-in-waiting, Palmerston found that it was his 'province to amuse Albert' and they 'had a great deal of agreeable talk about German politics & other matters'. The Prince, Palmerston judged, 'may be a Tory about England though I do not believe it, but about Germany he is quite a liberal, & all for having constitutions every where & looking to them as a source of national strength & union and not at all as Metternich views them, as sources of danger'. It was, it would seem, a propitious interview and Palmerston wrote home to Emily to say that 'Nothing however can be more amiable than Albert & the Queen are, and in many respects the trip will certainly be useful.'[6] This was not a view Palmerston would hold for very long and over the course of the following five and a half years the royal couple's mild reservations about Palmerston's tenancy of the Foreign Office hardened into outright hostility. Beyond the narrow confines of the Palace and Westminster, however, Palmerston's return to office was widely received as a welcome change from the Aberdeen years. Even papers traditionally hostile to the Whigs, such as the ultra-Tory *Standard*, found grounds, in the moral conscience evidenced in his speeches against slavery, for praising Palmerston's restoration to the Foreign Office.[7] *The Times* was glad that Palmerston had been willing to make 'personal sacrifices' in order to return to office,[8] although of course this was as much a criticism of Grey and Ellice as an unequivocal endorsement of Palmerston himself. Yet some sections of the press seemed willing to give Palmerston a third chance at the Foreign Office and only a little over a month into the life of the new government, the progressive *Daily News* suggested that 'the light which emanates from Downing-street in August is much more full of clearness and truth' than had been the case when Aberdeen had been Foreign Secretary.[9]

Given the circumstances surrounding the fall of Peel's government it was inevitable that commercial policy questions should occupy a high place in ministers' minds. Richard Cobden, who had peremptorily renounced any ambition for office for himself, had nonetheless impressed on Russell at the beginning of July the importance of '*not los[ing] the free-trade wind*' and argued that by 'spreading your sails to the free-trade gale at the outset of your voyage, you will acquire a prestige and support with the English public which will help your other measures'.[10] Russell showed Cobden's letter to Palmerston who dismissed it as the production of 'a man whose whole heart & soul has been engrossed for some years by a single question';[11] he doubted Cobden's claims that free trade was the only subject that interested 'the English mind'. There had been no doubt in Palmerston's thinking that in returning to office he was 'necessary' at the Foreign Office; this was where Britain's prestige was at stake and whatever he heard from Stewart and Kincaid in Ireland, or listened to in the House about the necessity of free trade, he was more inclined to agree with, or be influenced by, accounts that came from Europe than those from Sligo or London; 'the difficulties of the present situation', as William Russell had written to Lord John from Berlin in January, were all part of a 'dangerous contest' for influence and control on the continent.[12] As Clarendon reported while visiting the Duke of Bedford, elder brother of Lord John Russell, according to the Duke: 'the country gentlemen about here who in general know & care nothing about foreign affairs are all indignant at the conduct of Louis Philippe & at the Bedford Races the other day it was much more discussed than the horses or the corn laws or the bad potatoes'. The talk at the racecourse was about Spain, and Palmerston found one of the most pressing diplomatic questions with which he was obliged to deal on his return to office took him back to familiar ground in the Iberian Peninsula.

The contest among the European powers for influence in the Iberian Peninsula, which throughout the 1830s had appeared a microcosm of the wider clash between absolutism and liberalism, or at least was often so presented, had, by 1846, acquired a much more overt *realpolitik* dimension. The question centred on the marriages of Isabella, the fifteen-year-old Queen of Spain, and her younger sister, Luisa. Two suitors competed for Isabella's hand: Francisco, the Duke of Cadiz, and Enrique, the Duke of Seville. Meeting at Eu in the autumn of 1843 France and Britain had agreed that, once Isabella had married and produced an heir (or preferably heirs), Britain would relax its opposition to the French plans to marry Luisa to the Duke of Montpensier, Louis Philippe's son (an arrangement which would, in the event of Luisa succeeding to the Spanish throne should Isabella die without issue, have effectively united the French and Spanish thrones). To complicate matters, however, the Queen Mother, Christina, preferred to see one of her daughters married to Leopold of Saxe-Coburg. To this Guizot had retorted that in such a case the French government would regard any agreement made at Eu void and would press for a Montpensier marriage, either to Isabella herself, or to Luisa irrespective of the Queen's maternal condition. Although Aberdeen had professed himself willing to talk candidly with Palmerston in handing over to him in the summer of 1846, he appears to have been unforthcoming on the growing tensions between Britain and France over the Spanish marriages. When he came back to office in July, Palmerston preferred the prospect of a marriage between Isabella and the Duke of Seville, largely because of Seville's connections with the English Liberal Party,[13] but he did so without especial fervour and the government was open to a possible Coburg alliance. By August, however, Palmerston recognised that a breach between Britain and France was increasingly likely: Christina's support for Coburg, he thought, lacked parliamentary and popular backing in Spain, where there was too much of a disposition to 'bow to the dictates of France' and though he acknowledged that this strengthened France's position, he was unwilling to do anything that might 'crush their [the Spanish government's] already broken spirit'.[14] Guizot was not slow to exploit a change in government in Britain and Palmerston's evident ambivalence (or relative ignorance) on the issue with the aim of subverting the Eu 'agreement' and stealing a march on Britain in the peninsula. He argued that the Russell government was intriguing to pave the way for a Coburg marriage and had broken the agreements previously made with Aberdeen and hitherto respected by France.[15] In September news reached Britain that Isabella would marry Cadiz in October and, at the same time, Montpensier would marry Luisa (when the weddings did take place, on 10 October, they were separated by only a quarter of an hour, allowing the French to claim that they had respected the understanding that the Montpensier marriage would not take place before Isabella's).

Palmerston had initially thought the French announcement was 'a little diplomacy' and the Montpensier marriage could not take place 'for some little time to come'; he preferred to treat it as 'the announcement of an intention' than as 'the declaration of a decision'.[16] Russell responded with a more realistic interpretation: Louis Philippe, he told Palmerston on 6 September, was seeking to make Montpensier heir to, and ultimately occupant of, the Spanish throne.[17] And there was little reason for the British government to trust to internal Spanish opposition to French aggrandisement: Clarendon reported that though popular feeling in Madrid was hostile to Montpensier, he had little confidence in its vitality and reports recently received intimated that 'the people will submit to the marriage as to any other act of domestic or foreign tyranny to which they are accustomed'.[18] He counselled against British support for 'any foolish enterprise' of the Progresistas in Spain and urged Palmerston to beware of falling further into the French trap and provoking a quarrel between France and the new Whig government.[19] If Palmerston had been insufficiently alert to the manoeuvring of France in Spain, however, he quickly revised his opinions. The French, he wrote on 10 September, had 'carried their point by boldness, decision and promptitude'; the British government, by contrast, had 'been defeated by our timidity, hesitation and delay'. Too much 'shilli shallying' and standing 'in awe of France' had handed Paris the initiative and as 'always with France if others are firm they stop or recede; if others recede or faulter they advance or rush on'. He regretted that Britain had not backed the Coburg marriage with more vigour: if it had not prevented the Montpensier marriage, it would at least have rendered it 'less injurious'. Implicitly shifting some of the blame to Aberdeen and Peel, however, Palmerston noted that the Whigs were too recently returned to office to have sufficiently mastered the subject, 'its bearings . . . and former transactions about it'. As a result, they had, he said, been 'too much afraid of France' and had underestimated the duplicity of the French government. He proposed a series of remonstrances and protests, but as he admitted, having 'knock[ed] us down', the French government would be ready to make an apology to 'pacify us'; it appears he accepted an early diplomatic defeat and took this as a warning to reinforce Britain's national defences.[20] Russell disagreed that Britain should have backed the Coburg marriage – it would, he said, have involved Britain too much in the internal affairs of Spain to support a marriage that would have enjoyed little domestic support and would probably have exacerbated various tensions in Europe – but he agreed on the need to authorise Bulwer, Britain's minister to Spain, 'to hold language of displeasure'. He was willing, too, to intimate a preparedness to defend Spanish independence (by unspecified means) in the event of Luisa actually succeeding to the Spanish crown.[21] But he also agreed with Palmerston that relations with France under Aberdeen's watch had been handled too casually. Too often, Russell and Palmerston discovered, agreements between Guizot and Aberdeen representing formal diplomatic engagements had been dealt with via private correspondence. On being handed one of Guizot's letters by Jarnac, Palmerston had commented simply, 'Guizot writes a very good hand'; he had not readily appreciated that it was regarded in Paris as an official document. Following an interview with the French ambassador, in which he had vented his frustration at France's conduct, Russell worried that the government had no record of agreements that were 'to be the foundation of such grave proceedings as the Queen of Spain's marriage'. He had been shaken in his hopes that Britain could 'preserve the most friendly intimacy with France' and he urged Palmerston to adopt more conventional, and rigorous, diplomatic communication. In the meantime he hoped, simply, that 'the Spaniards will not bear Montpensier for king', being 'too Spanish for that' and looked to insurrection, perhaps under Don Carlos, to limit French advances.[22] It was further evidence of the uncertainty of diplomacy by such informal means that Aberdeen was said to be 'dreadfully shocked & disappointed' by Louis Philippe's conduct.[23]

Both Victoria and Albert were alarmed by French diplomatic manoeuvres and saw it as their role (as Walter Bagehot would later define the functions of the monarch) to be consulted, to encourage and to warn. Initially the Queen had concurred in Palmerston's general view of events in Spain,[24] but when news had reached the royal party on board their yacht that Isabella was to marry Cadiz and Luisa would wed Montpensier, Victoria complained bitterly of the turn events had taken; the French, she said, had 'behaved *very* unhandsomely', and though she did not think Britain could prevent the Montpensier marriage, she hoped at least to be able to delay it.[25] However, she also thought Palmerston had done much to make things worse (as, indeed, did his critics in the Cabinet, such as Grey and Wood).[26] 'If our dear Aberdeen was still at his post,' she wrote to her uncle the King of the Belgians, 'the whole thing would not have happened; for he would *not* have forced Enriquito (which enraged Christine), and secondly, Guizot would not have *escamoté* Aberdeen with the wish of triumphing over him as he has done over Palmerston, who has behaved most openly and fairly towards France, I must say, in this affair. But say what one will, it is he again who indirectly gets us into a squabble with France!' Yet, Victoria concluded, Palmerston's want of tact and sense of propriety could be easily overcome: 'Lord Palmerston,' she declared, 'is quite ready to be guided by us.'[27] The Queen endorsed Palmerston's and Russell's protests, and urged that Russia, Austria and Prussia should be informed of France's conduct in hopes that Paris might become diplomatically encircled. But she opposed any plans to foment insurrection in Spain: she wanted to see *'no* revolutions' there, 'for they are a most unjustifiable practice most unfortunately *in fashion* in the peninsula.'[28] In high political circles, Palmerston was thought to have been a tempting target for French intrigue given the widespread wariness of him (and in spite of his supposed bridge-building efforts prior to resuming office), and in this sense he had exacerbated tensions that Aberdeen's policy had held in abeyance; yet there was also agreement that, even supposing this to be the case, Palmerston had been the victim more of reputation than action and had done nothing since July to warrant the deterioration in Franco-British relations that had become evident by the autumn. Even Charles Wood was drawn to concede that it was the 'misconduct' of France, in the face of Palmerston's 'perfectly fair & proper conduct towards them', that had caused the present problems; indeed, he told Palmerston, he hoped recent events 'will convince all who see what has passed that even on former occasions blame has sometimes been laid on the wrong shoulders'. It was further consolation that the Concert of Europe would also see the 'knavery' of Britain's neighbours.[29]

When France published private British dispatches on the issue, which included some frank, not to say undiplomatic, comments on Christina, it was widely accepted that French activity in Spain was in part a strategy designed to discredit the new British government, and specifically Palmerston. On 14 October Palmerston told the French ambassador, Jarnac, that these personal attacks had no impact in Britain (or rather the reverse of what was intended by causing the government and country at large to rally to the Foreign Secretary), and if the aim had been to undermine him, it would be well for the French government to remember that British foreign policy was not, in fact, determined by Palmerston alone. Jarnac reported the conversation to Guizot and noted that it was surprising to see Palmerston grown much more personally hostile; he added that though the Cabinet backed Palmerston for the moment, he doubted it would do so for ever.[30] Yet Palmerston was concerned not just to correct any misapprehensions in France but also to restore and reinforce his own position at home. He reported the same meeting with Jarnac to Russell in tones much more colourful than he had used to Jarnac himself. As he explained, he had told the ambassador:

That I well know that great pains had been taken by some persons both at home & abroad to represent me as actuated by passion instead of by policy, & by personal impulse instead of by a regard for national interests; as a systematic hater of France, & lover of war; and as a disturber of the peace of Europe. That these imputations were totally false & groundless and were made only to serve purposes which it was easy to understand; but that let them be made by whomsoever they might, I should always resent them.[31]

Russell in turn wrote to Jarnac, reaffirming Palmerston's good standing within the government, of his reliance on Palmerston's 'sagacious perception of the true interests of his country' and his complete agreement with his Foreign Secretary on all matters relating to Britain's foreign relations.[32] A diplomatic crisis that threatened initially to damage Palmerston was gradually being turned round by him to one which redounded to his credit. Palmerston was glad to exploit a growing Francophobia in Britain to strengthen his own position (not least by contrast with Aberdeen and Peel) and, by encouraging the Queen in her criticism of Guizot, to tie her to his own line of policy. Peel had been at Windsor at the end of September and afterwards made particular efforts to make sure Russell knew that he, Aberdeen and Graham were indignant at French conduct in Spain; it is reasonable to assume he said similar things to the Queen. Palmerston was gratified to learn his opponents' erstwhile faith in French policy had been weakened.[33] Aberdeen, he noted, continued to be 'very charitable to Guizot',[34] but there was no mistaking the fact that the *entente cordiale* of the earlier 1840s looked much less sincere and worth sustaining. Aberdeen's 'system of making himself under secretary to Guizot has been injurious to British interests all over the world', Palmerston lamented in December.[35]

If the Spanish marriages question had, to a large extent, bolstered Palmerston's position in ministerial and royal circles by the end of 1846, it offered too an important platform to consolidate his wider reputation with the British public as a patriotic and steadfast defender of the national interest. In early October, Russell reported that the Sheriff of London had expressed the growing doubts of the City about the value of a 'special friendship' with France; and though 'people' had previously regarded a close relationship between Britain and France as a 'great security to peace', said the Sheriff, they 'are now beginning to think that such intimacies have embarrassments which might otherwise have been avoided'.[36] This was grist to the Palmerstonian mill. The Sheriff's views were, said Palmerston, 'very sensible', but what else was to be expected, he asked, having thrown 'a comparatively inexperienced honest minded open-hearted young woman into personal contact with a hoary and accomplished intriguer, with nobody to see fair play except a good natured, easy tempered, apathetic and yielding man like our friend Aberdeen'?[37] Clarendon urged Palmerston to make his position more public. Charles Greville had offered to write a pamphlet that in 'narrating facts' would 'expose'

Guizot and Louis Philippe (should Palmerston want him to), but, Clarendon thought, better still would be a press campaign. Palmerston's known contacts with the *Morning Chronicle*, he said, diminished the impact of any attack made through that journal, but he offered to help Palmerston get articles into *The Times* which would not only be good for 'enlightening the public' but also, given that paper's stature, tell to great effect in France.[38] John Thaddeus Delane, editor of *The Times*, was at first wary of becoming an instrument of Palmerstonian policy, but he came to acknowledge the (national) need to support the Foreign Secretary.[39]

At the formation of Russell's government, Palmerston had been cautiously welcomed back by many newspapers. The *Daily News* suggested that hostility to Palmerston in certain quarters when he had last been at the Foreign Office had been ultimately detrimental to British interests: 'The clamour against the Palmerston policy, instead of having an exclusive effect upon his lordship, had a prospective effect upon Lord Aberdeen; giving him a kind of *carte blanche* for letting down the pride and allowing the interests and the influence of the country to ooze away', an editorial in late August argued. 'The worst effect, indeed, of the Palmerston extreme was, that it enabled the Aberdeen extreme to pass without comment.' While Palmerstonian bellicosity had thrown the country 'into a fever', therefore, it had subsequently been 'so blooded and lowered' by Aberdeen 'that she has lain like a patient on a sick bed, weak apathetic; recovering but without vigour or sense to pursue her duties or support her rights', as had been the case in North America in the early 1840s, the paper noted.[40] It was an equivocal endorsement, but there was, it seems, an appetite for a certain robustness as an antidote to Aberdeen's perceived timidity: as the *Economist* put it in September, Palmerston 'is a man of high spirit and great firmness, and about the least likely statesman living to allow any power in Europe to take a sharp advantage of him'.[41]

Despite this, Palmerston's handling of affairs in Spain and relations with France had quickly attracted adverse comment. The Tory-leaning *Standard* had been the most severe of his newspaper critics. On 19 September it had said that Britain should do nothing in Spain: 'What the French Government, or any other Government, may do in a country like Spain, concerns us no more than the doings of a gentleman who may be indiscreet enough to mix himself in a street riot concerns the observer from a drawing room window.' Whether the mob be brought to order or not, the paper said, was a matter of indifference.[42] Indeed, the *Standard* maintained, the British people were never more desirous of good relations with France than at present and it mocked Palmerston's presumption in protesting against the Montpensier marriage as 'an extremely impertinent proceeding' on a question which had no bearing at all on Britain. Yet, having made the protest, if it was not followed up by preparations for war, the policy would be 'a disgraceful compromise of the honour of the country'. It was some consolation that Russell and Grey were in place to keep the 'incendiary Foreign Secretary' (who had been 'hankering unceasingly' for war with

France for the past six years) in some sort of order.[43] The *Standard's* hostility was predictable, but even papers more moderate, or even those well disposed to Palmerston, entertained misgivings about involvement in the peninsula. The *Manchester Guardian* thought the less Palmerston interfered in Spain the 'greater satisfaction' he would give at home since this was 'a matter of perfect indifference' to British interests.[44] Even the pro-Palmerston *Globe*, when it finally expressed an opinion on the Spanish marriages, pointed out, almost wearily, that 'this marriage policy' had been pursued 'for centuries' between France and Spain and admitted that it did not rate the question as one of particular importance 'in an international point of view'; an 'abstinence from everything like family influence' and 'the maintenance of a steady friendship with Spain, without reference to any particular party' was about as far as the *Globe* went in working out a line of policy.[45] The *Morning Post* concluded that Palmerston had been outwitted by his '*ci-devant* ally' France and imagined that Louis Philippe 'chuckles mightily in his addresses in victimising his Lordship so easily'. Though conceding that Palmerston was committed to making 'a very bad state of affairs as little calamitous and disgraceful as possible', the *Post* maintained that he had handled affairs poorly.[46] In part these journals were judging on the basis of imperfect intelligence: Palmerston himself said nothing in Parliament on the matter and much editorial comment drew for its inspiration on pre-existing prejudice and biased continental reports. Opinion softened, somewhat, once, as *The Times* put it in November, 'The sinking tide has ... disclosed rocks and shoals about our course, over which we floated a few months ago in confidence and safety. . . . We are not so unreasonable or so unjust as to impute to Lord Palmerston evils which he could not prevent and cannot repair.' The French government, it concluded, had used Palmerston's return to the Foreign Office 'to effect a stroke of policy under a pretence of a counter-intrigue on the part of England'.[47] The *Standard* continued to censure Palmerston, criticising 'this "Gunpowder" minister' and 'aged fop' for his 'officious coxcombry' in his treatment of France, but even this instrument of an emergent 'Country Party' (or the Protectionist opposition) was drawn to admit that Aberdeen had 'betrayed' agreements made at Eu in 1843 and that the change from Aberdeen to Palmerston was 'not so very bad after all', and both, with their 'soft heads', had 'cheated themselves'.[48]

The shifting opinion was perceptible, if gradual. The *Post*, still critical of Palmerston's policy, pointed out in November that much of the negative assessments derived from hostile overseas journals, such as *La Presse*, which projected into the courts of Europe (successfully, according to the *Post*), an image of London as 'the *point de mire* of all the revolutions of Europe, and Lord Palmerston to be considered by them as the "Messiah on whom they rely for the accomplishment of all their *projets de bouleversement*"'.[49] It was against this background, then, that the *Daily News* issued a rallying call to the public. 'If the country must take an interest in its foreign policy and influence, must make a hero or a demon of him who conducts that policy, we do humbly suggest that it would be much better for the country to rally behind the minister of spirit than the minister of humiliation.' Significantly, this editorial continued by underlining the perceived import of that opinion: 'Foreign countries and provinces know well the freedom of our form of government, are well aware where true power and sovereignty reside, and feel, that it is with the spirit of the British public they have to deal. Provided that this be over-mild, be humble, be prepared to offer one cheek to the blow after having suffered it on the other, foreign rivals will laugh at the resentment of a minister, nay will brave it with audacity, and success, as the King of the French has just done at Madrid.' These were the grounds upon which Palmerston was to be supported.[50] Such were the grounds in part, too, on which Palmerston needed popular backing.

Yet, as *The Times* argued – in denial of claims made in the *Standard* that it was writing under Palmerston's influence – press support was earned, not commanded. 'On these independent terms the support we may lend to a statesman when we think his policy national and wise is the more worth his acceptance, inasmuch as he knows it to be spontaneous and sincere; and if we are obliged to record our dissent, it may be worth while for such a statesman to ask himself which of the two conflicting lines of policy has the real support of the nation.'[51] Up to this point, Palmerston had exploited certain newspapers largely as a means of feeding or leaking information to a wider audience. Henceforth, he would become much more active in using the press to form opinion. The experiences of the winter of 1845 and the six months leading up to the formation of Russell's government had shown that Palmerston could not rely on Whig support, and, significantly, this had been widely reported in the press at the time. And although the Queen was (reluctantly) agreeable to Palmerston's policy on Spain, relations with the Victorian court were never again to be so close as they had been in the later 1830s. Occasional reference was still made to Palmerston's indiscretions of that earlier period – both public and private (such as his alleged attempted seduction of Mrs Brand, one of the Queen's ladies-in-waiting, at Windsor) – but under Albert's guidance the monarch was becoming more assertive in her supervision of foreign policy.

Technically, any dispatch sent abroad was sent in the sovereign's name. Constitutionally, therefore, the monarch had a right to review (and approve or amend) diplomatic correspondence before it was sent. Whereas Aberdeen had been, on the whole, willing to accommodate Victoria's views (or at least he had treated any divergence from his and the monarch's own opinions with delicacy),[52] Palmerston proved less willing to yield to royal influence. He did not feel obliged to wait for the Queen's acquiescence in all letters he wrote, partly because he knew that it would not always be forthcoming, partly because he found it too cumbersome a procedure to observe. It was not the first such complaint that Victoria made, then, when she remonstrated in April 1847 that she had 'several times asked Lord Palmerston through Lord John Russell, &

personally, to see that the drafts to our foreign ministers are not dispatched *previous* to their being submitted to the Queen; notwithstanding, this is still done'.[53] Where the Queen's surveillance of draft dispatches identified issues that needed further clarification, or highlighted orthographic mistakes, Palmerston admitted that this was often beneficial.[54] Even so, Prince Albert intended the Palace to do more than proof-read dispatches. He expected Palmerston to furnish them with enough material to be able to make informed judgements,[55] yet in pursuit of this Albert also maintained a regular correspondence not only with other members of the Cabinet, but also with European sovereigns, and this placed an increasing strain on relations between Palmerston and the court.[56] Victoria and Albert saw Palmerston as a minister dangerously prone to threaten war and insufficiently attentive to the monarch's counsel. Palmerston, for his part, thought the Queen too easily influenced (and misled) by 'persons who are hostile to her government, and who wish to poison her mind with distrust of her ministers; and in this way, she is constantly suffering under groundless uneasiness'.[57] By 1848 Russell was receiving summonses to attend the Queen to hear her complaints against Palmerston and the royal couple had begun to keep a dossier on his diplomatic misdemeanours.[58] Victoria complained that Palmerston meddled too much in the party politics of foreign countries and on one occasion accused him of behaving 'like a naughty child'.[59] Rather than Palmerston's policies, which appeared to her to destabilise the status quo, the Queen continued to press for non-intervention and the preservation of established authority, reflecting a sort of Hanoverian reactionary spirit, the chief author of which it was not difficult to identify.

Lady Palmerston warned Palmerston that he contradicted the Queen's 'notions too boldly';[60] yet though the Queen tolerated early Palmerstonian lapses in not sending dispatches in good time,[61] her patience was soon exhausted. Her warnings to Palmerston not to allow dispatches to be sent prior to approval again were made to little effect and complaints continued to rain in on both Russell and Palmerston throughout the life of the Russell government. Though he usually met these reprimands penitently, Palmerston was not above a certain petulant childishness in his rejoinder. 'The Queen spoke to me the other day about the drafts sent to her for her approval,' Russell wrote to Palmerston in February 1849, 'that they were sometimes sent at the bottom of a box, which she did not conceive required immediate attention: That sometimes they were sent as immediate & the messenger ordered to wait when there was no reason for hurry; but above all that they were sent to her for approval before I had seen them, & while they were still liable to alterations suggested by me, or by the Cabinet.'[62] Palmerston, quite legitimately, pointed out that the business of the Foreign Office had multiplied to such an extent that it was not always practicable to wait for the outcome of royal (and often also of Cabinet) deliberations. The Foreign Secretary wrote to one diplomat in the spring of 1848 that he should not be surprised if he did not hear from Palmerston by every messenger; rather he should wonder how Palmerston managed to write at all given the 'avalanche of despatches from every part of the world which come down upon me daily, and which must be read' and 'the number of interviews which I cannot avoid giving every day of the week'.[63] It was similarly impossible, he said, to comply with the Queen's demands for perpetual and complete consultation on diplomatic business. And as he observed to Russell in reply to one of the Queen's periodic chastisements:

> You are very expeditious & regular, but she often keeps drafts a long time, and as despatches cannot be sent off every day, like letters by the post, it often happens that the delay of two or three days by preventing a despatch from going by one periodical opportunity involves a delay of several days further; and when events are going on at a hard gallop, ones instructions become rather stale before they reach their destination. . . . But if you & the Queen wish it I can alter the present arrangement & order all drafts to go first to you, & not to the Queen till after you have returned them but this will reduce my flint gun to a matchlock. The number of despatches received & sent out in 1848 was upwards of 29,000. The number in 1828 was a little above 10,000.[64]

Russell clearly grew weary of mediating between the Foreign Office and the Palace and in 1848 asked Palmerston to 'save the Queen anxiety, & me some trouble by giving your reasons before, & not after an important dispatch is sent'.[65]

What is remarkable about this period is that Palmerston not only survived in office, but prospered. It must have seemed to George Julian Harney, as he ventured down to Tiverton in the summer of 1847 to 'get at' Palmerston at the general election, that the moment was propitious for pulling down the Foreign Secretary. Harney, a leading figure in the Chartist movement, had never seen Palmerston – when he spoke briefly with Palmerston before the hustings he had no idea with whom he chatted[66] – but he arrived forearmed with a stout critique of Palmerstonian policy to put before the electorate and expose Palmerston as unfit for Parliament, let alone the Foreign Office. Palmerston looked on Harney's challenge as a minor diversion. 'I have been so little with my constituents of late,' he told Russell, 'that I am advised to make a personal canvass although I have no opponent but a certain Mr Harney a Chartist who announces his intention of proving on the hustings that I am not, and that he is, a fit person to represent Tiverton. Such a contest is more likely to be amusing than dangerous.'[67]

Harney arrived three days before the nomination was due, and attempted to whip up the electors with Chartist speeches and general charges against Palmerston. Palmerston declined an invitation to join Harney at a pre-hustings meeting to discuss his foreign policy, but flattered his opponent by saying that he was sure 'that the observations you may think it right to make upon those matters will be made in the fair spirit of legitimate political hostility'.[68] By the third and final speech, Harney had succeeded, it seemed, in winning the popular support of the people: 'The town was now in a very lively state; some thousands were at the meeting, and the enthusiasm of the Chartists rose to the highest pitch when Mr Harney concluded a lengthy and impassioned appeal . . . – "Tonight we sleep upon our arms; to-morrow we march to battle and victory!" '[69] The 'effect was electrical; one mighty roar of applause showed the delight and determination of the people', observed a partisan pamphlet after-wards.[70] Harney had adverted to issues that resonated with a Chartist agenda, but he reserved his most powerful rhetoric for an assault on Palmerston's discreditable conduct. At the hustings, Harney promised, 'I will prove him to be devoid of true patriotism, a breaker of pledges, and a foe to the liberties of the people, whose dearest rights he will trample in the dust', promises that were, apparently, met with 'tremendous cheering'.[71] This was an attempt not just to disparage Palmerston's policies, but to undermine Palmerston's reputa-tion as a defender of liberalism and of constitutional rights.

On the day of the election, Palmerston led the three candidates (Heathcoat, Harney and himself), and his proposer and seconder, to the hustings, preceded by the town band and looking 'jubilant as usual – as if going to a pleasant picnic rather than to a passage of arms with a political antagonist'. Heathcoat spoke first, and though he was subsequently returned, played little other role in the drama of the day. Following Heathcoat, Palmerston should have spoken next but he deferred to Harney on the grounds that it made more sense for him to reply to Harney's attack than attempt to anticipate it.[72] Harney's supporters had initially opposed this proceeding but it was agreed that Harney should have a second speech in which, having attacked Palmerston, he could discuss those reforms he deemed 'necessary for the welfare of the country'.[73] Harney's attack on Palmerston, lasting for more than two hours, ranged over the whole of the Foreign Secretary's ministerial career and endeavoured first to damn him by association with the governments headed by Spencer Perceval ('a constitutional tyrant'), Canning ('a clever jester, a talented buffoon, the able and brilliant flunkey of the aristocracy'), Wellington (the ally 'of despotism') and Melbourne (leader of 'the profligate Whig Government'), before entering into a careful and minute criticism of Palmerston's foreign policy since 1830. When Harney concluded by implying Palmerston had also been complicit in recent City frauds, however, he is said to have 'roused Lord Palmerston's wrath' and Palmerston 'set himself to the task of reply with unwonted vigour', launching an hour-long defence of government policy and critique of the Charter.[74] Even in later life, Palmerston is said to have remembered Harney, not unkindly, as having given him 'a dressing down'.[75]

Palmerston 'was received with mingled cheers and groans' when he stood to answer Harney.[76] Harney's speech, Palmerston declared, was in many respects unobjectionable, but there were certain grounds upon which he took exception.

Firstly, he sought to remedy a misrepresentation, that 'I displayed a want of due feeling and sympathy for the misfortunes of the lower classes' in the House of Commons. Harney, he claimed, 'knows that what he has stated is not true (cries of "Oh, oh," and "Hear, hear")', and the subject had been imperfectly discussed because it was raised just at the close of the parliamentary session. Against Harney's other charges, Palmerston defended himself, and 'twitted' Harney 'with being a Tory in disguise'. He denied that his Irish estates yielded increased incomes, despite his attempts to improve them; he asserted that he was 'a decided advocate of reform', but that he wished to see it introduced 'by agitation of mind, and not by the agitation of physical force'; he acknowledged his political debt to Canning, but stressed the 'honour to his country' of Canning's conduct; he declared that he drew no distinction between Ireland and England nor Irish and English and fully supported attempts to relieve the distress caused by the famine; and he identified himself as a champion of factory, health and educational reform.[77] But he focused for the rest of his speech on foreign policy, his acknowledged specialism:

> Now, when I say that he knows nothing of the matters he has been talking of, all I mean is, that he appears to me to have got by rote a certain number of empty declamatory phrases (great laughter and interruption), a jargon and jingle of words – (Renewed laughter and loud cheers) – which have no reference to facts, which have no bearing upon anything that has happened, and that his statements are founded on a total misconception of the history of the last twelve or fourteen years. Mr Harney is of opinion that the great object and the grand result of my foreign policy has been the establishment of tyranny and despotism all over the world – (A voice, 'So it has,' and laughter) – and the suppression of the liberties of the people.

This Palmerston found amusing, since, as he continued, 'I have been accused all over Europe of being the great instigator of revolution – (Laughter) – the friend and champion of all popular insurrections, the enemy of all constituted authorities', and this way of thinking, he said, was founded on 'matters which are not really matters of opinion'. Harney's attacks on the substance of Palmerstonian politics, on his conduct of foreign policy, despite the momentary displays of popular approval, were lively in their linguistic construction, but limited in their actual impact. Yet they revealed a risk to Palmerston, who was counting on carrying opinion with him as he presented Britain as a beacon of liberalism in Europe. Harney's rhetorical badinage over liberal policies in the 1830s had been the prelude to a promised dissection of Palmerston's maladroit handling of policy since returning to office in 1846. Here Harney identified three issues in international – specifically European – affairs on which to challenge Palmerston. In Poland, and particularly in the extinction of Cracow as a free and independent state following its annexation to Austria in November 1846, Harney identified a breach of the Treaty of Vienna and alleged that when Palmerston had told the House of Commons (in August) that he believed the Austrian occupation of Cracow was temporary, and when he had finally written in protest, towards the end of the year, he had done so claiming he could not believe the Eastern powers would countenance such a fundamental breach of the treaty over such a relative trifle as Cracow. Yet, Harney said, when Palmerston had written this 'cringing rubbish' he knew that Cracow had been confiscated and the Vienna agreement thereby ignored. It was, he said, a temporary triumph for despotism (temporary since there was an inextinguishable devotion to liberty in Poland which would ensure that the country would again be free). But, significantly, Harney sought to tie Palmerston to the 'tyrants' who had 'shed oceans of blood' in Poland, by his complicity in, or failure to stand up to, Austrian aggrandisement. 'It was a part well done to make the British lion play the part of the blood-lapping wolf of Austria,' he said, to loud Tivertonian cheers.[78]

Yet while Palmerston (and other members of the government) had been alarmed by events in Poland in late 1846, pragmatism had seemed to dictate a policy of reluctant acquiescence. In August Palmerston had told the House that though a 'great and a noble people', Britain could offer no more support to Poland than was provided for under the terms of Vienna, and those terms, he pointed out, rested on joint action by the powers to defend Cracow (therefore Britain should not act alone now); he also intimated that when Austria had originally occupied Cracow, it was in response to known 'plots and conspiracies' that threatened Poland's neighbours and that, under the terms agreed in 1815, entitled Austria to intervene. He promised active British efforts to restore the independence of Cracow once the present crisis had passed, yet Palmerston also pointed out that though some MPs were calling for immediate armed intervention, from a military point of view Britain's chances of success in such a war were uncertain.[79] Harney was correct, in so far as Palmerston had been disinclined to act, but Palmerston himself had at the time maintained not that this breach of Vienna was unimportant, but that more pressing questions, in western Europe, demanded certain concessions in the east. Treating the actual annexation of Cracow as hypothetical – which Harney had decried as 'cringing' – Palmerston argued in fact gave Britain greater freedom of action. As he put it to Russell:

I confess it seems to me that with a view to our relations with Austria it would be far better that we should state our opinions as bearing upon a question which we may officially assume to be yet undecided rather than that we should at once have to protest against a measure announced to us as taken. By the first course at least we gain time for the coming to some understanding about the Spanish question by the latter course we are driven at once into argumentative conflict with Austria, or we must leave unnoticed a measure which in Parliament we could not defend ourselves for not protesting against.[80]

Russell had agreed that Britain was obliged to uphold Vienna and so 'we lament the extinction of a free city', but, he added, 'in the present situation of affairs we ought carefully to avoid any step which our crafty neighbour [France] might take advantage of to say, "We are as you are conservatives; England wishes to promote jacobinism and anarchy; it is your interest to join with us, & if we keep down revolution in Spain, you ought to be thankful to us." '[81]

Though the professed constitutionalist credentials of the Whig ministry raised an expectation that the government would protest against Austrian conduct, the risk of thus encouraging an alignment between France and the Eastern courts was too great to contemplate. The Queen worried about the implications for German states if they were to be surrounded by two powers, France and Russia, who were growing vociferous in their contempt for 'les clauses honteuses' of the Vienna settlement,[82] while Russell told Palmerston that if Russia was to take advantage of instability in central Europe and proceed to annex the Duchy of Warsaw (as was thought possible), it would be necessary for Britain to act.[83] Yet even when framing the Queen's speech for the opening of Parliament in January 1847, Palmerston was still keen to avoid, if possible, any rupture with Austria or Russia.[84]

Palmerston's response to events in Cracow, then, was affected by a delicate balance of contradictory considerations. As the *Morning Post* underlined the point in December 1846, any policy on Poland would of necessity have a significant Montpensier dimension, as France exploited the unsettled nature of European alignments to advance on Spain, while Russia and Austria were flexing their muscles in central and eastern Europe.[85] Palmerston argued that Britain could not take on Austria, Russia and (perhaps) Prussia combined, could not sanction the destruction of the Vienna settlement and could not divert its attention from French threats in the Iberian Peninsula. Yet these were conflicting objectives: whichever line Britain took over Cracow it seemed to Palmerston that France would use it as a means of driving a wedge between Britain and the rest of Europe – casting Britain either as a champion of anarchy or as a strategic rival to Austrian and Russian influence on their own borders; in either case France would seek Eastern support for its challenge to Britain in Spain. Thus, Palmerston argued that Britain should bide its time and avoid, if possible, an overt clash with Austria and Russia over Polish annexation. This was in essence what he told the House in March 1847 when he argued that Britain should not 'pass strong resolutions' in Parliament condemning the Eastern powers since he did not see how they could 'be followed up by some decisive step'; empty threats, he pointed out, would tarnish British honour and dignity.[86] By tying British policy in 1846 and 1847 to a strict reading of 1815 and to subsequent revisions, Palmerston also hoped to disarm Tory opponents by pointing out that these treaties had more to do with Castlereagh, Aberdeen and the Tories than with himself and the Whigs.[87] The difficulty, at home, as Harney's speech highlighted, was that in bowing to *realpolitik* constraints on his policy, Palmerston was seen, in certain quarters, to have forsaken his claims to represent liberal and constitutional government.

Harney made similar attempts to undermine Palmerston's liberal credentials in turning to the other two questions on which he said Palmerston had let his country down since the summer of 1846: those of Portugal and in Spain. In October 1846 the Portuguese Queen, Donna Maria, dismissed her government and introduced a series of repressive measures attacking personal freedoms and the liberty of the press. The ensuing civil war between the royal government and a 'liberal', popular, junta caused Palmerston to worry that Spain would be induced to intervene to stabilise the throne of a neighbour. Neither Spain, nor, by extension, France, really wished to see instability in Portugal and both were induced in the spring of 1847 to act with Britain to bring the Portuguese conflict to an end with a jointly mediated amnesty and reintroduction of a constitution. It was a diplomatic move driven by strategic interest, and though Palmerston's official biographer later tried to maintain that it was also a triumph for liberal principles over despotic ('Lord Palmerston was enabled to secure to the Portuguese nation those concessions which would not have been made if Spain had interfered singly at the request of the Absolutist party'), even he was obliged to concede that it was equally important from Britain's point of view to have limited Spanish influence in Portugal.[88] It was this latter point, implying that Palmerston's policy had been anti-Spanish more than pro-(liberal)-Portuguese, that Harney put to the people of Tiverton. Donna Maria, Harney said, was 'one of the noble lord's liberal pets', but her record in government showed her to be no respecter of constitutions: 'Dicer's oaths are of more value than Donna Maria's. She will swear to any number of Charters or Constitutions under compulsion, and violate every pledge the moment she can safely do so.' Palmerston's recent policy there, Harney maintained, displayed a marked disregard for popular sentiment: what remained of Donna Maria's authority (and Harney said it was not much) existed 'because the cannon of the English fleet pointed against the people'. 'Never was there a clearer case of national pronouncement against bad government. Yet the noble lord interfered to crush the patriots, at a moment too, when, in spite of our fleet in the Tagus, a last blow by the insurgents would certainly have sent Donna Maria packing to Windsor Castle. The noble lord will no doubt take credit to himself for having put an end to a civil war without bloodshed. But I ask if, even though without shedding blood you condemn a nation to slavery, is that nothing, is that any slight offence?'[89]

The irony of the charge was probably not lost on Palmerston: he had, in the autumn of 1846, regularly been subject to Queen Victoria's injunctions to tone down his dispatches which, she felt, as she wrote on one occasion in late November, 'must give the impression that we entirely espouse the cause of the rebels whose conduct is, to say the least, illegal & very reprehensible' and she criticised him for treating the Portuguese 'nation & the opposition as one & the same thing'.[90] The Queen rejoiced at news of Maria's forces' military advances in January 1847 and urged on Palmerston the need for 'moderation' in putting an end to the war.[91] Yet Palmerston, Victoria thought, continued to write in a manner which the Portuguese government would 'construe into an over great solicitude for the insurgents'.[92] Palmerston, however, in private correspondence, was clear that events in Portugal were not part of an ideological contest and he refused to act 'after the fashion of Austria & Russia' in intervening or arbitrating between the two sides. Certainly, he said, there was no obligation under the terms of the Quadruple Alliance of 1834 to act; perhaps if foreign forces threatened Maria's throne Britain might be able to invoke that agreement, but he saw no evidence of such external threats.[93] Cabinet colleagues agreed. Lansdowne spoke of using Britain's 'moral influence' to secure peace in Portugal but thought there was no case, at that moment, to go further.[94] Russell concurred that there was no 'foreign enemy' threatening the country and even if Maria had 'outraged public opinion' and reduced Portugal to an 'embarrassing and pitiable' state, the Quadruple Alliance, though couched in the language of liberalism, was in fact no more than a commitment to aid the Queen to expel Dom Miguel from Portugal, and Miguel was not on this occasion officially involved. There was, he concluded, no 'clear case for interference even by the spirit of the Quadruple Treaty'. The risk of a Spanish ascendancy at Lisbon was real enough, and so Russell argued for the joint action with Spain and France to stabilise Portugal; but there was obviously no appetite to turn this into a war of principles.[95] As Palmerston put the matter in August in a letter to Russell shortly after the general election, 'perhaps after all we may succeed, not in making things go just as we could wish, but at least in preventing them from going as ill as they otherwise would do'. He feared in particular a union of Spain and Portugal and the consequent loss of British leverage in the peninsula if instead of leaning to Britain, Portugal was annexed to Spain which might well itself become 'a satellite of France'. An 'Iberian Republic' was too much of an uncertain entity to be considered a viable alternative. Losing ground in Portugal, Palmerston said, would threaten British commercial, political, military and naval interests: the only safeguard against a hostile west European coast, from France to Portugal, was an independent Portugal in an 'intimate & protected state of alliance with England'.[96] Palmerston was willing to support, or tolerate, Maria's government if that seemed, as it did from the reports received, most likely to underpin stability. Qualms about the liberality of the Queen's government were swept aside on the grounds that no legal basis for unilateral interference existed. *The Times*, at Clarendon's bidding, had agreed to adhere to the view that 'we cld have done nothing but what we have done' in Portugal,[97] and the only significant press criticism of Palmerston's handling of the Portuguese civil war at the time had been, predictably, in the high Tory papers. The *Standard*, for instance, had maintained that Palmerston meant to involve Britain in the civil war (or, indeed, any war: 'Only give Lord Palmerston a war and he is "anybody's customer",' it had observed in one editorial on Portugal) and tried to present him as 'not . . . popular with any class' in Britain and the architect of policies hostile to peace everywhere in Europe.[98]

Harney's speech had picked over the civil war in Portugal selectively and presented the conflict in the peninsula as a straightforward clash between liberalism and despotism. This was fair so far as the characters of the two sides went; but it did not acknowledge the practical constraints (whether genuine or not) within which ministers and much of the newspaper press accepted that British policy was framed. Nor did it credit Palmerston with the sympathetic view of the Junta's grievances which he had displayed in his early private and draft diplomatic correspondence dealing with the matter. Yet when he had spoken on the issue at Westminster – and not until June 1847 did he make a significant parliamentary statement on Portugal – Palmerston had himself emphasised the limits on his freedom of manoeuvre and above all the importance of bringing the war to an end.[99] To an already excited crowd in Tiverton, however, the imagined analogies drawn by Harney with arbitrary governmental suppression of popular freedoms in Britain had simplified the issue and drawn a superficial but warmly endorsed hustings criticism of Palmerston. Likewise, turning in the final part of his election address to recent commercial dealings in Spain, Harney pointed to what he argued showed the disingenuousness of Palmerston's declared support for free trade, and by implication his lack of real concern for the material welfare of the poorer classes. Palmerston's threat to engage British military might to enforce demands for payment of debts owing to Spanish bond-holders in Britain was, said Harney, unjustifiable. Deploying the language of class conflict, Harney explained: 'These Spanish bondholders are English capitalists, who lent some millions of money to the government of Spain, not, as has been represented, because they were anxious to help the people of that country to obtain "Liberal institutions," but because they were promised a higher rate of interest than they could get at home. That money had been derived from the labour of the English people.' This was the stuff of classic Chartist invective: investing British capital overseas had inhibited the cultivation and development of domestic agriculture and industry and contributed to the growing divide between classes in Britain. Palmerston's foreign policy, therefore, said Harney, was the instrument of the rich and not the defender of the poor.[100] Palmerston had taken great offence at this in his reply, and although Harney partially retracted the charge when he spoke again, after Palmerston, the fact that the initial accusation was met with 'immense cheering' suggests a certain receptivity on the part of the audience. From the point of view of Palmerston's cultivation of an image of himself as defender of popular rights and interests, this was a significant blow.

Like his opponent, however, Palmerston retired from the front of the hustings at the end of his speech, 'amid loud and prolonged cheering'.[101] Harney won a show-of-hands poll on the day with a majority support of two-thirds of the audience (occasioning the 'most indescribable tumult of cheering' which 'continued for a long time'),[102] but until put to the test of an official ballot, which Harney declined to contest on the grounds that the existing franchise excluded 'the majority of adult male inhabitants of the borough',[103] the victory was somewhat illusory, though in a subsequent published version of his speech he styled himself 'the People's Member for Tiverton'.[104] Perhaps the show of hands demonstrated a groundswell of support among the disenfranchised, but it was from this same body that Palmerston also received loud and prolonged cheers. When the contest was put to a ballot, Palmerston secured 117 votes to come second (as usual) to Heathcoat with 147 while Harney, who refused to participate, officially polled 0. The Tiverton election of 1847 had been more than the amusement Palmerston had apparently expected. At the very least it illustrated the fickle nature of public opinion, and the imperfect means by which it was expressed.

Harney had been able to present himself, plausibly, as 'the friend of the people' and yet Palmerston had apparently elicited a popular endorsement of his political standing. Crucially, however attractive Harney's arguments might have been to his audience, Palmerston's authority (even if it was partly the theatrical demonstration of that authority) somehow exploited a sense that he could offer more convincing leadership, that while (unlike Harney) he did not pretend to be one of the people, he nevertheless argued that he was acting for them (just as Dugald Stewart would have advised). Ultimately, and interestingly in the light of the reported cheering of his performance, Harney's charges against Palmerston's illiberal and unpatriotic conduct did not stick, and even though doubts were still expressed in certain middle-class, educated circles about Palmerston's sincerity,[105] his ability to flatter extra-parliamentary audiences continued to buttress his position. However, though he had been triumphant at Tiverton in 1847, that election had also illustrated the capricious nature of popular support and the need to pay greater attention to courting favourable opinion. It was through foreign policy, and specifically the further elaboration of his English, national, liberal constitutionalist persona, that Palmerston was able to sustain a parliamentary position that seemed at frequent intervals during the late 1840s a particularly vulnerable one.

Although Harney had won fleeting applause for his criticism of the outward appearances of Palmerstonian foreign policy in the Iberian Peninsula and Cracow, Palmerston knew that there were larger stakes – both tangible and intangible – to be played for. What Harney had glossed over was the perceived threat to Britain posed by a resurgent and assertive France. Palmerston was more influenced by criticism that was both sustained and reasoned than by momentary confrontations and in response to allegations that he had been outwitted over the Spanish marriages by France, he argued that this served only to underline the need for a strong-arm and confident, pragmatic rejoinder. Ideally his foreign policy would defend popular liberties (or be presented as so doing), but before this it would uphold British strategic and commercial interests. In September 1846 Palmerston had drawn attention to Russell of the value of physical demonstrations of strength, suggesting that a British naval presence off the coast of Spain would have helped check France: 'This sort of demonstration often tells upon a negotiation; and it would do no harm at the Tuileries if any orders about fitting out line of battle ships could be given in our dockyards, & mentioned in the newspapers, even if no active or real steps were taken to carry them into effect.'[106] By the end of the year Palmerston began to point to the lamentable state of British coastal defences and the country's vulnerability to attack. Until the situation was attended to, he said, 'this Empire is existing only by sufferance and by the tolerance of the other powers; and our weakness being better known to others than it is felt by ourselves, tends greatly to encourage foreign states to do things calculated to expose us either to war or to deep humiliation.'[107] A poorly defended Britain would be susceptible to invasion and a militarily reticent Britain would be marginalised diplomatically; but domestically, being the minister seen to address those deficiencies would convey a powerful impression to the country at large. Palmerston's concerns about national defence were generally well received in government,[108] but he continued to write alarmist letters to colleagues about France. Some of these colleagues, such as Charles Wood, thought the threat was entirely of Palmerston's own making – 'all the foolish alarm about [a French] invasion', he told Hobhouse, 'was caused by Palmerston's correspondence & perpetual broils'[109] – but in fact such concerns pre-dated the Russell ministry, and Cabinet doubts about expanded national defence arrangements were motivated largely by economic considerations and reservations about how this might also raise the tricky political question of a national militia.[110] Palmerston continued to highlight the cross-Channel danger. There may well be 'a great mass of quiet money making men' in France, he wrote to Russell, but there were also 'an immense number of ardent spirits' bent on war with Britain. This was a private letter to the Prime Minister yet it would not be long before such sentiments – the primary need to act firmly to check overseas aggression – were more widely seen as defining something of Palmerston's spirit and policy.

Palmerston's foreign policy was becoming more nuanced – or rather he was more conscious of the tensions between *realpolitik* and *idealpolitik* and the need to accommodate these conflicting pressures. On the one hand was an impulse to promulgate liberal government in Europe, a position underpinned by the rhetoric of Whig Enlightenment thought and buttressed by a recognition of the fact that constitutional governments in Europe would be potentially more amenable, or malleable, to British will (especially if Britain had succeeded in positioning itself symbolically at the forefront of liberal reformist politics). This, so far as it went, was sincere enough. Palmerston favoured constitutional regimes from an intellectual point of view – Dugald Stewart had taught him that accountable and reformable government would better withstand the demands of increasingly modern societies for a wider distribution of power – and experience had often tended to confirm this: Belgium, Spain, Portugal and Greece, for example, all fitted a Palmerstonian or Whig narrative of progressive accommodation of radical demands within carefully reformed, broadly liberal, systems of government. By contrast autocratic regimes, whatever they did at home (and Palmerston rarely troubled to consider this unless he thought British domestic or diplomatic capital could be made from exposing abuses of power in such countries among their own populations), were unstable international partners, which is to say they were frequently perceived to be aggressively expansionist. (The British Empire, though doing much the same, was justified on the hubristic grounds that its expansion was just, not to say necessary, and quite possibly providentially ordained.) Austria, Russia and Prussia, for example, though they could appear potentially useful allies (witness Palmerston's evanescent disposition to treat Metternich's Austria sympathetically in the 1830s) were, in the event, more often rivals for power and influence. And, as if to underline the point, France's political see-sawing between monarchical and parliamentary government was reflected in the rapid waxing and waning of the *entente cordiale*.

So, a second consideration in foreign policy formulation, one which counterbalanced and could outweigh a desire to stimulate freedom, self-determination and liberal government, was a cold assessment of material and strategic self-interest. Palmerstonian foreign policy was and has (both at the time and subsequently) frequently been deemed idiosyncratic or even schizophrenic. This is a superficial judgement, but while it is possible to maintain that a (sometimes pretty thin) thread of Victorian Whig-Liberal thought ran through that foreign policy, it was always conditional upon a favourable calculation of material interests. Yet if that ideological gloss had its limitations in the framing of policy, it should not be discounted as a significant feature of that policy in its execution. Liberal, constitutional, regimes were always preferred by Palmerston, firstly as the outward expression of a Whiggish notion of 'improvement', and, secondly, but also concomitantly, as more (internally) stable diplomatic partners. If the 'real' commitment to the advance and consolidation of liberal government was limited, however, the avowed pursuit of, and support for, that ideal continued to yield domestic benefits, at least rhetorically. Any assessment of Palmerston's foreign policy must take account of the domestic background to that policy and those aspects of it designed primarily for British (popular) consumption alongside a consideration of its more strictly international dimension. Though the government remained for the moment secure in

Parliament, Palmerston felt, in the spring of 1847, that Peel was only about three years away from being able to offer a viable alternative ministry: if the threat was in the future, it was not so far so that the current administration could afford to be complacent, on any front.[111] This is seen clearly in Palmerston's handling of affairs in Italy since his return to the Foreign Office in 1846.

On 30 July 1846 Palmerston had written to Russell about the imminent crisis facing the Papal States. Italy, he said, was 'the weak part of Europe' and would probably be the cause of the next European war. Papal misrule in Italy had been sustained, he continued, only by physical force and the absence of external protest. Yet a society that had known relative peace and security (prior to French invasion) could not be expected to tolerate such a situation indefinitely, and indeed in the years since 1815 'discontent has more than once been . . . manifested by overt acts' in the Italian peninsula. A policy of inaction on Britain's part, however, was dangerous, thought Palmerston: France could and probably would intervene in support of any uprising against papal authority (justifying it as a good liberal cause) and, as well as handing France a lead in central European affairs, this would not be without wider consequences:

Austria *would* interfere, and could scarcely help doing so, even though not very efficiently backed by Russia; France and Austria would then fight each other in Italy, and France would have all the Italians on her side. But the war, begun in Italy, would probably spread to Germany, and at all events, we can have no wish to see Austria broken down and France aggrandised, and the military vanity and love of conquest of the French revived and strengthened by success.

The obvious and essential policy for the new Whig ministry in Britain, said Palmerston, was to offer unequivocal support to the new Pope, Pius IX (who had been elected at just about the moment the Whigs returned to office in Britain), 'in effecting reforms which every enlightened member of the Roman government has long seen and acknowledged to be necessary'.[112] Backing the new Pope was a policy born of diverse interests: a strategic desire to preserve some sort of equilibrium among the great powers alongside an ideological commitment to support a new liberal regime in Italy that would pacify and stabilise the population there (thus also reducing the risk of a major conflagration) while also satisfying the British people that the Whig government was committed to defending popular liberties. The controversy, such as it was, arose, as Donald Southgate pointed out, from Austria's horror and bemusement at witnessing a British minister preaching constitutionalism on Italian soil.[113]

Russell had agreed completely. Any attempt to concert great power action over Italy would necessarily fissure over national ambitions (not least Austria's) while bolstering the Pope's independent power would be more likely to secure 'the peace & happiness of Italy'.[114] More than this, added Palmerston, given the precarious state of affairs in the Iberian Peninsula, Britain would further benefit from acting firmly in Italy and not giving the impression of reliance on other parties, least of all on France.[115] As France began to play down the liberal tone of its foreign policy in an effort to tempt Austria into an anti-British alliance over Spain, and as Austria and Britain diverged over Cracow in the autumn and winter or 1846–47, it became easier for Palmerston and Britain to identify a common interest with the reforming Pius IX and by the beginning of 1847 Britain stood practically alone as a supporter of the Pope. Thus did supposedly Protestant Britain begin to find cause to laud the 'good Pope'.[116] As recent scholarship has suggested, this British backing for Pius IX is not so anomalous as traditional readings of frequently unsympathetic British attitudes to the Catholic Church might have suggested. It is clear that Palmerston and Russell hoped to negate French and Austrian influence in Italy and thereby stabilise central Europe, and also head off a Franco-Austrian combination against Britain in the Iberian Peninsula. Conventionally, this strategic imperative to use Italy to offset divergences with France and Austria elsewhere and thus underwrite a fragile diplomatic position has been taken as grounds enough to justify Palmerston and Russell's interest in Pius's reforms and their decision to send the Earl of Minto, the Lord Privy Seal (and Russell's father-in-law) on a special mission to offer unofficial backing to the Pope in 1847.[117] This certainly sits well with much of the evidence – diplomatic and clerical (the latter also inducing the Pope to regard the idea favourably)[118] – on which the government apparently based its calculations.[119] The proposal had first been aired in April 1847 but it was the summer before Minto was dispatched. With Austria flexing its military muscles in Ferrara in July and August 1847 in an attempt to quash papal attempts to assert independence through the Pope's recently formed civic guard, the case for British intervention to bolster Pius seemed strong (especially since France equivocated, torn between a desire to support liberal reforms in Italy and a hope of securing Austrian backing for its Iberian contest with Britain).[120] There was, Minto was told explicitly, no (official) appetite for becoming embroiled in wider Italian political questions: Russell made it clear that, in whatever political form, Britain 'disapprove[d] of the movement for Italian Unity'.[121] Yet closer to home, a friendlier relationship with the Pope might also, the reasoning went, alleviate growing tensions in Ireland.

When Palmerston presented the case for the mission to the Queen (who was highly sceptical of the merits of establishing diplomatic relations with the Pope), he stressed first of all the strategic advantages. Taking in Switzerland *en route* to Rome in order to measure demands for reform there Minto was 'to exhort them to abstain from all violent acts, and from any extreme measures which could afford either to Austria or to France any pretext for interference by force of arms'. (Palmerston evidently regarded liberal demands for change in Switzerland as significant more in terms of raising the prospect of Austro-French conflict than as a marker for European constitutional reform.)[122] Minto would promote a similarly moderate course in communications with the governments in Turin and Florence: he would urge them to look for closer relations with Britain but avoid any rupture with Austria or France. On this foundation would Minto encourage the Pope to continue his programme of domestic reform, with British support, and open up the prospect of formal political and commercial relations between the papal government and Britain. Palmerston concluded his case for the mission by adverting to the implications for the government's position in Ireland: 'Lord Minto would endeavour to obtain from the Pope,' he wrote, 'the exertion of his spiritual authority over the Catholic priesthood of Ireland to induce them to abstain from repeal agitation, and to urge them not to embarrass but rather to assist Your Majesty's government in the measures which they may plan for the improvement, and for the better government of Ireland.'[123] As Clarendon, the government's viceroy in Ireland, observed, disabusing the Pope of his apprehensions regarding British policy in Ireland and Irish priests' interference in politics, which, he said, 'has been presented to him in a far too favourable and *religious* light', would be useful.[124] Prince Albert, who had been wary when the idea of the mission was first suggested, had, meanwhile, found reason to welcome an initiative that promised to promote civilisation and liberty (prime British exports, he argued),[125] and with public opinion in Britain apparently keenly supportive of the Pope (as a liberal reformer),[126] the projected mission seemed likely to kill a good many birds with one fairly modest stone.

There are grounds for arguing that the objectives of this mission were, or increasingly became, defined in British more than continental terms. In the autumn of 1847 Clarendon wrote extensive memoranda and letters about the implications of Minto's assignment for Ireland, and specifically the government's position there. In a country ravaged by famine and in which the influence of the clergy was near total (and not, he suggested, necessarily benign), Clarendon argued, only papal intervention would remedy a 'state of things degrading to religion, striking at the root of all government, and of social order and improvement' which, he maintained, was exacerbated by the political activity of the priesthood.[127] Indeed, it has been suggested that the closer Minto got to Rome in the autumn of 1847, the more important was this Irish dimension.[128] Having reached Rome on 4 November, Minto's early communications with the Pope certainly dealt extensively with Ireland.[129] Within a fortnight of his arrival, Minto reported to Russell that the Pope and his Secretary of State, Cardinal Gabrielle Ferretti, were 'plain dealing men' who 'know & strongly feel how much they owe to our support, and how necessary it still is to them and I think they are quite ready to do justice to our motives. The influence of the English name is now so great in Italy, that they look as much for my assistance in tempering the views of their own public, as in averting danger from without. And every day brings fresh proofs of the confidence with which we are regarded by all classes in the country.'[130] Palmerston enthused about the prospects for spreading continental peace on the back of commercial ties between Britain and Italy and said that fostering an independent spirit in the peninsula would 'make that country no longer a prize to be fought for'.[131]

The mission did arouse concerns, however. Palmerston's brother-in-law Fred Lamb worried that the Pope would draw the conclusion that Britain was 'on the verge of turning Catholic herself, with all these conversions to Puseyism', while Lady Palmerston thought that as news of Minto's mission leaked out through the press the British public would judge Russell and Minto (though not Palmerston) to have been 'imprudent' and stories of a 'rapprochement with the Pope' reported in hostile papers such as the *Standard* were, she said, 'meant to frighten people out of their senses'.[132] It was, she maintained, a plot by Ellice and Grey to undermine the government generally and Palmerston personally (Grey in particular, Lady Palmerston said, was 'sly' and 'always has an object in everything he does').[133] Such suspicions surrounding the mission no doubt found their way into parliamentary thinking when, in early 1848, moves were made to formalise relations with the Vatican. Concern about accrediting a Catholic clergyman to the Court of St James and moves to avoid such an arrangement served to underline the difficulty inherent in reconciling ministries underpinned respectively by spiritual and political interests. Palmerston himself viewed formal relations with the papal court as potentially problematic. Writing to Clarendon in March 1848 he observed: 'I am convinced by my diplomatic experience that there would be no end to the embarrassments and inconveniences which we should suffer from having a Roman priest invested with diplomatic privilege holding his court in London being surrounded by English and Irish Catholics . . . & capable of becoming an engine of political intrigue to serve all kinds of foreign interests.'[134]

Whatever the primary looked-for results of Minto's mission, it was soon overtaken by events that caused Palmerston to moderate his faith in Pius's commitment to reform and to give greater attention to conventional territorial and strategic concerns. In January 1848 Minto was witness to some of the first stirrings of unrest that would eventually destabilise the continent. An insurrection at Palermo had been designed by the Sicilians to press the King of Naples into adopting the constitution of 1812. Both sides, the King and his disaffected subjects, appealed first to the British chargé d'affaires at Naples, Lord Napier, and then to Minto, to mediate. Palmerston, who had hoped that papal reforms would spread throughout the Italian states and quiet the more extreme demands for reform, saw in the events of early 1848 grounds to doubt whether Pius was up to the task of forcing through the necessary measures. 'Events have gone too fast for such a slow sailor as he is,' he wrote. 'I only hope he will not be swamped by the swell in the wake of those who have outstripped him, for this would perhaps bring the Austrians into the Roman states; and then we should have a regular European row.'[135] There was not time enough for either party to do anything, however, before revolution in Paris, as Ashley put it, provided 'the spark that set fire to all that was combustible in Italy'.[136]

The year 1848 marked a profound shift in European politics and the so-called year of revolutions, ushering in ideological ferment and political upheaval, was bound to have important ramifications for Palmerston. If the disturbances to the European order of the previous couple of years had stretched Palmerston's commitment to a liberal foreign policy, the events of 1846 and 1847, as Ashley put it, 'formed but a fit prelude to the storm which broke over Europe in 1848'.[137] By the end of the year Palmerston had become, so Philip Guedalla thought, 'more than ever . . . a European figure. Perhaps there were no others left. The waters of 1848 had submerged so many of his equals.'[138]

Prompted by events in Italy Palmerston sent Britain's representatives there a circular memorandum in January 1848 outlining his view of affairs. He said that in the prevailing uncertain circumstances it would be easy for 'sinister efforts' to stir up fears on both sides and provoke a more dangerous series of demands and reprisals than was already in prospect. It was important, he warned, for all parties to adopt a moderate course and he instructed his agents to point out to ministers in Italy

> that the direction of the progress of reform and improvement is still in the hands of the sovereigns, but that it is now too late for them to attempt to obstruct reasonable progress; and that resistance to moderate petitions is sure to lead ere long to the necessity of yielding to irresistible demands. That it is better for a government to frame its measures of improvement with timely deliberation, and to grant them with the grace of spontaneous concession, than to be compelled to adopt, on the sudden, changes perhaps insufficiently matured, and which, being wrung from them by the pressure of imperious circumstances, invert the natural order of things, and being of the nature of a capitulation of the sovereign to the subject, may not always be a sure foundation for permanent harmony between the crown and the people.

The 'popular leaders' who were ranged against the established ministries, Palmerston said, should be advised along similar lines. 'You should tell them', he wrote,

> that force put upon the inclinations of their sovereigns will produce ill-will and repugnance, which must lead their rulers, on their part, to be constantly looking out for an opportunity of shaking off the yoke which they may have been obliged to bear. That mutual distrust will thus be created between the governors and the governed. That this distrust will break out in overt acts on each side, intended perhaps defensively by

those by whom done, but regarded as offensive by the other party. That open discord will thence ensue, and foreign interference may be the ultimate result.[139]

These statements go a long way to defining the fundamental underpinnings of Palmerston's view of European affairs at this time: prudent change was necessary and desirable both of itself and as a security against more extreme and subversive shifts. In other words, this represented a Palmerstonian blend of principle and pragmatism that would, in the unsettled years of the later 1840s, characterise his approach to foreign affairs. If he required an illustration of the threats to the established order, Palmerston need only look to France where he became particularly interested in understanding just how Louis Philippe's supposed abuse of power had resulted in the toppling of the Orléans monarchy.[140] Yet though he had a general sense of the broad movements in European political culture and how Britain ought to regard them, he had not, in statements such as those issued to diplomats stationed in Italy, fashioned a policy that would reconcile British interests with continental realities.

Though British diplomatic attention at the beginning of 1848 may have been focused on Italian states, it was Paris that soon became the locus of political change. In February the self-indulgent government of Louis Philippe was toppled in favour of a more liberal system, founded as the Second Republic. 'Strange that a king who owed his crown to a revolution brought about by royal blindness and obstinacy should have lost it by exactly the same means,' reflected Palmerston.[141] To Palmerston it seemed that everything was cast into the crucible: ideological contest and strategic rivalries were all thrown into sharp relief, creating a moment to test the meanings of Palmerstonian politics. Following months of fraught relations between Britain and France there was, by 1848, little overt interest at the Foreign Office in an *entente cordiale* that was grounded in a common political heritage. But amidst tumbling thrones and collapsing governments across continental Europe as the spirit of the French Revolution reached the capitals of all major European powers (except Russia), there was an emergent and revitalised willingness to forge closer relations between the two countries, though now that projected connection rested on a more pragmatic assessment of Britain's material interests. 'Our principles of action are to acknowledge whatever rule may be established with apparent prospect of permanency but none other,' Palmerston told Britain's ambassador in Paris. The overriding objectives, he continued, were friendship and 'extended commercial intercourse' between Britain and France and peaceful relations between France and the rest of Europe. So long as France demonstrated no external ambitions and was left alone by the other powers, Palmerston anticipated a significant improvement in Franco-British relations.[142]

While France under Thiers seemed a potentially more amenable ally, Palmerston cast one eye to possible wider unrest if France and the ideas emanating from it were not kept within bounds. At the end of February Palmerston warned that a 'general war seems to be impending' and was worried that the French army might soon be invading Belgium and the Netherlands. The whole question of peace or war in Europe, he said, 'is now in the hands of the French government'. 'I grieve at the prospect of a republic in France,' he explained, 'for I fear that it must lead to war in Europe and fresh agitation in England. Large republics seem to be essentially and inherently aggressive, and the aggressions of the French will be resisted by the rest of Europe, and that is war; while on the other hand, the example of universal suffrage in France will set our non-voting population agog, and will create a demand for an inconvenient extension of the suffrage ballot, and other mischievous things.'[143] Whether recent history justified Palmerston's claim that a monarchy was a better safeguard of peace than a republic, he swam with the current rather than against it since, as he told Westmorland at the time, 'we must deal with things as they are, and not as we would wish to have them'.[144] If this was an endorsement of liberal change, it was a decidedly ambivalent one. In March, for example, Palmerston warned the Colonial Secretary, Grey, not to take a French threat for granted:

> The present govt of France in the person of Lamartine is certainly much more friendly to England than the late govt was in the persons of Louis Philippe and Guizot, who were more bent on reducing and crippling the power of England than any men who have governed France since Napoleon Bounaparte; but there is an underplot going on in Paris, and the Ledru Rollin Party if they had their way would soon do things which we should be unable to stand. It would be imprudent therefore in the uncertain state of things in France to consider ourselves secure from the necessity of having to defend ourselves, and it may be worth your while to consider whether you would reinforce the garrison of the Mauritius by some of the troops no longer wanted at the Cape. By things which we could not stand I mean distinctly things bearing upon the internal affairs of this country.[145]

Louis Napoleon's ascendancy by the end of the year, however, seemed to reassure many members of Russell's Whig ministry that the new government in France was at least made up of moderates, mindful of the interests of private property, of order and of the rule of law; moreover, a benevolent attitude towards the Second Republic seemed to Palmerston the best way of protecting Britain's commercial interests by avoiding any further disruption of the continent by intervention in French affairs. Though Aberdeen continued to supply Guizot with 'evidence' of Palmerston's dishonesty, and though Guizot appears to have suspected that Palmerston's embrace of France was lukewarm,[146] relations between the two countries did grow closer over the course of the year. Fears in British government circles that the French revolutionary spirit might infect British or Irish radical movements subsided with the failure of Chartist agitators to press their agenda of parliamentary reform to any effect in the spring; as Palmerston wrote to Normanby the day after the anticlimactic London demonstration of 10 April 1848: 'Yesterday was a glorious day, the Waterloo of peace and order', and one which would, he added, 'produce a good and calming effect all over this and the Sister Island'. There had been no need for the special constables to 'make an example of any whiskered or bearded rioter' by 'mash[ing] them to jelly'.[147] Anxiety about French republicanism gave way to a growing feeling among Britain's ruling elite, having avoided the social turmoil endured by much of continental Europe, of a certain politico-cultural superiority.[148] Such confidence in the Second Republic was not exclusively an elite view: significantly in an era of growing extra-parliamentary influence, even on foreign policy-making, it is perhaps interesting to note that beyond Westminster, too, there was a sense that the new government in Paris would pursue a more pacific, conciliatory course.[149] France, then, under Louis Napoleon, was a power Britain could work with: cooperation seemed to promise (relative) stability while hostile commentators could content themselves to some extent with thinking that 1848 had revealed France to be a weaker, junior, partner to Britain on the international stage.

Palmerston had never shied from an opportunity to mock France and the French. The levity in his treatment of events of early 1848, however, masked a genuine anxiety regarding both domestic ramifications and, externally, the balance of power. If Louis Napoleon's regime proved an unthreatening neighbour, that did not diminish Palmerston's wider concern to ensure that radical change elsewhere did not usher in a period of conflict. His reservations about unbounded change and his determination to support only moderate liberal reforms were highlighted throughout this year of revolutions.

The events of 1848 tested Palmerston's position and political courage on all fronts. His support for constitutional regimes just about withstood claims that he was fomenting revolution or thinking only in *realpolitik* terms, but the prominence of foreign questions brought Palmerston's handling of them to the forefront of political life. At the beginning of the year John Hobhouse, the President of the Board of Control, had expressed the concerns of many Cabinet members that Palmerston's diplomatic correspondence was 'couched in a language that ought never to be addressed to an independent state', while he appeared to encourage Britain's diplomatic corps (especially, he thought, Bulwer, Normanby and Lyons), to 'mix themselves up a good deal too much with the internal politics of the country to which they are sent'.[150] Had it not been for the weaknesses that marked Russell's premiership, notably his inability to impose a clear line on his subordinate colleagues (even allowing Palmerston to regard himself as at least the Prime Minister's equal in Cabinet, if not something more), Palmerston's tenure of the Foreign Office might have been brought into question. Russell effectively admitted to colleagues that he could not control Palmerston,[151] and when Lord

Grey discovered that Palmerston was sending out diplomatic letters without even consulting Russell, let alone the rest of the Cabinet, on matters of great importance in European affairs, he complained that this represented a 'very lamentable weakness' on Russell's part. 'Had P[almerston] played such a prank in my father's administrat'n,' he wrote in his diary, 'he wd have been dismissed without ceremony, nor can I conceive any Prime Minister submitting to such conduct without requiring it to be so punished.'[152] In May 1848, when Grey wrote this entry in his journal, Palmerston was under pressure within government following the expulsion of Bulwer from Madrid for having offended the Spanish government in seemingly intriguing, at Palmerston's behest, to uphold constitutional government and champion the Progresista cause. Bulwer had been implicated in designs to reintroduce Leopold of Saxe-Coburg's name to the list of possible suitors to Queen Isabella, allegedly with Palmerston's approval. Ministers felt he had taken a high-handed and unwarranted tone in trying to impose a government on Spain and had breached his own declared commitment to non-intervention. Hobhouse later complained that ministers 'knew nothing of the Bulwer correspondence until it was over – nor did the Cabinet know that Bulwer's conduct had received the approbation of the government until we saw the fact in the papers laid before Parliament.'[153] Fred Lamb warned Palmerston that Bulwer 'can never now do any good' and was quite unfit for employment while Emily worried about the consequences if Palmerston 'should go & act the knight errant to screen Bulwer if he is attacked – & really such a man does not deserve that you should put yourself in any scrape for him – he is a blackguard in feeling & in conduct'. Yet Palmerston saw in insults offered to Bulwer a direct challenge to his own policy and he stood behind the minister whom Lamb had dismissed as 'being so déconsidéré by the crapuleux life he leads'.[154]

Grey was not alone in thinking Palmerston would have to resign over the Bulwer affair particularly once, in early May, it had attracted parliamentary censure (led in the House of Lords by Stanley). This latest (but not unprecedented) 'sensation' caused by Palmerston's policy prompted Grey to think 'that it must have led either to Palmerston's retirement or the break up of the Govt. – the former wd. have given me infinite satisfact'n.'[155] Palmerston's critics seemed to be lining up to knock him down. The Queen clearly thought (or hoped) Palmerston's position had become untenable. 'When the Queen considers the position we had in Spain,' she wrote to Palmerston in June, 'and what it ought to have been after the constitution of the French Republic when we had no rival to fight and ought to have enjoyed the entire confidence and friendship of Spain, and compares this to the state into which our relations with that country have been brought, she cannot help being struck how much matters have been mismanaged.'[156] Surveying the state of affairs from the Palace, the royal couple were alarmed by the sight of European neighbours convulsed by revolution. In July 1848 the Queen set out for Palmerston the grounds of her growing unease:

She cannot conceal from him that she is ashamed of the policy we are pursuing in the Italian controversy, in abetting wrong, & this for the object of gaining *influence* in Italy. The Queen does not consider influence so gained as an advantage & though this influence is acquired to do good, she is afraid that the fear of losing it again will always stand in the way of this. At least in the countries where the greatest stress has been laid on that influence, & the greatest exertions made for it, the *least good* has been done; the Queen means in Spain, Portugal and Greece. Neither is there any kind of consistency in the line we take about Italy & that we follow with regard to Schleswick; both cases are perfectly alike (with the difference perhaps that there is a question of right mixed up in that of Schleswick); whilst we upbraid *Prussia*, caution her &c., we say *nothing to Charles Albert* except that if he did not wish to take all the Emperor of Austria's Italian dominions, we would not lay *any obstacles* in the way of his moderation.[157]

A few months later Victoria remarked how Britain was seeking to force Austria to give up her 'lawful possessions', and this seemed especially dangerous when the parallels with Ireland and even with Canada and Malta and other British territories seemed so obvious. British actions ought really in all instances, she suggested, to be governed by the simple principle of treating others as one would wish to be treated by them.[158] In September she explained to Russell that she 'had no confidence' in Palmerston and that she was 'seriously anxious and uneasy for the welfare of the country and for the peace of Europe in general', worrying 'from one day to another as to what might happen',[159] though it was also admitted that personal animosity as well as political differences drove these attacks on Palmerston.[160] Lady Palmerston, for her part, became incensed by what she saw as Victoria's gracelessness:

I am angry with the Queen for not being more courteous, the[?] little wretch!! I am sure she is very angry with you!! I am afraid you contradict her notions too boldly you fancy she will hear reason, when in fact all you say only proves to her that you are determined to act in the line which she disapproves, & which she still thinks wrong. I am sure it would be better if you *said* less to her – even if you *act* as you think best. I often think there is too much knight errantry in your ways. You always think you can convince people by arguments & she has not reflection or time enough to feel the force of them – therefore the strength of your arguments, & all the explanations you give only prove to her how deeply imbued you are in what she calls error & how impossible it is for her to make any effect upon you.

I should treat what she says more lightly and courteously, and not enter into argument with her but lead her on gently by letting her believe you have both the same opinions in fact & the same wishes but take sometimes different ways of carrying them out.[161]

However, rather than damage Palmerston's reputation, the events of 1848 had, arguably, made him a more prominent and indeed resilient figure. Russell refused to bend to ministerial and royal pressure to do something about Palmerston. He claimed that he had 'always approved in the main of the foreign policy of Lord Palmerston', and told the Queen that he was 'quite ready to resign my office, but I could not make Lord Palmerston the scapegoat for the sins which will be imputed to the Government in the late negotiations'.[162] Russell's unwillingness to dismiss his Foreign Secretary was more than an attempt to behave honourably; he well knew that whatever concerns might be raised around the Cabinet table and at court about the government's European policy, Palmerston was doing much in the interval to consolidate his popular association with liberal government at both the parliamentary and extra-parliamentary levels and this was making him an essential pillar of government strength. It helped, no doubt, that Palmerston's parliamentary opponents were largely ineffective at this time, but Palmerston took advantage of set-piece parliamentary contests to underline his continued political vitality.

In 1847 David Urquhart had entered Parliament at the general election, standing as a Tory but doing so in part with measured backing from Chartists who liked his commitment to free trade and fiscal prudence but remained unsure about his vehement Russophobia (even Harney had refused to attack Palmerston as a Russian agent).[163] Though he articulated a broad-based critique of Whig government,[164] Urquhart's principal target was foreign policy and specifically Palmerston. At Westminster Urquhart found few kindred spirits, but one such was Thomas Anstey, a Catholic barrister representing Youghal (County Cork) in the Liberal interest. Anstey does not appear to have been a political ideologue and his support was comparatively easily bought – in later years a little Palmerstonian flattery won him back again[165] – but in February 1848 Urquhart persuaded him to launch what was designed to be a set-piece demolition of Palmerston's position. Anstey duly introduced a motion for the production of papers dealing with British foreign policy since 1830 as a preliminary to an impeachment of Palmerston.[166]

When Palmerston rose in the House of Commons on 1 March to defend his record he delivered a speech which deflected the charges brought and implied by Anstey's motion and which has subsequently been interpreted as a defining exposition of Palmerstonian politics. Anstey's original motion specified forty charges, but Palmerston waved them aside with the comment that his opponent had 'skipped about from transaction to transaction, and jumbled the various matters adverted to in his notice in such a manner, that the topics of his speech might be likened to the confused mass of luggage brought to the Custom-house by some of the continental steamboats, when no man knows where he is to find his own'.[167] In a speech filling over sixty columns of *Hansard*, and lasting almost five hours,[168] Palmerston picked Anstey's motion apart, while reserving to himself the privilege of keeping secret details of diplomatic transactions, thereby allowing himself scope for general sweeping statements rather than intricate and dry analysis of obscure details.[169] On most points he argued simply that Anstey's motion was founded on a lack of knowledge and he mocked suggestions that he was 'such a determined instrument in the hands of Russia', pointing to Anstey's own observation that 'from 1830 to 1839, during the nine years in which I was in the office I have now the honour to hold, there had been such mutual distrust between the English and the Russian Governments that it was necessary Baron Brunnow should be sent as Ambassador to represent the real views of the Emperor, in order to remove that distrust' as evidence enough of the emptiness of the claims. His conduct of policy was and always had been guided, he said finally, by the simple maxim that Britain had no eternal allies and no perpetual enemies, only interests that were eternal and perpetual. Even where his policy might have been open to question, Palmerston argued that it had tended to acquire validity through popular approval; he continued to regard public opinion as occupying a significant place in the political system. Thus he concluded his defence against Anstey's motion by appropriating to himself the patriotic appeal of an earlier Foreign Secretary: 'And if I might be allowed to express in one sentence the principle which I think ought to guide an English Minister, I would adopt the expression of Canning, and say that with every British Minister the interests of England ought to be the shibboleth of his policy.'[170] The *Standard* claimed that Palmerston's speech had 'left the case pretty much where it was before',[171] but that journal had been consistently hostile to Palmerston and would not be expected to acknowledge a performance that had struck a chord with a large constituency beyond Parliament as well as within its bounds. Most newspapers gave the result to Palmerston on points and both Anstey and Urquhart found themselves thereafter the objects of parliamentary ridicule.[172] Palmerston later claimed that Louis Philippe had subsidised Urquhart and Anstey, as well as the Urquhartite *Portfolio*, to the tune of £60,000 in order to 'demolish' the Foreign Secretary.[173] The allegation was unsubstantiated, but revealed the depth of Palmerston's suspicion of the French King and government.

Nor could Disraeli, who spoke from the opposition benches, seemingly find a way to undermine Palmerston's apparent parliamentary ascendancy. He regarded Bulwer's dismissal from Madrid as 'a gross outrage' which had been 'inflicted upon this country', and used it as the starting point for an attack on the whole system of a liberal foreign policy. 'My objection to liberalism is this – that it is the introduction into the practical business of life of the highest kind – namely, politics – of philosophical ideas instead of political principles', he told the House in June. Palmerston, he acknowledged, was 'the great prophet of liberalism in foreign affairs', and indeed was 'the most able expounder' of the strain of liberalism embodied in the Quadruple Alliance of 1834 'which has been the characteristic of the foreign policy of England now for too many years'. Yet in allocating responsibility for this system, and for this 'sentimental' approach to politics, Disraeli pointed at Liberal governments, not Palmerston himself. 'I am exceedingly loth to assent to any vote which singles out the noble Lord [Palmerston] as a Member of the Government who has followed a policy so pernicious to this country,' argued Disraeli. 'We ought to strike at the system, and not at the individual.'[174] The following month Disraeli pointed to the dangers of allowing 'the sentimental principle' to 'develop the principle of nationality' which, looking to the Italian states, Disraeli saw as likely to 'resolve Europe into its original elements, and . . . not leave any social or political system in existence in the form which it now assumes'.[175] Confused and weak policies, Disraeli felt, but not Palmerston, were lowering the country's standing. With parliamentary opponents exonerating him for the perceived shortcomings of government policy it was not surprising that Palmerston was able to manufacture a commanding position at Westminster. If a year later Disraeli found that the published papers on Italy had 'somewhat lowered my opinion of Palmerston', the fact that Palmerston had been 'fortunate' and undeservedly '*felix*',[176] owed a good deal to the inability of opponents to subject him to meaningful parliamentary scrutiny.

Thus, while debates in Parliament in 1848 became mired in uncertainty about who was responsible (and for what), in the country at large opinion was influenced more by current events than confused parliamentary critiques. When he looked at what Palmerston's recent policy in Europe, and especially in Italy, meant for contemporary politics, Ambrose Brewin, one of Palmerston's constituents (and son-in-law of Tiverton's other MP, Heathcoat) observed that so long as he adhered to religious liberty his policy would do much to advance liberal interests:

Pray my Lord, do not forget '*religious liberty*' in these new charters and the laws wh must spring out of them. Time will come when this will perhaps determine the continuance of the charters themselves. If these good people wish to copy the British constitution do not allow them to leave out the foundation or basis. It is leaving out 'Hamlet'. May your Lordship's mind be as forcibly bent on achieving religious *liberty* wherever British influence extends as it has been to put down Negro slavery. And what cannot you now do in Italy and Spain! Old Cromwell would not let such an opportunity pass and I trust your Lordship will not do less. With religious liberty and the freedom of the press those two fine peninsulas may ere *very* long assume another position and begin to understand the principles of self-government.

Brewin was sure, he concluded, that Palmerston's 'last hours will be sweetened by having helped towards this great work'.[177] Another of Palmerston's correspondents, 'A Constituent', who had been an elector for the University of Cambridge when Palmerston had represented that seat, wrote to Palmerston in June that he found 'in every part of Europe, that you were the representative of my inviolability and dignity as an Englishman'. It was, said this anonymous correspondent, Palmerston's good fortune to stand in the popular mind as the wise interpreter of international affairs and the sound defender of national honour and interest: 'First as to yourself. The English people trouble themselves very little about foreign politics. This arises partly from the low estimation in which they hold all foreigners; but principally from the neglected state of general education. The masses know so little of the geographical division of Europe, that the great majority of them might reverse the position of the Alps and the Pyrenees, or annex Spain to Italy or Germany. So they wisely avoid discussions of these subjects. Yet they fully recognize in you the protector of constitutional freedom on the continent; and they consider England's honour and interests safe in your hands.'[178]

By the end of the year Palmerston felt confident that recent events signalled the ascendancy of constitutional principles. The situation in Italy, he thought, was uncertain but elsewhere he saw reason to be pleased. The abdication of 'the idiot Emperor of Austria, & the remuneration of his bigotted [sic] brother' were, he told his brother William, 'a great event and give a chance that Austria may be reconstructed solidly upon a constitutional principle'. The King of Prussia, he continued, had 'cut the knot by dissolving his Constituent Assembly, and giving his people a constitution. His scheme has many defects, but some of them may perhaps be attended afterwards by the Parliament which he has constituted.' The situation in France, where talk was of Louis Napoleon becoming President, though that remained as yet uncertain, Palmerston thought held out the prospect of positive effects within a few months' time: 'in the long run, and indeed before next summer is over it will have some very sensible effect. I should not be sorry if it ended in Louis Napoleon being made Emperor, & thus ridding us of both branches of the Bourbons; but the adherents of that family certainly imagine that they will be able to get rid of Louis Nap and set up a Bourbon in his stead.'[179] And while he had been willing to offer the Pope support in 1847, the latter's declining power was viewed by Palmerston as only to the good: 'It seems quite clear that the Pope never can again be what he has been, and that his spiritual power will be much diminished by the curtailment or loss of his temporal authority. This is surely a good thing for Europe both Catholic & Protestant and if it ends in very much nationalizing and localizing the Catholic Church in every country, that alone will be a great point gained, & will be a material step in the progress of human society.'[180]

It is debatable how far the events of 1848 really vindicated Palmerston's earlier 'liberal' policies. If that turbulent year had witnessed the rise of constitutionalist principles, it owed little to Palmerston's initiatives. By the same token, however, he had long since identified himself with a reforming spirit and he continued to position himself rhetorically at the forefront of the drive for moderate advances in constitutional governance. Though the uprisings in continental Europe were too violent and too radical to sit comfortably with Palmerston's essentially high Whig preference for modest change, characterised by aristocratic concession more than popular appropriation of power, in Britain the growing association in the popular mind of Palmerston with progressive improvement strengthened his claims to represent 'the people'. By the late 1840s, therefore, Palmerston could, and did, argue that his foreign policy suited the mood of the nation and this helped to consolidate his position at the Foreign Office. Sir James Graham, a leading figure among the increasingly disaffected Peelite wing of the Conservative party, thought this a dangerous personal ascendancy. In an effort to bolster the government, Russell had attempted to woo more liberal members of the opposition to join his government but in response to such an overture Graham had identified two obstacles to his joining the Cabinet. The first was a difference over fiscal policy; the second was Palmerston who, he wrote in a letter to Peel, 'has had too much and too long his own way to yield either to the influence of his colleagues or to the control of public opinion'.[181] If Graham was right then this served only to underline the effectiveness of Palmerston's cultivation of a liberal, patriotic image: Palmerston's enhanced standing was of his own manufacture and, Graham's comment implies, within Palmerston's control; or perhaps more significantly, increasingly beyond the control of the public ministers or the crown.

This was not inconsequential. Foreign policy had become an ever greater source of Cabinet disagreement, and erstwhile factionalism threatened to pull the government apart anew. A 'Grey faction', identified by Lord Minto as comprising Lord Grey, Sir George Grey and Sir Charles Wood (the stumbling blocks to the formation of a Whig ministry in December 1845) and now also Sir Francis Baring, Lord Carlisle (who had been, until 1848, Lord Morpeth) and possibly Henry Labouchere, stood ranged against Palmerston and his allies Russell, Lansdowne, Lord Campbell and Minto himself.[182] Grey grew vociferous in his calls for Russell to 'interfere more regularly' in Palmerston's handling of foreign affairs,[183] yet it was clear that Palmerston was becoming too powerful to be undermined or removed so easily.

Grey tried to work up a minor 'scandal' in early 1849 to force Palmerston out yet succeeded only in demonstrating how entrenched the Foreign Secretary had in fact become. In the autumn of 1848 an arms manufacturer and supplier to the government, whose own stocks were running low, had asked whether a recently completed order delivered to the British War Office might be returned to be used to fulfil an order for arms from rebels in Sicily. Palmerston had sanctioned the request since the recent receipt of the guns had created a surplus in the government's arsenal, but when news of the transaction was published in *The Times* in January 1849 it was taken by European conservatives as evidence that Palmerston was encouraging and even instigating revolution in Europe.[184] Palmerston denied any wrongdoing: 'It would perhaps have been better if I had

said no instead of yes to the question put to me by the Ordnance in Sept last;'
he wrote to Charles Wood, 'but I conceive there is a wide difference between
letting a contractor have back some guns which he had furnished & which were
not immediately wanted & which he was to replace by others, or supplying at
the expense of the public guns from our own stores.'[185]

Wood, however, along with Grey and George Grey, argued for Palmerston's
dismissal, though they took care not to make this look like a repeat of 'what
happened in Dec/45'.[186] Yet, as Grey recorded when the Cabinet met to discuss
the matter, 'There was then some vague discuss'n in wh I was to the last degree
disgusted by the apparent insensibility of the Cabinet to the gravity of the case &
to the disgraceful figure the Govt will make in pleading "inadvertence" as the
excuse for such a proceeding. I endeavoured to treat the matter somewhat more
seriously & to show how bad a posit'n we shd be placed in but nobody backed
me.'[187] Grey thought that the 'foolish and ignorant manner in wh he has been
attacked has almost set on its legs a policy for which I fear the case is not really
so good as it has appeared',[188] but the majority of the Cabinet did not dare to cast
aside a clear asset. In some respects it was Palmerston's presence that underwrote
the continuance of Russell's government, which might easily have been overthrown by a coordinated opposition. However, Conservative divisions also
gifted the government continual reprieves in Parliament and once the Peelite
Lord Aberdeen had stated that he would not endorse an alignment with the
Protectionist element, the Conservatives had no real candidate to challenge or
replace Palmerston at the Foreign Office. Edward Stanley lamented in May 1849
that 'Lord Aberdeen's final alienation from us makes it useless to displace
Palmerston', effectively acknowledging Palmerston's commanding hold over
foreign policy and, by extension, over the future of the government.[189]

Events certainly favoured Palmerston. Domestically the apparent weakness
of his parliamentary and ministerial rivals allowed much of his policy to pass
largely unhindered. Externally he was able to construct a narrative of political
affairs that linked a liberal stand against assorted autocratic abuses of power
and privilege directly with a patriotic defence of British people and interests.
In January 1850 rumours of a renewed Miguellite assault on Portugal began to
circulate in London (in fact Palmerston had been monitoring events there,
with some concern, for a number of months already).[190] Palmerston told the
Portuguese Minister in London, Baron Torre de Moncorvo, that 'all I hear of
that country leads me to believe that the nation is much dissatisfied with the
present government, & with its way of conducting affairs; and if the
Portugueze nation is thus dissatisfied we are equally so'; but, as he continued,
this was more to do with 'acts of injustice that are daily committed in Portugal
against British subjects (and some of those acts sanctioned by the Prime
Minister himself) and the hostility to every thing English, which is displayed
by all the people in authority' than to ideological concerns. Indeed, he threatened British opposition to a nominally liberal government if that government

paid insufficient attention to British interests. 'Therefore even if it were not for other reasons intirely out of the question that we should again take any active measure to interfere in any contest which may henceforward arise in Portugal between the Miguellites and the adherents of the present government,' he continued, 'the conduct of the present government towards England and the English would take away from us the slightest wish to stir a finger in its support.'[191] When a Dr Gincinto Achilli was imprisoned in Rome by the Inquisition at about the same time, Palmerston made clear that British opinion would not stand for a perceived injustice and whatever faith the Pope might have placed in Britain's friendly disposition following the Minto mission, that was not to be counted on unconditionally. 'The Pope is evidently not aware of the intense interest which this case is exciting both in England and in Scotland, and of the great injury which it is doing to the Papal government in public opinion in this country,' Palmerston wrote to his brother in Naples, 'and the public opinion of England is a matter not wholly to be disregarded even by an Italian sovereign, because that public opinion must necessarily have great influence on the measures & conduct of the British govt.'[192] Thanking Palmerston for his interest in Achilli's case, the Evangelical Alliance sent him an address in March 1850 acknowledging 'the very important and valuable services which, in the exercise of a generous philanthropy and a sacred regard to the claims of truth and of conscience, combined with a comprehensive and discriminating wisdom, worthy of his exalted and responsible position, his Lordship has been enabled to render, and which, by the blessings of Divine Providence, have, at length, been happily crowned with complete success.'[193] Together these apparently small episodes reveal a good deal of how Palmerston approached policy at this time. The recognition of his providentially inspired conduct was not limited to the Evangelical community; such high-flown constructions of his position resonated among many different constituencies in Britain. In May 1850 'a commercial traveller' wrote from Portsmouth attempting to represent what he took to be public feeling:

> I think it only right that you should know the feeling of the people gener-ally of this country toward you at such a time as this & more particularly when the leading paper of the day is so mis-representing every thing connected with the foreign policy of the country. Sensible Englishmen are proud my lord to think they have so experienced & excellent a statesman filling the office you now do – you may depend you have their entire confidence. I visit many towns & converse with numbers & I can safely say my lord your foreign policy is approved by the very great majority & we all trust (as we feel sure) you will for many many years continue to serve the country in your present official situation. The Times paper perhaps in the pay of the despots does not represent the opinions of the people of this country on foreign questions.[194]

Similarly, James Birch, editor of the *World* newspaper, wrote to correct the misleading impression of Palmerston's position generated by articles in *The Times*. 'It is impossible now to penetrate into any circle – high or low – to travel by land or water – whether you enter the aristocratic club – or the humble free and easy or *sans souce* [*sic*] of the artisan – the mart of commerce – or the threepenny omnibus – without hearing the policy of Lord Palmerston discussed – and as much as it is discussed – warmly applauded,' he told Palmerston in the summer. 'Your Lordship I do believe is now one of the most popular ministers that ever swayed the destiny of affairs in England.'[195] That supposed popularity derived in large measure from Palmerston's careful exploitation of, or fortuitous profiting from, a parliamentary squabble over the government's policy in Greece. It also represented, for Palmerston, a welcome relief from a period of unabated royal sniping.

The first half of the year had seen renewed efforts by the Queen and Prince to engineer Palmerston's removal. In February Victoria had returned, in her letters to Russell, to the theme of Palmerston's perceived unreliability, but though Russell might have been growing weary of the continued battle between the Palace and the Foreign Office he saw no grounds on which to dismiss Palmerston at this point. The Queen and Prince maintained a regular contact with loyal figures such as Aberdeen, who also supplied them with intelligence from his European friends ('I think it of importance, in the multitude of erroneous and conflicting accounts which are received, that they should sometimes see the statements of an able, impartial and clear sighted observer,' he explained to Guizot a few months later),[196] and so royal disquiet was not allayed by Russell's reassurances. As Albert wrote in the spring, though Palmerston was 'an able politician', he was also 'a man of expediency, of easy temper, no very high standard of honour and not a grain of moral feeling. He is consequently quite unscrupulous as to any line of policy that he is to follow, or any means he is to use as long as they lead to his ends.' The Prince thought Palmerston 'self-willed and impatient of any control of his own [department]', and that this arose from his 'personal conceit'. Palmerstonian policy, said the Prince, was marked by 'bullying', and though he conceded that Palmerston was often fortunate, 'success failing, he steers without a compass and makes one almost doubt his sagacity'.[197] In the face of such sustained carping Russell had apparently relented by May, telling Palmerston that he had informed the Queen that ('without imputing blame to you') he would try in the near future to shift Palmerston to another department (allowing, he said, the government to pursue 'the same line of foreign policy, without giving the same offence').[198]

Events again saved Palmerston. What Drouyn de Lhuys, the French ambassador in London, had dismissed in February as 'une tempête dans un verre d'eau' in Greece became, in fact, a minor cause célèbre. Britain had for some time past been pursuing claims for pecuniary compensation against the Greek government, but as Palmerston pointed out, 'King Otho is the enfant gati de l'absolutismo, and therefore all the arbitrary courts are in convulsions at what we have been doing; but it is our long forbearance, and not our precipitation that deserves remark.' Yet, he was determined that other nations should see in Britain's steadfast demands for redress of grievances a warning not to 'turn a deaf ear to our demands & think to wear us out by refusals or evasions'.[199] The specific grounds for 'redress' were founded on the apparent pecuniary losses of two individuals, but Palmerston's position should also be read in the context of a growing frustration with the Greek government which, so reports reaching the Foreign Office said, had been systematically abusing and misappropriating British funds given to support that government.[200] The British government had lodged a demand for £8,500 from the government in Athens as compensation principally for losses sustained by two British subjects, David Pacifico and George Finlay, in 1847 and 1836 respectively.[201] It was widely understood that these demands were exaggerated. Pacifico's request for compensation in particular, as made through the British government, rested on a tenuous claim to British citizenship and grossly inflated estimates of the value of property he had lost in anti-Semitic riots in Athens in 1847. Some, such as Lord Aberdeen, worried that Palmerston's high-handed treatment of Greece, which France attempted to mediate, would damage not only Britain's standing in Europe but specifically the *entente cordiale*, though there is little evidence of lasting ill-feeling in Paris.[202] However when Palmerston ordered a naval blockade of the Greek capital the mood among his parliamentary critics hardened. Lord Stanley introduced a motion in the House of Lords in June censuring the Foreign Secretary's recent conduct, claiming it had profoundly damaged Britain's relations with other powers. Lansdowne, speaking for the government, defended Palmerston on the grounds that the House of Commons, which spoke (significantly) for the 'the mercantile and manufacturing interests of the country', backed recent policy and suggested that if there had been any negative fallout from Palmerston's protection of British subjects overseas, that would prove to be temporary; all countries, he said, could be expected to behave similarly. Despite this apparent support for Palmerston, however, Stanley's motion passed by a margin of 37 votes.[203] In the Cabinet ministers agreed that this defeat might signal the end of the government and it was resolved that they would treat a Commons response as effectively a vote of confidence in the ministry. Palmerston's conduct over Pacifico was, after all, inspired by a view of policy which had long held sway in Whig Cabinets and with which many were associated from earlier years.[204] Earl Grey, who had voted against Stanley's motion in the Lords debate, later thought this move 'a great error',[205] largely, presumably, because it handed Palmerston a clear opportunity to retrieve a vulnerable personal as well as political position.

Before the Lords debate, George Shee had thought Palmerston's prospects in the Upper House were doubtful since there 'a strong, disciplined, phalanx of uncompromising and in part unprincipled men, who have objects quite distinct from the merits of the question' were lined up to make capital from the issue. In the House of Commons, however, with a measure of fair play he anticipated that his friend would 'come off with flying colours'.[206] Shee's optimism was well-judged; a motion proposed by John Arthur Roebuck commending Palmerston's conduct gave Palmerston the platform from which to deliver a lengthy speech in which he took care to represent the attack on the government's policy as one very much on him personally, and which culminated with his oft-quoted eulogy to British liberalism and the freedom of its people:

> I therefore fearlessly challenge the verdict which this House, as repre-
> senting a political, a commercial, a constitutional country, is to give on
> the question now brought before it; whether the principles on which the
> foreign policy of Her Majesty's Government has been conducted, and the
> sense of duty which has led us to think ourselves bound to afford protec-
> tion to our fellow subjects abroad, are proper and fitting guides for those
> who are charged with the Government of England; and whether, as the
> Roman, in days of old, held himself free from indignity, when he could
> say *Civis Romanus sum*; so also a British subject, in whatever land he may
> be, shall feel confident that the watchful eye and the strong arm of
> England, will protect him against injustice and wrong.[207]

Gladstone found the reference distasteful but on the opposition benches Disraeli, who appeared reluctant to attack Palmerston (despite clear prompting from his colleagues in the Lords), did little to press home the victory achieved in the Upper House a fortnight earlier. Principled opposition in the form of Cobdenite critiques of bellicose diplomacy attracted few members into the lobby. The resultant victory for the government by 310 to 264 votes was widely interpreted as a victory for Palmerston personally, even if it was, as A.J.P. Taylor put it, 'more in the nature of a caution not to do it again than a triumphant acquittal'.[208] Conservatives and Radicals complained among themselves that an opportunity to damage Palmerston had been thrown up – whether through in-fighting or lack of focus in debate[209] – but the public reaction to Palmerston's 'vindication' suggested, or was taken to indicate, widespread support for his approach. His speech had been loudly cheered from the gallery and when he left the House crowds had gathered to applaud him.[210] Earl Grey, no doubt with some regret, acknowledged that the recent debate had left Palmerston 'the most popular man in the country'.[211]

Just as important as the parliamentary debate itself was the *ex post facto* analysis and response beyond Westminster. This was, it should be borne in mind, one of the few memorable, quotable and exciting of Palmerston's parliamentary performances and, bearing, as it was made to appear, on the interests of every member of the population, it attracted considerable comment. Palmerston himself had deemed his speech a sufficiently important statement of his general principles to issue it to all clerks at the Foreign Office, and there is evidence that some diplomatic agents took the speech as a benchmark for their overseas conduct (and by acting in accordance with the Don Pacifico 'ethos' hoping to attract the favourable notice of the Foreign Secretary).[212] Among the wider population, Palmerston's by now well established connections with certain papers ensured that a favourable gloss was put on the result. 'Lord Palmerston, the House of Commons, and the Nation, are henceforth at one,' declared the ever-loyal *Globe*, and, with a deft Palmerstonian stroke, tied the defence of the individual liberties and sovereignty of the British people to broader currents of ideological conflict. Although the last two decades might not have demonstrated a consistent linking of the interests of 'the people' with the course of parliamentary politics at home, the recent debate, it said,

> awoke a sentiment through the length and breadth of England, to which we have been strangers since the days of Free-trade and the Reform-bill. The nation was outraged at the assumption that its contented apathy should be identified either with acquiescence in the Absolutist reaction, or indifference to the spread of German and Italian Constitutionalism. The great seats of manufacturing industry became aware that they were fighting for their own cause in supporting a Minister whose protecting arm was over every one of his countrymen, at the Court of the most arbitrary despot, or amid the mobs of the most unbridled democracy; and last night the House of Commons worthily answered the call of its constituents, by a vote which has silenced and shattered all the elaborate intrigues of these foreign exiles and their English confederates.[213]

Reaction to the issue, said the *Globe*, demonstrated 'the national affection and respect' for Palmerston and it praised his resolve to represent those who 'are determined to hold fast by their love of liberal institutions in foreign as well as in domestic politics'.[214] It was all a welcome change from the '*remplissage*' of Aberdeen's diluted protests.[215] The Commons vote, as well as highlighting the ascendancy of democratic opinion, did much to bolster the country's 'liberal influence abroad', according to the *Daily News*.[216] Elsewhere, while Cobdenite 'Manchester School' politics were supposed to speak for the commercial interest, an editorial in the *Manchester Guardian* in fact made clear that community's growing identification with the sort of uncompromising policies offered by Palmerston:

> The merchants of this neighbourhood are largely embarked in foreign commerce, and have numerous establishments scattered over the world, in countries under every variety of government, and in every stage of civilisation. We imagine they will not hear with much satisfaction that, in the deliberate opinion of the British House of Lords, they are entitled to,

and must expect to receive, no other protection, in their persons or their property, than that which they can obtain from a due enforcement of whatever law may happen to exist for the time in the country in which their establishments are.[217]

As the paper pointed out a few days later, 'the rights of individuals and of nations, are the same' and thus Palmerston's defence of Pacifico augured well for the future safeguarding of more broadly defined national commercial interests.[218] Letters to the paper further underlined the support for Palmerston, with many correspondents arguing that Cobden and Bright had forgotten the purpose of the debate and had instead tried to use the issue for party gain.[219] Such criticism of opposition members, Radical and Tory, for trying to turn a question of national honour into one of party intrigue simply highlighted the extent to which the issue had come to be seen in many quarters as about Palmerston as a patriotic hero.[220]

Though *The Times* mocked Palmerston's incarnation as the 'English Minister' who had 'represented with unrivalled spirit and success the interests and the opinions of this country' and preferred to see him instead as a quarrelsome and provocative figure,[221] and while the *Chronicle* feared that the debate had proved little or nothing about the real questions involved,[222] such arguments seemed to run counter to the prevailing mood. The Protectionist *Standard* maintained that if put to the country at large Palmerston's 'clap-trap phrases' would have had little effect, but there was little evidence of that at the time.[223] A pamphlet published by 'a Greek Gentleman' derided Palmerston's speech as having 'touched the sublime of clap-trap' and though he had, he said, previously supported Palmerston, he could not but regard the current episode as revealing Palmerston's lack of real understanding of affairs in Greece and his willingness, in search of a cheap victory, to endanger the peace of Europe.[224] It was quite true that Palmerston had taken liberties in his presentation of the case: as *The Times* had previously observed, Palmerston had himself shown 'so little confidence' in the accuracy of Pacifico's claims as to raise doubts about his commitment to it,[225] yet few really thought this issue was exclusively one about Greece. The debate was interpreted most widely as a commentary on Britain's 'greatness' and Palmerston's determination to defend it.

It was also, by extension, about saving Palmerston's career. Tributes to Palmerston's abilities were voiced around the country. The editor of the *Sun* newspaper described Palmerston as 'one of the manliest intellects in England; one of the noblest statesmen in all Europe, perhaps the wisest and certainly the most accomplished diplomatist who ever directed the foreign affairs of our country', and who carried with him 'the hearty sympathies of the people'.[226] From Yorkshire Palmerston was promised the support of all liberal papers as the minister who, his correspondent said, 'stands higher than ever in the estimation of his countrymen'.[227] A variety of newspaper editors and writers sent

Palmerston clippings from their papers to express their support of a patriotic, manly, national minister.[228] The performance had, apparently, won Palmerston many new adherents, as one writer explained:

> Your Lordship has indeed heard the triumphant cheers of the senate and of the club, but not less grateful would it have been to your Lordship to have heard, as day by day I have heard, from men of various shades of political opinion, and of all grades of mercantile pursuits, the most emphatic expressions of admiration and delight, in reference to Your Lordship's memorable speech – which contained an exposition of policy that made many converts, by its eloquent force & conclusive argument.[229]

Charles Greville judged that the apparent endorsement of Palmerston's conduct had made him 'so great in the Cabinet, and so popular in the country, and made the Government itself so strong, that if he turns over a new leaf, takes a lesson from all that has happened, and renounces his offensive manners and changes his mode of proceeding abroad, he may consider his tenure of office perfectly secure'.[230] Palmerston did not scruple to press home a demonstrable advantage. If support for him was not universal it was, as articulated and understood at Westminster, sufficiently widespread to solidify his position. Some time after the June debate Palmerston returned to one of Russell's earlier letters and wrote on the back of it:

> Towards the end of the session Ld John again brought the subject [of Palmerston's proposed removal from the Foreign Office] forward & proposed to me a change of office. I replied that after what had passed in the House of Commons on Roebuck's motion and after the general and decided approbation of my policy & conduct which had been expressed from one end of the country to the other by all the Liberal Party it was quite impossible for me to consent to any such arrangement. To do so would be to pass condemnation on myself after I had received a public approval, and to say that I thought the Hs of Lords which had blamed me was in the right, and the House of Commons which had approved me was in the wrong. I said that . . . if it was any convenience to the government I was ready now as I had been after the vote in the Lords, to relieve my colleagues of all difficulty by retiring altogether, but that if I remained in the govt I could not give up the Foreign Office.
>
> Ld John said that he wished me to remain a member of the govt, and he afterwards said that the Queen had consented thereto.[231]

Palmerston described the Don Pacifico debate in a letter to William as 'a shot fired by a foreign conspiracy' but he revelled in the way it had ricocheted in his favour: 'they have rendered me for the present the most popular minister that for a very long course of time has held my office' and only a sense of decorum had dictated that a modest Reform Club dinner be held to mark the triumph; there would have been enough enthusiasm, he said, for a dinner for a thousand people in Covent Garden.[232]

Lord Aberdeen remained less convinced of Palmerston's triumph: the Lords' censure, he told Guizot, had been 'not fatal to the existence of the government', but he also thought that it had 'not been reversed by the decision of the House of Commons'. However, there had been more than one event of political consequence during those days in early July. On the final night of the debate in the House of Commons, Robert Peel had died following a fall from his horse and this had left the parties, especially those on the opposition benches, in flux: Aberdeen said that though the recent attack on Palmerston had brought opposition factions together and though there remained no fundamental differences of opinion (free trade versus protectionism notwithstanding), the breach remained 'as irreconcilable as ever'.[233] If only because there was no obvious government-in-waiting, this all served to strengthen the position of ministers, not least Palmerston. Palmerston's opponents, indeed, seemed to be disappearing from the scene at convenient moments. A few weeks after Peel's death, at the beginning of September, he wrote to his brother with news of another demise: 'The death of Louis Philippe delivers me from my most artful and inveterate enemy whose position gave him in many ways the power to injure me and though I am sorry for the death of Peel from personal regard and because it is no doubt a great loss to the country, yet as far as my own political position is concerned I do not think that he was ever disposed to do me any good turn'.[234]

Though there were suggestions of a ministerial reshuffle towards the end of the year, perhaps even under a new head, Lord Lansdowne,[235] it appeared to Lord Aberdeen, in the wake of a turbulent political twelve months, that little had changed or probably would change for the foreseeable future. He told his friend Guizot: 'You may be sure that our foreign policy will continue to be as dishonest and as undignified as ever, although perhaps a little more prudent. I think the great business of our session, if war should happily be avoided, will be confined to domestick affairs. Financial and religious questions will occupy us largely'.[236] It was, as much as anything else, an acknowledgement of not only a Whig but a Palmerstonian ascendancy. Such was implicit also in Disraeli's suggestion in early 1851 that a Conservative union with Palmerston was both possible and desirable. 'Palmerston was a man who bore no malice, who liked office, whose tendencies were Conservative, and who would find no difficulty in throwing over former colleagues,' Disraeli is reported to have said to Derby, 'especially as he and Russell were not on the most cordial terms'.[237] Such discord was not, however, sufficient to rupture the Russell government when plans for a reconstruction were mooted in February 1851.[238]

At the beginning of 1851, therefore, the year of the Great Exhibition, Palmerston seemed as much a potent symbol of British fortitude and progress as any of the displays that would shortly be seen in the Crystal Palace. But in the aftermath of a close scrutiny of his policy, Palmerston may have been relieved that, as Aberdeen had suggested, foreign policy questions were not so volatile for a few months. Though he continued to press for improved coastal fortifications and defence provisions based on a perceived growing threat from France (which, under Louis Napoleon, was still very much an unknown quantity),[239] Palmerston was not particularly active during the early months of the year.[240] As he told the British Minister in Tuscany at the end of January, he did 'not anticipate any peril for the govt in any debates that are likely to come on, and I think we shall probably pass through the session without shipwreck.' In response to the Pope's plans to re-establish a Roman Catholic hierarchy in England and Wales, which fed continuing fears about a developing 'papal aggression', the government brought forward the Ecclesiastical Titles Bill, which would prevent Roman Catholic clergy adopting titles with British place names attached to them. This threatened some trouble, but though Palmerston thought the 'Roman Catholic hierarchy' might usefully be encouraged to avoid a confrontation with the British government over the titles, he was reluctant to press the Pope into aiding the government over the measure.[241] Instead he preferred to wait upon events and read into them a confirmation of Protestant supremacy and superiority. 'The people of this country bear with great composure mere differences in religious opinions,' he noted, being 'too much accustomed to such differences among Protestants themselves to look with any (real) hatred on such differences when exhibited between Protestants & Catholics; but the English nation are deeply impressed with the feeling that Catholic ascendancy and civil and political freedom are incompatible.' Meanwhile, he concluded, he thought 'the govt is pretty safe till next year. After the failures on the part of others to form a govt, it would be ridiculous for us to resign again unless the H of C were to vote a censure or a resolution of no confidence, and that is not likely to happen. There are few members who do not shrink from the prospect of an immediate dissolution and Stanley would be compelled to dissolve if he were forced to form a govt.'[242]

When, in the autumn of 1851, Palmerston 'availed himself of the leisure of the recess to pay his constituents a visit', he did so in buoyant mood. Addressing a public meeting in Tiverton, he said that in the recent past Britain had 'had to contend with great difficulties at home, and we have had to witness terrible convulsions abroad. Those domestic difficulties, by the blessing of Providence, have, to a certain degree, passed away – the convulsions abroad have, for the present, ceased. (Cheers.) And not only this, but that dreadful scourge, the scourge of famine, which ravaged so large a portion of the sister isle, has, if not entirely disappeared, been substantially diminished.' It was all, he insisted, a validation of Britain's pre-eminence which was founded on 'the great good sense, the goodness of heart, and the noble qualities which belong to the British nation' and which through the formal expression of public opinion became a force for good. Contrasting the British case with that of illiberal, primarily southern, European countries, Palmerston flattered his audience with demonstrations of their vicarious participation in the work of a providentially favoured world power.[243] Even the *Standard* found reason to commend Palmerston's conduct since July 1850, noting in December 1851 that it was 'unexampled' that there should have been 'an administration of foreign affairs uncriticised by the people or the Parliament for 18 months, including the half of one parliamentary session and the whole of another'.[244] Indeed, Palmerston still seemed to be riding the wave of popular support for his liberal policies, an apparent endorsement of his (self-proclaimed) position as defender of popular rights. At the end of November the Company of Merchants of Edinburgh, for example, noting Palmerston's efforts on behalf of political prisoners in Naples, paid tribute to his attempts 'to promote at once the cause of civil and religious liberty and to maintain the blessings of a secure and lasting peace', and, they hoped, he would 'continue his efforts in the cause of suffering humanity, in such way and manner as he may deem best for effecting the end in view, namely, obtaining for the subject deliverance from oppression and violence, and inducing the government to exercise its power with impartial justice tempered with mercy'.[245]

On 6 November 1851 Palmerston wrote to his brother a letter bristling with confidence about the government's position and claiming Derby had no desire to be Prime Minister (Derby was, said Palmerston, plagued by gout and preferred anyway the distractions of his 'large estate' to routine political labour). 'I do not see any rock ahead which is likely to wreck the government,' he wrote, giving a hostage to fortune that was exposed within a month.[246]

In December Lajos Kossuth, the leader of recent nationalist uprisings in Hungary, came to Britain on what amounted to a speaking tour of the country. In London Palmerston resolved to welcome Kossuth officially and when Cabinet colleagues objected on the grounds that this represented a potential diplomatic embarrassment, Palmerston responded by insisting that 'It is not as chief enemy of Austria that Kossuth has hitherto been looked upon, nor is it in that capacity that he is about to be received by the British nation. He has been regarded as a man who among others has stood up for the rights of his country'.[247] For Palmerston this was an opportunity to offer symbolic evidence of his identification with such laudable qualities. Draymen at Barclays Brewery in London had already given some hint of popular feeling about Austrian suppression of Hungarian rights and liberties when, in September 1850, they dumped the visiting Austrian general, Julius Jacob Haynau, in a water trough. Palmerston had, on that occasion, refused to offer an official apology to Vienna, to the chagrin of his colleagues. More recently, a deputation from Islington and Finsbury had impressed on Palmerston the level of popular approval of his defence of Hungarian interests,[248] reinforcing his sense that the public effectively endorsed his determination to receive Kossuth. He threatened to resign when Russell attempted to forbid the meeting with Kossuth,[249] and the Queen was 'deeply wounded' by his impertinence but all sides recognised that dismissing Palmerston would in effect be for the government to relinquish office.[250]

Only a few weeks later, however, Palmerston again tested his colleagues' tolerance of his independence of action and this time discovered its limits. On 2 December 1851, the anniversary of the Battle of Austerlitz, Louis Napoleon seized power in a *coup d'état*, making himself President for life; it was a clear bid for ultimate power and was confirmed one year later when he appointed himself Emperor and took the title of Napoleon III. Such overt aggrandisement caused some alarm among the British public. Ministers, too, were concerned when they heard from Lord Cowley that the new French President had declared that 'he was determined not to fall as Louis-Philippe had done by an extra-pacific policy; that he knew well that the instincts of France were military and domineering, and that he resolved to gratify them'.[251] Palmerston adopted a rather less hysterical point of view. Having welcomed the prospect of an extension of Napoleon's power as early as 1848 as a bulwark against a resurrection of Bourbon influence,[252] in 1851 he took the view that this was yet another necessary (if not altogether welcome) move to safeguard peace. As he wrote to his brother-in-law, Laurence Sulivan, it seemed that

> the course of events during the preceding period since the meeting of the assembly had placed the assembly & the President in such a state of antagonism that a conflict between them had obviously become inevitable and that it probably was true as asserted, that if the President had not dissolved the Assembly the Assembly would have tried to arrest him, & that it seemed to me to be better for France & for the tranquillity of Europe that the President should prevail over the Assembly than the Assembly over the President because the success of the Assembly who had no good candidate to offer for the government of France would probably lead to civil war.[253]

Accounts reaching Palmerston had convinced him that plots were afoot in Paris for an attack on Louis Napoleon and, as he put it some time later, these reports proved 'that if the President had not struck when he did he would himself have been knocked over'.[254] Thus Palmerston chose to signal his approval of Louis Napoleon's conduct when he met the French ambassador Walewski shortly afterwards. His Cabinet colleagues, however, thought this an unwarranted endorsement of an arbitrary abuse of power and called for Palmerston to be removed. Palmerston refused to yield on this point and, in effect, forced Russell to make a choice and on 17 December Russell wrote, 'with great reluctance', to ask for Palmerston's resignation. The 'complaints are too frequent, & too well founded', he explained, and while he maintained that he had in the past concurred and continued to 'concur in the foreign policy of which you have been the adviser', he had to 'observe that mis-understandings perpetually renewed, violations of prudence & decorum too frequently repeated have marred the effects which ought to have followed from a sound policy and able administration'.[255] Palmerston recognised that his position had become untenable within the existing government and he offered in reply to give up the seals of office whenever Russell liked, though he insisted that he had 'the satisfaction of thinking that the interests, the honor, the character, and the dignity of the country have not suffered' during his term of office.[256] Russell agreed unreservedly, he said.[257] It was perhaps less awkward to be gracious now that Palmerston's removal had become unavoidable. Palmerston believed that his going was not universally welcomed within the Cabinet,[258] but there were more ministers who agreed with Lord Truro that 'Palmerston's retirement is good',[259] than otherwise. Even Lord Minto, one of Palmerston's most loyal and consistent supporters, was forced to admit the 'painful conviction' that Palmerston's 'retirement had become inevitable'. It was both 'a public calamity' and 'a subject of private regret', he said, but it was inescapable.[260] In Paris Palmerston's fall was lamented by both the government and Louis Napoleon himself,[261] but removing Palmerston made little or no difference to the course or tone of British policy, something which Russell was at pains to stress across the Channel. In fact, according to Peter Borthwick of the *Morning Post*, who wrote to Palmerston at the time, when Russell met Walewski shortly after dismissing Palmerston he 'expressed himself in language *precisely similar in every respect* to that which had been originally held by your Lordship and the terms in which Walewski has conveyed the explanations of Lord John to his govt are to the full as warm as those in which he reported his first conversation with you'.[262] Indeed, if reports that reached Palmerston were true, Russell had done more than Palmerston to encourage the French ambassador to represent the British government as favourably disposed to Napoleon's actions. As Palmerston wrote in a lengthy account almost a year afterwards: 'Walewski dined with Lord John [on 5 Dec. 1851] and met there some other members of the Cabinet and that even said Count Walewsky to Lord John "upon that very sofa" (pointing to one in the room) "you expressed opinions if any thing stronger than what Lord Palmerston had said to me on the Wednesday [3 Dec.] and whereas I had contented myself with reporting what Lord Palmerston had said in a private letter . . ., I made what you had said the subject of an official despatch." '[263]

It is difficult to avoid the impression that Palmerston's endorsement of the coup was the occasion more than the direct cause of his removal from office, which rested as much on simmering personal antagonisms as on divergence over policy. Having got rid of Palmerston, however, no one wanted to admit responsibility for his fall. When Cabinet members had expressed alarm at his proposed reception of Kossuth, for example, there was supposed to be widespread opposition to the meeting. In fact Palmerston's position was privately supported by many of his colleagues. Russell, Lansdowne and Minto all thought that although receiving Kossuth would be liable to misrepresentation and would therefore be better avoided, they concluded that Palmerston did have a right to receive Kossuth in a private capacity.[264] In part, no doubt, they were concerned about having to face Palmerston as an opponent rather than trying to control him as a colleague,[265] and even Lord Grey admitted that there was not much of an appetite to force his removal at that point.[266]

In December it was stated officially that the government would not adopt a foreign policy different from that pursued by Palmerston, and both Clarendon and Grey found it odd that this episode should have been used as grounds for his dismissal when so many other opportunities of a similar nature had presented themselves over the previous five and a half years and been over-looked.[267] Some thought it was a move brought by royal command but though the Queen believed that affronts to the court had made Palmerston's position untenable,[268] and though she complained about the 'deviations from the principles laid down by the Cabinet for his conduct' and the 'personal and arbitrary perversion of the very nature and essence of those principles',[269] none of this was new. The Queen even acknowledged in private that pushing for Palmerston's removal in this manner would not be without difficulty: it would have been, she wrote in her journal, 'a most disagreeable task' and one 'not unattended with a small amount of danger, inasmuch as it would have put me too prominently forward'.[270] She tried to impress on Russell the need for a wholesale review of British policy since 1848, using Palmerston's removal as an excuse to examine matters afresh, but her lengthy appeal for a 'reconsideration' of principles generated little Cabinet interest.[271]

The *Daily News* thought the event simply further evidence of Cabinet in-fighting and suggested that Grey had been agitating for such a result since the formation of the ministry.[272] Grey himself, however, writing to Palmerston shortly after he had been ejected from the government, tried to cast the problem as a personal rivalry between Palmerston and Russell. He was surprised, he told Palmerston, 'that the difference was one which could not be settled without your retirement',[273] and in a letter to his friend Wood he suggested that though Russell had no option but to remove Palmerston, he thought the Prime Minister 'very much indeed to blame for allowing matters to come to such a pass as to create this necessity & thus inflict what I fear will be a mortal blow to the govt'.[274] In later years Russell said that he had acted in December 1851 in a fit of pique,[275] but if this was just an opportunity to do something he had long meditated on, it is unclear why that was judged the best (or only) moment to do it. If it had proved an awkward move, however, and although no one publicly celebrated Palmerston's retirement, Clarendon perhaps spoke for many of his colleagues when he observed that he was 'glad, however it has been made for as troublous times may be oncoming it is desireable [*sic*] not to have *all* the powers of Europe hostile to us and panting for our humiliation'.[276] But if many of the powers of Europe may have been gratified to see Palmerston gone, that was not necessarily the case closer to home. The government had just, after all, dismissed its most popular, patriotic and English minister.

At first Palmerston's approval of Napoleon's seizure of power appeared puzzling. One of his critics suggested that it only revealed his duplicity: 'are these the fitting achievements and habits of the Protestant, English, and Liberal statesman *par excellence*?' he asked.[277] Yet, encouraged by Palmerston himself, many others saw his departure as further evidence of European malevolence: Palmerston said that his removal was the result of 'a weak truckling to the hostile intrigues of the Orleans Family, Austria, Russia, Saxony & Bavaria & in some degree also the present Prussian Govt'.[278] When the news of Palmerston's dismissal reached the press, it was met with almost universal criticism.

The *Morning Post*, by now a loyal Palmerstonian journal, lamented that, in the 'present critical state of European affairs', the country had dispensed with a minster who stood 'in the very highest ranks of statesmanship'.[279] 'Public opinion will not be satisfied with light explanations of so great a misfortune;' an article observed, in response to suggestions that Palmerston had been sacrificed to the opinion of overseas courts, 'still less with explanations which attribute the result to unworthy or discreditable causes', more especially since it was Palmerston above all others to whom the longevity of the Russell government ought to be attributed.[280] Palmerston's only fault, said the *Post*, was 'that he loves his country so well, and serves his Sovereign so faithfully, that he prefers the independence of the one and the dignity of the other to the good or ill pleasure of certain foreign politicians',[281] and the paper's editor wrote privately to Palmerston to assure him that he was 'entitled well to the hearty service of every Englishman and I am desirous to be a faithful servant', even organising a number of 'confidence meetings' for Palmerston 'to express public gratitude for your administration of foreign affairs and public admiration for your character'.[282] That a sympathetic paper should have responded like this was not surprising, but even more critical titles were unsure about the merits of what had just passed. *The Times*, although thinking it was writing a political obituary, nonetheless applauded Palmerston's industry, courage and charm and steadfastly refrained from repeating the charges made against his foreign policy.[283] The Peelite *Morning Chronicle* described Palmerston's dismissal as a 'national humiliation'; he had been, the *Chronicle* said, 'the keystone of the arch' throughout the life of the government and was 'their only man of first-class ability; his policy, though dangerous always and injurious often, was at least bold, spirited, and not essentially un-English'.[284] The *Daily News* thought that, on balance, removing Palmerston at the current juncture was probably a dangerous move; and that although a periodic rotation of offices was beneficial, this was not the moment for such a reshuffle.[285] Even the *Standard* found Palmerston's departure 'the reverse of satisfactory' and argued that, with an eye to the undercurrent of tension between Grey and Palmerston, 'as Lord Palmerston was certainly the most able, and on every account the least unpopular member of the administration, the retirement of Lord Grey was more generally anticipated'.[286] The Grey faction, the *Standard* maintained, were 'Radicals and Revolutionists', 'ultra pro-Papists', and the dismissal of the true Protestant, Palmerston, was interpreted as a Catholic scheme, underlined, surely, by the appointment in Palmerston's place of Lord Granville, who was 'eminent for his pro-Romanist zeal'.[287] The contrast between Grey and Palmerston was referred to elsewhere. *Bell's Life in London*, a sporting paper, warned in early December:

> No, Lord John Russell, you had better get rid of *twenty Lord Grey's* [Palmerston's emphasis], and preserve the respect, obedience and loyalty of the Colonies, than sacrifice one Lord Palmerston, and with him sacrifice the sense of England's national independence. There is in England, and in such as are worthy of the name of Englishmen (the intriguers who are trying to coerce Lord John on this point are not worthy of it), no inclination to truckle to foreign domination of any kind.[288]

Revealing his interest in measuring his standing against public opinion, Palmerston collected and kept a wide range of newspaper cuttings and letters from around the country describing his dismissal. In them he saw that in many sections of the population he was seen as a patriotic hero, a Protestant defender of liberties, and a minister of ability. Such evidence of popular affection no doubt reinforced Palmerston's sense of his continuing political relevance. Some articles which he preserved, such as ones from the *Dundee Courier*, simply underlined the general bewilderment felt at his dismissal. Others, such as the Dublin-based *Warder*, worried that this was a bad time to hand an advantage to Catholic France and spoke of recent events as 'the most unseasonable exhibition of "the white feather," as of the most calamitous augury for the ultimate interests of peace'. In London, the *Morning Advertiser*, originally a publicans' paper, though by this time much more widely read, asked: 'Will Englishmen submit to this?', finding it hard to believe that they would acquiesce in the sacrifice of 'the most *English* Minister' ever to hold the seals of the foreign office being ' "basely" sacrificed to the despotic Courts of the Continent'. A letter to the *Lincolnshire Times* of February 1852 suggested that perhaps they would not.[289] Letters from private individuals told Palmerston that he was an English patriot and the only reliable defender of national honour. The mayor of Southampton even went so far as to dub Palmerston the 'People's Minister'.[290] This was not, apparently, a good moment to waste such a talent.[291]

On this solid basis of confidence Palmerston could invert the traditional antagonism towards France – and in December 1851 with a Bonaparte at the head of the French government there was a good deal of suspicion and unease – and still be held up as the defender of liberty and peace. Now that he had established himself, rhetorically, as the defender of these principles, public opinion could continue to believe that, however much the spectre of earlier Napoleonic menace might be resurrected, Palmerston still stood as the defender of the national interest. Though his dismissal in the face of such apparent popular outrage was a timely reminder of the limitations of popular support as a foundation for political eminence, it is far from the case that this represented an unqualified defeat for Palmerston. Russell's government, never strong, was beginning to look jaded and the Prime Minister had begun scouting about for new blood from among the Peelites.[292] Palmerston quickly began to represent his fall as something he might even have welcomed. He told Lansdowne that he had gone quietly in December so as to avoid damaging the reputation of the Queen, but he pointed out that although he was leaving a government in which he had been, apparently, an awkward fit, he had always carried public opinion with him.[293] This was still the case out of office, as he told his brother, and he claimed that he welcomed the chance to step out from Russell's shadow:

> John Russell's jealousy is of long standing. When Ld Grey came in in 1830 John Russell wanted to be Foreign Secretary instead of me, during the Syrian campaign when he was at the Home Office he was led by the Bear [Edward Ellice] & by Guizot into very active endeavours to thwart me, but luckily Charlie Napier & others brought the matter to a successful issue before these cabals could operate. For some time he has been annoyed at finding my name more mentioned at home & abroad in connection with our foreign policy than his, although he is Prime Minister, and his cold & reserved manner has rendered him less personally popular with our party generally than I have happened to be.[294]

Observers at the time were correct to sense that there was a growing friction between Palmerston and Russell as they jostled to assert pre-eminence within Whig–Liberal ranks. Very quickly Palmerston's supporters recast his dismissal as a liberation: freed from Russellite shackles Palmerston could now fulfil his destiny. The *Morning Advertiser* called for a very visible demonstration of this power shift when it suggested that the City of London, Russell's constituency, should sack Russell and replace him with Palmerston.[295] Liberal voters in Bristol, London and Glasgow all sought to be associated with this renaissance by inviting Palmerston to stand in their constituencies, approaches that were all politely declined.[296]

In January the *Leicestershire Mercury* (in another cutting kept by Palmerston) described how Palmerston's 'brilliancy' and 'genius' would soon be once again recognised and 'then shall we speedily see his lordship carried back to office on the shoulders of the people.'[297] Correspondents began to write in congratulatory terms of Palmerston's 'withdrawal' from the government; one letter from London described how, all over the city, and especially in the Lord Mayor's house, Palmerston's name was widely mentioned (' "Long live Palmerston", "Palmerston for ever" – "Vive Palmerston" ') and it was felt that it would not be long before Palmerston headed his own ministry.[298] The language of emancipation infused the writing of Palmerston's supporters: the Sheffield branch of the Rational Society, at a general meeting in January 1852, rejoiced 'in the liberation of Lord Palmerston from the thraldom of office'. One of his regular correspondents from Tiverton hoped that 'a little cessation of intense labour will give you fresh strength and recruit the effect of past toils'.[299] This was, it seemed, a criticial moment in British history. A clergyman from Kent expressed the hope that 'the talent, the energy, & the Protestantism of Lord Palmerston . . . [will] come to the rescue of England'.[300] The identification of Palmerston as a Protestant figurehead was repeated elsewhere: one writer enthused that with 'only the ace (the people) and knave of trumps in hand', Palmerston would be able to return to office as 'the guardian of the Protestant religion and the freedom of England'.[301] To a wider British audience concerned about issues of papal aggression and fearful of a perceived ascendancy of the Roman Catholic Church, Palmerston stood as a bulwark against absolutism and a defender of religious liberty.[302] Indeed, in some quarters calls were starting to be heard for Palmerston to become Prime Minister. He might have opposed franchise reform, but a Palmerston premiership would, it was suggested, represent progress and virtual representation of the people's true interests. As 'an Edinburgh Elector' warned in a letter to the *Edinburgh News*, for example:

> Thus the *Daily News* writes – 'Lord John Russell promises us a new reform Bill. Let us see what it will be like before we try to upset him in favour of one whose opinions on reform are far less known than those of the present Premier.'
>
> Electors, and people of Britain, beware of this piece of cunning and carry back Lord Palmerston as Premier to the Councils of Her Majesty and of the nation in favour of Kossuth, down-trodden nationalities, and the independence of this land from foreign dictation.[303]

There were, of course, dissentient voices too, but on one point all seemed to be agreed: Palmerston might have been down at the end of 1851 but he was certainly not out. As the *Guardian* concluded, he 'has acted with many sets of politicians; but there is one uniform characteristic of all his changes;– he always went forward;– he never took a step backward, and he will not do so now'.[304]

CHAPTER 10

THE PEOPLE'S MINISTER, 1852–1855

'The truth is, that for the last thirty years the principles of the foreign policy of this country have never varied. There may have been differences in the execution, according to the different hands intrusted with the direction of that policy: but the foundation of the foreign policy of this country has been, I repeat, for the last thirty years the same.'

Lord Aberdeen, speaking in the House of Lords, 27 December 1852[1]

TO SOME AT Westminster it appeared, as Lord Dufferin put it, that Palmerston had been 'completely floored' in December 1851 and, he observed a little over a month afterwards, 'people seem to think he is not likely to rise again'.[2] Those close to the government reassured themselves that the loss of Palmerston was not too serious a blow; indeed, that it might shore up an ageing administration. Lord Truro thought Palmerston had become 'too fond of popularity hunting to fit the Foreign Office & when he makes the good men of Tiverton his confidants, he incapacitates himself for that important situation'.[3] Clarendon had been quick to reassure the Prime Minister that the ministry would not suffer as a result of the rupture with Palmerston,[4] adding in January 1852: 'His friends and newspapers put about that he is the victim of a cabal, and this sustains him for a time; but if he fails to prove it he will sink in public opinion.'[5] Clarendon looked forward to some recovery of Britain's international standing having dispensed with Palmerstonian meddling overseas,[6] but what Clarendon and others failed to appreciate was the effect Palmerston's recent dismissal had had on the political nation where, outside the Cabinet and the closed doors of the Whig salons, Palmerston's departure was not so readily understood or applauded.

When he learned of Palmerston's dismissal, at the beginning of January 1852, Lord Howden wrote from Madrid to offer the new Foreign Secretary, Lord Granville, his resignation. He said that whatever the cause of Palmerston's 'retirement' it would be ascribed abroad to 'a direct concession to the reactionary spirit which is now riding roughshod over the world' and Howden's continued presence in Spain as an advocate of British interests would, he said, be 'useless, from it being supposed (however mistakenly) that the ground on which I stood has been cut from under my feet'.[7] Granville wrote back insisting 'that the policy of this country is unchanged with regard to its foreign relations' and that the foreign policy of the government was every bit as liberal as it had been under Palmerston (if not, indeed, more so).[8] Politicians on all sides struggled to make sense of what had happened in December. Aberdeen, though he found Louis Napoleon's recent conduct had surpassed that of Bonaparte 'in duplicity and hypocrisy', did not think that the change in the French government represented much of a threat to Britain. Palmerston's dismissal for endorsing the coup, therefore, seemed 'strange'. 'That the man who has supported revolutionary movements throughout Europe, should be dismissed in consequence of his approbation of arbitrary and despotick power seems whimsical,' he observed in a letter to Guizot. Though he thought Granville a reasonable replacement, Aberdeen speculated that the Russell government would not now last much longer.[9] From the back benches Palmerston agreed, though he thought it was Russell's determination 'to bid higher for radical support by his Reform plan' that would finish the ministry: 'the chances are,' he told Broughton, 'that the government will be wrecked on the Reform rock before the session has run much of its course; & perhaps it is best that things should take that turn.'[10] In fact, within a month Palmerston had brought the Russell government down himself. When, in February, Russell introduced a measure to develop the local militia, Palmerston thought it would be better if the arrangements were for a national, mobile, militia and moved an amendment to strike out the word 'local' from Russell's bill. The motion passed by 136 to 125 votes and amid considerable cheering which, Palmerston noted, was so vehement as to be of an 'almost insulting manner towards him', Russell resigned. Palmerston thought the Prime Minister had taken an easy exit to avoid a more difficult debate and likely defeat about war in the Cape, but he was still surprised by what had happened. The outcome was not intended, then, but nor was it unsatisfactory: 'I have had my tit for tat with John Russell,' he wrote to his brother afterwards.[11]

To many, Palmerston remained a potent political force. As the *Morning Post* said of his speech on the Militia Bill in February 1852, he had shown 'at once that he had sagacity to comprehend, and ability to meet, what parliament and the public felt to be the wish of the nation, and the necessity of the time'.[12] If Palmerston had defeated Russell, however, he had not supplanted him at the head of the Whigs and Liberals, and there was certainly little chance of the Queen turning to Palmerston to form a government after what had passed between them during the previous five years. It seemed that the political world was in flux and, as Algernon Borthwick, son of the *Morning Post* editor Peter, had observed in the middle of the previous December, anticipating the end of the Russell government, in any future arrangement 'coalition must be the order of the day'. To Borthwick it seemed that 'any body may coalesce with any body else' and he foresaw any possible combination of Radicals, Peelites and

Protectionists as viable; crucially he also saw Palmerston as a comfortable fit within any permutation: 'I see no principles that stand in the way,' he wrote, 'for the truth is that no one has any, except Lord P. I see no impediment to their *all* joining him.'[13] When Russell resigned on 20 February, it was Lord Derby who received the commission to form a new government, but his Protectionist administration always carried about it the air of impermanence.

As Borthwick had suggested, it seemed that Palmerston's erstwhile Whig ties were no bar to overtures to him to join the Conservatives and, having accepted the Queen's commission, Derby approached Palmerston with an offer of a place in the government. 'It would be a source of great gratification to me,' he wrote, 'if this event afforded me an opportunity of renewing the ties of office with one with whom as a colleague I never had a difference, and whose abilities I have since experienced in many a keen encounter, when circumstances have thrown us into adverse ranks, but without ever, I hope, impairing the feelings of personal regard, which I have never ceased to entertain for you.'[14] Palmerston lost no time in telling Derby that the question of protectionism made this impossible.[15] It was the cheapness of food that had, in large measure, staved off revolution in Britain in recent years, said Palmerston, and even though Derby had said that he would not introduce definite protectionist measures without the mandate of a general election victory, Palmerston insisted that this remained an 'insurmountable obstacle' to union. Furthermore, while indisposed to support advanced measures for parliamentary reform, Palmerston was more receptive to proposals for moderate franchise extension than was Derby. According to Palmerston's record of their meeting, Derby appears to have struck a cautious note; he would bring forward only those measures he judged 'of pressing importance' and he would look for a dissolution and general election at the earliest opportunity. To Derby this appeared the surest way of securing a stable parliamentary position for a new government; by the same token it was offering Palmerston a political transfer for limited gain and large potential sacrifice. It was clear too, from what Derby said, that Palmerston's return to office would meet with immediate royal opposition. So there was never any serious discussion of what place Palmerston might have filled. It seemed to Palmerston that Derby planned to offer him the Chancellorship of the Exchequer and though Palmerston said that he was happy to relinquish claims to the Foreign Office, he preferred, on balance, to take 'some refreshing rest at grass'.[16]

Palmerston's position at Westminster throughout 1852 was an interesting one. His separation from the Whigs seemed unlikely to be resolved soon while Derby, whose government was never convincing as a durable proposition, continued to hope that Palmerston might be induced to join the Tories.[17] More than one overture was made during these months,[18] but though he showed 'marked benevolence' towards the Derby government and maintained a close and friendly correspondence with the new Foreign Secretary, Malmesbury,[19] there was never any real likelihood of his joining it. If economic policy went a long way towards distinguishing the parties at this time, Palmerston not only felt that protectionism was an insuperable obstacle to union with Derby but, as the session progressed, he began to doubt the government's own coherence over financial matters (he thought when Disraeli spoke on finance in late April that he was disingenuously trying to take credit for sound economic management under Peel and Russell which at the time the Protectionists had loudly criticised). He judged it 'a real public advantage that the Tory party has come into office, and has an opportunity of seeing & learning & judging as responsible ministers many things of which in opposition they had very imperfect knowledge & conceptions', but though he thought the government was performing 'better than was expected of them', by the end of April he concluded that without 'some material reinforcement' they would not last until Christmas.[20] However, coalition with Peelite or Liberal groups was as unrealistic as ever and Palmerston was not prepared to jeopardise his own position for the sake of uncertain political rewards:

> I believe the Derby govt will rather calculate upon inducing me to join them when protection has had its public funeral; on this point of course I am studiously silent; but I have no intention or inclination to inlist [sic] under Derby's banner. I do not think highly of him as a statesman, and I suspect that there are many matters on which he & I should not agree. Besides after having acted for 22 years with the Whigs, & after having gained by & while acting with them any little political reputation I may have acquired, it would not answer nor be at all agreable to me to go slap over to the opposite camp, and this merely on account of a freak of Johnny Russell's, which the whole Whig party regretted & condemned. Moreover I am in no great hurry to return to hard work, & should not dislike a little more holyday.

By the same token, however, Palmerston was not willing to resubmit to serving under Russell. Though the two had, he said, repaired personal relations, he had 'lost all political confidence' in Lord John and 'it would be a very pressing public emergency' that would induce him to consider joining a new Russell administration. Russell had by his 'frolic' of February lost ground among Whigs, said Palmerston, but though he believed the majority of Whigs would be glad to see him replace Russell as their leader, it was not easy to 'reduce to the second place a public man who for many years has occupied the first place', and Lord John 'cannot be put upon the shelf'. Palmerston was evidently weighing up a bid to head his own government, but despite the apparent dearth of available talent he was modest about his own prospects. 'If I was sent for', he told his brother, 'which from the feeling towards me at court, is highly unlikely, I should have some difficulty in forming a govt, but I think I could do it; and though I should be conscious that I am wanting in many of the requisite qualifications for the post of Prime Minister, yet I think on the whole my deficiencies are not greater than those of Derby & John Russell, or of any other person who at present could be chosen for such a duty.'[21] Nonetheless, when he returned to the subject in June, he judged the 'best arrangement that could be made' would be a Lansdowne government under which he and Russell and other Whigs could serve alongside 'the best of the Peelites' on equal terms; Lansdowne, however, was said to be unwilling to undertake such a role.[22]

Yet Palmerston was not altogether unhappy with the political situation. 'As I have no office which other people want,' he wrote to William, 'nobody abuses me in order to knock me down; while both the govt and the Liberals wishing to get me on their side are vying with each other in civilities. This is all very well as long as it lasts, and after five years and a half of galley slave labour I find it not disagreable [sic] to have some command of my time.'[23] The Queen and Prince, he admitted, remained hostile, though polite, but in all other regards he perceived himself to be in a strong and strengthening position: 'the public, the press, the Parliament, & political parties', he said, were 'all well disposed & civil'. He professed his enjoyment at being 'free to act independently' and he thought his expressed opinions 'have generally been lucky enough to meet with concurrence'. All of which, he believed, placed him in an enviable position whereby all sides were bidding for his allegiance.[24]

Palmerston thought himself well placed in the summer of 1852 to take advantage of any shifts in the political landscape and the view was widely held. He was not the leading candidate to replace Derby, but as Nassau Senior, the political economist, noted at this time, Palmerston's name was mentioned alongside those of Lansdowne, Newcastle, Russell, Granville, Clarendon and Sir James Graham as possible premiers. The only thing Senior felt confident of predicting was that Palmerston would never again return to the Foreign Office since it was reported that even Palmerston himself admitted that 'his general unpopularity in Europe unfits him for that post'.[25] At the general election in early July, the Tories were despondent – Disraeli 'said they were watching the elections as the Egyptians did the Nile[,] they had no doubt of its rising – but the doubt was whether it would rise high enough'[26] – while Palmerston's stock, it seemed, rose. He had received offers to stand for other seats but preferred the security of 'a good & safe seat' in Tiverton where, though he was 'questioned' by the local butcher and Chartist, William Rowcliffe, no third candidate meant that he and Heathcoat were returned unopposed.[27] Palmerston interpreted the election as a verdict on free trade, which had, he said, 'contributed so much to the comfort, welfare and happiness of the great mass of the nation'. He stood, he said, as a free trader in more than just pure economic terms; that policy was but part of a more general 'principle of steadily progressive improvement' which had led to the reform of public life under the Whigs during the past three decades.[28] Lady Palmerston observed with pride how her husband's election speeches had charmed the political world.[29] Though he felt himself riding high, Palmerston continued to dismiss talk of his becoming Prime Minister, saying that only Lansdowne could unite the factious Whig party,[30] but he could not help noticing that 'many people & more than might have been supposed talk of me as the next minister'.[31]

None of this arrested speculation that Palmerston might yet join the Protectionists and the idea recurred in the autumn when, as Charles Greville noted, there was 'a strong conviction' at Westminster that Palmerston would join Derby 'provided the latter will give him a decent opportunity for so doing'.[32] Although Derby reported to Malmesbury that he thought 'Palmerston was ready to join us as soon as he saw we were safe', it is not known how seriously the notion of union was actually taken.[33] George Cornewall Lewis thought that by admitting Palmerston to his Cabinet, 'Ld Derby would find not only that he had got a master, but a master who made him feel his servitude every day – & rode him with a sharp bit & a hard hand',[34] and there is evidence that Derby was concerned about undermining his leadership in this way.[35] Rumours among the Protectionists suggested Palmerston had even joined the Peelites, but though Malmesbury was open to the idea of welcoming Palmerston into the Cabinet, even as a single addition, Derby worried about losing control of his government.[36] There was, however, a suggestion that Derby was using Palmerston for his own purposes: when he heard 'vague speculation' that Derby was about to offer Palmerston the Home Office, Sir James Graham thought it unsurprising: Palmerston, he thought, could easily fit into a Tory ministry, but bringing him in would give Derby a clear pretext for 'shelving at once protection and D'Israeli'.[37] For his part Palmerston had never encouraged or entered seriously into such political conjectures, except in so far as it advanced his real interest to consolidate and fortify his position among the Whigs and vis-à-vis Russell.

As the Derby administration stumbled to its fall in the autumn of 1852, attention in the press turned in earnest to the question of its replacement. Russell was dismissed as unfit again to become Prime Minister by the *Morning Post*: between him and that station were now 'raised up obstructions permanent and insurmountable', primarily popular and parliamentary distrust.[38] Palmerston, however, that paper said, held a very strong hand as one who 'in his present independent position, enjoys a wider popularity, and exercises a larger and more wholesome influence on the European mind, than any other living man'. On this ground, the *Post* argued, he need 'make no approaches to any party in the State . . . for to him "*Tout vient à propos*", whether he wait or not'.[39] In such an apparently strong position, then, Palmerston had all before him: Ashley would later describe Palmerston as 'indispensable', a politician whom a 'general though undefined feeling among the public had already marked . . . out as the coming man'.[40] In September Palmerston told the Duke of Bedford, elder brother of the former Whig Prime Minister, that he 'could not serve again under John Russell', but he held out the prospect of Whig reunion if that were under the leadership of a third party, such as Lansdowne.[41] It was a further three months, however, before a new government would be constituted, by which time it was Aberdeen who was seeking to form a coalition of Whigs and Peelites to unseat the Protectionists, though given the entrenched opinions within these groups it would be no easy task.[42] To some, Palmerston's course was difficult to predict. He might yet 'throw aside the part of a "juvenile Whig"', thought Graham and if Palmerston were to reinvent himself, then nothing, Graham continued, 'will now surprise me; and like a country clown I go to London *gaping*, and asking with my mouth wide open what I am to see next!'[43]

During December Lansdowne made concerted efforts to persuade leading Whigs to join the government and though Palmerston was initially wary, he became an enthusiast for the project, while refusing any suggestion of a return to the Foreign Office for himself, urging Clarendon to take that post. For himself, he said, he would agree to nothing more than to take the seals of the less demanding Home Office. It may have been genuinely a case of fatigue, or perhaps a realisation that he had made too many enemies, both at home and abroad, ever to be able effectively to run British foreign policy again,[44] but Palmerston was resolute: at Lansdowne's urging, Palmerston had 'consented to take [the] Home Office', but he was adamant that 'Nothing sh[oul]d induce me to go back to [the] Foreign Office.'[45] He reassured himself that either of the proposed candidates for the Foreign Office, Clarendon or Russell, would safeguard the liberal legacy and check the influence of Aberdeen. In any case, Palmerston thought, with regard to France, which he still saw as Britain's principal international rival, 'that with common prudence, & common good fortune we are safe for 1853 and I should hope for 1854' and though this 'interval' should be used 'in preparing actively permanent means of defence', this was something in which he could still claim a legitimate ministerial interest from his new position at the Home Office.[46] Many former Whig friends and colleagues had been excluded from the new administration, but, Palmerston argued, these omissions were a necessary price to pay for a durable government.[47]

To many, taking the Home Office was a curious and backward step for Palmerston. The Duke of Argyll felt that Palmerston had made a great sacrifice 'of personal feeling to public duty'. Not only had the Foreign Office been given to Russell ('the Minister who had summarily dismissed him from it'), but Palmerston now served 'under the leadership of a statesman whose arguments against his own policy he had described in the House of Commons as "antiquated imbecility"'.[48] Shaftesbury, too, confided in his diary that Palmerston's acceptance of office, in direct contradiction of everything he had said previously, surprised him greatly; he believed Palmerston had in some way been duped by Aberdeen and Russell, who had 'wanted to gag P.; and they have succeeded; they have bound the wild one between two tame elephants'.[49] Historians have often been just as surprised. David Roberts, author of the only study specifically of Palmerston's tenure of the Home Office, judged it 'one of the most humdrum of departments' and presented the appointment as a demotion, pointing out that the 'proud Foreign Secretary who had snubbed the crowned heads of Europe now haggled with vestrymen about their sewers'.[50] Jasper Ridley explained the move as motivated principally by pecuniary considerations: the Palmerstons, he observed, 'were beginning to feel the pinch without a ministerial salary', and the Home Office was simply the least objectionable post on offer.[51] And so Palmerston's tenure of the Home Office has often been treated as something of a curious aside in which biographers, obliged to include a chapter on the 'Home Office years', have tended to present a brief list of the measures overseen at that department between 1852 and 1855 before moving swiftly, and with some relief, on to more familiar Palmerstonian territory. Ridley even entitled his chapter: 'Home Secretary: the Eastern Question', while Southgate's account of 'the policies and politics of Palmerston', ignored Palmerston's work at the Home Office altogether and presented these years exclusively in terms of foreign affairs and disputes over foreign policy.[52]

Yet there is evidence that Palmerston had been thinking about a turn to domestic business for some months. When, in November 1850, it had been suggested that Lansdowne attempt to form a new government to replace the ailing Russell ministry, Palmerston had explained in a letter to his brother that in such a case Russell would have the Foreign Office and Palmerston would move to the Home Office and take the lead of the House of Commons. 'To say the truth,' he had told William at the time, 'but this you need not mention to any one, I should in any case much prefer the Home Office to going back to the immense labour of the Foreign Office. J'y ai été as the Frenchman said of fox hunting.'[53] By 1852 there were further grounds, both personal and political, for thinking of taking a new brief. 'It does not do for a man to pass his whole life in one department,' he wrote to William, 'and the Home Office deals with the concerns of the country internally, and brings one in contact with one's fellow-countrymen, besides which it gives one more influence in regard to the militia and the defences of the country.'[54] Palmerston's appointment to the Home Office was seen by many at the time as a test of his political character: after years of vacillation, would he now show himself to be a Liberal or a Tory?[55] Palmerston himself, defending his decision to accept the post, suggested that after twelve months of 'acting the part of a rope dancer & much astonishing the public by my individual performances and feats', now was the time, for practical reasons, to cease playing the part of 'a reckless adventurer' and commit to the cause of 'the great Liberal party, (not in the H. of Cms, nor at Brooks's nor at the Reform Club) but in the United Kingdom' and to fulfil his duty to his Tiverton constituents.[56] This professed commitment to 'the great Liberal party' is important. Palmerston had expressed his concern in a letter to Sulivan that standing outside this new alliance of Peelites and Whigs would have left him 'in a little agreeable political solitude'.[57] Southgate is no doubt justified in claiming that it was 'the extravagances of his foreign policy' that most appealed to Liberal opinion,[58] but it was not all. It is important to weigh carefully Palmerston's contribution to domestic politics in these years for he demonstrated a far more sincere and dynamic interest in the work of the Home Secretary than has often been allowed and in so doing was able both to advance his own claims to eminence within liberal circles and also, though he would not have known this in advance, to take refuge in the Home Office when the fallout from the ill-managed Crimean War showered on Downing Street.

There were also, perhaps, more personal issues mixed up in Palmerston's attitude to the work of the Home Office. In August 1852 Emily had contracted cholera. Palmerston had recently returned from visiting his estates in Ireland and had gone down to Tiverton in order to see his constituents: it was here that, on 26 August, he received a letter from Emily's daughter Minny reporting that her mother was 'a good deal pulled' by 'a very severe attack of the English cholera' and though the prescription of laudanum by Dr Latham, the family physician, was leading to some improvement, Emily remained in a state of 'great exhaustion'. Latham was 'anxious but hopeful' but it took time to overcome the disease and for two or three weeks in late summer Palmerston, who had rushed back to London immediately, spent a good deal of his time sitting up with Emily, reading prayers and consulting with Latham.[59] Though Palmerston himself made no connection between this personal experience and public duty, days and nights spent at Emily's side may conceivably have sharpened his interest in questions of public health.

Far from seeing the Home Office as an unimportant political backwater, Palmerston addressed himself to the work of the department with the energy that had characterised his work at the Foreign Office, though the duties, as he had hoped, were less arduous. A little over three months into his new appointment, Palmerston found:

The mere routine business of the Home Office is as far as that consists in daily correspondence, is very far lighter than that of the Foreign Office but during a session of Parliament the whole day of the Secy of State up to the time when he must go to the Hs of Cns is taken up by deputations of all kinds and interviews with members of Parliament militia colonels &c. But on the whole it is a much easier office than the Foreign, and in truth I really would not on any consideration undertake again an office so unceasingly laborious every day of the year as that of foreign affairs. I shall be able to do some good in the Home Office. I am shutting up all the grave yards in London, a measure authorized by an Act of last session, and absolutely required for preservation of the health of the town. There is a company who are going to make two great tunnels under London fifty feet below the surface one north the other south of the Thames running nearly alongside the river beginning someway above the town & ending some way below it. These tunnels are to be the receptacles into which all the sewers & drains of London are to be discharged so that nothing is to go into the Thames, and the contents of these tunnels are at the point of termination to be dried & converted into manure to be sold to agriculturalists as home made guano. I shall try to compel at least the tall chimneys to burn their own smoke and I should like to put down beer shops and to let shopkeepers sell beer like oil & vinegar & treacle to be carried home & drunk with wives & children.[60]

His achievements at the Home Office, however, speak of more than mere industry. Addressing his constituents in Tiverton in January 1853 Palmerston had insisted that not only did he have no interest in returning to the Foreign Office, but that in taking the Home Office he had accepted 'that office which I was most desirous to fill'.[61] During the life of the government Palmerston oversaw the introduction of the Factory Act of 1853, which while not fulfilling all of the hopes of reformers such as Shaftesbury, did go some way towards improving industrial working conditions, especially for children. He also attempted to pass legislation which would have confirmed the rights of trade unions to combine for lawful purposes as laid down in an Act of 1825 (although he resisted trade union demands for the legalisation of peaceful picketing) and, more successfully, introduced the Truck Act under the terms of which workers were entitled to payment in money, rather than goods or tokens for employers' own shops. Palmerston also sought to improve the condition of society, both environmentally and morally. He pioneered legislation aimed at curbing pollution with the weak but well-intentioned Smoke Abatement Act in August 1853, and reform of the Board of Health in 1854, for example, and throughout was a firm friend of the temperance societies. Nor did he shy away from the thorny problems associated with prisons and their reform.[62]

David Roberts judged Palmerston's reforming record to have been a 'partial success', though this is as much a verdict, in Roberts's view, on the 'weak coalition ministry of Lord Aberdeen' and the deep-rooted 'entrenched interests and widespread evils' of mid-Victorian society. It may or may not be evidence of Palmerston's shortcomings that he did not achieve more at the Home Office; but what is important is that, in taking the seals of that department, Palmerston had been obliged 'to define his basic social philosophy'. Roberts is vague on this, though, suggesting that Palmerston had a genuine sympathy for 'the masses' but distrusted them and that in the end his 'social outlook was paternalistic'.[63] This is fine so far as it goes, but Palmerston's record deserves to be read a little more carefully. In Jonathan Parry's narrative of the 'rise and fall' of Liberal government in the Victorian period it is Palmerston's domestic record, both at the Home Office and subsequently at the head of his own ministry, as much as his popular ebullient foreign policy, that helped establish his claims to leadership of Liberal politics. With Liberal forces in the mid-1850s in need of a clear focus,

Parry discerned three competing strategies: Russellite schemes for a Liberal–
Radical coalition based on constitutional and religious reform; a Peelite-
inspired 'programme of economy and good administration'; or, the 'most
successful' in the event, a Palmerstonian third way.[64] Significantly, in fashioning
this third way, it was in his approach to Home Office work that Palmerston did
much to distance himself from the perceived Whiggish social exclusiveness of
his aristocratic liberal colleagues.[65]

Palmerston's attitude to questions of public health revealed his interest in
'improvement' underpinned by a rationalist view of the role of religion in matters
of welfare and science. In the autumn of 1853 cholera swept Britain. Famously, in
the October, Palmerston received, and rejected, an appeal from the Edinburgh
Presbytery calling for a national fast in response to the 'mysterious epidemic'.[66]
Palmerston's response was that while there could 'be no doubt that manifestations
of humble resignation to the divine will & sincere ack[nowled]gements of human
unworthiness are never more appropriate than when it has pleased providence to
afflict mankind with some severe visitation', there were no grounds at that time to
warrant a fast. 'The maker of the universe has established certain laws of nature
for the planet in wh we live & the weal or woe of mankind depends upon the
observance or the neglect of those laws', he continued. It was 'exposure to those
noxious influences' caused by decomposing matter in cities that made sickness
'almost inevitable', but the remedy, he said, was human not divine, or at least it was
'the duty of man to attend to those laws of nature & to exert the faculties which
providence has thus given to man for his own welfare'. The current epidemic was
not a punishment for man's sins, but 'an awful warning given to the people of this
realm that they have too much neglected their duty in this respect & that those
persons with whom it rested to purify towns & cities & to prevent or to remove
the causes of disease have not been sufficiently active in regard to such matters'.
Civic works, especially in poorer areas which were most in need of 'purification
and improvement' were, Palmerston said, the surest means to ward off pestilence
and death. Only once man had done all in his powers for his own improvement,
he concluded, should he 'invoke the blessings of heaven to give effect to his exertions'.[67] When a Suffolk clergyman wrote afterwards to protest that Palmerston
had ignored the fact that the cholera epidemic afflicted middle- as much as
working-class communities and so was a divine judgement on man's sins after all
and not a symptom of inner-city slum living, Palmerston merely acknowledged
receipt of the letter; he was unmoved by a lengthy recitation of Old Testament
examples of the propriety of a fast day to slay the disease.[68] Though there was
some press criticism, for the most part it seemed that the newspapers (and hence
public opinion) were on the side of the Home Secretary and the rationalists, even
if, as it is said some 'free wits' claimed, the erstwhile Foreign Secretary had taken
to treating Heaven as a foreign power.[69]

Instead of submitting to a punitive divinity, Palmerston preferred to emphasise the capacity for self-directed human improvement. Combating disease was

a duty, not an opportunity for aggrandisement – he dismissed as unworthy an enquiry from one individual about a pecuniary reward for a cure for cholera – and from the Home Office he directed that afflicted areas be carefully monitored, urging factory inspectors to educate industrial communities, so far as possible, about the disease. Meanwhile Palmerston monitored rates of infection from Board of Health data and used what influence he had to expedite drainage works sanctioned by Parliament.[70] The Home Secretary even drew up his own plans for drainage works in London, ordering the metropolitan districts by urgency of need and sending his proposed programme of works to the Commissioner of Sewers.[71] There is evidence of a centralising tendency in this work, too, indicating an important aspect of Palmerston's conception of the role of the state which again echoed the general philosophical framework adopted from Dugald Stewart. In part this was a straightforward issue of efficiency: as Palmerston put it when discussing metropolitan sewers, there was a strong case for making the area one large administrative district rather than several small ones. Cholera, after all, he said, was no respecter of civic boundaries.[72] More than this, however, Palmerston advocated the benefits of a paternalist state, for moral as well as economic reasons. When inhabitants of Dundee complained to the Home Secretary that because of restrictions brought in in response to cholera they were no longer permitted to keep pigs in the city, Palmerston noted that, so long as the whole country was threatened by 'an awful pestilence', he was sure 'that they will feel that considerations of private & individual convenience & advantage ought to give way to considerations of public health and they ought especially to bear in mind that in every place in which the cholera has appeared it is the poorer classes that have been its first & greatest victims and they are therefore more specially benefitted by any measures of prevention which tend to remove causes of disease'.[73] When he learned that in Ryde ratepayers were not implementing drainage and cleaning measures laid out in the Health of Towns Act, Palmerston observed that they would have only themselves to blame if the town subsequently fell victim to the disease.[74] Such laxity demonstrated the need for state paternalism. The expense of dealing with an epidemic far exceeded the costs of preventing one, he argued,[75] and if local municipalities could not see that, then Palmerston wanted central government to take a more prominent role. When water company vested interests and hostile engineers and local councillors found their opposition to the impositions of the General Board of Health echoed in Parliament by the Protectionists (the 'party of dirt', as Palmerston called them) in the summer of 1854 resulting in the discontinuation of the Board, Palmerston simply created a new Board, under his supervision, and headed by one man.[76] Though some contemporaries were surprised that Palmerston appointed Benjamin Hall, one of the old Board's chief critics, to lead the new one, others, such as Russell, regarded Hall as 'a sort of tool of Palmerston's',[77] and it is evident that the Home Secretary intended that Hall should make the Board effective since, as he wrote,

Our English tradesman ... has a great notion of his own sagacity, and
cannot bear anything that may lead to the imposition of a rate, and they
will often as at Newcastle see their neighbours perish around them and
risk the lives of their wives and children and their own rather than ward
off the danger by arrangements which might involve a six penny rate,
forgetting or not knowing that in the end such measures would be a real
economy.[78]

The sanitary and public health reforms achieved during Palmerston's tenure
of the Home Office may have been unremarkable,[79] but Palmerston's determination to tackle the cholera epidemic at all, and to do so with drains and clean
water rather than prayers, is revealing. Although the science of environmental
contamination was not yet particularly advanced, Palmerston was an active
Home Secretary in his attempts to control pollution and improve general
living conditions. He pursued vigorously schemes for smoke abatement,
directing the Board of Health to investigate as fully as possible all means for
the prevention of smoke pollution in the summer of 1854 (in an attempt to
shore up the limited powers afforded by the Smoke Nuisance Abatement Act
of 1853),[80] and lectured any industrialists and manufacturers who protested
against such measures on the evils of smoke belched into urban skies.[81] Edwin
Chadwick commended Palmerston on having brought 'a new and widely
extended public attention to the subject'.[82] Palmerston also pressed for cleaner
water supplies in cities and instituted inquiries into lodging-house conditions.
Alongside his ongoing attempts to advance sanitary provision and arrest the
spread of disease (his monitoring of cholera outbreaks in particular continued
after he had left the Home Office)[83] such measures were designed to effect
some improvement in the 'condition of England' question.[84] To Shaftesbury at
least, Palmerston's work yielded some positive results: 'Your smoke-bill will be
highly beneficial;' he wrote in August 1853, '& I rejoice to see that the factory-
bill has escaped all the quicksands. It is remarkable; for this very same proposition, when made by myself in the H of Commons, was stoutly resisted by Sir
G. Grey & Bright, and afterwards by Derby & Walpole.'[85]

Responsibility for enforcing the smoke abatement measures and monitoring
the state of lodging houses, and other environmental measures, at least in
London to which much of these measures were seen primarily to apply,
devolved mainly on the Metropolitan Police. Though he criticised the handwriting of police reports as vigorously as he had that of clerks at the War and
Foreign Offices (and now used his position in domestic politics to press the
Board of Education to address the execrable handwriting of the middle and
lower orders),[86] Palmerston showed some sympathy for the position of these
public servants and argued for changes to ameliorate the working conditions
of police officers: reduced hours on the beat, longer periods of rest, freedom to
attend church services (out of uniform) on Sundays, better pay and, above all,

a larger police force to handle the growing burden of work.[87] Palmerston took a particular interest in those questions that touched on social order. In an age described in one novel set during this period as 'eminently favourable to the growth of all roguery which is careful enough to keep up appearances',[88] it was evident to patrician politicians such as Palmerston that society required careful supervision. If Palmerston was exercising his social conscience, therefore, he was doing so from a position informed by the prevailing prejudices of Victorian society at mid-century.

In August 1853 George Wake, a Hampshire neighbour of Palmerston's, wrote to the Home Secretary in great alarm over the damaging effects of public drunkenness among those frequenting public houses. Palmerston concurred in Wake's apprehensions and forwarded Wake's letter to the Treasury as evidence of the concerns of a 'respectable & intelligent gentleman'. Palmerston's own view was that 'the beer houses licensed to sell beer to be drunk on the premises are the haunts of thieves and the preparatory schools for prostitutes, and are among the most active causes of demoralization for the lower classes'.[89] With such widespread opportunities for the corruption of morals, society must be protected from those evils; indeed, in some ways, at least with respect to the poorer elements within it, society needed to be protected from itself. Palmerston was in no doubt that bad character and morals were created by environment and circumstance, and were not inherited or innate. In a speech to farm labourers at Romsey in 1854, Palmerston claimed that all children were born good and only bad education and bad associations corrupted the mind. To many, it seemed a direct challenge to the doctrine of original sin and caused some little controversy.[90] Palmerston had no such grand theological dissertation in mind, however; in a speech that was being made to agricultural labourers he was trying rather more prosaically simply to emphasise the importance of recognising the difference between what was generally 'good' and what was generally 'bad', urging them ultimately to avoid the 'two rocks' upon which they might be wrecked – the tobacco shop and the beer shop – and telling his listeners that 'But for these twin devices of the foe it is impossible to say how far the pure nature of man might go in the path of perfection'.[91] There was nothing new in this Palmerstonian view of society. Twenty-five years earlier, in November 1829, while visiting Ireland where he observed growing tensions between landlord and tenant, he had written in a notebook:

It would undoubtedly in such a state of things become necessary to check disorder & to punish crime; but if I were called upon to devise means of future prevention, I should say to the gentlemen, give me your assistance; but give it in the way in which by the very principles of human nature I must be most effective. Relax somewhat from your military position; unbend a little from the sternness of your attitude; make acquaintance with the peasantry, try if possible, even to make them your friends, you may fail at first, & with some; but in the long run, & with many you will succeed; convince them that you have their welfare & happiness at heart, & that their interests & yours are identified; do not abandon your rights, but harrass [*sic*] not the people by enforcing them beyond reason; & discretion; above all be rigidly just in your minutest dealings with the people; who whatever they may do themselves, are singularly keen sighted in their perceptions as to the conduct of others; and whatever may be your abstract predilection for large farms & wealthy tenants, do not hastily, and abruptly & I will add cruelly hurry to this arrangement by the wholesale expulsion of hundreds of families, who when thus driven out from the habitation of their fathers, have no refuge from despair; & must go perish by the ditches of the road and at the edges of the morass.

There is no effect without a cause; mankind are born ignorant, & illiterate, and rude, & unpolished; but they are not born cruel & ferocious. Robbers, incendiaries, and murderers are the offspring of society, & not of uncultivated nature; – and where we see a people ferocious & demoralized we may read in their vices the manner in which they have been dealt with, as surely as we can trace in the restiveness of an unruly horse the defects of its early management.[92]

There were nuances in Palmerston's social policies that have led some commentators to regard him as inconsistent or lacking a coherent ideological outlook. On the one hand he seemed humane, progressive and 'modern'; on the other reactionary and small minded. Thus, for example, he wanted to improve conditions for convicts in prisons, but he did not want them released back into British society. On 10 October 1854 Palmerston visited Parkhurst prison on the Isle of Wight where he was appalled by the conditions in which prisoners were kept. The cells, he judged, were not 'sufficiently ventilated' and he found the air felt 'very close & oppressive even when the door was open'. Investigating further, he learned of the poor sanitary conditions that were damaging the inmates' health. On his return to London he pressed for improvements to be made. He had found some of the boys held at Parkhurst whose 'countenances were good and their conduct was said to be good also' and Palmerston thought they would have been better sent to 'some reformatory school' rather than detained in the prison. Yet, however concerned or even progressive he might have seemed on the matter of prison conditions, he concluded his report on this visit with the note: 'I think [the] Colonial Office should be asked whether a certain number of the Parkhurst boys might not at the end of their terms of confinement be sent to the Australian colonies. I fear that being discharged at home they are likely . . . to fall back into a fresh system of offence.'[93] The question is, who was Palmerston looking to protect: the respectable classes from the unrespectable and criminal elements, or the disadvantaged from the conditions that had created their offending behaviour? Perhaps neither, or rather both: removing abuses in society would advance the interests of all sections of the community. It would create the conditions for the ordered, hierarchical society to which Palmerston aspired.

Reform was the watchword of Palmerston's tenure of the Home Office. Given his conviction that environment played a crucial role in determining character and conduct, it was logical that he should also pay close attention to working conditions. He was particularly keen to enact measures to regulate child labour in factories and mines. Some years before, he had borne witness to the arduous labour of factory work. During debates on Ashley's bill to reduce children's working hours (to ten per day) in February 1844 a deputation had called on Palmerston to solicit his support for the measure. Having finally gained access to Palmerston's house they found him in good humour but indisposed to believe that conditions were as bad as represented: 'I am led to understand the machinery does all the work without the aid of the children, attention to the spindles only being required,' he told them. To convince Palmerston, the delegates set about mocking up a spinning mule using the Palmerstons' dining furniture and while they simulated the operation of the mule, Palmerston and one of his footmen pushed a couple of 'large lounging chairs' the length of the imaginary 'stretch' of spun yarn, mimicking the toil of driving the machine engine. 'Surely this must be an exaggeration of the labour of factory workers,' a visibly tired Palmerston said after a few lengths. Yet he had been touched by the notion that children routinely undertook such work and as his visitors provided further physical evidence of the hardships endured by factory workers, Palmerston concluded that he could 'no longer withhold my support from your cause'. The delegation had left a more marked impression on Palmerston than they had on either Russell or Grey whom they had visited before calling on Palmerston, and these factory reformers regarded Palmerston from that point as a genuine friend of the 'poor factory child'.[94] Palmerston entered the Home Office, then, well informed about the struggles of working children. Although his attempts to force factory and mine owners to make their places of work safer for their employees enjoyed limited success, while no doubt setting important precedents,[95] Palmerston did achieve something tangible with regard to the hours worked by children. During 1853 he pressed for reduced working hours for children in factories and successfully introduced legislation prohibiting those aged under twelve, already limited to six hours' work per day, from working at all after 6p.m.[96] By excluding child labour from night shifts, this measure effectively meant a ten-hour day for adult workers too since many of the machines could not be operated without being tended to by children.

It was, it has been argued, humane considerations more than economic ones that directed Palmerston's conduct.[97] Yet, there was a balance to be struck between state intervention and the free operation of the economy. Though he was anxious to regulate conditions from the point of view of safety and welfare, such interventions were not designed to impede the market forces of supply and demand. Palmerston was, therefore, intolerant of industrial strike action. National prosperity demanded the continued competitiveness of British manufacturing. In 1853 a number of strikes were staged, particularly in the north of England where demands among some strikers were for a 10 per cent increase in wages. As the strikes dragged on through the autumn and winter, Palmerston grew increasingly frustrated. He fully approved of the handing out of punishments to those who tried to prevent willing workers from breaking strikes and drew up plans for the use of the militia in combating industrial unrest.[98] Though intelligence reaching the Home Office suggested that both owners and workers knew that wages were too low, Palmerston maintained that it was agitators who 'compelled workers to strike on the pretence that those wages were not enough.'[99] In response to one memorial from striking workers in December, Palmerston commented that he could not be other than warmly sympathetic to the feelings of the strikers who, he said, had been led to believe they were the victims of injustice and who were certainly, as a result of the strike action, suffering severe privations. However, as a member of the government, he maintained that he had no 'right or power to interfere in the matter'. Only the market could offer a remedy, so long as that market operated justly:

> The cost of production in regard to labour means the price of the necessaries of life, & the proportion of demand & supply must depend very much upon the periodical fluctuations of trade. It is greatly to be wished that both the working men & their employers would allow these general causes to act silently & gradually in equitably adjusting from time to time the proper rates of the money reward for labour and it is scarcely to be doubted that by forbearance on both sides, & by mutual & reciprocal good feeling these arrangements might generally be effected without a recourse to such injurious methods as strikes & lock outs.

Strikes, he continued, deprived workers of their wages and thus the means of subsistence and damaged British industry by handing to overseas producers a competitive advantage that might not be easily overcome afterwards, especially if the volatility of the British labour force encouraged capital investment to flow abroad, as was already happening, he noted, with British manufacturing establishments now to be found in Belgium, France and Mexico.[100] Because he could see effects of the 'artificial arrangements of society' which gave rise to inequality, Palmerston would legislate to protect the well-being of the population, but it was not necessarily 'inconsistent' for him still to champion the principles of free trade.[101]

As a result of his work at the Home Office, and informed no doubt by his experiences as a landlord in Hampshire and, especially, Ireland, Palmerston's hierarchical view of society was clearly articulated. A benevolent government (of the enlightened and well-informed) ruled in the interests of a commercially active middle class, while remaining mindful of, and attentive to, the interests of a working class humble enough to know its place and grateful enough to offer in return its (unofficial) endorsement of the government's conduct. Palmerston's view of society found its perfect expression in the social structures of the military. As he told Parliament in 1854, the militia was 'a valuable social element, in as much as it brought the gentry . . . in contact with the lower and working classes . . . and it cemented the bonds of union, which should always unite them, by common pursuits, common associations, and common objects'.[102] At the Home Office and subsequently he was able to elaborate on this view of society and government responsibility. Yet whatever might be read into Palmerston's domestic reforms in terms of his view of society and its relationship with government, much of his popular appeal continued to rest on a sense that he was a patriotic figure capable of representing English values. The emphasis on Englishness is important and was brought into sharp relief when Palmerston visited Scotland in the early autumn of 1853.

In late September 1853 Palmerston arrived in Glasgow. He had spent the previous nine days in Scotland, attending the Queen at Balmoral, and had earlier that day received the freedom of the Guild Incorporation of Perth in recognition 'particularly of the firm, manly, independent and truly British spirit uniformly displayed by his Lordship, more especially when in the management of the foreign relations of the United Kingdom'.[103] That night he lodged at the Queen's Hotel in Glasgow and at eleven o'clock the following morning was taken by the Lord Provost to see the Cathedral College. From there they went to the City Chambers at noon, where upwards of 2,000 people had gathered to witness Palmerston receive the freedom of the city. Fortified by fruit and wine, Palmerston then paid visits to Higginbotham's Cotton Handkerchief manufactory and to a couple of ironworks, including that of David Napier (inventor of the steam hammer), leaving Glasgow for Carlisle on the eight o'clock train having first dined once again with the Lord Provost. It was, on the surface, an unremarkable episode in Victorian civic politics, and having been cheered in George Square and at the ironworks by the people of Glasgow, Palmerston no doubt left feeling his place in the affections of the second city of the Empire was secure.[104] He left behind a minor political storm, however, which revealed much about the meaning and value of Palmerston's cultivation of the image of himself as 'the intensest Englishman in English public life'.[105] By the early 1850s a decade and a half at the Foreign Office and his current incumbency of the Home Office had cemented Palmerston's place in public life. For a minister approaching seventy years of age it was perhaps ironic that he should be described (in September 1854) as '"the coming man" in the legislature', but, as one newspaper portrait pointed out, '[t]he country expects much from him.[106] So it was not especially surprising that a major city such as Glasgow should have chosen to pay tribute to the Home Secretary.

In his formal speech presenting Palmerston with the freedom, the Lord Provost said Palmerston was 'considered by your countrymen as the greatest statesman of the age, and the most distinguished public man of your day', and highlighted 'the courage and determination you have so often displayed in protecting the interests and the privileges of your countrymen abroad . . . [and] the manner in which you have upheld the honour and maintained the dignity of your Sovereign and your country', all of which was met with loud cheering from the assembled crowd. Palmerston's speech in reply offered a conventional tribute to the strengths and virtues of the people of Glasgow and of the country he served. However, his apparent lack of sensitivity to the diversity and character of that country was betrayed in this address. As he declared at one point, the moral leadership exhibited by the country in its foreign policy, 'must be a great satisfaction to the people of this country, and more peculiarly the inhabitants of Glasgow, because I know that in no place more than here has a deeper interest been felt in that sacred cause [suppression of the slave trade] – (cheers) – that must be a great satisfaction to the people of England'. His speech was littered with references to England's successes and the virtues of the English: it was 'the power of England' that reverberated around the world, and if it was the 'British' navy that had recently compelled the Brazilian government to put an end to the slave trade, it was the 'people of England' whom the Brazilians should thank; Scotland, he observed, had of late undergone 'vast improvement' and stood as a 'bright example' to 'all Europe in regard to everything connected with the civilisation of man', but his eulogy to the 'unflinching perseverance' of 'the Scottish nation' was itself presented as simply a vindication of the superior virtues of the united British, or English, Empire to which it belonged.[107]

This generated what would become a sustained attack on Palmerston's Anglo-centrism (and ultimately also that of others including John Bright and to a lesser degree Gladstone and Disraeli) by a Glasgow solicitor, William Burns, a member of the recently formed (though ultimately short-lived) National Association for the Vindication of Scottish Rights.[108] Having read reports of Palmerston's speech, Burns took Palmerston to task, charging him with a failure to recognise the position of Scotland within the Union. Palmerston for his part felt he had made due acknowledgement of the distinct role, as he saw it, Scotland had played in the history of Britain, telling his Glasgow audience that 'I say it without compliment, that if there is one portion of the united empire which more than another is distinguished for this great and eminent quality of steady and unflinching perseverance, undoubtedly it is the Scottish nation', that Scotland represented a model for the 'civilisation of man', 'intellectual improvement' and 'material and physical welfare'.[109] But he was guilty as charged by Burns of conflating 'England' and 'Britain' not only in his speech but in his world view. Burns laid forth his complaint more fully in a letter to *The Times* in October 1853:

If I am asked the question, – of what consequence is all this, and why attach so much importance to a name? I might answer that I decline to discuss such a question; that I appeal to 'the law and the testimony upon the subject, as between England and Scotland, in the shape of the Treaty [of 1707]; that I am entitled to assume, from the terms of that Treaty itself, independently of its *significant history*, that importance was attached to the clauses I have quoted; and that I deny the right of one party to a contract to violate its terms, on the plea of their being unimportant. I maintain that, by this system of *merging* Scotland in England, in place of carrying out the spirit of the contract betwixt them – by stripping the people of this country of their own name, and seeking to invest them with another *repugnant to all the facts and associations of their past history*, in place of assuming the common ground on which they had agreed to stand – you rob them of a *birthright* of inestimable value.[110]

Palmerston's response, made only once he realised that Burns would not be ignored, was made via the Under-Secretary at the Home Office, Henry Fitzroy, who relayed 'Palmerston's assurance that, in using the words "English," "Englishman," "England," his Lordship meant no disparagement to Scotland, Ireland or Wales; but only used that form of speech which is usually and conveniently adopted, in speaking of the United Kingdom and its inhabitants'.[111] This did not satisfy Burns who went on to publish a number of pamphlets in the 1850s and 1860s on the core question, as he himself put it, of *What's in a Name?*[112] It did not help that Palmerston's apologists (which included many of the London papers, and particularly *The Times*) stoked the grievance by suggesting that the Channel Islands would have as much right to feel slighted as Scotland did over this matter.[113] However, it was not just the London press that found Burns's concerns exaggerated. The *Citizen*, for example, was quick to mock him:

Although Scotch ourselves, to the backbone, a funny Scotchman is to us as amusing as a funny Englishman. For instance, the 'North Briton,' who wrote a long letter in the *Times* to Lord Palmerston must be an exceedingly amusing person. His complaint about the conventional use of the word 'England' for 'Britain' is very comical indeed. Everybody, except this 'North Briton,' knows that the term 'England' is used for 'Great Britain,' just as 'gray hairs' is used to signify 'old age,' or, 'the crown' to signify 'the sovereign' or 'the monarchy.' It belongs to a well-known figure of speech, called, we believe, *synecdoche*, whereby a part is put for the whole. To describe the inhabitants of 'these islands' as 'English' is simply a means of escaping from clumsy reiterations of the term 'British,' or from any such inelegant and cumbersome periphrasis as 'United Kingdomites.' Besides, who does not know that England would not be England at all, unless it included Scotland? The complaint, therefore, is a blunder. The indignation of the 'North Briton' is clean thrown away and we can laugh ha! ha! ha! with the *Times*.[114]

More substantially, another pamphleteer critic, while recognising the insult of Palmerston's language, felt Burns had made a faulty attack, and sought instead to resurrect debates about Scotland having been 'bought and sold for English gold': 'If our fiery Bannockburn patriots, and valorous "North Britons," would confine themselves to rational and palpable grievances, Scotland would get up a tolerably strong demonstration, in the language of pounds, shillings, and pence.'[115]

The core issue for the NAVSR and Scottish nationalists of this period had been the familiar question of how the stateless nation of Scotland might be accommodated within the supposed nation-state of Great Britain. This was an institutional argument as much as a dispute about identity, as recognised in one Association pamphlet in 1854.[116] Colin Kidd has demonstrated how British constitutional history since 1707 had been plagued by the failure at the inception of the Union to create a shared British political culture, a discrepancy in the relations between the two countries felt more acutely in Scotland than in England.[117] It is worth noting, however, that the NAVSR was not anti-Union: self-government and self-administration, argued the Association, were 'not incompatible with the Union', while it was argued that it was precisely because Scotland had benefited (economically) from the Union that redress of the perceived slights to Scotland's position were all the more urgent.[118] However, attacking Palmerston for his (mis)-use of the label 'English' diverted attention from the grievance of affording proper recognition to the diversity of the British state. 'England' had become synonymous with 'Britain', something not universally accepted, but acknowledged to a greater or lesser extent on both sides of the border; but this was a double-edged issue. Certainly the confused state of nomenclature spoke of the Anglicisation of British political culture, but it also pointed to an appropriation or application of certain values that transcended state boundaries and legislatures but which had nonetheless frequently attracted the appellation 'English'. Thus could a Scottish patriot demand redress of grievances occasioned by the inequalities enshrined in the Union of 1707, yet simultaneously acknowledge and adopt the values of the greater British Empire that happened to be termed 'English'. It is significant that it was in the imperial sphere, that is outwith the geographical bounds of the island of Great Britain, that many Scots profited by and welcomed the establishment of Britain, even perhaps making the project a distinctly Scottish enterprise. Thus, the 'English' Empire very quickly became, during the course of the eighteenth century, the 'British' Empire, as large numbers of Scots and Irish 'penetrated' the Empire 'by stealth' after 1707.[119] Yet if a meaningful 'British' identity was being created as part of the Empire, the absence of such an identity at home was felt all the more acutely. Within the Empire, the existence of an avowedly English institutional structure (in which legal and commercial regulations based on English models predominated) did not prevent a genuinely British imperial experience; and however much English gold might have been spent in Edinburgh in 1707, there remained in socio-economic terms a relatively united Britain by the nineteenth century evidenced by the growth in trade, capital flows and emigration across the border as Scottish innovation, labour and capital helped drive the British industrial revolution.[120] In terms of a British constitution, however, not only did it famously not exist on paper, but it did not exist in practice: analyses of British government in the Victorian period adopted an unequivocally 'south British' focus, most notably, though not exclusively, in Walter Bagehot's *English Constitution* published in 1867.[121]

Burns's attempt to remedy the imbalance through linguistic adaptation did not strike a chord with all Scots. 'A Scotchman', in a letter to *The Times* of 25 October 1853, replying to Burns' letter to Palmerston published in the paper under the nom de plume 'A North Briton', observed that he was 'really very heartily ashamed that so many of my countrymen should write such nonsense with reference to Scotland's (supposed) grievances'. While admitting that there was 'some ground for the complaint that not sufficient is done by the general Government in favour of northern public institutions', nonetheless the 'puerilities and exaggerations as are contained in the letter of the "North Briton" which appeared in *The Times* . . . only serve to throw ridicule on the whole matter'. This writer heartily approved of the *Times'* 'badinage' in response to Burns's letter. After all, he argued, 'Who does not feel that the words "England" and "Englishmen" may frequently be most properly applied to the United Kingdom, and to the entire body of the inhabitants, simply on the very intelligible ground of the more important part standing for the whole?' Burns, the correspondent assured the paper, was widely ridiculed and the claims for the vindication of Scottish rights was 'the cry . . . of a very few'.[122] Burns's attack on Palmerston's Englishness when published in *The Times* provoked a brief though illuminating series of letters to the editor. Albeit an imperfect guide to the state of national feeling at the time, the points raised are worthy of notice. Echoing the 'Scotchman's' riposte, 'A Glasgow Merchant' sought to underline the marginality of the NAVSR: 'as far as this locality is concerned', he wrote, 'the "Association for the Vindication of Scottish Rights" is simply laughed to scorn. Most mercantile men here regard it as a ridiculous parody upon our Irish neighbours – the best proof of which is a reference to the committee-list published by the association, which hardly contains the name of one merchant of any mark or likelihood in this city'. Carefully drawing a line between the Edinburgh lawyers whom he suspected of wanting 'a repeal of the Union' and 'more salaried Government appointments', this west-coast merchant was hopeful 'that people of sense throughout the three kingdoms will not suppose that the class to which I belong is in any way taking a part in this hungry howl'.[123] Even an apologist for Burns, in a letter to *The Times*, confessed that he was unable to 'arrive at an exact understanding of the writer's [i.e. Burns's] object', though he trusted to the sagacity of the Scottish people, 'an eminently metaphysical people, and that, like Smith's *Wealth of Nations*, much golden ore may be contained in the letter, visible only to the initiated, and to be duly worked out when "Scotland's opportunity comes"'.[124] Elsewhere, a London-based Scot, John Cumming, preferred to talk of 'Scottish duties': he foresaw, he said, 'the beginning of a great battle for Scottish rights and nationality. It may, or may not be, well founded; but as one brick laid on this ground is a better prophecy of success than 20 castles built in the air, will you allow me to suggest to your eloquent correspondents, "North Briton," "Scotchman, &c.," the precedence of Scottish duties to Scottish rights?' This was mere opportunism: Cumming was himself involved in the London-based Caledonian Asylum ('for the education, primarily, of the children of orphans of soldiers and sailors, natives of Scotland, who have fought in our country's defence') and the Scottish Hospital ('for the relief of the indigent Scotch poor') and was hoping to turn outraged patriotism into subscriptions of two guineas a year for the benefit of Scots in London.[125] Others rebuked Burns simply for his lack of empathy with the mood in Scotland: 'his lucubrations', wrote one, 'have been read by his countrymen generally with scorn and contempt'.[126] A Welsh nationalist pointed out the apparent poverty of Burns's case:

> . . . in spite of all this hectoring and blustering, we benighted individuals in this part of the world cannot help thinking that Scotchmen monopolize far more than their legitimate proportion of the good things which the Imperial Parliament has to bestow.
>
> With a Scotchman for Prime Minister, a Scotchman for the Lord Privy Seal, a more than half Scotchman for Chancellor of the Exchequer, a Scotchman for Governor-General of India, and with a Scotchman swarming in every department of State, to say nothing of every other portion of Her Majesty's wide-spread dominions, it does certainly argue the possession of no small degree of modest assurance – I suppose I must not call it impudence – in any one of the race to talk of disregard, insult, and neglect.
>
> If they, of all people, have any grounds for their charge, then what might *we* not say – the descendants of the aborigines of the island, the patient, much enduring vilified Welch – our country traduced, our language stigmatised, and our very name a byword and a laughing stock among these proud, self-sufficient, English?[127]

Whether or not an Anglo-centric bias in nineteenth-century public life marginalised Scotland within the British state and British political culture, there is no doubt that Palmerston was an English patriot before he was a British one and brought to politics a certain Anglo-centrism founded on prejudice as well as laziness or ignorance. He resisted, for example, any suggestion in the 1850s that Scotland should have a Secretary of State, arguing that Scottish affairs were simply 'a part of the business of the British Home-Secretary'.[128] And in 1853–54, as Russell brought forward his plans for franchise reform, Palmerston was at pains to point out, revealingly, that 'England will not be satisfied, if it is to the advantage of Ireland and Scotland'.[129]

Whereas Queen Victoria was able to project and reflect back 'a wide range of identities and traditions' to appear simultaneously British, imperial and Scottish without prejudicing or privileging one over any other,[130] Palmerston was not so adept. Yet certainly he was neither the first nor the last politician to be guilty of a sloppy use of language. Salisbury was warned in the later nineteenth century about his use of 'England' when he meant 'Britain' and in 1890 it was still necessary for a Scottish Home Rule Association pamphlet to offer *A Protest against the mis-use of the terms 'England' and 'English' for 'Britain' and 'British', its empire, its people and institutions*.[131]

But arguably the point at issue is a subtler but more important one. Burns worried about the problem of accommodating Scottishness and Englishness within Britishness, yet these were themselves not necessarily singular, constant identities. As Kidd points out, in eighteenth-century Scottish political culture 'a defensiveness about the rights of Scots as equal partners within the Union, which manifested itself, for instance, in agitations for a Scottish militia, coexisted with the desires of historically minded politicians, jurists and literati who saw the opportunities presented by incorporation to remedy some of the defects in Scottish institutions, to "complete the Union". Thus despite a recognition of their distinct North British personality, Scotland's modern Whig historians adopted an Anglo-British institutional identity'.[132] And as Kidd has further observed, while nineteenth-century Scotland's inheritance of this 'assimilationist Anglo-British identity' might have been increasingly challenged by moves to reassert Scottish distinctiveness – of which the NAVSR is an obvious example – politically the assimilation appeared to continue in the 'age of reform': 'Furthermore,' he argues, 'British absorption in the nascent science of race gave rise to an overarching Teutonist identity highlighting the shared ethnic characteristics of the Saxon English and their Lowland cousins.'[133]

Yet looking beyond a shared 'institutional' identity, there are problems on the English side as well. There was, it might be said, no meaningful sense of Englishness at this time either and regional identities were stronger than any identification with the whole of England by those living south of the border.[134] Rather than something bound by geographical boundaries and adopting language about the subjugation of certain interests to the political will of another, therefore, the sort of 'Englishness' with which Palmerston identified and was associated in this period might be seen as a value system. As Paul

Langford has observed, implicitly recognising that 'identifying' Englishness meant something more than locating a physical position:

> The English themselves had some difficulty with Britishness. . . . But accepting that being British might involve some lessening of what it was to be English, was far more controversial. In periods when the expansion of the English state stimulated a commitment to a wider British identity, including the eighteenth and early nineteenth centuries, it did little to erode a deeper stratum of commitment to the language of Englishness. Indeed Britishness as an expression had to wait until the late nineteenth century, if the dictionaries are to be believed. And to be un-British was unexpressed until later still. But un-English was a term in use from at least the late seventeenth century. Nor was it arcane or arch usage. When Fenimore Cooper visited Britain in the 1830s he noted 'They have a custom here of saying that such and such an act is *un-English*.'[135]

This Englishness might even have a diverse and accommodating identity, a character that could be absorbed over time. Englishness in this view embodied the virtues of liberty and democracy, of hard work and material accumulation. The English had a developing 'consciousness of their own modernity'.[136] All of which might not be unhelpful in understanding Palmerston's position in the 1850s and 1860s. As Jonathan Parry has convincingly argued, English constitutionalism was central to notions of that Englishness and furthermore, when 'patriotism, in all its manifestations, was the major bond between Liberals, Palmerston, "the English mastiff", was without doubt the best representative of that patriotism'.[137] 'Englishness' to Palmerston meant the possession of certain values, applicable to the whole of Britain and not England exclusively. In place of a rigid anti-Catholic prejudice,[138] though without its complete eradication, a national consciousness could now be forged more simply by representing Britain as more liberal, tolerant and wealthy than continental rivals. It was, arguably, the values of liberal, constitutional, even providentially favoured government that Palmerston's audiences in Scotland applauded. These values might have been described as 'English', but that did not necessarily alienate all non-English parts of Great Britain.

This English 'inclusiveness' – what Palmerston perceived to be a valuable yet vicarious participation (that transcended distinctions of social class) in the advance of the liberal and progressive principles that Britain embodied – was regarded as a meaningful compensation for the lack of direct political representation at home. The two positions were not, for Palmerston, incompatible. However much Palmerston argued for, and even legislated for, an inclusive and coherent, ordered society, that society was as yet, he maintained, not one adequately prepared for political equality across classes. Palmerston remained profoundly wary of any scheme to extend political rights to the masses and despite his supposedly more socially inclusive aspirations, he was a consistent opponent of Russell's plans for franchise extension throughout his political career. So far as he ever accepted the need for change, it was more on the grounds, as the *Daily News* had put it in December 1851, of 'yielding to the inevitable necessity of parliamentary reform than zealously supporting it'.[139] Tories, such as Palmerston's son-in-law Shaftesbury, feared that any reduction in the franchise qualification would 'cause the greatest alarm' by binding employers 'hand and foot to the mercy of their operatives'. A substantial property qualification was, therefore, the only safeguard of the system: 'The franchise would be based altogether on possession & enjoyment of property; the parties, by their conduct & thrift, have given proofs of an orderly, decent, steady, & judicious, character; they are, in some measure, above bribery; & all would feel that a high & just tribute was paid both to the value & dignity of *honest labour*.' Palmerston was of much the same opinion and though some have taken this as evidence of his conservative (and Tory) sympathies, in fact it represents a fairly mainstream (aristocratic) view, as acknowledged by Shaftesbury.[140]

Palmerston therefore resisted strenuously Lord John Russell's plans, put forward in the winter of 1853–54, for a reduction in the borough franchise qualification to £6. Although the existence of a larger number of electors might in itself pose little or no risk to the security of the constitution, what Palmerston did 'think objectionable is the admission of a great number of electors of a lower class in regard to intelligence, property and independence'. He feared intimidation, manipulation and corruption would increase with the creation of a larger, and necessarily financially poorer and politically illiterate, electorate; but, more seriously, he worried that the stability of the existing system of representation, in which power was delegated to responsible ministers (what Dugald Stewart would have referred to as 'select councils'), would be jeopardised by the proposed reforms. He warned Russell that his proposals would 'establish in England a struggle similar to that which prevails in Ireland between the priests and the landlord', drawing a parallel, respectively, with radical agitators and industrial employers in England who would, he argued, exercise considerable sway over poorer voters. 'A low class of electors may naturally be expected to chuse a low class of representatives,' he warned Russell, 'but even where men of a superior kind are chosen, these men insensibly and unavoidably adapt their language, their tone, and their votes, to the lowest class of electors, if that class is numerous; just as actors are led to neglect the boxes and the pit, and to play for the shilling gallery.'[141] With an eye to the militant elements stirring up workers' passions in the north, Palmerston feared that Russell's plans for a more broadly based franchise risked bringing into the Commons men 'who would be following impulses not congenial to our institutions' and 'incapable of taking large views', for the sake of some little 'fleeting popularity among the lower classes' and in defiance of 'the intelligent & respectable classes whose good opinion is most to be valued'. This was, he added, no time, amid industrial unrest at home and looming war in the East, to destabilise the government.[142] To introduce reform measures at that moment, said Palmerston, was 'at variance with the plainest principles of parliamentary tactics' since there was no necessity for 'great & sweeping changes in the constitutional organization of . . . [the] country'. 'These six pound voters will be coerced on the one hand by their leaders to vote for Chartist or ultra Radical candidates, and on the other hand will be urged by their employers to vote for some other person; they will be between the hammer & anvil like the Irish peasant, & will cry loudly for ballot as their only protection, or where this struggle may arise they will sell themselves to the highest bidder,' Palmerston wrote in a vigorously argued letter to the Prime Minister, echoing his previously expressed doubts about the working man's independence and reliability. 'Can it be expected that men who murder their children to get nine pounds to be spent in drink will not sell their vote for whatever they can get for it?' he asked.[143] Aberdeen claimed Palmerston's objections placed him in 'a most embarrassing position' since the bill had already been sanctioned by the Cabinet,[144] but there was sufficient unease within the government to warrant a postponement of the measure. Palmerston protested that Russell and Graham subsequently used the delay to whip up 'an artificial excitement in the country' for the measure and, though Aberdeen denied the claim, any suggestion of Cabinet disunity was serious for a government on the verge of declaring war on Russia.[145]

Far from making Palmerston a Regency throwback, however, this tends only to strengthen his claims to stand as symbol of the age. His Whiggish reserve reassured many traditionalists, and while he did not share Russell's mature tastes for electoral reform, and certainly occupied a position that fell short of Radical demands for a more representative system of government, he was able to buy off such critics with a vicarious role in his popular (though not necessarily populist) foreign policy and showy demonstrations and assertions of patriotism. It was this peculiar combination of populism, constitutional conservatism and bombastic nationalism that made his temporary resignation from the government in December 1853 so significant.

Ostensibly Palmerston quit the Cabinet over Russell's plans for parliamentary reform. In December 1853 Russell's Reform plans were still under serious consideration and it is evident that Palmerston was growing increasingly frustrated that ministers were presenting the Cabinet as united on the issue. Palmerston stressed to Charles Wood that he was 'not one of the agreers' and that he had protested regularly against the proposals.[146] By this time Palmerston appears to have decided to leave the government, even though he had 'matters in hand which I should much wish to bring to a conclusion' at the Home Office.[147] He 'could not be *dragged* through *the dirt* by Lord *John*', he said. Aberdeen, Russell and Graham agreed that Palmerston's specific objections to the terms of the Reform Bill were 'fatal to the principles of the proposed measure' and on this point Palmerston resigned. There was much ill feeling on both sides: Palmerston felt somewhat betrayed that a private letter to his friend Lansdowne had been communicated to Aberdeen, Russell and Graham and that this letter had, in turn, been taken by them as an official (and insulting) commentary on their measure and conduct. Yet, as Charles Wood noted at the time, matters had reached an impasse and it was unlikely any compromise could have been reached between the factions. However, as Wood also appreciated, this was not simply a political disagreement: 'It is quite clear,' he wrote in his journal, 'that a good deal of personal feeling has been mixed up in the business. Palmerston for different reasons has had on former occasions in former years differences of opinion with all the other 3 actors in this trans-action, and I think no conciliatory spirit was shown by anybody.'[148] It was the differences with Russell that were especially important.

Palmerston's objections to Russellite reforms were sincere enough, yet ministerial colleagues realised that though this was the stated ground of disagreement, it would be widely apprehended instead as marking a diver-gence over foreign policy. Shaftesbury noted that the 'indifference in many cases, & the antipathy in others, to Reform is singular; not a meeting, not a letter, not a speech, scarcely an article in behalf of it!'[149] It seemed peculiar, therefore, that the Cabinet should have split over this issue. Yet, as Earl Grey observed, though Reform was put forward to explain the resignation, 'the world will believe (as I confess I shall too) that it has some connect[io]n at least with foreign politics.'[150] Other ministers thought the same. Clarendon explained to Lord Cowley that while they might insist that Palmerston's depar-ture had everything to do with parliamentary reform and nothing to do with foreign policy, 'we may swear that till we are black in the face and nobody will believe it either at home or abroad'.[151] In the press it was widely asserted that talk of disagreements over Reform were indeed disingenuous.[152]

While Prince Albert worried that Palmerston was manoeuvring himself into a position to assume the leadership of the opposition and force himself on the Queen as premier, he had misinterpreted Palmerston's underlying aims.[153] Two factors are important to an understanding of Palmerston's position in December 1853. Firstly Palmerston knew that his persistent opposition to the government's foreign policy had rendered – or would soon render – his posi-tion untenable. Yet there was also an opportunity to be seized given that his declarations in favour of a more assertive foreign policy (towards Russia) were increasingly seen as articulations of a line of policy that would have been more 'successful' than that urged by Aberdeen; that is to say, it would have checked Russian expansion into the Ottoman Empire and underlined Britain's contin-uing relevance in the region. However, and this was Palmerston's second consideration, Russell had, for much of 1853, shared Palmerston's views and been almost as much an advocate of a more hawkish policy as Palmerston himself. If Palmerston was to supplant Russell unequivocally as leader of the Whigs and Liberals then he needed to force a breach with Lord John. A confrontation over Reform, therefore, had the added benefit for Palmerston that it placed him and Russell in opposite camps. As Prince Albert commented a few weeks later, Palmerston had 'been playing a deep game all along'.[154]

Looking back a decade and a half later, Walter Bagehot described Aberdeen's 1852 government as 'the ablest we have had, perhaps, since the Reform Act', but it was also, he noted, 'a cabinet not only adapted, but eminently adapted, for every sort of difficulty save the one that it had to meet'.[155] A renewed crisis in the Ottoman Empire revealed the underlying tensions within the Cabinet and, in particular, brought Palmerston back to debates on foreign policy. In fact, he had never really forsaken his interest in external policy and was, from a very early point in the life of this government, a member of the de facto inner Cabinet on foreign policy, comprising, in addition to Palmerston himself, Aberdeen, Russell, Clarendon and Graham.[156] Nor, indeed, had the public ceased to regard him as a Foreign Minister. *The Times*, from correspondence between Clarendon, the Foreign Secretary, and Henry Reeve of that paper, was well aware that Palmerston continued to be outspoken in the Cabinet on matters of foreign policy.[157] The *Economist*, meanwhile, suggested in October 1853 that the government's foreign policy was necessarily validated by Palmerston's endorsement of it, and if the *Standard* had earlier in the year suggested something different in arguing that Palmerston should have been more active in foreign policy formulation, both papers essentially agreed that Palmerston's judgement in foreign affairs was important, if not, indeed, being the thing that demonstrated his continued political relevance.[158] As Palmerston apparently occupied himself mainly with domestic reforms, therefore, one anonymous correspondent complained that by his inaction on the international stage he seemed tamely to be selling out European liberties to Russian absolutism and appealed for him 'to flash out as of yore'. Palmerston's friends, his correspondent said, 'did ever hope better things of you' and they looked forward to Palmerston's emancipation from 'the tame elephants' in the Cabinet.[159]

Palmerston was not, however, a passive member of the government. He told Clarendon that he thought him a capable Foreign Secretary,[160] but at the same time Palmerston still felt it necessary to do something given that Clarendon had been 'put into the position of a general who, having taken the command of an army one day, should be called upon to go into action the next, before he had made himself acquainted with the qualities, habits and dispositions of his officers, and before he had had time to sound the tactics of his opponents; and who, moreover, should find himself fettered by a council of war some of whose members were of the slow-march school'.[161] Aberdeen, who never quite shook off the idea that Palmerston was always looking for an opportunity to undermine him as Prime Minister, would become irritated by Palmerston's influence over the Foreign Secretary,[162] while by the summer Clarendon was said to be constantly 'mediating between Aberdeen and Palmerston, whose ancient and habitual ideas of foreign policy are brought by this business into antagonism'.[163]

The growing concern over foreign policy was motivated by renewed crisis in the East. Since the high point of tensions in 1839–41, there had been an uneasy peace in the region. While no one great power regarded the Ottoman Empire as robust, what had been demonstrated during the 1830s was that none of them could manage its decline single-handedly. Equally, Russia, as the most dynamic of the powers in its schemes to usurp Turkish rule, was unable to reach an agreement with either France or Austria, its most obvious partners (against Britain) in any carve-up of the Ottoman Empire. Yet while Britain could not be diplomatically encircled, Peel and Aberdeen had proven themselves receptive to Russian overtures and in 1844 had reached some sort of understanding with the Tsar that provided for cooperation in the event of an attack on, and/or collapse of, Ottoman rule. The terms of this agreement remained vague, even when Count Nesselrode produced a memorandum of understanding at the end of that summer's discussions. Although the note asserted, repeatedly, common Russo-British interest in the future of the Ottoman Empire and made general observations on maintaining its integrity so far as that remained possible, it offered no specification of what constituted a threat to Ottoman rule, or how the understanding between Britain and Russia would translate into division of the territory in the event of the Empire's collapse.[164] Both sides, however, took the agreement to represent a genuine settlement, even, perhaps, in the Tsar's case, a formal alliance. Yet it was, in fact, nothing more than an informal understanding; in Britain at least whatever validity it had did not extend beyond the life of the Peel government when it fell in 1846. There was evidence enough in Franco-British opposition to Russian demands that Polish revolutionaries be extradited from Turkey in the later 1840s, when Palmerston was at the Foreign Office, to give the lie to the notion that any agreement made in 1844 between Russia and Britain signalled a genuine or lasting union.[165] However, as disputed claims to the Holy Places in Palestine again drew the powers into confrontation in the East, Russia continued to look to Britain for support, particularly once Aberdeen had returned to office at the end of 1852. In Britain the developing crisis did not initially provoke particular concern. Palmerston, in taking the Home Office, had already implicitly dismissed this dispute over the Holy Places, which had begun under his watch, as no real crisis and once Aberdeen's Cabinet assembled, its members apparently did not regard the Eastern question as urgent or especially serious. The Duke of Argyll thought that the government's Eastern policy would not be a source of internal controversy since 'the basis of our policy in any revival of the Eastern Question rested on maxims of policy on which all the members of that Cabinet had long been thoroughly agreed', referring back to concurrence in Palmerstonian policy of 1839–41.[166] Although the Nesselrode Memorandum was a dubious foundation for agreement, the Tsar's apparent desire to continue to work on the basis that the agreement held good gave ministers in Britain 'no reason to believe that . . . [the Tsar] contemplated a different course of policy', and, Argyll claimed later, 'we had every right to entertain that unsuspecting confidence in European peace which was undoubtedly the attitude of all our minds during the earlier months of 1853'.[167] While the new government privileged discussion of budget arrangements over foreign affairs, only Palmerston, according to Argyll, entertained any concerns about the fate of Turkey, but these doubts were hardly raised at the time.[168] By the autumn of 1853 Palmerston was making his opposition to partition of the Ottoman Empire perfectly clear; Turkey was not an exhausted power, he said, and 'the activity, spirit & the energy, moral & physical, military & political which the Turks have displayed in dealing with their present crisis, must surely convince any impartial & unprejudiced person that Turkey is not a dead or dying body, but that on the contrary it possesses powers of life & national resources which render it worth maintaining as a useful element in the European balance'.[169] Thus, he maintained, the Ottoman Empire still had an important stabilising role to play in the balance of power:

> We maintain the integrity & independence of Turkey not for the love & affection for the Turks, but because we prefer the existing state of things there, to any other state of things which at present wd be humanly possible, and because the interest political and commercial of England & of Europe would be dangerously injured by the destruction of that integrity and independence. For these reasons we have undertaken to defend Turkey against Russia, and we could not sacrifice those great interests by abandoning Turkey to her fate merely because the Turkish govt might not take our advice. . . . Things have in truth come to such a pass that the real conflict is between Russia on the one hand & England & France on the other, much more than between Russia & Turkey, & unless England & France are prepared to sink down into the condition of second rate powers they *must* prevail, by negotiation if possible, but by force of arms if necessary.[170]

Yet these statements were made in private letters to the Foreign Secretary, Clarendon, in September and October. Up to this point, though Palmerston criticised government policy, he had preferred to acquiesce in it rather than undermine the ministry.[171] He could seek some reassurance in the presence at Constantinople of Stratford Canning, a diplomat with strong Palmerstonian sympathies,[172] yet by the summer it was clear that the Cabinet was becoming divided.[173]

To Palmerston the issue was centred on limiting Russian encroachments on Ottoman sovereignty. In May Russia had claimed the right to protect the Orthodox Christians within the Ottoman Empire, a demand which had been rejected by the Porte at Constantinople. Sensing an impending clash between Russia and Turkey, the British and French dispatched warships to Besika Bay, just outside the Dardanelles, in June, effectively offering Franco-British support to Turkey in a clash with Russia. The Porte officially rejected the Russian claims on 16 June, and on 3 July Russian forces entered the Ottoman Empire. This effectively escalated the question into a direct contest between the great powers.[174] Palmerston, claiming to represent British interests, both strategic and popular, urged that the British navy should be sent immediately to obstruct Russian forces.[175] Aberdeen, who told Palmerston that in 'a case of this kind I dread popular support', disagreed. As the Cabinet debated the merits of naval intervention, Aberdeen's insistence on a negotiated settlement gradually won ground. Palmerston conceded in July 'that it is better even to submit to insult than to endanger the pending negotiation by throwing into it any fresh element of difficulty which could afford the pettifogging & quibbling govt with which we have to deal any pretence for rejecting proposals in themselves unobjectionable and I am willing to share the responsibility of such a course though contrary to my first opinions'.[176] Yet though the Cabinet was agreed, it was obviously not united. Palmerston continued to grumble about the timidity of British policy and Aberdeen's willingness to be dictated to by Russia. The British and French, he maintained, had a perfect right to enter the Bosphorus, especially since that was at Turkey's invitation, while Russia, in protesting, he said acted the part of 'the robber who declares that he will not leave the house until the policeman shall have first retired from the courtyard'.[177] For Aberdeen and the Peelites in the government it was perhaps fortunate that the parliamentary session was drawing to a close; Palmerston, 'the sworn ally of Turkey and Mahometanism', as Graham put it, was gaining considerable support from the opposition benches, although his speeches on the subject risked alienating France, which, while united with Britain in its opposition to Russian influence in Constantinople, was at the same time keen to establish its own authority there.[178]

The roots of the coalition were exposed as Peelites and Whigs split, broadly, though not completely, into doves and hawks over the question of how vigorously to resist Russian incursions into Ottoman territory. For the most part prime ministerial authority and Peelite numerical superiority gave an ascendancy to Aberdeen's wait-and-see, pacific, policy and dissent around the Cabinet table was largely suppressed in the interests of preserving a government that had, as Aberdeen himself argued in September, 'carried many useful and important measures; . . . and although a coalition of very different materials, we have adhered well together'.[179] By this stage, however, the Prime Minister was evidently becoming weary of the incessant labour of office and the quarrelling among his colleagues. He complained in a letter to Princess Lieven of being 'chained to the oar',[180] while to Guizot he spoke of his growing sense of fatigue: 'For myself I believe I may say, according to your French phrase, that I have accomplished my mission. I have brought persons to act cordially together who were formerly hostile, or estranged; and publick success has created personal union. I hope the principle of cohesion is now established; and that it is not forbidden to think of retirement.'[181] On 4 September Aberdeen noted that during a Cabinet meeting to discuss the crisis in the East, Palmerston and Russell, the acknowledged leaders of Whig opinion on the matter, had not been 'unreasonably pugnacious' and indeed had been 'rather constrained'.[182] Though they disagreed, it was still, arguably, important for all concerned to preserve the government. For Palmerston, though this was in part about avoiding a rift at a critical juncture in the crisis in which war seemed imminent, it was also about an ongoing rivalry with Russell. Palmerston and Russell might have been agreed that Aberdeen's policy made too many concessions to Russia and that Britain should offer a more robust challenge to Russian expansionism; they were not, however, agreed about much else. Argyll described them as 'very far from being close allies. Sometimes their views coincided, but as often they disagreed, and it was evident from Palmerston's manner that old scores had been by no means forgotten.'[183] The Disraelian newspaper, the *Press*, meanwhile, published a shrewd piece of satirical drama entitled 'A card party at the Foreign Office', that nicely captured the ministerial discordance:

ABERDEEN: Shuffle, Clarendon.
CLARENDON: You are always making me shuffle. It's Palmerston's lead.
PALMERSTON: I wish it was.
LORD JOHN RUSSELL: I've followed your lead, Palmerston.
PALMERSTON: And won the trick. It's a way people have who do as I bid them. If somebody I know had trumped Menshikoff's ultimatum with Dundas's Broadside, as I advised, we four should not be sitting in a back office in the first week of September instead of shooting partridges. However, we won't talk of that, or the Premier will go revoking to the damage of Clarendon's peace of mind.
ABERDEEN: I wish ye'd just play. Dinna talk so much.
PALMERSTON: You never see me put out.
ABERDEEN (spitefully): Not since Christmas twelvemonth.
PALMERSTON (laughing): Very good, very good indeed. Who says the old gentleman's memory is failing? Christmas had a February after it, hadn't it, Russell?
RUSSELL: Never mind. You play the deuce?
PALMERSTON: I did, though I ought not to say so.[184]

Clarendon admitted that in attempting 'to reconcile the discordant views' of Aberdeen, Russell and Palmerston he was framing a policy that was never what he himself approved.[185] It was misleading, therefore, for Aberdeen to claim in his letters to the Queen that though debates in Cabinet were lively, there was, in the end, 'a degree of unanimity'.[186] The disagreements might have been expressed politely, but Aberdeen's own account to Graham betrayed the fragmentation of his administration: 'Gladstone, active and energetic for peace; Argyll, Herbert, C. Wood, and Granville, all in the same sense. Newcastle, not quite so much so, but good; Lansdowne, not so warlike as formerly; Lord John warlike enough, but subdued in tone; Palmerston urged his views persever-ingly, but not disagreeably. The Chancellor said little, but was cordially peaceful.'[187] When Turkey declared war on Russia on 4 October the absence of a clear line of policy from London led Lord Minto, who was at the time in Turin, to observe that the prevailing view outside Britain was that 'our aid is no longer to be counted on in the cause of freedom or independence'.[188]

The outbreak of war in the East seemed to validate Palmerston's long-standing insistence on the need for a clear brake on Russia. As opinion in the Cabinet swung to Palmerston, even Aberdeen conceded that British military action was likely. For Palmerston, however, while the vindication of his position was gratifying, it was also a vindication of those other ministers who had shared his reservations about the Peelite policy. There was domestic political capital to be had from this turn of events and it seemed that Russell might just as easily reap a political reward if he could dissociate himself from the government and establish himself as the one whose interpretation had finally been borne out by events. On 3 October Aberdeen thought Russell was looking for a ground on which to leave the government (indeed, that he had been for some weeks)[189] and that now 'this will not be difficult to find'. Russell, he said, was 'more warlike than ever', and the Prime Minister did not doubt 'that Lord John will seek, and of course will find, an opportunity of breaking off on a popular ground, instead of one ridiculously untenable'. Aberdeen's view that Palmerston would 'undoubtedly ... do the same' failed to acknowledge that Palmerston and Russell were not looking to act in concert, but Aberdeen was right to see that the government's two leading Whigs would now want to uncouple them-selves from it.[190] It was 'pour les beaux yeux de Master Johnny', as Prince Albert put it, therefore, and to forestall Russell's resignation, that Aberdeen was keen to bring forward a measure for franchise reform in late 1853.[191]

With Russell effectively tied to the government again, the way was clear for Palmerston to seize the initiative. By resigning over Reform he broke the connection with Russell; by allowing the country at large to believe that it was based on his objections to the government's foreign policy he played up to Protectionist demands in Parliament for a more aggressive policy (thus lending credence to suspicions that he planned to form his own government) and to popular calls in the country at large for a more steadfast and patriotic defence of national interests.

In the event, Palmerston's separation from the government was temporary. Only a couple of days after quitting, Palmerston admitted, in private, that he 'rather repented of the step he had taken' and had not intended his threatened resignation to be treated as a final decision; he was 'in short not averse to a "transaction" if possible'. This had been reported, third-hand, to Charles Wood who lost no time in passing the intelligence on to Aberdeen. Yet, as Wood noted, Palmerston himself thought a reconciliation 'next to impossible' given the strength of ministerial feeling against him (not least, and significantly, Russell's intransigent insistence that Palmerston's conduct had been 'treacherous'), and Wood agreed, commenting that he was 'not sanguine' about the matter. On 20 December Wood and Lady Palmerston discussed the affair; Palmerston, she reported, felt he was being forced out but they both agreed that Palmerston had done much to bring this situation on himself; they also agreed on the need to heal the breach. Wood undertook to write to Lansdowne, with whom Russell was staying, to urge efforts to encourage Russell to relent; the Clarendons 'implored' Lady Palmerston to work on Palmerston in the same spirit. Meanwhile Gladstone and Aberdeen both wrote to Russell setting out the case for reconciliation.[192]

The significance of Palmerston's departure was measured largely in diplomatic terms. The *Standard* had reported almost immediately how, in Paris, Palmerston's resignation was read as ominous for the continuation of Franco-British combined action against Russia.[193] As letters flew between ministers discussing whether and how to bring Palmerston back in, Wood noted that Walewski, the French ambassador, was said to be 'furious' over the government's apparent paralysis while Louis Napoleon, who considered Palmerston 'his only real friend' in Britain, was increasingly disposed to listen to Austrian suggestions that a pro-Orléanist Aberdeen was playing France for a fool in the East.[194] Clarendon, meanwhile, worried that the Tsar would interpret these events as a 'licence' simply to disregard Britain.[195] Graham complained that yielding to Palmerston would weaken the government's credibility, and Grey afterwards complained that there could 'never be a good understanding again between Palmerston & some of his colleagues', but the majority of the Cabinet was united in the view that Palmerston had to be reincorporated into their ranks, if only because, as Aberdeen argued when they debated this, that was less potentially damaging than leaving him, and the government's disagreements, outside the Cabinet. Whether the Queen's objections to Palmerston's return would have materially swayed the Cabinet is doubtful; in the event the messenger who was charged with conveying 'a long letter' detailing Victoria's concerns to the Cabinet got drunk and did not deliver it in time for ministers to consider it.[196] Thus Palmerston was invited to return. His erstwhile colleagues thought it could be done on the grounds of Reform only by allowing Palmerston to retract his resignation on the basis that he had erroneously thought a definite decision had been taken on the measure. But though Aberdeen tried to negotiate Palmerston's return on these terms, Palmerston made it clear that he re-entered the Cabinet only because they had agreed, in his absence, to send a fleet, along with the French navy, into the Black Sea, something he had taken the trouble to have confirmed by the French ambassador before agreeing to return to the government.[197] Russell, predictably, was unhappy. On 24 December, as Palmerston was brought back, Lady John summoned Charles Wood to hear how,

> Lord John was very much annoyed at my having seen Lady Palmerston, that we were truckling to him, and that a great deal too much had been said in public imputing blame of haste. I said that nothing had been [done] to entreat Palmerston to come back, for they had made the move; that I thought for Lord John's character the reconciliation was most necessary; – that many of us and the world thought he had been precipitate in turning Palmerston [out] in 1851, and that what would be considered a repetition of the same course in 1853, would injure his character much. It might not be just, but such would be the effect. She said that she thought he ought to have seen Palmerston in 1851. I replied, if he had, it probably would not have happened. She said that I was not aware of the danger we were running of forcing him out, by doing what we believed was really for the good purpose of keeping the government together.[198]

The fact was that whether by long-standing design or short-term opportunism, Palmerston had, as Aberdeen recognised early on, 'made a very dextrous move'.[199] At the time that he quit the government, Palmerston was informed by one independent MP that he could expect the support of seven-eighths of the Conservative party plus many nonpartisan members if he became Prime Minister.[200] Subsequent historical analyses have cast doubt on Palmerston's ability at this time to steal the lead of the Tory opposition and face down the Aberdeen government,[201] but, as Prince Albert observed, Palmerston had succeeded in making all sides declare their admiration for him: 'The best of the joke is,' wrote the Prince on 24 December, 'that, because he went out, the Opposition journals extolled him to the skies, in order to damage the Ministry, and now the Ministerial journals have to do so, in order to justify the reconciliation.'[202]

It had been clear to ministers that Palmerston's remaining outside the government jeopardised good relations with France and there had been particular concern to avoid making this domestic rupture into a diplomatic crisis. There was also a recognition that on these grounds careless treatment of Palmerston could undermine what credibility the government had with the public, who again interpreted Palmerston's resignation as significant largely in terms of foreign affairs. The majority of newspapers had initially followed *The Times* in presenting the resignation as wholly unconnected with foreign policy disagreements, if only because for the previous few months Palmerston had, by remaining in the government, concurred in the official line. There was, it seemed, nothing new in December to justify a breach over external policy.[203] Even papers sympathetic to Palmerston, whether those that were personally loyal to him or Protectionist journals hoping to exploit the government fracture, while insisting that foreign policy differences had long been as significant as any over Reform, implicitly acknowledged that this was not a straight argument about the Eastern question.[204] Yet while his departure might have been attributed to mixed causes, his return was widely welcomed on the narrow lines that it would lead to 'a more worthy and active' policy in the East.[205] As the *Morning Chronicle* wrote: 'To a large class of politicians, who feel rather than reason – who admire rather than understand – the name of Palmerston is a symbol of pluck and public spirit – a sort of epitome of all that is most English in the English character. It was, indeed, amusing to see the pertinacity with which, for some time after the formation of the present Government, people refused to recognise him in his new post of Home Secretary.'[206] His exclusion or inclusion, therefore, was apprehended both at home and abroad as a statement on the government's willingness to execute an 'English', that is, in this case, bellicose, (and popular) foreign policy.[207]

Such was the febrile state of public feeling over the Eastern crisis, indeed, that in late January 1854 crowds gathered outside the Tower of London in the belief that they would witness the imprisonment for treason of Aberdeen and Prince Albert. As effigies of the two were burned by the crowd it mattered little to them that Aberdeen was starting to accept the necessity of adopting a more aggressive, 'Palmerstonian', policy and that Albert, far from being the agent of continental despotism and the author of Palmerston's recent removal from office (the latter a story propagated in the *Morning Advertiser* and elsewhere), had actually started to agree with Palmerston's view of Russia.[208] It was a dramatic and extreme, but not necessarily dissonant, articulation of public opinion.

Back in office Palmerston capitalised on his apparent victory in December and the demonstrable popular demand for a firm policy abroad and assumed a prominent role in discussions of the Eastern question which increasingly looked as if it would draw Britain directly into the conflict. Aberdeen continued to speak of and hope for peace, but members of the Cabinet were all, as Clarendon said of his own feelings, 'getting *in favor of war*'.[209] Aberdeen told Clarendon that he thought war unlikely but admitted that he had no real sense of the mood in the Cabinet.[210] In these circumstances Palmerston was able to seize the initiative; even Russell was drawn to concede that 'no one sees so quickly & so clearly in these matters' as the Home Secretary.[211] On 19 March Palmerston circulated his draft of a 'beau ideal' setting out plans for a recasting of European state boundaries in the aftermath of an anticipated British military victory over Russia that would not only help readjust the balance of power, but, crucially, tip it in Britain's favour.[212] It was Palmerston's delineation of Britain's aims and interests that underpinned the government's declaration of war shortly afterwards (Britain formally went to war on 27–28 March) more than any direction from the head of the government. As Clarendon noted a little while later, Palmerston was 'perpetually making new maps of Europe'.[213] It is noticeable that in Sir John Gilbert's depiction of *The Coalition Ministry*,

1854 (1855) it is Palmerston who is holding forth in the Cabinet, lecturing them while pointing to a map of the Near East. Aberdeen looks distant and disengaged, even defeated, while Clarendon, the Foreign Secretary, hovers in the background and the Secretary for War, the Duke of Newcastle, serves simply as a page-turner of the atlas for Palmerston.[214]

Aberdeen became an increasingly ineffective leader. Russell complained in May that the government was characterised by 'indecision' and showed no willingness, having gone to war, to press hard for victory.[215] The 'great want of all is a head of the English Cabinet', he said, and by the autumn of 1854 he concluded that Aberdeen had not 'at any time adequately performed the duties of Prime Minister'.[216] In Parliament the government was assailed from all sides: Cobdenite Radicals sought to draw attention to the problems of sustaining the Ottoman Empire and also the dangers of damaging British trading interests with Russia, while Tories grew exasperated by Aberdeen's constant vacillation.[217] Outside Parliament opinion seemed to be strongly in favour of a firm prosecution of the war on the grounds of upholding British honour and prestige (having entered the war it was necessary to win it) and in furtherance of traditional British commitment to defence of popular liberties (here the notion of protecting Ottoman Christians). As press criticism of the premier mounted, especially on the Tory side,[218] ministers became increasingly uneasy. In October the Duke of Argyll wrote to Clarendon expressing the concerns of many:

> What I dread is our going on without some purpose more definitely recognised – afraid of public opinion because we do not try to lead or guide it; – shy of each other because we do not know exactly each others' views. I do not believe that there is any difference which will prevent a practical conclusion, provided we try to come to it. But there is quite enough variety of *tendency* & of *feeling*, if we do not try, to keep our language various – our course unsteady – perhaps I ought rather to say, to prevent any definite course from being shaped at all. We shall then be at the mercy of tides; and our motion becomes a mere drift.[219]

The curious aspect of all this from a Palmerstonian perspective is the absence of a visible, or at least high-profile, lead from Palmerston himself. He appears to have done little to dampen speculation in Tory circles that he might still cross the floor and join Derby and Disraeli. The *Standard* made clear that Palmerston continued to be well regarded among the Protectionists and though Disraeli had denied at the beginning of the year that he was trying to bring Palmerston on board, some of Disraeli's colleagues perceived him as enjoying Palmerston's 'secret support' in debates as the country went to war.[220] There is evidence, too, that Palmerston was in close contact with Malmesbury and fed him information with which to probe (and possibly embarrass) the government in parliamentary debate.[221] Palmerston was not quite using the

Protectionists to criticise the government but nor was he putting himself forward as a proponent of the government's policy.

In part the explanation for this is to be found in the widespread anxiety about Aberdeen's failure to lead, as expressed by Russell. In part it was also based on an assumption, on Palmerston's side, that the argument about whether to go to war had been decided, in Palmerston's favour, in March. For much of 1854, therefore, the primary issue was how to manage the war; it was an administrative question and, as the letters and reports from the front that filled the newspapers amply demonstrated, a matter in which the government, and Britain, was falling short.[222] Palmerston did lead some aspects of policy – it was his decision to attack Sebastopol early, for example – but though he argued that Britain and France would 'lose caste in the world if they concluded the war with only a small result',[223] rather than aiming to capitalise on his strong position in the first three months of 1854 and take a leading role not just in foreign policy formulation but also in its execution, Palmerston seemed to take a step back.

To judge by newspaper reports, Palmerston evinced little or no interest in foreign affairs after March. Palmerston's name continued to appear in the leading newspapers' editorial columns, but this was almost always with reference to his work at the Home Office. There was much discussion of his reform of the Board of Health, his attention to the Poor Law, smoke abatement measures, the reform of prisons, of universities and of the police and to urban improvements such as new sewage systems.[224] Yet there was hardly any link made between Palmerston and the war. By the summer the *Standard* speculated that Palmerston's 'ominous silence' in Parliament suggested he was actually intriguing to replace the Prime Minister not support or undermine him.[225] By November *The Times* could not help wondering 'What is Lord Palmerston doing?'

> What does he think of the war? Would he have averted it? Would he have brought it earlier to a crisis? Is he gathering friends and concerting measures with a view to his old post?' We cannot undertake to answer all those questions, but the world may see at once one thing that Lord Palmerston is doing. Deep in the heart of the country, somewhere between the New Forest and Salisbury Plain, he is presiding over innocent rustic celebrities, delivering prizes to bucolic excellence, and teaching labourers how to be happy, and merry and wise.[226]

Given Palmerston's well-known connections with the newspaper press, it is tempting to suggest that he may have been deliberately exploiting these links to present an impression of industry at home. Ministerial colleagues, however, were far from convinced that he was busy at the Home Office. Wood recorded in April that Palmerston was said (by Sidney Herbert) to be 'losing ground every day by his ignorance and incapacity at the Home Office' while Granville said that Shaftesbury, who took full advantage of family ties to press his reform proposals on Palmerston, complained now that 'Palmerston always agreed to all he [Shaftesbury] proposed, gave instructions for its being done, and nobody ever heard of it again'.[227] Indeed, Shaftesbury himself felt that not only did Palmerston promise everything and do nothing, but that he 'actually destroys a great deal'.[228]

There was good reason for Palmerston to want to draw attention to his domestic reform record if he was to shore up his liberal credentials at home (and if he was thinking seriously at this stage about a bid for the premiership which would quite likely have required some measure of Radical support), but it was a risk nonetheless if that record showed diminishing rather than increasing industry. Certainly Home Office papers suggest that Palmerston was doing more in 1853 than he did in 1854, which tends to lend some credibility to the complaints of Shaftesbury and others. And for a minister whose reputation was built on assertive overseas policies, focusing on sewers and pollution during wartime struck some as, at best, a waste of his talents, at worst, a dereliction of duty. As the *Morning Herald* put it in June:

> Where is he now, when the destinies of the world are trembling in the balance? Pottering over sewers and squabbling about a county police. Let the noble lord the member for Tiverton beware; the favour of a great nation is never slighted with impunity, and the vexed people of England, however unwillingly, may be compelled to adopt the explanations tendered by Mr. Urquhart, and say that the greatest man at the present day in Britain does not dare to place himself at the head of his countrymen, because he fears to face the revelations which his promotion would render inevitable.[229]

David Urquhart had recently resurrected his charges against Palmerston but whatever criticisms might have been made of Palmerston's conduct, to accuse one of the government's most hawkish ministers of pro-Russian scheming was too tortuous an argument to have any real impact.[230] However, the *Herald*'s question, reprinted even in the decidedly pro-Palmerston journal the *Globe*, underlined the fragile status of any Palmerstonian claim to speak for 'the people'. There were many factors influencing Palmerston's outlook at this time. His advocacy of a firm and aggressive policy towards Russia had already caused a breach of sorts with the Peelites but had by the same token been well received in Whig, and Tory, circles and indeed by much of the country at large. However, it was unlikely that Palmerston would defect to the Protectionists and when he tried to take a lead among the Whigs, Russell was still in his way. In a letter written to her husband in 1854 Lady Palmerston captured something of the undercurrents that dominated these months at Westminster:

> Perhaps your meeting turned out for the best. Wm wrote . . . an account of it, and much like yours – saying that those people who rejected Horsman's proposal of ejecting Aberdeen evidently did so from the

notion that the only alternative was Johnny & the Whigs – and this they
thought even worse than Aberdeen. This is their difficulty that they
cannot in any way get hold of you – when they try to get you for War
Minister they catch Newcastle and when they try to catch you for Prime
Minister they fall into Johnnys hands which they dislike more than
Aberdeen. It is altogether a provoking position!!![231]

It is not unreasonable to argue that Palmerston was still concerned with
supplanting Russell among the Whigs and this too may have been part of his
calculations in 1854. While Palmerston did not give full vent to his views on
foreign policy, Russell emerged as the leading Cabinet rival to Aberdeen in
such matters. If dissent prior to March 1854 looked like wisdom, carping
within the Cabinet amid a disastrous military campaign looked like disloyalty.
As Russell's criticisms of Aberdeen's prime ministerial inadequacies continued,
Clarendon warned him that this served no useful purpose and only added to
the government's difficulties.[232] By the early summer, far from rallying disconcerted members of the government, Russell had done much to alienate them
by making his attacks on Aberdeen so frequent and so personal. As Minto,
Russell's father-in-law, observed in June:

> He is almost without support in the Cabinet. On great questions of
> foreign policy indeed Lansdowne, Palmerston and he, and I may add
> Granville, heartily agree, and in recent questions some of the Peelite
> members of the Cabinet entirely go with them. But as regards general
> support of him individually as the head of their party he can count upon
> none I think except Granville & I believe the Chancellor, & probably now
> George Grey, but on questions of foreign affairs the latter will bring him
> weakness rather than strength, and his most wretched speech at his elec-
> tion at Morpeth, as well as his conversation since has greatly lowered the
> estimate of the value of his accession to the government.[233]

As the *Morning Chronicle* pointed out in December, Palmerston and Russell
had 'been equally guilty of the "extreme folly" which is denounced; and they
are equally responsible for the "alarm and disgust" which the Ministerial
policy may call forth'.[234] Yet it was Russell on whom the Prince compiled a
dossier, detailing his actions to break up the government,[235] and Palmerston
whom the public seemed to identify as the sage interpreter of events and
defender of popular liberties. When he toured England in the summer, Lajos
Kossuth, the Hungarian nationalist, stirred up cheering crowds with emotive
rhetoric about the war that directly echoed Palmerstonian speeches.[236]

There remains, however, the question: why did Palmerston not try to take
charge of the War Office in 1854? This would have served as a platform from
which to address the apparent weakness of government policy by supplying

strong action and had Palmerston and not Newcastle occupied that office he would probably have obviated concerns that leaving a Peelite in that station betrayed a reluctance to prosecute the war vigorously.[237] Yet Palmerston did not appear to relish returning to an old hunting ground.

Although, as Prince Albert observed, 'the Country' thought him 'the only able War Minister',[238] and though he was reported (by Malmesbury) to be 'furious' not to have been given direction of the war at the outset,[239] Palmerston's actions did not suggest that he really wanted the post. It may not actually have ever been suggested that he should have it. According to Wood, Palmerston's claim to the department was dismissed by reason of 'a general opinion of his having lost ground in public estimation and of his inability for hard work'. In fact Russell was more seriously considered for the office, but he did not want to provoke a contest with Palmerston, especially since he did not have the backing of leading Peelites such as Aberdeen and Gladstone.[240] During 1854 Palmerston did not voice criticism of Newcastle, but as evidence of the War Office's unskilled management of the war became known public calls for better direction often mentioned Palmerston. In particular *The Times*, hitherto generally a friend to Aberdeen, switched allegiance: William Howard Russell's letters from the Crimea and Delane's own first-hand observations disclosed the hardships endured by British soldiers and the paper joined the campaign behind Palmerston.[241]

Towards the end of the year the subject of replacing Newcastle was again raised. Russell actually argued for Palmerston to have the appointment since the office required someone 'who from experience of military details, from inherent vigour of mind, & from weight with the H. of Commons can be expected to guide the great operations of war with authority and success'.[242] Aberdeen said Palmerston was too old, though this was most likely a cover for deeper, party-based, antagonisms.[243] Palmerston for his own part evinced no interest in the change of office but this was as much about ongoing internecine struggles as anything else. In early December he noted that 'Clarendon said that as the matter now stands, Aberdeen declares that if Newcastle is forced out he Aberdeen will resign, while on the other hand he Clarendon fears that John Russell will say that he will leave the govt if Newcastle does not give up the conduct of the war. Clarendon seemed to think this an intrigue got up for the purpose of breaking up the govt and getting John Russell back as Prime Minister.'[244] Such an intrigue, if it existed, was ambitious; to Prince Albert, for example, it was 'certain that not one of the present Cabinet could now serve under Lord John'.[245] On the other hand, as Clarendon pointed out in a letter to his wife, Palmerston's decision to endorse or replace Newcastle could have serious ramifications, for 'if P (wch is not likely) was to condemn Newcastle then I see nothing for it but a break up & as that wd destroy the confidence of France & crush the nascent vitality of Austria & be worth a dozen victories to Russia it wd I think fulfill all the conditions of treason'.[246] Charles Wood thought that though Palmerston spoke a great deal about military and defence matters, he had very little expertise in the area, arguing that Palmerston 'only said, there must be an army, there must be so and so done, but never gave a thought to where men were to come from, or how many there were available'. Aberdeen, meanwhile, argued against moving Palmerston on the grounds that 'it would tend to indispose Austria'.[247] Palmerston only put himself forward for the War Office when Russell threatened to smash the government by resigning in January 1855.

By that time, however, Palmerston's position was an altogether stronger one and as Russell advised the Queen, 'the country wanted Lord Palmerston either as War Minister or Prime Minister'.[248] If talk of Palmerston's claims to the premiership had seemed premature in 1852, by late 1854 they were being debated much more seriously. One favourable pen portrait in September pointed out that Palmerston's 'importance is felt so much in the whole kingdom, by almost all parties, that he is looked upon as the only one to be an efficient English premier'. That his party affiliations were sometimes ambiguous was, said this journalist, a source of strength since he could, as a 'peculiarly masculine' and English minister, unite feeling across the political spectrum. 'The country expects much from him,' the article concluded: 'We believe that he is "the coming man" in the legislature. It is possible that circumstances may shortly bring about such changes as to place him where he ought to be, in the government of this great country'.[249] Hostile pamphlets were published, such as *Palmerston for Premier!* (1854), which rehearsed Urquhartite claims that Palmerston had been intriguing throughout his career for 'the union of England and Russia' and argued that placing him in Aberdeen's office would encourage Russia 'to strike her grand blow for universal empire!',[250] and *Palmerston in Three Epochs* (1854), which accused Palmerston of pursuing policies that were 'un-English', and of being the voice of 'false Liberalism' and a 'Captain of Shams',[251] but they seemed out of tune with the majority feeling in favour of war. Even in areas of the country where support for the war had generally been weakest, such as among Manchester's commercial classes who were traditionally thought to favour the pacific approaches of Cobden and Bright, opinion by the end of 1854 had swung towards bellicosity.[252]

Palmerston had spent the second half of November 1854 in France, consulting with Louis Napoleon (now Napoleon III) on the war and re-affirming his close personal relations with the French Emperor. Palmerston had arrived in Paris, observed Abraham Hayward, a journalist for the *Morning Chronicle*, in 'high spirits' and though many Parisians were said to have believed that Palmerston was on an official visit, Hayward reported he was there only 'to amuse himself'. Yet while Hayward thought 'foreign affairs never looked more gloomy', Palmerston 'was speaking very cheerily about results'.[253] Following a series of dinners, soirées and military reviews during which he held discussions with the Emperor and leading members of the French government, Palmerston had reassured himself of their 'very good opinions on the subject of the war', and of their 'acting towards us with perfect fairness, openness & good faith'.[254] Following Palmerston's return to London, the Emperor continued to correspond with him about military plans and movements in the East, and Palmerston reciprocated – significant given that formally Palmerston had no direct control over such matters.[255]

Both at home and abroad, therefore, Palmerston was increasingly associated with leadership of the government. Yet when the Radical MP John Arthur Roebuck's motion for a committee of inquiry into the war led, on 30 January 1855, to the resignation of Aberdeen's ministry, the Queen was determined 'to exhaust everything before they send for Palmerston'.[256] Derby was again commissioned to form a government and he went straight to Palmerston to solicit his participation, but after some deliberation, and having ascertained that leading former colleagues including Gladstone, Sidney Herbert, Clarendon and Lansdowne were averse to collaborating with the Protectionists, Palmerston declined the offer. It was, he said, 'a ministry of 14 days'.[257] The Queen turned next to Russell. Initially Palmerston seemed willing to support this attempt, agreeing to take the lead of the House of Commons (Russell was to take a seat in the Lords) combined with his old post at the Home Office. Yet few other heavyweight figures were willing to serve under Russell – Clarendon, Lansdowne, Graham and most Peelites refused – and even before Russell gave up the commission, the Queen had begun sounding out Palmerston himself for the premiership. 'I know this would be very objectionable in many respects, and personally not agreeable to me,' she wrote in a memorandum,

> but *I* think of *nothing* but the country, and the preservation of its institutions, and *my own* personal feelings would be sunk if only the efficiency of the government could be obtained. *If* the *Peelites* and *Whigs* would serve *under* Lord Palmerston, *I should not* apprehend the consequences – for they would restrain him from mischief, and Palmerston *himself* in *that position* would feel the weight and responsibility of *such a position* in a manner that would make him feel very differently to what he has hitherto done, as a subordinate.[258]

On 4 February, Russell having failed, Palmerston was commissioned to form a government. He wrote immediately to Lansdowne, Aberdeen, Clarendon and Gladstone for support though only Lansdowne backed him unequivocally; Clarendon thought the plan depended on Peelite support which was uncertain, as evidenced by Gladstone's request for time to think the matter over. On 5 February the Peelite faction announced their unwillingness to participate and Palmerston spent a good deal of time talking to Whig friends about 'forming a purely Whig ministry'. Such was the uncertainty of the situation, however, that by that evening, Gladstone and other leading Peelites were thought to have changed their mind and Palmerston repeated the overture to them. Matters were still not settled on the morning of 6 February and, as Palmerston recorded in his diary, only a late interjection by Aberdeen facilitated the formation of Palmerston's first government:

> Queen came to town at 11. I went to her at Palace at one, reported refusal of Peelites & left with her their letters. She appointed me to go again at 5, she returning to Windsor at ½ past 6. Aberdeen came to me at two & said his friends wd join if he would say he had confidence in the foreign policy of the govt. He said to me he could hardly declare he had confidence in himself for he had never expected to be head of a ministry carrying on war against Russia; but concluded we should continue the foreign policy on which we had been acting. I said certainly. He asked would I make destruction of Sebastopol a sine qua non condition of peace, I said I thought limitation of Russian fleet in Black Sea a more important stipulation, and that we could not make destruction of Sebastopol a sine qua non unless we had taken it & had destroyed it ourselves. He was satisfied & promised answer before 5. He went back to Graham's meeting, just before 5 I recd a note from him saying I might assure the Queen that the great object wd be accomplished, and I also received a letter from Gladstone saying he would join. I reported this to the Queen at 5, and after a conversation of an hour with her & the Prince I kissed hands as First Lord of Treasury – received back letters of Gladstone, Argyll & Herbert declining which I had left with her in morning & left with her my letter to Gladstone. From Palace to Lansdowne whom I understood to promise to be organ of govt in Hs of Lords.[259]

The Queen, who was not overly pleased with the appointment, explained to her uncle that she had 'had *no* other alternative'.[260] As Palmerston put it in a letter to his brother, in the space of ten days Aberdeen, Derby and Russell 'all gave way like straw before the winds', and only Aberdeen's discredited status as a war leader, Derby's consciousness of his party's 'unfitness to govern' and Russell's diminished credibility (he had abandoned the government in January) had pushed Palmerston forward. As he admitted, a month earlier the prospect of his being Prime Minister 'was one of the most improbable events' but now, with the backing of the country and the support (however grudging) of the court, he was, 'for the moment l'inevitable'. He promised a firm policy against Russia in the search for peace, but as he acknowledged, his position was not altogether secure. Among the 'body of the Whigs' he saw much discontent at the continuation in office of many Peelites and though Palmerston felt his government depended on them, he looked ahead to the need to dissolve the government at the end of the current session.[261] Though in private Palmerston was careful to qualify the strength of his new position, beyond Westminster his appointment was widely welcomed. As Wood observed, the 'country never would be satisfied till Palmerston had tried his hand',[262] while many newspapers heralded him as a national saviour; the *Morning Post* and the *Globe* suggested Palmerston was the only minister capable of rescuing the country from its current crisis and even the Peelite *Morning Chronicle* conceded that had he not been able to form a government, 'his failure would have been a national misfortune'.[263] From Paris, Napoleon III wrote to congratulate Palmerston and spoke not only of his personal satisfaction at seeing Palmerston at the head of the British government, but of the new premier as the only person capable, if it were possible at all, of repairing the alliance between Britain and France.[264] Expectations were high, therefore, and as *Punch* exclaimed as Palmerston took up the reigns of power: 'Now for it!'[265]

CHAPTER 11

THE MORTAL MINISTER, 1855–1859

'P'
Stands for Palmerstone,
Who will his duty do,
Kill Puseyites and Jackabites,
And all the Russian crew.

Street ballad, 'The Political Alphabet for 1855'[1]

LORD BROUGHTON (FORMERLY John Cam Hobhouse) viewed Palmerston's accession to the premiership in 1855 as the culmination of a steady progression to that station. His flattering account of Palmerston's triumph resonated with a significant body of opinion that had for some time regarded the minister, despite his advancing years, as 'the coming man'. As Broughton put it: 'Gibbon said of Charles Fox that he rose by slow degrees to be the most accomplished debater that the world ever saw. And in like manner, it may be said of Lord Palmerston that, step by step, sometimes ascending quickly, at other times, almost stationary, but never falling back, after the longest official career on record, [he] reached the highest post of honor & power to which an Englishman can aspire.' Palmerston had been a late developer. Not until 1850, said Broughton, had Palmerston 'put forth all his powers, & showed of what he was capable', and if Palmerston's political genius was to shine in difficult circumstances, then his enhanced popularity following his dismissal at the end of 1851 and his 'increased influence' that had quickly made itself felt in Parliament a few weeks later, had underlined his political pre-eminence. It was his 'wisdom' and the 'propriety of his condescension' to join Aberdeen in 1852 that had made that government possible and now, having stood by it 'manfully, to the last, with his usual courageous loyalty', Palmerston came forward to do his duty and take up the reins of government in his own name.[2] Although written only a few months after Palmerston had formed his first government Broughton's account was symptomatic of a tendency to give Palmerston's rise to the premiership a sheen of inevitability. Jasper Ridley, therefore, was quite justified in writing of 'the Palmerston myth' that developed at this time as the (middle-class) public apparently concluded, as one journalist put it, 'that Palmerston was the man to whom the business of war could be committed, and in whose hands the name of England was safe'.[3] In fact the formation of this apparently long-anticipated political configuration was a difficult process.

As Lord Stanley had observed as his father's attempts to re-create a government in January and February foundered, Palmerston's position was not an unequivocally strong one; for all his self-declared inexorability, there were many, both within and outside his own political circle, who seemed unenthusiastic about his prospects. Disraeli, for example, told Lord Stanley that he 'thought that Palmerston would be deterred by age, infirmity, and the consciousness of an overrated reputation, from undertaking the Government'; indeed, it seemed to the Protectionists, even as late as the end of January, that it was far more likely that Palmerston would simply accept the lead of the House of Commons in a reconstituted Derby government than stake a claim to the premiership himself. Stanley concurred: Palmerston, he thought, lacked the necessary experience to head a government, having 'never yet been more than a departmental minister', but more than any political objection to Palmerston was his evidently 'failing' health and overtaxed reputation, both of which, he said, would collapse within short time and no Palmerston ministry would outlast the session of 1856. In any case, said Stanley, the Whigs were 'drawing together under Russell' and would be against Palmerston, as were the Protectionists, so long as they held their nerve, while 'the Radicals under Bright hated P. if possible worse than the court did'. Palmerston's only tangible support, Stanley judged, was 'the country' but though large, that constituency was also decidedly fickle and would 'expect impossibilities'. If the newspapers were any sort of guide to the mood of the nation, then that mood was clearly divided: *The Times*, the *Morning Post* and *Morning Chronicle*, for example, seemed broadly Palmerstonian and while this support was significant and probably meant that Palmerston just about managed it in this quarter, he was up against the not insubstantial dissenting voices of the *Morning Herald* which backed Derby, the *Daily News* which tried to defend Russell's position and the Peelite *Morning Chronicle* which simply lamented Aberdeen's demise. *The Times*, said Stanley, was 'Palmerstonian only in deference to the feeling of the moment' and was thus an ally of circumstance rather than conviction. There was some politicking in this, but Stanley was right in so far as Palmerston's prospects remained uncertain.[4]

If Palmerston's attempt at a government was one apparently beset by difficulties, however, those obstacles were gradually surmounted. An attempt by Russell to rally Whig forces to his side was rumoured to have elicited only three acceptances from potential ministers and by the beginning of February 'Palmerston's name was in all mouths'.[5] Having received his commission, Palmerston began the task in earnest of recruiting a Cabinet. Despite the scepticism displayed in Stanley's account concerning parliamentary support for Palmerston he was able, essentially, to reconstruct the coalition of Whigs and

Peelites that had carried the Aberdonian banner. Only Gladstone remained a problem: his opposition to Palmerston was profound, but so too was the perceived importance of his inclusion in any non-Protectionist government. A satirical take on their relationship in Aberdeen's Cabinet published in the *Press* in January 1854 had presented Palmerston and Gladstone as uncomfortable allies: with Gladstone and Palmerston adopting the roles of Horace and Lydia in a classical pastiche, Palmerston concluded their imagined lyrical duet by rejecting the charms of a Disraelian alliance in the interest of government stability:

> Though he is versed in Tory arts,
> And thou'rt, I fear, a ratting Raddy,
> Still, *till our Coalition parts*,
> I'll live and die colleagued with GLADDY.[6]

Twelve months later, little had changed in their mutual regard. For Philip Guedalla, 'two such opposites were scarcely to be found in the whole garden of English public life' and though 'they worked on', they did so 'as strange a pair as the winds and waves of politics have ever brought together'.[7] Yet the political differences can be overstated. Palmerston and Gladstone were not so very far apart politically, at least in a parliamentary sense – in 1852 Gladstone had viewed Palmerston's membership of the Aberdeen government as an essential bulwark against the Conservative opposition just as Palmerston now viewed Gladstone as an essential member of his government[8] – but on a personal level there was no great intimacy and though they were both broadly 'liberal' they were not always in accord. So long as there was a Conservative opposition or government to face, those latter differences could be subsumed by a common interest in liberal progress; when it came to one or other of them directing that liberal progress, however, the tensions acquired a more significant aspect. As far back as 1846 Gladstone had dismissed Palmerston as 'the anti-progress minister' and though that view might have been tempered over the ensuing years, a lingering doubt remained.[9] When Russell had resigned from the Aberdeen government in January 1855, provoking the current 'crisis', Gladstone noted how Palmerston's reply to Russell's statement to the House of Commons had done nothing to rally or steel liberal forces. 'Palmerston's reply to him was wretched,' he wrote. 'It produced in the House, that is in so much of the House as would otherwise have been favourable, a flatness and deadness of spirit towards the government which was indescribable: and Charles Wood with a marked expression of face said while it was going on, "And this is to be our leader!"'[10]

Initially Gladstone had attempted to head off a Palmerston administration by appealing to Palmerston himself to take a longer view of affairs. Much as Stanley had suggested, Gladstone argued that Palmerston's position was not as

strong as it appeared, telling the would-be premier that though his government would 'certainly start amidst immense clapping of hands', this would not
offset the fact that his parliamentary position would be an unstable one. It was
no doubt Gladstone's own prejudices that encouraged him to believe
Palmerston concurred.[11] Though Gladstone feared the adverse consequences
of Palmerston's replacing Aberdeen at a critical moment in international affairs
(the very reverse expectation of much popular clamour for just such a switch,
apparently), he did not deny Palmerston's central importance to a Liberal
government but he preferred Clarendon or Lansdowne (even if in the latter
case that might signal a turn to 'a homogeneous Whig government') rather
than coalition under Palmerston.[12] Though he admitted that Palmerston and
Aberdeen differed only in the sense that they represented 'distinct forms of the
same principles connected with different habits and temperaments', Gladstone
would not go so far as to regard them as interchangeable leaders.[13] On 4
February, as the news of Russell's abortive attempt to form a government
filtered through, Gladstone maintained that the Peelite response to the
Palmerstonian overture that would certainly follow must be 'in the negative'.
Despite the initial promise of Whig–Peelite union under Aberdeen in the early
1850s, Gladstone was now increasingly pessimistic about Liberal prospects: in
a conversation with Newcastle he concluded that it was probably better for
Derby to form the next government; that might mean Palmerston taking the
lead in the Commons, but though, 'like the light cavalry at Balaklava – we saw
our doom', he thought '*that* was a risk that might be run'.[14] On the same day
that he wrote all this, however, Gladstone had received an invitation from
Palmerston to remain at the Treasury in a Palmerston government. Aberdeen,
who told Gladstone that 'his *velléités* seemed to lean rather to *our* joining',[15]
encouraged Peelites to throw their lot in with Palmerston, but for his own
part Aberdeen made clear that he would himself stand outside the ministry.
In the space of forty-eight politically intense hours, the matter was kicked
back and forth by the Peelites and though Gladstone placed great emphasis
on Aberdeen's counsel, he could not shake completely his anxieties about
Palmerston: 'The truth is the world is drunk about a Palmerston government:'
he wrote on 5 February, 'and if we humour it in its drunkenness it will rightly
refuse to admit the excuse when restored to soberness it condemns what we
have done.'[16] So it was an equivocal acceptance of office that Gladstone sent to
Palmerston on 6 February, hedged about with statements of loyalty to
Aberdeen and, politically, to the maintenance of Peelite fiscal prudence and the
integrity of the Church of England.[17]

With his opponents numerous and his allies wavering, Palmerston's government was seemingly built on shaky foundations. The truth was that
Palmerston's rise to the premiership was not quite 'inevitable', but in a period
weighed down, politically, by what Angus Hawkins has described as 'a surfeit of
leadership' and the resultant party confusion at Westminster, Palmerston

emerged as the most feasible minister. Palmerston was, as Hawkins suggested, thrown forward as 'the temporary arbitrator of immediate differences',[18] and his first government, of 1855–58, had to steer a delicate course in Parliament between and among the fragments of Tory, Peelite, Whig and Radical group-ings. At the same time, a good deal was expected of Palmerston, the new broom which would, as *Punch* predicted, tidy up after the ministerial 'imbecility' of the Aberdeen years.[19] It was, as Broughton described the situation, a lot to ask:

> Had Lord Palmerston been possessed of ten times the energy, courage, experience, skill, & honesty of purpose, which are known to belong to him, there would have been little or no chance of his giving both satisfac-tion to the Parliament & people of England. A great deal too much was expected of him. It was thought, not said, that he would not only rectify all errors & reform all abuses of the existing system, but that he would change the system itself, and act upon an entirely new plan of govern-ment. The Cabinet, and all places in the executive plan of government were to be remodelled, merit was to be the sole passport to power, useless offices were to be abolished, jarring offices to be reconciled or consoli-dated. In short, the wise maxim 'the best man for the best place' was to be the watchword of the new minister, and all national calamities, as well as all private injustice were to cease.[20]

Though there was much to do on the domestic front, immediate attention in government circles was directed to foreign affairs. Palmerston became Prime Minister in the midst of, and largely because of, a war and the resolution of that conflict was a pressing concern. Within a couple of days of entering on his new duties, Palmerston had written a private letter to Napoleon III to assure the French Emperor of his commitment to the two countries' alliance, opening up a personal, unofficial, channel of communication between Downing Street and the Tuileries.[21] It was an early sign of an ongoing Palmerstonian commitment to the entente, but it was also an indication that the Peelites' 'great fears of the French influence over and through Palmerston' were not necessarily groundless.[22] When the new Cabinet met for the first time on 9 February Palmerston's apparent lack of leadership further unnerved the Peelite element. 'It did not relieve the gloom of my impressions,' wrote Gladstone of this meeting. 'Though it was a first Cabinet we were as I reported to Graham in the evening more acephalous than ever: less order, less unity of purpose: Charles Wood had twice cried, "*Will* the Cabinet decide *something* upon *some* point?" Palmerston, though he had appeared more *éveillé* than usual, had taken no lead.' At that meeting Palmerston had introduced three topics: the recall of Lord Raglan from the Crimea, a proposed purchase of 25,000 rifles from America, and the committee for inquiry into the war called for by Roebuck the month before. On the first of these Gladstone thought Palmerston had no real notion of what he hoped to achieve, of the second he expressed incredulity that Palmerston thought this administrative decision merited political discussion and on the question of the committee he seemed to regard the matter as not something to be taken seriously.[23] On this last point Palmerston underestimated the fragility of Cabinet unity and within days Gladstone had quit the government over the issue.

Parliamentary demands for the committee were loud and insistent and though Palmerston was himself hesitant about acquiescing, he maintained that compliance with the popular will was the only sensible course: refusal would lead to defeat, a parliamentary dissolution would be 'ruinous' and to throw up the reins of government within a fortnight of taking them up would make ministers 'the laughing stock of the country'. Gladstone, however, regarded such a committee as of dubious constitutionality and an unwarranted attack on Aberdeen's reputation; he had furthermore, so he thought, secured from Palmerston a promise to resist demands for the committee before agreeing to join the government.[24] Gladstone's friends and supporters of Liberalism had urged Gladstone not to throw over Palmerston's fledgling ministry lightly: whatever his faults, Palmerston was seen by many as a recognisable and prominent leader (in contrast to Aberdeen's invisibility) and, as Richard Monckton Milnes, a former Peelite and now Liberal MP, and friend of Gladstone's, pointed out in a private letter, it would 'go but a small way towards a vigorous united action if there were to be rival coteries at the Carlton and at Brooks's'; indeed, such acrimony in clubland, he said, would 'render any effective administration of affairs impossible'.[25] Despite Milnes's advice that the Peelites had insufficient resources to stand as a distinct party and only the ability to embarrass the government, Gladstone was apparently unmoved. As Palmerston and his Whig allies clearly intended to grant the committee on the war Gladstone resigned, along with fellow Peelites Sir James Graham (who had remained at the Admiralty as First Lord) and Sidney Herbert (who had taken charge of the Colonial Office under a new arrangement of the War and Colonial portfolios). Beyond the Cabinet, several Peelite ministers followed suit.[26] This was less than three weeks after accepting office, and Gladstone made sure that the royal couple understood that the government was sinking: it stood on 'tender ground' and would not last a year, he told the Prince a week after resigning.[27] The government, he insisted, had no head and though Palmerston was 'an eminent member of it', and controlled many important questions, he did not dominate on all and, fatally from Gladstone's point of view, Palmerston lacked 'that peculiar guiding influence which my experience of Sir R. Peel taught me to associate with the idea of premiership and which was not wholly wanting in Lord Aberdeen'.[28] Even Palmerston's political friends regretted his continued efforts to lead the country. Lord Granville, for example, told Gladstone that he had 'always anticipated that Palmerston would die with a great fame *unless* he came to lead the House of Commons or to be Prime Minister'.[29] Well might Disraeli write at the end of February that 'the political volcano still heaves and vomits forth its lava'.[30]

This 'first concoction' of Palmerston's Cabinet, as Broughton put it, 'was not fortunate'. By the same token, there was certainly no doubt in Broughton's mind that the Peelite defection was odd; it was barely credible, he thought, that they should have entered into government without a clear intimation of Palmerston's intentions in this direction. The rapid rise and fall of this first assemblage did at least give Palmerston the opportunity of, or force him into, making a clear break with Aberdeen's ministry.[31] On 9 March Palmerston reported to his brother that 'I have had a very harassing work of it to fill up all the vacant places. It is so difficult to find men fit to be appointed & willing to accept while there are shoals unfit, & pressing for appointments but I have nearly done.'[32] Such an apparent dearth of talent notwithstanding, Palmerston had used the enforced reshuffle as an opportunity to shore up the government's Whig foundations. While this ministry would, within the space of a few months, be opened to representatives of the middle classes with the accession to the Cabinet of Matthew Talbot Baines in December 1855 (something actually first mooted in early February),[33] Palmerston's reworking of his parliamentary resources in late February suggests an inclination to consolidate the position of aristocratic Whiggery; if not his natural ally, at least a body of politicians with whom he was familiar and knew he could work. Thus, Gladstone was replaced at the Exchequer by Sir George Cornewall Lewis, Russell took Herbert's seat at the Colonial Office and Sir Charles Wood was moved from the Board of Control to fill the vacancy created by Graham's departure; the further accessions of Stanley of Alderley (to the Presidency of the Board of Trade) and Robert Vernon Smith (to replace Wood at the Board of Control) underscored the Cabinet's Whig credentials. Disraeli, watching from the opposition benches, had speculated whether Palmerston would opt for 'a man of the people' such as Baines ('for popularity') or go for an 'exclusively Whig and family-party'; the Whig option, he thought, would provoke open warfare between ministers and erstwhile Peelite colleagues.[34] Acutely aware of the dangers of appearing to prevaricate in the midst of a crisis, however – frequent changes of important offices, Lewis, one of the recent accessions to the Cabinet, had observed shortly afterwards, 'seem to betoken levity of purpose'[35] – Palmerston had been keen to stabilise his Cabinet as quickly as possible and this would most effectively be achieved by turning to the Whigs; or at least a Whig ministry offered the prospect of fewer internecine quarrels and damaging compromises.[36] For the moment, Palmerston's priority was simply to form a durable government. Southgate thought this evidence of Palmerston's loyalty to his own class (the aristocracy),[37] but while this was Palmerston's natural milieu his reshuffling of ministers was driven much more by expediency. He had decided before the Peelite resignations had taken place that it would probably serve his purposes to dissolve Parliament at the end of the current session and go to the country for his own mandate, at that point because he thought his position strong and likely to remain so. If the second half of February had raised doubts about the security of that position, the arguments for a dissolution remained compelling.[38] This was therefore a Cabinet designed to get through the coming months with as little difficulty as was possible.

There is about this first couple of months of Palmerston's first government less the air of comfortable inevitability and more a sense of 'make do and mend', until either the country emerged from the storm of war into calmer waters, or a stronger leader materialised. Palmerston seemed a shadow of his former rumbustious self. Disraeli had mocked him as a broken-down relic – 'ginger beer and not champagne', he had said – whose growing deafness, deteriorating sight and 'false teeth, which would fall out of his mouth when speaking, if he did not hesitate and halt so in his talk', suggested he would not satisfy the country's demand for vigorous leadership.[39] Even sympathetic observers thought Palmerston was past his best. 'People think Lord Pam has lost his *dash* and courage, and looks old', Lady Cowper wrote at the end of February. 'He is subdued; is very blind, and wont wear spectacles. He pulls out glasses occasionally and says he has got something they call "clearers". But he has behaved admirably, with the greatest forbearance and kindness to everyone, tho' I fear he is not popular, except out of doors among the people, who say he is a true Englishman.'[40] It is true that Palmerston was growing old and his physical powers were diminishing – he is reported to have been caught napping in the House on more than one occasion and while still more than capable of turning a nice phrase, he sometimes delivered his speeches semi-coherently – but Palmerston was far from being a spent force.[41] Presiding over a government subject to a number of ministerial changes – in the space of ten months between February and November 1855, for example, he appointed four different Secretaries of State for the Colonies – Palmerston would deputise for colleagues during such transitions and in the case of the Colonial Office in particular, carried the work of that department himself (and indeed cleared the backlog of work there)[42] while Russell was attending the Vienna conference in the spring.[43] At the same time, he oversaw improvements to his home at Broadlands during the summer, continued to keep a close eye on his investments and racing concerns and took a personal interest in reforms ranging from reorganising the paths in London parks to messengers' salaries, as well as to protecting Smithfield market from redevelopment, safeguarding landlord rights in Prince Edward Island and securing the promotion of a Dublin clergyman.[44] Whatever ailments afflicted him (and Disraeli certainly exaggerated), Palmerston had lost none of his appetite for hard work. 'The mistake people made was to expect so much from him', Lord Cowper thought in April, 'and they were certain to be disappointed; but he works hard and has not yet got into any scrape, which is a great deal to say for any Prime Minister.'[45]

If Palmerston's diligence was not in doubt, what was less clear was just what his role was. Palmerston had cultivated a formidable reputation over the previous twenty-five years for his ability to command a department and offer a robust analysis of affairs from a close scrutiny and understanding of the papers that crossed his desk. He was now, however, effectively a minister without portfolio and it has been noted in several studies that this hampered his ability to control government policy and action. Southgate, whose book examined Palmerston's career for evidence of its Churchillian, or even Chathamite, qualities (seemingly an ability to exercise near total control over a government at war), found Palmerston wanting at this juncture: 'No pretence can be made that he was very effective as a war leader,' he concluded.[46] John Vincent judged that the Admiralty and the War Office kept the Prime Minister out of their business (Palmerston must have found it difficult to argue against such departmental territoriality) and reduced Palmerston to advising his Foreign Secretary, Clarendon, who was receptive to 'guidance'.[47] And as Palmerston had recognised in 1854, in the midst of war it was direction of the military that mattered more than control of diplomacy. The new prime ministerial broom had, apparently, little to do but sweep the parliamentary floor of someone else's war. There is something in such views, but Palmerston should not be discounted as an impotent figure: there remained a Palmerstonian position, and Palmerstonian activity, that preclude any premature abrogation of his political influence and impact.

Arguably, from a diplomatic point of view, there were good reasons to avoid direct association with the political dimensions of the conflict. In March, Russell, the new Colonial Secretary, had been dispatched to Vienna to represent Britain at a conference convened to search for a negotiated settlement to hostilities. Palmerston insisted that any such resolution must satisfy the far-reaching objectives that underpinned the original British decision to go to war. The Ottoman Empire was to be preserved and its position strengthened both by reinforcing Constantinople's own political position and that of its tributary states in the Balkans and by imposing limitations on Russia's reach into the Black Sea region and reaffirming the principle of free navigation of the Danube. Yet although Russia had agreed to negotiate on these points, even as he wrote instructions to Russell in late March Palmerston doubted whether a conference could achieve a satisfactory peace. While 'some few people here would applaud us for making a peace on almost any conditions', he wrote, 'yet the bulk of the nation would soon see through the flimsy veil which we should have endeavoured to [use to] disguise entire failure in attaining the objects for which we undertook the war, and we should receive the general condemnation which we should rightly deserve'.[48] Palmerston was not so wide of the mark in thinking the Tsar unlikely to make any substantial concessions or long-term promises in the Near East. The conference broke up after a final meeting on 26 April, having managed only to draw up proposals based on an Austrian plan that would have allowed Russia to maintain a presence in the Black Sea (the proposal was for a reduced fleet presence, but a presence nonetheless), and therefore effectively nullifying broader Franco-British objectives designed to buttress the Ottoman government's independent position in the region. Russell returned to London in the curious position of having intimated at Vienna that these terms were acceptable to Britain yet of being unwilling to argue for the arrangement when he presented the details to the Cabinet. The French Emperor rejected the terms in May and in July Russell even went so far as to denigrate the Vienna proposals in a House of Commons debate on the question. When he was shown to have subscribed to them himself at Vienna he exposed the government to ridicule: Palmerston thought it 'very embarrassing' and he doubted Russell's ability to overcome the great prejudice now mounting against him.[49] Russell's resignation a short while afterwards saved Palmerston's ministry from a potentially fatal vote of confidence.

At Westminster the conflict had all along divided the House. John Vincent has analysed the parliamentary dimension to Palmerston's management of the Crimean War.[50] Given the fluidity of Liberal identity at Westminster the importance of this aspect hardly needs stressing. What is significant, however, is the conclusion that Palmerston was to a large extent buffeted by parliamentary moods over the war, but also that he managed to survive. With ongoing efforts to effect a negotiated settlement in the spring, the House preferred to press for peace, but the failure of the Vienna meeting to produce a settlement, combined with a growing confidence in British military capabilities, saw a more hawkish mood develop, briefly, before news of the failure to capture Sebastopol in June filtered back home and turned attention, again, to considerations of peace more than war. Palmerston's primary objective, as he wrote to Lady Palmerston in July (in the middle of the Russell 'affair'), was 'to satisfy the House & the country that the govt is in earnest in the prosecution of the war, and that there is no party in the Cabinet hankering after a dishonourable peace. This I believe to be the truth and this is what we shall have to state.'[51] With crowds gathering to protest at the government's handling of the crisis, some sense of activity was required.[52] At the same time, Palmerston's private letters on the subject of taking the battle to Russia at Sweaburg reveal his own doubts about Britain's ability to overwhelm Russia's quantitative military superiority.[53] Despite such anxieties, Palmerston was able to ride the tides of parliamentary feeling largely because neither the government's supporters, nor its opponents, had a particularly clear, or at least fixed, policy.

Russell's departure from the government in July certainly weakened the ministry (could a Whig government exist without him?) and no one was quite sure whether he would advocate a bellicose or pacific course now that he was free to adopt his own line (Russell's various statements on the matter suggest he preferred to keep a foot in both camps). Meanwhile the military position in the Crimea by late summer looked uncertain, and as Sir George Cornewall Lewis pointed out, the fate of the government was to be determined in the trenches around Sebastopol. Palmerston's government seemed in an anomalous position:

as Vincent points out, it was a War Ministry that had no victories to celebrate; it was a Whig ministry lacking loyal Whig backing; and it was led by a Prime Minister who drew much of his strength from popular backing but who could not, in the face of the pacific temper of the House, hope to mobilise popular enthusiasm for a vigorous war effort. All the while Russell hovered as a possible alternative leader. The fall of Sebastopol at the end of September, therefore, at least gave the government some succour though this hard-won victory only underlined the extent to which Palmerston must now, however reluctantly, acquiesce in opposition demands for peace and no more war, which over the following six months Palmerston's government was to work towards.

In an analysis of the parliamentary constraints under which Palmerston's government arrived at this result, the tension between Palmerston's popular image as an effective War Minister and leader and the reality of his parliamentary limitations are clearly highlighted, and the very fact of his having survived appears a remarkable one. No doubt in a strictly parliamentary, high political, view this is the case. Yet however important this 'parliamentary dimension', it is only one facet of Palmerston's war. Most accounts agree that Palmerston was effective in his efforts to improve logistical efficiency of the military departments (notably in terms of supplies and sanitary provisions for the army) and the usefulness of these contributions has been generally acknowledged, even if their importance within the grand narrative of the (frequently inept) prosecution of the war is downplayed.[54] This, however, is to underestimate the significance of such efforts to an understanding of Palmerston's conception of the role he could fulfil and, more broadly, what this war had come to represent to Palmerston. The war was undoubtedly one of enormous strategic consequence; it was also, as has not gone unnoticed, a test of Britain's 'greatness' – of the institutions, power and influence of a progressive liberal nation.[55] On this front there was considerable evidence of Britain's shortcomings. Palmerston was addressing himself to these issues, it should be remembered, not only as the *realpolitik* Foreign Minister of popular (historical) caricature, but also as a domestic politician fully impressed by the gravity of the social and environmental problems bound up in the 'condition of England question'. The Palmerstonian, liberal, mindset saw this war, therefore, as much more than a high political debate about war and peace; it was, equally, a platform on which to examine continuing concerns about 'progress' and 'improvement'.

From the outset Palmerston had laid particular emphasis on the lamentable condition of Britain's forces in the Crimea just as much as on the execrable attempts to prosecute a great power conflict. His willingness to commission a committee of inquiry in February, then, despite his protested reservations about it in Cabinet debates with Gladstone and the Peelites during the very early days of the government, sat perfectly comfortably with his view that, as he had put it in a memorandum in January, current problems in the Crimea had nothing to do with extraneous factors such as the weather and had everything to do with human incompetence: 'The true cause lies in the apathy and indifference the neglect, the incapacity, the want of forsight [*sic*] the want of thought, the want of resource on the part of men in authority in the Crimea, and I should fear, in the want of sufficiently stimulating, peremptory and directing instructions to those men from home.'[56] He was also, in supporting calls for such a committee, acting in a manner which information reaching him from supporters around the country suggested would win favour with the general population: even George Cornewall Lewis, who opposed any inquiry, noted that it was 'impossible to be blind' to popular demands for such an investigation.[57] Thus was Palmerston highly active in his attention to matters of munitions supplies (he took a close interest in details of the cannon, rifles and shells that were used in the conflict) as well as to questions of army health: he had been impressed by W.H. Russell's accounts of the poor conditions in the Crimea and as a friend of the Nightingale family was not spared details of Florence's findings regarding such matters. Palmerston issued direct personal instructions, for example, concerning clothing provisions for soldiers and when cholera struck in the summer he insisted on twice-daily health inspections on the front line and a series of measures to ensure the cleanliness of military camps.[58] Within a short time, Palmerston's government had reformed the army's land transport arrangements and instituted a 'corps of scavengers' to 'remove all the filth' in the camps while sanitary commissioners were appointed to monitor conditions in camps and hospitals. In remodelling the army's medical departments and reviewing all aspects of the supply of materials Palmerston hoped 'to establish a better order of things in the Crimea'.[59] There is evidence that he informed himself about the poor conditions endured by soldiers and about the shortcomings of military leadership from sources beyond the official records and among his papers are handwritten notes copying extracts from letters written by front-line soldiers.[60]

If the fall of Sebastopol on 8 September did not represent an outright victory over Russia, it did at least give grounds on which Palmerston could argue for an ascendancy of the western alliance of, primarily, Britain and France (though by the autumn Palmerston was, in private, growing increasingly doubtful of French commitment to the effort).[61] Palmerston pointed immediately, therefore, to recent events as evidence not simply of military gains, but more significantly of the continued advance of liberal constitutional principles in Europe. Palmerston's wide-ranging ambitions for a *beau idéal* restructuring of European power balances were, arguably, not realisable *in toto*. Furthermore, given that, in material terms, the military advances that had been made had been achieved by allied forces comprised overwhelmingly of French and Sardinian, rather than British, soldiers (of almost a quarter of a million allied troops in the Crimea at this time only about 45,000 were British),[62] it was perhaps advantageous to talk of a shared liberal mission and to gloss over the details of military matters. Yet, despite these reservations, there was a genuine, meaningful, perhaps even overriding, ideological contest bound up in the war. Taking Sebastopol, Palmerston told an audience at Melbourne in Derbyshire, had been 'a triumph', but more than that Britain had, he said, 'struck a mortal blow at an enemy whose aggressive policy threatened the whole world' and 'Sebastopol has succumbed to the valour of the allies, and right has thus triumphed over wrong.' It had been a hard won and costly victory, he conceded, but 'it is a consolation to those who have lost relatives and friends in this contest, in support of liberty against despotism, that their names will be enrolled in the annals of fame, and will be associated with the imperishable glories of their country'.[63] At Romsey, against a backdrop of an arch bearing the legend 'Palmerston the true friend of liberty and peace', the Prime Minister spoke of the recent military victory (against a superior force) as evidence of something bigger:

> We are presenting to the world one of the noblest spectacles which it is possible for nations to exhibit. Here are the two greatest nations of the world – I say it without vanity and without exaggeration, but without one particle of diminution, that England and France, standing as they do at the head of everything that dignifies human nature, are presenting to the world the noblest possible spectacle of two great people casting into the shade of oblivion all former jealousies and rivalships and extinct animosities, and uniting for purposes generous and, as far as any sordid motives are concerned, entirely disinterested; looking for no trumpery or profit or gain, territorial or otherwise, for themselves, but seeking simply to establish the liberty of the world, in which they are deeply interested, upon a solid and permanent foundation, and making sacrifices, not wantonly or for abstract principles, but for sound political considerations.[64]

Both speeches – that made at Melbourne and that at Romsey – were widely reprinted in the regional newspapers and helped generate an alternative framework within which the conflict could be discussed. If parliamentary debates were essentially ideologically stale and turned largely on personal and party political rivalries, then the significance of Palmerston's attention to the wider meaning of the war is clear. Parliamentary preferences for peace inhibited Palmerston from overtly embracing a bellicose feeling in the country at large, but his focus on 'efficiency' and his cross-class rhetoric of the war as a vindication of Western (notably British) notions of improvement and progress represented a means by which to connect with his constituency beyond Westminster. In an address to the House of Commons in February he had laid out his view of this common patriotic endeavour:

> Talk to me of the aristocracy of England! Why, look to that glorious charge of the cavalry at Balaclava – look to that charge where the noblest and wealthiest of the land rode foremost, followed by heroic men from

the lowest classes of the community, each rivalling the other in bravery, neither the peer who led nor the trooper who followed being distinguished one from the other. In that glorious band there were the sons of the gentry of England; leading were the noblest of the land, and following were the representatives of the people of this country.[65]

It was a slightly more positive formulation than Tennyson's of the doomed heroism of the 600 cavalrymen who charged into the valley of death, but though Tennyson saw the pathos in the situation of those who, not reasoning why, simply did and died, there is a similar intimation in his poem of the nobility of a shared patriotic commitment to a worthy goal. In stressing the common purpose of the aristocracy, the gentry and the 'humble classes' in prosecuting the war, Palmerston was able simultaneously to do much to deflect the criticisms of the inefficiency and nepotism of aristocratic government that were gaining ground at this time under the banner of the Administrative Reform Association.[66]

It was against this background that Palmerston changed his mind about a dissolution in the autumn; not because he feared defeat, but because his government seemed adequately settled and faced few great problems (the capture of Sebastopol appears to have infused the ministry with a renewed sense of momentum). As Lewis observed, the government's opponents were in disarray. He dismissed talk of a Disraeli–Gladstone coalition, but the fact that such an alliance was being talked of, fairly seriously, points to a continued lack of genuine ideological coherence on the opposition benches that far outweighed any disagreements among the Whigs in government. Even if old Conservative divisions were being temporarily papered over by a common aversion to Palmerston, this did not signify the party unity that would have been essential for any alternative government to function: it is implausible to argue that Gladstone and Disraeli could have served together as ministerial colleagues. Thus, Lewis wrote to Palmerston: 'The government stands well in the country, & none of the other three parties, the Derbyites, the Peelites, & the Manchesterites, are in good odour or good condition. The two latter are unpopular, the former are divided.' More than this, as Lewis continued, the government's prospects looked favourable. With prices for agricultural produce high there would be no foothold for protectionist arguments and with trade and employment both buoyant, Lewis presented an optimistic assessment of the economy. Ireland, too, he pointed out was 'quiet' and offered opponents no ammunition with which to attack the government. Even though the Liberals had no direct electoral mandate, Lewis argued, now was not the best time to go to the country: the House seemed disposed to 'follow the changes of public opinion, without reference to the circumstances under which it was elected'. After all, by 'dissolving now, we deprive ourselves of a great card which may be played next session, if the House proves intractable, or some unforeseen crisis arrives – we cut down a stone which may be kept hanging over their heads until a real emergency arises.'[67] Lewis's optimism was arguably overstated: by his own admission the Bank of England was reporting a run on bullion reserves and he anticipated 'much uneasiness in the City'. The government's own finances were 'in a good state' and fiscal pressures were undoubtedly caused by factors beyond the government's control, but it might have been to trust a little too much to fortune to act, as Lewis advised, 'the part of bystanders, & watch the course of events.'[68] As Palmerston, believing there was little the government 'could do to stave off the evil', replied: 'Let us hope.'[69] And if reports were to be believed, there was perhaps something to hope for. Thomas Milner Gibson, a Radical MP, reported in November that he had been in Brooks's, the Whig-Liberal club, recently where he had 'found it the fashion to denounce Lord John Russell, & to say "that his new wife has softened his brain". Palmerston is the idol and the war is to be carried on with vigour until Russia goes on her knees and sues for peace.'[70]

Palmerston continued to press for firmness in any negotiated peace settlement – Russia, he told Clarendon in February 1856, '*must* have peace' and would eventually be brought to agree to British terms so long as France and Britain held their nerve[71] – but Cabinet colleagues were more cautious and hoped to soften some of the stipulations Palmerston sought to impose on Russia.[72] Talk in the clubs, especially liberal strongholds such as Brooks's, suggested that outside the Cabinet many still feared that Palmerston hankered after a decisive military victory and would seek to undermine initiatives aimed at a negotiated peace, but such suspicions were, in the event, ill founded.[73] Palmerston may have preferred 'to trip up the thing' (as Milner Gibson put it) but he had been reined in by his colleagues. And, furthermore, with France an apparently unreliable partner, Palmerston had presumably no particular desire to spin out a conflict that relied on a military alliance with a power which he did not, in the final analysis, completely trust. Explaining his acquiescence in the French plan to hold the peace congress at Paris (and not his suggested venue, Brussels) Palmerston stressed the advantage of being physically close to Napoleon III and able to subvert any undue 'Russian' feeling within the wider French political and diplomatic elite. Walewski, for example, was thought to be too sympathetic to the Tsar while, as Palmerston told Emily, 'We have indeed need of all the firmness we can command, not against our foes but against our French friends who are behaving as ill as is well possible. Did you read an article in the Times three days ago about stockjobbing statesmen who would welcome another Waterloo for their country if it would raise the funds. It was severe, but too true.'[74] So when the congress convened to settle the conflict in February, Britain's representatives, Clarendon, the Foreign Secretary, and Cowley, the ambassador to France, spoke on behalf of a government that was basically committed to a negotiated settlement. According to Anthony Panizzi, an Italian refugee close to the Palmerstons, everyone thought Palmerston the best choice to attend the meetings in person, but that, observed Lady Palmerston, was 'impossible' and at least Clarendon could go 'as the next best hand'.[75] In its negotiations at Paris Lewis felt the government had the backing of Parliament: 'The sour discontented unsettled feeling of last session has disappeared – & the spirit of mischief is muzzled. This change is owing to the taking of Sebastopol. The temper of the House was evidently on the whole pacific – they seemed disposed in favour of a peace upon the proposed terms.'[76]

During the course of the congress meetings, some concessions were made to Russian demands to retain a presence in the Crimea and Circassia, and the Tsar was forced into only a partial retreat from Bessarabia, but Russian fleets were expelled from the Black Sea and this represented a major setback to Russian influence and satisfied Britain and France that the war was being concluded to their advantage (or at least to Russia's disadvantage). With Russia patently weakened by the war, the Peace of Paris, though an imperfect resolution of the dispute, at least brought the conflict to a conclusion and, from Palmerston's point of view, did so with some measure of honour. 'Palmerston, wonderful man!' Clarendon observed at the time, 'is not only pleased with the Peace but it is extremely doubtful whether our army might not have been destroyed by disease if we had attempted an expedition to Asia Minor, and whether we might not have been beaten on our own element at Cronstadt, so there is no discontent in that quarter, and the Cabinet generally are satisfied. It remains to be seen what the public will say to the conditions.'[77]

Palmerston feared the conclusion of peace would open his government to renewed hostilities in Parliament, but when the peace terms were debated in the House of Commons in May the exchanges were described by Lewis as 'dull', and the House 'flat', as all sides acceded to the terms agreed at Paris.[78] It seemed that Palmerston's stock was rising but he remained acutely aware of the fact that his administration was built on foundations that could easily be weakened, both in Parliament, where Liberal unity remained fragile, and diplomatically, where Russian attempts to subvert or weaken the Paris settlement threatened to discredit the peace (Palmerston made clear his dissatisfaction with Russian behaviour in a meeting with the Russian ambassador in August).[79] It was necessary to consolidate his position with the country at large, and to test public attitudes to the peace. Although he identified the middle classes as the main community to be cultivated, it is significant that in discussing the peace Palmerston felt it important to make a direct connection with the whole nation.

Towards the end of the year, Palmerston visited the north-west of England where his speeches continued the theme of national unity in support of a noble cause. In Liverpool on 7 November Palmerston spoke to the assembled crowds of the gratification felt in government having witnessed 'during the continuance of the war in which we were unfortunately engaged, that a sense of the justice of the cause, that a sense of the necessity for the exertions which we called upon the country to make, overpowered, in the minds of the commercial community of this country, all considerations of private interests, and called forth from them that display of energetic patriotism which contributed so greatly to the success of the contest, and which reflected such honour upon the country at large'. It was the commercial classes in particular whom he applauded, identifying their willingness to underwrite the patriotic endeavours of the nation at large as evidence of 'that indomitable spirit of England'.[80] The day before, in Salford, he had said much the same thing to a similarly composed audience. Responding to the observations that his government had been formed 'in a moment of apparent difficulty', Palmerston downplayed that difficulty: since Britain was 'full of people of such energy and such high spirit, whose courage rises with the occasion, whose resources, both of wealth and ingenuity, are never-failing, and never inferior to the exigencies of the time, there is no difficulty which is real, or at least which is not sure to be surmounted'. Yet there was still an undercurrent of criticism, alluded to by Joseph Brotherton, Salford's MP, that suggested Palmerston was no peace minister but a bellicose one. This Palmerston addressed directly. It had been his overriding aim, he said, 'not to bring on war, but to prevent war; and rely upon it that that is the true policy for this country. It is the policy which has been pursued by all those statesmen of former times who have raised most highly the reputation of this country and most enjoyed the confidence of the people; it is the policy, be assured of it, which all enlightened statesmen will adopt, and which all intelligent people will justify and approve'.[81] This was an important statement of Palmerston's position. For commentators who have often preferred to focus on Palmerston's reputation for gunboat diplomacy, his avowed interest in peace can be easily overlooked or discounted. Given that this government was one preoccupied with international crises, it is ostensibly straightforward to portray Palmerston as a statesman disposed to pursue assertive, even aggressive foreign policies. Each year of the government's term seemed to be dominated by an overseas difficulty: 1855 was occupied largely with the war in the Crimea and its effects lasted well into 1856, despite its being finally 'settled'; late 1856 and 1857 saw renewed tensions in Britain's relations with China and in the summer of 1857 there was the beginning of imperial instability and difficulties in India; in 1858, the final year of this government's life, as well as ongoing concerns about India, the fallout from an attempted assassination of Napoleon III raised tricky questions about the state of Franco-British relations. Palmerston's government seemingly lived and died in the diplomatic sphere. Yet these were all episodes Palmerston's government had to respond to, not ones that it had created. As will be seen, had Palmerston been able to set the government's own agenda, arguments about his appetites for peace and war would have been quite different. As it was, however, much of Palmerston's, and the government's, time was occupied with managing external emergencies.

In late 1856 a relatively minor incident in southern China quickly escalated into a major conflict encapsulating a wide range of economic and political issues.[82] The source of the dispute is readily identified. On 3 October the *Arrow*, a Chinese lorcha (a type of schooner) sailed into the harbour at Canton and cast anchor. The ship was Chinese owned and crewed by Chinese sailors but had been registered by its owner in Hong Kong which meant that it was entitled to sail under a British flag and British protection. The captain of the *Arrow*, a young Irishman named Thomas Kennedy, had been appointed as a nominal master on the grounds that this would lend weight to the ship's claims to British protection (Kennedy was subsequently described unproblematically by the British authorities as English). On 8 October the owner of a Chinese cargo ship who happened to be in Canton identified a member of the *Arrow*'s crew as one of a gang of pirates who had attacked his vessel a month or so earlier and he called in the harbour authorities. The local marine police boarded the *Arrow* and took the ship's crew into custody. This much is not in doubt. Kennedy, who was at the time breakfasting with other 'captains of convenience' aboard a nearby ship, hurried over to the *Arrow* where, he would later claim, he saw the Chinese authorities haul down the British flag as they arrested the crew. In doing so, it was now claimed, the Chinese police had violated international maritime law in ignoring the *Arrow*'s proper claim to British protection and, in the process, 'insulted' the British flag and, by extension, the British nation and empire. The impetuous and abrasive British consul, Harry Parkes, lost no time in remonstrating with the Chinese authorities and wrote immediately to Commissioner Yeh. The *Arrow*, 'an English lorcha', he said, had been forcibly boarded that morning 'and regardless of the remonstrances of her master, an Englishman', the Chinese officers had 'seized, bound and carried off twelve of her Chinese crew, and hauled down the English colours which were then flying'. Kennedy had not in fact been on board at the time, but the assertion that the 'English colours' had been hauled down was more controversial. The police officers insisted that no flag had been flying; indeed, to have flown a Union flag while docked in port would have contravened British naval custom. Parkes's inquiries left him in no doubt on the matter, however, and he demanded 'that an insult so publicly committed must be equally publicly atoned'. There is little doubt that Parkes was an unreliable witness: his attempts to ascertain what had happened on the morning of 8 October were flawed at best, and recent accounts have shown that his gathering and presentation of evidence were highly partial and selective. It is suggested, indeed, that the insult for which he sought atonement was in fact a personal one: the injury to his pride caused by his inability to secure the immediate return of the sailors from the police himself. Parkes, however, persuaded Britain's plenipotentiary in China and governor of Hong Kong, Sir John Bowring, of the 'insult' and the matter rapidly grew more serious. By the end of October Bowring had instructed the British naval forces to begin bombarding Canton, and shelling and skirmishes continued in and around the city, with varying degrees of intensity (at the height of the conflict shells were being fired on Canton every ten minutes), until February 1857.

Bowring acted independently, but no doubt justified his actions to himself by recollecting how Palmerston had dealt with Don Pacifico's claims against Greece a decade earlier. Thus, despite the fact that the *Arrow*'s British registration was void (it had not been renewed on 27 September when it expired), despite the fact that no hard evidence of a direct 'insult' to the British flag was provided (at best the case rested on contestable testimony), and despite the fact that the *Arrow*'s implication in acts of piracy seemed sustainable, this attempt by the Chinese authorities to prosecute criminal behaviour had sparked a major conflict between Britain and China that affected, too, the commercial and material interests of both France and the USA.[83]

Palmerston, however, remained sanguine, telling Laurence Sulivan in January 1857 that public affairs looked 'well' and there were no threats on the horizon. 'Of course there will be plenty of work,' he added, 'and no lack of disposition in some quarters to take advantage of any opportunity to harrass [*sic*] the Govt, but we have the Country with us, and our most difficult foreign questions have been settled or will be so.'[84] The government's opponents were looking for an occasion to topple the ministry and the news from China arrived, contrary to what Palmerston told his brother-in-law, amid potentially testing parliamentary circumstances. In mid-December Derby suggested in a letter to Malmesbury that Palmerston was 'a Conservative Minister working with Radical tools and keeping up a show of Liberalism in his foreign policy';[85] it must have seemed that there was much to aim at in attacking him.

Although he had been a sometime admirer of the Prime Minister, by late 1856 Disraeli was determined to overthrow Palmerston, not least because the latter's apparent willingness to extend the conflict in the Crimea on liberal principles had caused Disraeli to reconsider his erstwhile support for Palmerston's policy against Russia.[86] With the intention of stirring up ill feeling, Disraeli visited Paris at the end of 1856 in order to try to discredit Palmerston with Napoleon III, only to find that the French Emperor was 'entirely with Palmerston' and viewed the British Tories as 'his hereditary enemies'. Unsuccessful though Disraeli had been in his interviews with Napoleon, however, he did gain something from the trip. At the Paris Embassy he met an unpaid attaché, Ralph Earle (later described as 'a man of considerable ambition and no scruples') who, sharing what he took to be the Disraelian objective of exposing the 'villainy' of Palmerston, undertook to supply documents relating to a secret treaty signed between Britain, France and Austria in December 1854. Under the terms of this agreement, by which Britain and France had hoped to draw Austria into the Crimean War, France had given a guarantee of 'good behaviour' in Italy by not encouraging revolutionary intrigue there. Since Austria did not in the end become involved in the war, the treaty was, in effect, redundant within a couple of years. Disraeli thought he could use this document as evidence of Palmerston's disingenuousness in championing Italian independence in public while there existed a secret treaty guaranteeing 'to

Austria the whole of her Italian dominions'. Disraeli brought the matter to the House in early 1857 and succeeded at least in exposing the fact that Palmerston had no recollection of the treaty. Greville recorded:

> The defeat which Disraeli sustained the other night was turned the night before last into something like a triumph, and Palmerston found himself in a disagreeable position. Disraeli had asserted that a treaty had been concluded between France and Austria for certain ends and at a certain time. Palmerston flatly contradicted him, and with great insolence of manner, especially insisting that it was nothing but a Convention, and that conditional, which *never had been signed*. Two nights after Palmerston came down to the House, and in a very jaunty way said he must correct his former statement, and inform the House he had just discovered that the Convention *had been signed*. Great triumph naturally on the part of Disraeli, who poured forth a rather violent invective. Then Palmerston lost his temper and retorted that Disraeli was trying to cover an ignominious retreat by vapouring. This language, under the circumstances of the case, was very imprudent and very improper, and (unlike what he had ever experienced before) he sat down without a single cheer, his own people even not venturing to challenge the approbation of the House in a matter in which, though Disraeli was not right, Palmerston was so clearly wrong. What business had he to make such a mistake? for he ought to have been perfectly and accurately informed of every detail connected with foreign affairs.[87]

Disraeli's 'victory', then, such as it was, had been won only on account of Palmerston's failing memory concerning the business of an office for which, it might be worth remembering, he did not hold the seals either in December 1854 or in 1857. It was not much of a parliamentary challenge, therefore, and Palmerston may have been justified on these grounds in dismissing his opponents' harassments in early 1857. Yet although Disraeli had been taken in by a diplomat on the make, elsewhere criticism was mounting based on more careful and potentially damaging grounds.

Those Peelites who had deserted Palmerston in 1855, notably Gladstone and Sir James Graham, had been growing noticeably more critical of the government during 1856. As Gladstone put it in a letter to Graham at the end of November 1856, they could expect of Palmerston only 'a foreign policy keeping us in perpetual hot water; large establishments which will undoubtedly be needed to sustain it; the utter ruin of the financial policy of 1853; and general legislative inefficiency'.[88] Palmerston might have expected little else from the Peelites, but the significant feature of this sense of disquiet was that it was shared by Derby's Protectionists and was drawing them – not least, and remarkably, Disraeli and Gladstone – into something approaching a concert. In February 1857 Gladstone

met Derby and told him that he 'deliberately disapproved of the government of
Lord Palmerston, and was prepared and desirous to aid in any proper measures
which might lead to its displacement'. So strong were his misgivings, he said, that
he 'was content to act thus without inquiring who was to follow'; any government but the present one, he continued, 'would govern with less prejudice to the
public interests'. Derby, with a little more reserve, concurred and even began to
speak of Conservative reunion.[89] Palmerston, Gladstone felt, was leading the
Liberals away from a true liberal course: 'I can neither give even the most qualified adhesion to the ministry of Lord Palmerston', he told Sidney Herbert in
March 1857, 'nor follow the liberal party in the abandonment of the very principles and pledges which were original and principal bonds of union with it.'[90]
Gladstone's concerns took parliamentary form in two prominent attacks on the
government in 1857. At the beginning of the year, he attempted to discredit the
government's fiscal policy through a thorough critique of the Chancellor,
Cornewall Lewis's, handling of the income tax. Lewis, an extremely able politician, sidestepped Gladstone's attack with a budget that harked back to Peelite
remedies with a reduced fixed rate, and in Parliament in late February the
attempts of Gladstone and Disraeli to censure government financial policy were
defeated by a comfortable majority. But although such attempts failed to land a
blow on the government, it was evident that the government's opponents were
lining up to take other shots. Gladstone, for example, also attacked the ministry's
attempts to liberalise divorce law, not least as it seemed to represent an unnecessary and unwelcome trespass by the state on the rights and position of the
Church. Such was the situation when news of the bombardment of Canton came
to be dissected by MPs. As James Wilson, Financial Secretary at the Treasury
commented on 22 February, 'Matters look very queer about China. I doubt
whether we shall come off so well on that subject.'[91] His misgivings were, to some
extent, warranted.

The Times had been the first newspaper to report on events at Canton, and
it did not receive the news until the very end of 1856. A hurried note was
inserted into the paper on 29 December and was followed, on 2 January, by a
fuller report and editorial comment. The paper endorsed Parkes's and
Bowring's conduct, and in this respect has been seen also to have served as a
semi-official mouthpiece of the government.[92] The language used by The
Times to justify naval bombardment of the Chinese port is significant. Yeh's
conduct was described as 'throughout arrogant and insulting' and in response
to such an official attitude it was said to have been necessary to assert British
superiority, cultural, material and economic: 'to tolerate such treatment as this
would be entirely to forfeit the position acquired by the war of 1842, and to
announce ourselves to the Chinese – always sufficiently ready to grasp at such
admissions – as a nation devoid of honour and self-respect, and ready, in the
pursuit of material wealth, to pocket any affront and submit to any indignity'.
The issue, in the view of The Times, was a commercial one: all Britain required,

it said, was 'liberty and security for our commerce' – but that required Britain to 'teach' its partner better mercantile manners.[93] Thus, Britain's robust response was entirely justified. In a further editorial, which spoke of 'the ridiculous pride of an ignorant race' and 'a tottering dynasty and a decaying system', China and Chinese society were presented as in need of (Western) modernisation: Britain's 'rights' to trade in Chinese ports were not only secured by treaty and military superiority, but were part of 'natural law'. The naval bombardment of Canton was even discussed in terms of the 'moderation' shown by the British admiral, Seymour, who had directed it. Though this was apparently a trade question, the dispute with China was also made to fit into the paradigm of western imperial progress:

> China must be brought into full communication with the civilized world, and the task of dragging her from seclusion can be best performed by Englishmen. In the interest, therefore, of humanity and civilization we ought not to let this matter drop. . . . We should, then, prepare at once to assert our position and to enforce the right of civilized nations to free commerce and communication with every part of this vast territory. There is no use in treating with such a Power as if it belonged to the enlightened communities of Europe.[94]

The *Morning Post*, a Palmerstonian paper of some years' standing, adopted a similarly hostile view of China and, like *The Times*, used tropes of civilisation and barbarism in its treatment of the affair. Thus, Britain must act with determination against 'an insincere, distrustful, and arrogant people'; there was 'no way', it said, 'of reaching the heart of China but by the sword' and, in speaking specifically of Yeh, the *Post* argued that to 'yield to a savage of this kind were to imperil our interests, not only in the East, but in every part of the world'.[95]

Yet while there was a popular appetite for such chauvinism, it was not universal. A good many papers, especially (and not surprisingly) those with Peelite leanings, thought Yeh's position reasonable and the British one unsustainable. The *Morning Chronicle*, for instance, maintained that Yeh had 'acted with much dignity and forbearance, and a lofty sense of duty' and if the object of British policy was to secure commercial interests, that should not be hedged about with specious arguments about moral improvement. Thus, the *Daily News* argued, 'a more rash, overbearing, and tyrannical exercise of power has rarely been recorded' than the bombardment of Canton, an event which represented the 'prostitution' of British power. It was 'a bad and a base' action, said the *News*, 'a wanton waste of human life at the shrine of a false etiquette and mistaken policy'.[96] In a similar vein, *Punch* produced an extensive satire of Parkes's bullying.[97]

Britain's relations with China had for some years, of course, been sensitive, and debates in the 1850s, about commerce and civilisation, evoked in particular those of the late 1830s and early 1840s. Like the earlier conflict with China in the late 1830s, usually referred to as the First Opium War, relations with China were intimately bound up with questions of trade, economics and empire. Palmerston had always made clear that in trading with China, largely in the opium market, he was far more interested in protecting the doctrine of free trade than in moral and health arguments about the nature of that trade.[98] Thus had Palmerston backed aggressive measures that led to the First Opium War (1840–42), and the Treaty of Nanking (1842) that sought to regularise that trade, when he was Foreign Secretary under Melbourne.[99]

In the 1850s, then, the issue for many was how the actions of Bowring in Canton would impact on the trade and imperial interests Britain had in the region. As the Duke of Argyll noted, the situation risked 'throw[ing] into confusion the whole system on which our commerce rested in that part of the world'.[100] When the question came before the House of Commons at the end of February, it was this mercantile aspect that was uppermost in the minds of those censuring the government (Cobden and Disraeli) and defending it (notably Palmerston), but the wider discussion of the matter in terms of honour and prestige had a notable effect on the structure of parliamentary debates. Palmerston, though he regarded the matter as pre-eminently about freedom of trade and was concerned that the bombardment of Canton might jeopardise that, also recognised that this was an issue that had come to be framed, in a large part of the public mind, in terms of a clash of cultures. He did not shy from efforts to inflame patriotic feeling when he spoke towards the end of the debate, denigrating Yeh as an 'inhuman monster' and speculating on the misfortunes that would befall British interest in the East if the country allowed itself to be cowed by China.[101] Palmerston's opponents were unimpressed: Greville thought his speech 'very dull in the first part, and very bow-wow in the second; not very judicious, on the whole bad, and it certainly failed to decide any doubtful votes in his favor'.[102] Milner Gibson, commenting on the government's priorities, lamented that the old Liberal motto of 'Peace, Retrenchment and Reform' had become 'Bombardment of Canton and no Reform',[103] while Disraeli, scenting victory in the division lobby, invited Palmerston to go to the country on a platform of 'No Reform! New Taxes! Canton Blazing! Persia invaded!'[104]

The opportunity to defeat the government on a genuinely controversial issue was irresistible. The Chancellor, Lewis, conceded at the end of the first day of the debate that the opposition had the best of the argument and it was already 'anticipated that there will be a large majority agst the govt'. Though he discerned 'some reaction of feeling in favour of the govt' the following day, it was obvious that the debate was running away from ministers.[105] The defeat, when it came on 3 March, was by a margin of only 16, but the implication was clear: the government had been profoundly weakened. The following day the Cabinet agreed on the need to go to the country and on 5 March announced the dissolution of Parliament.[106] The prospect of a general election energised parties on all sides. Aberdeen wrote to his friend Guizot in the middle of March describing the 'excitement' of the moment but conceded that Palmerston's opponents would need to tread carefully in attacking the Prime Minister: any attempt 'to overthrow the man who is thought to have triumphed over Russia', he feared, was liable to incur the resentment of the public.[107] While Aberdeen evinced a hope that 'the truth will be known' and Palmerston would be ejected, the mood among the Palmerstonians was reported to be just as optimistic. The American ambassador to London, George Mifflin Dallas, wrote on 16 March that ministers 'are confident of a triumph, and indications are thus far strongly in their favor. Lord Palmerston's personal popularity has some resemblance to that of General Jackson: his partisans concede his violence and his arrogance, but call them an excess of patriotism. Bluster seems, in all countries, to have its charms for the mass.'[108]

On 19 March the Lord Mayor of London hosted a dinner at the Mansion House for politicians and the diplomatic corps, a formal political event that attracted more interest now that an election drew close. Palmerston 'had a strikingly good reception',[109] and in his speech showed that he was going over the heads of politicians to allow the people to reverse the recent faulty verdict of the House of Commons. Deploying rhetoric strikingly reminiscent of his more famous parliamentary speeches of March 1848 and July 1850, Palmerston spoke of his commitment to 'peace abroad' and 'progressive improvement at home' but peace, he said, 'with honour, peace with safety, peace with the maintenance of our national rights, peace with security to our fellow countrymen abroad'.[110] Shortly afterwards, in a letter to his Tiverton constituents, Palmerston presented the election as a direct judgement on individuals and appealed to voters to return him and his colleagues, who had good claims to their confidence, over 'that aggregation of hitherto discordant elements' who had recently outvoted them in Parliament.[111]

Even Palmerston's opponents were obliged to concede that, in calling the election at that point, Palmerston had effectively made it a contest that turned on the extent to which the electorate supported the premier personally. In his address to electors in Buckingham, Disraeli suggested that being devoid of ideas and principles, Palmerston had tried to distract the people with foreign politics. 'His external system is turbulent and aggressive that his rule at home may be tranquil and unassailed,' said Disraeli, and this meant little more than high expenditure, high taxation and little social improvement. It was not a source of strength, then, thought Disraeli, that Palmerston's only claim to the confidence of the people was his name: 'Such arts and resources may suit the despotic ruler of a Continental State exhausted by revolutions, but they do not become a British Minister governing a country proud, free, and progressive, animated by glorious traditions, and aspiring to future excellence.'[112] Given that these were very like the rhetorical flourishes with which Palmerston had long embellished his vision of Britain as an advanced and liberal state, however, it is tempting to agree with Lord Shaftesbury that this contest was developing into one that did indeed revolve around the question, 'Were you, or were you not? are you, or are you not, for Palmerston?'[113] Disraeli returned to the issue in his private correspondence. 'Public appeals made in favor of a *name*, & not a *policy*, are convenient, but at the same time, deceptive,' he wrote on 23 March. 'A man returned pledged to support Palmerston, really means nothing, for there is always the proper mental reservation, when Palmerston, in his, the pledger's opinion, is not wrong. It is not like a specific measure, the ballot &c., wh: admits of no shuffling.'[114]

It was perhaps the fault of politicians themselves for allowing the election to be perceived as a plebiscite on Palmerston. The Cabinet had reassured itself as the government headed for defeat in March that the Prime Minister's popularity remained 'red hot' (as Clarendon put it),[115] and clearly the Protectionists felt the need to deal with Palmerston's personal attraction to electors. Yet, analyses of the election itself have suggested a quite different picture on the ground. Angus Hawkins has argued that local issues, always more important in general elections than is usually acknowledged, played an unusually significant role in this election. Furthermore, there were fewer candidates standing in 1857, and, with the exception of 1847, there were more uncontested seats than at any election since 1832. Such data are hardly suggestive of an animated contest and Hawkins has found little real interest in Palmerston in most constituencies: Palmerstonianism, he said, was 'peripheral' to the election results.[116] In the event, even Disraeli thought that Palmerston's name had not 'really carried a single vote,'[117] and more than a Palmerston victory, the result of the 1857 election was a defeat for the Tories who had yet to be forgiven by the country, Disraeli reflected, for 'shrinking from responsibility in the spring of 1855'.[118]

Palmerston and his ministers on the whole preferred a superficial reading of the election as the endorsement of a statesman 'in the heyday of his popularity'.[119] Granville, for example, thought the result was based entirely on Palmerston's appeal and demonstrated that the 'whole country in England and Scotland is Palmerstonian'.[120] Argyll wrote later that 'our foes were scattered like chaff before the wind, and the peace party and the Manchester party were wiped out of the House of Commons'.[121] For the most part, Palmerston's biographers have agreed with these judgements.[122] Nevertheless, Palmerston still possessed a powerful ability to manipulate the narrative of politics through the press. To the majority of electors the election may indeed have turned on local issues, but newspapers did not give voice to those concerns. During the election, Palmerston had been able to exercise considerable influence in his own favour through *The Times* and, by extension, through the varied ranks of the regional press which frequently took a lead from that paper. In this way, complained Richard Cobden, Palmerston had '*made greater use of that means of creating an artificial public opinion than any minister since the time of*

Bolingbroke'.[123] This manipulation of the national (that is, London) press helped generate what has been described as a 'Palmerston mania' throughout much of the country and in an election that should have served up rich pickings for the peace interest (if this really was about the government's handling of the war) the journalistic bias was overwhelmingly Palmerstonian. Cobden had early on in the campaign urged 'the peace people to send lecturers as soon as possible into the *boroughs* to lay before the constituencies the real merits of the Chinese question. – Think of this. – *Palmerston will die hard*', but there is little evidence of such efforts having had much impact.[124] As the metropolitan press lauded what it took to be patriotic Palmerstonian bellicosity, peace campaigners such as Cobden were derided for their willingness, as *Punch* put it, 'To make old England's colours lie/In degradation low, boys'.[125] Cobden had been trying to use the recently established *Morning Star* throughout the parliamentary debates to stimulate extra-parliamentary feeling, but to little effect.[126] Although in January Cobden had thought he perceived 'some sign of a conscience in the newspapers upon this Canton outrage, & it is pleasant to see the Times draw in its horns after having backed up as usual the atrocity',[127] these sentiments had seemingly evaporated by March. Only the more radical journals such as *Reynold's Newspaper* sought to attack Palmerstonian 'stupidity' and 'brutishness', but these critiques failed to make much impression on the wider discussion of the election and seemed out of tune with public opinion as refracted through the lens of the larger papers.[128] Malmesbury complained that Palmerston had exploited the fact that his opponents could not answer him in Parliament to distort treatment of the China debate through the press (where, presumably, though he attempted to answer Palmerston through this medium, Malmesbury knew he was dealing with a more sophisticated handler of newspapers). Palmerston replied that he had simply 'used a right which I do not deem myself deprived of by my official position', and in giving vent to his opinions in public had, he said, 'nothing to retract or to qualify'.[129]

In the wake of an election result that generated a clear non-Conservative majority and a ringing endorsement of the Prime Minister personally, ministers returned to Westminster in April 1857 confident of a smoother parliamentary ride. Yet almost immediately the government was thrust afresh into a crisis that originated again, geographically, a long way from Britain, though this time politically and constitutionally much closer to home, in India. It is striking that the subject of the British Empire rarely figured prominently in Palmerston's world view, unless and except where imperial issues impacted on Britain's influence as a great power; he lacked, as Douglas Peers puts it, 'an intellectually robust philosophy of empire and its responsibilities', efforts to suppress the slave trade excepted.[130] (Free) trade remained of paramount importance and so long as that appeared to operate smoothly enough, Palmerston demonstrated no particular interest in its mechanisms. Only when conflagrations, such as had recently been witnessed in China, threatened to disrupt British commercial interests did

Palmerston take what might be termed an active interest in imperial matters. So far as Palmerston reflected on imperial questions, he did so within the conventional paradigm of Victorian notions of security and civilisation. India, for example, he described as a territory surrounded by a multitude of potentially hostile powers and interests and a country inhabited by a population that was 'scarcely half civilized' and which it was an important British duty to improve by education, justice, industry and prosperity. The task of the British Governor-General was made all the more difficult, he thought, by the 'religious prejudices' of Hindus and Muslims that posed 'obstacles to the progress of European civilization'. Significantly, these notes on India were made only in response to difficulties in the 1830s and 1840s in Afghanistan and were part of a wider commentary on the problems faced by Lord Auckland as Governor-General between 1836 and 1842. India, and the Empire more generally, engaged Palmerston's interest only when he perceived that it affected Britain's international security or generated domestic political problems.[131] At all other times, as it has been suggested, Palmerston was no doubt happy not to encourage too much reflection on British policy in India for fear that such attention would reawaken debates about policy in neighbouring regions such as Afghanistan, Persia and China.[132]

It was not until late June that news of uprisings in India reached Britain and by then the rebellion was already more than a month and a half old. A new type of cartridge had been supplied to soldiers which, in the course of use, had to be bitten. The cartridges, however, were greased with a fat that was believed to be from pigs and cows and the demand that Indian soldiers use them was rapidly interpreted as a deliberate assault by the British on the Hindu and Muslim religions. In early May eighty-five Indian soldiers in Meerut refused to use the new cartridges and were swiftly court-martialled and sentenced to ten years' imprisonment. Simmering unrest which had seen regular incendiary protests now grew into open revolt, 'in all its unsuspected strength', as a report in The Times put it, and on 10 May soldiers at Meerut killed British officers, liberated their colleagues, and marched on Delhi. News of the uprising spread rapidly through northern India and within a month Delhi had been taken and Cawnpore was besieged; by the time this news reached London, Cawnpore had been surrendered by the British and four days later the city of Lucknow was under siege. Accounts published in the British press stressed the violence of the uprising: in Meerut, 'every English man, woman, or child, that fell in the way of the mutineers was pitilessly massacred', reported The Times and these 'bloody scenes' were repeated, it said, in Delhi, where the 'indiscriminate massacre' was conducted 'remorseless[ly]'. The very survival of British imperial rule in India was at stake and The Times called for 'action – sharp, stern, and decisive'.[133] In Britain these events were regarded as a mutiny; in India as something akin to a war of independence.

As news of the 'mutiny' reached Britain in the summer of 1857, however, Palmerston played down the gravity of the situation. Many colleagues found the Prime Minister's almost casual attitude trying, but although Palmerston acknowledged that matters required attention he did not see it as a crisis. In private he was more candid, though still measured: the 'last accounts from India are most distressing quite sickening as to the numbers of people including women & children who have been the victims of these savage barbarians', he wrote in a letter to Emily at the end of August. Britain must continue, therefore, to send troops, he said, not only to put down the rebellion but also because recent (unsubstantiated) reports suggested that the rebels were in receipt of Russian financial and political assistance.[134] Yet despite the apparent sense of moral outrage and fear of Russian intrigue (the latter an exaggerated fear), little government time was devoted to India until the autumn and winter. Then, predictably, the Cabinet's interest was driven by the economic consequences of imperial instability. In October and November the Chancellor of the Exchequer, Lewis, wrote a number of letters to Palmerston highlighting the detrimental effects external instability was having on the domestic economy and finances. The combined effects of recent events in India and American and French financial speculations had, he said, put 'pressure upon our money market greater than has occurred at any time since the formation of your government'.[135] The impending crisis looked likely to be worse than anything seen since 1847, Lewis warned, and though the roots of the problem lay in the economic crash in America, events in India were exacerbating its effects.[136] Banks across the country were on the verge of collapse, he said, and the Bank of England had not the resources to bail them all out.[137] Although government subsidies to the Indian government had been 'hitherto trifling' and the government remained able to offer a temporary credit facility of £500,000 to the East India Company, Lewis's letters conveyed a genuine anxiety about the country's ability to remain financially stable and secure.[138] It was this concern about the vulnerability of British finances in a turbulent international context that drove the Cabinet to address the question of Indian government more than any great interest in the moral welfare of the Indian population. This was always, for Palmerston and his government, a question to be debated and resolved in London on British terms.

Resolving the tensions in imperial government meant a fundamental shift in the way that power was exercised. At the beginning of October Palmerston announced his decision that the government of India by the East India Company must be terminated, a view that had been encouraged by ministerial colleagues.[139] Even those ministers who remained sceptical, among whose ranks was the Foreign Secretary Clarendon, acknowledged that though they disliked dismantling the Company, the existing state of things could not be sustained.[140] The decision to abolish the Company was finally taken in a Cabinet committee on 25 November,[141] and by mid-December a plan for the government of India to replace the East India Company had been drawn up. 'I think it will do very well,' wrote Palmerston, 'and every body is coming round to a conviction that the Company cannot be maintained.'[142] By 17 December Palmerston had drafted the heads of agreement that would abolish the East India Company and place Indian government under the direct authority of the crown, with a president and council 'to be established as part of the executive and responsible government of this country'. This was also to include most military departments, while financial matters, though managed in India, were to be subject to scrutiny by the Westminster Parliament (as, indeed, had been the case previously).[143] The Company's directors, while not overtly hostile to the plan (they took it 'more in sorrow than in anger')[144] did tell Lewis when he met them that they thought their record not a bad one.[145] When the Company presented a petition in the new year ('an able & skilfully composed document'), however, raising questions about the proposed changes, Lewis thought that pushing through such vast alterations to the system of imperial government so rapidly risked the government's good standing with the public. The petition, he said, had persuaded many in Britain that a 'more purely English' system of government, and one 'more adverse to the natives' would make putting down the rebellion more difficult. More than this, however, Lewis feared that so long as the details of the proposed changes remained unpublished, allegations that the new plan was simply a means by which to transfer patronage in India from the middle classes to the aristocracy weakened the government on a number of fronts. The plan's enemies, he said, were 'sure not to spare the black paint in their picture'. Sensing that politicians sitting on the opposition benches were looking for ways to use this as another stick with which to beat the government, Lewis urged Palmerston to bide his time and ascertain the true level of backbench support before presenting an 'urgent' case on which victory was uncertain.[146] Palmerston, however, insisted that the process must be kept moving forward; above all Britain needed to maintain its authority in India and this meant that power must be transferred. Even if his concerns about Russian activity in India in the summer of 1857 were unfounded, Palmerston was keen not to show a weak hand to Russia in playing the 'great game' in Asia and wanted to use this as an occasion to underline Britain's continued strong presence in the region. In an immediate reply to Lewis he wrote: 'The settlement of India means the total extinction of the revolt; that must be effected chiefly by military means and by the moral impression to be produced on the people of India, the military means can best be wielded by the Queen's government, and the moral impression will best be created by the Queen's name.' Any stalling would be for party political advantage, not to resolve the issues at stake, he maintained.[147]

Whatever doubts might have been entertained about the popular reception of the government's proposals, within Parliament the mood was in the ministry's favour, though even members of the Cabinet were surprised by the size of the majority that supported them when the House divided on 18 February.[148] Events, however, were again to define the government's fortunes. On the evening of the government's victory over the India Bill, Sir Richard Bethell, the Attorney-General, said to Palmerston that like the Roman consuls he ought, in moments of triumph, to have someone to remind him that he 'was as a minister mortal'. As Palmerston noted in his diary: 'The result of the next night shewed that no such reminder was needed.'[149]

The defeat on 19 February was inflicted on Palmerston's government for its perceived willingness to submit to French dictation at a time when France's pacific intentions could not, some felt, be taken for granted. On 14 January an attempt had been made on the lives of the Emperor and Empress of France as they drove to the Opera in Paris. Although Napoleon and Eugénie escaped serious injury, the bombs that had been thrown at their carriage did kill twenty bystanders. When it was discovered that one of the perpetrators, Felice Orsini, an Italian republican, had links with the Italian refugee community in London, and that the bombs used in the attack had been made in England, the French government was outraged that a supposed friendly neighbour was, as it saw it, sheltering assassins. In a letter to the French ambassador in London, Persigny, the French Foreign Minister, Walewski, presented strong demands for British action that would avert 'a repetition of such guilty enterprises by affording us a guarantee of security which no state can refuse to a neighbouring state, and which we are authorized to expect from an ally'. Although the British government made no official reply to Walewski, the Cabinet did acknowledge the legitimacy of the request.[150]

On 23 January Palmerston produced a lengthy memorandum which he circulated to members of the Cabinet. The implications of the assassination attempt were clear: 'The late atrocious crime committed at Paris by Italians who had been for some time refugees in England has created throughout France the most violent resentment against England,' he wrote, 'and has spread throughout Europe an opinion about England derogatory to our national character. We are represented and deemed the deliberate and intentional protectors of revolutionists and assassins pretending to shield our selves under constitutional difficulties, but in truth actuated by a base desire to reduce other countries to confusion & anarchy under a notion that our own prosperity and relative power would thereby be increased.' Even if these were, as Palmerston put it, the opinions of 'the ignorant and vulgar', they were 'perfectly natural' and 'would have been ours in as great a degree' had the situation been reversed (though he also felt that a persistent resentment about 1815 continued to animate French opinion). As a 'remedy', Palmerston proposed a series of new measures: the government was to have the right, for the next five years, to expel by order of a Secretary of State any foreigner suspected of plotting against a foreign power or its ruler and this expulsion would then be subject to (secret) parliamentary scrutiny. As a quid pro quo, Palmerston proposed requiring of the French government that it 'leave off' sending disruptive elements in French society to Britain; such undesirables could instead, he suggested, 'be sent . . . to the United States as easily as to England the only difference being that the longer passage would be a little more expensive.'[151]

At best the Cabinet was divided over Palmerston's proposals. Clarendon and Granville were the most enthusiastic supporters of the measure, but their enthusiasm was muted: both agreed that something had to be done to preserve Britain's reputation abroad, but, as Clarendon pointed out, it was doubtful whether these new powers would have been effective against Orsini had they been in place earlier.[152] Others, who gave general backing to the argument that the government needed to do something to avoid being seen as 'protecting a workshop of assassins', worried that Palmerston's measures would cause embarrassments – where, asked Stanley of Alderley, would the government draw the line between freedom of expression and 'actual conspiracies'? – while arbitrary expulsions of refugees would weaken Britain's claim to be regarded as a tolerant power.[153] The rest of the Cabinet were overtly hostile to the plan. The mechanism was cumbersome – how, wondered Lewis, could a minister execute these powers knowing that he would then have to face parliamentary sanction? – but also faulty in principle: 'In all previous Alien Acts the object has been to protect ourselves against foreigners who might promote sedition among our own people. No alien act was ever intended to protect a foreign govt.'[154] Labouchere agreed: the measure would be ineffectual, dishonourable and 'odious to the people of this country'.[155] In passing legislation that it would be impossible to act upon, Britain would simply open itself to more virulent criticism by disappointed foreign powers, argued the Lord Chancellor Cranworth.[156] If ministers were hesitant, however, they knew they must offer some response and at the end of January, a week after having first discussed Palmerston's paper, the Cabinet agreed, as Lewis recorded, 'to bring in a Bill making it a felony instead of a misdemeanour to conspire against the person of a foreign sovereign'.[157] It took a further four days of argument to finalise the terms of the bill they would present to Parliament.[158]

The opening exchanges in the debate in the House of Commons seemed to go in the government's favour. Lord John Russell's attempt to make this an issue of Liberal discord was ineffective and Palmerston and Sir George Grey, the Home Secretary, were thought to have had the upper hand. The first reading of the bill was secured with a majority of 200. As the debates wore on and the bill came up for a second reading, however, the result seemed less certain. Between the first and second readings, news reached Britain that addresses by the French army to Napoleon III had been framed in terms that could be perceived as threatening to Britain. Although not official French policy, it unnerved many British MPs to read in the French newspapers that some members of the French military viewed Britain as a sanctuary for assassins and were arguing that 'the infamous haunt in which such infernal machinations were planned should be destroyed forever'.[159] As Lewis recorded in his journal on 19 February: 'The feeling of the House was hostile, & there was a prevalent impression that the honour of the country had not been adequately sustained.' When Milner Gibson introduced an amendment criticising the government for the way it had handled its communications with France over the matter, Derbyites and Peelites combined to defeat the government by nineteen votes. 'There was', said Lewis, 'little expectation of this result on either side',[160] but, observed Palmerston, 'the temper of the House' was 'adverse',[161] and yet again the government had suffered a defeat over its handling of a foreign crisis not of its own making, by a margin very similar to that of a year earlier, and the conclusion drawn was the same. On 20 February Palmerston consulted the Cabinet and found no appetite to fight on as a government. Late in the afternoon Palmerston went to the Palace and tendered his resignation, which the Queen accepted reluctantly.[162] Lewis dined with the Queen and Prince the following evening and found that they 'evidently both regretted' the resignation, but they also pointed to 'the declining energy & increasing unfitness of Ld Palmerston'. Lewis believed that the change of government – Palmerston was replaced by Derby – was 'a matter of sincere regret to the Queen and Prince' but also thought the country unhappy with the result. Although the late government had lost ground for its 'want of *spirit* (as it is called) in our conduct towards France in reference to the treatment of refugees', Lewis thought this only temporary: 'this feeling is superficial & limited;' he noted, 'it does not extend to the general character & conduct of the govt & with this exception I believe that we possessed the general confidence of the country'.[163]

Palmerston took the setback with apparent equanimity. 'Well here are the ups and downs of public and parliamentary life, a majority of 145 one night for the government and the next a majority of 19 against the government,' he wrote to Emily.

> The way it happened was that many of our friends relying on the majority of 200 for bringing in the Conspiracy Bill, and the majority of 145 on Thursday night took leave of absence and went into the country for Friday Saturday & Sunday. The Derbyites on the contrary came to an understanding with Milner Gibson the Radicals & the Peelites and gathered together their forces to take us by surprize. Added to this a considerable amount of angry feeling had been got up in the House and the country about the pretended dictation of the French government, and the want of sufficient energy on the part of the government shewn by not answering Walewskys dispatch. Milner Gibson made a speech which had great effect upon a House prepared to vote with him, and Gladstone's speech was also a dextrous appeal to popular passions we had clearly the best of the argument, but they got the best of the vote.[164]

Many of Palmerston's opponents thought this the end of Palmerston's political career. Writing to Guizot, Lord Aberdeen said that the resignation of the government had taken the political world by surprise, but, he continued, 'the fall of Lord Palmerston has been for some time imminent, notwithstanding his great majorities'. Palmerston's long-proclaimed popularity had been 'without any solid foundation' and had now disappeared. It was 'whimsical', thought Aberdeen, 'that the man who for so many years had reproached me for unworthy concessions to foreign powers, should have been overthrown in consequence of a similar accusation'. As he speculated on future ministerial arrangements, Palmerston's name was conspicuous by its absence from Aberdeen's calculations.[165] Significantly, it is said that Tiverton, Palmerston's own constituency, was the only place that sent a memorial of support for Palmerston's position.[166] It seemed that the 'people's minister' had lost much of his former popular backing.

On some levels, Palmerston welcomed a respite from official labour. Lewis found him in 'good spirits' only days after announcing the resignation.[167] The liberal forces in Parliament were battered and fractious and some breathing space to regroup was to be welcomed. The previous three years had also been demanding ones personally and, as many at the time observed, Palmerston was starting to look jaded. His health was increasingly poor and he suffered in particular more frequent attacks of gout. At the end of 1857, Palmerston inserted a note at the back of his diary in which he was unusually candid about his physical condition:

> I had a good deal of ill health this year. I had in Sept 1856 a blow on my right shin by an office box falling on it. This being neglected became a wound. In January of this year I had gout at Broadlands, & then soriasis [sic] on the wounded leg. These two hung about me till far on in the spring. In October at Broadlands I had an attack of shingles which lasted more or less till Christmas, and at first was very painful and depressing.

As he noted, 'these ailments never prevented me from business as usual', and he had only missed two days in the House of Commons during the late session, but Palmerston was becoming more aware of his frailties.[168] Within his family circle these had not been easy years either. Lady Palmerston had been unwell during the summer of 1857 and although not a serious illness, it had evidently caused some consternation within the family.[169] The year before, in 1856, Palmerston had lost his brother William and the blow was a serious one. It left Palmerston, the eldest of the Temple children, now the last surviving of them: Mary had died at the age of only two while Elizabeth had died in 1837 and Frances the year after. Palmerston had been close to all of his adult siblings but with William, whether by virtue of simple longevity or because they both lived much of their lives in the diplomatic world, the bond always seemed closest. By the summer of 1856, William's health was failing and Palmerston urged him to leave Naples during the hot weather and place himself under the care of his physician. William set off for London at the end of July and arrived in early August to take up rooms in a hotel which Palmerston had arranged for him. Palmerston was reassured that his brother had been able to make the journey in such short time but when he consulted William's doctor, Roskelli, on 4 August he found that Roskelli was 'very uneasy' about his patient. Palmerston was evidently shaken and placed hopes in the ability of his own doctor, William Ferguson, to treat what Palmerston had diagnosed as 'a derangement of the liver, and an affection of the mucous membrane'. Less than three weeks later, however, on 24 July, William died.[170] The 'breaking of ties that began with one's earliest childhood must always cause a bitter pang', Palmerston wrote to Emily, 'but to say the truth, I have never since my brother's return indulged any but the most momentary hope that there could be a possibility of recovery, and it has been a great affliction to witness his distress and discomfort, which however did not amount to absolute pain'.[171] William's collection of antiquities was donated to the British Museum; his shares in Welsh Slate were now placed in trust for the daughters of Laurence and Elizabeth Sulivan, and Palmerston henceforth administered that income on their behalf along with his own investment. The remainder of William's estate, valued in the region of £35,000, seems to have passed to Palmerston.[172]

It had taken a number of years but by mid-century Palmerston's rackety finances had been put in order and the inheritance from William was but an augmentation to an increasingly comfortable position. It is evident from his estate business in Hampshire that Palmerston felt financially secure. In October 1858 he bought a public house, The Fox, near Broadlands, for £435 and in the same month he exchanged some property with Winchester College which enlarged his estate holdings around Romsey. The following summer, in June 1859, he bought Moor Court Farm for £20,000.[173] These transactions suggest Palmerston was consolidating his position as landlord for social as much as economic gain. It was his investments in Wales and, to some extent, Ireland that generated the larger profits on which this security rested. It was no doubt with this in mind that Palmerston took advantage of his retirement from office in 1858 to reacquaint himself with these areas.

At the beginning of August Palmerston left London to visit Wales, and then the west coast of Ireland. Writing to Emily he observed that 'It was amusing to trace in the figures & faces & doings of the people on the platforms the transition I was making through the country, from the civilized company at Euston Sq. to the bustling & sharp faced people in the manufacturing districts to the broad platter faced & pot bellied ale sodden men and women too in North Wales'.[174] There was, evidently, an English bias to Palmerston's Englishness. Yet he remained a British figure measured by his material interests. North Wales, he thought, 'very beautiful to drive through', but declared he 'should hate to live in it and be shut up in a deep valley'. From a commercial point of view he found everything equally satisfactory. At Porthmadog he visited 'our port and wharf' which provided 'very satisfactory' shipping facilities for the nearby Welsh Slate Company quarries at Tan y Bwlch and that evening talked 'slate at a great rate' over dinner with his local agents.[175] The quarries themselves were now on a sound footing and Palmerston, having spent five hours one afternoon inspecting the site above and below ground in the company of the managers, Messrs Williams and Chessie (who he thought managed the business 'exceedingly well'),[176] wrote an enthusiastic report to Emily:

> We found the workings carried on in a very judicious manner. We have about 300 workmen, which is a far less number in proportion to the work done, than the numbers employed by Pennant & Assheton Smith [owners of another local quarry], and owing to our economical system of management, and to the better quality of our slate, we make a profit of 20 shillings a ton upon the slate we sell while their profit is only about ten shillings a ton but then they beat us immensely in the quantity they make and sell. However I have good right to rejoice at having entered into this speculation for my share in it gives me between seven & eight thousand a year, besides from three to four hundred a year made over to each of my three nieces and I see no reason to fear that this profit will not continue the same during the remaining twenty years of our lease; while there is every chance of a renewal of the lease for twenty years more, with a fair prospect of equal profit during that time. My shares in this quarry will therefore pay off all the mortgages on my landed property, and leave moreover a good income to those who come after us after freeing the income of my landed property from the annual charges of the interest of the mortgages.[177]

The bequest of William's four Welsh Slate shares to the Sulivan girls was, therefore, a valuable one. Although the investment had looked questionable when it was made in 1825, the quarries were now yielding handsome profits as Palmerston intimated to Emily. Between April 1857 and December 1864, the period for which there is a surviving record of Palmerston's income from his Welsh Slate investment, the dividend per share never fell below £70, and in July 1860 it reached a peak of £200, generating an annual income on his twenty-four shares of between £7,200 and almost £13,500. In total Palmerston received £78,480 from these shares during this eight-year period, an average of almost £10,000 per annum, and although an imperfect snapshot of his financial condition, this does point to Palmerston's much greater solvency in later life.[178]

Having found all well in Wales, Palmerston travelled on to Ireland, reaching the west coast by 9 August. Here, too, he saw returns on his earlier investments. From Cliffony he described for Emily the changed face of the estate:

> I rode today all over these 1,000 Irish acres which when I first came here were like the sandy deserts of Africa, with the exception of the heat, and are

now almost all green, some parts covered with a strong sward of grass others pretty well covered with bent and a mixture of grass. It was a mighty operation to plant 1,000 Irish acres, nearly 1,300 English acres by dibbling each plant in by hand as you would plant cabbages in a small kitchen garden, and it has taken many long years to produce the highly satisfactory result which I witnessed today satisfactory not only to the eye of the beholder, but to the pocket of the landlord, for these sand hills that were now feed a great number of cattle which pay me 35 shillings a head for permission to graze, and grown as the grass & bent now are, the grazing of the cattle is good for the grass. I have had a great many petitions, but nothing to compare with those I used to have. The lands being squared and every man having been obliged to build his house (of course with assistance from me) on his own holding, & every holding having access to a road without interference with any other holding, almost all causes of quarrel have disappeared, except those which produce family squabbles.

As he continued, the revenue generated by rents had increased from a figure of £4,467 in 1824 to £7,370 in 1857. While some of this increase was due to the expiration of old leases which could then be renewed on more profitable terms, Palmerston estimated that at least half of the increase in rental income was attributable to the improvements he had financed over the years such as new road building, and to more continued squaring of rentable plots.[179]

Palmerston's interest in Ireland remained essentially an economic one. Sectarian tensions he had only ever regarded as matters to be treated in social and not theological terms, though these differences remained one of the chief reasons why Palmerston thought Ireland deserved special treatment within the structure of government.[180] In the late 1850s – even though in diplomatic terms the temporal power of the Pope remained controversial – Palmerston viewed the passions aroused by this in Ireland as something to be settled locally, and then ignored. When Catholic priests in Ireland began gathering in late 1859, for example, to protest against what they saw as hostile treatment of the Pope, Palmerston responded by advising George Cornewall Lewis that they should be allowed to make their 'violent speeches against the oppressors of the Pope' and should be permitted to send loyal addresses to Rome. 'They will only make themselves more and more ridiculous, and will more and more widen the breach which is beginning to open between the priests & the laity of the Irish Catholics,' he wrote. 'The fate of the Pope will be decided in the Congress [to confirm the Villafranca agreement between Austria and France], and the divisions of the Congress will in no degree be influenced by the ravings & rantings of Irish demagogues. It is a good thing to let men's passions evaporate in speeches, unless what they say should be so treasonable that respect for our institutions would make it the duty of a government not to allow what is said to pass by unnoticed.'[181]

Palmerston had never been, it has often been noticed, a particularly religious or pious figure.[182] Shaftesbury's comments that Palmerston did 'not know, in theology, Moses from Sydney Smith' and that 'as for the wants, the feelings, the views, the hopes and fears, of the country, and particularly the religious part of it, they are as strange to him as the interior of Japan', have long been taken as evidence, from someone who should have known, that Palmerston took no real account of religious feeling. It might have been true that the vicar of Romsey was the only clergyman with whom Palmerston spoke regularly, and even then not all that often, but it is misleading to take Shaftesbury at his oft-quoted word.[183] Shaftesbury himself, a year after writing this criticism, noted that Palmerston had 'yielded, in graceful manner, to the religious feelings of the country'.[184] Clearly Palmerston's religious sensibilities were not to be abruptly dismissed. Palmerston's interest in religion was real and sincere, but it was also pragmatic: he was not interested in the finer points of theology and though himself, broadly, Anglican, he entertained no hostility to other denominations on doctrinal grounds. His conception of religion was always framed by a conviction that faith should be a harmonising not fracturing agent in society. Thus he was, as John Wolffe concluded, anti-clerical but not anti-religious.[185] Yet the perception that religious policy was a Palmerstonian blind spot has encouraged an emphasis in many accounts on the role of Lord Shaftesbury – one of the Victorian period's more devout figures and Palmerston's son-in-law – suggesting that he had a significant, defining, influence on Palmerston's handling of religious matters during his premiership. Given the unusually high number of ecclesiastical appointments that it fell to Palmerston to make during his two premierships between 1855 and 1865, Shaftesbury's unofficial position as his adviser on these matters has been elevated to that of 'the bishop-maker' in many traditional accounts.[186] Palmerston did rely on Shaftesbury's counsel – only one episcopal appointment was made by him without consulting his son-in-law[187] – but Palmerston was not, as some narratives might imply, a puppet dancing to Shaftesbury's evangelical tune. The appointment of William Thomson to the bishopric of York in 1862, indeed, was made in spite of Shaftesbury's declared preference for Samuel Waldegrave.[188]

Long experience of the divisive and inflammatory potential of religious differences in both foreign affairs and closer to home (notably in Ireland) had instilled in Palmerston a predilection for guiding religious policy along lines best designed to promote social harmony. He preferred to search for common denominators rather than attempt to impose (potentially disruptive) ideological conformity. It was not the role of government, Palmerston maintained, to decide religious policy, except where religious questions impacted on matters of social order. He approached his responsibility to make clerical appointments, therefore, as 'his *political* duty' and is said to have 'disclaimed altogether any religious duty' in this regard.[189] If religion could be used to influence or guide opinion, it was to be supported, thought Palmerston, because it could thereby achieve worthwhile socio-political not spiritual ends.

Palmerston, as he had demonstrated on his Irish estates, saw tolerance not only as a critical feature of any religious policy, but also as one which meshed neatly with his perception of national identity: even if the rhetoric in which that was usually couched was of Protestant providentialism, just as important were the adjectives such as 'liberal' and 'benevolent' which often went with it. Palmerston made his position clear very early on in his premiership. Speaking in March 1855 on the subject of education in Scotland, he argued that while it was important to respect denominational differences, it was 'very desirable' that children should not 'be brought up in religious antagonism to each other'.[190] Again, with respect to Ireland, Palmerston opposed plans to repeal the grant awarded to support the Catholic colleges at Maynooth, which he had supported when Peel proposed increasing the grant in 1845. He had no patience with the arguments of High Church Protestantism that this would weaken the Established Church (and presumably therefore also the fabric of society). Protestants, he told Parliament, 'do not, in any degree, sacrifice their own principles, or act in treachery to the religion they profess, by affording to the priesthood of a large portion of their fellow-countrymen the means of an education at home, thus imparting in them . . . feelings of attachment to their country'.[191] It is significant that these two examples come from non-English parts of the United Kingdom and underline Palmerston's desire to achieve some measure of national harmony, in which project religion could be an important contributory factor.

Between 1855 and 1865 Palmerston made twenty-five appointments to bishoprics or archbishoprics and a further ten to deaneries. It was an unprecedented number to fall to one minister to manage.[192] It is through these appointments that Palmerston's attitude to religion – and to the further promotion of his desire for cross-class cohesion – can be assessed. Palmerston maintained that in making clerical appointments he was not interested in political gain. His object, as he put it on one occasion, was 'to choose the best man I could find' without reference to political interest.[193] Writing after Palmerston's death, Shaftesbury remembered how Palmerston had 'ever sought for good and proper men' in his episcopal appointments. '"If the man is a good man," he often said, "I don't care what his political opinions are. Certainly I would rather not name a bishop who would make party speeches and attacks on the government in the House of Lords; but short of that, let him do as he likes." "I am a very lucky man," he remarked to me; "luckier than most ministers. I have no sons, grandsons, or nephews to stuff into the Church; and so far as all that is concerned, I can do what I think is right".' As Shaftesbury added, Palmerston's notion of a 'good and proper man' was one 'who would go on well with the nonconformists. He had a very special dislike of every form of clerical assumption.'[194] Palmerston preferred to strengthen the position of the

Church by introducing better leaders rather than by attempting structural reform of the institution. A parliamentary battle with both High Church and Radical interests over the relatively trivial Bishops of London and Durham Resignation Bill in 1856, which would have allowed those two bishops to resign on health grounds, had demonstrated the extent to which attempts to meddle with the constitution of the Church, in however minor and necessary a manner, could be used to sow division in ecclesiastical ranks.[195]

Palmerston had, in Shaftesbury, an adviser whose outlook was broadly compatible with his own.[196] Shaftesbury's suggestions from the evangelical wing did much to support Palmerston's drive for administrative efficiency, but the fact that he and Palmerston shared a preference for 'practical divinity' over 'speculative divinity'[197] does not indicate Shaftesburian dictation of religious policy. Palmerston regarded a bishop's role as essentially a practical one: he looked for men who would be active in their pastoral duties, who would avoid conflict within the Church and, at the same time, not alienate dissenters. Low Churchmen, therefore, were better suited to Palmerston's taste and they were, significantly, much closer to the working- and middle-class mainstream. These men, said Palmerston, were 'more forbearing towards their high church bretheren, and are at peace with the dissenters'. At all events, he wanted 'not to pick out persons of extreme opinions'.[198] When Shaftesbury wrote to Palmerston to recommend certain candidates for vacant deaneries in late 1856, then, the terms he used were precisely those by which Palmerston judged matters himself:

> You must have perceived that the country will, no longer, submit to the old type of bishops. It requires men drawn from the larger parishes; men of great activity & experience; men with the disposition to live on friendly terms with their clergy, & to be very busy in all things relating to the temporal & spiritual interests of the working-classes; men, in fact, who, as bishops, will work with no less vigour and effect, than they did as parish-priests.
>
> Well then, this demand necessarily excludes a 'learned' bench, learned in the sense of profound & minute research, detailed scholarship, and the power of keeping pace with the theological literature of the times. They may have abundant knowledge of all that is primarily necessary, but they must, in fact, subsist on what they acquire before 30 years of age.
>
> Bishops, such as these, will rivet the Church in the affections of the people, will secure the establishment, & promote true & sound religion. But they cannot, from their own resources, contend with the heresies, and difficulties of the day; and manifest all the specialities and precision of learning that would be exhibited by a German professor.
>
> Now, many a learned man, who is fit to be a dean, is wholly unfit to be such a bishop as the country (I thank God for it) requires.

As a dean he may study; keep watch & ward in his library; read & write without interruption; eat deservedly the bread of the Church, and defend her & the truth against all assailants.

Reserve, then, your deaneries (with exceptions of course) for *learned* men, and your bishopricks for *active* men. Be assured that, thus, you will please the country; do honour to yourself; & good to the Church.[199]

In championing (or defending) the position of dissent, Palmerston knew that he was reinforcing the position of those who spoke for what were, in general terms, working-and middle-class interests in the face of a traditionally High Church, upper-class establishment. It was just as important that candidates for clerical posts would not divide opinion outside the Church as that internal discord should be avoided. Thus, when he recommended William Broderick for the deanery of Canterbury in February 1857, Shaftesbury did so on the grounds that Broderick was 'neither high church, nor low, but well regarded by both extremes', whereas other candidates for the position, such as Henry Alford and William Palmer, would neither of them 'be what is called "a popular" appointment, because they are not known to the great mass of the middling classes'.[200] Although appointments made during Palmerston's second premiership displayed a greater sensitivity to High Church interests (not least for reasons of Cabinet harmony, given that Gladstone was in the government), taken as a whole, Palmerston's appointments effectively balanced High and Low Church representation on the episcopal bench and though there were always voices of discontent, this was, as Wolffe argued, a 'logical and sensible recognition of the growing internal pluralism of the church'.[201]

Despite Palmerston's insistence that these appointments were not political, they did, perhaps inevitably, bring some electoral advantage and political gain. 'The first appointments', Shaftesbury wrote in his diary in late 1865, 'were so successful that they influenced elections, turned votes in the House of Commons, and raised around him a strong party in the country'. On visits to the north of England in 1858, according to Shaftesbury, Palmerston had been met everywhere 'with vast favour' which Palmerston had ascribed in part to the appointments he had made in the Church. In Parliament, indeed, many Tory critics, such as Lord Derby, were drawn to accuse Palmerston not only of betraying the Church of England, by promoting an Evangelical-inspired 'false peace and . . . false union' within the Church, but of doing so for party political advantage.[202] This was fair in the sense that Palmerston identified the separation of Church and state as an important symbol of liberal progress and a counterpoint to Tory stasis, but he never really saw this as a truly party political issue. For Palmerston it was liberal progress with a small 'l' and therefore something that stood above party contests. Palmerston wanted a polity in which all religious feeling was accommodated but in which government was not driven by religious interest. When he conceded to concerns (from across the religious spectrum) about Sabbath observance in 1856 and agreed to discontinue recreations which he had championed, such as allowing military bands to play in London parks on Sunday afternoons, he did so on the grounds that the desirability of avoiding religious conflict outweighed the benefits of increased recreational opportunities for the people. The concerts, for example, Palmerston said, had been intended as an 'innocent' diversion for the working classes and were 'no desecration of the Sabbath' but he acquiesced in their termination on the grounds that, 'in a free country like this', 'it was not the duty of the government to run counter to . . . so large a number of the community . . . entitled to respect'.[203] The decision was democratic more than it was religious.

Palmerston's supposed antagonism to Roman Catholicism was evident only when he perceived that sectarian tensions or religious differences were adversely affecting diplomacy or domestic social stability. On no occasion did he retreat from his support for Catholic emancipation in the late 1820s.[204] Reflecting towards the end of his career, Palmerston thought his record in religious matters a positive one. In April 1864 he wrote to the Queen:

> In a body among the ranks of which such diversities of theological opinion exist, as in the ranks of the Church of England, it is perfectly impossible that any choice for dignities can be made which shall be approved by all parties, but Viscount Palmerston has the satisfaction of knowing, by many communications made to him by wholly disinterested persons, and by persons of many different political parties, that his recommendations to your Majesty for ecclesiastical appointments have been generally approved; and it has been acknowledged by all that these recommendations have not been suggested by personal partialities, or what is vulgarly called the spirit of job, but have arisen from an earnest desire to promote the character and interests of the Church.[205]

Accounts of Palmerston's premierships, however, have frequently dismissed his real interest in questions such as ecclesiastical appointments on the grounds that these issues did not resonate with the crude stereotypes of Palmerston's amoral or immoral gunboat diplomacy, and given that traditional narratives have been able to focus on a first premiership dominated by foreign affairs, notably in the Near and Far East, the domestic record of the 1855–58 government has received somewhat meagre attention from Palmerston's biographers. Only recently has it generated a little more interest among historians of Victorian liberalism. Yet when Lord Aberdeen pointed to the irony of Palmerston's fall from favour in February 1858 over a matter of foreign policy, he highlighted a key point about the late government. As Palmerston's ministry lurched from crisis to crisis on the international stage, this obscured the fact that Palmerston himself remained a liberal figure whose inclination, had external events not dictated otherwise, was to focus on a political agenda that spoke of domestic progress and improvement. In his election address to voters in March 1857, for example, having emphasised the importance of settling foreign crises, Palmerston had also stressed his commitment to domestic advancement: 'At home,' he had said, 'our guiding principles will be judicious and well-regulated economy, progressive improvement in all that concerns the welfare of the nation, the continued diffusion of education among the people, and such well-considered reforms as from time to time may be required by changes of circumstances and by the increasing growth of intelligence.'[206]

Palmerston used his first premiership to consolidate the reformist record of his tenure of the Home Office. His government pursued, for example, education reforms that, in reviewing school curricula, sought to place greater emphasis on science, modern languages and mathematics, thereby making the education provided more useful and relevant to the needs of the time. In reforming divorce law in 1857 through the Matrimonial Causes Bill, despite considerable opposition from Gladstone in Parliament, Palmerston – and it was Palmerston who drove the measure through, refusing to prorogue Parliament until it had accepted the bill – made divorce a civil rather than religious question.[207] There was evidence, too, of a more professional and increasingly meritocratic ethos in the execution of public duty. Based on the report of the Northcote Trevelyan investigation of the civil service published in 1854, there was some modest reform of the creaking bureaucratic machine (an institution satirised at about this time in Charles Dickens's description of the workings of the Circumlocution Office[208]) and the civil service was to some extent opened up by the introduction of competitive entry and the establishment, for example, in 1855 of the Civil Service Commission. Palmerston still took a very hierarchical view of society and placed a good deal of emphasis on wealth, personal standing and social distinction as qualifications for public office,[209] but his attitude was softening in line with the more commercial, earned-rather-than-inherited culture of mid-Victorian society. Through the cultivation of an air of disinterested (even professional) government by way of limited use of patronage (limited at least when compared with his predecessors' use of such privilege); and through the introduction to government of a body of more modern politicians, professional and skilled rather than simply high-born, Palmerston effectively weakened the aristocracy's hitherto hegemonic grip on power. His was a government driven by aspirations of efficient administration and if that meant that Palmerston was not a dramatic and highly active reformer, he was, in his careful way, committed nonetheless to moderate change so long as that was safe and likely to last.[210] When W.L. Burn, writing in 1964, dismissed thoughts of labelling the 'age of equipoise' the 'age of Palmerston' he did so because he thought Palmerston lacked 'the sober, serious, conscious thoughtfulness so characteristic of the age he lived into', and because of 'the sense that there was, at the bottom of him, a moral vacuum'.[211] While Burn reflected pretty accurately the prevailing view among many mid-twentieth-century historians, however, he perpetuated a fundamental misinterpretation of Palmerston. Although revisionist suggestions that Palmerston was an advanced reformer who self-consciously shaped Britain for a more democratic future have been criticised for exaggerating his intentions, Palmerston was, and his premierships demonstrate that he was, genuinely interested in liberal progress.[212]

Speaking to audiences in the north of England in November 1856, Palmerston had made quite clear the liberal principles that underpinned his government's outlook. In Liverpool he praised the local civic commitment to education for the working classes, noting that, significantly, no duty was 'more important' or 'more interesting', or 'attended with more permanent and general benefit' than 'the spread of education and the diffusion of information among the lower classes'. Providing working people with such means of improvement enabled them to develop their 'moral and intellectual faculties' and to be raised 'as citizens in the scale of civilization'. Just as private individuals strove for 'progressive improvement' in their own affairs, so too, he said, should the nation. It was, he argued, the role of government to 'endeavour to be perpetually ameliorating those laws and institutions which, being human, cannot be perfect, but which, according to the progress of society and the change of circumstance must be continually in need of emendation and extension'. (It may be worth reflecting that this rhetoric echoed to a significant degree that of Dugald Stewart half a century earlier.) A country that demonstrably promoted the 'intellectual advancement of the country' and 'welfare of all classes' was one that exercised a 'potent influence' in the world, Palmerston observed.[213] He added to this, in Manchester, tributes to the commercial and technological advances that had served Britain well in its international struggles and, in a broader view, underpinned the country's growing prosperity, happiness and influence.[214]

This is evidence of a Palmerstonian commitment to improvement and progress, of a pursuit of progress that cut across social classes and grounds and on which Palmerston should be seen as a sincere liberal reformer. If this was a *mentalité*, or an ethos, more than a prescription for (immediate) action, it is no less significant as a signal of Palmerston's conception of government and approach to its execution. His natural conservatism checked radical change, but his genuine interest in a specific notion of progress is important. Thus, David Steele is partially right in identifying Palmerston as a progressive liberal figure, but his portrait of Palmerston as a democrat remains an overstated one. For one of the most obvious measures of democratic taste, parliamentary reform, Palmerston's appetite remained limited. He continued to regard property as the basic qualification of any claim to enfranchisement and entertained real misgivings about universal suffrage.[215] This was one domestic reform he had worked hard to contain within the Cabinet. While he acknowledged that colleagues and liberal supporters in Parliament were strongly in favour of some proposal for Reform, Palmerston did 'not intend to be forced driven or hustled by friend or foe into any premature declarations or details'.[216]

However, while Palmerston had a clear sense of the shape of a liberal programme, it was not universally shared. So in early 1858 he had been relieved to hand over to Derby the task of marshalling a political faction into a governing majority. Yet, despite the frustrations of trying to mould Whig, Liberal and Radical into some vaguely coherent body, this was not mere political manoeuvring. Palmerston found very rapidly that Derby's government jarred, ideologically, with his own vision of national government and progress. It was entirely in keeping with the Palmerstonian agenda, therefore, that his efforts in the months spent in opposition during 1858 and 1859 were directed above all at reconstituting a genuine liberal presence at Westminster. His critics had been quick to write Palmerston off in the spring of 1858, but a period of rest from government duty and an inspiration to reassert liberal dominance soon revitalised him. When Nassau Senior visited Broadlands in January 1859, for example, in contrast to the widely retailed image of fatigue and failing health he found Palmerston 'in wonderful vigor of mind and body' and he saw 'no symptoms of age, except that he dyes his hair and whiskers'.[217]

Later commentators saw Palmerston's ability to hold the Liberal party together as owing a good deal to the force of his personality which allowed him to paper over many of the ideological cracks.[218] Out of office, however, Palmerston faced several internal party obstacles to maintaining this façade of liberal unity. On one side, Peelites such as Gladstone seemed to place more emphasis on being conservative than on being liberal. Writing to Bright as soon as Derby had been appointed to replace Palmerston in February, Gladstone stressed that for the honour of Parliament and the country, he felt it essential to support the new government as an antidote to Palmerston's late ministry.[219] This Gladstonian hostility to Palmerston did not diminish as the year wore on. Much of it, thought Lewis, dated from the 'inexplicable offence' of the 1857 election, but the 'animosity' ran deeper than that. What was clear to Lewis, writing in October, however, was that the 'pains which he [Gladstone] takes in anonymous writing to support the present govt shews that he wishes them well, & probably contemplates joining them, at some future time'.[220] Manchester School radicalism, voiced in particular by Richard Cobden and John Bright, had long positioned itself in overt opposition to Palmerston and defeats at the election of 1857 had done nothing to draw feeling in this quarter closer to Palmerston either. Yet this branch of radicalism had central place in liberal politics. Charles Wood might have described Bright as 'on the verge of insanity' towards the end of the year,[221] but it was marginalising a significant non-Tory constituency to perpetuate or sustain the division.

More pressing in 1858 was the need to address the gulf that existed between Palmerston and Lord John Russell. Russell remained just as suspicious of Palmerston as ever: he thought Palmerston had, during his late government, subverted national and imperial interests to serve his own vanity and Russell feared, as he put it in January 1858, the new dangers that Palmerston's 'levity and presumption may bring upon us'. Russell's only concern was to make sure that any opposition to Palmerston was reasoned and could not be dismissed as a 'factious combination against him'.[222]

When Palmerston met Lord Granville, George Grey, Charles Wood and George Cornewall Lewis in early March they agreed that the former government must 'be as quiet as possible' and 'avoid all appearance of faction', but also that they must open communications with Russell. Wood was sceptical, but most knew that a simmering tension between the two leading figures in parliamentary liberal circles could only ever be damaging to them all. Russell, as Lewis noted afterwards, 'wishes to set up for himself as leader of the Liberal party in opposition; he is extremely jealous of Palmerston, & much alienated from his former friends. It was agreed that we must do nothing which cd make him suppose that we wished him to surrender his independence, & assume an inferior position with respect to Palmerston, & we parted with the understanding that I shd this week call upon him at Richmond, & in the course of conversation give him to understand that we wished, as far as we could, to act with him, if he did not repudiate us'.[223] On 10 March Lewis met Russell and they discussed how each would respond to the major issues of the coming session. There seemed to be no major disagreements between them on financial questions; likewise both parties were agreed that they should oppose Roebuck's recent motion for the abolition of the Lord Lieutenancy of Ireland unless and until Irish government could be placed under the control of the Home Office. They did not agree over plans for the reform of Indian government – Russell preferring some sort of elected council to be constructed – but it appears neither Lewis nor Russell was willing to press differences here to the extent of dashing all hopes of a future Palmerstonian–Russellite concert. Lewis and Russell parted with an agreement that these discussions should continue regularly and even if there was no imminent reconciliation in prospect, Lewis was gratified by Russell's 'friendly, easy & open' manner.[224] By the end of March Palmerston and Russell had even managed to speak amicably to each other, though as Palmerston remarked of their conversation after a dinner hosted by the Duchess of Sutherland for the express purpose of bringing him together with Russell, 'Johnny' had been 'civil & friendly but wavering'.[225] Although the two sides were now speaking, and in broad agreement on the most general points, they were not yet united over a common liberal agenda. Palmerston, meanwhile, had thrown off his initial willingness to give Derby a run at government and by the end of March was aiming to eject the fledgling ministry. He found its India Bill objectionable and worried about leaving questions of future parliamentary reform in its hands. On these points his erstwhile Cabinet colleagues were in agreement.[226] Russell, too, concurred and Palmerston even began to talk of a 'concert of cooperation with John Russell' that would 'tend to please and unite the Liberal party' at Westminster.[227] Palmerston, however, assumed that he would lead this concert and he underestimated the depth of Russell's antipathy towards him. Russell had, indeed, shared other Liberals' determination to oppose the government's plans for Indian government, and had drafted several resolutions to modify those plans, but he had proposed revisions of the government bill with a view to keeping Derby in power and there were even rumours circulating that he had drafted the amendments in consultation with the government for fear that, should he enter into a common attack alongside Palmerston which unseated the government, 'he shd raise the question of another Palmerston ministry'.[228]

Neither Palmerston nor Russell was willing to make any great concession to the other and any reunion was likely to represent the ascendancy of one over the other rather than a peaceable reconciliation. Thus, as the question of the future government of India remained a prominent issue at Westminster in the spring of 1858, it appeared on the Liberal side that it was becoming a site of internecine warfare more than a debate about how to reform colonial governance. Thomas Milner Gibson, for example, complained that Palmerston was trying to engineer a defeat of the government's plans purely for the purpose of effecting his own return to the premiership.[229] Yet within certain Whig and Liberal circles, some thought this was precisely what Palmerston was being encouraged to do: Sir Thomas Erskine Perry, a moderate Radical MP, lamented the fact that the Liberal interest was insufficiently focused on the issue of India itself, as he observed in mid-April:

> It seems to me that a great many supporters of the late govt are egging Ld Palmerston on to have a trial of strength with Lord John, & the India bill is suggested as the battle ground. Lord Palmerston appears to me to have shown the greatest discretion & tact hitherto in avoiding anything like faction, but if he hears nothing but clamour from his supporters urging him to a particular course it is improbable that he will be able long to resist it. I confess I think any division which should tend to group the Palmerstonians on one side, & Lord John and his friends on the other, would be a great misfortune.[230]

Acting as an intermediary, Lewis thought Russell inclined to be conciliatory,[231] but Palmerston, though he continued to hope for Russell's 'accession to our ranks' (it is significant that the effort would have to be Russell's), was not prepared to welcome him back at any cost. Within Parliament, he explained to Lewis, the Liberal party was all for Russell's return, but outside Parliament 'the great majority of Liberals ... are perpetually warning us against having anything to do with him'. Thus, bringing Russell back would be both a source of strength and of weakness; only because his current focus of attention was on defeating Derby in Parliament did Palmerston think Russell worth accommodating, but even here he feared alienating liberal conservative support.[232] As Wood noted, the long-term survival of Derby's government was uncertain so it was important to gather Liberal forces together; but this must be on a durable foundation, he stressed, and that meant including Russell.[233] Yet despite this heralded convergence of liberal factions, by May it still seemed a long way off. Milner Gibson thought it very possible that the government would fall and Palmerston would attempt to replace it with a coalition of Conservatives and Whigs, leaving Russell outside to lead a Liberal opposition. Palmerston gave no indication that he would pursue such a course, but Gibson was quite right in thinking there was no combination of Palmerston and Russell in sight.[234] As Palmerston's political friends tried to muster potential colleagues for a new government one thing was clear: an overture to Russell 'would be useless'.[235] Russell was, said Nassau Senior in the summer, 'very anti-Palmerstonian' and was planning to return to power at the head of his own administration.[236] Whatever signs there were in private of Palmerston and Russell coming together to create a coherent opposition, in public, in Parliament, they worked apart.[237]

This condition of Liberal fragmentation therefore persisted: neither Palmerston nor Russell (no other figure was a credible leader) could offer a homogenising vision around which all groups could coalesce. As George Cornewall Lewis summarised the situation in early August in his diary:

> Since the resignation of Ld Palmerston's govt, the Liberal party has been in a disorganized state, & the disunion is as great now as it was in March. The personal alienation between Ld Palmerston & Ld J. Russell is diminished, but the real rivalry remains. Graham, Gladstone, & Bright view Ld Palmerston with feelings of the bitterest animosity, chiefly on account of the dissolution & election of 1857. The rank & file of the party think that Ld Palmerston is more Tory than liberal in his tendencies, & they distrust Ld John on account of his conduct to his colleagues, on former occasions; his course moreover in suggesting the mode of proceeding by resolutions which enabled the govt to withdraw their India bill is disapproved by many liberals who were willing to abstain from any active hostility.
>
> Agst [sic] the govt on the whole, the personal jealousies & alienations among the liberal party are such as to deprive it of all compact strength, & to offer a fair prospect of stability to the present govt, if they can satisfy their own supporters, & avoid internal differences.[238]

By the end of 1858 Russell's determination to forge a non-Palmerstonian liberal identity seemed to be underlined by his enthusiasm for new plans for parliamentary reform that were designed, it seemed to Lewis, to underpin a bid for leadership of the party and which Palmerston was not willing to discuss.[239]

In January 1859 George Cornewall Lewis confessed to feeling 'much uneasiness as to the course which Lds Palmerston & J. Russell will take about the

Italian question' when Parliament reconvened.[240] With France and Austria growing increasingly assertive in their claims to influence in Italy a new international crisis threatened further to destabilise British Liberal politics at home. In fact the letters exchanged by Palmerston and Russell over this issue do not suggest that Italy served to exacerbate existing tensions.[241] The issue that did continue to separate them was parliamentary reform. Derby's government put forward a modest proposal for Reform in early 1859 in response to the evident popular demand for further change, a demand that had been whipped up in part by people like John Bright who had been touring the country at the turn of the year stirring up feeling on the question. At the beginning of March Russell announced that he planned to call a meeting of the Liberal party to consider Reform. Palmerston and Russell discussed the grounds on which the government's measure should be opposed and even the terms of an alternative proposal, managing to sketch out a broad platform on which they could agree.[242] However, neither was willing or confident enough to drop his guard and offer the other a chance to claim unequivocally leadership of the Liberal party. When the Reform question was debated in Parliament, therefore, Palmerston was adamant that Russell should not be able to use the issue, however much they were agreed on their opposition to Derby's proposals, to try to turn the government out; Palmerston was not yet convinced that if a new Prime Minister was sought in the spring of 1859 he would automatically be chosen for that role over Russell.[243] This is perhaps evident in Lady Palmerston's efforts to link a 'Palmerstonian' identity to a 'liberal' one; in March 1859 there was 'really a new state of things' in political life, she said, and she worried that the 'mixed party on our side' may see 'blue & orange fuse into some other colour or sink into white'.[244]

By the same token, it was clear that Derby's government could disintegrate at any moment. Palmerston thought the government's leaders had 'taken a great liking for office' and would cling on for as long as they could, but as Aberdeen admitted in April, the government 'cannot be considered in an efficient state'.[245] Palmerston's sparring with Russell over party leadership risked appearing irresponsible if the Conservatives were indeed on the verge of collapse. Charles Wood thought there was no point trying to overturn the government so long as the Liberals remained 'broken up into fragments with more of mutual repulsion than tendency to approximate'.[246]

In May there was finally some evidence of Palmerston and Russell looking earnestly for a common *modus vivendi* and even *modus operandi*. While they could agree that they did not like Derby's plan for Reform, any attempt to devise a detailed scheme of their own would only aggravate tensions between them. Palmerston, for his part, maintained that there was 'no feeling in favor of an extensive Reform, either among the constituencies or the working classes' and he suggested that a number of Liberals in borough seats would actually have lost their places at the last election had they come out in favour of a reduction in the franchise qualification.[247] It was obvious to observers that Palmerston and Russell would not find an accommodation on these grounds and the choice still seemed to be between the two men.[248] For this reason Palmerston was reluctant to force the matter to a choice. Thus, in challenging the government he suggested to Russell, via Lewis as intermediary, that in attacking Derby they should avoid direct assaults on issues of Reform or foreign policy, but focus instead on a straightforward vote of no confidence. To this Russell assented.[249] By the end of May they had agreed that in any future change of government and in the interests of Liberal harmony they would work together and serve in the other's Cabinet, leaving the choice, nominally, in the hands of the Queen.[250] They would not agree to work under anyone else, which, significantly, would, for the foreseeable future, keep Liberal politics in the hands of those who were either by background or instinct, or both, Whiggish in their outlook, but this arrangement did overcome the impasse. When Derby's government was defeated over its Reform plans, therefore, the government resigned and called a general election. Palmerston paid Russell a visit on 2 June and proposed summoning a meeting of the Liberal party to consolidate this new unity of purpose and although Russell continued to harbour resentments dating from the split with Palmerston in 1855, he agreed to attend the meeting which was organised for 6 June at Willis's Rooms in St James's, London.[251] At the meeting, Palmerston spoke first, outlining the need to step up to the challenge of replacing Derby's government which had, he insisted, forfeited the confidence of the country. He told the audience of over 270 Liberals that the only 'manly and straightforward course' was to accept the challenge to form a new government. Russell addressed the meeting next and in speaking of the Liberal party laid emphasis on the need for 'the three great sections of that party – the old Whigs, the Peelites, and the advanced Liberals' to be represented in any future Liberal government. Other speakers also took up the theme of recent Liberal discord. John Bright sought to sink 'minor differences' (though before he did so finally could not resist a quick jibe at Palmerstonian foreign policy) and John Roebuck said that he 'felt no confidence in the sudden change which had taken place in the relations between Lord Palmerston and Lord John Russell', but according to Lewis this sniping 'made little impression. Overall the tone of the meeting was conciliatory and constructive and Palmerston's and Russell's public reconciliation seemed to be well received.'[252] Afterwards Palmerston declared the 'result of [the] meeting highly satisfactory'.[253]

At the election held later in March the Liberals were returned with a majority. Contrary to expectations the Queen turned first to Lord Granville to form a government and though he entertained reservations about it, Palmerston agreed he would support Granville if the latter could establish a ministry.[254] However, once it became clear that Granville would not be able to fulfil the commission (not least because, as Clarendon pointed out, it was thought Palmerston would soon try to subvert a Granville ministry),[255] Palmerston was charged with forming his second government. 'It will be one of the great objects of the government so formed,' he told his constituents in Tiverton, 'to preserve for this country the blessings of peace; and to take advantage of any favourable opportunity that may present itself to exert the moral influence of Great Britain to assist in restoring peace to the continent of Europe.'[256]

CHAPTER 12

THE PRIME MINISTER, 1859–1865

As yon agéd oak still grows,
Spreading branches strong and shady,
Autumn's storms and Winter's snows
Do but make its hold more steady;
So in years matur'd and sound,
PALMERSTON! in youth-like health,
Shed thine influence around –
Peace and Plenty, Might and Wealth.

Friend of 'Industry and Art,'
Help of all who do their duty,
To our Op'ning-day impart
Thoughts of joy 'mid scenes of beauty.
Long be thou the People's friend!
Long thy smile their labours cheer!
Till thine own great work shall end,
And thou seek a brighter sphere.

from 'Ode to Viscount Palmerston, K.G., to be sung at the opening
of the Romsey Exhibition' [?April 1862][1]

THAT THE QUEEN turned to Granville before appointing Palmerston, ahead of
Russell, to form a government in the summer of 1859 is itself sufficient
evidence of the fact that Palmerston's return to the premiership was far from
inevitable. The negotiations between Palmerston and Russell during the earlier
part of the year had been important in so far as they had facilitated some sort
of Liberal rapprochement in June, but Palmerston's own position was much
less certain than his conduct indicated. He had been forced from office in
1858, in part, because the public thought he was unduly compliant in his dealings with France. Thus, when in November of that year Palmerston (along
with Clarendon) stayed as a guest of the French Emperor, many thought he
had committed political suicide. The press lambasted him for availing himself
of Napoleon's hospitality at such a moment.[2] The criticism was short-lived, but

it was a reminder to the 'people's minister' that he could not take the people's support for granted.

If Palmerston had successfully negotiated a potentially difficult period in opposition and preserved a position at the forefront of Liberal politics, however, he faced a tricky task in forming a new ministry in June 1859. In 1855 he had at least had the advantage of being able to offer something new; in 1859 his earlier administration was still a recent memory. He had told Argyll in August 1858 that, having been unceremoniously turned out of government, a swift return to office was not likely;[3] the restoration to power a year later, therefore, seemed to represent a pretty rapid (and unanticipated) comeback. Forming a non-Tory, Liberal, government in 1859 was no easy task. Promises and conciliatory gestures had been made at Willis's Rooms, but turning those opposition sentiments into a tangible and meaningful foundation for government required some skill. The only grouping within Parliament with whom Palmerston had made clear he was unwilling to coalesce was Derby's Protectionists. In May, in an attempt to subvert the fragile reunion between Palmerston and Russell, Disraeli had proposed to Palmerston that he join forces with Derby in government, offering by way of inducement control of foreign policy and the opportunity to 'dictate the terms' of any Reform measure. It was a proposal, however, that Disraeli made on the grounds that it would strengthen Conservative government.[4] Palmerston, whose conservatism was only ever of the small 'c' variety, was not disposed to throw up his liberal credentials and perceived ascendancy within Liberal circles for such a reward. Nonetheless, following the 1859 general election, which had left the Conservatives with around 300 seats in the House of Commons, any arrangement that excluded them looked likely to be, as Disraeli observed, a government without a majority (the only candidate capable of drawing together Conservative and Whig members, Disraeli thought, was Lord Stanley).[5] Having ruled out joining Derby and Disraeli, Palmerston needed to attract a diverse range of Liberal members to his government if he was to outnumber the opposition. Russell, of course, had to be accommodated, but so too did the Peelites (and that meant, above all, finding common ground with Gladstone), while the support of Radical MPs would also be necessary, and they had made it clear that they would 'never consent to the Sir W. Molesworth dodge again' (whereby such support had apparently been bought cheaply by the Aberdeen coalition through the appointment of the Radical Molesworth to the government), since, as Bright had told Palmerston, they judged that 'one place in Cabinet was worse than none'.[6] Disraeli thought the task beyond the new Prime Minister: 'the difficulties of Ld Palmerston are so great,' he wrote on 16 June, 'that the new Ministry, instead of being formed on the boasted broad basis, will be merely a refaceimento of the old Palmerston clique. That won't last long, & only can subsist by our support'.[7]

Accommodating Russell, and those Whigs who identified themselves most closely with him, was, comparatively speaking, the most straightforward of Palmerston's tasks. Although he would have preferred to place Clarendon back at the Foreign Office, Russell insisted on the post for himself and Palmerston, who knew that he must have Russell on board, acquiesced. It meant that he lost the ministerial services of his friend and ally Clarendon, but what he gained with the Russellite and Whig accession was, from a political point of view, much more valuable. One of the building blocks of a second Palmerston government was in place. Adding the second and third, the Peelite and Radical, was more difficult and Palmerston was forced to make further concessions to secure their support.

Palmerston had asked George Cornewall Lewis to return to the Exchequer as soon as he began assembling his new Cabinet, but when, later the same day, he discovered that this was the prize Gladstone demanded if he was to join the government, Palmerston withdrew the offer to Lewis, making him instead Home Secretary, and appointed Gladstone as his Chancellor.[8] The rapprochement with Gladstone represented an important turning point in Liberal politics, though there had been signs of a gradual thaw in relations (or revision of attitudes) for a while. Though he continued to distance himself from Palmerston personally, Gladstone had for some months been retreating from a position of outright hostility. 'It was true', he told Lord Aberdeen and Sir James Graham in May 1858, 'I had no broad differences of principle from the party opposite; on the whole perhaps I differed more from Lord Palmerston than from almost any one, and this was more on account of his temper and views of public conduct, than of any political opinions. Nay more, it would be hard to show broad differences of public principle between the government and the bench opposite.' It was largely, he said, a reverence for 'public sentiment' which would be 'shocked' if he joined again with Palmerston that kept them on opposite sides of the House.[9] As a recent Gladstone biographer has pointed out, the only thing separating Palmerston and Gladstone by this time was personality. But with no obvious point of union with the Protectionist Tories, Gladstone was obliged to look more sympathetically at Palmerston's leadership of parliamentary Liberalism if he wanted to play a leading role in political life.[10] The desire to participate in government was evidently a powerful one: 'He must be a very bad minister indeed, who does not do ten times the good to the country when he is in office than he would do when he is out of it,' observed Gladstone.[11]

Gladstone's decision to join Palmerston's government in 1859, therefore, is not altogether anomalous. Palmerston's apparent enthusiasm for Italian independence did much to provide Gladstone with an easy rationale for joining a Liberal ministry, but as the new Chancellor of the Exchequer argued, the alignment was a perfectly natural one: 'I am in real and close harmony of sentiment with the new premier, and the new foreign secretary,' he told told Sir William Heathcote three days after joining the Cabinet.[12] When Gladstone wrote 'It may be better or less bad that war should come *now*, than that the ails of Italy should go on festering and should accumulate more and more. . . . The worst is, that as matters now stand, war may easily pass into European confusion', Donald

Southgate concluded that 'Only the style identifies the writer as Gladstone rather than Palmerston.'[13] Palmerstonian sympathy for Italian unification, or at least opposition to Austrian rule there, no doubt helped – famously Gladstone's return from the Ionian Islands via Italy is supposed to have impressed on him the importance of this cause – but as Gladstone later explained, there was more to his decision to join Palmerston than support for Italy:

> When I took my present office in 1859, I had several negative and several positive reasons for accepting it. Of the first, there were these. There had been differences and collisions, but there were no resentments. I felt myself to be mischievous in an isolated position, outside the regular party organization of parliament. And I was aware of no differences of opinion or tendency likely to disturb the new government. Then on the positive side. I felt sure that in finance there was still much useful work to be done. I was desirous to co-operate in settling the question of the franchise, and failed to anticipate the disaster that it was to undergo. My friends were enlisted, or I knew would enlist: Sir James Graham indeed declining office, but taking his position in the party. And the overwhelming interest and weight of the Italian question, and of our foreign policy in connection with it, joined to my entire mistrust of the former government in relation to it, led me to decide without one moment's hesitation.[14]

With Gladstone in the Cabinet, bringing in other leading Peelites was fairly straightforward. The Duke of Newcastle took the Colonial Office while Sidney Herbert became Secretary for War. Some of Palmerston's friends thought he had compromised too much, however. George Shee, for example, welcomed a Palmerston government but expressed some unease at its composition:

> *Now*, however, your government appears to have been formed, and, rejoicing as I do, at *your* position within it, I may now say that I view the formation with *great* alarm. *John Russell* at the FO, *Gladstone* at the *Exchequer*, and the D of *Somerset* at the *Admy* are *formidable* nominations, pregnant with mischief to the country, and, what is worse, people say that they were *dictated* by the *first* of that triumvirate.
>
> If you have allowed him to assume the power that has been attributed to him, you have I fear much imperilled your own stability and, if so, your only course I think will be to secure a *strong thoroughgoing majority* in your Cabinet, and then to *turn* that *hedgehog* as soon as possible out of your nest. Your own interest and what, to you, will be more important your *country's* interest, requires this at your hands and fervently do I hope that whatever course you may determine to pursue may contribute to the increase of your own fame and the extrication of us all from the complicated difficulties with which we are surrounded.

Palmerston replied that he thought his government was a 'good & strong one that will work well'.[15] It was not Russellite dictation that threatened Palmerston's administration; if anything, the risk came from the multiplicity of voices and competing interests he was bringing together. In addition to Whigs and Peelites, Palmerston also courted erstwhile Radical critics. Thomas Milner Gibson, who had been one of Palmerston's most vehement detractors over the Conspiracy to Murder Bill in 1858, 'handsomely consented to waive all former differences and to become a member of the new cabinet' and, with this apparent evidence of reconciliation, Palmerston hoped to induce Richard Cobden, a more significant potential recruit, to do the same.[16] Palmerston knew that if he could persuade Cobden to join the government he would secure valuable Radical support, but this was never likely to be an easy negotiation. Shaftesbury believed John Bright would make sure Cobden refused, and foresaw only difficulties in Palmerston's bringing in Manchester School politicians, though he agreed that Palmerston must at least be seen to make an offer to them (he thought Bright himself should be approached too), if only as a 'quietus'.[17]

Palmerston opened with an offer at the end of June to make Cobden President of the Board of Trade. Cobden, who received the offer as he disembarked in Liverpool, having just returned from America, professed surprise and also some bewilderment in the face of the diverse but earnest entreaties he received at the same time to accept the post. 'Indeed almost without exception every body, radicals peace men & all, are trying to persuade me to it,' Cobden wrote to his wife. Given his well-known and publicly stated antipathy to Palmerstonian politics Cobden thought everyone had 'gone mad' and that should he accept Palmerston's offer, he would 'ruin' himself and 'ultimately lose the confidence of the very men who are in this moment of excitement urging me to enter his Cabinet'. It would be, he concluded, a 'monstrous course' and he resolved to refuse to join, but by the same token he would, he said, 'give Lord Palmerston's governt all the aid in my power so long as Gibson is in the Cabinet, & if Palmerston keeps out of war & acts decently on the Reform question I don't intend to quarrel with him on trifles'.[18] On reaching London at the beginning of July, Cobden called on Palmerston and explained, candidly, that he must decline on the grounds that, as he told the premier, 'I believed you to be warlike, intermeddling [sic], & quarrelsome, & that your policy was calculated to embroil us with foreign nations; – & at the same time I have expressed a general want of confidence in your domestic politics.' Palmerston tried to rise above personal differences and impress on Cobden the need for, effectively, a national government. If Cobden felt such unease with Palmerstonian policies, argued Palmerston, he could do more to moderate them within the Cabinet, where they were formed, than in Parliament where they were merely presented (it was an interesting admission of the extent to which Palmerston disregarded the House as a factor in the formulation of policy). The offer, said Palmerston, was not made for any other reason than to secure a viable government. 'Recollect,' he told Cobden, 'I don't offer you the seat from any desire of my own to change my colleagues – If left to me, I would of course rather have gone on as before with my old friends. – I offer you the seat because you have a right to it.'[19] Cobden, however, was resolute, though in parting he accepted an invitation to a party hosted by Lady Palmerston the next evening, at which he discovered that a politician who had refused office under Palmerston was considered a 'great monster' and the 'women stared at me, & brought their friend to look at me through their glasses'.[20] Since Cobden had turned down the Board of Trade, Palmerston offered it to Milner Gibson and in a bid to further broaden the basis of his government also appointed C.P. Villiers, another Cobdenite Radical, to the presidency of the Poor Law Board.

Evelyn Ashley maintained that this not only marked the formation of Palmerston's second ministry but, from this point, and for the next 'six years he was accepted by the country as the minister of the nation, and almost occupied a position removed from the chances of party strife'.[21] Ashley's was an optimistic assessment, made, as he admitted, too close to the events to be written with an 'absence of reserve on the part of the historian', but while he overstated the level of popular acceptance of Palmerstonian hegemony at Westminster and elsewhere, there was a growing sense that Palmerston had become, at very nearly seventy-five years of age, something of a national political fixture. To a large extent this impression of solidity and of *presence* was important in explaining Palmerston's continuing relevance and his ability to draw diverse interests together to create a second government.

Much as Palmerston's first premiership had opened amid European conflict, so too, in 1859, was the political agenda dominated by European tensions. Although considerable attention had been devoted to domestic issues, notably parliamentary reform, during the period of manoeuvring among the Liberal factions, an equally important issue separating the Liberals and Tories was the future of the Italian states. With France and Austria again competing for influence in the Italian peninsula, balance of power concerns once more merged with familiar ideological debates about conservatism and liberal constitutionalism.

Like so many of the arrangements made at Vienna in 1815, the settlement of the Italian states proved not to be permanent. In 1815 the priority had been to secure the peninsula against French aggrandisement and therefore provision had been made to strengthen the position of Piedmont, which shared a border with France, while Lombardy and Venetia were confirmed as Austrian possessions. These northern states were the principal focus of attention in 1815; no party at that congress considered Italian unification (or even Italian nationalism) as especially important. So while the Vienna settlement might have addressed the immediate strategic concerns of the powers, it paid little attention to the sovereign rights of those states. However, during the years following 1815, and notably in 1848 and 1849, it became clear that demands within the Italian states for liberal reforms were becoming more urgent; it was equally clear that Austria was determined to quell those demands whenever they arose, and Italian republicans and patriots came to regard Austria as chief among the obstacles to Italian progress, which increasingly also meant some sort of unification. Yet if Austria was the enemy of liberal reform, Italian reformers remained uncertain how, without a great power ally, Austria's commanding influence in the north could be overcome. The only Italian state in which attempted reforms had been consolidated at this time was Piedmont. Elsewhere Austrian-inspired reactionaryism and outright military activity had reversed such temporary constitutional advances as had been made. Thereafter, and particularly once Count Cavour became Prime Minister in 1852 and extended the programme of reforms of Piedmontese government, Piedmont's reputation as a beacon of constitutionalism grew throughout the Italian peninsula and the rest of Europe. It was Cavour's Piedmont that had allied with Britain and France in the liberal interest during the Crimean War and although Palmerston had not been keen to become too closely drawn into Italian affairs, Napoleon III's France did come to see the Kingdom of Piedmont-Sardinia as a natural ally both in the cause of the extending of liberal government and, more importantly, in its strategic rivalry with Austria in central Europe.[22]

'Events,' wrote Cavour in 1857, 'have led Piedmont to take up a definite and firm position in Italy.' It was a position, moreover, in which, since 'Providence has willed that Piedmont alone in Italy should be free and independent, Piedmont must use her freedom and independence to plead before Europe the cause of the unhappy peninsula.'[23] While some within Piedmont interpreted this as a justification for Piedmontese aggrandisement rather than a benevolent mission of liberation, the underpinning need in either case was defeat of Austria. This appealed to France, and in July 1858 at Plombières Napoleon III and Cavour met to discuss their common interest in driving Austria out of Italy. They agreed, as Cavour reported their discussions, on the need to provoke a war with Austria; on what grounds, however, they were less certain. Crucially, France and Piedmont needed to make sure that any conflict was limited to the three principal belligerents: Britain and Russia, they agreed, must not be given grounds on which to justify their own intervention. They thought that existing popular discontent in Modena might be agitated (by Piedmont) to the point where the Duke of Modena would offer an insult to Piedmont and call on Austria to help suppress opposition, in response to which Cavour would be entitled to turn to Paris for support. Such a cause, they calculated, would be popular in Britain and, since Derby's government was a 'slave' to public opinion, Britain would remain neutral while Prussian 'antipathy to the Austrians' would prevent any opposition from that quarter. Both Napoleon III and Cavour were confident enough in the plan as a *casus belli* and of their likely victory over Austria to start planning a post-conflict division of spoils, in which Lombardy and Venetia would be annexed to Piedmont (with the expectation of further gains as other states were liberated from indirect Austrian control) while France would claim Savoy, and perhaps also Nice, from Piedmont. Neither side discussed Italian unification; the objective was, for both parties, understood in strictly *realpolitik* terms, but as Cavour acknowledged, 'National sentiment in Italy is stronger than Liberal opinion' and it was therefore in Piedmont's interest, and also in that of France, to ensure that the contest also had a national identity and was not lost to 'despotic' forces such as the King of Naples who might pick up the Italian cause against Austria if Piedmont and France failed.[24]

In early 1859 it was obvious to outside observers that something was afoot in northern Italy. Victor Emmanuel, the King of Piedmont-Sardinia, spoke of the 'cry of pain' heard throughout Italy when he opened his parliament in January; meanwhile at the end of the month Prince Napoleon, Napoleon III's cousin, married Princess Clotilde, daughter of Victor Emmanuel, as part of the plans drawn up at Plombières and an unambiguous sign of Franco-Piedmontese accord. In early February a pamphlet entitled *L'Empereur Napoléon III et l'Italie*, arguing for an Italian federation, appeared in Paris and removed all doubt that the two parties were seeking to engineer a crisis.[25] In Britain the Derby government, which had long entertained Austrian sympathies,[26] spoke of remaining neutral so far as possible. When it became clear that diplomatic remedies would not heal the breach, however, Malmesbury, Derby's Foreign Secretary, did not hide the government's determination to stand against France and Piedmont. 'France having always been a curse to Europe, we look upon it as the will of God, and resign ourselves to the torment, but... that Europe should be deluged with blood for the personal ambition of an Italian attorney and a tambour-major, like Cavour and his master, is intolerable,' he wrote to Britain's ambassador in Paris, Lord Cowley.[27] If it came to war, and Malmesbury hoped it would not, Britain would take up arms against France.[28]

When Nassau Senior asked Palmerston in January 1859 'what there was to prevent L. Napoleon from attacking Austria in Italy', Palmerston answered 'nothing', but also said that he thought that, all the same, 'we shall be quiet'.[29] In fact Palmerston was deeply torn over events in Italy. A war between Austria and France had long been something Palmerston had strived to avoid; by the same token the anticipated war not only promised to weaken an international rival, Austria, but also offered a means to outbid a domestic one, Russell. This was just the time, it should not be forgotten, that Palmerston and Russell were negotiating possible Liberal reunion, but Palmerston knew that on the subject of parliamentary reform Russell had a better claim on Radical support than he did himself. A clear Liberal stand over Italy, therefore, offered Palmerston the chance to reaffirm his own reformist credentials without having to make unpalatable concessions to domestic franchise demands.[30] Thus Palmerston emphasised his sympathy with Austria's opponents, even if he did so with qualifications. 'As for myself,' he wrote to Granville in January, 'I am very Austrian north of the Alps, but very anti-Austrian south of the Alps. The Austrians have no business in Italy, and they are a public nuisance there. They govern their own provinces ill, and are the props & encouragers of bad government in all the other states of the Peninsula, except in Piemont [*sic*], where fortunately they have no influence.' Any rights the Austrians did have in Italy, he said, dated back no further than 1815, but certainly Austria had overstepped even those rights by its military occupation of the Papal States. 'I should therefore rejoice and feel relieved,' he continued, 'if Italy up to the Tyrol were freed from Austrian domination and military occupation.' By the same token, however, he acknowledged that driving Austria from Italy would not be done 'without a desperate struggle' and while achieving that would be desirable, if it led to the weakening of Austria in central Europe, where both Russia and Hungary might then be tempted to offer further challenges to Austrian authority, there was much to be feared in a possible consequent 'dismemberment' of Austria.[31] Not only did this make the debate in Britain in part an ideological one, it also made it a party political one. Malmesbury hoped to persuade Palmerston not to escalate matters: he regretted that Palmerston's and Russell's names were 'used freely by Cavour & his partisans among the people he is trying to delude & who are ignorant of our political principles in England,'[32] but among Palmerston's political friends there was a growing consensus that this was an issue on which the government had to be opposed. The issue was not straight-forward, however. While Liberals generally agreed that Austria should not be supported, there were also concerns about the longer-term effects of Austria being weakened, and of what France might do if it gained a foothold in Italy at Austria's expense. 'It is easier to begin a great war in Europe than to limit its range or foresee its results,' Sir Charles Wood observed.[33]

Unforeseen results or not, the increasingly tense situation between France, Piedmont and Austria finally erupted into war in April 1859. Wood still considered the circumstances to be precarious: there was little doubt that Austria would be defeated, he thought, but it would be a bloody conflict. More ominous for Wood was the augmentation of French power and influence. 'Napoleon Jerome [*sic*] the bridegroom', he said, was sure to be installed in 'some Italian principality' and in central Europe he thought France was enjoying a disturbing ascendancy. Reports in the British press at the time suggested that France and Russia had entered into an accord to stabilise both their positions; this Wood only partially dismissed: 'I have no belief in a treaty between France & Russia so large in its engagements as the Times asserts,' he wrote to Palmerston at the beginning of May, 'but there can be no doubt that they are acting against Austria like two greyhounds against a hare; only the hare is a very slow one, and the northern greyhound has a lame leg owing to a severe beating which he received not long ago.'[34] Palmerston, however, was, by virtue of the fact that his wariness of Austria outweighed his doubts about France, becoming more pro-Italian. Although he expressed, formally, a prefer-ence for neutrality and above all for not being dragged in on the side of

Austria, when he took to the hustings in Tiverton in June he used language very similar to that in which he had written to Granville in January about pushing the Austrians north of the Alps.[35] The election results, which left the Conservatives in a relatively strong position, did not suggest that the country had been much influenced by events in Italy, but so far as the public was perceived to have formed an opinion on the matter, it was thought to be suspicious of Derby's Austrian leanings.

Scarcely had Palmerston become Prime Minister in June, however, than the Italian question changed dramatically. At the beginning of that month, everything appeared to be going in France's and Piedmont's favour. Decisive victories at Magenta and Solferino had placed France in a commanding position, but significantly this was perceived in Britain as a French triumph, not a Franco-Piedmontese one. Immediately, therefore, the Italian question seemed to portend the French ascendancy so long feared by British ministers. It was impossible for Palmerston's government to adopt a clear, unproblematic, view of events. Greville captured something of the mood towards the end of June when he wrote:

> The sentiments of people here are of a very mixed and almost contradictory character, for they are on the whole Anti-Austrian, Anti-French, and though more indulgent than they deserve to the Sardinians, not favorable to them. The most earnest and general desire is that we should keep out of the mêlée, and any termination of the war would be hailed with gladness, because we should thereby be relieved from our apprehensions of being involved in it. We should not be sorry to see the Austrians driven out of Italy for good and all, though most people would regret that the Emperor L[ouis] N[apoleon] should be triumphant, and that such a course of perfidy, falsehood, and selfish ambition should be crowned with success.[36]

Palmerston's new Cabinet gave every appearance of embodying these tensions and uncertainties. As Prince Albert observed, the government was one 'which exactly suits Louis Napoleon', by which he meant it lacked a clear united outlook. 'Palmerston is anti-Austrian, pro-Italian, and especially pro-Napoleon,' he explained to the Prince Regent of Prussia; 'Lord John is anti-French, but strongly pro-Italian; Sidney Herbert, Granville, the Duke of Newcastle, Sir George Cornewall Lewis, and Lord Elgin are anti-French and on the whole pro-Austrian; Gladstone is violently pro-Italian. Sir George Grey, Sir Charles Wood, Mr Cardwell, and the Duke of Argyll are quite neutral. Mr Milner Gibson admires Mazzini [the Italian republican] and Kossuth [the Hungarian nationalist] and was a bosom friend of Orsini . . .!'[37] While members of the Cabinet worried about French aggrandisement, the consequences of a weakened Austria and the uncertainties of war, Palmerston, Russell and Gladstone gave British foreign policy a pro-Italian, liberal constitutionalist sheen. If the Queen and Prince Albert opposed this 'pro-Italian triumvirate', that did nothing to alter Palmerston's view.[38] What did affect Palmerston's assessment was the unexpected decision of Napoleon III to sue for peace in July. Despite French military successes in June, early the following month Persigny, the French ambassador to London, approached Palmerston to propose a British brokered armistice (on terms suggested by France, specifically that in return for peace, France would allow Austria to retain, effectively, possession of Venetia and Modena by placing those two states under a nominally independent Austrian sovereign). Palmerston rejected the idea. Britain, he said, must remain wary of becoming embroiled in a complicated question, not least because to accept Persigny's suggestion would be to enter into the affair on terms sketched out by one of the belligerents. Britain was under no obligation to endorse the French terms and in particular, as he pointed out in a letter to Russell, 'It is to be observed that we are not told that this scheme has the assent of the Sardinians nor of the Italians generally'. Palmerston was anxious to avoid any suggestion that Britain had been complicit in 'having succeeded to rivet on Italy a remnant of Austrian shackles, and of having betrayed and disappointed the Italians at the very moment when their prospects were the brightest'. As Palmerston concluded: 'If the French Emperor is tired of his war, and finds the job tougher than he expected, let him make what proposals he pleases, and to whomsoever he pleases; but let them be made as from himself formally and officially, and let him not ask us to father his suggestions, and make ourselves answerable for them.'[39]

Perhaps because he anticipated that Palmerston would be unwilling to agree to present French terms, Napoleon III had anyway proposed an armistice to Austria directly which on 6 July was accepted in Vienna. Five days later a provisional peace treaty was signed between the French and Austrian emperors at Villafranca. With Austria thus keeping hold of Venetia (which it had been expected, before Napoleon III started talking of an armistice, would fall to France) the British government was wrong-footed. Palmerston was firm in his condemnation of the settlement. By allowing Austria a role in an Italian confederation, he said, 'toute l'Italie est livrée pieds et mains lies à l'Autriche'; Austria, he insisted, must be kept out of Italy and confined within Austrian borders. It was also, he told Persigny, detrimental to French honour to make such concessions and, unless Austria was fully excluded from Italian affairs, French blood would have been shed in vain and Napoleon's glory would be short-lived.[40] Palmerston denied that this signified overt hostility towards Austria. He was, he said, 'an enemy to bad government, to oppression and tyranny; and, unfortunately, the Austrian rule in Italy, as else-where, has been marked by those evils'. However, while he confessed himself on these grounds an 'enemy' of Austria and wished to see Italy 'freed from the Austrian yoke', this was a specific and not universal dislike of that country. 'I wish with all my heart she would change her system, and conciliate the goodwill of her subjects,' he wrote to Cowley, 'for I hold a great and powerful Austrian empire north of the Alps to be of the utmost importance for the general interests of Europe.' What Palmerston was most concerned about was how the fallout from Villafranca would play in an Italian context. Just as he lamented the continued Austrian presence in Italy, so too did he hope France would not forget that the crisis had initially been raised amid calls for 'Italy free from the alps to the Adriatic' and 'l'Italie rendue à elle même'. So long as 'the Italians are left to themselves', he concluded, 'all will go well'.[41] In some respects, therefore, and despite his protested opposition to it, Villafranca was a blessing for Palmerston: as Jasper Ridley suggested, it allowed him to express his fears about France without appearing to abandon Italy or seem sympathetic towards Austria.[42]

During the late summer and autumn the Cabinet and royal couple tried to rein in Palmerston and Russell in their Italian policy, but they were moving gradually away from a position of neutrality on the issue. By the end of the year the matter threatened to divide and even shatter the government. Palmerston and Russell started to argue more forcefully that Britain should consider a formal engagement with France in Italy and offer material support to Piedmont in its struggle against Austria. While the positive impulse, to encourage liberal progress in the Italian peninsula, was relatively uncontroversial, the negative one, to oppose Austria, was the opposite. Even among the enthusiasts for Palmerstonian–Russellite strategy, there was a concern to make sure that such an alliance would not serve to extend French interest and influence in Italy.[43] When the topic was debated in Cabinet in January it emerged that it was both a complicated and a controversial subject. Palmerston made his own position clear: firstly, France acting alone in support of Italian liberation (and possibly federation) swung the balance of power in central Europe too much in favour of Paris; secondly, the cause that French intervention was ostensibly designed to support, Italian freedom, was a good one which Britain, as a liberal power, should also sponsor; and, thirdly, Austria, whose position and activities had to a large extent provoked or exacerbated the current crisis, should be pushed back within its own boundaries.

In a memorandum prepared for Cabinet colleagues, Palmerston dismissed the notion that Britain could stand aside: leaving 'to others the task of settling as they like the affairs of the continent of Europe', he wrote, 'has not been the policy of the wisest and greatest statesmen who have taken part in the government of this country'. The current crisis, he said, was of fundamental interest to Britain: 'what is at issue is not the interests of the Emperor Napoleon, but the interests of the people of Italy, and, through them, the welfare and peace of Europe.' Looking forward to an anticipated congress to deal with the subject, Palmerston argued that the foundation of Britain's policy was that 'the people of Italy, and especially of central Italy, should be left free to determine their own condition of political existence.' This, he continued, would be most effectively achieved by entering into an understanding with France and Sardinia, and that without delay. Such an arrangement would of necessity have an anti-Austrian character, but irresolution now would only make war more, not less, likely by encouraging Austria to under-estimate the strength of opposition which it would face. Palmerston dismissed suggestions that Napoleon III was an unsteady ally and argued unequivocally for a Franco–Sardinian–British 'triple league [which] would better deserve the title of holy alliance than the league which bore that name'.[44] Britain could not, Palmerston explained in a letter to George Cornewall Lewis on 6 January, wait for an overt act of aggression on the part of Austria before entering into any sort of agreement with France (though his memorandum had spoken of Sardinia as well as France as partners, his correspondence underlines the fact that this remained primarily a great power concern). He and Russell, he said, wanted to 'prevent Austrian violence, and not to punish it', and therefore Austria needed to know that it would face opposition if it pursued an aggressive policy. 'I cannot conceive how there can be two opinions as to the sound policy of such a course,' said Palmerston. Not to resist possible violence would be irresponsible but this did not mean, he stressed, that Britain would be entering into a 'permanent guarantee of any thing or any body'. By the same token, leaving France to act alone, in which case the central Italian states would see France alone as a guardian protector against Austria, was undesirable. If Prince Napoleon was, as seemed eminently feasible, installed at the head of a union of Sardinia and the duchies of central Italy, then France would be placed in a strong, and unchecked, position in the peninsula. Palmerston effectively staked his administration's survival on the question; if Russell's proposal for an agreement with France was not endorsed by the Cabinet, Palmerston foretold – in a letter to Lewis – the departure of the Foreign Secretary and the consequent collapse of the government.[45] He repeated the argument in letters to other members of the Cabinet at the same time.[46] Cabinet colleagues, however, remained sceptical. Lewis replied to Palmerston's letter that the situation was 'one of great nicety & difficulty', but he could not support any written engagement with France made to guarantee central Italy against foreign intervention without prior aggression on the part of Austria.[47]

There was, as a letter from Shaftesbury made clear, a good deal at stake for Palmerston in terms of his standing in the country. If the government appeared to sanction French conduct, public opinion would judge it harshly: Napoleon III's demands for the surrender of Savoy and Nice appeared to belie claims that French intervention had been made to secure Italian freedom; and if he appeared too close to France, then Palmerston risked compromising his liberal reputation. Shaftesbury enumerated the situation in stark terms:

1. The country will consider the act as a return to the old system of dealing with nations like flocks of sheep, and handing them over as articles of barter and exchange.
2. It would be the surrender of a *free* people to a *despotic* rule; of a people in enjoyment of *religious liberty*, to an empire where it is professed, & violated.

3. It would beget in all minds an apprehension that this was a revival of the French policy to attain 'natural boundaries'. The acquisition of Savoy might be followed by an effort to effect the acquisition of the Rhine.

4. It would render your administration unpopular to the greatest extent.[48]

In the event, Palmerston and Russell had relented and adopted Persigny's proposed compromise that Britain simply required that neither France nor Austria should interfere in Italy. Palmerston did little during the course of 1860 to advance materially the cause of Italian independence and unification, other than to oppose Garibaldi's drive to secure Naples for Victor Emmanuel, in spite of his initial fears that this would benefit France as the chief ally of Victor Emmanuel's Sardinia. On this, to a large extent, rested Palmerston's reputation as an architect of Italian unity.[49] In fact, so long as Italy was stable and Austria's influence was diminished, Palmerston, and the Cabinet, seemed generally satisfied and attention to the Italian crisis gradually shifted away from the Italian states themselves.[50] Palmerston continued to regard Austria, in the Italian context at least, as 'a malignant fiend',[51] and his regard for Italy was certainly sincere: as he said in reply to an address from the people of Capua in southern Italy in the spring of 1862, he took 'a lively interest in the welfare and prosperity of the Italian nation'; an interest that was widely acknowledged and welcomed throughout the Italian states.[52] However, although this concern for Italian liberties was genuine enough, it had been superseded by less idealistic concerns about Britain's relations with France which had been thrown into sharp relief by events in the peninsula. By the spring of 1860 the Italian question had become, to a very great extent, 'a phrase blazoned on a French banner'.[53] On 1 March Napoleon III had stated in public that he did intend to claim Nice and Savoy for France and this was an issue far more pressing for Palmerston than a principled stand on Italian rights. In an interview with Count Flahault, the French ambassador, on 27 March, Palmerston made plain his views of French policy at that moment:

I said distrust might be founded on either of two grounds, either upon the supposition of intentional deceit, or upon such a frequent change of purpose, and of conduct as to shew that no reliance could be placed upon the continuance of the intentions or policy of the moment, & Ct F. must admit that without imputing the first, there is ample ground for a feeling founded on the second consideration. Ct. F. said his great object was to prevent war between the two countries I said that I feared the Emperor & Thouvenal had schemes & views which tended to bring about that result, & might array Europe against France. Ct. F. did not fear that, but was apprehensive that irritation on both sides might bring on war between England & France. I said that I was most anxious to prevent such a war but if it was forced upon England, England would fearlessly accept it, whether in conjunction with a confederated alliance or singly and by herself; that the nation would rise and rally as one man; & though speaking to a Frenchman I ought perhaps not to say so, yet I could not refrain from observing that the examples of history led me to conclude that the result of conflict between English and French upon any thing like equal terms would not be unsatisfactory to the former.[54]

France remained, for Palmerston, the leading foreign power: alternately, and sometimes simultaneously, a rival and an ally. The Crimean War had revived notions of an entente but that was not a permanent arrangement. Even during the conflict, an indiscreet story spread by the King of Sardinia, Victor Emmanuel, reported that Palmerston had 'said that His Imperial Majesty [Napoleon III] was in the hands of a parcel of adventurers, that he could not stand up against them, and that yielding to their exigencies, he was ready to conclude an ignominious peace – that England did not care a fig for the French – that the Emperor might withdraw his army from the Crimea if he liked' and that only Britain (in collaboration with Sardinia) could steer the war to 'an honourable conclusion'. Napoleon was reported to have been both 'hurt' and 'annoyed'.[55] As soon as the ink was dry on the Treaty of Paris in 1856, Palmerston began speculating that France would again look across the Channel with a view to aggression. When he saw France buying more ships in the summer of 1856, for example, he worried that they might be 'turned to any bad purpose', by which he meant sent up the Thames.[56] He had already watched, a few years earlier, as the port at Cherbourg underwent extensive redevelopment which, as reports filtering back to London in 1851 had suggested, were undertaken with a view to challenging British naval mastery.[57] Significant sums were indeed being spent in Cherbourg at that time on 'works for defence',[58] although as ministers in Paris had been at pains to point out, the Paris government had no hostile intentions and, indeed, financial records suggest that between the mid-1840s and mid-1850s, naval expenditure in France actually fell by around 16 per cent.[59] The numbers were less exciting than the images, however, and the perception remained in the minds of many that there was, whatever temporary arrangements had been made in the face of a common Russian enemy, an underlying French threat to British national security. The concerns about the development of Cherbourg were still in Palmerston's thoughts in 1857 and though he said that he trusted the French Emperor personally, still Napoleon was 'not immortal' and had himself told Palmerston when the two met at Osborne that 'the feeling in France towards England was not good, and that a quarrel with us would be popular there'.[60] Just as importantly, Cowley reported from Paris in late 1857 that Palmerston's speeches at this time, which talked of a growing French threat to Britain, 'raised the indignation of these ridiculously susceptible people', and he suggested that certain figures in Paris, notably Walewski, were keen to 'poison the Emperor's mind, not only against Palmerston, but against England'.[61] Such, then, was the atmosphere of mutual suspicion that many key figures felt themselves to be operating within. On the British side they could point to a more tangible cause for concern too. Napoleon's plans in the aftermath of the Crimean War for a re-drafted map of Europe – in which borders were shifted eastwards allowing France to appropriate much of Belgium, Savoy and the Rhineland, while creating loose federal structures in Italy and Germany where France would be able to exercise indirect influence if not control – would be underpinned by a dramatically reinvigorated French naval capability. As Lord Aberdeen observed in a letter to Guizot in March 1858, in the aftermath of public debates about the Orsini plot, there was a tangible atmosphere of fear and suspicion about France in Britain:

> I think I have scarcely ever known such a rapid change in the public mind, as has recently taken place. It appeared as if all ranks vied with each other in the fulsome adulation of the Emperor. Our periodical press was the most base and abject of all. Now, every thing is changed. Notwithstanding the amicable settlement of the differences connected with the Conspiracy Bill, and the concessions made by the French government, a sore feeling remains, and the Emperor has become universally unpopular. People here regard the state of France with much alarm. It is difficult to believe that the present state of suspicion and severity should endure; but the consequence of any crisis can only I fear be such at present as to lead to the most gloomy apprehensions.[62]

The threat to Britain was clear but made far more explicit in 1860 when the French ambassador told the British government bluntly that if British support for the French over unification of the Danubian Principalities were not forthcoming, then British dockyards, and thus by extension British power, would be destroyed.[63] The full import of the redevelopment of Cherbourg was now obvious as both countries embarked on an arms race, which had no fixed point of real antagonism, by way of mutual self-definition and in order to lay claim to international relevance. Palmerston, particularly once returned to office in 1859, played up the Franco-British rivalry to justify high levels of defence expenditure in the face of loud demands for retrenchment and greater economy (not least from the Chancellor, William Gladstone). Only by neutralising, or countering, the French challenge, it was argued, could Britain regain an independent voice in international affairs, a significant matter, it was maintained, as France sought to extend its influence in Italy.[64]

Lord Cowley, Britain's ambassador in Paris, and Napoleon together smoothed ruffled feathers, and Disraeli, back in office briefly until Palmerston returned in 1859, talked of an *entente cordiale* again in Parliament, yet the dominant mood remained one of suspicion. Renewed war scares and further tension over Italy suggest relations were still not close. Palmerston, indeed, seemed in many respects determined to heighten tensions between the two countries. As Sir John Trelawny observed from the back benches in 1860 when proposals for strengthening Britain's coastal fortifications were under review, 'It was remarkable that Palmerston threw off all diplomatic reserve & plainly indicated where danger lies – viz, in France.' It was felt that Palmerston's increasingly belligerent tone towards France, warning of naval threats and critical of Italian intervention, might well be taken in France 'as a menace'.[65] Palmerston, however, was reacting to perceived French aggression: as he had recorded in his diary in March 1860, there had been a 'scene' at the Tuileries in which Napoleon had publicly chastised the British ambassador, Lord Cowley, over Britain's policy towards the projected annexation of Savoy and had declared that 'it was impossible to maintain friendly relations with England'.[66]

Yet there was no war between Britain and France and relations even at this critical juncture were not so unequivocally hostile as narratives of a naval race might imply. Palmerston, the gunboat diplomat and populist minister, need not have looked too far for popular backing for a showdown with France – as even Lord Aberdeen's correspondence with Guizot had acknowledged.[67] Nonetheless, Palmerston insisted throughout, whatever he might have said in the Commons about naval and military rivalries, that 'in spite of conflicting interests which might place England at variance . . . with France and the United States, the ties of commercial interest are too strong to be broken'.[68] Palmerston's faith in free trade was of long standing and it was a principle he held to; indeed, at just this time he even went so far as to tell the Russian ambassador that if it was the aim of any country 'to secure a good understanding with England, they ought to liberalize their commercial system'.[69] The commercial treaty between Britain and France brokered by Richard Cobden in 1860, therefore, was fundamental to preserving good relations between the two countries. It was, however, a political prescription and not an economic one. As Cobden himself put it in a letter to the French Minister of Commerce, 'England had, since 1846, renounced the principle of commercial treaties; &, with no other power than France, & with no less motive than to strengthen the alliance of the French & English nations, would such a policy have been revived.'[70]

Although Richard Cobden had declined Palmerston's offer to join the government in 1859, he was prevailed upon to conduct negotiations with France for a commercial treaty between the two countries. He had long complained of the perilous state of relations which, he feared, could easily lead to war. Writing to his friend Michel Chevalier, a French politician and likeminded free-marketeer, Cobden had expressed his concern that though Palmerston and Russell refuted the widespread calls for a showdown with France, they were simultaneously stoking the war scares by investing heavily in armaments. 'The effect of this inconsistency between the words and acts of our ministers,' he wrote, 'is to cause even greater suspicion & ill feeling than if we had some ground of quarrel on some intelligible question at issue between the countries.'[71] This was the field, then, in which Cobden came to see that he might make a contribution to the government. In October he reported a meeting with the Prime Minister and Foreign Secretary to his friend Henry Ashworth. He had tried, he said, 'to convince them how unsatisfactory our relations with France are, & how necessary it is that something should be done to change the warlike tone into which we are drifting. The difficulty is to make people whose minds have been running for half a century in other grooves feel the importance of these questions of political economy.'[72] He thought Gladstone understood the argument better, but Palmerston proved receptive and authorised Cobden to open discussions in Paris. In a meeting with Napoleon III at the end of October Cobden argued that liberalising trade would not only be commercially advantageous to both countries, but would reduce spending on arms and improve diplomatic relations; 'the governments of both countries,' he said, 'professing as they did to be friendly, would be responsible if not blameable, were nothing done to try to put an end to this state of things.'[73] At the same time, Cobden reported back to Gladstone that he thought Napoleon III would agree, principally 'from a desire to conciliate & draw closer the bonds with *us*, than from any sufficient conviction of its great necessity for his own country.'[74]

In January 1860 a commercial treaty – frequently referred to as the Cobden–Chevalier Treaty in recognition of the efforts of its chief authors – was signed, but it took several months of further negotiations to fine-tune the details. The treaty did not automatically restore Franco-British trust, however: Cobden had cause frequently to complain, as he put it in July 1860, of how the 'extraordinary military & warlike displays of the last few months have also tended to diminish the hopes which were at first entertained in connexion with the Treaty',[75] but this simply underlined the extent to which the commercial arrangement was not providing tangible assurances of mutual good faith quickly enough. The tariff reductions that were finally agreed in 1860 did play a part in averting Franco-British conflict, and to some extent set the stage for a period of harmonious relations, but both countries found the agreement less commercially useful than had been hoped, and it was ultimately abandoned in the 1880s.[76] Palmerston had reservations about the apparent imbalances within the agreement for mutual tariff reductions at the time and wondered how he might sell the idea to Parliament and the British public, but he suppressed his doubts on the basis that a commercial agreement would offset other potentially damaging areas of disagreement.

It was because relations between the two countries were fragile and balanced delicately between peace and war that Palmerston reluctantly acquiesced in the French annexation of Savoy and Nice in 1860. Yet, for all the contemporary fears that this was the harbinger of further French expansionism, it is reported by Lord Malmesbury that Palmerston not only knew of Napoleon's intention to claim these territories as reward for French intervention as early as November 1858 but that he 'entered into the plan completely'.[77] Indeed, Palmerston insisted in a speech to Parliament that French conduct in Italy only confirmed Napoleon's much earlier stated intention to preserve peace, not wage war in Europe: 'I do not hold,' Palmerston insisted, 'that . . . what took place in Italy last year . . . was any departure from that principle . . . France undertook a noble enterprise . . . freeing Italy from foreign domination – aye . . . French domination included . . .'.[78]

Palmerston may have had his reservations about France under Napoleon III, but he was more worried about what or who might follow the Empire or the Emperor. Thus his defence-building concerns were against future threats more than present dangers. Anxieties about a naval challenge from France – it was feared by 1859–60 that the French navy might actually exceed the British in both size and sophistication[79] – were part of a much broader concern about Britain's ebbing world power. There was certainly considerable alarm in Britain in the late 1850s and early 1860s over a potential conflict with France, causing Tennyson to issue his famous call to 'Riflemen, form!' in *The Times*,[80] and even the Queen was drawn to complain angrily in May 1860:

> Really it is too bad! *No* country, no human being would ever dream of *disturbing* or *attacking* France; every one would be glad to see her pros-perous; but *she* must needs disturb every quarter of the Globe and try to make mischief and set every one by the ears; and, of course, it will end some day in a *regular crusade* against *the universal disturber of the world!* It is really monstrous![81]

Yet projected naval and military threats need not be taken at face value. If Palmerstonian foreign policy was about anything it was about pragmatic checks and balances. His insistence on Britain having 'no eternal allies' and 'no perpetual enemies', only interests that 'are eternal and perpetual' has become a platitude, but Palmerston did see this as an important foundation for his poli-tics. As he reminded Clarendon in 1859, 'Governments and nations are less influenced by resentment for former antagonism or by gratitude for former services than by considerations of present or prospective interest.'[82]

France, and specifically France under Napoleon III, was a known quantity. Commercial ties and common security concerns (notably containment of Russia) were enough to underpin a common bond in a changing world. Palmerston might not have liked the balance of power in Europe at all times, but it was more familiar and broadly manageable than the unknown ramifica-tions of a growing American world role as civil war upset the status quo in America, where Britain had important economic interests too, of course. There was perhaps reason to see the benefit of a cordial understanding with

Britain's close neighbour across the Channel, therefore: as Palmerston put it in 1865, clearly with concerns about the possible spread of American democracy to Europe if Europe seemed weak, a goodwill visit to Britain by the French navy had several benefits, including: 'a most wholesome effect in Yankee land, where they [demonstrations of friendship between Britain and France] will be taken as indications of a closer union than in fact . . . exists, and . . . will thus tend to disincline the Yankees from aggression on us'.[83] In a period of instability in North America, Palmerston was keen to convey the impression that 'the Yankees will be all the less likely to give trouble in Canada or Mexico'.[84] It may have been that this overarching concern of maintaining an entente ultimately distracted Britain, and France, from the only slightly longer term challenge of Prussia,[85] but nonetheless Franco-British harmony seemed the best guarantor of the international relevance and influence of both countries. As Trelawny commented in 1861, it was largely external affairs that kept Palmerston's ministry in power: the 'Govt is mainly sustained by their foreign policy', he wrote, '& the great apprehensions most men now have of the effect of change at this moment. America, France, Italy, Poland, Hungary – danger everywhere. Who is to open the ball in this dance of death?'[86]

A reading of Palmerston's handling of the Italian question in 1859 and 1860 suggests that his approach to foreign policy continued to mix considerations of *ideal-* and *realpolitik*. In late 1860 Palmerston and George Cornewall Lewis exchanged a short series of letters which reveals something of the principles underpinning Palmerston's approach to foreign policy and some of the arguments in his own Cabinet with which he had to deal during these years. Writing on 22 November, Palmerston referred to Lewis's having 'broached . . . a political heresy', one which Palmerston hoped was only raised as a 'conversational paradox':

> You said you dissented from the maxim that prevention is better than cure, and that you thought that instead of trying to prevent an evil we ought to wait till it had happened and should then apply the proper remedy. Now I beg to submit that the prevention of evil is the proper function of statesmen and diplomatists, and that the correction of evil calls forth the action of generals and admirals; evils are prevented by the pen, but are corrected by the sword; they are prevented by ink shed but can be corrected only by bloodshed; the first is an operation of peace, the second an action of war.

There were, he said, 'endless instances' of crises that might have been avoided by pre-emptive and decisive action, though significantly the only examples he cited were of the shortcomings of the foreign policies of the Duke of Wellington (whose timidity in 1830 allowed France to gain Algeria which in the event of war with France 'will give us trouble and cause us much expense') and Lord Aberdeen (whose prevarication encouraged Russia to invade the Crimean region in the early 1850s); it was, he said, 'needless to multiply examples to prove what appear to me to be self evident propositions'.[87] It did not matter, Lewis replied, that France possessed Algeria, and to worry about preventing all possible future adversities was unrealistic for a power such as Britain with so many diverse interests around the globe. It was unnecessary to be so active, he said: 'Generally, I think that our foreign policy is too timorous, that we are apt to be scared by bugbears, & that we underrate the power of England & the fear of it entertained by foreign nations.' Direct action, he concluded, should only be considered where there was evidence of a 'proximate & certain evil'.[88] On such grounds did Lewis counsel non-intervention in Italy in December; and Palmerston agreed that with the future conduct of Austria and France being so uncertain, 'it would be better that we should be free to act according to circumstances at the time'.[89]

Palmerston's approach to foreign policy in the 1860s, then, was a pragmatic one. In part this is because he was dealing with a rapidly changing world in which familiar debates about liberal constitutional and autocratic monarchical government were giving way to nation-state formations that were not based only on an ideological expression of national sentiment, but increasingly also on developing military-industrial complexes. Palmerston, growing weary, having more than the Foreign Office to think about and aware of the relative decline of British power and influence (whatever Lewis might have said), chose his battles more selectively in these later years.

The growing tensions within the United States of America underlined the difficulties facing Palmerston in adopting a strong, and effective, line of policy. Palmerston had long regarded the United States with ill-disguised disdain, as both a threat to British interests in North America and as a possible inspiration to republicanism in Europe. Thus, he welcomed a visible Franco-British rapprochement in 1865 as a counterpoint to radicalism in 'Yankee land'. As Palmerston had put it in a letter to Lewis a few years previously, 'the state of things in the *Dis*united States . . . affords an instructive illustration of the blessings of a republican form of government for anything larger than a Swiss canton or a Hanse town district'.[90] By the 1860s, however, attitudes towards America could not be formed so superficially. Abraham Lincoln's election to the presidency of the United States in 1860 had provoked South Carolina to announce its secession from the Union in December and within four months ten other Southern slave-owning states had followed suit. It raised, as Lewis observed to Palmerston, tricky diplomatic questions, particularly, 'what constitutes the identity of a state, with respect to the obligation of treaties'. Just as in Europe, where it would be hard to argue that a treaty negotiated with Sardinia only could subsequently be held to apply to a united Italy, Lewis asked whether there could be any continuity in Britain's relations with the United States if the Union was disrupted: 'if all the slave states secede,' he wrote in

January 1861, 'it will not be easy to maintain that the remaining states represent the Union with which treaties were made. All this will be embarrassing
with reference to treaties involving the slave trade.'[91] It was not just a long-
standing commitment to suppression of the slave trade that was at issue,
however: Britain had important commercial links with America, not least in
the textile industry, which it was essential to preserve. As Palmerston acknowledged, Britain was in a difficult position: it had an interest in the outcome of
the developing conflict, but little grounds on which to justify interference.
Writing to Edward Ellice in May 1861 he said:

> There would, moreover, be great difficulty in suggesting any basis of
> arrangement to which both parties could agree, and which it would not
> be repugnant to English feelings and principles to propose. We could not
> well mix ourselves up with the acknowledgement of slavery and the prin-
> ciple that a slave escaping to a free soil state should be followed, claimed,
> and recovered, like a horse or an ox. We might possibly propose that the
> North and South should separate amicably; that they should make some
> boundary line, to be agreed upon, the line of separation between them;
> and that each confederation should be free to make for its own internal
> affairs and concerns such laws as it might think fit – the two confedera-
> tions entering, however, into certain mutual arrangements as to trade and
> commerce with each other.[92]

But Palmerston knew that Britain had no grounds on which to suggest such a
settlement. Doing nothing, however, was equally problematic.

Britain's 'relations with the Washington government are in a ticklish condition', Palmerston noted in August 1861. 'No reliance can be placed on Seward
[the US Secretary of State] & Lincoln from week to week', and the 'only security
we can have against wrong, insult & aggression on their part must consist in our
being strong in our provinces, and in our squadron off their coast.'[93] There was
no clear line to be derived from domestic opinion either. Radical feeling,
looking first and foremost at the slavery issue, tended to back the Northern
states, and certainly within the Cabinet the Duke of Argyll, Villiers and Milner
Gibson spoke up for the Unionists, as did Cobden and Bright from outside the
government and, it seemed, this was a sentiment shared widely out of doors.
Traditionally, more conservative interests were thought to have preferred the
Confederacy, seeing in Southern society something more akin to the hierarchical aristocratic milieu within which they felt comfortable and viewing
Northerners as dangerous republicans and democrats. Within the Cabinet,
even liberal figures, such as Gladstone and Russell, favoured the South.[94] In fact
the divisions within British opinion were not so neat as this model implies, but
divisions did exist.[95] Palmerston's instinct was to back the South since his fear
of democracy outweighed his distaste for slavery and both considerations were

secondary to a cold assessment of material interest which suggested that the South would break away and Britain needed to maintain good relations with those states. While not going so far as to recognise the Confederacy as an independent state, Palmerston and Russell agreed to recognise the Confederates as belligerents, but even this lent to the South a legitimacy resented by Seward and Lincoln who interpreted it as a definite statement of partisan preference. It was, however, a decision made without sentiment: the North seemed to be in the weaker position. Confederate successes at Bull's Run and Missouri convinced Lewis by the summer of 1861 that the Northerners would 'find their hands too full, to attempt an attack upon Canada' and, determined to focus resources and efforts on the Confederacy, 'Their eyes will be turned southward not northward'. He counselled caution, but not anxiety.[96] As long as Britain made clear its willingness to take Washington on, it seemed that, for the moment, a direct confrontation could be avoided.[97]

Palmerston, therefore, led his government into an increasingly pragmatic, pro-Southern, position, not from any sense of a shared aristocratic interest and discounting any ideological dimension to the conflict based on the slavery question. 'It is in the highest degree likely that the North will not be able to subdue the South,' he wrote in a memorandum dated 20 October, 'and it is no doubt certain that if the Southern Union is established as an independent state it would afford a valuable and extensive market for British manufactures but the operations of the war have as yet been too indecisive to warrant an acknowledgement of the Southern Union.'[98] Palmerston's closest Cabinet allies in foreign policy matters, Russell and Gladstone, and especially Gladstone, shared these Southern sympathies, although officially Britain remained neutral. In an attempt to make something of this known disposition in Britain (and in France), however, the Confederate government dispatched two envoys, James Murray Mason and John Slidell, to solicit support in Europe.

In November 1861 Mason and Slidell boarded the British passenger ship the *Trent* in Cuba, bound for England. When Palmerston learned that a Northern vessel, the *James Adger*, had put in to Southampton and planned to intercept the *Trent* when it reached home and forcibly remove Mason and Slidell, he objected that this would be an illegal act and an unwarranted assault on British freedom of action. Although Palmerston protested about the plan to the United States ambassador, Charles Francis Adams, events overtook him. Before the *Trent* could be arrested by the *James Adger*, a second Northern vessel, the *San Jacinto*, returning to America from Africa, stopped the *Trent*, and, without any orders to do so, removed Mason and Slidell and took them back to the United States. Here was a definite 'insult' to the British flag. There would have been only very dubious grounds on which to protest against an interception made by the *James Adger* – Britain had claimed similar rights of interception against American ships in 1812 and so ironically if the proposed action of the *Adger* had infringed any interpretation of international law it was the American and not British one – but the unauthorised mid-ocean actions of the *San Jacinto* did seem, to law officers in Britain, more obviously illegal and confrontational.[99] Palmerston thought the North was spoiling for a fight with Britain and preparing to attack at a perceived weak spot, in Canada. (France, he said, had no obvious 'vulnerable point' and therefore was treated with 'great respect' by Seward.)[100] Lewis, with whom Palmerston corresponded frequently on this subject, agreed that war with the North was 'inevitable'.[101]

Palmerston made preparations to prohibit the supply of armaments to the North.[102] If this was not an explicit reversal of British neutrality, it was nonetheless an action designed to emphasise the antagonism felt within the Cabinet towards the Washington government. Palmerston was frustrated, however, that Lincoln did not seem to be taking the British government's anger seriously: 'the Yankees,' he complained, were 'in a fool's paradise about the Trent affair, which Lincoln told a Canadian, that the Federal Govt would have no difficulty in "getting along with".'[103] However much he blustered, Palmerston knew that it was important to avoid a real conflict. The *Trent* affair was resolved, ultimately, with a fudged settlement whereby Britain demanded the liberation of Slidell and Mason, but, thanks to an intervention by the dying Prince Albert, the demand noted that the Washington government had not authorised the *San Jacinto* to seize the Confederate envoys, allowing the North to end the dispute without losing face. Palmerston writing to his Sligo neighbour Robert Gore-Booth at this moment about Sligo estate matters, concluded his letter with a note about the dispute with America. 'We have at last a satisfactory conclusion of the Trent Affair,' he said, 'and we all must rejoice at the maintenance of peace with the United or rather disunited States; but if we had been driven to war, we should I think have given them a lesson which they would not soon have forgotten.'[104] It was the sort of letter he could write to a friend far removed from the scene of action, but Palmerston knew Britain's international position was not quite so secure.

The consequences of the *Trent* affair were important. Only slow transatlantic communications, according to some accounts, prevented the bad feeling and high passions generated on both sides from escalating the dispute into open war between Britain and the North.[105] Palmerston's government was, certainly, by the beginning of 1862, more overtly hostile to the North than at any time previously. Palmerston thought war was quite likely, because, as he had put it in a letter to Russell in December 1861, 'nations and especially republican nations or nations in which the masses influence or direct the destinies of the country are swayed much more by passion than by interest'.[106] During 1862, however, the character of the war changed dramatically. In February the North secured its first notable military victory over the South, capturing New Orleans and making a significant inroad thereby into the heart of the Confederacy. This made the controversy in the summer of 1862 over Britain's alleged breach of its stated neutrality all the more significant. A ship ordered by the Confederacy was built on Merseyside and before the government could, at the bidding of the North, prevent its dispatch, the *Alabama* was delivered into the Southern navy. In sanctioning this material assistance to the South (as it was perceived in the North at least), the British government was held partly responsible for the considerable damage that vessel would go on to inflict on Northern forces over the next two years. Palmerston's government, despite its protestations of disinterestedness, seemed to be offering unequivocal backing to the South – and Gladstone in particular was talking ever more freely of the need to recognise, formally, the Confederacy as an independent government – at a time when the course of the war seemed uncertain, or at least the anticipated Southern victory seemed less assured. Palmerston worried that this would redound to Britain's discredit and disadvantage, whether the North won or not. 'The war will end in the separation of the South from North', of that much he remained sure, but as he also noted, at the end of 1862: 'The North will want compensation and some triumph over somebody to wipe away the stain of failure in the civil war. The invasion of Canada if it could be followed by the conquest of the province would satisfy both requirements, and if we were unprepared for resistance the temptation might be overpowering.'[107] The following autumn he judged that risk diminished, but still present, and he urged caution in order not to stir up aggressive feeling.[108] At all events, he would not sanction the sending of British troops to New Zealand, where the government also faced challenges to its position, at the expense of maintaining sufficient forces on hand to hold the Unionists in check in North America.[109] Palmerston worried, too, that the conflict might be brought much closer to home. He had not hesitated to identify the influence of 'exiled Irishmen' (through the newspapers which they controlled in the Northern states) on Federalists' policy.[110] In 1865 he was concerned that this Irish dimension might yet drag Britain and the United States into conflict, even after the civil war had come to an end in the spring. In late September he expressed his fears to Earl de Grey, the Secretary of State for War: 'The American assault on Ireland under the name of Fenianism may now be held to have failed, but the snake is only scotched and not killed. It is far from improbable that the American conspirators may try to obtain in our North-American Provinces compensation for their defeat in Ireland.'[111] This, in part, explains why he shifted his allegiance in favour of the North midway through the war. With a Northern victory increasingly likely by the summer of 1863, it made sense to conciliate the probable victor. Fortuitously, Lincoln had made his Emancipation Proclamation which had come into effect at the beginning of 1863. With the war now one that could be interpreted as a conflict fought explicitly over the issue of slavery, it was possible for Palmerston to argue that a Liberal government in Britain, which had all along opposed slavery and the slave trade, should align itself with the side now talking openly of the importance of freeing slaves.

Palmerston's policy in North America vacillated according to whom he thought would win. But he used liberal justifications to underpin his shifting position. In the beginning it was possible to argue that supporting the South was about offering backing to the cause of states' rights of self determination. Once Lincoln made explicit reference to slavery, Palmerston could make this the ground on which to manoeuvre Britain behind the Northern states. In each case, conveniently, liberal arguments brought Britain to the side that enjoyed the upper hand in the war. Pragmatic, even cynical, it might have been, but above all Palmerston knew that this was making the best of a weak position. Britain could, as had been recognised from the outset, do little to influence the outcome of the conflict. Neither side was appealing to Palmerston: the North was worryingly democratic, the South's pro-slavery position jarred with his liberalism. This was, as Palmerston saw, a situation in which Britain had much to lose and little to win: economic interests in America, imperial interests in Canada and a delicate situation in Ireland meant that Palmerston was pushed into a policy of wait-and-see in the hope that this would not alienate either side once the war was concluded. Recent accounts have credited Palmerston with having pursued a wise and successful policy. By reining in Russell's and Gladstone's support for the South, Palmerston avoided a potentially ruinous conflict with the North.[112] And by restraining the much more enthusiastically pro-Southern Napoleon III, Palmerston gained some credit in Northern circles for having moderated antagonistic European feeling.[113] Significantly, too, he managed generally to pursue a line of policy that accorded with British public opinion. In the early months of the war he had run up against a pro-Northern feeling in the press and among Cobdenite critics – Cobden had used the *Star* to advocate a critical line on the conduct of the Confederacy[114] – but by 1863 Palmerston's changing view blunted the criticisms of his earlier policy.

It was evident that in relation to foreign policy Palmerston was operating on increasingly unfamiliar terms. Events in continental Europe did little to counter the impression that Britain was losing ground. The limitations of British power were further exposed in central Europe at the same time as war in America revealed the extent to which Palmerston was riding the diplomatic waves, not steering through them. The crisis that blew up around the duchies of Schleswig and Holstein was notoriously complicated.

Mr Mellish [a senior clerk in the Foreign Office] was deeply versed in German politics. Some one once asked Lord Palmerston to explain to him the question of the Danish Duchies. Lord Palmerston replied, 'There are only two people who understand the question – myself and Mellish of the Foreign Office.' The other said that he thought Mr Mellish was dead. Lord Palmerston rejoined, 'In that case, I am the only person who understands the question.'[115]

The status of these north European duchies had been a source of dispute since the 1840s. In the wake of the revolutions of 1848, insurrectionists in Schleswig and Holstein, in an attempt to free themselves from the Danish crown, appealed to the German Confederation for support, which was given. In a series of agreements made in the early 1850s it was supposed that a restructuring of the Danish monarchy had been settled that would allow the duchies some measure of independence. In fact the relationship remained a highly ambiguous one. It was possible, therefore, for the Danish King, Frederick VII, in March 1863 to feel justified in issuing a patent which, although it did acknowledge Holstein's special position, maintained that Schleswig remained firmly under the Danish crown. The German Confederation was outraged and in Britain Russell and Palmerston advised the King to withdraw the document on the grounds that this was not really a plausible interpretation of the 1852 Treaty of London. That treaty, as a British Foreign Office memorandum noted, was a weak document: the contracting parties had all exchanged ratifications with Denmark, but not with each other, meaning that there were several interpretations of the terms in existence.[116] Palmerston, however, wanted above all to make sure that German intervention was avoided. He spoke in the House of Commons on 23 July of the danger to Europe of any threat to Danish independence and intimated that Britain would come to Denmark's aid in the event of such an attack.[117] In a memorandum composed a couple of days later he explained:

> It is impossible for any man who looks at the map of Europe, and who knows the great interest which the powers of Europe feel in the independence of the Danish monarchy to shut his eyes to the fact that war begun about a pretty quarrel concerning the institutions of Holstein would in all probability not end where it began, but might draw after it consequences which all the parties who began it would have been exceedingly sorry to have caused.
>
> As I have said we intirely concur with him and with every reasonable man in Europe including those in France & Russia in desiring that the independence the integrity and the rights of Denmark may be maintained.
>
> We are convinced, I am convinced at least, that if any violent attempt were made to overthrow those rights and to interfere with that independence, those who made the attempt would find in the result that it would not be Denmark alone with which they would have to contend.
>
> Fitzgerald has said if the government would say that under pretext of federal rights the German Confederation were not to interfere with the rights of the Danish Crown, and if France & Russia held similar language the danger to which he had adverted might be obviated.[118]

Emboldened by declarations of support at Westminster, however, rather than heeding the proffered warnings, the Danish parliament proceeded to ratify the patent on 13 November 1863. Just two days later, Frederick VII died. He was succeeded by Christian of Glucksbürg, as had been agreed would happen during the negotiations of 1852 at London, but the Duke of Augustenburg, whose father had renounced his family's claim to the duchies, came forward now insisting that his father's renunciation was not binding on him and asserting his title to the duchies. Liberals in Germany supported Augustenburg, as did Queen Victoria (Albert had always said the Augustenburg claim was a good one), but importantly Otto von Bismarck in Prussia saw an opportunity to exploit uncertainty in the duchies to advance Prussian interests, in particular to secure control of the port of Kiel. Bismarck was given a favourable hearing in Vienna where the Austrian government recognised that if it acquiesced in the secession of Schleswig and Holstein from Denmark, it might find that used as a precedent by Venetia to demand independence from Austria. In late December 1863 the German Confederation sent troops to occupy Holstein in the name of the Duke of Augustenburg and in January 1864 formally renounced the 1852 treaty. Having failed to settle the question on the terms agreed in 1852 (which had granted Holstein some autonomy), therefore, Bismarck's Prussia, along with Austria, proceeded to enter the duchies themselves on 1 February.

In Britain there was considerable sympathy for Denmark's position, and the Danish government looked to Britain for material support. If the details of the crisis were difficult to explain, what did strike a warning note was the fact that two great powers were threatening to overwhelm a small state at a strategically sensitive point. There was much talk of the need for a Franco-British negotiated armistice, but Palmerston was sceptical: as he explained in a letter to Russell, he thought France would participate only if it could secure some territorial gain in return, while if an attempt at a brokered peace failed, 'to enter into a military conflict with all Germany on continental ground would be a serious undertaking', and one which, he thought, would end in Germany's favour. It would be unwise, therefore, to push France and Prussia into open conflict, he concluded, and, on the whole, he thought it 'best for us to wait a while before taking any strong step in these matters'.[119] Important though Danish independence was, Palmerston thought the time of year, the 'smallness' of the British army and the 'great risk of failure in a struggle with all Germany' militated against direct action. Were the conflict to take to the seas, he thought, Britain might be better circumstanced, but this was fundamentally a land-based contest.[120]

A conference of the interested powers was held in London in April, but it achieved little and the armistice it arranged in May lasted only just over a month. In the face of overwhelming military force, the Danish government surrendered Schleswig, Holstein and Lauenberg to Germany at Vienna shortly afterwards. Palmerston had been mocked in the House of Commons for his inability to deliver British support to Denmark, although many, such as Cobden, were pleased to see British interventionism finally curtailed. Palmerston complained of the injustice of the situation. The Danes, he admitted to Gladstone, 'were in the wrong in the beginning and have been wrong in the end', but he thought they had been 'most unjustly used by the Germans'.[121] Writing to the King of the Belgians at the end of August 1864 he observed: 'It was, however, an unworthy abuse of power by Austria and Prussia to take advantage of their superior enlightenment and strength to crush an antagonist so utterly incapable of successful resistance; and the events of this Danish war do not form a page in German history which any honourable or generous German hereafter will look back upon without a blush.'[122]

But he could do little to alter events. Palmerston used Bismarck's own writings as evidence of a Prussian conspiracy. An essay written by the Prussian Chancellor on the subject of 'alliances' Palmerston described as 'an impudent vainglorious & boastful pamphlet intended to inlist Prussian sympathies in support of a ministry likely to be defeated in Parliament; to coax France by visions of Prussian assistance to promote the ambitious projects of France; to intimidate Austria by representing her [as] unable to stand alone, and to keep Russia quiet & friendly, and finally to destroy the influence of England on the continent by representing her as incapable of any exertion. The pamphlet is however ably written for its purpose.'[123] Bismarck did not entertain the sort of hostility towards Britain attributed to him by Palmerston, but it was convenient for Palmerston to be able to explain an obviously weakening British position as the result of such apparent malevolence. There was no escaping the conclusion, however, that by the end of his life and career Palmerston's foreign policy had lost a good deal of its force. If this was gratifying to his long-term critics such as Cobden, the satisfaction was no doubt tempered by the fact that this was not something Palmerston had consciously effected, but was simply the result of shifting power balances, which were not in themselves signifiers of a more pacific era. In February 1864 Lord Derby, speaking in Parliament, had criticised the government's foreign policy for its failure to respect the government's stated principle of non-intervention:

> Now, my Lords, as to non-intervention in the internal affairs of other countries, when I look around me I fail to see what country there is in the internal affairs of which the noble Earl [Russell] and Her Majesty's Government have not interfered. *Nihil intactum reliquit, nihil tetigit quod* – I cannot say *non ornavit*, but *non conturbavit*. Or the foreign policy of the noble Earl, as far as the principle of non-intervention is concerned, may be summed up in two short homely but expressive words – 'meddle and muddle.' During the whole course of the noble Earl's diplomatic correspondence, wherever he has interfered – and he has interfered everywhere – he has been lecturing, scolding, blustering, and retreating.[124]

The ridicule was directed at Russell, but Palmerston was just as much an architect of the mocked policies as his Foreign Secretary. In pointing to the disposition to lecture, scold, bluster and retreat, however, Derby highlighted

Britain's inability to do much more. It is said that one of Palmerston's maxims in foreign affairs was that any country would always give up three out of any four questions at issue; the successful powers managed not to reveal which three.[125] This had worked for Palmerston to some extent over a number of years and, buttressed by highly visible demonstrations of power, such as, perhaps most obviously, that directed at Athens over Don Pacifico, Palmerston had managed to mask the relative decline of British leverage with a flamboyant diplomacy. In the 1860s, however, fewer statesmen were willing to listen. Bismarck's Prussia and Lincoln's United States both saw that Palmerston was trying to punch above Britain's weight and they called his bluff.

Whatever disagreements and difficulties there might have been over foreign policy, crucially they did not serve to jeopardise one of the Cabinet's most delicate accessions in 1859, that of the Peelites, and specifically Gladstone. Gladstone, indeed, appeared generally content on this front. In September 1859 he had reported to his wife that he had 'been well pleased on the whole with the tone of the Cabinet: there is a good disposition to consider the case [China?] with its difficulties which are many, and they (P. included in some degree) do not take the hand over head view which was presented in the newspapers – and happily there is no perceptible tendency of opinions to decide according to our former controversy. The ground was quite new.' The following month he noted with some satisfaction that 'Altogether the pacific element predominates in the Cabinet as far as policy is concerned.'[126] While foreign policy, and specifically agreement over Italy, was probably not alone sufficient to heal the breach between Gladstone and Palmerston, it did at least help facilitate Gladstone's return to the Liberal fold.[127] By all accounts, the personal relations between the two were still somewhat cool. Palmerston, says Edgar Feuchtwanger, 'probably disliked Gladstone rather strongly, but usually managed to hide it. He thought the best way to handle him was to bully him a bit; and after lengthy outpourings by Gladstone in Cabinet, Palmerston would say: "Now my Lords and Gentlemen, let us go to business." '[128] Gladstone himself in 1863 complained that Palmerston had been 'bumptious . . . in his tone' in Cabinet.[129] And Palmerston was known to feel of Gladstone that 'He is a dangerous man, keep him in Oxford and he is partially muzzled; but send him elsewhere and he will run wild.'[130]

Palmerston was necessary to Gladstone and Gladstone was necessary to Palmerston. Indeed, it is argued in some quarters that it was Gladstone's fiscal policy that represented the real success of this government: as Cobden told Gladstone himself in 1863: 'I consider that you alone have kept the party together so long by your great budgets.'[131] These budgets were not uncontroversial, however, and had the potential, as Palmerston recognised, to unsettle, if not scuttle, the ministry. Gladstone brought to the Treasury a Peelite commitment to financial prudence and a determination to balance the government's accounts. He had also promised, in 1853 when Chancellor in

Aberdeen's government, that he would abolish income tax, a duty which, in 1860 when he was called on to draft his first budget under Palmerston, stood at ninepence in the pound, by far the highest rate yet levied for what was only ever supposed to have been a wartime tax. Yet when Gladstone presented his proposed measures to the Cabinet in January 1860 he suggested that the income tax should actually be increased, to tenpence, an augmentation of revenue which, when added to an existing surplus of £5 million, could be used to abolish paper duties, a measure which would, among other things, make newspapers considerably cheaper and could therefore be put forward as a good liberal measure to advance the interests of the wider population. Radical opinion in the Cabinet favoured Gladstone's plan to abolish the paper duties, but George Cornewall Lewis, Palmerston's former Chancellor, and Charles Wood, voted against the plans, preferring to retain the commitment to reducing (or abolishing), rather than increasing, income tax rates.[132] Some argued that if the government wanted to court popularity through its fiscal policies, it would do so more effectively by reducing duties on tea not paper.[133] The real debate, however, centred not so much on where to save, but on what to spend. Gladstone's desire to balance the budget was a political as well as economic consideration, inspired in part, since much of the demand for increases in expenditure was for armaments and fortifications, by a sympathy with (Cobdenite) pacifism. On the other side of the Cabinet table, Palmerston argued that in the prevailing international circumstances where war seemed possible, or at least it was important to show France that Britain was ready for conflict if provoked, this was not the time to pare back spending on defence provision and military preparedness. Gladstone did not deny the importance of defence provisions, but he thought Palmerston's enthusiasm in this direction was as much offensive as defensive. 'I would ask you however to consider,' he had written to Palmerston in the previous November, 'whether it is really wise to continue the present outlay on so great a scale for the building of more maritime castles which we call line of battle ships & which seem to be constructed on the principle precisely opposite to that of all land fortifications, and to aim at presenting as large a surface as possible to the destroying fire of an enemy.' Claiming that his intention was not to achieve 'the reduction of our outlay on building as a whole', but rather to make that expenditure more effective, and genuinely defensive, Gladstone was evidently concerned to make sure that spending in this quarter would not underwrite an aggressive foreign policy which he found both politically and economically unpalatable.[134] By early 1860 his position had hardened and he told Palmerston in February, for example, that he would not entertain proposals for an increased loan to augment fortifications.[135]

Palmerston was not opposed to repealing the paper duties. He had, after all, long recognised the usefulness of a cheap and widely disseminated newspaper press, and argued in support of Gladstone that it was 'the right thing to do',[136] but he also knew that the measure was damaging to Liberal unity and it was on these grounds that he urged on Gladstone the desirability of postponing the measure until 1861.[137] On 5 May, as the bill for repealing the paper duties was coming up for a third reading in Parliament, Palmerston tried once more to broker a compromise in the Cabinet. In a meeting to discuss the 'state of our finances & [the] state of affairs in Europe', he argued that, in spite of a projected shortfall of £1.5 million in the government's accounts by the end of the year, there should be 'No reduction of military and naval expenditure' and the paper duties bill should be dropped. Yet the majority in the Cabinet sided with Gladstone.[138] When the proposal was debated in the House of Commons three days later, Gladstone's bill scraped through with a majority of only nine votes. Lewis thought that with 'better management of the debate, the opposition wd probably have obtained a majority'.[139] With Palmerston known to be shaky in support of his Chancellor, and the narrowness of the Commons victory in mind, the government was decidedly nervous about the progress of the bill when it went to the House of Lords where it was known there was a strong inclination to throw the measure out. On 21 May the Lords delivered a clear verdict on the plan, defeating Gladstone's bill by 89 votes, with 26 Liberal peers voting against the government and 44 staying away unpaired.[140] This defeat raised a constitutional problem: could the House of Lords overturn the decision of the House of Commons on this bill? Some in the Cabinet thought they should resign in order 'to mark their disapprobation of the conduct of the House of Lords' but as the days passed it became clear that there was not much of an appetite, either in government or in the Commons, for a fight with the Lords. As Gladstone continued to look for a way to get his bill through both Houses, his support within the Cabinet gradually ebbed away. By July only Milner Gibson and the Duke of Argyll were willing to speak up for Gladstone's scheme.[141] Gladstone spoke of resigning, but it was obvious that to do so would simply be to place himself in political isolation.[142] For Palmerston, this made his position easier: Gladstone's divisive measure could be shelved without a confrontation between the two of them and the exposure of Gladstone's weakened position meant that Palmerston had less reason to fear Peelite dissent within his ministry. Liberals had, on the whole, backed Palmerston rather than Gladstone, even if that was for pragmatic parliamentary rather than ideological reasons and Gladstone had, in joining Palmerston in 1859, effectively given up any possible accommodation with the Tories. It is striking that a Cabinet was held in July, 'in Gladstone's absence, upon the fortification question, with respect to the mode of framing the scheme'. That ministers 'agreed to limit the demand for the sum requested during the current year' did not do much to alter the fact that Gladstone's stock was visibly diminished.[143]

The following year Gladstone again brought proposals for tax cuts and a resignation threat to the Cabinet table, but his bluster was just that. The Conservatives had already, through Malmesbury, told Palmerston that if

Gladstone resigned over the budget they would support the government; as Palmerston noted, '& at all events [they] will make no attempt to turn us out this session, unless we make war against Austria', and this in the knowledge that some Radicals, led by Bright, had told the Conservatives in turn that if they had chosen to unseat Palmerston they would have given them 'two years of office'.[144] When Gladstone's proposed budget for 1861 was discussed in Cabinet he found very little backing for his renewed attempt to repeal the paper duties, which he justified in part by pointing to a £2 million surplus in the coffers. Only Milner Gibson endorsed Gladstone's plan; the rest of the Cabinet talked up the merits of income tax and tea duty reductions. As Lewis recorded, the Cabinet was far from united: eight members argued for a reduction in the income tax, six for a lower duty on tea and two, Gladstone and Milner Gibson, for the abolition of paper duties. Lewis said the Cabinet separated on 12 April 'in a state of complete uncertainty' about its course and it seemed the Chancellor, who had indicated that he was prepared to quit over the issue, was expected to do just that. The following day, however, Gladstone returned to the Cabinet offering a compromise: he would cut income tax by one penny and still repeal the paper duty. After 'some discussion', this was adopted as government policy.[145] Colleagues had, between the meetings on 12 and 13 April, apparently persuaded Gladstone to relax his demands and effect a compromise, not least because events in Europe made it desirable to maintain Cabinet solidarity.[146] Certainly Palmerston had made it clear that he 'did not mean the fate of my administration to depend on [the] fate of his budget'.[147] The parliamentary debate on Gladstone's 1861 budget was less intense than that of 1860 only in the sense that it no longer provoked discussion of precedents; the one thing the Cabinet had agreed was that it would back a single finance bill, that would be passed *in toto* or not at all, in order to circumvent any opposition from peers. Otherwise, the budget was again a hard fought issue in Parliament.

Gladstone's principles of fiscal management were certainly prudent and popular with Radicals, and his budgets did, as Cobden observed, do much to underwrite Palmerston's government's claims to be acting in the Liberal interest, not least by underlining the commitment to free trade and liberalisation of commerce. Significantly, however, within government, this was not a platform from which Gladstone could mount a challenge to Palmerston's dominant position at the head of parliamentary Liberalism. Gladstone knew that he could not defeat the ageing Palmerston, who remained impossibly popular, and that he must simply wait to outlive him, for having now thrown in his lot with the Liberals his political future could only lie within that party. As he admitted, revealingly, in 1861 when struggling with Palmerston over expenditure, 'Up to a certain point, I must certainly make a stand';[148] but evidently he would not press it beyond that 'certain point'. Although the early 1860s are often recorded as having been a time of tension between the two ministers, not least over spending where Palmerston's projects jarred with

Gladstone's Peelite thriftiness (Gladstone complained to his wife in 1864 that 'What is really painful is to believe that he will not agree unless through apprehension, his own leanings and desires being in favour of a large and not a moderate expenditure'),[149] perhaps they were not really so far apart, beyond the evident personal dislike.

Gladstone had long since sought in public to distance himself from Palmerston, arguing in 1856, for example, that Palmerston's foreign policy since 1834 had 'scarcely had the approbation of a single British statesman', but he was obliged to concede that, 'whether from its manliness or from the sound and affectation of it, it has beyond all doubt been eminently agreeable to those who form the masses of the ten-pound constituency, and to those who reflect that constituency in the press'.[150] Yet the difference was frequently one of style as much as substance. Following Palmerston's death, Gladstone could not avoid acknowledging Palmerston's contributions, conceding in his third Midlothian speech in 1879 that the name of Palmerston 'will ever be honoured by those who recollect the erection of the kingdom of Belgium, and the union of the disjointed provinces of Italy'.[151]

Gladstone may have professed to mistrust Palmerston's courting popularity and his appeals to and accommodation of the 'people', but here again they were not so far apart. While Gladstone's celebrated 1864 declaration that every man 'who is not presumably incapacitated by some consideration of personal unfitness or of political danger, is morally entitled to come within the pale of the constitution' might have infuriated Palmerston, Gladstone's elaboration on his meaning was arguably one that Palmerston himself would have acknowledged as reasonable: by 'capacity', Gladstone explained, he meant 'self-command, self-control, respect for order, patience under suffering, confidence in the law, regard for superiors'.[152] And as David Steele has shown convincingly, while Gladstone may have shared contemporary suspicion of Palmerstonian appeals to the public, he too, certainly once 'unmuzzled', did just as much stumping around the country as Palmerston; and though it is the People's William who is remembered for taking politics to the masses, it was the People's Minister who introduced Gladstone to this technique. As Steele demonstrates, Palmerston and Gladstone between them visited most of Britain, spoke to the people about social order, free trade, empire and foreign policy, spreading the same or a similar message and sharing a common sense of the importance of going beyond Westminster.[153]

Another key aspect of the Liberal agenda was traditionally in the field of parliamentary reform. George Jacob Holyoake, a Radical and not Palmerston's greatest admirer, observed of the Prime Minister's attitude to this issue that he 'never said he was the enemy of Reform, but he never "felt like" promoting it'.[154] In notes made some time in 1860–61, at the time when Gladstone's financial policy had provoked a minor constitutional crisis over parliamentary procedure and precedent, Palmerston turned to John Hatsell's four-volume *Precedents of Proceedings in the House of Commons* (1776–96) from which he drafted some brief notes on the relationship between the Upper and Lower Houses. Of the House of Lords, he wrote:

> The conclusion to be drawn from the history of all these transactions is, that it should be the endeavour of both houses, and of every member of each house of parliament to take care in their proceedings not to transgress those boundaries which the constitution has wisely allotted to them, or to interfere in those matters which by the rules and practice of Parliament in former ages are not within their jurisdiction for the rights & privileges of Parliament are interwoven with the earliest establishment of government in this country.

Turning to the House of Commons he added:

> The sole and exclusive right of beginning all aids and charges upon the people and not suffering any alteration to be made by the lords is sufficiently guarded by the claims as here expressed, & it does not seem to be either for their honor or advantage to push the matter further and by asserting principles which may be subjects of doubt & discussion thereby to weaken their claim to those clear and indubitable rights which are vested in them by the constitution, and have been confirmed to them by the constant and uniform practice of Parliament.[155]

A reading of these notes makes it clear that Palmerston did not regard the institution as in need of further reform. There is an underlying faith in the efficiency of a proven system and of the established safeguards of long use and tradition. It is not insignificant that Palmerston's chosen authority on matters of parliamentary procedure was an eighteenth-century one.[156] Palmerston's wariness of making concessions to the poor and altering the political system had not been modified over the years. 'What can be the use of urging candidates to declare for ballot and other things which the present government never can agree to?' he had asked Granville in March 1857. 'They are only storing up causes of disruption of the party. Such pledges are wholly unnecessary for [the success] of any liberal candidate.'[157] If any changes were to be made, he reflected in another letter on Boxing Day 1859, they would have to be introduced as a necessary evil and not as a positive improvement:

> Our great difficulty will arise from the enormous quantity of additional votes which any lowering of the borough franchise will create in the large manufacturing towns practically disenfranchising the present electors, and at all events reducing to political nullities all the wealthy and intelligent men in those seats of manufacture and trade thus undoing that which it was one of the great merits of the Reform Bill of 1832 to do. But

lower the borough franchise we must, and perhaps by restrictions as to a certain period of residence before registration we may be able to mitigate the evil otherwise we shall be giving up the representation of the great towns to the trades unions.[158]

Gladstone continued to argue that Reform was a vital issue but the broad consensus in the Cabinet was that, in the midst of other crises, this could be put to one side. Palmerston dismissed Gladstone's calls for the government either to introduce a measure of parliamentary reform or to resign (on the grounds that they had 'come in on Reform') as an attempt to divert attention from his difficulties over the budget in 1860 and his unwillingness to subscribe to increased spending on defence.[159] The emphasis on change during this ministry, therefore, was on piecemeal reform of specific abuses rather than wholesale change of the system.[160] Following the lack of success of Russell's Reform bill of March 1860, in June the Cabinet had agreed to postpone any possible measure until at least the next session and when the subject was raised again in November it was obvious that there was little support for the issue. Significantly, even Russell was reluctant to press for Reform. As Lewis recorded in his diary, towards the end of a Cabinet meeting in mid-November:

the question of reform was propounded by Ld J. Russell. He requested Ld Palmerston to state his opinion. The latter gave his opinion at some length, defending the introduction of a Reform bill by the govt in [the] next session. Ld John then said that he had a clear opinion on the question, & this was, that it was *not* desirable to bring in a bill. He stated that the country did not appear to wish for ulterior reform, that the liberal members who had opposed the £6 borough franchise appeared to retain the confidence of their constituents, & that he was the last person who ought to complain of the country being satisfied with the act of 1832. All the rest of the Cabinet, without exception, acquiesced in this view, & the question was thus decided.[161]

This was perfectly in keeping with Palmerston's tastes. When discussing proposed changes to the county franchise in January 1860, Palmerston observed that the government would be 'taking a leap in the dark'. More voters, he said, meant more expenses, but also a reduction in the quality of the electoral base: 'the more respectable part of a very large constituency' would simply abstain, judging their votes ineffectual. Thus 'wealth and intelligence' would give way to the hegemony of the 'lowest class', who would be susceptible to bribery and (perhaps even worse) would fall 'under the dictation of the socialist leaders of the trade unions'.[162] When Gladstone opened up the question of allowing all capable men to come within the pale of the constitution in May 1864, Palmerston shared the 'unfavourable impression' which he thought

Gladstone's speech had made on the Liberal party. He thought the enthusiasm of the *Observer* for Gladstone's speech a curiosity:

> Mr Gladstone's doctrine which the Observer praises that every sane man has a moral right to a vote goes straight to universal suffrage which not even the most vehement Reformer has hitherto advocated. Moreover if every sane man has that right why does it not also belong to every sane woman who is equally affected by legislation & taxation.
>
> The fact is that a vote is not a *right* but a *trust*. All the nation cannot by possibility be brought together to vote and therefore a selected few are appointed by law to perform this function for the rest and the publicity attached to the performance of this trust is a security that it will be responsibly performed.[163]

The argument came straight from Dugald Stewart's lectures, backed by Palmerston's years of parliamentary experience. Palmerston still preferred to fend off demands for parliamentary reform and calls for active popular participation in politics by emphasising the vicarious participation (and therefore effective representation) already enjoyed by the majority of the population. Much as he had during the 1840s and 1850s, he continued to rely on a perceived popular identification of and with himself as a man for (if not quite of) the people and to buy off support for the more radical reform agenda with flattery and the rhetoric of inclusivity.

In August 1864 Palmerston was invited to Bradford to lay the foundation stone of the new Exchange building. George Jacob Holyoake, then editor of the *English Leader* later recorded how he had endeavoured to encourage the working classes not to be duped by Palmerstonian overtures. The leading figures within the working classes, Holyoake said, successfully broadcast the message that Palmerston was no friend to their interests. One such address, as Holyoake recorded it, asked:

> But will it be wise on your part – who are as yet unenfranchised, and mainly so through the influence of this Minister's antagonistic policy – to greet him with demonstrations of gladness? What has he ever done to merit it? Nothing . . . . working men, would it not be more manly and becoming to exhibit, in some measure, your disappointment at the manner in which your claims have been received – not by hisses and groans – but by a dignified and significant abstinence from all cheering, or other noisy demonstrations of joy?

When Palmerston visited, then, according to Holyoake, he was 'touched and pained' to find that the proposed cheer in his honour was not taken up by the people, leaving the Prime Minister 'standing as it were alone in that vast and voiceless crowd'.[164] Holyoake, however, was not an altogether impartial observer. According to *The Times*, although there had indeed been a meeting to discuss Palmerston's reception, that meeting had not been 'numerously attended' and 'the meeting was by no means unanimous' in its determination to oppose Palmerston. There were, reportedly, many interjections and disagreements and amid the 'uproar' at least one person present said it was the 'indifference' of the people themselves and not Palmerston that had held back change. An address complaining of Palmerston's failure to honour what were taken to be solid promises of reform made in June 1859 was drafted and placards were prepared for the visit, but the impact of this attempt to challenge Palmerston was diminished by official moves to prevent any presentation to him and by the outbursts of off-message individuals, such as the one who was reported to have shouted 'Europe's hope and England's glory!' as Palmerston climbed into a waiting carriage. The official reception was 'most cordial' and if the cheering in Peel Park as Palmerston passed had been 'not very demonstrative, it was amply made up for by unmistakeable enthusiasm manifested along the entire route' to the Exchange. In his speeches at the Exchange and afterwards at the official dinner Palmerston spoke fully of the warmth of his reception and of his pride at celebrating commercial progress and prosperity. In contrast to statesmen in 'despotic countries', he said, it was his 'good fortune' to have mixed with his fellow countrymen on 'easy terms' and to have 'see[n] their faces and show[n] one's own'.[165]

While a ceremonial visit and some high-flown rhetoric were obviously not accepted by all members of the unenfranchised classes as a substitute for formal representation, by the same token, Palmerston did have grounds on which to believe that there still existed some sense of popular deference by which unenfranchised opinion could be kept in hand without actively or overtly opposing or challenging it. By striking up a rapport with a sizeable portion of the population, therefore, Palmerston was able to reassure himself that he was satisfying his own liberal instincts for directing government in their interests (why would they generally cheer him if they did not agree that he did so?) without undermining the efficacy of that government by recklessly handing power to people (as yet) unprepared to exercise it. Palmerston's instinct was to consolidate his relationship with the people. His natural milieu was southern English but he would make periodic efforts to connect with those inhabiting the more northerly reaches of the country where he could test his standing with the wider population and reaffirm his liberal and popular reputation.

In late 1860 Richard Monckton Milnes had arranged one such visit for Palmerston to Yorkshire. By the time the visit came to be made, in October, Milnes rather regretted the effort – 'As my liking for him has very much gone off,' he wrote, 'I take this rather as a *corvée* than as a pleasure. It will cost me some money and anxiety, and the honour does not much touch me now' – but the tour went ahead and Palmerston enjoyed 'a triumphal progress' in the north country.[166] Arriving at Leeds he was mobbed by supporters at the railway station and in a progress over the course of a week he was welcomed warmly in all parts of the county, both on political grounds and personally; in Fairburn, just outside Pontefract where Palmerston owned a small estate, one elderly tenant commented on seeing her landlord again that 'He was a handsome man when he came afore, that is he was younger like, for he's very handsome now, you know, for his time.'[167] Only illness marred the visit: a cold which Lady Palmerston picked up during the trip was made worse by having to sleep in a damp bed at one of the houses they stayed in and they skipped a planned final visit to Wakefield (her illness was to last until late December, giving the lie to suggestions that the Palmerstons had simply had enough of the trip before its scheduled conclusion).[168]

The most important public aspects of the visit were the receptions in the larger towns of Leeds and Pontefract where local people were able to demonstrate their appreciation of the premier, and he, in turn, was able to talk up his liberal credentials. Commercial issues were of central concern to Yorkshire industrial communities and Palmerston was pressed in Leeds not to abandon plans to reform bankruptcy laws that would help secure the position of creditors. To such requests Palmerston was happy to accede, although he did seek to avert detailed technical discussion of the issues (admitting with regard to the bankruptcy bill that he had not read it himself and relied on a précis from the Attorney-General picking out the key points).[169] The greater part of the visit, however, was consumed by traditional civic and institutional addresses which praised Palmerston for his liberal policies at home and abroad over the past thirty years, which Palmerston happily accepted and took as an invitation to remind his audiences of his efforts in these directions particularly in terms of the promotion of religious liberty, the suppression of slavery, the spread of free trade, liberal reforms of local government and a general advance towards greater political freedom, both at home and elsewhere (he spoke particularly of Belgium, Spain, Portugal and Italy as examples of British-inspired liberal progress). Such well-rehearsed and predictable set-pieces were no doubt gratifying, but ultimately unexceptional. What does make such visits and speeches interesting is the way in which Palmerston used them as a platform to expound more fully on his conception of social and political improvement. Crucially, Palmerston's notion of advance rested on education. Speaking at the Leeds Mechanics' Institute and Literary Society he argued that rational and scientific understanding were central to progress. Having spoken about the importance of a subject like geology to an understanding of one's environment, Palmerston continued:

But there is no reason why the working classes should not learn the general outlines of a still further science, and be taught the main principles of the organization of the universe. There is no reason why they should not be taught that those innumerable bright spots which bespangle the sky on a clear night are not simply ornaments of the

Heavens, but that they consist of millions of suns, larger, many of them, far than our earth, surrounded by a planetary system like ours, and extending to such an infinity of space that, whereas the light which comes from our sun, which is 95,000,000 miles from the earth, reaches us in eight minutes, the light from some of these distant suns is calculated to have been hundreds, and in some cases thousands of years in reaching the earth. These contemplations are useful and healthful to the human mind. They inspire us with an awful respect and sentiment of the vast powers, of the vast wisdom, and the beneficence of that Almighty Being by whom the great and wonderful expanse of creation has been formed. And while, on the other hand, these contemplations, enlarging the human mind, must tend to abate the pride and vanity of prosperity, so, on the other hand, they must tend to calm and console those who may be labouring under adversity, by letting them see that the affairs of this world form but a small and minute part of the general dispensation of the Almighty, and that all these great arrangements, whatever their partial and temporary effect, are destined in the main for ultimate and permanent good.

Thus, education would improve men's minds, but it would also help harmonise society by giving its members a sense of their place in the wider scheme of things. What made Britain a more stable country than many others, he insisted, was that with an appreciation of 'order', 'Every rank knows its own position; it is neither jealous of those above nor does it treat without proper respect those who happen to be below it.'[170] It was 'the arrangement of Providence' he said, that societies should always comprise both rich and poor members, but it was a mark of any individual community's degree of civilisation how those different parts interacted; that he saw evidence, as he did speaking to the Leeds Ragged School and Shoeblack Brigade, of a benevolent attitude among the wealthy towards the poor was a sign of advance in Britain. This common vision of improvement, he said, meant that children who were otherwise disadvantaged could still learn 'early habits of industry, early habits of order, early instruction of a moral and religious description' that would result in 'their success in life'. Education, then, by which Palmerston meant personal improvement and social progress, would underpin stability:

In moral and intellectual matters we may take as examples the means employed in physical and material matters. If you want to dry up a morass, and to get rid of the noxious exhalations from an unhealthy district, you do not simply go and pump out the water which lies stagnant on the surface of the ground, but you go to the source of the evil, to the heads of the springs which percolate through this marshy district, and by turning them into new channels, diverting them from the country which they have impregnated, you lead them into healthy currents for the uses of mankind, and at the same time turn that which was only a noxious morass into profitable, fertile, and healthy land. (Cheers.) In the same way, I should say, you should intercept the sources of crime at the fountain head. Inculcate, early, in the minds of the children of the country maxims of religious and moral principles. (Cheers.) Teach them betimes the value and importance of rules, regulations, and order; teach the child, even in his school hours, to be obedient to certain regulations, and you will find that when he becomes a man he will be equally ready to submit to the laws of his country, and to maintain order in the society of which he is a member. (Cheers.)[171]

This was essentially a development of Palmerston's reflections on the theme of original sin delivered in Romsey in 1854 and repeated again thereafter, such as in December 1859 when he had told the Labourers' Encouragement Society in Romsey that

> I would particularly impress upon you the importance of attending to the manner in which you rear your children. Impressions made in early life we all know are lasting, and there are no impressions that go deeper into the mind of a child than those which he receives from his parents in his tender years. As the twig is bent, so the tree will grow. Those who are employed out of doors all day long have fewer opportunities than others of attending to the instruction of their children; but you, all of you, have moments which you can devote to that purpose, and you should not omit any opportunity which family intercourse affords you to impress strongly upon your children the distinction between right and wrong.[172]

It was also precisely the principle on which he had himself acted on his estates in Sligo where he had, since his first visit there, identified education as one of the most important means by which to reform the lives of his tenants. It was a matter for self-congratulation, as he told an audience in Pontefract during his 1860 visit, that commercial prosperity had liberated Britain from the fears of 'an anxious future' and instead placed the country on a secure and peaceable footing:

> It is, indeed, a useful lesson to all who are disposed to read it; it shows how the progress of enlightenment, the progress of intellect, the diffusion of knowledge, the increase of civilization, and the augmentation of civil and political liberty lead to personal and collective security – how that great aggregate, by increasing the security of property and affording a safe development for industry, tends to multiply the happiness of the people, to increase the wealth and power of the country, and to conduce to all those improvements in society which more and more qualify man to fill the dignified position which his Creator destined for him in this world.[173]

It was fitting, given his stated enthusiasm for education, then, that Palmerston should be elected as Rector of the University of Glasgow in November 1862.[174] In the spring of 1863 Palmerston visited Scotland, firstly to be installed as Rector at Glasgow and also to receive the freedom of the City of Edinburgh and an honorary doctorate from Edinburgh University. In his speech at Glasgow, on the importance of education, Palmerston also made sure that he did not repeat his mistake of 1853 by conflating unproblematically England with Scotland; instead he stressed their separate as well as shared interests.[175] Likewise, at Edinburgh, Palmerston said:

> Gentlemen, local pride and tradition have an inestimable value. *You, the people of Scotland*, are now part of a great nation – the nation which inhabits the UNITED KINGDOM; but *long may you continue to treasure up in your hearts your own peculiar traditions, history, and glory*; and, though you will be, as I know you will be, for ever loyal and affectionate to our common sovereign, and in kindly brotherhood with other portions of the union, yet *continue in your hearts to be Scotsmen*, and cherish in your minds, and in your recollections, all those glorious traditions which are connected with your peculiar portion of the BRITISH ISLAND.[176]

His erstwhile critics seemed satisfied: W.L. Burns observed that, 'This was really a more complete retraction than if Lord Palmerston had confessed his error in the most express terms.'[177] Overall, the 1863 visit to Scotland appears to have been a triumph. As Evelyn Ashley, who had accompanied Palmerston on the trip as his personal secretary, described it, Palmerston had been 'received everywhere with marked enthusiasm. As he went down the Clyde in a small steamer to Greenock, both banks of the river were lined with thousands of workmen, who had left their work to catch a glimpse of the Premier on the paddlebox, and to cheer him as he passed.'[178] Palmerston himself was delighted with his reception: 'My ears are still ringing with and almost deafened by the cheers which have accompanied us wherever we have been, whether driving walking, in doors or out of doors,' he told Lady Palmerston afterwards, adding in another letter: 'If I was as vain as John Russell or as self sufficient as Gladstone, I should return to you quite unbearable from conceit at the wonderful reception I have met with from all classes in Scotland but I bear it all meekly though with much inward gratification.'[179]

At Greenock, the town dignitaries were keen to applaud Palmerston's 'chivalrous patriotism' and, tellingly, in the light of Burns's concerns about the Palmerstonian threat to Scottish identity, preferred to 'rejoice to believe that the confidence which the whole nation reposes in your Lordship, is, in no small measure, shared by other peoples, less happily circumstanced than we are, who have learned from your Lordship's enlightened rule to admire our political institutions, and to look to Britain for ready sympathy and moral support in their struggles for national independence.'[180] Indeed, Palmerston was celebrated in some quarters for his efforts (or attainments) in actually reconciling the peoples living to the north and south of the border. The *North British Daily Mail*, for example, suggested on the occasion of his 1863 visit to Glasgow that

> Personal regard, beyond a question, we feel for him, but there is no need for indulgence in his case. 'It is well known,' said his Lordship, 'that Scotchmen have warm hearts, and that, when they like, they like to good purpose.' Englishmen who really know Scotchmen know this, and are always forward to declare that some of the truest friends they have ever been fortunate enough to find have been Scotchmen; but the number of Englishmen who do really know Scotchmen is very small; and, therefore, for the enlightenment of the Englishmen who don't, we are glad that the Premier has scouted the calumnious characterisation we are generally condemned to in the South – to wit, that we are a cold, cheese-paringly cautious race.[181]

Palmerston certainly made efforts in the course of 1863 to affirm the positive aspects of 'Scottish nationality', but he did so in the terms of British civilisation that by now characterised all of his outdoor speeches. Scotland, he said in a visit later that year, 'is a country remarkable for the educated intelligence of its people, for the high state of scientific agriculture there practised, for the great prosperity of its manufacturing industry, and for its success in commercial enterprise', and for this reason was a country that stood 'high in the respect and esteem of the civilized world'.[182] It was, arguably, the values of liberal, constitutional, even providentially favoured government that Palmerston's audiences in Scotland applauded. These values might have been described as 'English', but that did not necessarily alienate all non-English parts of Great Britain. His reception in Greenock, after all, had been made on the grounds that he was a liberal and unifying force in Britain:

> ... in common with all our fellow countrymen, we are proud of a MINISTER, who, by his penetration and sagacity, his firm yet liberal foreign policy, his commanding administrative talents, and his chivalrous patriotism, has maintained the honour and pre-eminence of the country in times of anxiety and danger, strengthened and extended our pacific relations with Foreign Governments, and taught the humblest subject of the Queen to confide in the British flag as a sure protection to life and property in every region of the globe. ...
>
> Among many signal benefits for which this favoured Nation is indebted to Divine Providence, we esteem it not the least valuable, that we have at the helm of public affairs in these critical times a Nobleman who combines with the unabated ardour and energy of his earlier years the ripe wisdom and experience of a veteran Statesman.[183]

It may have been hyperbole, but it was an image that resonated in many parts of Britain. Alongside the rhetoric, an important part of Palmerston's appeal lay in his dynamism and vigour.

On 8 November 1863, Palmerston recorded in his diary the details of an odd encounter earlier that day:

> Walking down Park overtaken by stout man with black whiskers and large eyes stared at me in the face as he passed, I stared fully at him. He fell back & followed me. I stopped till he overtook me I looking round at trees. He stopped and stared me rudely in face I stared at him again after a few seconds he touched my [sic] hat & walked on, & I saw no more of him.[184]

It was testament to Palmerston's vitality that, at the age of seventy-nine, he was prepared to face down a stranger in the street. The state of the premier's health had been a subject for comment among many of those who knew him for a number of years. It was well known that Palmerston had long been a sufferer from gout, but much of his supposed popularity derived from a perception that he was an energetic sportsman, something with which many people, even if they were largely politically illiterate, could identify on some level.[185] His love of boxing, for example, and his enthusiasm for some bouts and keen interest in the sport generally allowed observers to attach certain manly characteristics to Palmerston out of which he could fashion part of his public persona. When Thomas Sayers and John Heenan slugged it out for two hours and twenty minutes in a bare-knuckle fight for the unofficial world boxing championship in Hampshire on 17 April 1860, such was the intensity of the match that it brought the whole (illegal) sport under review.[186] The fight had ended technically as a draw but amid such scenes of confusion, claim and counter-claim and with such damaging effects on the health of the protagonists (it was effectively the end of Sayers's illustrious career in the ring) as to raise calls for such matches to be banned. As the issue came before the House of Commons, Palmerston encouraged his Home Secretary, Lewis, who had suggested that everyone who had been present at the fight might be prosecuted for participating in an unlawful assembly, not to join the attacks on the sport:

> I hope that in answering Ewart today about the law on pugilistic encounters, you will not give encouragement to the cry which some well meaning people are trying to get up against boxing matches. It is surely better that as no law can prevent men from quarrelling they should settle their quarrels with fists rather than with bowie knives or stilettos.
>
> As to the late fight instead of its being a disgusting exhibition, it seems to me to have been a noble display of manly courage & physical endurance honorable [sic] to the race to which the two champions belong.[187]

Though he had avoided 'pugilistic encounters' himself, at least since his schooldays, Palmerston remained an active sportsman, and in particular a keen horseman, famously galloping over to Harrow School to deliver prizes towards the end of his life, but in fact always an enthusiast for such exercise, making rides an important part of his daily schedule. Even in later life, Palmerston's appetite for vigorous physical exertion remained undimmed. As Abraham Hayward noted on one occasion in August 1856, 'Lord Palmerston was in the highest health and spirits. After taking his ride on Saturday, he came down to me as I was fishing on the lake from a boat, took the oars, and rowed for half an hour.'[188] Though there were signs that Palmerston was ageing, and that he was taking longer to recover from periodic ailments, on the whole his health held up during his later years. In October 1861 Clarendon reported to Cowley in Paris that the Prime Minister was wearing well: 'I assure you,' he wrote, 'that for the last twenty years you have not seen Palmerston look as he does now. The warmer breezes have agreed with him wonderfully, the sea has washed all the dye out of his whiskers and given him a bright colour of his own, and altogether he looks, and I am sure he feels, as if he did not care one straw for any man or thing on earth.'[189] In late 1861 reports were in circulation that a particularly severe attack of gout had laid Palmerston low, but though it was admitted that he was in a good deal of pain, by the end of the year his friends were relieved to find that there was 'no longer any ground for immediate anxiety on his account'. At all events, as Ashley reported, Palmerston would not be diverted from his work.[190] Clarendon thought the Tories had been exaggerating the rumours for political effect. 'The last canard was that he could keep nothing on his stomach, but as P. is not a man to work hard for such a *return* as that, it's pleasant to know that his appetite is as ever.'[191] Such periods of illness were becoming more frequent, but were always short-lived. George Jacob Holyoake could still be impressed by Palmerston's 'buoyancy': 'Shortly before his death,' Holyoake wrote, 'when he was more than 80, I watched him crossing Palace Yard, one summer evening, when the House was up early. Cabs were running about wildly, but he dodged them with agility, and went on foot to Cambridge House, in Piccadilly, where he resided.'[192]

It was such visible energy on Palmerston's part that lent just about enough credibility to suggestions that he had been caught in an adulterous relationship with a Mrs O'Kane in 1863. The allegation was that, in June 1863, Margaret O'Kane, wife of the Irish radical journalist Timothy Joseph O'Kane,[193] had visited Palmerston at home to discuss a political matter, only to be seduced by him. The adultery, Timothy maintained, had continued for some time afterwards and in October 1863 he petitioned for a divorce, citing Palmerston as co-respondent and demanding £20,000 in damages. It was a clear attempt at extortion, observed Clarendon, worked up by O'Kane's 'unscrupulous attorney'. The scandal was widely commented on, but Clarendon thought Palmerston would 'pull through': it was, he wrote to Cowley, 'a disagreeable business, but still I can't believe that "the old lad" is destined to have such a miserable end to his career'.[194] Palmerston's lawyer, Nicholl, thought the case would never come to trial, but Palmerston found it frustrating to have to wait for the matter to be concluded, or rather for 'the conspiracy' to 'be exposed'.[195] When it became clear that Margaret O'Kane was lukewarm on the case, and that the O'Kanes' marriage was of dubious legal status, Palmerston obtained an order in chambers requiring O'Kane to prove the marriage was valid, which he did not do.[196] On these grounds the case collapsed and on 4 February 1864 a judge dismissed the case 'wild "with contempt"', as Palmerston noted in his diary.[197] The case was, in itself, a farce, but in the varied reaction to it, Palmerston might be said to have benefited from O'Kane's action. Gladstone and the Liberal party whips had fretted over the impact of the allegations on Palmerston's and, by extension the party's, reputation with Nonconformists and with the electorate. Their worries were misplaced. As Derby and Disraeli recognised, the case had the potential to enhance Palmerston's popularity, and they even suggested the affair had been a deliberate Palmerston scheme to that very end. The wits might have asked whether 'though the lady was certainly Kane, . . . was Palmerston Abel?' The country, while laughing at the claims, seemed to judge that in most matters he was.[198] A verse composed on the scandal in 1863 titled 'Lord Palmerston / He is a clever man / And they won't get over him' underlined the popular affection for a national minister. Several turgid verses of doggerel concluded:

Here's jolly good luck to Palmerston,
    And although near fourscore,
We hope that he may live in health,
    For twenty years or more;
We could not find a better,
    If we hunted through the land,
Then here's success to Palmerston,
    He's a regular good old man.[199]

It was perhaps unsurprising that, for a minister who had played on his physical strength and charms throughout much of his life, his decline should be widely treated in such a way as to sustain the image. Palmerston might have been undeniably 'Old Pam', but there were many who liked to think that there still lurked behind the wooden teeth and greying whiskers something of the old 'Lord Cupid'. Populist writers at least have been drawn to accounts of Palmerston's death as the result of, or at least having occurred in the midst of, one final fling with a maid, on the billiard table, at Brocket Hall.[200] Palmerston's reputation for womanising has lent just about enough credibility to such stories for the rumours to persist. Indeed, for those hagiographers as well as scandal-mongers for whom Palmerston remained a larger-than-life, 'full-blooded male', the image perhaps added suitable colour to their portrait of a cavalier lover and politician. Yet the reality is far removed from such gossipy narratives. Palmerston died on 18 October 1865 following months of ill health, surrounded by family and physicians intent on creating for him an appropriately pious and very Victorian melodramatic deathbed.

Palmerston had been in indifferent health for some time. He had been plagued by periodic afflictions of gout during his later life, but by the mid-1860s there was no doubt that Palmerston's health was declining rapidly and more seriously than at any previous period. In April 1865 his physician, Dr Ferguson, diagnosed haematuria and 'catarrh of the bladder' after Palmerston had been 'riding a rough horse' which had caused pain and 'great distress' and 'reduced his strength considerably'. In the summer Ferguson died and after briefly consulting a Dr Watson, Palmerston turned to Dr Protheroe Smith who prescribed 'tonics and astringents' combined with 'generous diet and rest' which caused some improvement in Palmerston's condition, particularly once the parliamentary session ended and he was able to retire to Brocket Hall.[201] He explained his retreat from public life on the grounds that his 'old' and 'disagreeable enemy' gout had struck again, but even then he was concerned that reports of his poor health should not make their way into the newspapers.[202] Smith took care to monitor the 'quantity as well as quality of pus and . . . character of the secretion' in Palmerston's urine and prescribed nightly doses of laudanum together with regular fresh air and the avoidance of 'every thing whether it be in diet, horse-exercise or any thing else which in any way produce local irritation or general derangement of health'. Although anxious that his patient was not rallying as quickly as he would have hoped, Smith did think, as he put it in August, that 'Considering the chronic nature & long continuance of the malady there is every reason to be satisfied with the improvement heretofore attained.'[203] The infection of the bladder seemed to be improving and other symptoms, such as the 'brown thick fur' that had been covering Palmerston's tongue, had cleared. Although he continued to avoid horse-riding, Palmerston, evidently sensing some recovery himself, was in the habit of taking regular drives in his carriage but on 9 October, as the weather began to turn much colder, he caught a cold during one such outing. His doctors had long feared the effects of the autumn weather and were no doubt frustrated that Palmerston spent an hour and a half 'undressing and dawdling and would take his bath as usual' rather than going straight to bed. Very quickly Palmerston's condition became serious again: the bladder infection returned, accompanied by 'abdominal and dorsal pains', an irregular heartbeat, renewed furring of the tongue and a loss of appetite. For the next few days Palmerston rallied and collapsed alternately (on 13 October Clarendon had thought he 'was looking quite rosy'),[204] but by the end of the week three doctors, Smith, Watson and Burrows, had all examined him and found him to be, more or less, improving, though there remained cause for concern. News of Palmerston's illness spread and it became clear that he was not likely to recover: the Prince of Wales noted that 'He will be a great loss to the country & to his party but of course at 81 he could not be expected to last very long.'[205] On Tuesday 17 October Palmerston took what turned out to be a final turn for the worse and 'symptoms of great prostration set in'. Palmerston's 'intellect remained unimpaired to the last', but his fading pulse and uneasy breathing signalled an imminent demise.[206] At a quarter to eleven on the morning of 18 October, Palmerston died. The official cause of death was noted as catarrah of the bladder and abscess of the kidney.[207]

As Palmerston declined before them, his doctors and family contrived to make his death a 'good' one.[208] The Evangelical Smith did not confine his role simply to medical matters: having 'anxiously watched for an opportunity of bringing before my patient the saving truths of salvation and ascertaining his belief in them', as soon as Palmerston rallied somewhat on 15 October Smith decided that the 'fitting occasion' had arrived. It being Sunday he proposed that they 'think of the Lord Jesus Christ, who as it were on a Sunday rose from the dead'. Palmerston assented and Smith proceeded to ascertain Palmerston's faith, and, after a period of catechising, Smith was reassured 'of the sincerity of his belief'.[209] When, on 17 October, Smith informed Palmerston that he was indeed dying, Smith suggested that it was 'the Lord's will that your very useful career on earth should terminate' and, he continued, Palmerston must place his faith and trust in the Lord in order that he might be saved. Palmerston was too weary to reply, but Smith would not let the matter drop; he discerned that Palmerston had bowed his head in assent and told him that if that was to be a sign of agreement, then he should 'do nothing else', to which Palmerston 'closed his eyes and remained quiet'. This satisfied Smith, but in the morning of the 18th, as it became clear Palmerston did not have much time left, Smith, Shaftesbury and William Cowper took it in turns to pray at his bedside. Thus, noted Smith, 'during the rest of the fatal morning till death robbed the world of its great master – kind prayer and consolatory texts of Scripture were uttered by familiar voices in his hearing' and as Palmerston breathed his last 'all around his couch were in earnest prayer'.[210] The theatrical aspect of Palmerston's death was certainly designed for the comfort of his family and attendants, not Palmerston himself who was practically unconscious throughout his final hours. Shaftesbury found in the spectacle evidence of God's goodness and concluded that Palmerston had been a great 'instrument . . . in the hands of the Almighty'. Searching for evidence of Palmerston's own piety, William Cowper, Shaftesbury and Smith in particular took his immobility as evidence of assent and approval of their prayers.[211] The remaining members of Palmerston's family, Emily and the children and grandchildren, mourned with less marked religiosity in an adjoining room.

Palmerston left an estate valued by probate at almost £97,000.[212] Broadlands, by now a valuable and profitable estate, went to Emily for life and on her death in 1869 passed, according to the terms of Palmerston's will, to William Cowper, the second of the Cowper children, the first, George Augustus, having already inherited the title and estates of the Cowper earldom on the death of Emily's first husband. When William Cowper (elevated to the peerage as Mount Temple, a nod in the second part of the title to his biological link to Palmerston) died in 1888 the estate passed to Evelyn Ashley, second son of the Shaftesburys, their eldest son, Anthony, succeeding to the Shaftesbury inheritance. Palmerston had always been particularly fond of the Shaftesbury family: Minny he thought a sunbeam whenever she entered a room;[213] the Shaftesbury children he described as 'the most delightful children I ever saw . . . so cheerful, so sensible, so affectionate and behaving on all occasions with such propriety'.[214] Thus far did Palmerston's prescriptions keep the estate within the family he felt close to. When Evelyn Ashley died in 1907 the estate passed to his son Wilfred, an MP, and it was through his daughter, Edwina, that Broadlands would come to be associated in the twentieth century with the Mountbatten family.[215]

Georgiana Cowper, William's wife, thought Palmerston 'could not have done better', dying as he did 'in the Zenith of his glory' and before he had 'begun to go down hill'.[216] To Lady Westmorland 'his death completes the extraordinary happiness of his life', possessed as he was of all his faculties and 'everything that can make life pleasant'.[217] Emily was inwardly distraught at her loss but 'calm and resigned' and took comfort from having survived her husband: 'she feels,' Lady Holland noted at the time, 'she was essential to him, which is perfectly true.' This was not, however, merely a personal tragedy. It was undeniably the end of an era. Lady Holland lamented that Palmerston was 'the last of the set I remember at Holland House when I entered it',[218] but this was more than the final instalment in the history of salon-based Whiggery. Condolence books were inscribed to Lady Palmerston from around the country expressing the apparent mood of national loss: as one such from the City of Manchester put it: 'the memory of the late distinguished statesman will long live in the recollection of his grateful fellow-countrymen from the conviction that it has been mainly owing to the wisdom which has characterized the administration over which he has so long presided that this country has long continued to enjoy, and under circumstances of peculiar difficulty and peril, the inestimable blessings of peace.'[219] Gladstone, who was 'stunned' by the news, observed on the day of Palmerston's death that 'Tomorrow all England will be ringing of it, and the world will echo England.'[220] From Paris, the French Emperor and government duly expressed regret at the loss of an eminent European statesman. The memory of his years of service would reverberate around the world, said Drouyn de Lhuys, the French Foreign Minister, and nowhere more so than in France where it was understood that it was Palmerston, who had been the first to recognise the important shift in French politics in 1851, who had done so much to establish friendly and secure relations between the two countries and to disseminate the liberal ideas that united the two polities.[221]

Yet there were suggestions that Palmerston's posthumous reputation owed as much to good luck as to great attributes. A year after his death the *Pall Mall Gazette* noted:

> When we turn from considering the consequences of Lord PALMERSTON's death to a more deliberate revision of the judgements formerly passed upon his character and public services, there seems little to correct in the appreciations generally uttered a year ago. A popularity so long continued, and growing to the very last, proves the possession of many fine qualities. Such unclouded success in the slippery and contested arena of politics argues remarkable skill. But surely the attribute which chiefly distinguishes him in the roll of our statesmen is his good fortune. We say this with no inclination to disparage our English statesman whom the whole course and end of his life has crowned. *Fortunam reverenter habemus.* But the very highest order of deserts never runs a career so smooth. Our deepest gratitude and love are due to those who have bought them at a price. Lord PALMERSTON never had the supreme honour of making the foes of a great cause his own. The temperament which preserved him from enmity during his life denied him the power of bequeathing passionate regret. We may still for a long time miss him in Parliament. We may wish that Mr GLADSTONE possessed a little of his tact and geniality. But it cannot be long before his memory will begin to fade, as that of the shrewdest men and the pleasantest fellows *will* fade; and when the generation which has quizzed his *canniness* and cheered his pluck passes away, it will not be easy to understand how Lord PALMERSTON achieved and maintained so long his pre-eminent authority in English life.[222]

The judgement was in some respects a perceptive one. Palmerston's legacy was certainly ambiguous and his historical profile has frequently been obscured by the more prominent figures of Gladstone and Disraeli standing in the foreground. Historians have been left to debate whether he was a Liberal, a Tory, or perhaps just a Palmerstonian, often recording an open verdict. This is unfortunate on a number of levels. It fails to take account of the lasting impact Palmerston had on Victorian politics and society and therefore risks exaggerating, at Palmerston's expense, the influence of later Victorian politicians in the process of making Britain more 'modern'.

To many later commentators Palmerston seemed an awkward fit in the Victorian cultural and political scene.[223] The impression that Palmerston was a man out of tune with his times goes to the heart of debates about his place in Victorian Britain: whether he was an incurable reactionary or, by contrast, a progressive visionary. He was often taken to be, as Philip Guedalla put it in

1926, 'the last candle of the eighteenth century', a throwback to a bygone age, yet, as E.D. Steele has more recently suggested, his later career might sustain a quite different interpretation, in which he is presented as the possessor of a 'genius for adaptation' whose governments in the 1850s and 1860s were in fact a 'conscious introduction to the new era' of democratic politics.[224] In fact, Palmerston does not quite fit either formulation. He was neither the anachronistic symbol of an earlier age who had outlived his usefulness and relevance, nor was he the conscious, self-styled harbinger of late Victorian democracy and modernity. His reputation lies somewhere between the two extremes; he was neither behind nor ahead of his times, but very much of them. His commitment to social reform and his determination to address the 'condition of England question' on some level suggests that there was not quite a 'moral vacuum' at the bottom of him; his wariness of the masses and his limited conception of the nature and value of democratic politics, however, speak of his innate Whiggish, and very mid-Victorian, conservatism. Walter Bagehot would describe this as an ignoble legacy. Palmerston, he said, 'a little degraded us by preaching a doctrine just below our own standard – a doctrine not enough below us to repel us much, but yet enough below us to harm us by augmenting a worldliness which needed no addition and by diminishing a love of principle and philosophy which did not want deduction'.[225] This, though, was to expect of Palmerston more than he could reasonably deliver. Palmerston embodied the mid-century equilibrium; his were the politics of balance and stability, of careful accommodation of change where necessary but of not pursuing reckless and premature innovation for its own sake. As he had told an audience in Leeds in 1860:

> though rapid and pen-stroke improvements may suit despotic countries where the Executive government is all in all, where the nation is bound to obey those impulses which come from above, yet in a country like this, where the whole nation participates in the function of government, and where public opinion is as powerful as the edicts of the Premier's authority, time and delay are often necessary for the accomplishment of good and useful legislation. If improvements and reforms are not fully discussed, if all the objections on one side and the other are not put forward before the mind of every reflecting man, if public opinion is not fully prepared for the change, the good, great as it may be, which may result from this change is not fully and properly accomplished.[226]

Such moderation, however, did not mean inaction, but rather a commitment to stability and the preservation of a certain 'equipoise'.

LEGACY

Happy in his mental and physical condition, and in the circumstances of his life, he may be considered, like the Roman statesman, felix etiam opportunitate mortis.
The Saturday Review, 21 October 1865

SIR JOHN TRELAWNY observed in 1862, not altogether approvingly: 'Lord Palmerston has the happy gift of saying tonight what no one expects, but a great majority will agree to tomorrow morning. He has a manner, too, which conciliates his bitterest opponents. While his geniality cannot fail to please, it is not quite satisfactory to those who have been in the habit of attaching great importance to laws, customs, Institutions or policy, in affecting the current of a Nation's History, to reflect that the personal qualities of one man carry every one captive.'[1] This sense of political ease has sometimes led to suggestions that Palmerston seemed always to sail with a favourable wind and enjoyed a charmed life. On hearing of the Prime Minister's death in October 1865, for example, John Wodehouse (later first earl of Kimberley), observed: 'If ever a man could be pronounced fortunate both in his life & death Lord Palmerston is the man.'[2] The supposed element of luck in Palmerston's career has not gone unnoticed.[3] Thus, for example, the argument goes, the effective division of the continent in 1830 on ideological lines, following the French Revolution in July, seemed to place Britain in the position of holding the balance between the forces of autocratic and liberal government which Palmerston could manage by a mix of alliances, threats and conferences. With the benefit of operating within governments whose interests lay elsewhere (such as Grey's concern with parliamentary reform) or led by ministers, such as Melbourne, who exercised limited control over the Foreign Office and a young Queen who, at least for a while, deferred to her Foreign Secretary, Palmerston developed a commanding control of his department. Although the limitations of British power were starting to become apparent, Palmerston could turn episodes such as the granting of independence to Belgium (a matter largely settled in principle before Palmerston came to office) or the establishment of the Quadruple Alliance in 1834 into a 'public triumph at little cost' (so at least John Charmley has said of the latter) while a general policy of bluff was rarely called since

France and Russia, 'the two countries whose ambitions he feared the most', never found common cause because of fundamental differences of ideology. Even in the face of apparent reverses, such as in his policy on the Spanish marriages question in the 1840s or Don Pacifico in the 1850s, Palmerston survived and turned setbacks into successes, if only by passing responsibility to others. 'Palmerston was not averse to taking the credit for events over which he had little control; for him "the connection between publicity and diplomacy was fundamental; an unsung triumph was only half a triumph".' Foreign events favoured Palmerston at home, too, his ability to reunite the Liberal party in 1859 owing much to the coincidental drive for Italian independence providing a common rallying point for disparate liberal interests. Even where Palmerston appeared to exhaust his good fortune, as over Schleswig-Holstein, 'time softened the impact . . . and lent a tincture of rose to "Pam's" earlier triumphs.'[4] To the argument might be added the disharmony among Palmerston's opponents, such as Derby and Disraeli, and, furthermore, Palmerston's ability simply to outlast his principal rivals, some of whom, such as Sir Robert Peel or Prince Albert, died at opportune moments.

There is no doubt some substance to such an argument: since Palmerston was not omnipotent, a measure of good fortune did make his political dominance possible. But it is inadequate if that is taken to suggest that Palmerston lacked purpose or ability to pursue a particular course. As Gladstone acknowledged, 'it was the force of will, the sense of duty, and the determination not to give in, that enabled him to make himself a model for all of us who yet remain to follow him', while Disraeli praised Palmerston's combination 'in the highest degree [of] two qualities which we seldom find united – energy and experience'.[5] Yet if Palmerston was widely acknowledged to have been a significant political presence, quite how that was to be interpreted in the years following his death was not always certain.

Palmerston's last words were, reportedly, 'Die, my dear Doctor, that's the last thing I shall do!'[6] Death was, of course, Palmerston's final mortal act but it was not, in a sense, the last thing he did. Since 1865 his reputation and legacy have continued to divide opinion among politicians and historians alike. There was at the time, and subsequently, a pretty widespread sense that Palmerston's passing marked the end of an era: 'We shall never look upon his like again,' observed Walter Bagehot in an obituary in *The Economist*.[7] To the German essayist Dr Geffcken, writing about Palmerston some years later: 'the feeling was universal that with him ended an epoch in English public life – an epoch during which England had truly held her place in the council of the nations, and had attained a mighty internal development; and it was felt that after him began the time of democratic innovations at home, and of unsteady guidance abroad, – the era, in short, of the *Epigoni*.'[8] Yet, equally, there were others who have seen in Palmerston not just a figure who gave a shape to British foreign policy long after his death, but also a more or less direct inspiration to politicians such as Benjamin Disraeli. Whatever the significance of Palmerston's death, there is similar disagreement over just what had been lost. Eulogists and hagiographers were quick to publish obituaries and essays stressing Palmerston's impact for the greater good while antagonists, such as Palmerston's erstwhile critics in Urquhartite circles, were equally swift with the publication of *Materials for the True History of Lord Palmerston* designed to show his malign and corrupt record.[9]

From a historical perspective, Palmerston has been relatively ill served by biographers. The official *Life*, a joint production of Sir Henry Bulwer (who wrote the first three volumes) and Evelyn Ashley (who authored the final two and later revised the whole for a two-volume abridged edition) was, in effect, little more than a carefully selected and annotated edition of Palmerston's most interesting or quotable letters. Palmerston's private life was discreetly left in the shade and most attention was given to his dominance in foreign affairs. Reviewers noted that Bulwer's contributions were the most enlightening since his 'remarks' were not only elegantly written but were based on his own experiences as a diplomat during much of the period he was writing about. The *Annual Register* suggested these volumes were in fact 'more or less unconsciously' a 'fragment of autobiography'.[10] Ashley, by contrast, 'suppressed himself' much more (according to the *Daily News*), but as a result the quality of the analysis was thought to suffer and Ashley, who had for some years been Palmerston's private secretary, was, it was suggested in some quarters, perhaps too close to his subject to really do it justice.[11] What was apparent, however, whatever the literary merits of the work, was that this was a biography written with a view to articulating a (still valid) Palmerstonian alternative to Gladstonian liberalism.[12] Bulwer and Ashley's *Life* was coloured from the outset by the determination of its authors to make it a contribution to ongoing debates about Victorian liberalism in the 1870s. It remained the only accessible source for Palmerston's private papers, however imperfectly chosen and presented (anything especially inflammatory about France was expunged, for example), and thus was used as the raw building blocks of many later studies. Anthony Trollope was not the first, or last, to take Ashley (the two-volume edition) 'as my guide to his general life' when composing his own biography of Palmerston.[13] While such studies may have revealed something of contemporary interpretations of Palmerston, they added nothing of substance to an understanding of Palmerston's life, career and impact, although biographers such as the Marquis of Lorne were able to add a few amusing anecdotes to flesh out the character of their subject.[14]

Scholarship on Palmerston, such as it was, focused narrowly on using Palmerston as a medium through which to write about a fast disappearing British (or frequently more specifically English) golden age of power, prosperity and progress. Thus, for example, to Bagehot Palmerston was very much a man of the world and, importantly, of his times, while *The Times* noted in its obituary that 'There never was a statesman who more truly represented England than Lord Palmerston', one of the few statesmen in British history 'who in times of great difficulty have rendered England prosperous at home and famous abroad'.[15] But as the limitations of Britain's international power and prestige seemed ever more apparent to late nineteenth-century observers, this 'achievement' appeared even more significant and indicative of Palmerston's place in history and not the present. Even less friendly studies took it for granted that Palmerston was a symbol of a passing, if not a past, age. Thus when Philip Guedalla published his biography in 1926 he did not essentially revise the generally accepted view of Palmerston when he suggested that with Palmerston's death in 1865 'the last candle of the eighteenth century was out'.[16] Guedalla's work, however, though elegantly written, was not a reliable book and has justly been described as more a work of art than a rigorous biography.[17] Ten years later Herbert Bell produced a valuable two-volume study, but he had no access to Palmerston's private papers and little interest in Palmerston's activities beyond the diplomatic sphere.[18] The narrow interest in Palmerston as an international statesman was reflected in the fact that the next major Palmerston study was Sir Charles Webster's *Foreign Policy of Palmerston, 1830–1841*, published in 1951. Although Webster did use some material from the Palmerston archive, this was a classic example of technical diplomatic history and it did nothing to explain the broader contours of Palmerstonian politics or indeed Palmerston himself.

By the mid-twentieth century, therefore, the limited conception of Palmerston as a Foreign Minister had produced a number of unbalanced accounts and thus could A.J.P. Taylor suggest in 1954, with only secondary sources to inform him, that 'Very little has been written, or ever will be, about . . . [Palmerston's] place in British political life, for it is an empty one.' In so far as domestic concerns appeared important, it was in the need to acknowledge that Palmerston 'owe[d] his success solely to public opinion' (and even 'ended his life its prisoner') but that, fundamentally, 'he did not voice any great principle or idea'.[19] It was entirely in keeping with this developing historiographical trend that Donald Southgate's 1966 study of '*The Most English Minister . . .': The Policies and Politics of Palmerston*, another book based exclusively on published sources, should offer a study of Victorian politics rather than a biographical treatment. Indeed, Southgate's analysis only begins in 1829 and it omits periods of Palmerston's life when he was not in office. Jasper Ridley's well-written though not particularly academic *Lord Palmerston* of 1970 did flesh Palmerston out a little, but the limitations of a study based on published official records and secondary texts were evident once again. Palmerston had, a century after his death, become a two-dimensional caricature of a bellicose Foreign Minister.

Kenneth Bourne's lengthy study of Palmerston's early years was a major departure in Palmerston studies. For the first time since Bulwer and Ashley had done so, a biographer had trawled through Palmerston's private papers and had recognised the importance of domestic politics and even Palmerston's private life to an understanding of this significant but still imperfectly perceived figure. Yet though Bourne pointed to a number of important new approaches to Palmerston, his unfinished study left the portrait an incomplete one. Suggesting that there was, however, a serious domestic politician lurking behind the gunboat diplomat did at least pave the way for historians such as E.D. Steele to look afresh at Palmerston's later career and suggest that not only were there, *pace* A.J.P. Taylor, some great principles or ideas to consider, but that Palmerston had pushed Britain consciously and deliberately towards a democratic future.

For all their limitations, studies of Palmerston written since the 1930s had, it is true, begun to acknowledge something more substantial in Palmerstonian politics, but the identification of that something remained vague and even speculative. Thus, for example, in his closing remarks, Bell suggested that Palmerston could 'best be understood' as 'an exponent of early and mid-nine-teenth century nationalism', in which 'he showed the lack of moderation of a bigot'. In his pursuit of pre-eminence for Britain, however, Palmerston, in Bell's view, evolved a system of 'moral nationalism' in which public opinion and popular liberties were made central to the direction of the national interest; that he found, in effect, 'the force of public opinion a great fact and made it a great doctrine'.[20] What remained unclear was whether this pointed to a recognition of the need to play to public opinion for tactical reasons or was an acknowledgement of a shifting political balance towards something more inclusive, if not indeed democratic. Southgate, some time later, preferred to emphasise the cautionary aspect of Palmerstonian politics, arguing that all along Palmerston had acted as a check to liberalism, his death transferring the 'onus of providing a brake for Liberalism from No. 10 Downing Street to the Whig aristocracy and the smoking room of the House of Commons'.[21] But if Palmerston had held the forces of change in abeyance, or moderated their excesses, he was not necessarily hostile to political progress. Thus has Steele more recently suggested that, quoting G.C. Lewis, Palmerston's distinctive contribution to politics was to foster 'an aristocratic-democratic representative constitution'. Indeed, judged Steele,

> In saying of Palmerston 'he devoted more time and ability to . . . under-standing the people than any democratic politician of his age', the *Daily News* . . . recognized that his ministries were a conscious introduction to a new era. If not a good party man, he fashioned the instrument which served Gladstone well: a Liberalism whose unifying idea and function – social harmony in pursuit of ordered change – he had redefined and emphasized. Disraeli and, with more success, Lord Salisbury tried to acquire this Palmerstonian inheritance.[22]

It is instructive to consider the way in which Palmerston was appropriated, or rejected, following his death in order to make some sense of this problematic legacy. Gladstone, in party terms, had the best claim to inherit Palmerston's mantle, but although he supplied the necessary eulogies to his predecessor, he did so in terms replete with qualifications. He could not shake the feeling that, as he had put it in 1856, Palmerston's foreign policies, where they had found favour, had done so only among the rowdier sections of the public and press.[23] It was not a reputation Gladstone wished for himself. Yet in rejecting what he took to be the brash chauvinism of Palmerston's showier foreign policy (in 1850 Palmerston may have proclaimed *civis Romanus sum* but as Gladstone pointed out that was to link Britain with an aggressive and enslaving ancient empire), Gladstone obscured Palmerston's contribution to liberalism. Disraeli was far less scrupulous about adopting Palmerston's patriotic rhetoric, but not his liberal ideals, and using this as the basis for populist appeals to the prejudices of the British people.

It has become a commonplace to see in Disraeli's novels evidence of his personal outlook; thus in reading *Endymion*, when Lady Montfort observes approvingly that Lord Roehampton, whom Disraeli had modelled on Palmerston, 'does not care a rush whether the revenue increases or declines. He is thinking of real politics: foreign affairs; maintaining our power in Europe', Lord Blake was happy to conclude that Disraeli 'always regarded foreign policy as the most important and fascinating task of the statesman'.[24] At the time Disraeli wrote *Endymion*, in the late 1870s,[25] his politics were indeed deeply coloured by his attention to external policy, most vividly in his cultivation of a sense of British imperial grandeur, and his commitment to preserving some sort of balance of power, problematically though significantly, for example, asserting in 1875 that he would 'settle' the Eastern question that had 'haunted Europe for a century'.[26] In considering this patriotic and *realpolitik* attitude, it has become almost a platitude to argue that Disraeli was one of the natural 'heirs of the Palmerstonian tradition',[27] laying claim to the legacy of Palmerston's blustering foreign policy, and indeed in many ways defining that legacy (even if that was in large part only because Gladstone did not). Paul Smith has rightly cautioned that the 'common idea that he [Disraeli] donned Palmerston's mantle in foreign policy is accurate only if the cut of that cloth is properly recognised and his reservations about some of its gaudier trimmings noted'.[28] Yet by the 1870s, to which period this comment relates, Disraeli was able not simply to don the Palmerstonian mantle, but to define it. Freed from the need to operate in the shadow of, or in opposition to, the figure he in many ways sought to emulate, Disraeli could indeed happily trim away the gaudier embellishments of Palmerstonism and create a Disraelian policy. This had important implications for Palmerston's posthumous reputation, particularly since Gladstone did not much want to associate himself with Palmerston, and Palmerston's own official biographers were doing what they could to make that separation clear to a late Victorian audience.

One of Palmerston's few quotable statements, perhaps rather too quotable, was his dictum of 1848 that Britain had no eternal allies and no perpetual enemies.[29] It has subsequently become a historical justification for diplomatic intransigence, or at least determination; to take one example, as Alan Bullock put it in his biography of the post-war Foreign Secretary Ernest Bevin, 'the familiar picture of a truculent Bevin angrily declaring "I won't 'ave it",' brought to mind an image of 'Palmerston in a cloth cap'.[30] The image of Palmerston as a steadfast defender of national interests, unencumbered by troublesome obligations and ideological commitments, has had an important impact: the perceived absence of such forthright Palmerstonian rhetoric in Japanese diplomacy since 1945, for example, has led one recent commentator to observe that 'Japan has not had what could be properly called a foreign policy' at all.[31] More recently, Palmerston has been appropriated by American neoconservatism as part of a shorthand justification for an assertive foreign policy.[32] This crude caricaturing of Palmerston as a bullying gunboat diplomat has served largely to confirm or enhance his status among groups on the political right. The problem, of course, is a selective reading of Palmerston's career and legacy. As one of the more astute commentators on such casual links between contemporary right-wing politics and Palmerstonism observed: 'In a famous speech of the nineteenth-century British prime minister, Lord Palmerston, the realist credo found its most eloquent spokesman: "We have no eternal allies and we have no perpetual enemies. Our interests are eternal and perpetual, and those interests it is our duty to follow." But later in that same speech, Palmerston went on to explain that the policy of Britain was also "to be the champion of justice and right: pursuing that course with moderation and prudence, not becoming the Quixote of the world, but giving her moral sanction and support wherever she thinks justice is, and whenever she thinks that wrong has been done."'[33] Palmerston was much more than an unthinking gunboat diplomat and although he formulated his foreign policy with a certain flamboyance, much as he lived his life, this should not mask his attempts to create an intelligent and coherent political doctrine and to express that through his foreign policy. As Gladstone observed in a speech to Parliament shortly after Palmerston's death: 'He had the power to stir up angry passions, but he chose, like the sea-god in the *Æneid*, rather to pacify.'[34]

In 1936 the historians Sir Charles Webster and E.L. Woodward argued in the letters pages of *The Times* over the sincerity of Palmerston's conduct in Spain a century earlier, agreeing ultimately that whatever its defects, Palmerston's foreign policy was at least driven by a genuine concern to guard constitutionalism in Europe against despotism.[35] Still, apparently, Britain was believed to exercise some sway in the world, and as such a Palmerstonian legacy was a reminder of an obligation to do good with that influence. Inter-war commentators perhaps exaggerated the ability of Britain to achieve much, but if they had overestimated Britain's influence in the 1930s, the limits of that power were much more clearly in evidence a decade later. As E.H. Carr observed in 1946:

> When Palmerston banged the despatch box with his fist and made provocative speeches, the effect was due not to the weight of the fist or the strength of the language, but to the overwhelming preponderance of the British navy and to the willingness of the British Government to use it. Today the idea apparently still prevails that to bang the despatch box with a fist twice as weighty as Palmerston's and to use language twice as strong will compensate for the lack of British preponderance in ships and air squadrons and military divisions. This view is both seductive and dangerous; it encourages the comfortable belief, which played so much havoc in British foreign policy between the wars, that words can be a substitute for deeds.[36]

Yet Carr's words of caution fell on many deaf ears. The memory of Palmerstonian grandstanding, as Britain moved closer to Europe in the 1960s and 1970s in particular, seemed to illustrate how far Britain's stock had fallen in recent times, while in the 1980s and 1990s he seemed to serve as a role model for patriotic adventurism in the Falklands or for 'punching above Britain's weight' in the chancelleries of Europe.

In the late twentieth century and early twenty-first, then, Palmerston has come to represent no-nonsense *realpolitik* foreign policy. This is not wholly accurate and fails adequately to encapsulate the subtleties of Palmerston's foreign policy. Palmerston might just as easily, and properly should, have been taken as the root of a more liberal tradition in British foreign policy that stressed his commitment to the principles of freedom and constitutionalism for Europe, much as Webster and Woodward suggested. As Anthony Howe has argued, by the mid-nineteenth century Palmerston was increasingly coming to represent not the vested interests of old money and aristocratic privilege, but 'the international concerns of the liberal bourgeoisie', and his concerns were motivated less by conceptions of vested interests than by important middle-class attitudes. Support for Italy, to take but one example, mobilised a latent Protestantism in the English middle class, while simultaneously standing as a model for the working class's search for political emancipation.[37]

Palmerston's attempts to present his foreign policy underpinned by a belief in constitutional government were, to some extent, about how Britain interacted with foreign powers. But it was equally a means by which Palmerston, who spent much of his career at the Foreign Office or dealing with external questions, was able to demonstrate to the British people that he was a defender of their interests. The rhetorical constructions of Britain on the international stage certainly produced a powerful narrative of improvement which played well to domestic audiences eager for a vicarious role in the liberal and progressive mission or project in which Britain seemed to be engaged. But in Palmerston's case, though the rhetoric could hide inconsistencies, he was not insincere. Palmerston's commitment to liberal advancement – increased freedom, increased liberty, moral and environmental improvement – was genuine, but for him power was exercised on the people's behalf by an enlightened, forward-looking but moderate elite. That this was often elaborated to imply an English, or British, superiority over European neighbours was something Palmerston did not shy away from, but which has sometimes tended to confuse under-standings of his primary purpose.

ABBREVIATIONS

Ashley	Evelyn Ashley, *The Life of Henry John Temple, Viscount Palmerston, 1846–1865*, 2 vols. (London: Richard Bentley, 1876)
BDL	*Benjamin Disraeli Letters*, 7 vols. [to date] (Toronto: University of Toronto Press, 1982–2004): vols. I–II (1815–34; 1835–37), ed. J.A.W. Gunn, J. Matthews, D.M. Schurman and M.G. Wiebe; vols. III–V (1838–41; 1842–47; 1848–51), ed. M. G. Wiebe, J. B. Conacher, J. Matthews and M. S. Millar; vol.VI (1852–56), ed. M. G. Wiebe, M.S. Millar and A. P. Robson; vol. VII (1857–59), ed. M. G. Wiebe, M.S. Millar, A. P. Robson and E. Hawman
Bell	H.C.F. Bell, *Lord Palmerston*, 2 vols. (London: Longmans, Green, 1936)
BIY	Borthwick Institute, University of York
BL	British Library
BL, Add Ms	British Library, Additional Manuscripts
Bourne	Kenneth Bourne, *Palmerston: The Early Years, 1784–1841* (London: Allen Lane, 1982)
Bulwer	H. L. Bulwer, *The Life of Henry John Temple, Viscount Palmerston*, 3 vols (London: Richard Bentley, 1870–74)
Chamberlain	Muriel Chamberlain, *Lord Palmerston* (Cardiff: University of Wales Press, 1987)
Connell	Brian Connell, *Portrait of a Whig Peer: Compiled from the Papers of the Second Viscount Palmerston, 1739–1802* (London: André Deutsch, 1957)
EHR	*English Historical Review*
Greville Memoirs	*The Greville Memoirs, 1814–1860*, ed. Lytton Strachey and Roger Fulford, 8 vols. (London: Macmillan, 1938)
Guedalla	Philip Guedalla, *Palmerston* (London: Hodder & Stoughton, 1937 edn)
Hansard	*Hansard's Parliamentary Debates*
HJT	Henry John Temple, subsequently third Viscount Palmerston. (Abbreviation used in notes in the early chapters to distinguish Palmerston, the subject of this biography, from his father, the second Viscount Palmerston.)
HRO	Hampshire Record Office
LQV	*The Letters of Queen Victoria: A Selection from Her Majesty's Correspondence between the Years 1837 and 1861*, ed. A.C. Benson and Viscount Esher, 3 vols. (London: John Murray, 1907)
LQV II	*The Letters of Queen Victoria. Second Series. A Selection from Her Majesty's Correspondence and Journals between the Years 1862 and and 1885*, ed. G.E. Buckle, 3 vols. (London: John Murray, 1926–28)
NLS	National Library of Scotland
NLW	National Library of Wales
ODNB	*The Oxford Dictionary of National Biography* (Oxford: Oxford University Press, 2004 and online [oxforddnb.com])
Opinions	*Opinions and Policy of the Right Honourable Viscount Palmerston, G.C.B, M.P., &c. as Minister, Diplomatist, and Statesman, during more than forty years of public life. With a memoir by George Henry Francis* (London: Colburn, 1852).
PP	Palmerston Papers (Broadlands Papers), University of Southampton Library
PRONI	Public Record Office of Northern Ireland
PSL	*The Letters of the Third Viscount Palmerston to Laurence and Elizabeth Sulivan, 1804–1863*, ed. K. Bourne (London: RHS/Camden Fourth Series, Vol. 23, 1979)
Ridley	Jasper Ridley, *Lord Palmerston* (London: Constable, 1970)

RP	Russell Papers, The National Archives, Kew
Southgate	Donald Southgate, *'The Most English Minister . . .': The Policies and Politics of Palmerston* (London: Macmillan, 1966)
Steele	E.D. Steele, *Palmerston and Liberalism, 1855–1865* (Cambridge: Cambridge University Press, 1991)
TNA	The National Archives, Kew
Webster	Charles Webster, *The Foreign Policy of Palmerston, 1830–1841*, 2 vols. (London: G. Bell, 1969)
WSRO	West Sussex Record Office
WYAS	West Yorkshire Archive Service

NOTES

Introduction

1. W.E. Gladstone to Sir Anthony Panizzi, 18 Oct. 1865, PP, BR22(ii)/22/6.
2. *The Times*, 21 Oct. 1865.
3. Disraeli to Lady Londonderry, 2 Feb. 1855, quoted in W.F. Moneypenny and G.E. Buckle, *The Life of Benjamin Disraeli, Earl of Beaconsfield*, 2 vols. (rev. edn, London: John Murray, 1929), i, p. 1383.
4. On the fragility of Palmerston's health, see, for example, Queen Victoria to the King of the Belgians, 31 Dec. 1852, *LQV*, ii, pp. 522–3.
5. Writing to his brother shortly after his appointment as Prime Minister, Palmerston described himself as 'l'inévitable': Palmerston to William Temple, 15 Feb. 1855, PP, GC/TE/356.
6. Steele.
7. Palmerston to Aberdeen, 12 Feb. 1854, PP, HA/G/10.
8. The mayor of Southampton wrote to Palmerston describing him as the 'people's minister' in early 1852, shortly after Palmerston had been ejected from the government: R. Andrews to Palmerston, 26 Jan. 1852, PP, GMC/106.
9. Ridley, p. 528.
10. According to popular doggerel in Germany *c.*1848, 'Hat der Teufel einen Sohn / so heisst er sicher Palmerston' [If the devil has a son/his name is surely Palmerston]. See F.L. Müller, *Britain and the German Question: Perceptions of Nationalism and Political Reform, 1830–63* (Basingstoke: Palgrave, 2002), p. 57.
11. Edward M. Whitty, *The Governing Classes of Great Britain: Political Portraits* (London, 1859), p. 118.
12. Philip Guedalla, 'Lord Palmerston in Action', *Sunday Times*, 3 May 1936.
13. See, for example, the reviews by D.C. Moore in the *Journal of Modern History*, 56:1 (1984), 142–4; Valerie Cromwell in the *EHR*, 99 (1984), 398–401; and Kenneth Fielden in *History*, 69 (1984), 145.
14. Southgate, p. xv; Bourne, p. xiii.
15. Chamberlain, p. 1.
16. A comment written in Nov. 1829, included in a notebook containing newspaper cuttings, anecdotes, notes on Irish affairs, 1827–*c.*1832, PP, BR22(ii)/13, facing pp. 33–4.
17. J. Parry, *The Rise and Fall of Liberal Government in Victorian Britain*, (New Haven and London: Yale University Press, 1993), p. 194.
18. Extract from the *Edinburgh Review*, Jan. 1843, transcribed in Palmerston's hand, PP, M/154.
19. Arthur D. Elliot, *The Life of George Joachim Goschen, first Viscount Goschen, 1831–1907*, 2 vols. (London: Longmans, Green, 1911), i, p. 65.
20. From Palmerston's speech at the University of Edinburgh (where he had received an honourary LLD degree), April 1863, as printed in the *Edinburgh Evening Courant*, 2 Apr. 1863, PP, BR206/2.
21. George Henry Francis, 'Contemporary Orators, No. VIII: Lord Palmerston', *Fraser's Magazine*, 33: 195 (Mar. 1846), 319–20, quoted in Joseph S. Meisel, 'Humour and Insult in the House of Commons: The Case of Palmerston and Disraeli', *Parliamentary History*, 28:2 (2009), 234.
22. Henry Drummond Wolff, *Rambling Recollections*, 2 vols. (London: Macmillan, 1908), i, pp. 114–15.

Chapter 1 About Harry, 1784–1800

1. Clifford to H.L. Bulwer, 21 Sept. 1870, Bulwer, i, pp. x–xi.
2. James Hannay, 'The Family of Temple', *Cornhill Magazine*, 12 (1865), 749–60. Hannay adopts Walter Savage Landor's book title of 1853 for his quotation (p. 760). For a general history of the Temples, see also J. Dalton, *A Brief Notice of Viscount Palmerston, his Ancestors and Antecedents*.

From 'Genealogical Notices' of distinguished Ancient Irish Families (Dublin: W. Powell, 1857), esp. pp. 3–9.

3. Hannay, 'Family of Temple', 752, 755.
4. Elizabethanne Boran, 'Temple, Sir William (1554/5–1627)', *ODNB*.
5. Robert Dunlop, 'Temple, Sir John (1600–1677)', rev. Sean Kelsey, *ODNB*.
6. J.D. Davies, 'Temple, Sir William, baronet (1628–1699)', *ODNB*.
7. Stuart Handley, 'Temple, Sir John (1632–1705)', *ODNB*.
8. W.P. Courtney, 'Temple, Henry, first Viscount Palmerston (1672/3–1757), *ODNB*; Hannay, 'Family of Temple', 759; Connell, p. 22.
9. E.A. Smith, 'Temple, Henry, Palmerston (2nd Visc.) (1739–1802)', *ODNB*; Connell, p. 23.
10. Connell, *passim*; Bourne, pp. 1–3.
11. Connell, pp. 21; 212 (on Fox and Pitt).
12. Connell, pp. 94–100, 138–43. This is essentially an inversion of the story told by Bulwer of the meeting which had Palmerston falling in love with Mary having fallen from his horse and been taken to the Mee household to be treated: Bulwer, i, p. 4; Mabell, Countess of Airlie, *Lady Palmerston and her Times*, 2 vols. (London: Hodder & Stoughton, 1922), i, p. 31.
13. Sarah, daughter of Count Rumford, quoted in Connell, p. 20.
14. Ashley was mistaken in locating the birth at Broadlands (Evelyn Ashley, *The Life and Correspondence of Henry John Temple, Viscount Palmerston*, 2 vols. (London: Richard Bentley, 1879), i, p. 2. This information was added by Ashley to Bulwer's original text which formed the basis of Ashley's two-volume abridged edition of their combined five-volume *Life*, of which Bulwer had written the first three volumes.
15. Diary of Palmerston (2nd Visc.), 21 Oct. 1784, Connell, p. 156.
16. Guedalla, p. 13.
17. Connell, p. 157; Bourne, p. 2.
18. Quoted in Bourne, p. 3.
19. HJT to Lady Palmerston, 3 Feb. 1795, PP, BR22A/1b.
20. *Life and Letters of Sir Gilbert Elliot, first Earl of Minto from 1751 to 1806*, ed. the Countess of Minto, 3 vols. (London: Longmans, Green, 1874), i, p. 107 (from a letter dated 26 June 1786).
21. Lady Palmerston to Palmerston (2nd Visc.), 17 Dec. 1786, Connell, p. 169.
22. Palmerston (2nd Visc.) to Lady Palmerston, 24 Feb. 1795, Connell, p. 321 (referring to Harry's dancing at an earlier date).
23. *Life and Letters of Sir Gilbert Elliot, first Earl of Minto*, i, p. 98.
24. Connell, pp. 199, 209, 258, 296, 320.
25. Bourne, p. 3; Chamberlain, p. 10.
26. Lady Palmerston to Palmerston (2nd Visc.), 18 July 1791, Connell, pp. 228–9.
27. Bourne, p 3.
28. Connell, p. 260.
29. Bourne, p. 4.
30. Palmerston (2nd Visc.), journal, 15 Aug. 1792, Connell, p. 267
31. HJT to Lady Palmerston, 11 July 1794, PP, BR22A/1b (written from Munich); Connell, p. 293.
32. Ravizzotti is first mentioned as a member of the party in one of Lady Palmerston's letters to her brother written from Bellinzona on 18 July 1793 (Connell, p. 288).
33. Bourne, p. 6.
34. Ibid.
35. Palmerston, 10 Dec. 1794, Connell, p. 320.
36. HJT to Lady Palmerston, 25 Feb. 1795, PP, BR22A/1b.
37. HJT to Lady Palmerston, 'Londre samedi fevr 28 1795', PP, BR22A/1b.
38. HJT to Lady Palmerston, [n.d., ?Mar. 1795], 15 Mar. 1795, PP, BR22A/1b; Connell, p. 321.
39. Palmerston (2nd Visc.) to Lady Palmerston, 17 Mar. 1795, Connell, pp. 321–2.
40. Guedalla, p. 21.
41. W.T.J. Gunn, *The Harrow School Register, 1571–1800* (London: Longmans, Green, 1934), p. 154; Bourne, p. 6.
42. Percy M. Thornton, *Harrow School and its Surroundings* (London: W.H. Allen, 1885), pp. 196–7.
43. Ibid., p. 202.
44. Palmerston (2nd Visc.) to Lady Palmerston, 18, 26 May 1795, Connell, pp. 323–4.
45. Palmerston (2nd Visc.) to Lady Palmerston, 3 June 1795, Connell, pp. 324–5.
46. HJT to Lady Palmerston, 24 Oct. 1795, PP, BR22A/1d.
47. Thomas Bromley to Palmerston (2nd Visc.), 15 Oct. 1795, PP, BR22A/4.
48. Palmerston (2nd Visc.) to Lady Palmerston, 22 Feb. 1796, Connell, p. 325.
49. HJT to Lady Palmerston, 10 June 1795, PP, BR22A/1d.
50. HJT to Palmerston (2nd Visc.), 9 Dec. 1795, PP, BR22A/1d.

51. Bourne, p. 8.
52. Augustus Clifford to H.L. Bulwer, 21 Sept. 1870, Bulwer, i, pp. x–xi.
53. Connell, p. 420.
54. Marquis of Lorne, *Viscount Palmerston, KG* (London: Sampson Low, Marston, 1892), p. 2.
55. HJT to Lady Palmerston, 29 June 1800, PP, BR22A/1d.
56. Connell, pp. 420–1.
57. Francis George Hare to HJT, 5 Jan. 1798, PP, BR22(i)/1/4; HJT to Francis George Hare, 29 Mar. 1798, PP, BR22(i)/1/5.
58. HJT to Palmerston (2nd Visc.), 23 Oct. 1799, PP, BR22A/2.
59. HJT to Lady Palmerston, 1 Dec. 1799, PP, BR22A/1d.
60. HJT to Lady Palmerston, 11 May 1800, PP, BR22A/1d.
61. Bourne, p. 9.
62. HJT to Lady Palmerston, 29 June 1800, PP, BR22A/1d.
63. HJT to Lady Palmerston, 23 Mar. 1795 and HJT to Palmerston (2nd Visc.), 23 Oct. 1799, Connell, pp. 322, 424; HJT to Palmerston (2nd Visc.), 23 Oct. 1799, PP, BR22A/2.
64. HJT to Palmerston (2nd Visc.), 13 June 1800, PP, BR22A/2.
65. Thomas Bromley to Palmerston (2nd Visc.), 22 July 1800, PP, BR22A/4.
66. Thornton, *Harrow School*, pp. 300, 361.

Chapter 2 North and South, 1800–1806

1. Quoted in Spencer Walpole, *Life of Lord John Russell*, 2 vols. (London: Longmans, Green, 1891), i, p. 60.
2. Bourne, p. 11.
3. Palmerston (2nd Visc.) to Dugald Stewart, 19 June 1800, Connell, p. 426.
4. 'Autobiography' written by Palmerston for Lady Cowper, *c*.1838–39, PP, D/26, reprinted as 'Autobiographical sketch entire, as given to me – HLB' in Bulwer, i, pp. 367–83 (here p. 367).
5. Lady Minto to Minto, 21 Feb. 1802, *Life and Letters of Sir Gilbert Elliot, first Earl of Minto, from 1751 to 1806*, ed. the Countess of Minto, 3 vols. (London: Longmans, Green, 1874), iii, pp. 235–6.
6. S.H. Romilly, *Letters to 'Ivy' from the first Earl of Dudley* (London: Longmans, Green, 1905), p. 4.
7. Mackintosh, quoted in Bourne, p. 11.
8. Michael P. Brown, 'Stewart, Dugald (1753–1828)', *ODNB*; Gordon Macintyre, *Dugald Stewart: The Pride and Ornament of Scotland* (Brighton and Portland: Sussex Academic Press, 2003), esp. pp. 24–54.
9. Bourne, p. 12.
10. Stewart himself quoted the guinea and a half price to Lord Lansdowne in 1796: see Macintyre, *Dugald Stewart*, p. 106.
11. Notes by the second Viscount Palmerston on Edinburgh and Stewart, n.d. [1801?], PP, BR23AA/8/4.
12. Bourne, p. 13.
13. Palmerston (2nd Visc.) to Dugald Stewart, 19 June 1800, Connell, pp. 425–6.
14. Dugald Stewart to Palmerston (2nd Visc.), Connell, pp. 426–7. According to Connell this letter was a reply to Palmerston's of 19 June, but Connell (presumably mis-)dates Stewart's letter as 16 June 1800.
15. Connell, pp. 427–30.
16. Travel journal of HJT, 'London to Edinburgh via Lake District and Edinburgh to Inverary, 11 Sept.–30 Oct. 1800', PP, BR23A/1 (entry for 11 Oct. 1800).
17. HJT to Elizabeth Temple, 16 Oct. 1800, PP, BR24/1/14. (Stewart's nephew is not named in HJT's letter but there is a reference to Stewart's nephew Peter Miller living at Lothian House at this time in Macintyre, *Dugald Stewart*, p. 106. Miller would have been 18 not 20, according to Macintyre.)
18. Palmerston (2nd Visc.), journal, 7, 8, 9 Nov. 1800; Lady Palmerston, journal, 10 Nov. 1800, Connell, pp. 430–1.
19. HJT to Palmerston (2nd Visc.), 28 Nov. 1800, PP, BR22A/2.
20. Maria Edgeworth, *Moral Tales* (1801; London: Simpkin, Marshall, one vol. edn, 1853), pp. iv–v.
21. HJT to Palmerston (2nd Visc.), 18 Apr. 1801, PP, BR22/A/2.
22. HJT to Lady Palmerston, 20 Nov. 1800 and 28 Mar. 1801, PP, BR22A/1c.
23. [M. Stewart], *Memoir of the late Dugald Stewart, Esq., Author of the Philosophy of the Human Mind* (Edinburgh, 1838), p. 12.
24. HJT to Lady Palmerston, 16 Nov. 1800, PP, BR22A/1c.
25. James McCosh, *The Scottish Philosophy: Biographical, Expository, Critical, from Hutcheson to Hamilton* (London: Macmillan, 1875), p. 283.

26. HJT to Lady Palmerston, 28 Mar. 1801, PP, BR22A/1c.
27. HJT to Lady Palmerston, 15 May 1801, PP, BR22A/1c.
28. HJT to Palmerston (2nd Visc.), 28 Nov. 1800 and 10 Dec. 1800, PP, BR22A/2.
29. HJT to Palmerston (2nd Visc.), 10 Dec. 1800, PP, BR22A/2.
30. Bourne, p. 18.
31. HJT to Palmerston (2nd Visc.), 22 Mar. 1801, PP, BR22A/2.
32. HJT to Lady Palmerston, 28 Mar. 1801, PP, BR22A/1c.
33. Dugald Stewart to Mr Blanc, 27 Apr. 1801, PP, BR22(ii)/7.
34. HJT to Palmerston (2nd Visc.), 10 Dec. 1800, PP, BR22A/2.
35. Book of essays by 3rd Viscount Palmerston (bound volume), 1800–6, PP, BR22(ii)/6.
36. HJT to Palmerston (2nd Visc.), 22 Mar. 1801, PP, BR22A/2.
37. HJT to Lady Palmerston, 28 Mar. 1801, PP, BR22A/1c.
38. HJT to Lady Palmerston, 16 Nov. 1800, PP, BR22A/1c.
39. HJT to Lady Palmerston, 20 Nov. 1800, PP, BR22A/1c.
40. *Life and Letters of Sir Gilbert Elliot, first Earl of Minto*, iii, pp. 231–2.
41. HJT to Lady Palmerston, 15 May 1801, PP, BR22A/1c.
42. HJT to Palmerston (2nd Visc.), 28 Nov. 1800, PP, BR22A/2; HJT to Lady Palmerston, 15 May 1801, PP, BR22A/1c; Bourne, p. 15.
43. HJT to Palmerston (2nd Visc.), 22 Mar. 1801, PP, BR22A/2.
44. Palmerston (2nd Visc.) to HJT, 14 Apr. 1801, PP, BR22A/3.
45. See, for example, HJT to Palmerston (2nd Visc.), 18 Apr. 1801, Connell, p. 443. See also HJT to Lady Palmerston, 15 May 1801, PP, BR22A/1c.
46. Palmerston (2nd Visc.) to HJT, 14 Apr. 1801, PP, BR22A/3.
47. *Life and Letters of Sir Gilbert Elliot, first Earl of Minto*, iii, pp. 234–5.
48. Palmerston (2nd Visc.) to HJT, 6 Jan. 1802, PP, BR22A/3.
49. Connell, p. 457.
50. Palmerston's diary, 1859, PP, D/19 (5 Feb. 1859).
51. Minto to Lady Minto, 19 Apr. 1802, Connell, p. 458.
52. Connell, p. 458.
53. *Life and Letters of Sir Gilbert Elliot, first Earl of Minto*, iii, p. 118n.
54. Bell, i, p. 9.
55. Lady Palmerston to 1st Earl Malmesbury, 29 Apr. 1802, quoted in Connell, pp. 458–9.
56. Minto to Lady Minto, 3 June 1802, *Life and Letters of Sir Gilbert Elliot, first Earl of Minto*, iii, p. 251.
57. Bourne, pp. 14–15.
58. Palmerston's timetable at Edinburgh, sent as an enclosure to a letter to Frances Temple, 28 Feb. 1803, PP, BR24/4/3/enc.
59. Malmesbury to Palmerston, 23 Nov. 1802, PP, BR22(i)/5/2.
60. Quoted in McCosh, *Scottish Philosophy*, p. 281.
61. *The Journal of Walter Scott, from the Original Manuscript at Abbotsford*, 2 vols. (New York: Harper, 1890), ii, p. 201.
62. McCosh, *Scottish Philosophy*, p. 282.
63. J. Mackintosh, *Dissertation on the Progress of Ethical Philosophy* (2nd edn, 1837), quoted in Donald Winch, 'The System of the North: Dugald Stewart and his Pupils', in S. Collini, D. Winch and J. Burrow, *That Noble Science of Politics: A Study in Nineteenth-Century Intellectual History* (Cambridge: Cambridge University Press, 1983), p. 44.
64. Nicholas Phillipson, 'The Pursuit of Virtue in Scottish University Education: Dugald Stewart and Scottish Moral Philosophy in the Enlightenment', in N. Phillipson (ed.), *Universities, Society and the Future* (Edinburgh: Edinburgh University Press, 1983), p. 85.
65. McCosh, *Scottish Philosophy*, p. 277.
66. John Veitch, 'A Memoir of Dugald Stewart', in *The Collected Works of Dugald Stewart*, ed. Sir William Hamilton, 11 vols. (Edinburgh: Thomas Constable, 1854–60), x, pp. xxxix–xl.
67. Winch, 'The System of the North', p. 37.
68. See, for example, McCosh, *Scottish Philosophy*, p. 301.
69. Henry Cockburn, *Memorials of His Time* (Edinburgh: Adam and Charles Black, 1856), pp. 175–6.
70. *Outlines of Moral Philosophy* (1793), quoted in Winch, 'The System of the North', p. 26.
71. On Stewart's views on God, see Knud Haaksonssen, *Natural Law and Moral Philosophy, from Grotius to the Scottish Enlightenment* (Cambridge: Cambridge University Press, 1996), pp. 259–60.
72. Dugald Stewart, *Elements in the Philosophy of the Human Mind, Vol. I* (1792) in *The Collected Works of Dugald Stewart*, ii, p. 227.
73. Stewart, *Elements*, in *Works*, ii, pp. 222–3.
74. Ibid., pp. 224, 227.

75. Winch, 'The System of the North', p. 32.
76. Stewart, *Elements*, in *Works*, ii, pp. 228–9.
77. Ibid., p. 229.
78. Ibid., pp. 223, 229, 244–5.
79. *Notes from a Course of Lectures on Political Economy from Decr. 1802 to April 1803 given by D. Stewart, Mor. Prof. Edinburgh* [in the handwriting of HJT, 3rd Visc. Palmerston], p. 1, Edinburgh University Library, Mic.M.136.
80. Bell, i, pp. 7–8.
81. Stewart, *Lectures on Political Economy Vol. I* in *Works*, viii, pp. 16–17.
82. Stewart, *Dissertation Exhibiting the Progress of Metaphysical, Ethical and Political Philosophy since the Revival of Letters in Europe (1815–21)*, in *Works*, i, p. 22.
83. Stewart, *Lectures on Political Economy Vol. I*, in *Works*, viii, pp. 21–2.
84. Ibid., pp. 23–4.
85. Ibid., p. 35.
86. Stewart, *Lectures on Political Economy Vol. II*, in *Works*, ix, p. 357.
87. Ibid., p. 358.
88. Stewart, *Lectures on Political Economy Vol. I*, in *Works*, viii, p. 28.
89. Stewart, *Lectures on Political Economy Vol. II*, in *Works*, ix, p. 362.
90. Ibid., p. 374.
91. Ibid., p. 376.
92. Ibid., pp. 445–6.
93. Ibid., pp. 459–60.
94. Helen D'Arcy Stewart to Palmerston, 24 Apr. 1828, PP, BR22(i)/10.
95. Maria Stewart [daughter of Dugald Stewart] to Mrs Frances Bowles [Fanny Temple], 23 June 1828, PP, BR22(i)/10.
96. Helen D'Arcy Stewart to Palmerston, 28 July 1828, PP, BR22(i)/10.
97. *Hansard*, n.s., xx, 234–8 (10 Feb. 1828), 278 (12 Feb. 1828), 1237–53 (18 Mar. 1828), 1352–63 (19 Mar. 1828).
98. Palmerston to Helen D'Arcy Stewart, 4 Aug. 1828, PP, BR22(i)/10.
99. Palmerston, travel journal, 'Highlands of Scotland, 11 May–27 June 1803', PP, BR23A/2.
100. Malmesbury to Palmerston, 5 Mar. 1803, PP, BR22(i)/5/4.
101. 'Autobiography', Bulwer, i, pp. 367–8.
102. Bell, i, pp. 9–10.
103. Malmesbury to Palmerston, 6 Dec. 1803, PP, BR22(i)/5/6.
104. Lord Colchester, preface to *A Political Diary 1828–1830 by Edward Law, Lord Ellenborough*, ed. Lord Colchester, 2 vols. (London: Richard Bentley, 1881), i, pp. vi–vii.
105. Palmerston to Helen D'Arcy Stewart, Oct. 1803, PP, BR22(i)/13.
106. 'Autobiography', Bulwer, i, pp. 367–8.
107. Palmerston to Helen D'Arcy Stewart, Oct. 1803, PP, BR22(i)/13.
108. Edmund Outram to Palmerston, 8 June 1804, PP, BR22(i)/1/10.
109. Palmerston to Frances Temple, 10 June 1805, PP, BR24/6/8. See also Bourne, p. 35.
110. Palmerston to Frances Temple, 11 Feb. 1804, PP, BR24/5/2.
111. Palmerston to Frances Temple, 11 Nov. 1803, PP, BR24/4/13.
112. Malmesbury to Palmerston, 6 Dec. 1803, PP, BR22(i)/5/6.
113. Palmerston to Frances Temple, 11 Nov. 1803, PP, BR24/4/13.
114. Palmerston to Frances Temple, 7 Dec. 1803, PP, BR24/4/14.
115. Palmerston to Frances Temple, 24 Feb. 1804, PP, BR24/5/3.
116. Presumably Cardinal Henry Beaufort (1375?–1447).
117. Book of essays by 3rd Viscount Palmerston (bound volume), 1800–6, PP, BR22(ii)/6.
118. Vice-Admiral Sir Robert Calder had sailed back to Britain from the Mediterranean a few days earlier to stand trial and defend his reputation against charges of retreating before the enemy in August.
119. Palmerston to Frances Temple, 7 Nov. 1805, PP, BR24/6/12.
120. Palmerston to Elizabeth Temple, 19 Mar. 1804, PP, BR24/5/4; Palmerston to Frances Temple, 10 June 1805, PP, BR24/6/8.
121. Palmerston to Elizabeth Temple, 12 May 1805, PP, BR24/6/5.
122. Palmerston to Frances Temple, 7 Nov. 1805, PP, BR24/6/12.
123. Palmerston to Frances Temple, 10 June 1805, PP, BR24/6/8.
124. 'Autobiography', Bulwer, i, pp. 367–8.
125. *Life and Letters of Sir Gilbert Elliot, first Earl of Minto*, iii, p. 220.

Chapter 3 War and Peace, 1806–1828

1. Lady Minto to Lord Minto, 1812, quoted in *Lord Minto in India: Life and Letters of Gilbert Elliot, first Earl of Minto, from 1807 to 1814*, ed. the Countess of Minto (London: Longmans, Green, 1880), p. 331.
2. Palmerston's journal, 30 Dec. 1806; Bulwer, i, p. 41.
3. Palmerston to Frances Temple, 2 Dec. 1805, PP, BR24/6/13.
4. Lord Rosebery, *Pitt* (London: Macmillan, 1895), pp. 256–7.
5. 'Autobiography', Bulwer, i, pp. 367–8.
6. Bourne, p. 49.
7. Palmerston to Frances Temple, 23 Jan. 1806, PP, BR24/7/1.
8. Bulwer, i, p. 13.
9. John Ward to 'Ivy' [Helen D'Arcy Stewart], 'Saturday' [25 Jan. 1806], S.H. Romilly, *Letters to 'Ivy' from the first Earl of Dudley* (London: Longmans, Green, 1905), p. 35.
10. Palmerston's circular letter to voters, Cambridge University election, Jan. 1806, PP, BR195/108.
11. George Shee to Palmerston, 27 Jan. 1806, PP, GC/SH/72.
12. Palmerston to Frances Temple, 'Friday', Jan. 1806, PP, BR24/7/2; Frances Temple to Palmerston, 29 Jan. 1806, PP, BR22A/9; Shee to Palmerston, 27 Jan. 1806, PP, GC/SH/72.
13. Bourne, pp. 52–3.
14. Palmerston to Laurence Sulivan, 24 Jan. 1806, *PSL*, p. 49.
15. 'Autobiography', Bulwer, i, p. 368.
16. C.J. Wright, 'Fitzmaurice, Henry Petty, third marquess of Lansdowne (1780–1863)', *ODNB*.
17. Ridley, p. 20; Ellis Archer Wasson, 'Spencer, John Charles, Viscount Althorp and third earl Spencer (1782–1845)', *ODNB*.
18. Palmerston to Laurence Sulivan, 25 Jan. [24 Jan.] 1806; 25 Jan. 1806, *PSL*, pp. 49–50.
19. Palmerston to Laurence Sulivan, 28 Jan. 1806, Bulwer, i, pp. 14–17.
20. Palmerston to Laurence Sulivan, 26 Jan. 1806, *PSL*, p. 51.
21. Bourne, p. 54.
22. Henry Brougham to Zachary Macaulay, 1806, Marquis of Lorne, *Viscount Palmerston, KG* (London: Sampson Low, Marston, 1892), p. 9. Lorne cites the recipient of Brougham's letter as T.B. Macaulay but this is corrected in Bourne, p. 59, where the letter is identified as one written to Zachary Macaulay.
23. The second Viscount Palmerston had voted against Wilberforce's 1791 motion for abolition, describing it as 'blind enthusiastic zeal' that would be 'ineffectual and ruinous'. Palmerston had argued more sympathetically for gradual abolition but this found no favour in abolitionist circles. Bourne, p. 59.
24. Isaac Milner to Palmerston, 'Friday morning' [7 Feb. 1806], PP, SLT/1.
25. Isaac Milner (Dean of Carlisle) to William Wilberforce, 7 Feb. 1806, *The Correspondence of William Wilberforce*, ed. Robert Isaac Wilberforce and Samuel Wilberforce, 2 vols. (London: John Murray, 1840), ii, p. 68.
26. Francis Horner to J.A. Murray, 6–7 Feb. 1806, *The Horner Papers. Selections from the Letters and Miscellaneous Writings of Francis Horner, MP, 1795–1817*, ed. Kenneth Bourne and William Banks Taylor (Edinburgh: Edinburgh University Press, 1994), doc. 221 (p. 404).
27. Palmerston to Laurence Sulivan, 25 Jan. 1806, *PSL*, p. 51
28. Palmerston to Laurence Sulivan, 26 Jan. 1806, *PSL*, pp. 51–2.
29. Palmerston to Laurence Sulivan, 23 Feb. 1806, *PSL*, p. 54.
30. Palmerston to Laurence Sulivan, 29 Jan. 1806, *PSL*, p. 53.
31. Palmerston to Laurence Sulivan, 4 Feb. 1806, 'Wednesday evening [?5 Feb. 1806], *PSL*, pp. 55–6.
32. 'Autobiography', Bulwer, i, p. 368.
33. Malmesbury to Palmerston, 7 Feb. 1806, PP, BR22(i)/5/21.
34. Malmesbury to Palmerston, 8 Feb. 1806, PP, BR22(i)/5/22.
35. F. Cholmeley [a nephew of Sir Henry Englefield; Edinburgh contemporary] to Palmerston, 27 Feb. 1806, PP, BR22(i)/7.
36. Guedalla, p. 34.
37. Bell, i, pp. 12–14; Ridley, pp. 22–3.
38. Chamberlain, p. 19.
39. William Wilberforce to Rev. Thomas Gisborne, 11 Feb. 1806, *The Correspondence of William Wilberforce*, ii, p. 73.
40. Lady Amherst to Lady Malmesbury, 9 Feb. [1806], PP, BR195/108.
41. Ridley, p. 22.
42. Palmerston to George Shee, 17 July 1806, PP, GC/SH/137/1–2.
43. George Shee to Palmerston, 1 Aug. 1806, PP, GC/SH/75/1–2.
44. Palmerston's journal, 16 Sept. 1806, Bulwer, i, pp. 34–5.

45. Palmerston's journal, 15 July, 26 Aug., 5 Oct. 1806, Bulwer, i, pp. 26–7, 30–2, 40–1. The study by Gentz referred to by Palmerston must be *Fragments upon the Balance of Power in Europe* (London, 1806).
46. Palmerston to Frances Temple, 7 July 1806, PP, BR24/7/4.
47. Palmerston to Laurence Sulivan, 26 June 1806, *PSL*, pp. 56–7.
48. Palmerston to Laurence Sulivan, 16 July 1806, *PSL*, p. 59.
49. Palmerston to Laurence Sulivan, 17–25 Aug. 1806, *PSL*, p. 63.
50. Malmesbury to Palmerston, 25 Sept. 1806, PP, BR22(i)/5/27.
51. Palmerston to Laurence Sulivan, 17 Oct. [16 Oct.] 1806, *PSL*, pp. 67–8.
52. Palmerston to Laurence Sulivan, 19 Oct. 1806, *PSL*, pp. 68–70.
53. Palmerston to 'the Vice Chancellor and the rest of the senate of the University of Cambridge', [Oct. 1806], BR195/108.
54. *PSL*, pp. 68–9, n. 2.
55. Palmerston to Earl Percy 30 Oct. 1806, PP, BR195/108.
56. Lady Malmesbury to Palmerston, 22 Oct. 1806, PP, BR195/108.
57. Bourne, p. 68.
58. Malmesbury to Palmerston, 17 Oct. 1806, PP, BR195/108.
59. Bourne, pp. 68–9.
60. Bourne, pp. 68–71.
61. 'Autobiography', Bulwer, i, pp. 368–9.
62. Malmesbury to Palmerston, 20 Jan. 1807, PP, BR22(i)/5/35.
63. Minto to Palmerston, 22 Jan. 1807, PP, BR23/1/17/2.
64. Palmerston to Frances Temple, Feb. 1807, PP, BR24/7/7; Bourne, pp. 71–2.
65. Palmerston to Laurence Sulivan, Saturday evening [25 Apr. 1807], *PSL*, p. 79 and n. 1.
66. Mulgrave to Malmesbury, 1 Apr. 1807, PP, GC/MU/1.
67. 'Autobiography', Bulwer, i, p. 369.
68. Palmerston to Mulgrave, 2 Apr. 1807 (copy, endorsed on PP, GC/MU/1).
69. Lorne, *Palmerston*, p. 11
70. Bulwer, i, p. 79.
71. Lorne, *Palmerston*, p. 44.
72. Palmerston to Laurence Sulivan, Saturday evening [25 Apr. 1807], *PSL*, p. 79.
73. 'Autobiography', Bulwer, i, p. 369.
74. Palmerston to Laurence Sulivan, 28 Apr. 1807, *PSL*, pp. 79–80.
75. R.A. Melikan, 'Gibbs, Sir Vicary (1751–1820)', *ODNB*.
76. Palmerston to Laurence Sulivan, 30 Apr. 1807, *PSL*, pp. 80–1.
77. Adam Sedgwick to William Ainger, 4 May 1807, John Willis Clark and Thomas McKenny Hughes, *The Life and Letters of the Reverend Adam Sedgwick, Fellow of Trinity College, Cambridge, Prebendary of Norwich, Woodwardian Professor of Geology, 1818–1873*, 2 vols. (Cambridge: Cambridge University Press, 1890), i, p. 87.
78. Palmerston to Laurence Sulivan, 1 May 1807, *PSL*, p. 81 and n. 1.
79. 'Autobiography', Bulwer, i, p. 369.
80. Malmesbury to Palmerston, 2 May 1807, PP, BR22(i)/5/41.
81. Clark and Hughes, *Sedgwick*, i, p. 88.
82. Palmerston to Laurence Sulivan, 1/2 past 12 o'clock, Friday night [1 May 1807], *PSL*, pp. 83–4.
83. 'Autobiography', Bulwer, i, p. 369–70.
84. Ibid., p. 370.
85. Palmerston to Laurence Sulivan, 8 May 1807, Bulwer, i, p. 22.
86. Palmerston to Laurence Sulivan, 11 May 1897, *PSL*, p. 85.
87. 'Autobiography', Bulwer, i, p. 370.
88. Malmesbury to Palmerston, 4, 9 May 1807, PP, BR22(i)/5/42–3; 'Autobiography', Bulwer, i, p. 370.
89. Malmesbury to Palmerston, 7 Aug. 1807, PP, BR22(i)/5/44.
90. Malmesbury to Palmerston, 9 Aug. 1807, PP, BR22(i)/5/44.
91. Malmesbury to Palmerston, 13 Aug. 1807, PP, BR22(i)/5/45.
92. 'Autobiography', Bulwer, i, pp. 370–1.
93. *Opinions*, pp. 1–3; *Cobbett's Parliamentary Debates*, x, 300–1 (3 Feb. 1808).
94. Palmerston to Elizabeth Temple, 4 Feb. 1808, Bulwer, i, pp. 80–1.
95. Palmerston to Elizabeth Temple, 6 Feb. 1808, PP, BR24/8/6.
96. Bulwer, i, p. 81. The result of the vote was: For the motion 108; against 253. Palmerston thought that the 108 was a fair reflection of support on that side, but that 'we were less so than I expected. I thought we should have had three to one, but during this weather it is difficult to get people to come up to town' (Palmerston to Elizabeth Temple, 4 Feb. 1808, Bulwer, i, pp. 80–1).
97. Bulwer, i, p. 83.

98. Possibly the Argyll Rooms (to which Palmerston subscribed at this time: see Bourne, p. 181).

99. Walter Scott's epic poem, published in Feb. 1808.

100. Walter Scott, *The Lay of the Last Minstrel* (1805).

101. Lorne, *Palmerston*, pp. 14–15.

102. Ridley, pp. 31–3. On the Clarke/York scandal, see Owen Wheeler, *The War Office, Past and Present* (London: Methuen, 1914), pp. 74–84.

103. Robert Gildea, *Borders and Barricades: Europe 1800–1914* (Oxford: Oxford University Press, 2nd edn, 1996), p. 43.

104. Wendy Hinde, *George Canning* (Oxford: Blackwell, 1989 edn), p. 227.

105. Palmerston to Frances Temple, Sept. 1809, PP, BR24/10/9.

106. 'Autobiography', Bulwer, i, p. 371.

107. Palmerston to William Temple, 16 Oct. 1809, PP, GC/TE/137.

108. Palmerston to Malmesbury, 16 Oct. 1809, PP, GMC/1/1 and GC/MA/165/1–3.

109. Malmesbury to Palmerston, 17 Oct. 1809, PP, GMC/3 and GC/MA/165/enc.1.

110. William Temple to Palmerston, 17 Oct. 1809, PP, GMC/2.

111. Palmerston to Malmesbury, 18 Oct. 1809, PP, GMC/5/2.

112. Palmerston to Malmesbury, 23 Oct. 1809, PP, GC/MA/167.

113. Spencer Perceval to Palmerston, ? Oct. 1809, PP, GMC/11 (endorsement by Palmerston); Palmerston to Malmesbury, 25 Oct. 1809, PP, GC/MA/168.

114. Denis Gray, *Spencer Perceval: The Evangelical Prime Minister, 1762–1812* (Manchester: Manchester University Press, 1963), pp. 114, 129, 269.

115. Palmerston to Malmesbury, 27 Oct. 1809, PP, GMC/15; Spencer Perceval to Palmerston, 26 Oct. 1809, PP, GMC/13.

116. Palmerston to Frances Temple, 'Sunday', [24] Oct. 1809, PP, BR24/10/10. This letter was written two days before Palmerston's appointment at the War Office was confirmed.

117. Malmesbury to Palmerston, 30 Oct. 1809, PP, GC/MA/120.

118. Palmerston to Malmesbury, 9 Nov. 1809, Bulwer, i, pp. 107–8.

119. Palmerston to Frederick Robinson, 11 June 1826, Ripon Papers, BL Add Ms 40862, ff. 181–7.

120. Guedalla, p. 48.

121. Palmerston to Richard Wharton, 8 Nov. 1812, Palmerston Papers, BL, Add Ms 48418, ff. 13–14.

122. Guedalla, p. 45.

123. Select Committee on Army and Ordnance Expenditure, *Parliamentary Papers* 1850 (662) x, 1.

124. Charles M. Clode, *The Military Forces of the Crown: Their Administration and Government*, 2 vols. (London: John Murray, 1869), ii, p. 253.

125. Ibid., pp. 255–65.

126. Ridley, p. 38.

127. Memorandum by Palmerston [for the Prince Regent], 16 Aug. 1811, Palmerston Papers, BL Add Ms 48417, ff. 63 *et seq.*

128. Palmerston to Spencer Perceval, 30 Sept. 1810, Palmerston Papers, BL, Add Ms 48417, ff. 5–6.

129. Palmerston to Spencer Perceval, 13 Oct. 1810, ibid., ff. 7–8.

130. Palmerston to Spencer Perceval, 9 Dec. 1810, ibid., ff. 8–9.

131. Sir David Dundas to Palmerston, 2 Mar. 1811, forwarding a copy of a memorandum by Dundas submitted to the Prince Regent, Feb. 1811, ibid., ff. 23–45.

132. Memorandum [for the Prince Regent] by Palmerston, 16 Aug. 1811, ibid., ff. 45–69 [quotations from ff. 60–2].

133. Memorandum by HRH the Commander-in-Chief [Frederick, Duke of York], 23 Sept. 1811, ibid., ff. 88–107.

134. Observations of Spencer Perceval transmitted to the Commander-in-Chief and the Secretary at War (with enclosures from Lord Eldon, Lord Liverpool and Charles Yorke), 19 Dec. 1811, ibid., ff. 112–18.

135. Memorandum signed in duplicate by HRH the Prince Regent, and transmitted to the Commander-in-Chief and to the Secretary at War, 29 May 1812, ibid., f. 122. See also Liverpool Papers, BL, Add Ms 38194, ff. 1–16 for papers concerning the dispute dated between 30 Sept. 1810 and 2 June 1812 sent to Liverpool in the aftermath of Perceval's death providing a summary of the correspondence between Palmerston, Dundas, York and Perceval.

136. Palmerston to Liverpool, 21 Feb. 1814, Liverpool Papers, BL, Add Ms 38194, f. 26.

137. Palmerston to Lt Gen. Sir Harry Calvert, 27 June 1816, Palmerston Papers, BL, Add Ms 48418, ff. 60–1.

138. Palmerston to Liverpool, 14 Mar. 1820, PP, GC/LI/193.

139. Circular letter from Sir Herbert Taylor to officers commanding abroad, 20 Jan. 1823, PP, WO/14/5.

140. Palmerston to Sir Herbert Taylor, 22 Jan. 1823, PP, WO/14/6.

141. Sir Herbert Taylor to Palmerston, 24 Jan. 1823, PP, WO/14/7–8.
142. Palmerston to Sir Herbert Taylor, 25 Jan. 1823, PP, WO/14/9.
143. Palmerston to Sir Herbert Taylor, 25 Jan. 1823, PP, WO/15/11.
144. Palmerston to Liverpool, 6 Feb. 1823, Liverpool Papers, BL, Add Ms 38194, ff. 87–9.
145. Duke of York to Liverpool, 8 Feb. 1823, PP, WO/18/5–7. See also Palmerston to Liverpool, 10 and 12 Feb. 1823, PP, WO/18/8 and WO/18/10.
146. Memorandum by Liverpool, 13 Feb. 1823, PP, WO/18/12–13.
147. Palmerston to Sir Herbert Taylor, 24 May 1823, PP, WO/26/1–2 and May 1823, PP, WO/27.
148. See, for example, a memorandum by Palmerston, 4 May 1827, concerning the roles of Secretary at War and adjutant-general (PP, WO/46).
149. Palmerston to Howick (subs. Grey [3rd Earl]), 22 Dec. 1836, PP, GC/GR/2406.
150. Palmerston to Frederick Robinson, 11 Apr. 1826, Ripon Papers, BL, Add Ms 40862, ff. 168–9. As evidence of Palmerston's long-standing concern to reduce the cost of army clothing, see also: J. C. Herries to Palmerston, 23 Dec. 1812, and 10 June 181, Herries Papers, BL, Add Ms 57431, ff. 90–1 and *ibid.*, BL, Add Ms 57433, f. 25.
151. Bourne, p. 97.
152. J.C. Herries to Palmerston, Tuesday evening [12 Nov. 1811], Herries Papers, BL, Add Ms 57428, ff. 51–2.
153. Bourne, pp. 109–10.
154. Palmerston, House of Commons, 20 Mar. 1822, *Opinions*, p. 18.
155. Malmesbury to Palmerston, 4 Mar. 1810, PP, GC/MA/131. On the same theme, for the summer debate, see also Malmesbury to Palmerston, 28 July 1810, PP, GC/MA/141.
156. Lady Malmesbury's journal, Mar. 1810, quoted in Bourne, pp. 133–4.
157. Clark and Hughes, *Sedgwick*, i, pp. 108–9, quoting contemporary Tory opinion.
158. Palmerston, House of Commons, 26 Feb. 1816, *Opinions*, pp. 11–12.
159. Palmerston, House of Commons, 8 Mar. 1816, *Opinions*, pp. 12–13.
160. Palmerston, House of Commons, 25 Apr. 1816, *Opinions*, p. 13.
161. See, for example, J.C. Herries to Palmerston, 6 July 1826, Herries Papers, BL, Add Ms 57441, f. 126.
162. *The Times*, 9, 14 Mar. 1821.
163. *The Times*, 21 May 1821.
164. *The Times*, 5 June 1820.
165. Palmerston, House of Commons, 3 Mar. 1826, *Opinions*, pp. 33–4.
166. *The Times*, 25 Dec. 1821.
167. Michael Partridge, 'Palmerston and the War Office, 1809–1828', in David Brown and Miles Taylor (eds), *Palmerston Studies II* (Southampton: Hartley Institute, 2007), p. 5.
168. Palmerston to S. Lushington, 26 Nov. 1821, Palmerston Papers, BL, Add Ms 48419, ff. 42–5. The ten posts to be abolished were: one superintendent of accounts (at a salary of £1,200); two senior clerks (£1,000, £800); three inspectors, first class (two earning £800, one £700); one assistant and one junior clerk (£450, £300); one examiner, first class (£400); one junior clerk (£200). He also proposed a reduction in the salary of a law clerk from £500 to £400.
169. Palmerston to Frederick Robinson, 11 June 1826, Ripon Papers, BL, Add Ms 40862, ff. 181–7.
170. Bourne, p. 114. As Ellenborough noted, the process of reducing the costs of the militia and remedying pension fraud continued apace in 1829: see the entry in his diary for 8 Jan. 1829, *A Political Diary 1828–1830 by Edward Law, Lord Ellenborough*, ed. Lord Colchester, 2 vols. (London: Richard Bentley, 1881), i, p. 291.
171. *The Journal of Mrs Arbuthnot, 1820–1832*, ed. Francis Bamford and the Duke of Wellington, 2 vols. (London: Macmillan, 1950), ii, p. 190 (1 June 1828); Bourne, pp. 115, 132.
172. Mark Boyd, *Reminiscences of Fifty Years* (London: Longmans, Green, 1871), pp. 42–4.
173. Bourne, pp. 116, 118, 136.
174. Ridley, p. 61
175. Bulwer, i, p. 145.
176. On the initial complaint in 1821, see M. Foveaux to Palmerston, 8 Dec. 1821, PP, BL, Add Ms 48419, ff. 55–60. For the subsequent correspondence, see also *ibid.*, ff. 61–75.
177. Palmerston to Laurence Sulivan, 17 Dec. 1817, *PSL*, pp. 136–8.
178. Palmerston to Laurence Sulivan, 28 Oct. 1809, *PSL*, pp. 113–15.
179. Bourne, 'Introduction', *PSL*, pp. 18–19.
180. See, for example, *The Times*, 3 Mar. 1828.
181. Palmerston to William Merry, 8 Feb. 1828, PP, BL, Add Ms 48420, ff. 50–1. See also Palmerston to Merry, 11 Mar. 1828, *ibid.*
182. *The Times*, 17 Mar. 1828 (letter dated 13 Mar. 1828).
183. Bourne, p. 132.

184. Palmerston to Sir William Temple, 10 Apr. 1818, PP, GC/TE/156.
185. For accounts of the incident, in addition to Palmerston's letters to his brother, see *The Times*, 9, 10, 14, 16 Apr. 1818. A visitor at the War Office at the time of the attack later claimed Davies had cried 'You know my wrongs; he has killed *me*' (see *The Times*, 9 Apr. 1818).
186. *The Times*, 16 Apr. 1818.
187. Palmerston to Sir William Temple, 9 and 10 Apr. 1818, PP, GC/TE/155 and GC/TE/156.
188. Palmerston to Malmesbury, 10 Apr. 1818, *A Series of Letters of the first Earl of Malmesbury, his Family and Friends from 1745 to 1820*, ed. the Earl of Malmesbury, 2 vols. (London: Richard Bentley, 1870), ii, p. 524.
189. Palmerston's diary, entries for 8, 9, 10, 11, 12 Apr. 1818, PP, D/3.
190. Palmerston to Sir William Temple, 17 Apr. 1818, PP, GC/TE/157.
191. Palmerston to Sir William Temple, 26 May 1818, PP, GC/TE/158.
192. Lt David Davies to Palmerston, 14 July 1821, PP, GC/DA/11 and GC/DA/11/enc.1.
193. Memorandum by Palmerston, 3 July 1815, PP, BL, Add Ms 48418, ff. 48–50. See also H. Torrens to Palmerston, 5 July 1815 and Liverpool to Palmerston, 11 July 1815 both approving the proposals and the memorandum written by Palmerston to the Commander-in-Chief, 12 July 1815, formalising the plans (*ibid.*, ff. 50–5).
194. Palmerston to H. Torrens, 20 July 1815, PP, BL, Add Ms 48418, ff. 47–8.
195. Palmerston to Sidmouth, 8 Feb. 1816, ibid., f. 60.
196. Palmerston to Sir H. Taylor, 2 Feb. 1823, PP, BL, Add Ms 48419, f. 90; Sir H. Taylor to Palmerston, 13 Mar. 1826, PP, WO/33. Bourne, pp. 138–42.
197. Lady Sarah Spencer to Lord Spencer, 26 Oct. 1809, *Correspondence of Sarah Spencer, Lady Lyttelton, 1787–1870*, ed. Mrs H. Wyndham (London: John Murray, 1912), p. 85.

Chapter 4 The Making of Palmerston I: Lord Cupid, Irish Landlord

1. Ashley, ii, 316.
2. Palmerston's diary, 1829, PP, D/5.
3. Palmerston's diary, 1818, PP, D/3.
4. Palmerston's diary, 1819, PP, D/4.
5. A. Taylor, 'Palmerston and Radicalism, 1847–1865', *Journal of British Studies*, 33:2 (1994), 157–79, esp. 160–1.
6. Ridley, p. 42.
7. Ibid., pp. 42–4.
8. See esp. Bourne's chapter on 'The Ruling Passion', Bourne, pp. 181–226.
9. *The Journal of Mrs Arbuthnot, 1820–1832*, ed. Francis Bamford and the Duke of Wellington, 2 vols. (London: Macmillan, 1950), i, pp. 406, 409, 424 (July, 18 Nov. 1825).
10. This is taken from a file of 'Memoranda & Calculations about affairs & accounts', PP, BR207/1/2.
11. 'Short Statement of his Lordship's interest in his real estates', 'State and Estimate of the late Lord Palmerston's Personal Estate now remaining to be applied and of the Debts and Legacies unpaid, 5 Jan. 1811' and 'State of Residue of the late Lord Palmerston's Personal Estate and of the Proposed Application thereof', Nov. 1811, PP, BR207/1/9.
12. Bourne, p. 254.
13. In addition to the references to PP, BR207, see also the Account Books, which contain private statements of Palmerston's accounts with his solicitors Oddie, Oddie & Forster and their successors for the period Mar. 1806–Nov 1842: PP, BL, Add Ms 48584, ff. 1–62.
14. Palmerston had subsidised his former tutor's lifestyle since shortly after inheriting from his father and continued these payments thereafter. Ravizzotti had established a girls' school in Kensington but had run up debts of £500 through repairs made to and furnishing of the house, debts which by late 1804 he could no longer service. Palmerston instructed Ravizzotti not to make any further appeals to Lady Palmerston but sent him £50 as a temporary measure (13 Oct. 1804) and then made arrangements to pay Ravizzotti £200 to pay creditors and allow him time to make money to settle the rest of the debt. Palmerston asked Pelham (Dec. 1804) and Malmesbury (Dec. 1804) to sanction this – as his guardians, which they did (23 Dec. and 14 Dec. respectively). As Palmerston explained in his letter to Pelham: 'The sum I am aware is a large one, but then the withholding of it would almost certainly oblige Mr Gaetano to relinquish his present plans, in wh. the little he had saved has all been sunk and he and his family would come upon my hands so that in fact this money will in the end be economically laid out' (PP, BR22(i)/6).
15. PP, BR207/1/2.
16. [Anon.], Memo. about the Slate Quarry, n.d., c. 1883, PP, BR205/6/14. Evelyn Ashley, in an aide-memoire written in 1894, noted of the Welsh Slate Company that 'The company or partnership was first formed in 1825 under a lease given by Mr Oakley's uncle. It has ever since without break

or disagreement of any kind worked the quarries under successive leases. It was a losing concern to the partnership for nearly a quarter of a century and many of the original partners threw up their shares. A few, of whom Ld. Palmerston was one, held on all through these bad times. Royalties however were paid to the lessor during all this long time' (PP, BR187/12/1).

17. See Chapter 11, below.
18. The affair can be followed in *The Times*, 28 July, 5, 7 Aug., 21 Oct., 15, 18 Nov. 1826, 12 Mar. 1827. See also Bourne, p. 264.
19. Accounts 1834–38 (for English [Hampshire] estates), PP, BL, Add Ms 48586, ff. 1–83. In these accounts, the following records of excess income over expenditure are recorded: £1,359 18s. 1¼d. (1834); £1,164 17s. 5d. (1835); £1,784 7s. 0¾d. (1836); £2,148 13s. 3¼d. (1837); £2,851 1s. 0⅔d. (1838).
20. PP, BR207/1/2.
21. 'Memorandum of Income & Expenditure June 1830', PP, BR207/1/4.
22. R. Hayden, 'Health and Housing: Lord Palmerston as Hampshire Proprietor, *c*. 1807–1865', *Proceedings of the Hampshire Field Club and Archaeological Society*, 58 (2003), 256–7.
23. Bourne, p. 22.
24. In a letter of 29 Dec. 1810, Palmerston wrote: 'I enclose a draft for 50*l*, for clothing for the Romsey people as usual', quoted in Bulwer, i, p. 121.
25. See, for a brief discussion of Palmerston's life in Hampshire, Ridley, pp. 62–3.
26. Palmerston to William Temple, 17 July 1826, PP, GC/TE/179.
27. Palmerston to William Temple, 26 Nov. 1841, PP, GC/TE/294. In 1843 Palmerston wrote to his brother: 'Iliona, the mare I had last year is to run at Ascot, & may perhaps win me a good stake there; that is to say about 400£; But Ld G. Bentinck puts all such trifling matters into the shade; He has a horse to run for the Derby next week & if the horse wins, Ld George is to win upwards of sixty thousand pounds; how much he is to lose if his horse is beat I know not, but I presume he has hedged so as not to be a great sufferer even in that case' (Palmerston to William Temple, 29 May 1843, PP, GC/TE/306).
28. William Day, *William Day's Reminiscences of the Turf* (London: Richard Bentley, 1886), pp. 210–15 (quotations from pp. 215, 213, 210, 213).
29. Letter from Palmerston, 21 Apr. 1834, quoted in Bulwer, ii, p. 185.
30. J. R. Vincent, *The Formation of the Liberal Party, 1857–68* (London, Constable, 1966), pp. 146–8.
31. Ridley, pp. 65–6; Bourne, p. 157.
32. Bourne, p. 157.
33. See Ridley, pp. 71–5.
34. PP, BR195/4, Palmerston to Thomas Warner, 7 Oct. 1806. At this time Palmerston was himself seeking to be returned for Horsham at the coming election (in which ambition he was disappointed) under Tory patronage and was clearly motivated by a sense of party interest.
35. PP, BR195/13, Palmerston to Sir John Pollen, 19 Feb. 1820.
36. PP, BR195/18, Lord Portsmouth to Palmerston, 4 Mar. 1820.
37. Bulwer, i, p. 84 and *passim*.
38. Bourne, esp. pp. xiii, 22, 81, 231, 235, 258, 274–5, 292–9.
39. Roy Foster, for example, although suggesting that Palmerston had been 'a fairly exemplary, if absentee, Irish landlord', noted that while 'Some landlords saw the arrangement of a reliable passage, and the equipment of their emigrating tenants, as part of their duty; many more (notoriously Lord Palmerston) did not', R.F. Foster, *Modern Ireland, 1600–1972* (London: Penguin, 1988), p. 350.
40. Tyler Anbinder, 'Lord Palmerston and the Irish Famine Emigration', *Historical Journal*, 44: 2 (2001), 441–69; Desmond Norton, 'Lord Palmerston and the Irish Famine Emigration: A Rejoinder', *Historical Journal*, 46: 1 (2003), 155–65; Desmond Norton, *Landlords, Tenants, Famine: The Business of an Irish Land Agency in the 1840s* (Dublin: University College Dublin Press, 2006).
41. Anbinder, 'Lord Palmerston and the Irish Famine Emigration', 446. For Anbinder's descriptions of conditions on Palmerston's Ahamlish estate prior to 1845, drawn from published, official accounts, see 446–8.
42. Desmond Norton, 'On Lord Palmerston's Irish Estates in the 1840s', *EHR*, 119: 484 (2004), esp. 1256–8; Norton, 'Lord Palmerston and the Irish Famine Emigration: A Rejoinder', 156–8. See also his *Stewart and Kincaid, Irish Land Agents in the 1840s*, University College Dublin Centre for Economic Research Working Paper WP02/08 (Feb. 2002) for general background on estate management at this time.
43. Anbinder, 'Lord Palmerston and the Irish Famine Emigration', 450–4. Ironically, perhaps, a recent biographer of Gore-Booth noted that it was Palmerston who had served as something of a model of progressive landlordism to Gore-Booth in the 1820s and '30s. Of the apparently divergent

approaches to the famine in 1847, it is noted: 'If Sir Robert was irritated because he felt obliged to come to the assistance of Palmerston's tenants, there is no evidence of it among the surviving correspondence', Dermot James, *The Gore-Booths of Lissadell* (Dublin: Woodfield Press 2004), pp. 22, 33.

44. T. O'Rorke, *The History of Sligo: Town and County*, 2 vols. (Dublin, [?1890]), ii, pp. 29-30, 32.
45. Ibid., p. 32; Norton, 'On Lord Palmerston's Irish Estates,' 1,256.
46. PP, BR22(ii)/13, pp. 73-6. Palmerston's comments are deliberately satirical and his protest that in these references 'I am *of course* not now speaking of Ireland' was clearly sarcastic.
47. Hannah Corkran to Palmerston, 8 Sept. 1808, PP, BR147/3/3.
48. Hannah Corkran to Palmerston, 3 Mar. 1810, PP, BR147/3/13.
49. Robert Lyons to Palmerston, 5 Nov. 1813, PP, BR147/4/29.
50. Palmerston endorsed Lyons's letter (above, n. 49), with the note: 'Heard many complaints of him, but as the transactions were so long gone by & he had so many years ceased to be agent did not think worth while to inquire into them enough to form an opinion on them.' On the specific case underpinning Lyons's remonstrance, that of an Arthur McKenna, Palmerston had decided against McKenna's appeal for a renewed lease anyway (PP, BR147/4/29).
51. See, for example, R. Chambers to Palmerston, 25 Mar. 1809, PP, BR147/3/7.
52. Swan, a barrister, enjoyed a dubious reputation. In addition to his other responsibilities, he was Treasurer of the Irish Post Office, a position he abused by the sending and receiving of letters free of charge. This was a potentially not inconsiderable fraud. See Norton, *Landlords, Tenants, Famine*, p. 5.
53. G. Swan to Palmerston, 16 Mar. 1813, PP, BR147/4/2.
54. G. Swan to Palmerston, 12 Apr. 1814, PP, BR147/5/9/1.
55. Palmerston to the Tenants of Captain Jones's Estate in the Parish of Ahamlish, 24 Apr. 1826, PP, BR147/10/27/1.
56. Henry Stewart to Palmerston, 10 Nov. 1806, PP, BR149/1/1/2.
57. Palmerston to Charles O'Hara, 20 Jan. 1818, PP, BR147/6/1.
58. On the squaring of land in this period, see Desmond Norton, 'On Landlord-assisted Emigration from Some Irish Estates in the 1840s', *Agricultural History Review*, 53:1 (2005), 27-8 and Norton, 'On Lord Palmerston's Irish Estates', 1,256-7, 1,268-9.
59. J. Kincaid to Palmerston, 2 June 1837 [with Palmerston's endorsement on the wrapper], PP, BR145/9/15.
60. Norton, 'On Landlord-assisted Emigration', 28.
61. Palmerston to Elizabeth Temple, 12 Sept. 1808, Bulwer, i, pp. 85-8. See also *PSL*, pp. 104-5.
62. G. Swan to Palmerston, 30 Oct. 1820, PP, BR147/6/32.
63. Memorandum by G. Swan, Sept. 1822. An endorsement on this memorandum indicated that Palmerston approved the plan on 24 Nov. 1822.
64. For accounts of progress on the harbour see PP, BR147, *passim*. The 'dilatory' employee was a William England who was refused re-employment in April 1826 (W. England to Palmerston, 24 Apr. 1826, *ibid.*, BR147/10/30). Other examples of alleged corruption among workers are to be found in these papers.
65. Palmerston to Henry Townshend [secretary to Fisheries Board], 28 Oct. 1826 (draft copy), PP, BR147/10/63.
66. Henry Townshend to Palmerston, 7 Nov. 1826, PP, BR147/10/64; James Walker to Palmerston, 4 July 1829, BR145/2/30; E. Nicholson to Palmerston, 16 and 25 July 1829, BR145/2/28, BR150/9/29; H. Townshend to Palmerston, 2 Nov. 1829, BR145/2/5.
67. Draft advertisement by Palmerston for Mullaghmore harbour to be placed in Sligo and Fermanagh papers, Mar. 1828, PP, BR145/1/10.
68. For example, Herbert Clifford [the Sligo Coastguard] to Palmerston, 3 Dec. 1831, PP, BR145/4/14.
69. John Lynch to Palmerston, 5 Dec. 1831, PP, BR145/4/15.
70. James Walker to Palmerston, 24 Aug. 1835, PP, BR145/7/34.
71. J. Kincaid to Palmerston, 21 June 1837, PP, BR145/9/14/1.
72. See, for example, John Lynch to Palmerston, 25 Oct. 1845, PP, BR146/7/48.
73. W. Urwick to Palmerston, 18 June 1822, PP, BR147/7/16/2.
74. Palmerston to W. Urwick, 22 June 1822 (not sent), PP, BR147/7/16/2.
75. See, for example, reports on works submitted to Palmerston by agents, esp. PP, BR147.
76. List of 'Quantity of uncultivated Bog on my Sligo Estate', n.d. [1818-21]. The total figure given is: '2184A, 2R, 29P', PP, BR147/6/48.
77. Memorandum by Palmerston for Mr Nimmo: 'Instructions for surveying the bogs on my estate in Sligo with a view to drain & reclaim them', 12 Oct. 1824 (copy), PP, BR149/6/1/4.
78. See, for example, correspondence between Palmerston and his agents collected in PP, BR145, BR, BR146, BR147, BR148, BR149, BR150. The earliest listed letter dealing with bent planting is from James Walker, 26 May 1825 (BR147/9/28).

79. T.G.[?] Scott to Palmerston, 17 Nov. 1835, PP, BR145/7/46.

80. James Fraser, *Hand Book for Travellers in Ireland* (Dublin, 1854), quoted in Norton, *Landlords, Tenants, Famine*, p. 27.

81. Robert Stevenson to Palmerston, 16 Dec. 1835, PP, BR145/7/49 (Palmerston's endorsement quoted).

82. Palmerston to Daniel O'Connell, 30 Mar. 1836, PP, BR145/8/15.

83. Norton, *Landlords, Tenants, Famine*, p. 27.

84. Palmerston to William Temple, 27 Nov. 1827, PP, GC/TE/190.

85. William Bowles to Palmerston, 22 July 1835, PP, BR145/7/32.

86. J.R. Bertolacci to Sir Charles Trevelyan, 21 Nov. 1848, PP, BR146/10/18.

87. Address of Castlegarron Tenants, 22 Oct. 1840, PP, BR146/2/28.

88. O'Rorke, *History of Sligo*, ii, p. 36.

89. PP, BR22(ii)/13, pp. 68–9.

90. Palmerston to Frances Temple, 31 Aug. 1808, PP, BR24/8/15.

91. Palmerston to Laurence Sulivan, 17 Oct. 1828, *PSL*, p. 217.

92. *Western Luminary* [Sligo], 23 Nov. 1827 [Report of a dinner to John Lawless, extracts from the toast to Palmerston by Chairman, Revd Dr Burke].

93. Palmerston to Revd Dr Burke, 6 Nov. 1827, PP, BR147/11/26/1; also quoted in the *Western Luminary* [Sligo], 23 Nov. 1827. The extract quoted in the *Western Luminary* is an essentially accurate transcription.

94. Memo by G. Swan, 'Schools on Sligo Estate', Dec. 1819, PP, BR147/6/20/15.

95. G. Swan to Palmerston, 7 Jan. 1820, PP, BR147/6/23/1.

96. Revd Charles Hamilton to G. Swan, 19 Aug. 1823, PP, BR147/8/30/1.

97. See Lucinda Faniset to Palmerston, 19 Aug. 23, 29 Sept. 1823, PP, BR147/8/30/2–4.

98. PP, BR147/8/30/1.

99. Revd Charles Hamilton to Palmerston, 11 Oct. 1823, PP, BR147/8/32, with Palmerston's endorsement on the same.

100. Report by Graves Swan on the establishment of estate schools, May 1824, PP, BR150/5/6.

101. Note by Palmerston on estimates for schools in Sligo, Apr. 1825, PP, BR149/4/6.

102. O'Rorke, *History of Sligo*, ii, p. 36: 'At this time he [Palmerston] seems to have taken no thought about the ministers of the Catholic church, as if they were to count for nothing in his proceedings regarding their flocks; and even after he opened the school for his tenantry, he was so clear and decided on this point, that he writes: – "I have just got two schools on foot, but am at war with my priest, who, as usual, forbids the people to send their children. I know that if I was resident, I should beat him in a moment, and I hope to do so even though an absentee."'

103. Palmerston to Felix Conolly, 22 Nov. 1826, PP, BR147/10/65/2.

104. Revd Roger Burne to Palmerston, 15 Dec 1826, PP, BR147/10/77.

105. See Felix Conolly to Palmerston, 5 Jan. 1827, PP, BR147/11/2/1.

106. Palmerston to Felix Conolly, 10 Jan. 1827, PP, BR147/11/2/2.

107. A. Plunkett to Palmerston, 14 Nov. 1827, PP, BR147/11/26/2.

108. Norton, *Landlords, Tenants, Famine*, p. 27.

109. See, for example, PP, BR145/3/23, BR145/3/37, BR145/3/40, BR145/3/41, BR145/3/52/1–2, BR145/3/56.

110. See, for example, PP, BR145/3/23 and BR145/3/24 (Apr. 1830). In BR145/3/23, one girl is spoken of in this regard; in BR145/3/24 four boys; in both the teachers discuss whether the children really were deserving but it is evident that Palmerston decided for himself.

111. Isabella Soden to Palmerston, PP, BR145/3/37.

112. A. Jordan to Palmerston, 24 June 1830, PP, BR145/3/40.

113. James Stewart to Palmerston, 19 July 1830, PP, BR145/3/50.

114. See A. Jordan to Palmerston, 5 Aug. 1830, PP, BR145/3/55; Capt. J. Soden to Palmerston, 11 Aug. 1830, PP, BR145/3/54; William Jordan to Palmerston, PP, BR145/3/56; J. Soden to Palmerston, PP, BR145/3/62; Bishop Patrick Burke to Palmerston, PP, BR145/3/69.

115. Bourne, pp. 231, 274–5, 292–4.

116. Ibid., p. 235.

117. See Chapter 6.

118. Palmerston's diary, 1826–27, PP, D/25. The cover of this volume is inscribed 'Ireland 1826'; a newspaper cutting pasted inside is dated Aug. 1827; but apart from these indications, the entries are undated.

119. Palmerston to William Temple, 27 June 1828, PP, GC/TE/201.

120. Palmerston to William Temple, 9 Dec. 1828, PP, GC/TE/203.

Chapter 5 The Making of Palmerston II: The Politician

1. Edward Berens Blackburn to Palmerston, 15 Nov. 1823, PP, BR22(i)/9.
2. Palmerston to Fitzharris, 26 June 1815, *A Series of Letters of the first Earl of Malmesbury, his Family and Friends from 1745 to 1820*, ed. the Earl of Malmesbury, 2 vols. (London: Richard Bentley, 1870), ii, p. 449.
3. Palmerston's travel journals: France, 1815, 29 Aug.–7 Oct. 1815, PP, BR23A/3/1, p. 13 (1 Sept. 1815).
4. Palmerston's travel journals: France, 1815, PP, BR23A/3/1, pp. 30–1 (2 Sept.).
5. Aberdeen to Harrowby, 23 Sept. 1813; Aberdeen to Maria, Lady Hamilton, 22 Oct. 1813, quoted in Muriel E. Chamberlain, *Aberdeen: A Political Biography* (Harlow: Longman, 1983), pp. 126, 134–5.
6. Palmerston's travel journals: France, 1815, PP, BR23A/3/1, pp. 31–77 (3, 4, 5, 8–12 Sept. 1815). Quotation from p. 44 (5 Sept.).
7. Palmerston's travel journals: France, 1815, PP, BR23A/3/1, pp. 93–4 (19 Sept. 1815).
8. See Bourne, p. 190.
9. Palmerston's travel journals, PP, BR23A/4/2 (6 Oct. 1816).
10. Palmerston's travel journals: France, 1818, PP, BR23A/5, p. 1 (13 Oct. 1818). This description was excised from the published *Selections from Private Journals of Tours in France in 1815 and 1818 by the Right Honourable Viscount Palmerston, KG* (London: Richard Bentley, 1871), p. 38.
11. Palmerston, House of Commons, 8 Mar. 1816, *Opinions*, pp. 13–14.
12. Palmerston, House of Commons, 14 June 1820, *Opinions*, pp. 16–17.
13. Palmerston to William Temple, 21 Oct. 1817, PP, GC/TE/146.
14. Palmerston to Fitzharris, 1 Nov. 1819, *A Series of Letters of the first Earl of Malmesbury*, ii, pp. 531–2.
15. J.E. Cookson, *Lord Liverpool's Administration: The Crucial Years, 1815–1822* (Edinburgh and London: Scottish Academic Press, 1975), p. 37.
16. Bulwer, i, p. 150.
17. Palmerston to Laurence Sulivan, 15 Sept. 1809, *PSL*, p. 110.
18. Bourne, pp. 228–9.
19. Ibid., pp. 230–5.
20. Palmerston to Laurence Sulivan, 15 Sept. 1809, *PSL*, p. 112.
21. Palmerston to Laurence Sulivan, 5 Aug. 1810, *PSL*, p. 117.
22. Palmerston to Frances Temple, 4 Jan. 1810, PP, BR24/11/1.
23. 'Autobiography', Bulwer, i, p. 372.
24. Palmerston to Laurence Sulivan, 24 Mar. 1811, *PSL*, p. 120.
25. Bourne, pp. 240–1. R.A. Melikan, 'Gibbs, Sir Vicary (1751–1820)', *ODNB*. Palmerston mistakenly attributed Smyth's succession to Gibbs's death ('Autobiography', Bulwer, i, p. 373). In 1812 Palmerston wrote to Laurence Sulivan: 'I take it the only thing to be done will be to go down to Cambridge immediately and canvass the gyps & porters who probably are at present the chief occupiers of the colleges; but however I trust we shall not have much trouble this time as I do not anticipate a contest' (27 Sept. 1812), *PSL*, p. 125.
26. Palmerston to William Temple, 5 Dec. 1817, PP, GC/TE/151/1–2.
27. Palmerston to Liverpool, 15 Nov. 1820, Liverpool Papers, BL, Add Ms 38194, ff. 64–5.
28. Palmerston to Liverpool, 19 Mar. 1820, ibid., f. 66.
29. 'Autobiography', Bulwer, i, p. 373.
30. Palmerston, House of Commons, 1 Mar. 1813, *Opinions*, pp. 6–11.
31. Liverpool to Palmerston, 29 Nov. 1821, PP, GC/LI/190.
32. Palmerston to Liverpool, 30 Nov. 1821, Liverpool Papers, BL, Add Ms 38194, ff. 83–4.
33. Palmerston to Laurence Sulivan, 30 Nov. 1822, *PSL*, pp. 153–4.
34. Colchester to Charles Yorke, 30 Nov. 1822, *PSL*, p. 154 n.
35. Palmerston to George Canning, 28 Dec. 1822, Canning Papers, WYAS, Leeds, WYL 250/8/74.
36. Palmerston to Laurence Sulivan, 5 Oct. 1823, *PSL*, p. 167.
37. Palmerston to Laurence Sulivan, 7 Jan. 1825, *PSL*, p. 172.
38. Palmerston to William Temple, 2 Dec. 1825, PP, GC/TE/175.
39. Palmerston to Laurence Sulivan, 4 Dec. 1825, Bulwer, i, pp. 164–5.
40. See, for example, Palmerston to J.C. Hobhouse, 13 Dec. 1825, Broughton Papers, BL, Add Ms 36461, ff. 389–90.
41. A. Sedgwick to J.C. Hobhouse, 8 Jan. [1826], [commenting on Palmerston's letter to Hobhouse of 13 Dec. 1825], ibid.
42. Palmerston to George Canning, 22 Dec. 1825, Canning Papers, WYAS, Leeds, WYL 250/8/74.
43. Palmerston to William Temple, 23 Dec. 1825, PP, GC/TE/176.

44. Eldon to Palmerston, Dec. 1825, PP, GC/EL/1/enc.1 (see also Palmerston to Eldon, 26 Dec. 1825 GC/EL/1)

45. Palmerston to Bathurst, 12 Jan. 1826, PP, BR195/110. On 10 Jan. Bathurst had written to Palmerston explaining that he felt obliged, because of an 'intimate official connection', to support Goulburn: 'I must therefore, I am afraid, limit my exertions to him; not certainly on account of the part you have taken in the Catholic question as I think the University would reflect little credit on themselves, if they were to reject one who has so long served them with general good acceptance because he has temperately supported a question which their favourite member Mr Pitt originally introduced' (PP, BR195/110).

46. Bathurst to Palmerston, 15 Jan. 1826; Robert Peel to Palmerston, 15 Jan. 1826, PP, BR195/110.

47. Palmerston to Laurence Sulivan, 15 Jan. 1826, PSL, pp. 179–80.

48. Chester W. New, The Life of Henry Brougham to 1830 (Oxford: Clarendon Press, 1961), p. 307.

49. Adam Sedgwick to Ainger, 29 Dec. [1825], John Willis Clark and Thomas McKenny Hughes, The Life and Letters of the Reverend Adam Sedgwick, Fellow of Trinity College, Cambridge, Prebendary of Norwich, Woodwardian Professor of Geology, 1818-1873, 2 vols. (Cambridge: Cambridge University Press, 1890), i, pp. 268–9. Ainger voted for Copley and Bankes.

50. Palmerston to Laurence Sulivan, 31 Dec. 1824 [1825], PSL, pp. 177–9.

51. Palmerston to Liverpool, 19 Jan. 1826, PP, BR195/110.

52. Liverpool to Palmerston, 23 Jan 1826, PP, BR195/110.

53. Palmerston to Liverpool, 31 May 1826; Liverpool to Palmerston, 1 June 1826, PP, BR195/110.

54. Palmerston to Sir William Temple, 5 June 1826, PP, GC/TE/178.

55. For a digest of the result, including a breakdown of voting figures by college, see Henry Gunning, The poll for the election of a representative in Parliament for the University of Cambridge . . . 1826. Candidates Sir John S. Copley, M.A., Trinity College, Viscount Palmerston, M.A., St. John's College, William John Bankes, Esq., M.A., Trinity College, Right Hon. Henry Goulburn, M.A., Trinity College (Cambridge: J. & W.T. Clarke [London], 1826), pp. 5–45 and summary p. 46.

56. New, Brougham, p. 307.

57. Palmerston to Sir William Temple, 17 July 1826, PP, GC/TE/179.

58. 'Autobiography', Bulwer, i, p. 374.

59. See, for example, PP, BR195/111.

60. Palmerston to William Lamb, 19 Apr. 1827, GC/ME/507.

61. Bell, i, p. 56.

62. Bourne, pp. 251–2; Southgate, p. 3.

63. See the correspondence between Palmerston and George Canning, 26 Dec. 1822–15 July 1823, Canning Papers, WYAS, Leeds, WYL 250/8/74.

64. Memorandum by Palmerston on letter from Canning to Palmerston, 14 Apr. 1827, PP, GC/CA/80.

65. Edward Herries, Memoir of the Public Life of the Right Hon John Charles Herries in the Reigns of George III, George IV, William IV, and Victoria, 2 vols. (London: John Murray, 1880), i, p. 129.

66. 'Autobiography', Bulwer, i, p. 375.

67. Memorandum by Palmerston on letter from Canning to Palmerston, 14 Apr. 1827, PP, GC/CA/80. See also 'Autobiography', Bulwer, i, pp. 376–7. In the 'Autobiography' Palmerston wrote of the offer of the Governor-Generalship of India: 'I was not insensible to the splendour of the post which he was now proposing; that I felt what means it afforded for increasing one's fortune, for gratifying one's love of power, for affording scope for doing good upon a magnificent theatre of action; but my ambition was satisfied with my position at home. I happened not to have a family for whom I should be desirous of providing, and my health would not stand the climate of India.'

68. Palmerston to William Temple, 19 Apr. 1827, PP, GC/TE/185.

69. Palmerston to William Temple, 4 May 1827, PP, GC/TE/186.

70. Wendy Hinde, George Canning (Oxford: Blackwell, 1973), pp. 460–1.

71. Palmerston to Elizabeth Sulivan, 7 Aug. 1827, PSL, p. 190. This letter was written the day before Canning's death but that event was already widely anticipated.

72. Palmerston, House of Commons, 14 May 1828, Opinions, p. 59.

73. Palmerston to William Temple, 24 Aug. 1827, PP, GC/TE/188/1–2.

74. Henry Brougham to Palmerston, 26 Aug. 1827, PP, GC/BR/66.

75. Palmerston to William Temple, 19 Oct. 1827, PP, GC/TE/189.

76. P.J. Jupp, 'Robinson, Frederick John, first Viscount Goderich and first earl of Ripon (1782–1859)', ODNB.

77. Palmerston to Princess Lieven, vendredi [17 Aug. 1827], Lieven Papers, BL, Add Ms 47366, ff. 1–2.

78. 'Autobiography', Bulwer, i, pp. 377–8.

79. Palmerston to William Sturges Bourne, 30 Aug. 1827, PP, GMC/17.

80. Goderich to Palmerston, 30 Aug. 1827 (2 letters), PP, GC/GO/18 and GC/GO/19.

81. Goderich to Palmerston, 30 Aug. 1827, PP, GC/GO/19.

82. 'Narrative of Events from August 8 to Sepember 3, 1827, by Mr Herries', in Herries, *Memoir*, i, pp. 153–77.

83. Palmerston to Goderich, 18 Dec. 1827, PP, GC/GO/20/enc.1.

84. George Shee to Palmerston, 21 Dec. 1827, PP, GC/SH/84.

85. William Huskisson to Granville, 11 Jan. 1828, Huskisson Papers, BL, Add Ms 38754, ff. 80–3.

86. Palmerston's uncertainty was evident in a letter to William of 8 Jan. in which he described ministerial arrangements as being in 'a very unsettled state' and in consequence he had been 'still more anxious' to secure William's promotion 'while it was to be had from friends and colleagues' (PP, GC/TE/193).

87. George Shee to Palmerston, 12 Jan. 1828, PP, GC/SH/85.

88. 'Autobiography', Bulwer, i, p. 379.

89. Ibid.

90. Memorandum by Palmerston of an interview with the Duke of Wellington on change of government, 13 Jan. 1828, PP, GMC/18. These views were also related to Emily on the same day (Palmerston to Emily, Lady Cowper, 'Sunday' [13 Jan. 1828], PP, BR23AA/5/5).

91. Palmerston to Emily, Lady Cowper, 14 Jan. 1828, PP, BR23AA/5/1.

92. Salisbury to Lord Lytton, 9 Mar. 1877, Lady Gwendolen Cecil, *The Life of Robert, Marquis of Salisbury*, 4 vols. (London: Hodder & Stoughton, 1921–32), ii, p. 130.

93. See, for example, Huskisson's correspondence with Robert Peel at this time for a flavour of such 'Canningite' unity: Huskisson to Robert Peel and reply, 15 Jan. 1828, Huskisson Papers, BL, Add MS 38754, ff. 117–22.

94. Palmerston to William Temple, 18 Jan. 1828, PP, GC/TE/194.

95. William Huskisson to Charles Grant, 16 Jan. 1828, Palmerston to Huskisson, 17 Jan. 1828, Grant to Huskisson, 17 Jan. 1828, Huskisson to Wellington, 17 Jan. 1828, Huskisson Papers, BL, Add Ms 38754, ff. 124–5, 132–3, 133–4, 137–8.

96. Grant to Huskisson, 17 Jan. 1828, Huskisson Papers, BL, Add Ms 38754, ff. 150–1.

97. Palmerston to Huskisson, 'Friday' [18 Jan. 1828], ibid., ff. 152–3.

98. Memorandum by Palmerston, 18 Jan. 1828, PP, GMC/25.

99. Huskisson to Granville, 18 Jan. 1828, Huskisson Papers, BL, Add Ms 38754, ff. 162–5.

100. Memorandum by Palmerston on 'Substance of the understanding verbally come to in a Conversation at Apsley House, between Huskisson, Dudley, Grant & myself on one side & the Duke of Wellington on the other', 18 Jan. 1828, PP, GMC/24.

101. Palmerston to Emily, Lady Cowper, 21 Jan. 1828, PP, GMC/28.

102. Huskisson to Seaford, 25 Jan. 1828, Huskisson Papers, BL, Add Ms 38754, ff. 234–7.

103. Palmerston to William Temple, 25 Mar. 1828, PP, GC/TE/195.

104. Palmerston to Wellington, 6 Apr. 1828, PP, GC/WE/58. Palmerston forwarded this letter to Huskisson on 7 Apr. (Huskisson Papers, BL, Add Ms 38756, ff. 44–7). Five months earlier Palmerston had said something similar when he told his brother: 'the Treaty of London *must* be carried into effect Cost what it may, & oppose it who will' (Palmerston to William Temple, 4 Dec. 1827, PP, GC/TE/191).

105. Palmerston to William Temple, 19 May 1828, PP, GC/TE/198.

106. Palmerston to William Temple, 25 Apr. 1828, PP, GC/TE/196.

107. *A Political Diary 1828–30 by Edward Law, Lord Ellenborough*, ed. Lord Colchester, 2 vols. (London: Richard Bentley, 1881), i, pp. 106–7 (17 May 1828). Palmerston made only two relatively short contributions to the debate. On 13 May he objected to the issue of a pension for the Canning family being used to make party political points and on the following day observed that Canning's 'name would be venerated long after his detractors had been consigned to oblivion': *Hansard*, n.s., xix, 715, 722 (13, 14 May 1828).

108. *A Political Diary 1828–30 by Edward Law, Lord Ellenborough*, i, p. 113 (22 May 1828).

109. Ibid., i, pp. 116, 120–1 (23 May and 24 May 1828).

110. Palmerston also furnished Princess Lieven with glowing accounts of these events, believing they would 'interest' her. See: Palmerston to Princess Lieven, [20, 21, 24 (two letters), 25 May 1828], Lieven Papers, BL, Add Ms 47366, ff. 11–12, 13–14, 15–17, 18–19, 20.

111. George Robert Gleig, *Personal Reminiscences of the First Duke of Wellington* (Edinburgh and London: William Blackwood, 1904), pp. 41–2.

112. 'Autobiography', Bulwer, i, pp. 380–1.

113. Palmerston to William Temple, 8 June 1828, PP, GC/TE/200. In this letter Palmerston identified the following politicians in talking of an emerging parliamentary Liberal party: 'In the Hs of Cns we reckon the following, Huskisson, P., Lamb, Grant, Bourne, Harton, F. Lewis, Ld F. Leveson Gower, Ld Sandon, Ld Jermyn, Littleton of Staffordshire, Warrender, Ellis (Ld Seaford's son),

Wortley (Ld Wharncliffe's[)], Denison, Wm Lascelles (Ld Harewood's son), Acland, Ld Spencer Chichester, Lock (Ld Stafford's member), I. Fitzgerald (Ld Seaford's) Stratford Canning, Lennard, – Besides Spencer Perceval, Liddell (Ld Ravenworth's), Ld G. Bentinck, Morpeth, Normanby & others who are well disposed. In the Lords we have Dudley, Goderich, Seaford, Howard de Walden, Bristol, Morley, Haddington, Granville (who comes away from Paris), Stafford, Gower, Carlisle, Harrowby, Wharncliffe'.

114. Palmerston to Emily, Lady Cowper, 17 June 1828, PP, BR23AA/5/3.
115. Palmerston to Emily, Lady Cowper, 25 July 1828, PP, BR23AA/5/4.
116. Palmerston to William Temple, 26 Aug. 1828, PP, GC/TE/202.
117. Bereft of office and obvious party support, Palmerston, thought Jasper Ridley, 'acquired the art of Parliamentary eloquence in 1829 because it had suddenly become essential for him to do so' (Ridley, p. 98).
118. Notebook containing newspaper cuttings, anecdotes, notes on Irish affairs, 1827–c.1832, PP, BR22(ii)/13. Where Palmerston has dated these memoranda, they are from late 1829 (Nov. and Dec.); given the format of the book, it is reasonable to assume that the undated memoranda were written at the same time. One entry, discussing constitutional government ('There are some govts . . .') is dated 'Dec. 1830' but this appears between other entries dated Dec. 1829 and the dating might be taken to be a typographical error on Palmerston's part. The pagination of this volume is eccentric. Starting from the front (cover entitled 'Memoranda') Palmerston has written on the right-hand pages to the end of book (p. 86) and then returned to the facing pages (at p. 30; the left-hand pages up to p. 30 have been used for miscellaneous notes) where the memoranda continue. All notes referred to above come from pp. 13–80 and facing pp. 31–52. The quotation 'parcere subjectis et deballare superbos' is from Virgil's *Aeneid* and may be translated as 'spare the vanquished and subdue the proud'.
119. Palmerston to Emily, Lady Cowper, 3 Oct. 1829, PP, BR23AA/5/6.
120. Notably Donald Southgate who opened his study with a chapter on 'The emergence of Palmerston' (Southgate, pp. 1–18) which took this speech as its point of departure.
121. Palmerston to William Temple, 27 June 1828, PP, GC/TE/201.
122. Palmerston to William Temple, 6 May 1829, PP, GC/TE/204.
123. *Hansard*, 2nd ser., xxi, 1643–70 (1 June 1829).
124. Southgate, p. 7.
125. *Speech of Viscount Palmerston in the House of Commons on Monday, the first of June 1829 upon the motion of Sir James Mackintosh respecting the relations of England with Portugal* (London: J. Ridgway, 1829).
126. Henry Gally Knight to Palmerston, 6 June 1829, PP, MM/PO/20.
127. Memorandum of Points to be inquired into in the Session of 1830, June 1829, PP, MM/PO/23. Palmerston's list of papers to move was as follows:

Portugal
1. Complaints from Heytesbury & Lamb about Ld Beresford's Interference.
2. Complaints from British subjects in Portugal of treatment by Miguel; Representations made in consequence by English govt answers by Portuguese govt, and statement of dates of imprisonment & liberation in each case; & of compensation made by Portuguese govt.
3. Copies of all communications by British govt to English ambassador at Lisbon on our relations with Portugal from landing of Miguel to recall of our ambassador.
4. Any representations made by Spanish minister here or by D'Asseca[?] upon subject of Portuguese refugees at Plymouth towards end of year 1828.
5. Copies of any reports made by British consuls at Lisbon of the attempt made by Don Miguel upon the life of the Infanta Isabella.
6. Protocols of conferences while Miguel was in England.
7. Report about seizure of any Portguese out of any British ship leaving Terceira, by Miguel's blockading squadron in May or June 1829.

Spain
1. Copy of any application from Spain for our interference in defence of Cuba; and of any communications made by England to the American states with respect to our intentions to prevent an attack on that island.

Russia, Turkey & Greece
1. Copy of any instructions to Sir F. Adam to declare to the Greeks in 1829 that their blockade of northern Greece would not be respected by England, and of any report from Sir F. Adam of the proclamation which he issued on this subject.

    2. Copy of report made by the three ambassadors of France, Engnd & Russia, as to limits of Greece, her tribute, organization, &c.

128. Southgate, pp. 9–17.
129. See, for example, Henry Gally Knight to Palmerston, 6 June 1829, PP, MM/PO/20.
130. In 1860 Palmerston was sent a draft of a biography of himself by a publisher in which were passages claiming that Canning had 'made Palmerston a politician in reality and depth' and that after 1828 Palmerston had 'aimed at acquiring the reputation of being Mr Canning's successor'. Palmerston returned the manuscript with these passages scored out. See Bell, i, p. 59. For a recent essay on the subject of Palmerston's Canningite connections, see Stephen M. Lee, 'Palmerston and Canning', in David Brown and Miles Taylor (eds), *Palmerston Studies I* (Southampton: Hartley Institute, 2007), pp. 1–18.
131. Southgate, p. 17.
132. Palmerston to William Temple, 14 June 1829, Bulwer, i, pp. 333–9.
133. *Hansard*, 2nd ser., viii, 1453–4 (30 Apr. 1823).
134. *Hansard*, 2nd ser., xxi, 1643–70, quotation at 1668 (1 June 1829).
135. See, for example, George Shee to Palmerston, 16 Jan. 1828, PP, GC/SH/87 and enc.1. Shee enclosed a draft of 'as strong a govt all circumstances considered as the country could furnish' in which he proposed an arrangement of seven offices each to the Canningites and the ultras. Palmerston, in this scheme, was to have the Foreign Office, while the other Canningites were to be appointed as follows: Huskisson the Colonial Office, Melville the Home Office, Dudley to be Lord Privy Seal, Wellesley the Duchy of Lancaster, Wynne the Board of Control and Grant the Board of Trade. The remaining offices were to go to the Tories: Peel (Treasury and Exchequer); Eldon (Presidency of the Council); Duke of Wellington (Ordnance); Lyndhurst (Lord Chancellor); Bathurst (Mint); Dawson (Woods and Forests); and Goulburn (Secretary at War).
136. Bulwer, i, p. 340.
137. For example, Chamberlain, p. 41.
138. Bulwer, i, p. 346.
139. Palmerston to Emily, Lady Cowper, 25 Nov. 1829, PP, BR23AA/5/8. A month earlier, Palmerston had written in a similar vein, with regard to foreign affairs, to his brother: 'If our govt had any well understood regard for their own credit they would have taken the line of praising the moderation of the terms of the treaty, and saying that this moderation was the consequence of the tone they had assumed & the threats they had held out; & that if we had not had Gordon on the spot, and had not vapoured a little in London & Petersburgh, greater cessions would have been demanded from Turkey: to be sure this would not have been true, but that would have been no objection to a disciple of the Metternich school' (Palmerston to William Temple, 13 Oct. 1829, PP, GC/TE/206).
140. *Hansard*, 2nd ser., xxii, 566 (16 Feb. 1830).
141. Cf. *Mr Edmund Burke's Speeches at his Arrival at Bristol and at the Conclusion of the Poll [13 Oct., 3 Nov. 1774]* (London: J. Wilkie, 1774): 'Parliament is not a *congress* of ambassadors from different and hostile interests; which interests each must maintain, as an agent and advocate, against other agents and advocates; but Parliament is a *deliberative* assembly of *one* nation, with *one* interest, that of the whole; where, not local purposes, not local prejudices ought to guide, but the general good, resulting from the general reason of the whole.'
142. Palmerston to Princess Lieven, 19 June 1830, Lieven Papers, BL, Add Ms 47366, ff. 26–8.
143. *A Political Diary 1828–30 by Edward Law, Lord Ellenborough*, ii, pp. 306, 312, 316 (10, 15, 17 July 1830).
144. Memorandum by Palmerston, 1830, concerning offer made to join Wellington government in June 1830, PP, GMC/33/1–2.
145. *A Political Diary 1828–30 by Edward Law, Lord Ellenborough*, ii, p. 418 (6 Nov. 1830).
146. Palmerston to Charles Grant, 17 Aug. 1830, PP, GC/GL/220.
147. Palmerston to Huskisson, 3 Sept. 1830, PP, GC/HU/119.
148. Brougham, *The Result of the General Election; or, What has the Duke of Wellington gained by the dissolution?* (London, 1830).
149. Extract of a letter from Palmerston to Charles Grant, 25 Sept. 1830, PP, GMC/35.
150. Palmerston to Holland (3rd Baron), 12 Oct. 1830, Holland House Papers, BL, Add Ms 51599A, ff. 7–10. On the offer made and its refusal, see Clive to Palmerston, 1 Oct. 1830 and Palmerston's reply, 4 Oct. 1830, PP, GMC/36 and 37.
151. *A Political Diary 1828–30 by Edward Law, Lord Ellenborough*, ii, p. 440 (19 Nov. 1830).
152. Memorandum by Palmerston, 'Proposal made to me by the Duke of Wellington to join his Government', Oct 1830, PP, GMC/38. These views were repeated to Wellington at a short personal interview a fortnight later ('Mem. [by Palmerston] of interview with the Duke of Wellington

about political arrangements; in consequence of his note of this morning', Saturday 30 Oct. 1830, PP, GMC/42).

153. Huskisson to Palmerston, 3 Sept. 1830, PP, GC/HU/119.
154. *A Political Diary 1828–30 by Edward Law, Lord Ellenborough*, ii, pp. 362–3 (20 Sept. 1830).
155. 'Autobiography', Bulwer, i, p. 383.
156. *Hansard*, n.s., xix (2 June 1828). For Palmerston's account of this issue, see also Bulwer, i, pp. 253–67.
157. 'Autobiography', Bulwer, i, p. 383.
158. Bell, i, pp. 92–3.
159. Ridley, p. 104–6.
160. Bourne, pp. 330–1.
161. Webster, i, pp. 20–1.
162. Southgate, pp. 17–18.
163. Bulwer, ii, p. 17.
164. Palmerston to Elizabeth Sulivan, 18 Nov. 1830, *PSL*, p. 248.
165. Palmerston to Laurence Sulivan, 22 Dec. 1830, Bulwer, i, p. 385.

Chapter 6 The Whig Foreign Secretary, 1830–1834

1. [Palmerston], *The Reform Ministry, and the Reformed Parliament* (London: James Ridgway, 1833). [By Lords Althorp, Stanley and Palmerston and Sir James Graham. Ed. Sir Denis Le Marchant], p. 104.
2. Palmerston to William Temple, 9 Oct. 1830, PP, GC/TE/208.
3. Palmerston to Laurence Sulivan, 1 Aug. 1830, Mabell, Countess of Airlie, *Lady Palmerston and Her Times*, 2 vols. (London: Hodder & Stoughton, 1922), i, pp. 172–4.
4. Extract of letter from Palmerston to Charles Grant, 17 Aug. 1830, PP, GC/GL/220.
5. Palmerston to James Graham, 4 Aug. 1830, Graham Papers, BL, Add Ms 79705, ff. 3–4.
6. Bulwer, i, p. 359.
7. Ashley to Palmerston, 20 Nov. 1830, PP, GC/SH/2: 'The peculiarity of circumstances now attending party & the business of politics has, I know, greatly changed the grounds upon which public men of different, tho' approximating, opinions, must regulate their conduct. It has become a matter of feeling much more than of principle, to decide the acceptance or refusal of office; & feelings, perhaps unfortunately for the interests of mankind, maintain their spirit of exclusiveness, long after principles have ceased to present any distinction.

    'I regret sincerely that such views as these, delusive as they may be, should forbid me to undertake a change, which would be suited alike to my taste in public business, & to my personal gratification in the chief that I should officially serve – this last consideration will cause me more regret than the other. I shall hope however for a continuance of your friendship, which is so amiably displayed in an offer that I shall ever feel and acknowledge with gratitude.'
8. Memorandum by Palmerston, 18 Dec. 1836, PP, FO/B/3.
9. Palmerston to Russell, 20 Oct. 1839, Russell Papers, TNA, PRO/30/22 3D, ff. 83–5.
10. Bourne, pp. 422–5.
11. Bourne, in a chapter on 'The Foreign Office' (Bourne, pp. 408–98) provides a detailed administrative history of the Office during Palmerston's tenure. Specific references in this paragraph are taken from pp. 409, 416. Bourne's description of the practicalities of life at the Office may be supplemented by John Tilley and Stephen Gaselee, *The Foreign Office* (London: G.P. Putnam's, 1933), ch. 3.
12. Palmerston to Emily, Lady Cowper, 31 Dec. 1831, PP, BR23AA/5/23.
13. Palmerston to Heytesbury, 31 Dec 1830, Heytesbury Papers, BL, Add Ms 41560, ff. 235–8.
14. 'maladroit' is Muriel Chamberlain's term: see M.E. Chamberlain, *British Foreign Policy in the Age of Palmerston* (London: Longman, 1980), p. 35.
15. Webster, i, p. 99.
16. Palmerston to Melbourne, 1 Mar. 1836, PP, GC/ME/519.
17. Quoted in Webster, i, p. 107.
18. Palmerston to Heytesbury, 31 Dec. 1830, Heytesbury Papers, BL, Add Ms 41560, ff. 235–8.
19. See G. Le G. Norgate, 'Trench, Richard Le Poer, second earl of Clancarty (1767–1837)', rev. H.C.G. Matthew, *ODNB*, for background on Clancarty's diplomatic career.
20. Clancarty to Londonderry, 14 Feb. 1831, Castlereagh Papers, PRONI, D/3030/CC/28 (MIC/570/Reel 17/D/3030/CC/28).
21. From *Hansard*, 18 Feb. 1831, Ridley, p. 128.
22. Palmerston to Ponsonby, 15 Apr. 1831, Webster, i, p. 108.

23. Metternich to Apponyi in Paris, Vienna, 3 June 1831, *Memoirs of Prince Metternich*, ed. Prince Richard Metternich, trans. Gerard W. Smith, 5 vols. (London: Richard Bentley, 1880–82), v, p. 116.
24. Webster, i, pp. 117–18.
25. Ibid., p. 115.
26. 'Précis des négociations relatives à la séparation de la Belgique d'avec la Hollande, et à l'indépendance future du nouvel état', PP, MM/BE/95.
27. Bulwer, ii, p. 24 n.
28. Bourne, p. 336.
29. Palmerston to ?, 12 Nov. 1831, Webster, i, p. 111.
30. Palmerston to Granville, 21 Jan. 1831, Bulwer, ii, p. 31.
31. Lady Cowper to Devonshire, 'Sat' [8 Jan. 1831], Bourne, p. 334.
32. Palmerston to Sir Charles Bagot, 16 Nov. 1831, PP, GC/BA/213.
33. Webster, i, p. 111.
34. *Treaty relative to the Netherlands. Signed at London, November 15 1831. Presented to both Houses of Parliament, by Command of His Majesty, 1832.* A copy may be found in Palmerston's Papers, PP, MM/BE/36.
35. Bourne, p. 343.
36. Palmerston to Granville, 7 Jan. 1831, Bulwer, ii, pp. 28–9.
37. Palmerston to Granville, 27 Jan. 1831, Bulwer, ii, pp. 34–5; Palmerston to Granville, 2 Feb. 1831, Bulwer, ii, pp. 36–7.
38. Palmerston to Granville, 8 Feb. 1831, Bulwer, ii, p. 39; Palmerston to Granville, 15 Feb. 1831, Bulwer, ii, p. 41.
39. Palmerston to Granville, 15 Mar. 1831, Bulwer, ii, p. 52.
40. Palmerston to Granville, 18 Mar. 1831, Bulwer, ii, pp. 55–6; Palmerston to Granville, 25 Mar. 1831, Bulwer, ii, p. 60.
41. Palmerston to Granville, 31 May 1831, Bulwer, ii, pp. 81–5.
42. Palmerston to Holland (3rd Baron), 9 Apr. 1831, Holland House Papers, BL, Add Ms 51599A, ff. 31–3.
43. Palmerston to Granville, 17 Aug., 26 Aug. 1831, Bulwer, ii, pp. 109, 122.
44. Palmerston to Holland (3rd Baron), 31 Aug. 1831, Holland House Papers, BL, Add Ms 51599A, ff. 64–6.
45. Palmerston to Heytesbury, 26 Aug. 1831, Heytesbury Papers, BL, Add Ms 41562, ff. 64–6.
46. Palmerston to Sir F. Lamb, 10 Apr. 1832, Beauvale Papers, BL, Add Ms 60463, ff. 55–60.
47. See, for example, Metternich to Neumann, 21 Mar. 1832, *Metternich Memoirs*, v, pp. 218–19, speaking of the revolts in the Italian states: 'In fact, what the factions in the Legations want, is not to get good laws, but to shake off the Pontifical rule. As, however, their hopes are inconsistent with the general interests of Europe, this handful of men must resign themselves to obey. They will find neither Europe as a whole, nor any state taken individually, inclined to forward their personal views at the expense of the general political repose, and the internal tranquillity of the various states.'
48. Palmerston to Heytesbury, 22 Mar. 1831, Heytesbury Papers, BL, Add Ms 41561, ff. 111–15.
49. Palmerston to Holland (3rd Baron), 20 Mar. 1831, Holland House Papers, BL, Add Ms 51599A, ff. 24–9.
50. Palmerston to Holland (3rd Baron), 9 Apr. 1831, ibid., ff. 31–3.
51. Palmerston to Heytesbury, 23 Nov. 1831, Heytesbury Papers, BL, Add Ms 41562, ff. 151–5.
52. Holland to Palmerston, 21 May 1831, PP, GC/HO/68.
53. See: J.P. Parry, *The Rise and Fall of Liberal Government in Victorian Britain* (New Haven and London: Yale University Press, 1993), p. 93; E.A. Smith, *Lord Grey 1764–1845* (Oxford: Oxford University Press, 1990), p. 280.
54. Note by Palmerston on 'Notes by Ld. Holland on some F.O. Despatches', n.d., PP, GC/HO/137–8A. The letters from Holland can be found *ibid.*, GC/HO/62–136.
55. C.R. Middleton, *The Administration of British Foreign Policy, 1782–1846* (Durham, NC: Duke University Press, 1977), pp. 46–50.
56. Palmerston to Emily, Lady Cowper, 9 Jan. 1832, Lamb Papers, BL, Add Ms 45911, f. 71; Palmerston to F. Lamb, 6 Feb. 1832, Beauvale Papers, BL, Add Ms 60463, ff. 6–7.
57. Palmerston to Emily, Lady Cowper, 9 Jan. 1832, Lamb Papers, BL, Add Ms 45911, f. 71.
58. Metternich to Apponyi, 8 Jan. 1832, *Metternich Memoirs*, v, pp. 177–8.
59. Palmerston to General Goblet [representative of King Leopold in London], 22 Dec. 1831 [translated from the French original], Théodore Juste, *Memoirs of Leopold I, King of the Belgians, from unpublished documents*, trans. Robert Black, 2 vols. (London: Sampson Low, 1868), i, pp. 235–6.
60. Palmerston to Frederick Lamb, 19 Feb. 1832, Beauvale Papers, BL, Add Ms 60463, ff. 8–19.
61. Metternich to Ficquelmont, 29 Dec. 1831, *Metternich Memoirs*, v, pp. 150–1.

62. Palmerston to Frederick Lamb, 19 Feb. 1832, Beauvale Papers, BL, Add Ms 60463, ff. 8–19.
63. Palmerston to Frederick Lamb, 26 Feb. 1832, ibid., ff. 26–35.
64. Palmerston to Heytesbury, 15 Mar. 1832, Heytesbury Papers, BL, Add Ms 41563, ff. 110–17; Palmerston to Frederick Lamb, 7 Mar. 1832, Beauvale Papers, BL, Add Ms 60463, f. 36.
65. Palmerston to Heytesbury, 15, 17 Mar. 1832, Heytesbury Papers, BL, Add Ms 41563, ff. 110–17, 120. As the attempts to resolve the question continued into the summer of 1832, Palmerston complained that 'Russia is our great clog, and I foresee that we shall be obliged to shake her off & that France & England will have to send their combined squadron to blockade the Dutch Ports and my own *conviction* is that a fortnight's application of that screw would bring the King [of the Netherlands] & his merchants to a very reasonable temper of mind.' (Palmerston to Sir Charles Bagot, 5 June 1832, PP, GC/BA/234).
66. Palmerston to Granville, 3 Apr. 1832, Granville Papers (1st Earl), TNA, PRO 30/29/14/6, ff. 28–30.
67. Memorandum by Palmerston, 8 Apr. 1832, PP, MM/BE/38–9.
68. Palmerston to Frederick Lamb, 10 Apr. 1832, Beauvale Papers, BL, Add Ms 60463, ff. 55–60.
69. Metternich to Apponyi, 25 Jan. 1832, *Metternich Memoirs*, v, p. 180.
70. Metternich to Apponyi, 29 Feb. 1832, ibid., p. 184.
71. Metternich to Wessenberg, 21 Mar. 1832, ibid., pp. 226–7.
72. Metternich to Wessenberg, 6 Apr. 1832, ibid., p. 229.
73. Metternich to Neumann, 31 Oct. 1832, ibid., pp. 267–9.
74. Palmerston to Granville, 10 June 1831, Granville Papers (1st Earl), TNA, PRO 30/29/14/6, ff. 12–14.
75. Palmerston to Granville, 2 Aug. 1831, ibid., ff. 16–17.
76. Palmerston to Sir James Graham, 27 Oct. 1831, Graham Papers, BL, Add Ms 79705, ff. 32–4.
77. Palmerston to Emily, Lady Cowper, 15 Nov. 1831, PP, BR23AA/5/17.
78. Palmerston to Henry Addington, 10 Feb. 1832, PP, GC/AD/590.
79. Palmerston to Frederick Lamb, 19 Feb. 1832, Beauvale Papers, BL, Add Ms 60463, ff. 8–19.
80. Palmerston to Frederick Lamb, 11 Apr. 1832, ibid., ff. 61–6.
81. Palmerston to Frederick Lamb, 15 Apr. 1832, ibid., ff. 69–73.
82. Metternich to Schwarzenberg, 13 Oct. 1832, *Metternich Memoirs*, v, pp. 272–3, 277.
83. Metternich to Ficquelmont, 13 Oct. 1830, (confidential dispatch); Metternich to Trauttmansdorff, 8 Dec. 1832, ibid., pp. 56–7, 281–3.
84. Palmerston to Frederick Lamb, 4 Jan. 1833, BL, Add Ms 60464, ff. 6–16.
85. Palmerston to Emily, Lady Cowper, 27 Sept. 1832, PP, BR 23AA/5/26.
86. Metternich to Apponyi, 26 Jan. 1833, *Metternich Memoirs*, v, pp. 316–18.
87. Palmerston to Sir James Graham, 18 Jan. 1833, 5 July 1833, BL, Add Ms 79705, ff. 188–93; Add Ms 79706, ff. 25–7.
88. Palmerston to Frederick Lamb, 17 May 1833, BL, Add Ms 60464, ff. 91–3.
89. Palmerston to William Temple, 1833, PP, GC/TE/216.
90. Palmerston to Frederick Lamb, 4 Jan. 1833, Beauvale Papers, BL, Add Ms 60464, ff. 6–16.
91. Palmerston to Sir James Graham, 18 Jan. 1833, Graham Papers, BL, Add Ms 79705, ff. 188–93.
92. Palmerston to Frederick Lamb, 22 Mar. 1833, Beauvale Papers, BL, Add Ms 60464, f. 74.
93. Palmerston to Frederick Lamb, 22 Mar. 1833, ibid.; Palmerston to Sir James Graham, 12 July 1833, Graham Papers, BL, Add Ms 79706, ff. 28–9.
94. Palmerston to Frederick Lamb, 17 Jan. 1833, Beauvale Papers, BL, Add Ms 60464, ff. 32–7.
95. Palmerston to Frederick Lamb, 18 June 1833, Beauvale Papers, BL, Add Ms 60464, ff. 125–33.
96. Palmerston to Frederick Lamb, 17 Mar. 1833, Beauvale Papers, BL, Add Ms 60464, f. 66.
97. Webster, i, p. 200.
98. Southgate, p. 49.
99. Palmerston to Frederick Lamb, 18 June 1833, Beauvale Papers, BL, Add Ms 60464, ff. 125–33.
100. Palmerston, House of Commons, 2 Aug. 1832 (*Opinions*, p. 208).
101. Bourne, pp. 369–70.
102. Webster, i, p. 230.
103. Southgate, pp. 51–2.
104. Palmerston to Frederick Lamb, 3 Aug. 1832, Webster, i, p. 227.
105. Palmerston to Granville, 16 Sept. 1831, Bulwer, ii, p. 127.
106. Bourne, p. 367.
107. Webster, i, p. 236.
108. Palmerston to Frederick Lamb, 6 Apr. 1833, Beauvale Papers, BL, Add Ms 60464, ff. 81–3.
109. Palmerston to Frederick Lamb, 14 Nov. 1833, Beauvale Papers, BL, Add Ms 60464, ff. 182–91.
110. Metternich to Neumann, 31 Oct. 1832, *Metternich Memoirs*, v, p. 267.

111. Bell, i, p. 103.
112. Palmerston to Heytesbury, 23 Nov. 1831, Heytesbury Papers, BL, Add Ms 41562, ff. 164–70.
113. Palmerston to Frederick Lamb, 4 Jan. 1832, Beauvale Papers, BL, Add Ms 60464, ff. 2–5.
114. *Hansard*, 3rd ser., i, 610–11 (22 Nov. 1830).
115. Palmerston to Heytesbury, 2 Aug. 1831, Heytesbury Papers, BL, Add Ms 41562, ff. 29–30.
116. Grey to Princess Lieven, Sept. 1830, Smith, *Lord Grey*, p. 282.
117. Palmerston to Emily, Lady Cowper, 8 Oct. 1831, PP, BR23AA/5/9.
118. B. Frere to Palmerston, 25 Apr. 1831, PP, BR195/112.
119. Cf. the voting figures published in *The Times* (9 May 1831) which suggest that, contrary to Palmerston's assessment, the clergy were, relatively speaking, much more hostile to his candidature than the laity. The pollbook record of the result provides the following breakdown of votes: Goulburn: clergy 570 votes, laity 236, total 806; Peel: clergy 573, laity 232, total 805; Cavendish: clergy 323, laity 307, total 630; Palmerston: clergy 309, laity 301, total 610. See J.R. Vincent, *Pollbooks. How Victorians Voted* (Cambridge: Cambridge University Press, 1967), pp. 93–4.
120. Palmerston to Lady Holland, 'Sunday' [8 May 1831], Holland House Papers, BL, Add Ms 51600, ff. 7–8.
121. Bourne, pp. 506–8. The voting figures at the end of the poll were: Goulburn, 805; Peel, 804; Cavendish, 630; Palmerston, 610.
122. Palmerston paid £800 for Bletchingley, in the knowledge that it would be abolished within the year. When Edward Ellice wrote to ask Palmerston for a second payment of £800 for the seat he replied, revealing more than just his reluctance to pay more money: 'When I was returned for Bletchingley you told me that you should have to call upon me for £800, and that sum I paid but you never gave me the slightest hint that any further payment was agreed for, or would be expected from me. You say *seats* are not to be had for £800. To this I reply, that if by *seats*, is meant a seat for an ordinary Parliament with the chance of six years duration, you are right; but on the other hand, I have never heard of *£1,600 a year* being paid for a seat, even bought from a circumcised Jew' (Palmerston to Edward Ellice, 12 Mar. 1832, PP, GC/EL/20/enc.2).
123. Palmerston to Fred Gunning, 11 June 1832, PP, BR195/112.
124. Dr J. Lamb to Palmerston, 26 June 1832, PP, BR195/112. See also Bourne, pp. 535–6.
125. J. Wood to Palmerston, 17 Nov. 1832, PP, BR195/112.
126. Palmerston to James Graham, 6 July 1832, Graham Papers, BL, Add MS 79705, ff. 69–72.
127. Palmerston to Laurence Sulivan, 13 Feb. 1820, *PSL*, p. 148.
128. Bourne, p. 536.
129. William Temple to Palmerston, 23, 28 June, 1, 3 July 1832; William Lake to Palmerston, 22 July 1832, PP, BR195, pt.2 [Penryn and Falmouth, 1832]; printed address by William Temple 'To the Worthy and Independent Electors of Penryn', PP, BR195/114.
130. William Temple to Palmerston, 23 June 1832, PP, BR195/114.
131. William Lake to James Graham, 29 Sept. 1832, PP, BR195, pt. 2 [Penryn and Falmouth, 1832].
132. Bourne, p. 536.
133. PP, BR195, pt. 2 [Lambeth, 1832]; Holland to Palmerston, 20 July 1832, PP, GC/HO/84.
134. William Jones to Palmerston, 13 Sept. 1832, PP, BR195/30.
135. Palmerston to Richard Cannon, 14 Sept. 1832, PP, BR195, pt. 2 [Lambeth, 1832].
136. Palmerston to William Jones, 15 Sept. 1832, PP, BR195/33.
137. Palmerston to James Graham, 29 Sept. 1832, Graham Papers, BL, Add Ms 79705, ff. 132–3.
138. V. Bonham-Carter, *In a Liberal Tradition: A Social Biography, 1700–1950* (London: Constable, 1960), ch. 2.
139. John Bonham-Carter to F.T. Baring, 13 Sept. 1832, Bonham-Carter Papers, HRO, 94M72/F12.
140. John Bonham-Carter to Palmerston, 28 Sept. 1832, PP, BR195/34.
141. William Sloane Stanley to Palmerston, 29 Sept. 1832, PP, BR195/35.
142. James Graham to Palmerston, 10 Oct. 1832, PP, BR195/36.
143. Palmerston to John Bonham-Carter PP, BR195/37.
144. W.E Nightingale to Palmerston, 3 Oct. 1832 PP, BR195/38; Henry Holmes to Palmerston, 3 Oct. 1832, PP, BR195/39.
145. Palmerston to W.E. Nightingale, 5 Oct. 1832, PP, BR195/41.
146. Palmerston to W.E. Nightingale, 5 Oct. 1832, PP, BR195/42.
147. John Bonham-Carter to Palmerston, PP, BR195/43, 44.
148. Holland to Palmerston, 6 Oct. 1832, PP, GC/HO/86.
149. John Bonham-Carter to J.T. Baring, 4, 7 Nov. 1832, Bonham-Carter Papers, HRO, 94M72/F12.
150. Palmerston to W.E. Nightingale, 27 Nov. 1832, PP, BR 195/48. For a more detailed treatment of Palmerston and South Hampshire, see D. Brown, *Palmerston, South Hampshire and Electoral Politics, 1832–1835. Hampshire Papers, 26* (Winchester: Hampshire County Council, 2003).
151. Richard Davenport-Hines, 'Staunton, Sir George Thomas, second baronet (1781–1859)', *ODNB*.

152. G.T. Staunton, *Memoirs of the Chief Incidents of the Public Life of Sir George Thomas Staunton, Bart.* (Printed for private circulation, 1856), p. 110.
153. R. Stewart, *Party and Politics, 1830–1852* (1989), p. 38.
154. John Bonham-Carter to J.T. Baring, 4 Nov. 1832, Bonham-Carter Papers, HRO, 94M72/F12.
155. *Hampshire Advertiser*, 17 Nov. 1832.
156. Ibid.
157. Ibid., 24 Nov. 1832; see also election poster, PP, BR195/84.
158. H. Temperley, *British Antislavery, 1833–1870* (Harlow: Longman, 1972), p. 16.
159. J.R. Oldfield, 'Southampton and Anti-Slavery, 1823–1870', *Southern History*, 9 (1987), 91–2.
160. Ibid., 93–4.
161. Petition sent to Palmerston, 21 Nov. 1832, PP, BR195/46.
162. Palmerston to Robert Lindoe, 1 Dec. 1832, PP, BR195/51.
163. See, for example, Captain Badcock, RN, to Palmerston, 3 Dec. 1832, PP, BR195/52.
164. *Hampshire Advertiser*, 15 Dec. 1832.
165. Ibid., 22 Dec. 1832.
166. Palmerston to Sir H. Taylor, 23 Dec. 1832, PP, BR195/55.
167. Woodbine Parish to Palmerston, 15 Feb. 1833, PP, SLT/4.
168. I. Gross, 'The Abolition of Negro Slavery and British Parliamentary Politics, 1832–1833', *Historical Journal*, 23 (1980), 70, 82–3.
169. See, for example, *Hampshire Chronicle*, 6 May, 22 July, 12 Aug., 14 Oct. 1833.
170. Staunton, *Memoirs*, p. 200.
171. Webster, i, p. 257.
172. [David Urquhart], *England, France, Russia and Turkey* (3rd edn, London: James Ridgway, 1835), p. 83.
173. Palmerston to Prince Lieven, 10 Jan. 1831, Lieven Papers, BL, Add Ms 47263, ff. 61–2.
174. Palmerston to Dawkins, 30 Sept. 1834; Palmerston to Sir Edward Lyons, 21 Sept. 1835, Webster, i, pp. 271–2.
175. Palmerston to Granville, 3 June 1831, Granville Papers, TNA, PRO/30/29/14/6, ff. 9–11.
176. Webster, i, pp. 283–4.
177. M.S. Anderson, *The Eastern Question, 1774–1923: A Study in International Relations* (London: Macmillan, 1966), pp. 77–87; A.L. Macfie, *The Eastern Question, 1774–1923* (Harlow: Longman, rev. edn, 1996), pp. 20–1.
178. Palmerston to Granville, 29 Jan. 1833, M. Vereté, 'Palmerston and the Levant Crisis, 1832', in *From Palmerston to Balfour: Collected Essays of Meyir Vereté*, ed. Norman Rose (London: Frank Cass, 1992), p. 167.
179. Vereté, 'Palmerston and the Levant Crisis, 1832', p. 165; Webster, i, p. 257 *et seq.*; Bourne, pp. 375–6.
180. Webster, i, p. 259.
181. Palmerston to Arthur Aston, 23 Apr. 1833, PP, GC/AS/183.
182. Palmerston to Sir James Graham, Graham Papers, BL, Add Ms 79706, ff. 3–8.
183. Palmerston to Frederick Lamb, 2 May 1833, Beauvale Papers, BL, Add Ms 60464, ff. 84–90.
184. Palmerston to Frederick Lamb, 17 May 1833, ibid., ff. 91–3.
185. Palmerston to Frederick Lamb, 11 June 1833, ibid., ff. 119–20.
186. Palmerston to Frederick Lamb, 10 June 1833, ibid., ff. 107–18.
187. Palmerston to Sir James Graham, 2 Aug. 1833, Graham Papers, BL, Add Ms 79706, ff. 48–9.
188. Macfie, *The Eastern Question*, pp. 90–1.
189. Palmerston to Frederick Lamb, 17 Oct. 1833, Beauvale Papers, BL, Add Ms 60464, ff. 176–81.
190. Palmerston to Esterhazy, 20 Nov. 1833, PP, GC/ES/53.
191. Palmerston to Frederick Lamb, 10 Mar. 1834, Beauvale Papers, BL, Add Ms 60465, ff. 17–22.
192. Webster, i, p. 277.
193. Palmerston to Frederick Lamb, 22 Apr. 1834, Beauvale Papers, BL, Add Ms 60465, ff. 23–5.
194. Palmerston to William Temple, 21 Apr. 1834, PP, GC/TE/219.
195. Palmerston to Frederick Lamb, 22 Apr. 1834, Beauvale Papers, BL, Add Ms 60465, ff. 26–7.
196. Palmerston to William Temple, 12 May 1834, PP, GC/TE/221.
197. Palmerston to Frederick Lamb, 6 May 1834, Beauvale Papers, BL, Add Ms 60465, ff. 30–1.
198. E. A. Smith, 'Grey, Charles, second Earl Grey (1764–1845)', *ODNB*.
199. Bourne, p. 402.
200. Palmerston to Frederick Lamb, 30 May 1834, Beauvale Papers, BL, Add Ms 60465, ff. 38–41.
201. Palmerston to Frederick Lamb, 24 June 1834, ibid., ff. 42–3.
202. Palmerston to Melbourne, 12 July 1834, PP, GC/ME/508.
203. Palmerston to Melbourne, 30 Aug. 1834, PP, GC/ME/509.
204. *Hampshire Advertiser*, 29 Nov. 1834.
205. Ibid., 6 Dec. 1834.

206. *Hampshire Chronicle*, 8 Dec. 1834.
207. Ibid.
208. Palmerston to Elizabeth Sulivan, 28 Dec. 1834, *PSL*, p. 259 and 259 n. 2.
209. *Hampshire Advertiser*, 20 Dec. 1834, Election poster [Dec. 1834], Compton of Minstead Papers, HRO 12M60/91.
210. Election poster [Dec. 1834], Compton of Minstead Papers, HRO 12M60/91.
211. *Hampshire Advertiser*, 13 Dec. 1834
212. *Hampshire Chronicle*, 22 Dec. 1834, 29 Dec. 1834.
213. Palmerston to Elizabeth Sulivan, 28 Dec. 1834, *PSL*, pp. 259–60.
214. Results cards from the 1835 election, Compton of Minstead Papers, HRO 12M60/91.
215. Staunton, *Memoirs*, pp. 132, 135.
216. Palmerston to Elizabeth Sulivan, 18 Jan. 1835, *PSL*, pp. 260–1.
217. James Grant, *The Metropolitan Weekly and Provincial Press. Third and Concluding Volume of the History of the Newspaper Press* (London: George Routledge, 1872), p. 237.
218. Bourne, p. 480.
219. Grant, *The Metropolitan Weekly and Provincial Press*, p. 238.
220. Wellington to Sir Robert Peel, 1827, A. Aspinall, 'The Social Status of Journalists at the beginning of the 19th century', *Review of English Studies*, 21 (1945), 218.
221. See Peter Jupp, *British Politics on the Eve of Reform: The Duke of Wellington's Administration, 1828–30* (Basingstoke: Macmillan, 1998), pp. 347–52 for comments on differing Tory and Whig attitudes to the press in the later 1820s.
222. H. Brougham to Lady Cowper, 3 Sept. 1830, PP, GC/BR/68/2–3.
223. It is reported that Lord Holland, John Allen, Hobhouse, Normanby, Poulett Thomson, Le Marchant and others all contributed to the *Chronicle* while the Marquis of Londonderry corresponded with the *Herald*. See Hannah Barker, *Newspapers, Politics and English Society, 1695–1855* (Harlow: Longman, 2000), p. 87.
224. Malmesbury (1st Earl) to Palmerston, 1 Apr. 1810, PP, GC/MA/135.
225. Palmerston to Lady Cowper, 21 Sept. 1831, Lieven Papers, BL, Add Ms 47355, ff. 187–8. A key phrase in this letter – 'I can impel but I cannot control' – has frequently been misquoted as 'I can compel but I cannot control'.
226. On Palmerston's relationships with the press, see D. Brown, 'Compelling but not Controlling?: Palmerston and the Press, 1846–1855', *History*, 86 (Jan. 2001), 41–61.
227. Robert Adair to Palmerston, 3 Aug. 1832, PP, GC/AD/132.
228. John Maberley to Palmerston, 4 July 1834, PP, PRE/A/3.
229. Palmerston to William Temple, PP, GC/TE/226.

Chapter 7 Palmerston, *Rex* and Autocrat, 1835–1841

1. Disraeli to Sarah Disraeli, [22? June 1838], *BDL*, iii, 786.
2. Bell, i, p. 208.
3. Memorandum by Lord Grey on Wood's account of the failure to form a government, Dec. 1846, after Grey had seen the account in Apr. 1884 at Hickleton, Hickleton Papers, BIY, A8/1/6.
4. Charles Wood, political journal, 17 Apr. 1835, ibid., A8/1/1.
5. Bourne, p. 550.
6. Bell, i, pp. 199–200; 204.
7. N. Gash, *Reaction and Reconstruction in English Politics, 1832–52* (Oxford: Oxford University Press, 1965) and *idem, Aristocracy and People, 1815–1865* (London: Edward Arnold, 1979).
8. J. Parry, *The Rise and Fall of Liberal Government in Victorian Britain* (New Haven and London: Yale University Press, 1993), p. 128.
9. Russell to Lord Howick, 1 Feb. 1835 and to Grey, 1835, T.A. Jenkins, *The Liberal Ascendancy, 1830–1886* (Basingstoke: Macmillan, 1994), p. 25.
10. Russell to Melbourne, 10 Aug. 1837, ibid., p. 29.
11. See, for example, Palmerston to William Temple, 9 Jan. 1835, PP, GC/TE/233.
12. Palmerston's diary, 1835, PP, D/7. A copy of the letter from Lansdowne, Melbourne, Holland, Palmerston and Spring Rice to [2nd Earl] Grey, 11 Apr. 1835, may be found in PP, GC/ME/24/enc.1.
13. Note in Pam's hand on letter from Melbourne to Palmerston, 12 Apr. 1835, PP, GC/ME/24.
14. Palmerston to Chevalier de Moraes Sarmento, 6 Apr. 1835, Moraes Sarmento Papers, BL, Add Ms 63174, f. 10.
15. Grey to Melbourne, 14 Apr. 1835, PP, GC/ME/26/enc.1.
16. Postscript added by Palmerston to the letter from Grey to Melbourne, 14 Apr. 1835, PP, GC/ME/26/enc.1; Memorandum by Palmerston, 14 Apr. 1835, PP, GC/ME/26/enc.3.

17. Palmerston to Melbourne, 14 Apr. 1835, PP, GC/ME/26/enc.2.
18. Melbourne to Palmerston, and Palmerston's reply, both 15 Apr. 1835, PP, GC/ME/27 and GC/ME/27/enc.1.
19. Joseph Croucher to Palmerston, 24 Jan. 1835, PP, BR23/1/10/1 and Oddie, Foster and Lumley to Palmerston, Jan/Apr. [n.d., but endorsed by Palmerston 'Jany. Ap. 1835'], PP, BR23/1/10/2.
20. Cf. Palmerston's later address to his constituents in 1837: 'It has been stated that I came here in 1835 to purchase your borough. Now, Gentlemen, I really wish I were wealthy enough to purchase the borough of Tiverton, because knowing that you are honourable, honest, free and independent gentlemen as ever trod the face of God's earth, I am well convinced that the sum which would enable any man to purchase you, would buy a Principality anywhere, it would buy even some Kingdoms in Germany (A Voice: "It would buy all the Tories.")', quoted in F.J. Snell, *Palmerston's Borough: A Budget of Electioneering Anecdotes, Jokes, Squibs and Speeches* (London: Horace Marshall; and Tiverton: Gregory, Son and Tozer, 1894), p. 51.
21. Snell, *Palmerston's Borough*, p. 47.
22. Palmerston's printed election address: 'To the Free and Independent Electors of the Borough of Tiverton', 29 May 1835, PP, BR195/115.
23. Snell, *Palmerston's Borough*, p. 71.
24. Palmerston to William Temple, 2 June 1835, PP, GC/TE/237.
25. Palmerston to William Temple, 1 Aug. 1835, PP, GC/TE/238.
26. George Coles to Palmerston, 14 and 21 Jan. 1836, PP, BR23/1/7/1–2.
27. George Coles to Palmerston, 7 Feb. 1836, PP, BR23/1/7/3.
28. Correspondence between Francis Hole (mayor of Tiverton), Palmerston and Lord Lichfield (Postmaster-General), Oct.–Nov. 1836, PP, BR23/1/14/3–5.
29. Francis Hole to Palmerston, 14 Apr. 1837, PP, BR23/1/14/7.
30. Reported to his brother: Palmerston to William Temple, 1 Oct. 1835, PP, GC/TE/240.
31. Palmerston to William Temple, 1 July 1836, PP, GC/TE/247.
32. Palmerston to William Temple, 1 Aug. 1835, PP, GC/TE/238.
33. Palmerston to George Shee, 1 June 1837, Shee Papers, BL, Add Ms 60341, ff. 78–9.
34. Palmerston to Frederick Lamb, 12 June 1837, Beauvale Papers, BL, Add Ms 60465, ff. 120–3.
35. Palmerston to William Temple, 1 Sept. 1837, PP, GC/TE/263.
36. Palmerston to George Shee, 1 Aug. 1837, Shee Papers, BL, Add Ms 60341, ff. 80–1.
37. Palmerston to Frederick Lamb, 6 Sept. 1837, Beauvale Papers, BL, Add Ms 60465, ff. 130–5; Palmerston to George Shee, 10 Oct. 1837, Shee Papers, BL, Add Ms 60341, ff. 86–7.
38. Palmerston to William Temple, 1 Sept. 1837, PP, GC/TE/263.
39. See the letters from Queen Victoria to Palmerston, 1837, PP, RC/F/1–14.
40. Queen Victoria to Palmerston, 12 Aug. 1837, PP, RC/F/15/1.
41. Melbourne to Palmerston, 22 Nov. 1838, 14 Dec. 1840, PP, GC/ME/255 and 465.
42. Palmerston to William Temple, 24 Sept. 1839, PP, GC/TE/276.
43. Palmerston to William Temple, 14 Apr. 1838, PP, GC/TE/269.
44. Palmerston to William Temple, 11 Feb. 1840, PP, GC/TE/282.
45. Palmerston to William Temple, 13 Mar. 1840, PP, GC/TE/283.
46. *Greville Memoirs*, iv, p. 219 (27 Nov. 1839).
47. F. Eyck, *The Prince Consort: A Political Biography* (Boston, Mass., and Cambridge, 1959), p. 22, memorandum by George Anson (Albert's private secretary), Aug. 1840.
48. Aberdeen to Queen Victoria, 6 Jan. 1853, *LQV*, iii, p. 4.
49. Eyck, *Prince Consort*, p. 24, memorandum by Anson, 2 Jan. 1841.
50. See, for example, Melbourne to Palmerston, 17 Nov. 1836, PP, GC/ME/180.
51. Bourne, pp. 550–1.
52. Melbourne to Palmerston, 13 Jan. 1836, PP, GC/ME/66.
53. Melbourne to Palmerston, 10 Feb. 1836, PP, GC/ME/69.
54. Palmerston to Melbourne, 30 Oct. 1835, PP, GC/ME/514.
55. Palmerston to Melbourne, 31 Oct. 1835, PP, GC/ME/515.
56. Palmerston to Melbourne, Mar. 1836, Bell, i, p. 209.
57. Palmerston to Melbourne, 1 Mar. 1836, PP, GC/ME/519.
58. Bell, i, p. 209.
59. Palmerston to Frederick Lamb, 10 Apr. 1837, Beauvale Papers, BL, Add Ms 60465, ff. 103–6.
60. Bulwer, ii, pp. 221–3.
61. Palmerston to J.C. Hobhouse, 11 Nov. 1836, Broughton Papers, BL, Add Ms 46915, ff. 55–6.
62. Melbourne to Palmerston, 4 Mar. 1836, PP, GC/ME/77.
63. Palmerston to William Temple, 5 Mar. 1836, PP, GC/TE/243.
64. Palmerston to George Shee, 15 Mar. 1836, Shee Papers, BL, Add Ms 60341, ff. 36–7.
65. Palmerston to George Shee, 25 Mar. 1836, ibid., ff. 38–9.

66. Palmerston to Granville, 12 Mar. 1839, Granville Papers, TNA, PRO/30/29/14/6, ff. 77–8.
67. Palmerston to Arthur Aston, 4 Aug. 1836, PP, GC/AS/212.
68. Melbourne to Palmerston, 30 Aug. 1836, PP, GC/ME/120.
69. Melbourne to Palmerston, 14 Sept. 1836, PP, GC/ME/124.
70. Palmerston to Frederick Lamb, 24 Sept. 1836, Beauvale Papers, BL, Add Ms 60465, f. 77; Palmerston to George Shee, 24 Sept. 1836, Shee Papers, BL, Add Ms 60341, ff. 52–5.
71. Melbourne to Palmerston, 8 Oct. 1836, PP, GC/ME/131.
72. Palmerston to George Shee, 9 Dec. 1836, Shee Papers, BL Add Ms 60341, ff. 60–1.
73. Palmerston to George Shee, 13 Dec. 1836, ibid., ff. 62–3.
74. Palmerston, House of Commons, 10 Mar. 1837, *Opinions*, p. 330.
75. Ibid., pp. 329–33.
76. See, for example, Sir Thomas Buckler Lethbridge to Palmerston, 21 Apr. 1837, PP, GC/LE/10.
77. [Richard Ford], *An Historical Enquiry into the Unchangeable Character of a War in Spain* (London: John Murray, 1837), p. 1.
78. Palmerston to Arthur Aston, 24 Sept. 1840, PP, GC/AS/238.
79. *An Historical Enquiry into the Unchangeable Character of a War in Spain*, pp. 33–7, 58, 69–70.
80. Palmerston to William Temple, 31 Dec. 1836, PP, GC/TE/256.
81. [James Harris], *A Reply to the Pamphlet entitled 'The Policy of England towards Spain'. By a Nobleman* (London: J. Hatchard, 1837), pp. 32, 49–50.
82. Palmerston to George Shee, 10 Apr. 1837, Shee Papers, BL, Add Ms 60341, ff. 71–2.
83. Palmerston to Frederick Lamb, 6 Sept. 1837, Beauvale Papers, BL, Add Ms 60465, ff. 130–5.
84. Palmerston to Frederick Lamb, 12 June 1837, ibid., ff. 120–3.
85. Ridley, p. 215.
86. Snell, *Palmerston's Borough*, pp. 106–7.
87. George Coles to Palmerston, 27 Feb. 1836, and Thomas Capern to Palmerston, 29 Feb. 1836, PP, BR23/1/7/4.
88. Palmerston to George Shee, 1 and 18 Apr. 1836, Shee Papers, BL, Add Ms 60341, ff. 40–1, 42–3. Palmerston's diary, 7–12 Apr. 1836, PP, D/8.
89. George Coles to Palmerston, 23 July 1836, PP, BR23/1/7/14.
90. Palmerston to George Hadfield, 26 June 1836, PP, GC/HA/2.
91. Francis Hole to Palmerston, 21 July 1837, PP, BR23/1/14/10.
92. Snell, *Palmerston's Borough*, pp. 47–9; George Coles to Palmerston, July 1837, PP, BR23/1/8/2.
93. Snell, *Palmerston's Borough*, pp. 56, 58–9.
94. Charles Warren to Palmerston, 23 May 1838, PP, BR195/115. Enclosing a statement of expenses for the 1837 election, Warren wrote: 'tho' I, in common with your committee, regret the amount (circumstanced as we were, in having to contend against the lavish expenditure of the Tories, furnished from the Carlton Club, or some other source equally corrupt) it could not be expected very much less, but I hope & trust, that it will be some years before we get another election, and prior to it, the legislature will devise some means either by ballot, or other check, to bring the country into something like purity of voting.' The statement reveals that there were '4 poor voters who did not attend the dinner but had the money'. It was estimated that though high, the costs could have been greater still: 'Your committee consider that, by stipulating the sum to 10/6 per head, £200 has been saved. Mr Heathcoat's dinner the election before last when left to the publicans to charge as they pleased cost nearly £500.' The payments to individuals totalled £399 3s. 3d.; the dinner bill, £196 7s. 10d.
95. Palmerston to William Temple, 4 Aug. 1837, PP, GC/TE/262.
96. Palmerston's printed election address: 'To the Free and Independent Electors of the Borough of Tiverton', 10 July 1837, PP, BR195/115.
97. Palmerston to William Temple, 4 Aug. 1837, PP, GC/TE/262.
98. Palmerston's printed address, 'To the Free and Independent Electors of the Borough of Tiverton', 15 Aug. 1837, PP, BR195/115.
99. Snell, *Palmerston's Borough*, p. 67 (Snell's source is John Sharland).
100. *Greville Memoirs*, iv, pp. 82–3 (28 July 1838). Greville here reports the views of Denis Le Marchant.
101. Palmerston to William Temple, 28 Nov. 1834, PP, GC/TE/232.
102. George Cole to Palmerston, 29 July 1836, with Palmerston's minute dated '3/8-36' on reverse and enclosing 'Prospectuses for a new bi-weekly newspaper (Wednesday and Saturday), Aug. 1836, to be called *The Englishman*', PP, BR187/9/1–3.
103. Palmerston to Frederick Lamb, 5 Jan. 1834, Beauvale Papers, BL, Add Ms 60465, ff. 1–2.
104. In 1836, for example, Palmerston wrote a not untypical introduction of this sort for a Dr Lovell, 'a gentleman connected with the establishment of the Chronicle who is going to Lisbon to correspond with that paper. He is I understand a very intelligent & respectable man.' Palmerston to Lord Howard de Walden, 14 Apr. 1836, Howard de Walden Papers, BL, Add Ms 45176, ff.16–17.

105. Palmerston to William Temple, 6 Sept. 1839, PP, GC/TE/274.

106. See, for example, Anthony Mackenrot to Palmerston, 8 Oct. 1836 offering informations 'which are not, and cannot be furnished by the regular diplomatists from the Kings Ambassadors down to Consuls, and as it would be highly desirable both *officially* & *personally*, that your Lordship should be acquainted with certain facts respecting Lisbon and Madrid.' Palmerston rejected this approach on the grounds 'that as he is employed as correspondent of a paper whose political views & objects are directly at variance with those of H.M. Govt it seems to me that there would be a practical incongruity in my receiving communications from him' (Memo by Palmerston, 19 Oct. 1836 on above letter), PP, PRE/A/4 and enc. 1.

107. See, for example, to Lord Howard de Walden, 24 Sept. 1836 and 16 Oct. 1838, Howard de Walden Papers, BL, Add Ms 45176, ff. 36–7, 123–4.

108. The following figures are extracted from secret service accounts sent to Palmerston by the Audit Office, PP, FO/E/1–9. (The average spend calculations are my own.):

	Charge	*Discharge*	*Average spend (approx)*
20 Nov. 1830– 15 Nov. 1834	£126,133 5s. 4d.	£126,133 5s. 4d.	annual: £31,536 monthly: £2,628
29 Jan. 1835– 31 Dec. 1837	£95,202 2s. 10d.	£85,331 17s. 3d.	annual: £29,256 monthly: £2,438
6 July 1846– 1 July 1849	£111,762 17s. 9d.	£83,834 3s. 10d.	annual: £27,948 monthly: £2,329
1 July 1849– 26 Dec. 1851	£81,928 13s. 11d.	£81,928 13s. 11d.	annual: £32,772 monthly: £2,731

109. Palmerston to R.W. Lumley, 1 Oct. 1839, PP, BR22(ii)/14. Lumley was Palmerston's solicitor and on this occasion Palmerston was writing to him about libels recently perpetrated in *The Times* suggesting that Palmerston had misapplied secret service funds in 'bribing a Spanish general in the service of Don Carlos to betray his master'. He insisted that even if he had done this (he would swear an affidavit that he had not), it would have been no cause for censure – securing peace by such means would have been 'a very praise worthy act'. He did however rule out use of such funds for political assassination: 'though it may be right & proper to purchase peace; it must always be infamous to purchase murder'.

110. Palmerston to George Shee, 29 Nov. 1836, PP, GC/SH/109.

111. E Walter[?Ewalter] B. Congreve Laudale[?] to Palmerston, 11 Oct. 1838, PP, PRE/A/6.

112. Melbourne to Palmerston, 12 Sept. 1836, PP, GC/ME/123.

113. Melbourne to Palmerston, 16 Sept. 1836, PP, GC/ME/125.

114. Southgate, p. 119.

115. Holland to Palmerston, 30 Dec. 1835, PP, GC/HO/101.

116. See the copies of letters from Strangways to D. Urquhart, Dec. 1835, PP, FO/H/14.

117. Melbourne to Palmerston, 17 Feb. 1836, PP, GC/ME/73.

118. Melbourne to Palmerston, 5 Mar. 1836, PP, GC/ME/78.

119. M.H. Jenks, 'The Activities and Influence of David Urquhart, 1833–56, with Special Reference to the Affairs of the Near East' (unpublished PhD thesis, University of London, 1964), p. 205.

120. *Protest of Committees for the Examination of Diplomatic Documents, against the Treaty of 15th July,* 18 Sept. 1840, PP, FO/H/74/enc.1.

121. John Backhouse to Palmerston, 30 Sept. 1840, PP, GC/BA/16.

122. Further evidence of defamatory attacks came, for example, in a letter to Palmerston from Lord Ashley: 'I must give you an extract of a letter from Scotland. After stating that Mr Urquhart in the Coryphaeus of a set of fellows "who believe that Lord Palmerston is a gigantic traitor, & *in the pay of the Muscovite*," it proceeds "young Monteith lately Tory candidate for Glasgow has just published a pamphlet, which, if Palmerston chose to take notice of it in a court of law, would be pronounced the biggest of libels." These are charges that far exceed the licence allowed even in attacking a minister' (Ashley to Palmerston, 24 Oct. 1840, PP, GC/SH/13).

123. Legal opinions of the Attorney-General on what Palmerston has termed the 'Urquhart Conspiracy, 1840', PP, FO/H/79/1–4.

124. [David Urquhart], *England, France, Russia and Turkey* (3rd edn, London: James Ridgway, 1835), quotations from pp. 6–7, 62–3, 76, 107.

125. David Urquhart, *Diplomatic Transactions in Central Asia, from 1834 to 1839* (London: Thomas Brettell, 1841). The subtitle gives the purpose of the volume as an *Exposition of transactions in Central Asia, through which the independence of states, and the affections of people, barriers to the*

British possessions in India, have been sacrificed to Russia, by Henry John, Viscount Palmerston, Her Majesty's Principal Secretary of State for Foreign Affairs, constituting grounds for impeachment of that minister.

126. G.H. Bolsover, 'David Urquhart and the Eastern Question, 1833–37: A Study in Publicity and Diplomacy', *Journal of Modern History*, 8:4 (1936), 461.

127. Palmerston to William Temple, 16 Sept. 1838, PP, GC/TE/271.

128. Bourne, p. 304.

129. Melbourne to Palmerston, 12 Feb. 1836, PP, GC/ME/70.

130. Palmerston to Melbourne, 12 Jan. 1836, PP, CAB/28B and GC/ME/518.

131. Melbourne to Palmerston, 23 Jan. 1836, PP, GC/ME/67.

132. Palmerston to Holland, 11 Feb. 1836, PP, GC/HO/103/enc.2.

133. Palmerston to Frederick Lamb, 17 May 1836, Beauvale Papers, BL, Add Ms 60465, f. 58.

134. Palmerston to George Hodges, 2 Jan. 1838, PP, GC/HO/4.

135. Palmerston to J.C. Hobhouse, 9 May 1838, Broughton Papers, BL, Add Ms 46915, ff. 79–81.

136. Palmerston to Frederick Lamb, 22 May 1838, Beauvale Papers, BL, Add Ms 60466, ff. 36–9.

137. Palmerston to Frederick Lamb, 23 June 1838, ibid., ff. 40–3.

138. Palmerston to J.C. Hobhouse, 18 July 1838, Broughton Papers, BL, Add Ms 46915, ff. 93–4.

139. Palmerston to J.C. Hobhouse, 27 July 1838, ibid., ff. 163–4.

140. Palmerston to J.C. Hobhouse, 26 Sept. 1838, ibid., ff. 119–22.

141. Palmerston to J.C. Hobhouse, 29 Oct. 1838, ibid., ff. 133–4. Two days later Palmerston added in a letter to the same: 'If we establish one sovereign in eastern Affghanstan reigning over Caboul & Candahar, and another over the western country at Herat, in process of time they will quarrel & go to war, and if left to themselves the eastern man will look to us, and the western man to Persia & Russia. The only way to prevent this will be at once to place both in connection with and in dependence upon us. But I daresay that is Auckland's plan, or at least will be so, when he receives your last despatch.' (Palmerston to J.C. Hobhouse, 31 Oct. 1838, ibid., ff. 135–6.)

142. Palmerston to Frederick Lamb, 12 Feb. 1838, Beauvale Papers, BL, Add Ms 60466, ff. 10–15.

143. Palmerston to Frederick Lamb, 21 Mar. 1838, ibid., ff. 19–22.

144. Melbourne to Palmerston, 3 June 1838, PP, GC/ME/201.

145. Extract of a letter from Palmerston to Frederick Lamb, 23 July 1838, PP, MM/TU/11.

146. Palmerston to H.L. Bulwer, 13 Sept. 1838, Bulwer, ii, p. 285.

147. Frederic Fysh, *The Time of the End; or, The Sultan of Turkey the Wilful King, and Mehemet Ali the King of the South Pushing at Him, as Foretold by Daniel* (Bath: Binns and Goodwin; London: Simpkin, Marshall, 1839), pp. 13–14, 16, 20.

148. Palmerston to Clanricarde, 10 Oct. 1838, quoted Webster, ii, p. 594.

149. Palmerston to Granville, 5 and 8 June 1838, Bulwer, ii, pp. 266–9.

150. Extract of a letter from Palmerston to Frederick Lamb, 23 July 1838, PP, MM/TU/11.

151. George Hodges to Palmerston, 17 May [rec'd 31 May] 1838, PP, GC/HO/14. Hodges explained in this letter that: 'The strange and inconsistent measures of Prince Metternich have confirmed me in this opinion, for while on a late occasion already made known to your Lordship, he was proffering his good offices to Prince Miloseh [?Milŏs Obrenović, Prince of Serbia], and using me as the channel by which he made these communications the *inescapable* and *unaccredited*, but *paid* agents of Austria were exerting their best endeavours in conjunction with the Russian Consul and his party, to cut off from me every means of obtaining a knowledge of passing events, and they have even gone so far as to attempt to interrupt the friendly intercourse that existed between the Princess and myself and family.'

152. Southgate, pp. 117–18.

153. Palmerston to Frederick Lamb, 14 Apr. 1838, Beauvale Papers, BL, Add Ms 60466, ff. 26–31.

154. Palmerston to Granville, 10 June 1839, quoted in Harold Temperley, *England and the Near East: The Crimea* (1936; London: Frank Cass, 1964 edn), p. 89.

155. H.L. Bulwer to Palmerston, 30 July 1838, Bulwer, ii, p. 279.

156. Palmerston to Ponsonby, 6 Dec. 1833, Webster, ii, pp. 540–1.

157. Palmerston to H.L. Bulwer, 22 Sept. 1838, Bulwer, ii, p. 287.

158. John G. Kinnear, *Cairo, Petra, and Damascus in 1839. With remarks on the government of Mehemet Ali and on the present prospects of Syria* (London: John Murray, 1840), pp. viii and 307–40 (quotations from pp. viii, 311, 313, 333, 337–8).

159. M.S. Anderson, *The Eastern Question, 1774–1923* (London: Macmillan, 1966), p. 95.

160. Kinnear, *Cairo, Petra, and Damascus in 1839*, pp. 253–4.

161. Palmerston to Beauvale, 20 June 1839, Beauvale Papers, BL, Add Ms 60466, ff. 62–6.

162. Palmerston to Beauvale, 13 July 1839, ibid., ff. 67–9.

163. Palmerston to Beauvale, 1 Aug. 1839, ibid., ff. 79–83.

164. Palmerston to George Shee, 1 Aug. 1839, Shee Papers, BL, Add Ms 60341, ff. 154–5.

165. This description of the early stages of the crisis draws heavily on M.S. Anderson's analysis (*Eastern Question*, ch. 4, esp. pp. 95-9.) The description of Abdul Medjid as 'weak and stupid' is Anderson's (p. 95).

166. Quoted in Harold N. Ingle, *Nesselrode and the Russian Rapprochement with Britain, 1836-1844* (Berkeley and Los Angeles: University of California Press, 1976), p. 119.

167. Esterhazy to Palmerston, Sunday morning [2 Sept. 1838], PP, GC/ES/20.

168. Palmerston to H.L. Bulwer, 22 Sept. 1838, Bulwer, ii, p. 287.

169. Memorandum by Palmerston, 'Scheme of measures & operations for compelling Mehemet Ali to evacuate Syria', 19 Sept. 1839, PP, MM/TU/16.

170. Palmerston to William Temple, 24 Sept. 1839, PP, GC/TE/276.

171. Palmerston to Beauvale, 14 Sept. 1839, Beauvale Papers, BL, Add Ms 60466, ff. 94-8.

172. Anderson, *Eastern Question*, pp. 98-9.

173. Palmerston to J.C. Hobhouse, 30 Oct. 1839, Broughton Papers, BL, Add Ms 46915, ff. 179-80.

174. Quoted in Anderson, *Eastern Question*, p. 99.

175. As reported by George Shee in a letter to Palmerston written from Stuttgart, 23 Nov. 1839 (rec'd 12 Dec.), PP, GC/SH/114.

176. George Shee to Palmerston, 8/15 Dec. 1839, PP, GC/SH/119 and 120. Shee reported to Palmerston that he had said to Brunnow: 'If you wish to do business with the government, keep clear of their opponents. Court both sides & you will break down. With the Duke of Wellington you may converse. He is of much too high a character to suffer his party feelings to influence his foreign politics, and his opinions whether sound or not will at all events be honest, but Aberdeen & co have nothing to do with. Then again with regard to Lord Palmerston's colleagues, you may if you please talk with Melbourne & Lansdowne who understand such matters, & are moreover Lord P's personal friends, but of the others only two know anything of such subjects, Holland & Minto, and of these one wants discretion, & the other wants time. As for the rest, from Normanby to Macaulay, you may leave them alone, not to mention that such communications always wear an appearance of intrigue, which I am sure is opposite to your disposition, & would be prejudicial to your object.'

177. Palmerston to George Shee, 7 Nov. 1839, PP, GC/SH/138.

178. Palmerston to George Shee, 7 Dec. 183, Shee Papers, BL, Add Ms 60341, ff. 168-9.

179. Palmerston to Melbourne, 5 Dec. 1839, PP, GC/ME/329.

180. Anderson, *Eastern Question*, pp. 99-100.

181. Palmerston to George Shee, 7 Mar. 1840, Shee Papers, BL, Add Ms 60341, ff. 209-11.

182. Palmerston to George Shee, 12 Mar. 1840, ibid., ff. 172-4.

183. Palmerston to Beauvale, 28 Mar. 1840, Beauvale Papers, BL, Add Ms 60466, ff. 128-32.

184. Palmerston to Beauvale, 11 Apr. 1840, ibid., ff. 133-4.

185. Palmerston to George Hodges, 17 Feb. 1840, PP, GC/HO/55.

186. Palmerston to George Shee, 12 Mar. 1840, Shee Papers, BL, Add Ms 60341, ff. 172-4.

187. 'Translation from article in *Allgemeine Zeitung*, 28 Mar. or 16 Apr. 1840', Shee Papers, BL, Add Ms 60342, ff. 29-35. There is an unmistakable correlation between this article and Palmerston's letter to Shee of 12 Mar.

188. Anderson, *Eastern Question*, p. 100.

189. Melbourne told Palmerston on 7 June, for example: 'I think there is no doubt that a large majority of the Cabinet will go with your proposition. But they do it with fear, reluctantly & upon the ground that they are bound by what has already taken place' (PP, GC/ME/389).

190. Melbourne to Palmerston, 4 July 1840, PP, GC/ME/393.

191. Palmerston to William Temple, 27 July 1840, PP, GC/TE/288.

192. Palmerston to Melbourne, 5 July 1840, PP, GC/ME/536.

193. Melbourne to Palmerston, 6 July 1840, PP, GC/M/394. Palmerston's resignation was offered in a letter to Melbourne of 5 July 1840, see PP, GC/ME/535.

194. Melbourne to Palmerston, 7 and 8 July 1840, PP, GC/ME/395 and 396.

195. Palmerston to William Temple, 27 July 1840, PP, GC/TE/288.

196. Palmerston to Beauvale, 9 July 1840, Beauvale Papers, BL, Add Ms 60467, ff. 1-4.

197. Palmerston to William Temple, 27 July 1840, PP, GC/TE/288.

198. Anderson, *Eastern Question*, p. 101.

199. Palmerston to George Hodges, 1 Aug. 1840, PP, GC/HO/57.

200. Palmerston to George Hodges, 18 July 1840, PP, GC/HO/56.

201. Palmerston to Holland, 19 July 1840, PP, GC/HO/141.

202. Melbourne to Palmerston, 28 July 1840, PP, GC/ME/402.

203. Palmerston to William Temple, 27 July 1840, PP, GC/TE/288.

204. Melbourne to Palmerston, 14 Sept. 1840, PP, GC/ME/418.

205. Spencer to Melbourne, 7 Aug. 1840, PP, GC/ME/409/enc.1. Melbourne forwarded this letter to Palmerston on 8 Aug. (PP, GC/ME/409).

206. Palmerston to John Easthope, 31 Aug. 1840, Easthope Papers, BL, Add Ms 86842.
207. Palmerston to George Shee, 14 Aug. 1840, Shee Papers, BL, Add Ms 60341, ff. 184–5.
208. Palmerston to Charles Napier, 31 Aug. 1840, Napier Papers, BL, Add Ms 40038, f. 10.
209. Palmerston to Arthur Aston, 12 Sept. 1840, PP, GC/AS/237.
210. Russell to Melbourne, 24 Aug. 1840, PP, GC/ME/412/enc.1.
211. Melbourne to Palmerston, 10 Sept. 1840, PP, GC/ME/415.
212. Melbourne to Palmerston, 14 Sept. 1840, PP, GC/ME/418.
213. Melbourne to Palmerston, 16 and 19 Sept. 1840, PP, GC/ME/421 and 423.
214. Melbourne to Palmerston, 29 Sept. 1840, PP, GC/ME/429.
215. As Greville recorded in the late 1830s, Emily found the Queen wanting in tact, judgement and manners. For example: 'Much talk with Lady Cowper about the Queen, who was eloquent on her merits but admitted that She had faults and those in her position dangerous ones – obstinacy to wit, and a very high opinion of herself – which is unquestionably the truth, and accounts for the pertinacity with which She adhered to her purpose and held out against the Duke' (14 June 1839); 'She [Lady Cowper] lamented the obstinate character of the Queen, from which she thought that hereafter great evils may be apprehended. She said that her prejudices and antipathies were deep and strong, and her disposition very inflexible' (13 Nov. 1839), *Greville Memoirs*, iv, pp. 178, 217. Greville agreed.
216. Beauvale to Emily Palmerston, 30 Nov. 1840, Lamb Papers, BL, Add Ms 45552, ff. 105–8.
217. Emily Palmerston to Palmerston, [?2] Sept. 1840, Lamb Papers, BL, Add Ms 45553, f. 1.
218. Ashley to Palmerston, 2 Sept. 1840, PP, GC/SH/9.
219. Palmerston to Holland, 19 Sept. 1840, PP, GC/HO/142.
220. Melbourne to Palmerston, 17 Sept. 1840, PP, GC/ME/422.
221. Palmerston to J.C. Hobhouse, 29 Sept. 1840, Broughton Papers, BL, Add Ms 46915, ff. 221–2; Melbourne to Palmerston, 30 Sept. 1840, PP, GC/ME/430, enclosing notes from Lansdowne [enc.1] and Prince Albert [enc.2].
222. Palmerston to Charles Napier, Napier Papers, BL, Add Ms 40038, ff. 119–20.
223. Lansdowne to Melbourne, 'Sunday' [?7 Oct. 1840], PP, GC/ME/435/enc.1.
224. Charles Greville to Guizot, 4 Nov. 1840, Papiers Guizot, Archives Nationales, Paris, 42 AP 226/8 [163 MI 55]. See also Greville to Guizot, 'Sunday morning' [11 Oct. 1840] and 6 Nov. 1840, ibid., 42 AP 226/7 and 42 AP 226/9 [163 MI 55]. In similar vein, Ashley (quoting an unnamed informant) described an alleged agent acting to undermine Palmerston as follows: '"an English agent of Guizot (who has likewise made himself conspicuous as an intriguer elsewhere) but where manoeuvres are well known . . . there never was an unwashed man of all work, so baffled & put down as Edward Ellice – but the intriguer whom I have alluded to elsewhere is a certain Clerk of the Council – a *shrewd* fellow"' Ashley to Palmerston, 6 Oct. 1840, PP, GC/SH/12.
225. Charles Greville to Guizot, Tuesday evening [1840], Papiers Guizot, Archives Nationales, Paris, 42 AP 226/1 [163 MI 55].
226. Ashley to Palmerston, 3 Oct. 1840, PP, GC/SH/11.
227. Guizot to Palmerston, 13 Oct. 1840, PP, GC/GU/33.
228. Palmerston to Guizot, 14 Oct. 1840, Papiers Guizot, Archives Nationales, Paris, 42 AP 219/17 [163 MI 55].
229. Palmerston to John Easthope, 21 Sept. 1840, Easthope Papers, BL, Add Ms 86842. In this letter Palmerston counselled Easthope to 'be careful in saying anything upon the suggestion which occurred to me while I was talking to you, not to mention it as a thing to which we should by any means pledge ourselves to accede because events in Syria may very possibly take such a turn as would render such a concession unnecessary & therefore inexpedient; and moreover many opinions & wills would be requisitioned for any such arrangement.'
230. Palmerston to J.C. Hobhouse, 11 Oct. 1840, Broughton Papers, BL, Add Ms 46915, ff. 223–7.
231. Ibid.
232. Palmerston's endorsement on a letter from Melbourne, 12 Oct. 1840, PP, GC/ME/438.
233. Palmerston to Arthur Aston, 1 Oct. 1840, PP, GC/AS/239.
234. Russell to Palmerston, 24 Sept. 1840, PP, GC/RU/41.
235. Russell to Palmerston, 29 Sept. 1840, PP, GC/RU/42.
236. Russell to Palmerston, 7 Nov. 1840, PP, GC/RU/50. One of Russell's chief concerns had been the role of Lord Ponsonby, the British ambassador to the Porte. On 1 November he had written to the Prime Minister, Lord Melbourne, to warn that he could not remain a member of the government for much longer if Ponsonby continued at his post (Russell to Melbourne, 1 Nov. 1840, PP, GC/RU/48). In his letter to Palmerston of 7 Nov., however, Russell tacitly admitted defeat and conceded that 'it would be unjust & discouraging to all engaged to recall him, or send a special Embassy to the Porte'.
237. Minute in Palmerston's hand on letter from Russell to Palmerston, 7 Nov. 1840, PP, GC/RU/51.
238. Palmerston to J.C. Hobhouse, 11 Oct. 1840, Broughton Papers, BL, Add Ms 46915, ff. 223–7.
239. Palmerston to J.C. Hobhouse, 4 Nov. 1840, ibid., ff. 229–32.

240. King of the Belgians to Prince Albert, 26 Nov. 1840, *LQV*, i, pp. 247–8.
241. Lansdowne to Melbourne, 25 Oct. 1840, PP, GC/LA/57.
242. Palmerston to Beauvale, 27 Oct. 1840, Beauvale Papers, BL, Add Ms 60467, ff. 48–51.
243. Palmerston to Howard de Walden, 31 Oct. 1840, Howard de Walden Papers, BL, Add Ms 45176, ff. 162–4.
244. Palmerston to Beauvale, 4 Nov. 1840, Beauvale Papers, BL, Add Ms 60467, ff. 52–6.
245. Ashley to Palmerston, 9 Nov. 1840, PP, GC/SH/14.
246. Palmerston to J.C. Hobhouse, Beauvale Papers, BL, Add Ms 46915, ff. 233–5.
247. John Backhouse to Palmerston, 14 Sept. 1840, PP, GC/BA/15.
248. Lansdowne to Palmerston, 13 Nov. 1840, PP, GC/LA/59.
249. Palmerston to John Easthope, 21 Nov. 1840, Easthope Papers, BL, Add Ms 86842.
250. Palmerston to Beauvale, 24 Nov. 1840, Beauvale Papers, BL, Add Ms 60467, ff. 66–70.
251. Palmerston to George Shee, 25 Nov. 1840, Shee Papers, BL, Add Ms 60341, ff. 200–1.
252. Palmerston to Beauvale, 12 Dec. 1840, Beauvale Papers, BL, Add Ms 60467, ff. 86–7.
253. Palmerston to Beauvale, 26 Dec. 1840, ibid., ff. 91–6.
254. Palmerston to Howard de Walden, 5 Dec. 1840, Howard de Walden Papers, BL, Add Ms 45176, ff. 165–6.
255. Palmerston to Beauvale, 7 Jan. 1841, Beauvale Papers, Add Ms 60467, ff. 97–103.
256. Emily Palmerston to Palmerston, Monday [30 Nov. 1840], Lamb Papers, BL, Add Ms 45553, ff. 19–21.
257. Emily Palmerston to Palmerston, 1 Dec. 1840, ibid., ff. 22–7.
258. Ashley to Palmerston, 2 Dec. 1840, PP, GC/SH/15.
259. John Scanlan (editor of the *Observer*) to Palmerston, 31 Dec. 1840 and memo by Palmerston on a reply to Scanlan, 2 Jan. 1841, PP, PRE/A/9 and PRE/A/9/enc.1.
260. Yet, cf. Bernard Nelson's claim that 'The study of British diplomacy between 1815 and 1863 reveals how dangerously close the pursuit of this aspect of her foreign policy brought the [British] empire to disrupted diplomatic relations with the maritime nations of the world [esp. Portugal and the United States]', Bernard H. Nelson, 'The Slave Trade as a Factor in British Foreign Policy 1815–1862', *Journal of Negro History*, 27:2 (1942), 209. L.M. Bethell described negotiations with Portugal over the slave trade in the 1830s as 'once again the major concern of the British government' ('Britain, Portugal and the Suppression of the Brazilian Slave Trade: The Origins of Lord Palmerston's Act of 1839', *EHR*, 80 (1965), 767.
261. Palmerston, House of Commons, 18 May 1841 (Bulwer, ii, pp. 374–5).
262. Bethell, 'Britain, Portugal and the Suppression of the Brazilian Slave Trade', 761–9.
263. Palmerston to Lord Howard de Walden, 16 July 1836, Howard de Walden Papers, BL, Add Ms 45176, ff. 28–31.
264. Palmerston to Baron Torre de Moncorvo, 26 July 1836, Moraes Sarmento Papers, BL, Add Ms 63174, ff. 38–41.
265. Palmerston to Lord Howard de Walden, 30 July 1836, Howard de Walden Papers, BL, Add Ms 45176, ff. 32–3.
266. Palmerston to Baron Torre de Moncorvo, 26 July 1836, Moraes Sarmento Papers, BL, Add Ms 63174, ff. 38–41.
267. Palmerston to Lord Howard de Walden, 10[?16] Feb. 1838, Howard de Walden Papers, BL, Add Ms 45176, ff. 102–3.
268. T.F. Buxton to Palmerston, 29 May 1837, PP, SLT/8.
269. *Hansard*, 3rd ser., xxxviii, 1827 (6 July 1837).
270. Palmerston to J.C. Hobhouse, 25 July 1838, Broughton Papers, BL, Add Ms 46915, ff. 101–2.
271. Memorandum of a meeting held at the Foreign Office, 12 Dec. 1838, PP, SLT/13.
272. Palmerston to Lord Howard de Walden, 24 Jan. 1839, Howard de Walden Papers, BL, Add Ms 45176, ff. 131–3.
273. Bethell, 'Britain, Portugal and the Suppression of the Brazilian Slave Trade', 780–1.
274. Palmerston to Lord Howard de Walden, 21 Dec. 1839, Howard de Walden Papers, BL, Add Ms 45176, ff. 152–4.
275. Palmerston to Lord Howard de Walden, 5 Dec. 1840, ibid., ff. 165–6.
276. Answer to Address to Anti-Slavery Society, 18 Oct. 1842, PP, SLT/19.
277. Palmerston to William Temple, 13 Mar. 1840, PP, GC/TE/283.
278. Palmerston to William Temple, 27 July 1840, PP, GC/TE/288.
279. S. Walpole, *Life of Lord John Russell*, 2 vols. (London: Longmans, Green, 1891), i, p. 369.
280. *Greville Memoirs*, iv, p. 376 (11 May 1841).
281. Palmerston to George Shee, 16 July 1841, Shee Papers, BL, Add Ms 60341, ff. 218–21.
282. Palmerston to William Temple, 17 Aug. 1841, PP, GC/TE/293. Palmerston calculated the aggregate increase in the number of dispatches sent and received between 1828–29 (when Aberdeen

was at the Foreign Office) and 1839–40 to be twofold, from 22,000 to approximately 44,000. See also Palmerston to George Shee, 17 Aug 1841, Shee Papers, BL, Add Ms 60341, ff. 222–4.

283. Palmerston to William Temple, 17 Aug. 1841, PP, GC/TE/293.
284. Palmerston to George Shee, 17 Aug. 1841, Shee Papers, BL, Add Ms 60341, ff. 222–4.
285. *Greville Memoirs*, iv, p. 418 (29 Sept. 1841).
286. Palmerston to George Shee, 17 Aug. 1841, Shee Papers, BL, Add Ms 60341, ff. 222–4.
287. Bell titled his chapter dealing with the period 1841–46, 'Palmerston's longest "holiday" ', Bell, i, ch. xv, pp. 322–48.

Chapter 8 The Absentee, 1841–1846

1. PP, GC/TE/294.
2. Gladstone recorded a story told to him in 1838: 'He [Croker] had an admirable story of Lord Palmerston. He was engaged to dine with him at seven – whiled the time away with Peel at Harrow so that he came in at eight – found Lord Binning waiting and growling: he had been there an hour: and a quarter of an hour after he arrived, said Lord Binning, he heard horses at the door – "Oh it is Palmerston come in from his ride" – he went to the window – no it was Palmerston going out upon that quest! – he made his appearance at length. This story was told minutely but (it seemed) not accurately' (William Gladstone, 'Autobiographical Memorandum', 17 Feb. 1838, *The Prime Minister's Papers: W.E. Gladstone II: Autobiographical Memoranda, 1832–1845*, ed. John Brooke and Mary Sorensen (London: HMSO, 1972), p. 45). See also Bourne, p. 551.
3. Beauvale to Emily Palmerston, 19 Mar. 1840, Lamb Papers, BL, Add Ms 45552, ff. 93–4.
4. Palmerston to Beauvale, 15 Sept. 1841, Beauvale Papers, BL, Add Ms 60467, ff. 143–6.
5. Palmerston to William Temple, 6 Sept. 1839, PP, GC/TE/274.
6. Palmerston to George Shee, 12 Dec. 1838, Shee Papers, BL, Add Ms 60341, ff. 128–9.
7. Frederick Lamb to Emily Cowper, 5 Feb. 1839, Lamb Papers, BL, Add Ms 45552, ff. 40–1.
8. Palmerston to William Temple, 6 Sept. 1839, PP, GC/TE/274.
9. Frederick Lamb to Emily Cowper, 1 July 1837, Mabell, Countess of Airlie, *Lady Palmerston and her Times*, 2 vols. (London: Hodder & Stoughton, 1922), i, p. 194.
10. Mabell, Countess of Airlie, *Lady Palmerston and her Times*, i, p. 193.
11. Ibid., ii, p. 5.
12. Emily, Lady Cowper to Palmerston, 11 Oct. 1837, PP, BR22(i)/11.
13. Mabell, Countess of Airlie, *Lady Palmerston and her Times*, ii, pp. 30–1.
14. Palmerston to William Temple, 31 Oct. 1839, PP, GC/TE/279.
15. Palmerston to George Shee, 7 Dec. 1839, Shee Papers, BL, Add Ms 60341, ff. 168–9.
16. Palmerston to William Temple, 11 Sept. 1839, PP, GC/TE/275.
17. Palmerston to William Temple, 31 Oct. 1839, PP, GC/TE/279.
18. Mabell, Countess of Airlie, *Lady Palmerston and her Times*, ii, pp. 32–9.
19. Ibid., p. 41.
20. Palmerston to Emily Palmerston, 5 Sept. 1840, PP, BR23AA/1.
21. Emily Palmerston to Palmerston, n.d. [May–Nov. 1840] and 6 Dec. 1840, Lamb Papers, BL, Add Ms 45553, ff. 9–12 and 41–3.
22. Emily Palmerston to Palmerston, 24 Mar. 1841, ibid., ff. 53–5.
23. Emily Palmerston to Palmerston, 5 Sept. 1840, Mabell, Countess of Airlie, *Lady Palmerston and her Times*, ii, p. 44.
24. PP, BR23AA/2/1.
25. Abraham Hayward, *Selected Essays*, 2 vols. (London: Longmans, Green, 1878), ii, pp. 347–58 ('Lady Palmerston'), quotations from pp. 350, 351. This essay had been published as an obituary in *The Times*, 15 Sept. 1869. On Hayward's connection with Lady Palmerston, see K.D. Reynolds, *Aristocratic Women and Political Society in Victorian Britain* (Oxford: Oxford University Press, 1998), p. 177.
26. Mabell, Countess of Airlie, *Lady Palmerston and her Times*, ii, p. 43.
27. Ibid., p. 61.
28. Reynolds, *Aristocratic Women*, p. 154.
29. Hayward, *Selected Essays*, ii, p. 352.
30. Mabell, Countess of Airlie, *Lady Palmerston and her Times*, ii, pp. 42–3.
31. Lady Frances Balfour, *Ne Obliviscaris: Dinna Forget*, 2 vols. (London: Hodder & Stoughton, 1930), i, p. 195; ii, p. 149.
32. Emily Palmerston to Princess Lieven, 13 Nov. [1840], *The Lieven–Palmerston Correspondence, 1828–1856*, trans. and ed. Lord Sudley (London: John Murray, 1943), p. 197.
33. Reynolds, *Aristocratic Women*, pp. 176–8.
34. Mabell, Countess of Airlie, *Lady Palmerston and her Times*, ii, p. 66.

35. Palmerston to William Temple, 22 Mar. 1842, PP, GC/TE/298.
36. Palmerston to William Temple, 19 Jan./8 Feb. 1842, PP, GC/TE/295 and 22 Mar. 1842, PP, GC/TE/298.
37. Palmerston to William Temple, 29 May 1843, PP, GC/TE/306.
38. Palmerston to Sir Robert Gore-Booth, 24 Jan. 1841, Lissadell Papers, PRONI, D/4131/H/1.
39. Emily Palmerston to Palmerston, Jan. 1841, Lamb Papers, BL, Add Ms 45553, ff. 49–52.
40. Emily Palmerston to Palmerston, Wednesday [?Aug.] 1841, Mabell, Countess of Airlie, *Lady Palmerston and her Times*, ii, p. 68.
41. For brief details of the tour – primarily notes on itinerary and weather conditions – see the diary Palmerston kept, PP, BR22(ii)/17. Palmerston's observations on the progress of the slate mines from: Palmerston to William Temple, 26 Nov. 1841, PP, GC/TE/294.
42. Palmerston to William Temple, 26 Nov. 1841, PP, GC/TE/294.
43. J. Kincaid to Palmerston, 23 Sept. 1843, PP, BR144/9/21, enclosing cutting from the *Morning Chronicle*, n.d., but 6 Sept. according to letter from Kincaid.
44. Peter Gray, *Famine, Land and Politics: British Government and Irish Society, 1843–50* (Dublin: Irish Academic Press, 1999), p. 267.
45. Alexander Somerville, *Letters from Ireland during the Famine of 1847*, ed. K.D.M. Snell (Dublin: Irish Academic Press, 1994), p. 155. The *Letters* were first published in book form in 1852.
46. Cormac Ó Gráda, *Black '47 and Beyond: The Great Irish Famine in History, Economy, and Memory* (Princeton, NJ: Princeton University Press, 1999), pp. 23–4.
47. J. Kincaid to Palmerston, 13 Nov. 1845, PP, BR144/10/20.
48. For example: J. Kincaid to Palmerston, 4 June 1831, PP, BR145/4/3, reporting on famine in Mayo to the relief of which Palmerston contributed £50.
49. Desmond Norton, *Landlords, Tenants, Famine: the Business of an Irish Land Agency in the 1840s* (Dublin: University College Dublin Press, 2006), p. 46.
50. J. Kincaid to Palmerston, 6 Feb. 1846, PP, BR144/10/30.
51. Palmerston to William Temple, 13–18 May 1846, PP, GC/TE/315.
52. John Lynch to Palmerston, 7 June 1846, PP, BR149/12/8.
53. J. Kincaid to Palmerston, 6 Aug. 1846, PP, BR148/3/5.
54. John Lynch to Palmerston, 7 Aug. 1846, PP, BR148/3/6.
55. J. Kincaid to Palmerston, 20 Aug. 1846, PP, BR148/3/7.
56. J. Kincaid to Palmerston, 9 Sept. 1846, enclosing a cutting from an unidentified Sligo newspaper containing an account of the Relief Committee's meeting held on 1 Sept. and also reports of the complete failure of the potato crop, PP, BR148/3/9.
57. Lt. Col. H.W. Barton to Palmerston, 30 Sept. 1846, PP, BR148/3/11. Barton argued for a new fishing harbour at Tullaghan bay and hoped to persuade Palmerston to press the Board of Works to support the plan.
58. J. Kincaid to Palmerston, 24 Sept. 1846, PP, BR148/3/10.
59. J. Kincaid to Palmerston, 6 Oct. 1846, PP, BR148/3/12.
60. J. Kinkaid to Palmerston, 21 Oct. 1846, PP, BR148/3/14. According to one estimate (by the Revd Brennan), it would require 10 tons of grain per day to feed Palmerston's Ahamlish tenants. A cargo of 50 tons of Indian corn imported at the end of 1846 would not, therefore, last very long (Norton, *Landlords, Tenants, Famine*, pp. 47–8).
61. Revd Malachi Brennan to Palmerston, 24 Oct. 1846, PP, BR148/3/15.
62. J. Kincaid to Palmerston, 7 Nov. 1846 (enclosing newspaper cutting originally forwarded to Stewart and Kincaid by Malachi Brennan), PP, BR148/3/17. Palmerston endorsed the letter: 'Distress at Mullaghmore'.
63. Memorial of the Relief Committee for the Parishes of Ahamplish [*sic*] and Rossinver, County Sligo, sent to Palmerston, 10 Nov. 1846. The committee comprised: Sir Robert Gore-Booth (chairman), Revd H. St. George, Revd F. O'Reilly, Revd J.E. Greene, Revd M. Brennan, Revd D. Noon, Revd W. Jeffcott, Ormsby Jones Esq. J.P. and Lieutenant Hamilton. PP, BR148/3/18.
64. J. Kincaid to Palmerston, 21 Nov. 1846, PP, BR148/3/19.
65. Norton, *Landlords, Tenants, Famine*, pp. 49–50.
66. Ibid., p. 42.
67. J. Kincaid to Sir Robert Gore-Booth, 3 Feb. 1847, Lissadell Papers, PRONI, D/4131/H/8 [MIC/590/Reel 1/H/8/67–8].
68. J. Kincaid to Palmerston, 26 Mar. 1847, PP, BR146/9/3.
69. Palmerston to William Temple, 8 Mar. 1847, PP, GC/TE/317.
70. Palmerston to Sir Robert Gore-Booth, 22 Apr. 1847, Lissadell Papers, PRONI, D/4131/H/1.
71. List of emigrants sent out from Henry John Temple, third Viscount Palmerston's Sligo estates on the *Carrick, Transit* and *Spring Hill* to Quebec in Apr. 1847, PP, BR146/9/4

72. 'Names and Number of Passengers sent to America from Lord Palmerston's Estate in 1847', dated Dublin, 19 June 1847, PP, BR146/9/6.

73. Thomas Frederick Elliot to Palmerston, 3 July 1847 (of the Colonial Land Emigration Office, Westminster), enclosing and commenting on A.C. Buchanan [chief agent] to S. Walcote, 11 June 1847, Govt Emigration Office, Quebec, PP, BR146/9/8/1–2.

74. Contemporary copy of extract of letter from Chief Emigration Officer at Quebec sent in dispatch of James Bruce, eighth earl of Elgin, Governor-General of Canada, concerning the condition of the emigrants that had arrived at Quebec on the *Spring Hill*, enclosed in Lord Elgin's dispatch no. 76 of 11 Aug. 1847, PP, BR16/9/10.

75. Norton, *Landlords, Tenants, Famine*, p. 52.

76. M.H. Perley (HM Emigration Officer) to John S. Saunders, 2 Nov. 1847, PP, BR146/9/16/2 (forwarded to Palmerston by Earl Grey, 4 Dec. 1847, PP, BR146/9/16/1.

77. Norton, *Landlords, Tenants, Famine*, p. 53.

78. S. Maxwell to Stewart and Kincaid, 27 Nov. 1847, PP, BR146/9/17.

79. Tyler Anbinder, 'From Famine to Five Points: Lord Lansdowne's Irish Tenants Encounter North America's most Notorious Slum', *American Historical Review*, 107 (2002), 367.

80. For a copy of one such report, see the memorandum by Thomas Frederick Elliot of the Emigration Office, 27 Aug.–11 Nov. 1847, PP, BR146/9/13.

81. Stewart and Kincaid to Palmerston, 3 Dec. 1847, PP, BR146/9/15. According to some more recent estimates, the number of emigrants from Palmerston's estates – taking into account data suggesting the point of departure for some was Liverpool as well as Sligo – may have been nearer 2,500 (see Norton, *Landlords, Tenants, Famine*, p. 51, citing McTernan's calculations regarding Liverpool).

82. Stewart and Kincaid to Palmerston, 16 Dec. 1847, PP, BR1469/18. Cf. Tyler Anbinder's comment on this claim that 'it was cruel to send out emigrants whose only option upon arrival in Canada was residence in an almshouse or begging in the streets of St John', and that 'Stewart and Kincaid knew perfectly well that the emigrants' pleadings should not have been the deciding factor in determining whether or not the last ships should have sailed to America' (Tyler Anbinder, 'Lord Palmerston and the Irish Famine Emigration', *Historical Journal*, 44: 2 (2001), 464–5).

83. Desmond Norton, 'Lord Palmerston and the Irish Famine Emigration: A Rejoinder', *Historical Journal*, 46: 1 (2003), 163.

84. Norton, *Landlords, Tenants, Famine*, pp. 52–4. The quotation from the Stewart and Kincaid memo is given by Norton from archive material in his private possession.

85. Puncheon: a large cask for liquids, fish, etc. As a liquid measure it varied from 72 (beer) to 120 (whisky) gallons [*OED*].

86. Wm Kernaghan, 'Incidents & reminiscences of Lord Palmerston', n.d., PP, BR138/19. As Norton points out, this manuscript is watermarked 1870 (Norton, 'Lord Palmerston and the Irish Famine Emigration: A Rejoinder', 163).

87. J. Kincaid to Earl Grey (3rd Earl), 1 Mar. 1848, PP, BR150/7/1/2.

88. J. Kincaid to Palmerston, 1 June 1849, PP, BR148/3/22. ('Ornamental' is Kincaid's word).

89. According to Palmerston's agents, the Ahamlish population fell from 6,474 in 1841 to 4,877 in 1851, a reduction of 1,597 (J. Kincaid to Palmerston, 15 Feb. 1852, PP, BR146/11/12). Quoting the *Census of Ireland 1851* (1852), Norton gives the figures for the same place for the same period as 8,720 and 6,499 (Norton, *Landlords, Tenants, Famine*, p. 60). Whatever the discrepancies in absolute numbers, both estimates signify a 25 per cent reduction in the Ahamlish population overall.

90. Patrick Duffy, 'Emigrants and the Estate Office in the mid-Nineteenth Century: A Compassionate Relationship?', in E. Margaret Crawford (ed.), *The Hungry Stream: Essays on Emigration and Famine* (Belfast: Institute of Irish Studies, Queen's University Belfast, and the Centre for Emigration Studies, Ulster-American Folk Park, 1997), p. 72.

91. See Anbinder, 'From Famine to Five Points', 351–87.

92. Cf. also Cormac Ó Gráda's comments on mass emigration: while acknowledging the great limitations of this as a famine relief policy – the high number of deaths, the demographic and socio-economic imbalances in those emigrating – he concludes that as a whole (and including private as well as state- and landlord-assisted emigration): 'Still, emigration reduced famine mortality. Moreover, few of the emigrants returned when the crisis had passed, suggesting an asymmetry with other forms of disaster relief. While emigration did not target the poor as effectively as soup-kitchens or the public works, unlike them its effect went well beyond mere crisis-management. The famine emigration has often been seen as one of the great tragedies in Irish history, and in human terms this is of course correct. Nonetheless, in the long run this emigration played an important role in increasing the living standards of those who stayed behind' (*Ireland's Great Famine: Interdisciplinary Perspectives* (Dublin: University College Dublin Press, 2006), pp. 141–2).

93. Palmerston to J. Kincaid, 22 May 1851, PP, BR150/9/50.

94. J. Kincaid to Palmerston, 28 July 1851, enclosing a list of 'Labourers from the Right Honble Viscount Palmerston's Ahamlish Estate (Co. Sligo) prepared to emigrate to Mr Wadsworths Estate New York'. PP, BR146/11/4/1-2.

95. Charles Murray to Palmerston, 18 Apr. 1851, PP, BR146/11/4/3.

96. James S. Wadsworth to Stewart and Kincaid, 7 Sept. 1853 and J. Kincaid to Palmerston, 29 Sept. 1853, PP, BR149/12/18/1-2.

97. On this theme, see especially Peter Gray, *Famine, Land and Politics*.

98. Norton, *Landlords, Tenants, Famine*, p. 35.

99. T. O'Rorke, *The History of Sligo: Town and County*, 2 vols. (Dublin, [?1890]), ii, pp. 33, 35.

100. Anbinder, 'Lord Palmerston and the Irish Famine Emigration', 441-69.

101. Desmond Norton, 'On Landlord-assisted Emigration from some Irish Estates in the 1840s', *Agricultural History Review*, 53:1 (2005), esp. 25, 27, 38, 40.

102. Desmond Norton, 'On Lord Palmerston's Irish Estates in the 1840s', *EHR*, 119: 484 (2004), esp. 1255, 1271-3; Norton, *Landlords, Tenants, Famine*, pp. 56-61.

103. Emily Palmerston to Vere Foster, 1 May 1856, Foster of Glyde Papers, PRONI, D/3618/D/22/4.

104. Norton admits that the records are imperfect and numbers of emigrants are unknown, but he notes references to emigration from Palmerston's land, for example in newspaper reports and Stewart and Kincaid records, sporadically through the 1850s and early 1860s. The final instance noted by Norton dates from May 1862; *Landlords, Tenants, Famine*, p. 56.

105. W.A. Maguire, *The Downshire Estates in Ireland, 1801-1845: The Management of Irish Landed Estates in the Early Nineteenth Century* (Oxford: Clarendon Press, 1972), p. 71.

106. Norton, *Landlords, Tenants, Famine*, pp. 31, 34, 61-3.

107. Palmerston to Sir Robert Gore-Booth, 10 Apr. 1856, Lissadell Papers, PRONI, D/4131/H/1.

108. K. Theodore Hoppen, 'Landlords, Society and Electoral Politics in mid-Nineteenth-Century Ireland', in C.H.E. Philpin, *Nationalism and Popular Protest in Ireland* (Cambridge: Cambridge University Press, 1987), esp. pp. 289-98.

109. See, for example, Palmerston to Sir Robert Gore-Booth, 28 Mar. 1848 and 2 Apr. 1852, Lissadell Papers, PRONI, D4131/H/1.

110. Palmerston to William Temple, 5 Apr. 1844, PP, GC/TE/308.

111. Beauvale to Emily Palmerston, 19 July 1841, and n.d. 1841, Mabell, Countess of Airlie, *Lady Palmerston and her Times*, ii, pp. 63-4, 76-7.

112. Emily Palmerston to Palmerston, 'Wednesday' [Aug.] 1841, ibid., p. 68.

113. Palmerston to Melbourne, 26 Dec. 1845, *LQV*, ii, pp. 79-82.

114. Richard Monckton Milnes to Robert Peel, 24 Jan. 1841, T. Wemyss Reid, *The Life, Letters and Friendships of Richard Monckton Milnes, first Lord Houghton*, 2 vols. (London: Cassell, 1891), i, pp. 248-9.

115. *Greville Memoirs*, v, pp. 2, 9, 11, 13 (11 Jan., 1, 5[6], 11 Feb. 1842).

116. Southgate, p. 170.

117. Palmerston to John Easthope, 17 Oct. 1841, Easthope Papers, BL, Add Ms 86842.

118. Palmerston to John Easthope, 7 Dec. 1841, ibid.

119. Palmerston to William Temple, 4 Oct. 1843, PP, GC/TE/307.

120. Palmerston to John Easthope, 1 Dec. 1841, Easthope Papers, BL, Add Ms 86842.

121. Southgate, p. 171.

122. *Greville Memoirs*, v, p. 333 (14 July 1846).

123. Palmerston to John Easthope, 16 Jan. 1842, Easthope Papers, BL, Add Ms 86842.

124. Palmerston to John Easthope, 4 Nov. 1842, ibid. At about the same time, Palmerston applauded the *Chronicle*'s 'judicious' coverage of European rivalries as played out in Asia (to John Easthope, 25 Nov. 1842, ibid.).

125. Palmerston to William Temple, 25 Feb. 1842, PP, GC/TE/296.

126. George Brown Tindall, *America: A Narrative History* (2nd edn, New York: W.W. Norton, 1988), pp. 533-5.

127. Melbourne to Palmerston, 15 Dec. 1838, PP, GC/ME/260.

128. Palmerston to John Easthope, 1 Jan. 1841, Easthope Papers, BL, Add Ms 86842.

129. Palmerston to William Temple, 1 Sept. 1842, PP, GC/TE/303.

130. *Greville Memoirs*, v, p. 197 (18 Jan. 1845).

131. Palmerston to William Temple, 30 Sept. 1842, PP, GC/TE/304.

132. Russell to Melbourne, 4 Oct. 1842; Palmerston to Melbourne, 10 Oct. 1842, PP, GC/ME/494/enc.1.

133. *Greville Memoirs*, v, p. 29 (1 Sept. 1842).

134. Ibid., pp. 35, 38 (24 Sept. and 4-5 Oct. 1842).

135. Palmerston to J.C. Hobhouse, 5 Oct. 1843, Broughton Papers, BL, Add Ms 46915, ff. 285-8.

136. Palmerston to William Temple, 23 Oct. 1844, PP, GC/TE/309.

137. Palmerston to J.C. Hobhouse, 27 Nov. 1844, Broughton Papers, BL, Add Ms 46915, ff. 289–90.

138. Palmerston to William Temple, 26 July 1845, PP, BR26/8/2.

139. Palmerston to John Easthope, 15 Jan. 1845, Easthope Papers, BL, Add Ms 86842.

140. Richard Monckton Milnes to Guizot, 31 Aug. 1844, Reid, *The Life, Letters and Friendships of Richard Monckton Milnes*, i, pp. 333–4.

141. *Greville Memoirs*, v, p. 226 (21 Aug. 1845).

142. Palmerston to William Temple, 10 Dec. 1845 / 26 Jan. 1846, PP, GC/TE/311 [see part written 10 Dec. 1845].

143. *Greville Memoirs*, v, p. 252 (12 Dec. 1845).

144. Memorandum by Prince Albert, 20 Dec. 1845, *LQV*, II, pp. 69–71

145. Third Earl Grey, journal, 18 Dec. 1845, Grey Papers, (3rd Earl) Durham University Library C3/12; F.A. Dreyer, 'The Russell Administration, 1846–52' (unpublished D.Phil. thesis, University of St Andrews, 1962), p. 31.

146. *Lord Grey and Lord Palmerston – A Letter Addressed to Macaulay on the occasion of His Letter to M'Farlane, from a Free Trader* (London, 1846), pp. 18–19.

147. Shaftesbury diary, 22 Dec. 1845, PP, SHA/PD/4.

148. Howick to Palmerston, 26 Apr. 1843, PP, GC/GR/2382.

149. E. Twisleton to G.C. Lewis, 2 Jan. 1846, Harpton Court Mss, NLW, C/2508.

150. Grey (3rd Earl), journal, 18 Dec. 1845, Grey Papers, Durham University Library, C3/12.

151. Guizot to Aberdeen, 13 Nov. 1845, Papiers Guizot, Archives Nationales, Paris, 42 AP 211/122 [163 MI 51].

152. Guizot to Aberdeen, 12 Jan. 1845, ibid., AP 211/114 [163 MI 51].

153. Guizot to Aberdeen, 3 June 1845, ibid., AP 211/116 [163 MI 51].

154. *Greville Memoirs*, v, p. 62 (14 Dec. 1842). The French quotation may be translated as: 'I beg your pardon for my levity, but I assure you that I and all the people I see have been quite foolish in believing that the great successes in the East have been due to Sir R. Peel and his government. Apparently we are mistaken and I beg 1,000 pardons for our frivolousness.'

155. Ibid., pp. 143–4 (29 Nov. 1843). Earlier Greville had remarked that 'I never saw so much political bitterness as that which rankles in the hearts of himself [Palmerston] and his wife' (ibid., p. 35 (24 Sept. 1842)).

156. Palmerston to Melbourne, 26 Dec. 1845, PP, GC/ME/547.

157. Beauvale to Emily Palmerston, 5 Jan. 1846, Mabell, Countess of Airlie, *Lady Palmerston and her Times*, ii, p. 106.

158. Palmerston to John Easthope, 29 Dec. 1845, Easthope Papers, BL, Add Ms 86842; Palmerston to William Temple, 10 Dec. 1845 / 26 Jan. 1846, PP, GC/TE/311 [see part written 26 Jan. 1845].

159. Russell to Palmerston, 19 Dec. 1845, PP, GC/RU/99.

160. Memorandum by Prince Albert, 20 Dec. 1845, *LQV*, ii, pp. 72–3

161. Russell to Lady John Russell, 20, 21 Dec. 1845, S. Walpole, *The Life of Lord John Russell*, 2 vols (London, 1889), I, pp. 416, 417; *Greville Memoirs*, v, p. 256 (13 Dec. 1845), cf. ibid., p. 265 (21 Dec. 1845).

162. Palmerston to William Temple, 10 Apr. 1846, PP, GC/TE/314.

163. *Greville Memoirs*, iv, p. 417 (27 Sept. 1841).

164. Walpole, *The Life of Lord John Russell*, i, pp. 423–6, esp. Russell to Duncannon [Bessborough], 11 Apr. 1846, ibid., i, pp. 423–4, n. 1.

165. Memorandum by Lord Grey on Wood's account of the failure to form a government, Dec. 1846, after Grey had seen the account in Apr. 1884 at Hickleton, Hickleton Papers, BIY, A8/1/6.

166. Sir Robert Peel to Guizot, 18 Dec. 1845, Papiers Guizot, Archives Nationales, Paris, 42 AP 221/1 [163 MI 55].

167. See Palmerston's journal (incl. observations on tour of continent), 13 Aug.–4 Nov. 1844, PP, BR22(ii)/18. The tour took in, among other places, principally: Brussels, Cologne, Ems, Koblenz, Wiesbaden, Frankfurt, Fulda, Eisenach, Gotha, Leipzig, Berlin, Dresden, Prague and Hanover.

168. *Greville Memoirs*, v, pp. 201, 204 (28 Jan. and 4 Feb. 1845).

169. Palmerston to Melbourne, 26 Dec. 1845, PP, GC/ME/547.

170. As Beauvale wrote in Jan. 1846: 'In talking about Palmerston the Queen said to me that it was all in consequence of Syria and that the French had hardly yet got over it; no I said, nor never will, any more than they have got over Waterloo, but that is no reason for us to regret either one or the other, at which I had the satisfaction to see her chuckle with glee, and this gave me an opportunity to repeat to her what Thiers had said that he had no reason to be a friend to P. by whom he had been worsted but that did not prevent him from regarding him as the first statesman of this age and perhaps of any other. . . . All this and much more in the same strain was corresponded to with full harmony by the Queen' (Beauvale to Emily Palmerston, Jan. 1846, Lamb Papers, BL, Add Ms 45552, ff. 180–2; Mabell, Countess of Airlie, *Lady Palmerston and her Times*, ii, p. 105 dates this letter as 5 Jan.).

171. Palmerston to William Temple, 10 Apr. 1846, PP, GC/TE/314.
172. *Greville Memoirs*, v, p. 313 (23 Apr. 1846). Palmerston committed only one faux pas while in France, according to Greville, when he wrote to congratulate Louis Philippe on escaping an assassination attempt while the Palmerstons were in Paris. 'This was considered impertinent from a foreign statesman casually at Paris', explained Henry Reeve (ibid., v, p. 318 and n. 1).
173. Guizot to Aberdeen, 28 Apr. 1846, Papiers Guizot, Archives Nationales, Paris, 42 AP 211/124 [163 MI 51].
174. Palmerston to William Temple, 13 May 1846, PP, GC/TE/315.
175. *Greville Memoirs*, v, p. 285 (14 Jan. 1846).
176. Reported by Charles Wood (C. Wood to Russell, 1 July 1846 [?],Walpole, *The Life of Lord John Russell*, i, pp. 427–8).
177. T.F. Lewis to G.C. Lewis, 26 May 1846, Harpton Court Mss, NLW, C/609.
178. *Greville Memoirs*, v, p. 334 (14 July 1846).

Chapter 9 The Gunpowder Minister, 1846–1851

1. Cobden Papers, BL, Add Ms 43649, ff. 66–9; *The Letters of Richard Cobden: Volume One, 1815–1847*, ed. Anthony Howe et al. (Oxford: Oxford University Press, 2007), pp. 467–8.
2. Queen Victoria to the King of the Belgians, 14 July 1846, *LQV*, ii, p. 105.
3. Memorandum by Prince Albert, 6 July 1846, *LQV*, ii, pp. 101–3.
4. Charles Wood, political journal, 27 and 29 June 1846, Hickleton Papers, BIY, A8/1/2 (see also typescript 'Journals and Memoranda 1846–1867 by Sir Charles Wood afterwards Viscount Halifax', 2 vols., Hickleton Papers, A8).
5. Prince Albert to Palmerston, 9 Aug. 1846, *LQV*, ii, p. 113.
6. Palmerston to Emily Palmerston, 1 Sept. 1846, PP, BR23AA/1/2.
7. *Standard*, 11 July 1846.
8. *The Times*, 7 July 1846.
9. *Daily News*, 10 Aug. 1846.
10. Richard Cobden to Russell, 4 July 1846, RP, TNA, PRO 30/22/5B.
11. Palmerston to Russell, RP, TNA, PRO 30/22/5B, ff. 190–3.
12. William Russell to Russell, RP, TNA, PRO 30/22/5A, ff. 94–5.
13. Brian Connell, *Regina v. Palmerston: The Correspondence between Queen Victoria and her Foreign and Prime Minister, 1837–1865* (London: Evans Brothers, 1962), pp. 35–7.
14. Palmerston to Russell, 19 Aug. 1846, RP, TNA, PRO 30/22/5B, f. 386.
15. See Clarendon to Palmerston, 11 Oct. 1846, PP, GC/CL/463.
16. Palmerston to Russell, 3 Sept. 1846, RP, TNA, PRO 30/22/5C, ff. 27–8.
17. Russell to Palmerston, 6 Sept., 1846, PP, GC/RU/110.
18. Clarendon to Russell, 8 Sept. 1846, RP, TNA, PRO 30/22/5C, ff. 65–6.
19. Clarendon to Palmerston, 8 Sept. 1846, PP, GC/CL/457.
20. Palmerston to Russell, 10 Sept. 1846, RP, TNA, PRO 30/22/5C, ff. 102–3.
21. Russell to Palmerston, 13 Sept. 1846, PP, GC/RU/111.
22. Russell to Palmerston, 20 Sept. 1846, PP, GC/RU/114.
23. Clarendon to Palmerston, 4 Oct. 1846, PP, GC/CL/462.
24. Queen Victoria to Palmerston, 18 July 1846, PP, RC/F/262.
25. Queen Victoria to Palmerston, 10 Sept. 1846, PP, RC/F/271.
26. Grey, journal, 14 Sept. 1846, Grey Papers (3rd Earl), Durham University Library, C3/13: '[Wood] tells me that Palmerston has already managed to get upon very unpleasant terms indeed with the French Govt about this Spanish marriage. No doubt the French have behaved very ill but from Wood's account P's conduct & still more his language to M. de Jarnac have been very imprudent & the result is a very bad state of feeling indeed.'
27. Queen Victoria to the King of the Belgians, 14 Sept. 1846, *LQV*, ii, pp. 121–3.
28. Queen Victoria to Palmerston, 14 Sept., 1 Oct., 17 Nov. 1846, PP, RC/F/273, 277, 287.
29. Charles Wood to Palmerston, 10 Oct. and [n.d.] Oct. 1846, PP, GC/WO/16 and 17.
30. Jarnac to Guizot, 15 Oct. 1846, PP, MM/FR/13.
31. Palmerston to Russell, 25 Oct. 1846, RP, TNA, PRO 30/22/5D, ff. 289–90.
32. Russell to Jarnac, 26 Oct. 1846, RP, TNA, PRO 30/22/5d, ff. 302–5.
33. Palmerston to Emily Palmerston, 1 Oct. 1846, PP, BR23AA/1/5.
34. Palmerston to Russell, 20 Nov. 1846, RP, TNA, PRO 30/22/5E, ff. 140–1.
35. Palmerston to Russell, 8 Dec. 1846, RP, TNA, PRO 30/22/5F, ff. 96–7.
36. Russell to Palmerston, 4 Oct. 1846, PP, GC/RU/117.
37. Palmerston to Russell, 6 Oct. 1846, RP, TNA, PRO 30/22/5D, ff. 114–15.
38. Clarendon to Palmerston, 11 Oct. 1846, PP, GC/CL/463.

39. Clarendon to Palmerston, 9 Nov. 1846, PP, GC/CL/466.
40. *Daily News*, 29 Aug. 1846.
41. *Economist*, 12 Sept. 1846.
42. *Standard*, 19 Sept. 1846.
43. Ibid., 22, 26 Sept. 1846.
44. *Manchester Guardian*, 11, 19 Sept. 1846.
45. *Globe*, 10 Sept. 1846.
46. *Morning Post*, 24 Sept., 6, 12, 15 Oct. 1846.
47. *The Times*, 7 Nov. 1846.
48. *Standard*, 2, 27 Oct., 2, 3 Nov. 1846.
49. *Morning Post*, 12 Nov. 1846.
50. *Daily News*, 9 Nov. 1846.
51. *The Times*, 25 Nov. 1846.
52. Aberdeen to Queen Victoria, Jan. 1844, M. Charlot, *Victoria: The Young Queen* (Oxford: Blackwell, 1991), p. 302.
53. Queen Victoria to Palmerston, 17 Apr. 1847, PP, RC/F/316.
54. See, for example, Palmerston to Russell, 23 Aug. 1846, PP, GC/RU/985; and same to same, 6 Jan. 1847, RP, TNA, PRO 30/22/6A, ff. 56–8.
55. Prince Albert to Palmerston, 9 Aug. 1846, *LQV*, ii, p. 113.
56. F. Eyck, *The Prince Consort: A Political Biography of Prince Albert* (London: Chatto & Windus, 1959), pp. 58–9.
57. Palmerston to Russell, 25 Sept. 1848, RP, TNA, PRO 30/22/7D, ff. 115–17.
58. Connell, *Regina v. Palmerston*, p. 78.
59. Queen Victoria to Russell, 18 June 1848, ibid., p. 80.
60. Emily Palmerston to Palmerston, 1848, E. Longford, *Victoria, R.I.* (London: World Books, 1967 edn), p. 260.
61. Queen Victoria to Palmerston, 28 Nov. 1846, *LQV*, ii, p. 132.
62. Russell to Palmerston, 3 Feb. 1849, PP, GC/RU/253.
63. Palmerston to Normanby, 31 Mar. 1848, Ashley, ii, p. 78.
64. Palmerston to Russell, 18 Jan. 1849, RP, TNA, PRO 30/22/7F, ff. 343–5. On a later occasion, Palmerston suggested that if Russell and the Queen continued to demand a full supply of documents from the Foreign Office, 'he would 'require an additional clerk or two. You must be liberal & allow me that assistance', Palmerston to Russell, 13 Aug. 1850, RP, TNA, PRO 30/22/9E, ff. 80–1.
65. Russell to Palmerston, 1 Oct. 1848, PP, GC/RU/225.
66. Harney's own retrospective account, written in 1894, quoted in F. J. Snell, *Palmerston's Borough: A Budget of Electioneering Anecdotes, Jokes, Squibs and Speeches* (London: Horace Marshall; Tiverton: Gregory, Son & Tozer, 1894), pp. 89–90.
67. Palmerston to Russell, 25 July 1847, RP, PRO 30/22/6D, ff. 199–200.
68. Palmerston to George Julian Harney, 31 July 1847, PP, BR23/1/13/2.
69. Snell, *Palmerston's Borough*, p. 84.
70. *The Trial and Condemnation of Lord Viscount Palmerston, at Tiverton, Jul. 30, 1847, containing a verbatim report of the speech of G. Julian Harney, the People's Member for Tiverton* (London, 1847), p. 3.
71. Snell, *Palmerston's Borough*, p. 78.
72. Ibid., pp. 78–9.
73. *Trial and Condemnation*, p. 3.
74. Ibid., pp. 4–11; Snell, *Palmerston's Borough*, pp. 79–80, 85–6.
75. According to an anecdote recounted by Harney in 1894, quoted in Snell, *Palmerston's Borough*, p. 90.
76. *Trial and Condemnation*, p. 11.
77. *Speech of Lord Viscount Palmerston, Secretary of State for Foreign Affairs, to the Electors of Tiverton, on the 31st Jul. 1847* (London: Smith, Elder, 2nd edn, 1847), pp. 3–16; *Trial and Condemnation*, p. 11.
78. *Trial and Condemnation*, p. 9.
79. *Hansard*, 3rd ser., lxxxviii, 826–32 (17 Aug. 1846).
80. Palmerston to Russell, 13 Nov. 1846, RP, TNA, PRO 30/22/5E, ff. 92–3.
81. Russell to Palmerston, 14 Nov. 1846, PP, GC/RU/124.
82. Queen Victoria to Palmerston, 11 Dec. 1846, PP, RC/F/296.
83. Russell to Palmerston, 14 Dec. 1846, PP, GC/RU/129.
84. Palmerston to Russell, 17 Jan. 1847, RP, TNA, PRO 30/22/6A, ff. 157–8.
85. *Morning Post*, 12 Dec. 1846.
86. *Hansard*, 3rd ser., xci, 91–101 (16 Mar. 1847).

87. E.g., *Hansard*, 3rd ser., lxxxix, 163–4 (20 Jan. 1847).
88. Ashley, i, p. 17.
89. *Trial and Condemnation*, pp. 9–10.
90. Queen Victoria to Palmerston, 28 Nov. 1846, PP, RC/F/289.
91. Queen Victoria to Palmerston, 5 Jan. 1847, PP, RC/F/300.
92. Queen Victoria to Palmerston, 4 Feb. 1847, PP, RC/F/306.
93. Palmerston to Russell, 10 Feb. 1847, RP, TNA, PRO, 30/22/6B, ff. 57–60.
94. Lansdowne to Russell, 12 Feb. 1847, RP, TNA, PRO 30/22/6B, ff. 68–9.
95. Memo by Russell, 'Portugal', 13 Feb. 1847, RP, TNA, PRO 30/22/6B, ff. 70–3; Russell to Palmerston, 22 Mar. 1847, PP, GC/RU/140.
96. Palmerston to Russell, 9 Aug. 1847, RP, TNA, PRO 30/22/6E, ff. 67–70.
97. Clarendon to Russell, RP, TNA, PRO 30/22/6D, ff. 18–19.
98. *Standard*, 2, 16, 18, 23 Nov. 1846 (quotations from 18 and 23).
99. *Hansard*, 3rd ser., xciii, 663–6, 772–5, 1202–4 (17, 18 June, 5 July 1847).
100. *Trial and Condemnation*, p. 10.
101. Snell, *Palmerston's Borough*, pp. 22–3, 38.
102. *Trial and Condemnation*, p. 11.
103. Ibid., p. 12. Harney did, however, pledge in an open letter to 'The Electors and Non-Electors of Tiverton' of 10 Aug. 1847 to go to the poll 'whenever another election shall take place' (PP, BR195 pt. 2).
104. *Trial and Condemnation*.
105. Snooks (pseud.), *A letter to Lord Palmerston, on the 'Condition of England Question,' elicited by his speech to the electors of Tiverton* (London, 1847), pp. 25–6.
106. Palmerston to Russell, 27 Sept. 1846, RP, TNA, PRO 30/22/5C, ff. 344–5.
107. Memo by Palmerston, Dec. 1846, RP, TNA, PRO, 30/22/5F, ff. 11–28.
108. See, for example, Minto to Russell, 12 Dec. 1846 (2 letters), RP, TNA, PRO 30/22/5F, ff. 161–2, 165–6; Charles Wood to Palmerston, 26 Dec. 1846, PP, GC/WO/20. Minto suggested some modest alterations to Palmerston's plans, and Wood (as Chancellor) worried about costs, but neither dissented from the need to support strong military and defensive arrangements.
109. Broughton Diaries, 28 Jan. 1848, BL, Add Ms 43751.
110. M.S. Partridge, 'The Russell Cabinet and National Defence, 1846–1852', *History*, 72 (1987), 231–50.
111. Palmerston to William Temple, 8 Mar. 1847, PP, GC/TE/317. For the moment, Palmerston said, Bentinck, Stanley and Disraeli were 'not formidable as candidates for office'.
112. Palmerston to Russell, 30 July 1846, RP, TNA, PRO 30/22/5B, ff. 267–70.
113. Southgate, p. 205.
114. Russell to Palmerston, 30 July 1846, PP, GC/RU/103.
115. Palmerston to Russell, 14 Sept. 1846, RP, TNA, PRO 30/22/6F, ff. 73–6.
116. Saho Matsumoto-Best, *Britain and the Papacy in the Age of Revolution, 1846–1851* (Woodbridge Suffolk: Royal Historical Society/Boydell Press, 2003), pp. 1, 37.
117. See, for example, L.P. Wallace, 'Pius IX and Lord Palmerston, 1846–1849', in L.P. Wallace and W. C. Askew (eds), *Power, Public Opinion, and Diplomacy* (Durham, NC: Duke University Press, 1959), pp. 3–46.
118. Matsumoto-Best, *Britain and the Papacy*, pp. 62–8. Herbert Bell exaggerates the influence of the Pope on Palmerston when he suggests that the mission was essentially Pius's project taken up by Palmerston (Bell, i, p. 412).
119. See Matsumoto-Best, *Britain and the Papacy*, pp. 50–1. Matsumoto-Best highlights, for example, the correspondence of Lord Abercromby (from Turin), Bishop Nicholas Wiseman (vicar-apostolic of the London District) and Lord Shrewsbury.
120. Ibid., pp. 45–7.
121. Russell to Minto, 22 Sept. 1847, in Frederico Curato (ed.), *Gran Bretagna e Italia nei documenti della missione Minto*, 2 vols. (Rome: Instituto Storico Italiano, 1970), i, no. 26, p. 76. See also Matsumoto-Best, *Britain and the Papacy*, pp. 52–3.
122. See Palmerston's correspondence with Minto, Stratford Canning and Ponsonby, Nov.–Dec. 1847, in Ashley, i, pp. 7–16.
123. Palmerston to Queen Victoria, 31 Aug. 1847, *Missione Minto*, i, no. 9, pp. 44–5.
124. Clarendon to Russell, n.d., ibid., i, no. 10, pp. 48–9.
125. Prince Albert to Russell, 5 Sept. 1847, ibid., i, no. 13, pp. 51–3.
126. Matsumoto-Best, *Britain and the Papacy*, pp. 53–7.
127. Clarendon to Russell, 1 Oct. 1847, in *Missione Minto*, i, no. 30, pp. 81–5.
128. Matsumoto-Best, *Britain and the Papacy*, p. 60.
129. See, for example, Minto to Palmerston, 12 and 14 Nov. 1847 and 1 Dec. 1847, in *Missione Minto*, i, nos 98, 103 and 131, pp. 183–4, 190–4, 238–9.

130. Minto to Russell, 15 Nov. 1847, RP, TNA, PRO 30/22/6G, ff. 127-8.
131. Palmerston to Russell, 20 Nov. 1847, RP, TNA, PRO 30/22/6G, ff. 199-200.
132. Emily Palmerston to Palmerston, 'Wednesday' [15 Sept. 1847] (on leaked information) and 9 Nov. 1847 (on Lamb's fears), Lamb Papers, BL, Add Ms 45553, ff. 142-5, 157-9.
133. Emily Palmerston to Palmerston, 9 Sept. 1847, ibid., ff. 134-8.
134. Palmerston to Clarendon, 9 Mar. 1848, Bell, i, p. 417.
135. Palmerston to Minto, 24 Feb. 1848, Ashley, i, pp. 52-4.
136. Ashley, i, p. 54.
137. Ibid., p. 2.
138. Guedalla, p. 253.
139. Memorandum by Palmerston, Jan. 1848, in Ashley, i, pp. 3-4.
140. G.J. Billy, *Palmerston's Foreign Policy: 1848* (New York: Peter Lang, 1993), pp. 65-6. Normanby's account of recent events in Paris sent to Palmerston on 13 Mar. 1848 may have supplied a partial answer: 'The infatuation of the King during the whole of the debates on the Address was very remarkable. Several of the representatives of the smaller German Courts went to him with letters of condolence on Madame Adelaide's death, and to some he said, "Tell your master not to mind having popular assemblies; let them only learn to manage them as I manage mine; see the noise they are making now; I shall soon have them in hand again; they want me to get rid of Guizot; I will not do it. Can I possibly give a stronger proof of my power?" ' (Ashley, i, p. 74). Guizot's ministry, of course, had been obliged to resign in February.
141. Palmerston to Normanby, 26 Feb. 1848, Ashley, i, p. 77.
142. Palmerston to Normanby, 26 Feb. 1848, Ashley, i, pp. 76-8.
143. Palmerston to Normanby 27 and 28 Feb. 1848, Ashley, i, pp. 78-82.
144. Palmerston to Westmorland (Minister in Berlin), 29 Feb. 1848, in K. Bourne, *The Foreign Policy of Victorian England, 1830-1902* (Oxford: Clarendon Press, 1970), p. 291.
145. Palmerston to Grey (3rd Earl), 29 Mar. 1848, PP, GC/GR/2408.
146. See, for example: Aberdeen to Guizot, 29 July 1848 and Guizot to Aberdeen, 16 Aug. 1848, Papiers Guizot, Archives Nationales, Paris, 42 AP 211/5 and 42 AP 211/140 [163 MI 51].
147. Palmerston to Normanby, 11 Apr. 1848, Ashley, i, pp. 93-4.
148. Fabrice Bensimon, *Les Britanniques face à la révolution française de 1848* (Paris: L'Harmattan, 2000), p. 399: 'A travers ce qu'expriment les notables victoriens sur la révolution française de 1848, nous voyons l'Angleterre à laquelle ils aspirent: libérale, loyale, dominante, sûre d'elle, fière de ses traditions et respectueuse de ses clivages sociaux, avec ses classes laborieuses et ses élites éclairées'.
149. D. Brown, 'Palmerston and Anglo-French Relations, 1846-65', *Diplomacy and Statecraft*, 17:4 (2006), 679-80; R. Postgate and A. Vallance (eds), *Those Foreigners. The English People's Opinion on Foreign Affairs as reflected in their Newspapers since Waterloo* (London: Harrap, 1937), esp. pp. 61-2.
150. Broughton Diaries, 28 Jan. 1848, BL, Add Ms 43751.
151. Russell to Lansdowne, 2 Mar. 1848, Lansdowne Papers, BL, Lans. 3/43, f. 42.
152. Grey, journal, 5 May 1848, Grey Papers (3rd Earl), Durham University Library, C3/14.
153. Broughton Diaries, 3 June 1848, BL, Add Ms 43752.
154. Emily Palmerston to Palmerston, 30 Apr. 1848, Lamb Papers, BL, Add Ms 45553, ff. 186-9.
155. Grey, journal, 7 May 1848, Grey Papers (3rd Earl), Durham University Library, C3/14.
156. Queen Victoria to Palmerston, 15 June 1848, *LQV*, ii, 211-12.
157. Queen Victoria to Palmerston, 1 July 1848, PP, RC/F/371/1-2.
158. Queen Victoria to King of the Belgians, 10 Oct. 1848, *LQV*, ii, pp. 237-8.
159. Memorandum by the Queen Victoria, 19 Sept. 1848, *LQV*, ii, pp. 231-3.
160. Memorandum by Prince Albert, 3 Mar. 1850, *LQV*, ii, pp. 279-82.
161. Emily Palmerston to Palmerston, [19 Oct. 1848], Lamb Papers, BL, Add Ms 45553, ff. 198-201.
162. Russell to Queen Victoria, 22 Jan. 1849, *LQV*, ii, pp. 250-1; Russell to Prince Albert, 18 May 1850, ibid., p. 288.
163. During his speech at Tiverton in 1847 Harney had observed that with regard to Urquhart's accusations of Palmerston's Russianism, 'I never believed anything of the sort' (*Trial and Condemnation*, p. 8).
164. M. Taylor, 'The Old Radicalism and the New: David Urquhart and the Politics of Opposition, 1832-1867', in E.F. Biagini and A.J. Reid (eds), *Currents of Radicalism: Popular Radicalism, Organised Labour and Party Politics in Britain, 1850-1914* (Cambridge: Cambridge University Press, 1991), pp. 30-1.
165. Ridley, pp. 334, 524-5. Henry Drummond Wolff recorded that Anstey was flattered and 'delighted with his reception' when Palmerston greeted him warmly in the House of Commons coffee room (*Rambling Recollections*, 2 vols. (London: Macmillan, 1908), i, pp. 114-15).
166. *Hansard*, 3rd ser., xcvi, 291-311, 1132-242 (8, 23 Feb. 1848).

167. *Hansard*, 3rd ser., xcvii, 67 (1 Mar. 1848).
168. Palmerston's diary, 1 Mar. 1848, PP, D/10: 'I spoke from about one till near six'.
169. *Hansard*, 3rd ser., xcvii, 66–123 (1 Mar. 1848).
170. *Hansard*, 3rd ser., xcvii, 123 (1 Mar. 1848).
171. *Standard*, 2 Mar. 1848.
172. M.H. Jenks, 'The Activities and Influence of David Urquhart, 1833–56, with special reference to the affairs of the Near East' (unpublished PhD thesis, University of London, 1964), pp. 269–72.
173. Palmerston to William Temple, 24 July 1852, PP, GC/TE/346.
174. *Hansard*, 3rd ser., xcix, 388, 396–400 (5 June 1848).
175. *Hansard*, 3rd ser., ci, 147–63 (16 Aug. 1848).
176. Disraeli to Metternich, 2 Sept. 1849, *BDL*, v, 1874.
177. Ambrose Brewin to Palmerston, 6 Mar. 1848, PP, GC/BR/35.
178. 'A Constituent' to Palmerston, June 1848, PP, MPC/1523.
179. Palmerston to William Temple, 9 Dec. 1848, PP, GC/TE/322.
180. Palmerston to William Temple, 7 July 1849, PP, GC/TE/327.
181. Graham to Peel, 16 Jan. 1849, in F.A. Dreyer 'The Russell Administration, 1846–52' (unpublished D.Phil thesis, University of St Andrews, 1962), p. 148.
182. Minto, journal, 25 Oct. 1848, 7 Dec. 1848, 21 Apr. 1849, Minto Papers, NLS, Ms.11995.
183. Grey, journal, 15 Jan. 1849, Grey Papers (3rd Earl), Durham University Library, C3/14.
184. See Ridley, p. 354.
185. Palmerston to Charles Wood, 23 Jan. 1849, Hickleton Papers, BIY, A4/63/6.
186. Grey, journal, 16 and 18 Jan. 1849, Grey Papers (3rd Earl), Durham University Library, C3/14.
187. Grey, journal, 23 Jan. 1849, ibid.
188. Grey, journal, 1 Feb. 1849, ibid.
189. J. Vincent (ed.) *Disraeli, Derby and the Conservative Party: Journals and Memoirs of Edward Henry, Lord Stanley, 1849–1869* (Hassocks: Harvester Press, 1978), p. 8 (19 May 1849).
190. See, for example, Palmerston to Baron Torre de Moncorvo, 6 June and 29 Oct. 1849, Moraes Sarmento Papers, BL, Add Ms 63174, ff. 130–1, 135–6.
191. Palmerston to Baron Torre de Moncorvo, 8 Jan. 1850, ibid., ff. 137–8.
192. Palmerston to William Temple, 24 Jan. 1850, PP, GC/TE/332.
193. Address from Evangelical Alliance, 'rec'd 9 March 1850', PP, MM/IT/23.
194. 'A Commercial Traveller' to Palmerston, 22 May 1850, PP, MPC/1538.
195. James Birch to Palmerston, 13 June 1850, PP, MPC/1539.
196. Aberdeen to Guizot, 21 Jan. 1851, Papiers Guizot, Archives Nationales, Paris, 42 AP 211/34 [163 MI 51].
197. Albert to Russell, 2 Apr. 1850, in Connell, *Regina v. Palmerston*, p. 115.
198. Russell to Palmerston, 22 May 1850, PP, GC/RU/343.
199. Palmerston to William Temple, 15 Feb. 1850, PP, GC/TE/333.
200. See, for example, Sir Robert Gilmour Colquhoun [British Consul-General in Bucharest] to Palmerston, 20 May 1847, PP, BR22(i)/1/84, reporting on a meeting with the Hospodar. Colquhoun wrote: 'I replied to the Prince that Great Britain had given innumerable proofs not to Greece alone, but to many other powers, that she was by no means a harsh creditor; that so long as good faith was observed by the Greek government, so long as a proper use was made of the money furnished to that state by England, & the country was deriving benefit from it, the British government would forbear & had forborne from pressing the strict fulfilment of the bond. But, what has been the case? It has been proved that frauds to an enormous extent had been committed in the government departments; funds mis-applied from the purposes to which they had been destined, and turned into channels for the corrupting of persons who should have been above such iniquities, & that even falsified accounts had been presented to the chamber, to throw dust in the eyes of the foreign creditor, & induce him to forego pressing his due. That Great Britain finding her leniency misunderstood, her very funds employed to demoralize a country she had made such sacrifices to serve, & such a total want of faith & common honesty in her debtor felt bound to act as she was now doing – and I doubted not that even Greece herself would ere long see the good effects of our present measures – that with regard to the measures adopted by another power, England would not allow herself to be turned aside from what she felt to be her line of duty, that she had no one party to support more than another; her wishes were for the welfare of Greece as a nation, & not to support any particular set of men.'
201. Palmerston to Drouyn de Lhuys, 21 Apr. [reverse minuted as May] 1850, PP, GC/DR/15 and enc.1. Almost £3,000 of this total comprised interest charges on Finlay's losses (over fourteen years) and Pacifico's (over three years).
202. Aberdeen to Guizot, 13 May 1850, Papiers Guizot, Archives Nationales, Paris, 42 AP 211/30 [163 MI 51]; Drouyn de Lhuys to Lord Halperton, 17 May 1850, PP, GC/DR/9 [extract from letter written in Palmerston's hand].

203. For this extensive debate, see *Hansard*, 3rd ser., cxi, 1293–403 (17 June 1850).

204. In 1833, discussing proposed interference in Portugal to defend British wine merchants' interests, Palmerston had written to Sir James Graham: 'we have also a right nay indeed it is our duty, to protect the persons & property of British subjects all over the world, but none more especially in places where they are found by virtue of treaties with other states, and when the property at stake is so large as that at Villa Nova, it ceases to be an individual and becomes a national concern. All nations act upon this principle, & when opposite rights clash, there is cause of war legitimate. Why did we interfere between the Sultan & the Greeks, and between the Dutch & the Belgians, & lately between Mehemet & his sovereign? Not from any abstract right, but because national interests were in jeopardy, and the first right of all nations is self protection' (Palmerston to Sir James Graham, 5 July 1833, Graham Papers, BL, Add Ms 79706, ff. 25–7).

205. Grey, journal, 18 June 1850, Grey Papers (3rd Earl), Durham University Library, C3/15.

206. George Shee to Palmerston, 27 May 1850, PP, MM/GR/37.

207. *Hansard*, 3rd ser., cxii, 443–4 (24 June 1850).

208. A.J.P. Taylor, *The Trouble Makers: Dissent over Foreign Policy, 1792–1939* (Harmondsworth: Pelican, 1985 edn), p. 57.

209. D. Brown, *Palmerston and the Politics of Foreign Policy, 1846–55* (Manchester: Manchester University Press, 2002), pp. 110–19.

210. *Illustrated London News*, 29 June 1850.

211. *Greville Memoirs*, vi, p. 233 (1 July 1850).

212. Esmé Wingfield-Stratford, *This Was a Man. The Biography of the Honourable Edward Vesey Bligh, Diplomat – Parson – Squire* (London: Robert Hale, 1949), pp. 85–9; Drummond Wolff, *Rambling Recollections*, i, p. 118.

213. *Globe*, 29 June 1850.

214. Ibid., 26 June 1850.

215. Ibid., 27 June 1850.

216. *Daily News*, 22 July 1850.

217. *Manchester Guardian*, 29 June 1850.

218. Ibid., 3 July 1850.

219. See R. M. Keeling, 'Palmerston and the Pacifico Debate' (unpublished PhD dissertation, University of Missouri, Columbia, 1968), pp. 180–1.

220. *Morning Post*, 27 June 1850.

221. *The Times*, 22 June 1850.

222. *Morning Chronicle*, 27, 29 June 1850.

223. *Standard*, 29 June, 1 July, 20 Aug. 1850.

224. *On the Speech of Her Majesty's Foreign Secretary, delivered in the House of Commons Jun. 25, 1850. A letter to the Right Hon. Viscount Palmerston, in reference to the Greek Question, exclusive of His Lordship's general foreign policy. By a Greek Gentleman* (London, 1850), pp. 5, 6–8, 35.

225. *The Times*, 22 Feb. 1850, 20 May 1850.

226. Editor of the *Sun* to Col. Freeston, 30 May 1850, PP, MM/GR/38.

227. James Aspinall to Palmerston, 26 June 1850, PP, MM/GR/47; *Albion*, 24 June 1850, PP, MM/GR/47/enc.1.

228. John Henderson [editor of the *Renfrewshire Reformer and Glasgow Saturday Post*] to Palmerston, 30 June 1850, enclosing a copy of the paper, PP, MM/GR/49; *Sligo Champion*, June 1850, PP, MM/GR/50; R.O. Warwick [Pensioner of Greenwich Hospital] to Palmerston, 2 July 1850, PP, MM/GR/52; Abraham Jones Le Gras[?] to Palmerston, 8 July 1850, PP, MM/GR/54.

229. Edwin Budell to Palmerston, 24 July 1850, PP, MM/GR/59/1.

230. *Greville Memoirs*, vi, 233 (1 July 1850).

231. From a minute, in Palmerston's hand, on a letter from Russell, 22 May 1850, PP, GC/RU/343/enc.1.

232. Palmerston to William Temple, 8 July 1850, PP, GC/TE/334.

233. Aberdeen to Guizot, 12 July 1850, Papiers Guizot, Archives Nationales, Paris, 42 AP 211/31 [163 MI 51].

234. Palmerston to William Temple, 1 Sept. 1850, PP, GC/TE/335.

235. Palmerston to William Temple, 17 and [n.d.] Nov. 1850, PP, GC/TE/349 and 350 [second letter incomplete].

236. Aberdeen to Guizot, 1 Nov. 1850, Papiers Guizot, Archives Nationales, Paris, 42 AP 211/32 [163 MI 51].

237. Vincent (ed.) *Disraeli, Derby and the Conservative Party*, pp. 40–1 (16 Feb. 1851).

238. See correspondence on the proposed restructuring in PP, GMC/46.

239. See, for example, Aberdeen's comments to Guizot of 24 Jan. 1851: 'You may imagine that the proceedings of the French Assembly have been watched here with much interest. The unanimity

of our press, in the judgement pronounced upon these proceedings, is a remarkable circumstance, which I cannot easily explain. If we could trust the President, it would be intelligible enough; for if honest, he is undoubtedly a very ill used man. But our writers probably entertain as little doubt respecting his projects, as is felt elsewhere; and I can scarcely believe that the restoration of the Empire, with all its consequences, should generally be welcome to the people of this country. Our ministers may perhaps desire it, in order to promote their personal influence; but this would not regulate the language of our journals, and still less the popular voice. As these journals generally follow, while they affect to direct the publick, I suppose that the President must be regarded by us as an incarnation of Washington. This, certainly, is very far from being my opinion; but be this as it may, it cannot be denied that he has shewn firmness & decision; and that he has carried off the essential parts of victory. Believing him to look steadily to the attainment of Empire, it is clear that the removal of [General] Changarnier was indispensable at all risks. He knew well that he had nothing to hope from Changarnier at the critical period of the revision of the constitution, and he also knew how much may depend on the commander of the troops at that time' (Papiers Guizot, Archives Nationales, Paris, 42 AP 211/35 [163 MI 51]).

240. Palmerston to Charles Wood, 22, 24 Jan. 1851, Hickleton Papers, BIY, A4/63/12 and 13–13A; Extract from the *Moniteur*, 2 Mar. 1851, PP, MM/FR/21; Memo on defence of Cherbourg, PP, MM/FR/23/enc.1; Partridge, 'The Russell Cabinet and National Defence', 231–50; Brown, 'Palmerston and Anglo-French Relations, 1846–65', 680–2.
241. Palmerston to Richard Shiel, 28 Jan. 1851, PP, GC/SH/152.
242. Palmerston to Richard Shiel, 3 Apr. 1851, PP, GC/SH/153.
243. *Illustrated London News*, 27 Sept. 1851.
244. *Standard*, 26 Dec. 1851.
245. Address from the Company of Merchants of Edinburgh, 28 Nov. 1851, PP, MM/IT/29/enc.1.
246. Palmerston to William Temple, 6 Nov. 1851, PP, GC/TE/339.
247. Palmerston to Russell, 24 Oct. 1851, PP, GC/RU/430/enc.2.
248. Ridley, pp. 396–7.
249. Palmerston to Russell, 30 Oct. 1851, RP, PRO 30/22/9G(2), ff. 143–4.
250. Queen Victoria to Russell, 20 Nov. 1851, PP, GC/RU/440/enc.1.
251. Quoted in D. Newsome, *The Victorian World Picture: Perceptions and Introspections in an Age of Change* (London: John Murray, 1997), p. 102.
252. Palmerston to Sir William Temple, 9 Dec. 1848, PP, GC/TE/322: 'People seem still to think that Louis Napoleon will be President. That will not at first or for a certain time make any material change in the foreign policy of France; but in the long run, and indeed before next summer is over it will have some very sensible effect. I should not be sorry if it ended in Louis Napoleon being made Emperor, & thus ridding us of both branches of the Bourbons; but the adherents of that family certainly imagine that they will be able to get rid of Louis Nap and set up a Bourbon in his stead. . . .'
253. Palmerston to Laurence Sulivan, 26 Dec. 1851, *PSL*, pp. 298–9.
254. Palmerston, 'Memorandum of certain circumstances connected with the coup d'etat Decr. 1851', written 29 Sept. 1858, PP, MM/FR/27.
255. Russell to Palmerston, 17 Dec. 1851, PP, GC/RU/449, GC/RU/450/1–2.
256. Palmerston to Russell, 18 Dec. 1851, PP, GC/RU/1098.
257. Russell to Palmerston, 19 Dec. 1851, PP, GC/RU/453.
258. Note by Palmerston on letter from Russell to Palmerston, 22 Dec. 1851, PP, GC/RU/454.
259. Lord Truro to Russell, Jan. 1852, RP, TNA PRO 30/22/10A(1), f. 80.
260. Minto to Palmerston, 13 Jan. 1852, PP, GC/MI/501.
261. A. Lefèvre, 'La Chute de Palmerston (1851): la part de responsabilité française', *Revue d'histoire diplomatique*, 84 (1970), 94; Count Alexandre Walewski to Palmerston, 26 Dec. 1851, PP, GC/WA/13.
262. Peter Borthwick to Palmerston, 27 Dec. 1851, PP, GMC/47. For a fuller consideration of the domestic impact and consequences of this episode in Britain, see Brown, *Palmerston and the Politics of Foreign Policy*, pp. 119–29 and D. Brown, 'The Power of Public Opinion: Palmerston and the Crisis of December 1851', *Parliamentary History*, 20:3 (2001).
263. Palmerston to Lansdowne, first week in Oct. 1852, PP, GC/LA/74/enc.1.
264. Minto, journal, 1, 3 Nov. 1851, Minto Papers, NLS, Ms.11998.
265. Minto, journal, 27 Nov. 1851, ibid.
266. 'When the subject was brought before us I thought the Cabinet showed great weakness for though I believe every member of it disapproved exceedingly of what had been done this feeling was scarcely expressed except by Labouchere and myself', Grey, journal, 'Retrospect written 6 March 1852', Grey Papers (3rd Earl), C3/15.
267. Clarendon to Lansdowne, 25 Dec. 1851, Lansdowne Papers, BL, Lans. 3/32, f. 103; Grey journal, 'Retrospect written 6 March 1852', Grey Papers (3rd Earl), C3/15.

268. Queen Victoria to Russell, 31 Oct. 1851, *LQV*, ii, 325–7.

269. Queen Victoria to Russell, 28 Dec. 1851, *LQV*, ii, 351–2.

270. Queen Victoria's journal, 20 Dec. 1851, Connell, *Regina v. Palmerston*, p. 132.

271. Queen Victoria [memorandum/letter to Russell], 28 Dec. 1851, RP, TNA, PRO 30/29/31 (1).

272. *Daily News*, 2 Dec. 1851.

273. Grey to Palmerston, 23 Dec. 1851, PP, GMC/87.

274. Grey to Wood, 23 Dec. 1851, Hickleton Papers, BIY, A4/55/1.

275. Earl Russell, *Recollections and Suggestions, 1813–1873* (London: Longmans, Green, 1875), pp. 257–8. As G.P. Gooch suggests, however, it is likely that this 'judgement was inspired by the softening influence of time and by subsequent experience of harmonious co-operation' (G.P. Gooch (ed.), *The Later Correspondence of Lord John Russell, 1840–1878*, 2 vols. (London: Longmans, 1925), p. xxxv).

276. Clarendon to Lansdowne, 25 Dec. 1851, Lansdowne Papers, BL, Lans. 3/32, f. 103.

277. W. Wilks, *Palmerston in Three Epochs: A Comparison of Facts with Opinions* (London, 1854), p. 57.

278. Palmerston to William Temple, 22 Jan. 1852, PP, GC/TE/341.

279. *Morning Post*, 25 Dec. 1851.

280. Ibid., 26 Dec. 1851.

281. Ibid., 30 Dec. 1851.

282. Peter Borthwick to Palmerston, 27 Dec. 1851, PP, GMC/47.

283. *The Times*, 24 Dec. 1851.

284. *Morning Chronicle*, 25 Dec. 1851.

285. *Daily News*, 2, 25, 26 Dec. 1850.

286. *Standard*, 24 Dec. 1851.

287. Ibid., 26, 30 Dec. 1850.

288. *Bell's Life in London*, 7 Dec. 1851 (press cutting kept and annotated by Palmerston), PP, GMC/49.

289. *Dundee Courier*, Feb. 1852, PP, GMC/54/1–2; *Warder*, 26 Dec. 1851, PP, GMC/50; *Morning Advertiser*, 31 Dec. 1851, PP, GMC/51; *Lincolnshire Times*, Feb. 1852 (letter dated 20 Feb. 1852), PP, GMC/53.

290. R. Andrews to Palmerston, 26 Jan. 1852, PP, GMC/106. In a similar vein, also: R. Alston to Palmerston, 27 Dec. 1851, PP, GMC/51; Henry Berkeley [MP for Bristol] to Palmerston, 27 Dec. 1851, PP, GMC/65; George Coles [of Tiverton] to Palmerston, 2 Jan. 1852, PP, GMC/73; Edward Dawes [MP for the Isle of Wight] to Palmerston, 13 Jan. 1852, PP, GMC/77.

291. See J. Davidson, *The Fall of the Pope, and the Fate of the French President* (London and Aberdeen, 1852). Davidson sent this pamphlet to Palmerston on 17 Jan. 1852 (PP, GMC/76, GMC/76/enc.1).

292. Southgate, p. 291.

293. Palmerston to Lansdowne, Oct. 1852, Ashley, ii, p. 226.

294. Palmerston to William Temple, 22 Jan. 1852, PP, GC/TE/341.

295. *Morning Advertiser*, 7 Feb. 1852.

296. Mr Shaw (Honorary Secretary of the City of London Tradesman's Club) to Palmerston, 24 Jan. 1852 (with a copy of Palmerston's reply), PP, GMC/58; Henry Berkeley to Palmerston, 6 Jan. 1852 (with a copy of Palmerston's reply), PP, GMC/66; A. Drummond to Palmerston, 1 Jan. 1852 (with a copy of Palmerston's reply), PP, GMC/79.

297. *Leicestershire Mercury*, 24 Jan. 1852, PP, GMC/52.

298. Address by the Members of the Working Men's Institution of Leamington Priors, Warwickshire, 1 Jan. 1852, PP, GMC/92/enc.1; A. Kirkaldy to Palmerston, 29 Dec. 1851, PP, GMC/97.

299. Wm. Lawton (Secretary of the Sheffield Rational Society) to Palmerston, 7 Jan. 1852, PP, GMC/57; Ambrose Brewin to Palmerston, 6 Jan. 1852, PP, GMC/70.

300. Revd Clotworthy Gillmor to Palmerston, 6 Jan. 1852, PP, GMC/85.

301. John Wallis to Palmerston, 5 Jan. 1852, PP, GMC/122.

302. On the significance of these concerns, see, for example, D.E.D. Beales, *England and Italy, 1859–60* (London: Nelson, 1961), pp. 14, 19–20 and G.F.A. Best, 'Popular Protestantism in Victorian Britain', in R. Robson (ed.), *Ideas and Institutions of Victorian Britain* (London: G. Bell, 1967), p. 119.

303. PP, GMC/86/enc.2, letter 'To the Editor of the *Edinburgh News* from an Edinburgh Elector', 6 Jan. 1852, cut from the newspaper, with the quote from the *Daily News* highlighted [by Palmerston's pen?].

304. *Manchester Guardian*, 31 Dec. 1851.

Chapter 10 The People's Minister, 1852–1855

1. *Hansard*, 3rd ser., cxxiii, 1724 (27 Dec. 1852).

2. An observation made after the debate of 3 Feb. 1852 quoted A. Lyall, *The Life of the Marquis of Dufferin and Ava* (London: Nelson, 1905), p. 77.

3. Truro to Russell, Jan. 1852, Russell Papers, PRO, 30/22/10A(1), f. 80.

4. Clarendon to Russell, 26 Dec. 1851, G.P. Gooch (ed.), *The Later Correspondence of Lord John Russell, 1840-1878*, 2 vols. (London: Longmans, 1925), ii, p. 94.

5. Clarendon to Russell, 4 Jan. 1852, ibid., p. 96.

6. Clarendon to Russell, 22 Jan. 1852, ibid., pp. 97-9.

7. Howden to Granville, 8 Jan. 1852, Granville Papers (2nd Earl), TNA, PRO 30/29/20/9, ff. 125-32.

8. Granville to Howden, 18 Jan. 1852, ibid., ff. 145-8.

9. Aberdeen to Guizot, 26 Jan. 1852, Papiers Guizot, Archives Nationales, Paris, 42 AP 211/47 [163 MI 51].

10. Palmerston to Broughton, 30 Jan. 1852, Broughton Papers, BL, Add Ms 46915, ff. 339-40.

11. Palmerston to William Temple, 24 Feb. 1852, PP, GC/TE/342; Palmerston's diary, 20 Feb. 1852, PP, D/13.

12. *Morning Post*, 23 Feb. 1852.

13. Algernon Borthwick to Peter Borthwick, 13 Dec. 1852, Glenesk-Bathurst Papers, Brotherton Library, Leeds, MS.Dep.1990/1/1173.

14. Derby to Palmerston, 22 Feb. 1852, PP, GMC/129.

15. Palmerston's diary, 22 Feb. 1852, PP, D/13.

16. Palmerston, memorandum: 'Substance of my conversation with Ld Derby on 22nd Feby 1852 when he invited me to join the administration he was commissioned to form', 29 Mar. 1852, PP, GMC/130/1-2.

17. A. Hawkins, 'Lord Derby and Victorian Conservatism: A Reappraisal', *Parliamentary History*, 6 (1987), 287.

18. W.F. Moneypenny and G.E. Buckle, *The Life of Benjamin Disraeli, Earl of Beaconsfield*, 2 vols. (rev. edn., London, 1929), i, p. 1196.

19. Bell, ii, p. 61; Southgate, p. 310; Lord Malmesbury, *Memoirs of an Ex-Minister, An Autobiography*, 2 vols. (London: Longmans, Green, 1884), i, pp. 305, 317; Malmesbury (3rd Earl) to Palmerston, 2 Nov. 1852, PP, GC/MA/191.

20. Palmerston to William Temple, 30 Apr. 1852 PP, GC/TE/343.

21. Palmerston to William Temple, 30 Apr. 1852, PP, GC/TE/343.

22. Palmerston to William Temple, 20 June 1852, PP, GC/TE/345.

23. Palmerston to William Temple, 23 May 1852, PP, GC/TE/344.

24. Palmerston to William Temple, 20 June 1852, PP, GC/TE/345.

25. Nassau Senior to Monsieur Quetelet, 26 June 1852, Nassau Senior Manuscripts, NLW, C/357.

26. Emily Palmerston to Palmerston, 6 July 1852, Lamb Papers, BL, Add Ms 45554, ff. 64-5.

27. Palmerston to William Temple, 30 Apr. 1852, PP, GC/TE/343; Palmerston's diary, 7 July 1852, PP, D/13.

28. See Palmerston's printed address 'To the Electors of the Borough of Tiverton . . . 1 July 1852', PP, BR195/115.

29. Emily Palmerston to Palmerston, 8 July 1852, Lamb Papers, BL, Add Ms 45554, ff. 68-9.

30. Palmerston's diary, 22 July 1852, PP, D/13.

31. Palmerston to William Temple, 24 July 1852, PP, GC/TE/346.

32. Charles Greville to Clarendon, 21 Oct. 1852, quoted in H. Maxwell, *The Life and Letters of George William Frederick Fourth Earl of Clarendon*, 2 vols. (London: Edward Arnold, 1913), i, p. 350.

33. Malmesbury (3rd Earl), political journal, 24 Oct. 1852, Malmesbury Papers, HRO, 9M73/79.

34. Sir James Graham Papers, Bodleian Library, Oxford (microfilm), MS Film 124, Bundle 112, G.C. Lewis to Graham, 8 Sept. 1852.

35. See, for example, J.R. Vincent (ed.), *Disraeli, Derby and the Conservative Party: Journals and Memoirs of Edward Henry, Lord Stanley, 1849-1869* (Hassocks: Harvester Press, 1978), p. xiv.

36. Malmesbury (3rd Earl), political journal, 12, 21, 25, 28 Nov. 1852, Malmesbury Papers, HRO, 9M73/79.

37. Sir James Graham to George Cornewall Lewis, 1 Sept. 1852, Harpton Court Ms, NLW, C/700.

38. *Morning Post*, 4 Oct. 1852.

39. Ibid., 7 Oct. 1852.

40. Ashley, ii, p. 1.

41. Palmerston's diary, 15 Sept., 22 July 1852, PP, D/13.

42. See, for example, Sir James Graham to George Cornewall Lewis, 9 Sept. 1852, Harpton Court Ms, NLW, C/701: 'My view of the policy of the Opposition entirely coincides with yours. There ought to be no violence, no eagerness, no haste; but steady uncompromising adherence to right principles, and a bold assertion of them on every fitting occasion. The sails must not be trimmed to

catch Gladstone or Palmerston; while no exertion ought to be omitted in the hope of conciliating them and of carrying them with us.'

43. Sir James Graham to George Cornewall Lewis, 21 Oct. 1852, Harpton Court Ms, NLW, C/704.
44. Chamberlain, p. 80; Ridley, pp. 404–5.
45. Palmerston's diary, 20 Dec. 1852, PP, D/13.
46. Palmerston to Aberdeen, 10 Jan. 1853, Aberdeen Papers, BL, Add Ms 43069.
47. Palmerston to Broughton, 26 Dec. 1852, Broughton Papers, BL, Add Ms 46915, ff. 341–2.
48. George Douglas Campbell, Eighth Duke of Argyll, *Autobiography and Memoirs*, ed. Dowager Duchess of Argyll, 2 vols. (London: John Murray, 1906), i, pp. 378–89.
49. Shaftesbury's diary, 30 Dec. 1852, PP, SHA/PD/6.
50. D. Roberts, 'Lord Palmerston at the Home Office', *Historian*, 21: 1 (1958), 63.
51. Ridley, p. 405.
52. Ibid., pp. 406–24; Southgate, pp. 315–55. See also Chamberlain, pp. 77–90.
53. Palmerston to William Temple, Nov. 1850 [incomplete letter], PP, GC/TE/350.
54. Palmerston to William Temple, 22 Dec 1852, Ashley, ii, pp. 2–3.
55. Roberts, 'Palmerston at the Home Office', 65: 'Was the new Home Secretary, as the *Manchester Guardian* insisted, a liberal who supported all good reforms, or, as the *The Times* claimed, at heart a Tory? His work at the Home Office would, in part, answer that question.'
56. Palmerston to Laurence Sulivan, 31 Dec. 1852, PP, GC/SU/34.
57. Palmerston to Laurence Sulivan, 24 Dec. 1852, *PSL*, p. 304.
58. Southgate, p. 315.
59. Emily Shaftesbury to Palmerston, 25 Aug. 1852, enclosing note dictated by Latham on Lady Palmerston's health, Lamb Papers, BL, Add Ms 45548, ff. 174–6; Palmerston's diary, 24 Aug.–7 Sept. 1852 (*et seq.* for brief references to Emily's improvement), PP, D/13.
60. Palmerston to William Temple, 3 Apr. 1852, PP, GC/TE/353.
61. *Daily News*, 4 Jan. 1853.
62. On Palmerston's work at the Home Office, see Roberts, 'Palmerston at the Home Office'; Ridley, pp. 406–12; Chamberlain, pp. 80–3.
63. Roberts, 'Palmerston at the Home Office', 80.
64. J. Parry, *The Rise and Fall of Liberal Government in Victorian Britain* (New Haven and London: Yale University Press, 1993), p. 170.
65. Ibid., pp. 173–5.
66. W.H. Tweedie to Palmerston, 15 Oct. 1853, TNA, HO 45/4548.
67. Henry Fitzroy to W.H. Tweedie, 19 Oct. 1853, TNA, HO 103/12, ff. 240–1. This letter reproduces the text of Palmerston's draft reply written on the back of Tweedie's original letter and dated by Palmerston 17 Oct. 1853, TNA HO 45/4548.
68. W.B. Robinson to Palmerston, 11 Nov. 1853, TNA HO 45/4548.
69. Roberts, 'Palmerston at the Home Office', 71 (press comment); Ashley, ii, p. 15 (free wits).
70. See TNA HO 45/4548: George Charlton to Palmerston, 27 Sept. 1853, with note by Palmerston, 10 Oct. 1853; John Kincaid to Palmerston, 26 Sept. and 2 Dec. 1853, with notes by Palmerston, respectively, 2 Oct. and 8 Dec. 1853; note by Palmerston 5 Sept. 1853.
71. 'Directions for letter [to the] Commrs of Sewers', 10 Sept. 1853, TNA, HO 45/4765.
72. Memorandum by Palmerston, 19 Sept. 1853, TNA, HO 45/4765.
73. Note by Palmerston on a letter ([?from James Stark] received 30 Sept.), 2 Oct. 1853, TNA, HO 45/4548.
74. Note for the Board of Health by Palmerston, 27 Nov. 1853, TNA, HO 45/4580.
75. Note by Palmerston, 18 Dec. 1853, on letter from James Cooke 'and other ratepayers' of Gosport, 12/13 Dec. 1853, TNA, HO 45/4580.
76. Although this reconstruction of the Board was brought about by parliamentary defeat for a continuation as then constituted, the memoranda exchanged between Palmerston and Henry Waddington (Permanent Under-Secretary at the Home Office, 1848–67) between May and July 1854 indicate that though Palmerston intended to maintain the Board in its existing form, he was also keen to strengthen the personal control over its activities exercised by the Home Secretary (PP, HO/F/5/1–6).
77. Russell's description of Hall taken from an entry in Charles Wood, political journal, 25/26 Feb. 1854, Hickleton Papers, BIY, A8/1/2 (see also typescript 'Journals and Memoranda 1846–1867 by Sir Charles Wood afterwards Viscount Halifax', 2 vols., ibid., A8).
78. Palmerston to Benjamin Hall, 20 Aug. 1854, quoted Roberts, 'Palmerston at the Home Office', 77.
79. Roberts, 'Palmerston at the Home Office', 74–5.
80. *Parliamentary Papers* 1854 (1854), Consumption of Smoke, 20 July 1854.
81. Roberts, 'Palmerston at the Home Office', 75–6.
82. Edwin Chadwick to Palmerston, 3 Dec. 1853, PP, GC/CH/51.

83. See, for example, files on public health, dealing especially with sewers, sewage and cholera, 1854–58, PP, HA/F/6–10.
84. For a flavour of such inquiries and reform programmes, see: *Parliamentary Papers* 1852–53 (435), Common Lodging Houses; *Parliamentary Papers* 1854 (376) Metropolitan Sewers; *Parliamentary Papers* 1854 (394) Metropolitan Sewers; *Parliamentary Papers* 1854 (1776) Report of the Several Metropolitan Water Companies.
85. Shaftesbury to Palmerston, 23 Aug. 1853, PP, GC/SH/24.
86. Notes by Palmerston, 18 Feb.1853 TNA, HO 45/4641 and 21 May, 19 June 1854, TNA, HO 45/5280.
87. Notes and memoranda by Palmerston, Oct. 1854–Feb. 1855, TNA, HO 45/5698/1.
88. Wilkie Collins, *Armadale* (1864–66), Epilogue, ch. 1. The story is set in late 1851.
89. George Wake to Palmerston, 18 Aug. 1853, with Palmerston's notes, 22 Aug. 1853, TNA, HO 45/4973.
90. Ashley, ii, pp. 15–16.
91. Ibid., p. 16; Roberts, 'Palmerston at the Home Office', 79; *The Times*, 2 Nov. 1854.
92. Notebook containing newspaper cuttings, anecdotes, notes on Irish affairs, 1827–c.1832, PP, BR22(ii)/13, pp. 73–6.
93. Memorandum by Palmerston on 'Parkhurst Prisons', 10 Oct. 1854, PP, HA/N/10.
94. Philip Grant, *The History of Factory Legislation* (Manchester: John Heywood, 1866), pp. 70–2. Grant was a member of the delegation that called on Palmerston in 1844.
95. Roberts, 'Palmerston at the Home Office', 72–3.
96. See TNA, HO 45/4758.
97. Roberts, 'Palmerston at the Home Office', 66.
98. Palmerston, memoranda, 19 Sept., 3 Nov. 1853, TNA, HO 45/5128.
99. Palmerston to Aberdeen, 12 Feb. 1854, PP, HA/G/10.
100. Palmerston, memorandum, 22 Dec. 1853, TNA, HO 45/5128.
101. Roberts, 'Palmerston at the Home Office', 70.
102. *Hansard*, 3rd ser., cxxxvi (1854); Roberts, 'Palmerston at the Home Office', 79.
103. David Ross (Dean of the Guild Incorporation of Perth) to Palmerston, 21 Sept. 1853, PP, GC/RO/20.
104. Palmerston's diary, entries for 26, 27 Sept. 1853, PP, D/14. Palmerston identifies the ironworks as simply that of 'Napier', but it would seem most likely to be that of David Napier (see T.M. Devine, *The Scottish Nation, 1700–2000* (Harmondsworth: Penguin, 1999), pp. 256–7).
105. E.M. Whitty, *The Governing Classes of Great Britain: Political Portraits* (London, 1854), quoted in P. Langford, *Englishness Identified: Manners and Character, 1650–1850* (Oxford: Oxford University Press, 2000), pp. 20–1.
106. E. Davies to Palmerston, 16 Sept. 1854, PP, MPC/1561, enclosing newspaper cutting entitled 'Portrait Gallery of Eminent Living Men. Lord Palmerston, MP', PP, MPC/1561/enc.1.
107. The speeches were reprinted in the *Glasgow Constitutional*; Palmerston kept a cutting from a newspaper (unidentified) reprinting the *Constitutional*'s reports, PP, SP/B/3/1–4.
108. The NAVSR was founded in 1853 but struggled to establish itself as a powerful force in politics and was largely defunct by 1856, although one historian of Scottish nationalist politics in the later nineteenth and twentieth centuries identifies it as the 'ancestor of the SNP' (R.J. Finlay, *A Partnership for Good? Scottish Politics and the Union since 1880* (Edinburgh: John Donald, 1997), p. 4. Among the best accounts of the NAVSR are: H.J. Hanham, 'Mid-Century Scottish Nationalism: Romantic and Radical', in R. Robson (ed.), *Ideas and Institutions of Victorian Britain* (London: G. Bell, 1967), pp. 143–79, and Graeme Morton, *Unionist Nationalism: Governing Urban Scotland, 1830–1860* (East Linton: Tuckwell, 1999), pp. 135–54.
109. See PP, SP/B/3/1–4.
110. [William Burns], *Letter by a North Briton to Lord Palmerston, as published in the 'Times' of 22d October, 1863 [?1853]* (1863), pp. 7–8.
111. Henry Fitzroy to William Burns, 27 Oct. 1853. Burns published this letter in his own pamphlets: see [William Burns], *Scottish Rights and Honour Vindicated, in letters addressed to Viscount Palmerston, 'The Times', and 'Caledonian Mercury'. Dedicated to the People of Scotland, by a North Briton* (Glasgow, 1854), p. 3; [Burns], *Letter by a North Briton*, p. 9.
112. The most important of Burns's published pamphlets on this subject are: *Scottish Rights and Honour Vindicated; What's in a Name?* (Glasgow, 1860); *Letter by a North Briton; 'England' versus 'Britain'* (Glasgow, 1863); *The Question, how far the practice of substituting England for Britain, as the name of the United Kingdom, is legitimate in itself, or injurious to Scotland* (London, 1863); *'England' versus 'Great Britain'* (Glasgow, 1865); and *Address by William Burns to Glasgow St. Andrew's Society* (Glasgow, 1869).
113. See *Scotland and Her Calumniators* (Glasgow, 1858), p. 58. *The Times* made explicit the prejudices informing its treatment of Burns's case in 1859: see *The Times*, 27 Jan. 1859, p. 6, in which a

leading article opening with the plea, 'Will not somebody give poor old England a turn?', disparaged Burns's arguments as part of a broader appeal for a clearer sense of an English identity.

114. Burns, *What's in a Name?* p. 65, quoting the *Citizen*.
115. *Scotland and Her Calumniators*, p. 59.
116. *Tracts of the National Association for the Vindication of Scottish Rights, No. 3* (1854), quoted in Morton, *Unionist Nationalism*, p. 146.
117. C. Kidd, *Subverting Scotland's Past: Scottish Whig Historians and the Creation of an Anglo-British Identity, 1689–1830* (Cambridge: Cambridge University Press, 1993), pp. 33–50, 73.
118. See Finlay, *A Partnership for Good?*, pp. 18–19.
119. T.M. Devine, *Scotland's Empire, 1600–1815* (London: Penguin, 2003), p. xxvii and *passim*.
120. See, for example, Devine, *Scottish Nation*, pp. 249–73.
121. For some valuable indications of the state of political thought in mid-century Britain see A. Hawkins, ' "Parliamentary Government" and Victorian Political Parties, c.1830–c.1880', *EHR*, 104 (July 1989), 638–69.
122. 'A Scotchman', letter to *The Times*, 25 Oct. 1853, p. 8.
123. 'A Glasgow Merchant', letter to *The Times*, 26 Oct. 1853, p. 9.
124. 'Humphry', letter to *The Times*, 26 Oct. 1853, p. 9.
125. John Cumming, letter to *The Times*, 27 Oct. 1853, p. 11.
126. 'A Scotchman', letter to *The Times*, 27 Oct. 1853, p. 11.
127. 'Cambro Briton', letter to *The Times*, 27 Oct. 1853, p. 11. In 1853 the Prime Minister was Lord Aberdeen, the Lord Privy Seal the Duke of Argyll, the Chancellor of the Exchequer William Gladstone and the Governor-General of India the Marquis of Dalhousie. For reflections on Welsh–Scottish links and contacts, see the essay on 'Wales and the Scottish Connexion', in K. Robbins, *History, Religion and Identity in Modern Britain* (London: Hambledon, 1993), pp. 271–80.
128. The phrase is that used in 'The Union with England and Scottish Nationality', *North British Review*, 21 (Feb.–Aug. 1854), 89. See also Palmerston's speech on this question in 1858 in *Hansard*, 3rd ser., cols, 2142–46 (15 June 1858).
129. Memorandum by Palmerston on Parliamentary Reform, 1853–54, pp, HA/G/8.
130. R. Finlay, 'Queen Victoria and the Cult of Scottish Monarchy', in E.J. Cowan and R. Finlay (eds), *Scottish History: The Power of the Past* (Edinburgh: Edinburgh University Press, 2002), pp. 209–24.
131. Finlay, *A Partnership for Good?*, pp. 33 and 37 n. 38.
132. Kidd, *Subverting Scotland's Past*, pp. 98–9.
133. C. Kidd, 'Sentiment, Race and Revival: Scottish Identities in the Aftermath of Enlightenment', in L. Brockliss and D. Eastwood (eds), *A Union of Multiple Identities: The British Isles, c.1750–1850* (Manchester: Manchester University Press, 1997), p. 110.
134. E. Evans, 'Englishness and Britishness: National Identities, c.1790–c.1870', in Alexander Grant and Keith J. Stringer (eds), *Uniting the Kingdom? The Making of British History* (London: Routledge, 1995), *passim*.
135. Langford, *Englishness Identified*, pp. 13–14.
136. P. Mandler, 'The Consciousness of Modernity', in Martin Daunton and Bernhard Rieger (eds), *Meanings of Modernity: Britain from the Late-Victorian Era to World War II* (Oxford: Berg, 2001), pp. 119, 125, 126–8.
137. J.P. Parry, 'The Impact of Napoleon III on British Politics, 1851–1880', *Transactions of the Royal Historical Society*, 6th ser., 11 (2001), 170.
138. See L. Colley, *Britons: Forging the Nation, 1707–1837* (New Haven and London: Yale University Press, 1992), *passim*, for a discussion of anti-Catholicism as a feature of a 'forged' British identity.
139. *Daily News*, 29 Dec. 1851.
140. [Unsigned] memo: 'Lord Shaftesbury on Parliamentary Reform, Nov. 1853', PP, HA/G/3. According to this memo: 'All the press, excepting the Daily News, is against it; and every man, Whig, Tory, free-trade or Protectionist that I have met with, is equally hostile.'
141. Palmerston to Russell, 22 Jan. 1854, PP, CAB/60. Lansdowne and Molesworth both wrote to Palmerston expressing their agreement during his argument with Russell, 25 Jan. 1854 and [n.d.] 1854, PP, CAB/60/enc.1 and 2.
142. Palmerston to Russell, 29 Jan. 1854, RP, TNA, PRO 30/22/11C, ff. 110A–112.
143. Palmerston to Aberdeen, 12 Feb. 1854, PP, HA/G/10.
144. Aberdeen to Palmerston, 12 Feb. 1854, PP, HA/G/11.
145. Palmerston to Aberdeen, 2, 3 Mar. 1854; Aberdeen to Palmerston, 2, 4 Mar. 1854, PP, HA/G/12–15.
146. Palmerston to Charles Wood, 8 Dec. 1853, Hickleton Papers, BIY, A4/63/16.
147. Palmerston to Lansdowne, 8 Dec. 1853, Lansdowne Papers, BL, Lans. 3/42, f. 39.
148. Charles Wood, political journal, entry entitled: 'Crisis with Palmerston on the Reform bill, 1853, autumn and winter', Hickleton Papers, BIY, A8/1/2 (see also typescript 'Journals and Memoranda 1846–1867 by Sir Charles Wood afterwards Viscount Halifax', 2 vols., Hickleton Papers, B/Y, A8).

149. Shaftesbury's Diary, 21 Dec. 1853, PP, SHA/PD/6.
150. Grey, journal, 17 Dec. 1853, Grey Papers (3rd Earl) Durham University Library, C3/17.
151. Clarendon to Cowley, 16 Dec. 1853, Maxwell, *Clarendon*, ii, p. 35.
152. For example: *Standard*, 16 Dec. 1853; *Daily News*, 19 Dec. 1853.
153. Prince Albert to Aberdeen, 9 Dec. 1853; memorandum by Prince Albert, 16 Dec. 1853, *LQV*, ii, pp. 568–70.
154. Memorandum by Prince Albert, 26 Feb. 1854, quoted in F. Eyck, *The Prince Consort: a Political Biography of Prince Albert* (London: Chatto & Windus, 1959), p. 233.
155. W. Bagehot, *The English Constitution* [1867], ed. P. Smith (Cambridge: Cambridge University Press, 2001), p. 20.
156. D. Brown, *Palmerston and the Politics of Foreign Policy, 1846–55* (Manchester: Manchester University Press, 2002), p. 154.
157. See, for example, Clarendon to Reeve, 16 Dec. 1853, Clarendon Deposit, Bodleian Library, Oxford, MSS.Clar.dep.c.535, ff. 87–8. See also J.T. Delane to G. [Dasent], 4 Oct. 1853, Delane Papers, Times Newspapers Ltd Archive, News International Record Office, London, T.N.L., 5/39.
158. *Economist*, 1 Oct. 1853; *Standard*, 9 Feb. 1853.
159. 'Cadux' to Palmerston, 12 July 1853, PP, MPC/1554.
160. Palmerston to Clarendon, 31 July 1853, Clarendon Deposit, Bodleian Library, Oxford, MSS.Clar.dep.c.3, ff. 108–9.
161. Palmerston to Clarendon, 26 Aug. 1853, Maxwell, *Clarendon*, ii, p. 18.
162. Bell, ii, p. 90.
163. *Greville Memoirs*, vi, p. 430 (22 June 1853).
164. Palmerston kept a copy of this memorandum: PP, MM/RU/7.
165. M.S. Anderson, *The Eastern Question 1774–1923* (London: Macmillan, 1966), pp. 112–14.
166. Argyll, *Autobiography and Memoirs*, i, p. 441.
167. Ibid., pp. 442–3.
168. Ibid., pp. 445–6.
169. Palmerston to Clarendon, 12 Sept. 1853, PP, GC/CL/523/enc.1.
170. Palmerston to Clarendon, 14 Oct. 1853, PP, GC/CL/1371/1.
171. Argyll, *Autobiography and Memoirs*, i, pp. 455–6.
172. Brown, *Palmerston and the Politics of Foreign Policy*, pp. 162–3.
173. *Greville Memoirs*, vi, p. 430 (22 June 1853).
174. Anderson, *Eastern Question*, pp. 120–5.
175. Palmerston to Aberdeen, 4 July 1853, Aberdeen Papers, BL, Add Ms 43069.
176. Palmerston to Clarendon, 15 July 1853, Clarendon Deposit, Bodleian Library, Oxford, MSS.Clar.dep.c.3, ff. 98–9.
177. Memorandum circulated to members of the Cabinet by Palmerston, 12 July 1853, PP, GC/AB/304.
178. Graham to Clarendon, 14 July 1853, Clarendon Deposit, Bodleian Library, Oxford, MSS.Clar.dep.c.4, ff. 178–9; Graham to Clarendon, 16 Aug. 1853, Maxwell, *Clarendon*, ii, p. 16.
179. Aberdeen to Madame Lieven, 8 Sept. 1853, J.B. Conacher, *The Aberdeen Coalition, 1852–1855* (Cambridge: Cambridge University Press, 1968), pp. 172–3.
180. Aberdeen to Madame Lieven, 8 Sept. 1853, Conacher, *Aberdeen Coalition*, pp. 172–3.
181. Aberdeen to Guizot, 1 Sept. 1853, Papiers Guizot, Archives Nationales, Paris, 42 AP 211/50 [163 MI 51].
182. Aberdeen to Graham, 4 Sept. 1853, Graham Papers, Bodleian Library, Oxford (microfilm), MS Film 124, Bundle 114.
183. Argyll, *Autobiography and Memoirs*, i, p. 459. See also a satirical description of 'A Card Party at the Foreign Office' in the *Press*, 10 Sept. 1853.
184. *Press*, 10 Sept. 1853.
185. Clarendon to Wood, 20 Oct. 1853, Hickleton Papers, BIY, A4/57.
186. Aberdeen to Queen, *LQV*, ii, pp. 551–2.
187. Aberdeen to Graham, 8 Oct. 1853, Aberdeen Papers, BL, Add Ms 43191.
188. Minto, journal, 8 Oct. 1853, Minto Papers, NLS, MS 12000.
189. Aberdeen wrote to Graham on 22 Sept. 1853: 'it seems to me pretty clear that Lord John is determined to go. It is probable that on reflection, he found that the intention of leaving a government with whom he entirely agreed, and a place, which however exceptional, was of his own making, would put him in a ridiculous point of view, and was in fact an untenable position. It was therefore necessary to have some ground of difference; and this Turkish affair presented one, out of which some capital might be made into the bargain. He has made a bad hit this time; but he may be more successful on the next occasion' (Graham Papers, Bodleian Library, Oxford (microfilm), MS Film 124, Bundle 114).

190. Aberdeen to Graham, 3 Oct. 1853, ibid.
191. Memorandum by Prince Albert, 16 Dec. 1853, in J. Prest, *Lord John Russell* (London: Macmillan, 1972), p. 361.
192. Charles Wood, political journal, 19–20 Dec. 1853, Hickleton Papers, BIY, A8/1/2 (see also 'Journals and Memoranda 1846–1867 by Sir Charles Wood', ibid., A8).
193. *Standard*, 19 Dec. 1853.
194. Wood, political journal, 21 Dec. 1853, Hickleton Papers, BIY, A8/1/2 (see also 'Journals and Memoranda 1846–1867 by Sir Charles Wood', ibid., A8).
195. Clarendon to Cowley, 16 Dec. 1853, Maxwell, *Clarendon*, ii, p. 35.
196. Grey, journal, 31 Dec. 1853, Grey Papers (3rd Earl), C3/17; Wood, political journal, 22–23 Dec. 1853, Hickleton Papers, BIY, A8/1/2 (see also 'Journals and Memoranda 1846–1867 by Sir Charles Wood', ibid., A8).
197. Palmerston to Lansdowne, 24 Dec. 1853, PP, GC/LA/112; Palmerston to Aberdeen, 23 Dec. 1853, Aberdeen Papers, BL, Add Ms 43069.
198. Wood, political journal, 24 Dec. 1853, Hickleton Papers, BIY, A8/1/2 (see also 'Journals and Memoranda 1846–1867 by Sir Charles Wood', ibid., A8).
199. Aberdeen to Graham, 10 Dec. 1853, Conacher, *Aberdeen Coalition*, p. 221.
200. C.H. Frewen to Palmerston, 19 Dec. 1853, PP, GC/FR/7.
201. Kingsley Martin, *The Triumph of Lord Palmerston: A Study of Public Opinion in England before the Crimean War* (London: Hutchinson, 1963), p. 160.
202. Prince Albert, 24 Dec. 1853 [?], Bell, ii, p. 101.
203. See, for example, *The Times*, 16 Dec. 1853; *Economist*, 17 Dec. 1853; *Globe*, 16, 17 Dec. 1853; *Morning Chronicle*, 16 Dec. 1853.
204. See, for example, *Morning Post*, 17, 19 Dec. 1853.
205. Ibid., 26 Dec. 1853.
206. *Morning Chronicle*, 26 Dec. 1853.
207. Ibid., 27 Dec. 1853. *Standard*, 23, 26 Dec. 1853.
208. See Eyck, *Prince Consort*, p. 225; R. Williams, *The Contentious Crown: Public Discussion of the British Monarchy in the Reign of Queen Victoria* (Aldershot: Ashgate, 1997), pp. 99–103; Stanley Weintraub, *Albert: Uncrowned King* (London: John Murray, 1997), pp. 296–301.
209. Clarendon to Lady Clarendon, 2 Jan. 1854, in Maxwell, *Clarendon*, ii, p. 37; Conacher, *Aberdeen Coalition*, pp. 245, 261–3.
210. Aberdeen to Clarendon, 12 Feb. 1854, Clarendon Deposit, Bodleian Library, Oxford, Mss.Clar.dep.c.14, f. 12.
211. Russell to Clarendon, 15 Jan. 1854, Clarendon Deposit, Bodleian Library, Oxford, Mss.Clar.dep.c.15, ff. 311–12.
212. Memorandum by Palmerston, 19 Mar. 1854, RP, PRO 30/22/11/C, ff. 267–8.
213. Clarendon to Russell, 7 May 1854, Gooch (ed.), *The Later Correspondence of Lord John Russell, 1840–1878*, ii, p. 164.
214. Sir John Gilbert, *The Coalition Ministry, 1854* (1855), National Portrait Gallery, NPG 1125.
215. Russell to Aberdeen, 5 May 1854, RP, PRO 30/22/11D.
216. Russell to Clarendon, 12 May 1854, Clarendon Deposit, Bodleian Library, Oxford, Mss.Clar.dep.c.15, ff. 485–8; Russell to Clarendon, 12 Oct. 1854, ibid., ff. 679–80.
217. Brown, *Palmerston and the Politics of Foreign Policy*, pp. 192–3.
218. *Standard*, 9 Jan., 13 July, 2 Aug., 25 Sept. 1854.
219. Argyll to Clarendon, 25 Oct. 1854, Clarendon Deposit, Bodleian Library, Oxford, Mss.Clar.dep.c.14, ff. 706–15.
220. For example: *Standard*, 2 Aug. 1854; Disraeli to Ponsonby, 22 Jan. 1854, *BDL*, vi, 2624; Vincent (ed.), *Disraeli, Derby and the Conservative Party*, p. 123 (24 Mar. 1854).
221. Malmesbury, *Memoirs*, i, p. 433 (3, 11 May 1854); for an example of the parliamentary effect of this connection, cf. *Hansard*, 3rd ser., cxxxiii, 142–4 (11 May 1854).
222. See Olive Anderson, *A Liberal State at War: English Politics and Economics during the Crimean War* (London: Macmillan, 1967) for a useful treatment of the war as a test of British institutions (and, by implication, of British 'greatness').
223. Memorandum by Palmerston 'on the measures to be adopted against Russia', 15 June 1854, PP, CAB/65.
224. See articles in: the *Globe*, 10 Mar., 3 Apr., 11, 31 July, 5 Oct., 2 Nov. 1854; *Morning Chronicle*, 7, 11 Jan., 7 Feb., 17 Apr., 27 June, 8, 13, 20 July, 1, 3 Aug., 11 Sept. 1854; *Daily News*, 27 Jan., 24 Mar., 30 Aug., 18 Nov. 1854; *Standard*, 30, 31 Mar. 1854.
225. *Standard*, 1 Aug. 1854.
226. *The Times*, 2 Nov. 1854.

227. Wood, political journal, 11 Apr. 1854, Hickleton Papers, BIY, A8/1/2 (see also 'Journals and Memoranda 1846–1867 by Sir Charles Wood', ibid., A8).
228. Shaftesbury's Diary, 28 June 1854, PP, SHA/PD/6.
229. Quoted (approvingly) in the *Globe*, 10 June 1854.
230. For example: D. Urquhart, *The War of Ignorance: A Prognostication* (London, 1854) and *Recent Events in the East* (London, 1854).
231. Emily Palmerston to Palmerston, 'Tuesday', 1854, PP, BR 30/20.
232. See Conacher, *Aberdeen Coalition*, p. 492.
233. Minto, journal, 30 June 1854, Minto Papers, NLS, MS 12001.
234. *Morning Chronicle*, 7 Dec. 1854. Nevertheless, the Peelites did still see Russell as more important than Palmerston in this government's foreign policy debates, as a letter from Newcastle to Gladstone in Feb. 1855 illustrates in which Newcastle clearly labels the anti-Aberdonian faction within the Cabinet as 'the Russell section' (Newcastle to Gladstone, 5 Feb. 1855, Newcastle Papers, Nottingham University Library, NeC 10851/1/2).
235. G.B. Henderson, *Crimean War Diplomacy* (Glasgow: Glasgow University Press, 1947), p. 34.
236. *Authentic Report of Kossuth's Speeches on the War in the East and the Alliance with Austria, at Sheffield, Jun. 5, and at Nottingham, Jun. 12, 1854. Published by Himself* (London, 1854).
237. See *Daily News*, 17, 18 July 1854.
238. Memorandum by Prince Albert, 10 Apr. 1854, *LQV*, iii, pp. 27–8.
239. Malmesbury, *Memoirs*, i, pp. 435–6.
240. Wood, political journal, 'Question of who should have the War Department, 1854', Hickleton Papers, BIY, A8/1/2 (see also 'Journals and Memoranda 1846–1867 by Sir Charles Wood', ibid., A8).
241. L. Brown, *Victorian News and Newspapers* (Oxford: Oxford University Press, 1985), p. 235.
242. Russell to Aberdeen, 17 Nov. 1854, (copy), Newcastle Papers, Nottingham University Library, NeC 10295/1–2.
243. Aberdeen to Russell, 21 Nov. 1854, Aberdeen Papers, BL, Add Ms 43068.
244. Minute by Palmerston, 2 Dec. 1854 on letter from Clarendon to Palmerston, 30 Nov. 1854, PP, GC/CL/582.
245. Memorandum by Albert, 9 Dec. 1854, *LQV*, ii, p. 76.
246. Clarendon to Lady Clarendon, 5 Dec. 1854, Bodleian Library, Oxford, Mss. Eng.c.2085.
247. Charles Wood, political journal, 5 Dec. 1854, Hickleton Papers, BIY, A8/1/2 (see also 'Journals and Memoranda 1846–1867 by Sir Charles Wood', ibid., A8).
248. Memorandum by the Queen, [3 Feb. 1855?], *LQV*, iii, pp. 118–19.
249. E. Davies to Palmerston, 16 Sept. 1854, enclosing newspaper cutting entitled 'Portrait Gallery of Eminent Living Men. Lord Palmerston, MP', PP, MPC/1561 and enc.1.
250. [Anon.], *Palmerston for Premier! The claims of Lord Palmerston to fill the post of Prime Minister of England considered* (London, 1854), p. 42. For details of the charges made against Palmerston indicated, see esp. pp. 6–37.
251. Washington Wilks, *Palmerston in Three Epochs: A Comparison of Facts with Opinions* (London, 1854), pp. 62–3.
252. J. W. Hudson to Palmerston, 23 Dec. 1854, PP, GC/HU/53. When John Bright visited Manchester at this time, he required a police escort to defend him against protesters angry at his anti-interventionist stance over the war.
253. Abraham Hayward to his sisters, 22 Nov. 1854 and to Sir John Young, 28 Nov. 1854, *A Selection from the Correspondence of Abraham Hayward, QC, from 1832 to 1884*, ed. Henry E. Carlisle, 2 vols. (London: John Murray, 1886), i, pp. 224–5.
254. Palmerston to William Temple, 21 Nov. 1854, PP, GC/TE/354. For details of Palmerston's itinerary, see Palmerston's diary, 17 Nov.–1 Dec. 1854, PP, D/15.
255. See, for example, Louis Napoleon [Napoleon III] to Palmerston, 16 Dec. 1854 and Palmerston's reply, 21 Dec. 1854, PP, GC/NA/96 and GC/NA/96/enc.2.
256. Shaftesbury's Diary, 2 Feb. 1855, PP, SHA/PD/6.
257. Charles Wood, political journal, 31 Jan. 1855, Hickleton Papers, BIY, A8/1/4 (see also 'Journals and Memoranda 1846–1867 by Sir Charles Wood', ibid., A8).
258. Memorandum by Queen Victoria, 1 Feb. 1855, in Henderson, *Crimean War Diplomacy*, p. 81.
259. Palmerston's diary, 6 Feb. 1855, PP, D/16. For Palmerston's account of attempts to form a government by Derby and Russell, as well as his own, see ibid., 31 Jan.–5 Feb. 1855.
260. Queen Victoria to the King of the Belgians, 6 Feb. 1855, *LQV*, iii, p. 128.
261. Palmerston to William Temple, 15 Feb. 1855, PP, GC/TE/356.
262. Charles Wood, political journal, 6 Feb. 1855, Hickleton Papers, BIY, A8/1/4 (see also 'Journals and Memoranda 1846–1867 by Sir Charles Wood', ibid., A8).
263. *Morning Post*, 30 Jan. 1855; *Globe*, 5 Feb. 1855; *Morning Chronicle*, 7 Feb. 1855.
264. Louis Napoleon [Napoleon III] to Palmerston, 16 Feb. 1855, PP, GC/NA/97.
265. *Punch*, 28 (Jan/Feb. 1855), 65.

Chapter 11 The Mortal Minister, 1855-1859

1. 'The Political Alphabet for 1855', Harding Collection, Bodleian Library, Oxford, B.14 (355).
2. Broughton, 'An account of transactions occurring in the two last years but, more particularly, during the last session of Parliament', Broughton Papers, BL, Add Ms 47230, ff. 47–126, here ff. 76–81.
3. Ridley, p. 438. The journalist quoted is Pater Bayne of the *St Paul's Magazine* and is cited by Ridley as an illustration of this developing 'myth'.
4. Stanley, 'Memorandum on the Change of Ministry, January–February 1855', in John Vincent (ed.), *Disraeli, Derby and the Conservative Party: Journals and Memoirs of Edward Henry, Lord Stanley, 1849–1869* (Hassocks: Harvester Press, 1978), pp. 127–34; entries for 30 Jan. and 8 Feb. 1855 (pp. 130, 131, 132, 134).
5. Stanley, 'Memorandum on the Change of Ministry', entry for 2 Feb. 1855, pp. 132–3.
6. *Press*, 7 Jan. 1854.
7. P. Guedalla (ed.), *The Palmerston Papers: Gladstone and Palmerston, being the Correspondence of Lord Palmerston with Mr Gladstone, 1851–1865* (London: Victor Gollancz, 1928), p. 19.
8. Gladstone to Catherine Gladstone, 21 and 22 Dec. 1852, A. Tilney Bassett (ed.), *Gladstone to his Wife* (London: Methuen, 1936), pp. 95–6.
9. *The Prime Minister's Papers: W.E. Gladstone III: Autobiographical Memoranda, 1845–1866*, ed. John Brooke and Mary Sorensen (London: HMSO, 1978), p. 22 (10 July 1846).
10. Ibid., pp. 155–6 (26 Jan. 1855).
11. Ibid., pp. 156–7 (31 Jan. 1855).
12. Ibid., pp. 159–60 (2 Feb. 1855).
13. Ibid., p. 163 (3 Feb. 1855).
14. Ibid., p. 166 (4 Feb. 1855).
15. Ibid., p. 167 (4 Feb. 1855).
16. Ibid., p. 172 (5 Feb. 1855).
17. Gladstone to Palmerston, 6 Feb. 1855, PP, GC/GL/10.
18. Angus Hawkins, *Parliament, Party and the Art of Politics in Britain, 1855–59* (London: Macmillan, 1987), pp. 2, 20.
19. *Punch*, 3 Feb. 1855 ('The dirty doorstep'). This cartoon shows Palmerston as a boy, dustpan and brush in hand, ready to sweep the doorstep of 'Aberdeen, Newcastle, & Co.', which is littered with 'blunders', 'routine', 'precedent', 'incapacity', 'higgledy piggledy', 'delay', 'twaddle' and 'disorder'. 'P-lm-rst-n (an active lad)', says: 'Well! This is the greatest mess I ever saw at anybody's door.' 'Little Jack R-ss-ll', also standing on the doorstep, replies: 'Ah! I lived there once – but I was obliged to leave – it was such a very irregular family.'
20. Broughton, 'An account of transactions occurring in the two last years . . .', Broughton Papers, BL, Add Ms 47230, ff. 47–126, here ff. 89–92.
21. Palmerston to Louis Napoleon (Napoleon III), 8 Feb. 1855, PP, GC/NA/100.
22. *W.E. Gladstone III: Autobiographical Memoranda, 1845–1866*, p. 170 (5 Feb. 1855).
23. Ibid., p. 176 (10 Feb. 1855).
24. Ibid., pp. 180–2 (19 Feb. 1855).
25. Richard Monckton Milnes to William Gladstone, 12 Feb. 1855, in T. Wemyss Reid, *The Life, Letters and Friendships of Richard Monckton Milnes, first Lord Houghton*, 2 vols. (London: Cassell, 1891), i, pp. 501–2.
26. Southgate, p. 360.
27. *W.E. Gladstone III: Autobiographical Memoranda, 1845–1866*, p. 192 (28 Feb. 1855).
28. Ibid., p. 193 (Feb. 1855).
29. Ibid., p. 194 (3 Mar. 1855).
30. Disraeli to Frances Anne, Marchioness of Londonderry, 25 Feb. 1855, *Letters from Benjamin Disraeli to Frances Anne Marchioness of Londonderry, 1837–1861*, ed. the Marchioness of Londonderry (London: Macmillan, 1938), p. 147.
31. Broughton, 'An account of transactions occurring in the two last years . . .', Broughton Papers, BL, Add Ms 47230, ff. 47–126, here ff. 89–92.
32. Palmerston to William Temple, 9 Mar. 1855, PP, GC/TE/357.
33. Palmerston's diary, 3 Feb. 1855, PP, D/16: in a discussion of possible ministerial arrangements with Russell, there had been some talk of 'Baines to be in Cabinet as representing middle classes'.
34. Disraeli to Frances Anne, Marchioness of Londonderry, 25 Feb. 1855, *Letters from Benjamin Disraeli*, pp. 147–8.
35. G.C. Lewis to Palmerston, 16 Mar. 1855, PP, GC/LE/16.
36. Cf. the Duke of Newcastle's view that this was a crude scheme 'to resuscitate Whiggery pur et simple': Newcastle to Granville, 16 Apr. 1855, Granville Papers (2nd Earl), TNA, PRO 30/29/18/4, ff. 47–50.

37. Southgate, pp. 362-3.
38. Palmerston to William Temple, 15 Feb. 1855, Ashley, ii, p. 78.
39. Disraeli to Frances Anne, Marchioness of Londonderry, 2 Feb. 1855, W.F. Moneypenny and G.E. Buckle, *The Life of Benjamin Disraeli, Earl of Beaconsfield*, 2 vols. (rev. edn, London: John Murray, 1929), i, p. 1383.
40. Lady Cowper to Francis Cowper, 28 Feb. 1855, *Earl Cowper, K.G. A Memoir by his Wife* (Printed for private circulation, 1913), pp. 49-50.
41. Southgate, p. 375.
42. Palmerston to Granville, 15 Apr. 1855, Granville Papers (2nd Earl), TNA, PRO 30/29/18/3, ff. 23-4.
43. In October he was still 'disposing of the business of the Colonial Office till a new Secy of State is appointed' (Palmerston to William Temple, 24 Oct. 1855, PP, GC/TE/361).
44. J.R. Vincent, 'The Parliamentary Dimension of the Crimean War', *Transactions of the Royal Historical Society*, 5th ser., 31 (1981), 38-9.
45. Cowper to Francis Cowper, 30 Apr. 1855, *Earl Cowper, K.G.*, p. 66.
46. Southgate, p. 375.
47. Vincent, 'Parliamentary Dimension', 39.
48. Palmerston to Russell, 28 Mar. 1855, Ashley, ii, pp. 84-5.
49. Palmerston to Emily Palmerston, 11 July 1855, PP, BR23AA/1/13.
50. Vincent, 'Parliamentary Dimension'.
51. Palmerston to Emily Palmerston, 11 July 1855, PP, BR23AA/1/13.
52. Palmerston's diary, 15 July 1855, PP, D/16.
53. Palmerston to Charles Wood, 16 July 1855, Hickleton Papers, BIY, A4/63/37-37A.
54. For example: Southgate, pp. 372-4.
55. See, for example, for a detailed study of this issue: Olive Anderson, *A Liberal State at War: English Politics and Economics during the Crimean War* (London: Macmillan, 1967).
56. Memorandum by Palmerston, 20 Jan. 1855, PP, BR22(i)/1/96.
57. G.C. Lewis to Palmerston, 21 Feb. 1855, PP, GC/LE/15.
58. Ridley, p. 439.
59. Memo [by Palmerston] of measures taken to establish a better order of things in the Crimea, 1855, PP, MM/RU/30.
60. See, for example, note in Palmerston's hand 'from Camp before Sebastopol, 10 Jany 1856', PP, BR22(i)/1/98.
61. Palmerston to William Temple, 25 Aug. 1855, Ashley, ii, p. 100.
62. Ridley, p. 438.
63. *The Times*, 15 Sept. 1855.
64. Ibid., 6 Oct. 1855.
65. Palmerston, House of Commons, 19 Feb. 1855 (quoted Ridley, p. 441).
66. Steele, pp. 52-3
67. G.C. Lewis to Palmerston, 18 Sept. 1855, PP, GC/LE/35.
68. G.C. Lewis to Palmerston, 5 Oct. 1855, PP, GC/LE/42.
69. Palmerston to G.C. Lewis, 7 Oct. 1855, PP, GC/LE 177.
70. Thomas Milner Gibson to John Bright, 14 Nov. 1855, Bright Papers, BL, Add Ms 43388, ff. 56-7.
71. Palmerston to Clarendon, 29 Feb. 1856, Ridley, p. 451.
72. For an account of Cabinet discussions, see George Cornewall Lewis, diary, esp. entries for 23, 29 Jan. 1856, Harpton Court Ms, NLW, Ms 3570.
73. Thomas Milner Gibson to John Bright, 20 Jan. 1856, Bright Papers, BL, Add Ms 43388, ff. 58-9.
74. Palmerston to Emily Palmerston, 24 Jan. 1856, PP, BR23AA/1/16.
75. Emily Palmerston to Palmerston, Jan. 1856, Lamb Papers, BL, Add Ms 45554, ff. 111-12.
76. G.C. Lewis, diary, 31 Jan. 1856, Harpton Court Ms, NLW, Ms 3570.
77. Clarendon to Cowley, Mar. 1856, *The Paris Embassy during the Second Empire. Selections from the Papers of Henry Richard Charles Wellesley, 1st Earl Cowley, Ambassador at Paris, 1852-1867*, ed. F.A. Wellesley (London: Thornton Butterworth, 1928), p. 95.
78. G.C. Lewis, diary, 28 Apr., 5 May 1856, Harpton Court Ms, NLW, Ms 3570.
79. Memo by Palmerston of a meeting with Count Chreptovitch, 12 Aug. 1856, PP, MM/RU/35.
80. *The Times*, 8 Nov. 1856.
81. Ibid., 7 Nov. 1856.
82. John Wong argues that this episode should be treated as a world war; see J.Y. Wong, *Deadly Dreams: Opium, Imperialism, and the Arrow War (1856-1860) in China* (Cambridge: Cambridge University Press, 1998), p. 1 *et seq.*
83. This discussion draws heavily on Wong's account in *Deadly Dreams*, esp. pp. 43-66. For a transcript of Parkes's letter to Yeh of 8 Oct. 1856, see p. 47. For Wong's assessment of Parkes's and Bowring's personal roles see also chs 3 and 4.

84. Palmerston to Laurence Sulivan, 20 Jan. 1857, *PSL*, pp. 313–14.

85. Derby to Malmesbury, 15 Dec. 1856, Southgate, p. 419.

86. J.P. Parry, 'Disraeli and England', *Historical Journal*, 43, 3 (2000), 720–1.

87. This discussion of the secret treaty of 1854 and subsequent parliamentary debate of 1857 draws on the chapter 'Disraeli and Palmerston in 1857, or, the Dangers of Explanations in Parliament', in G.B. Henderson, *Crimean War Diplomacy and Other Historical Essays* (Glasgow, 1947), pp. 249–66. Quotations are taken specifically from pp. 249 [terms of treaty], 253 [Napoleon], 254 [Earle's character], 255 ['villainy' and terms of treaty], 263 [Greville].

88. Southgate, p. 420.

89. *W.E. Gladstone III: Autobiographical Memoranda, 1845–1866*, pp. 213–14 (4 Feb. 1857).

90. Gladstone to Sidney Herbert, 22 Mar. 1857, J. Morley, *The Life of William Ewart Gladstone*, 3 vols. (London: Macmillan, 1903), i, p. 566.

91. Quoted in Southgate, p. 421.

92. Wong, *Deadly Dreams*, pp. 153–6.

93. *The Times*, 2 Jan. 1856.

94. Ibid., 8 Jan. 1857.

95. *Morning Post*, 2, 5 Jan., 3 Feb. 1857, Wong, *Deadly Dreams*, pp. 157–8.

96. *Morning Chronicle*, 8 Jan. 1857; *Daily News*, 2, 9 Jan. 1857, Wong, *Deadly Dreams*, pp. 159–60.

97. Wong, *Deadly Dreams*, pp. 161–5.

98. Ridley, p. 460.

99. For a recent analysis of this episode, see Glenn Melancon, *Britain's China Policy and the Opium Crisis: Balancing Drugs, Violence and National Honour, 1833–1840* (Aldershot: Ashgate, 2003).

100. Quoted in Southgate, p. 422.

101. *Hansard*, 3rd ser., cxliv, 1812 *et seq.* (3 Mar. 1857); (Wong, pp. 201–2).

102. *Greville Memoirs*, vii, p. 276 (4 Mar. 1857); Hawkins, *Parliament, Party and the Art of Politics*, p. 61.

103. *Hansard*, 3rd ser., cxliv, 1745–52 (3 Mar. 1857).

104. Ibid., cxliv, 1840 (3 Mar. 1857).

105. G.C. Lewis, diary, 26, 27 Feb. 1857, Harpton Court Ms, NLW, Ms 3571.

106. G.C. Lewis, diary, 5 Mar. 1857, ibid.

107. Aberdeen to Guizot, 12 Mar. 1857, Papiers Guizot, Archives Nationales, Paris, 42 AP 211/63 [163 MI 51].

108. George Mifflin Dallas to J.P. Hutchinson, 16 Mar. 1857, *A series of letters from London written during the years 1856, '57, '58, '59 and '60. By George Mifflin Dallas, then minister of the United States at the British court*, ed. Julia Dallas, 2 vols. (Philadelphia: J.B. Lippincott, 1869), i, pp. 145–6.

109. G.C. Lewis, diary, 19 Mar. 1857, Harpton Court Ms, NLW, Ms 3571.

110. *The Times*, 21 Mar. 1857.

111. Ibid., 24 Mar. 1857.

112. Disraeli's address to the Electors of Buckingham, 17 Mar. 1857, *BDL*, vii, 2916.

113. Ridley, p. 470.

114. Disraeli to Sarah Brydges Willyams, 23 Mar. 1857, *BDL*, vii, 2918.

115. Quoted in Hawkins, *Parliament, Party and the Art of Politics*, p. 63.

116. Ibid., p. 64.

117. Disraeli to Sarah Disraeli, 13 Apr. 1857, *BDL*, vii, 2928.

118. Disraeli to Sir William Jolliffe, 29 Apr. 1857, ibid., 2935.

119. Ashley, ii, pp. 135–6.

120. Granville to Charles Canning, 8 Apr. 1857, Southgate, pp. 428–9.

121. George Douglas Campbell, Eighth Duke of Argyll, *Autobiography and Memoirs*, ed. Dowager Duchess of Argyll, 2 vols. (London: John Murray, 1906), ii, p. 74; Wong, *Deadly Dreams*, p. 250.

122. Ashley, ii, pp. 135–6; Southgate, pp. 428–9; Ridley, pp. 469–70.

123. Cobden to Henry Richard, 7 March 1857, Cobden Papers, BL, Add Ms 43658, ff. 269–71.

124. Richard Cobden to Joseph Sturge, 4 Mar. 1857, Sturge Papers, BL, Add Ms 43722, ff. 209–10.

125. *Punch*, 14 Mar. 1857; Wong, *Deadly Dreams*, p. 238.

126. See, for example, Richard Cobden to Henry Richard, 3, 7, 11, 15 Jan., 15 Feb. 1857, Cobden Papers, BL, Add Ms 43658, ff. 229–30, 231–2, 233–4, 241–2, 264–6.

127. Richard Cobden to Joseph Sturge, 16 Jan. 1857, BL, Add Ms 43722, ff. 202–3.

128. On this episode, Wong, *Deadly Dreams*, esp. pp. 153–73, 235–46.

129. Malmesbury (3rd Earl) to Palmerston, 25 Mar. 1857 and Palmerston's reply of the same date, PP, GC/MA/193 and enc.1.

130. Douglas M. Peers, '"He has a jolly way of looking at disasters": Palmerston and India in the mid-Nineteenth Century', in David Brown and Miles Taylor (eds), *Palmerston Studies II* (Southampton: Hartley Institute, 2007), p. 121; on the theme of Palmerston's lack of an 'imperial imagination', see ibid., pp. 119–43.

131. Memo by Palmerston on the role of the Governor-General of India, n.d., PP, MM/IN/4.
132. Peers, 'Palmerston and India', p. 124.
133. *The Times*, 27, 29 June 1857. See also: Ridley, pp. 473–4; Angus Hawkins, 'British Parliamentary Party Alignment and the Indian Issue, 1857–1858', *Journal of British Studies*, 23:2 (1984), 79–80.
134. Palmerston to Emily Palmerston, 29 Aug. 1857, PP, BR23AA/1/21.
135. G.C. Lewis to Palmerston, 13 Oct. 1857, PP, GC/LE/101.
136. G.C. Lewis, diary, 12 Oct. 1857, Harpton Court Ms, NLW, Ms 3572.
137. G.C. Lewis to Palmerston, 28 Oct., 3 Nov. 1857, PP, GC/LE/102 and 103.
138. G.C. Lewis to Palmerston, 8, 12 Nov. 1857, PP, GC/LE/104 and 105.
139. G.C. Lewis, diary, 2 Oct. 1857, Harpton Court Ms, NLW, Ms 3572.
140. G.C. Lewis, diary, 1–2 Nov. 1857, ibid.
141. G.C. Lewis, diary, 25 Nov. 1857, ibid.
142. Palmerston to Emily Palmerston, 15 Dec. 1857, PP, BR23AA/1/22.
143. Memorandum in Palmerston's hand, 'Heads of proposed arrangement for the future government of India, 17 Dec. 1857', PP, CAB/88B.
144. G.C. Lewis, diary, 21 Dec. 1857, Harpton Court Ms, NLW, Ms 3572.
145. See G.C. Lewis to Palmerston, 27 Dec. 1857, PP, GC/LE/107.
146. G.C. Lewis to Palmerston, 24 Jan. 1858, PP, GC/LE/110.
147. Palmerston to G.C. Lewis, 24 Jan. 1858, PP, GC/LE/201.
148. G.C. Lewis, diary, 18 Feb. 1858, Harpton Court Ms, NLW, Ms 3572.
149. Palmerston's diary, 18 Feb. 1858, PP, D/18.
150. Ashley, ii, pp. 142–3.
151. Memo by Palmerston on Conspiracy to Murder Bill, 23 Jan. 1858, PP, CAB/89.
152. Memoranda by Clarendon, 21 Jan. 1858 and Granville, n.d. [Jan. 1858], PP, CAB/90 and 101.
153. Memoranda by Panmure, 22 Jan. 1858, Clanricarde, n.d. [Jan. 1858], Stanley of Alderley, n.d. [Jan. 1858], and Argyll, n.d. [Jan. 1858], PP, CAB/92, 93, 94 and 99. Quotations from Stanley of Alderley.
154. Memo by G.C. Lewis, 22 Jan. 1858, PP, CAB/91.
155. Memo by Labouchere, n.d. [Jan. 1858], PP, CAB/95.
156. Memoranda by G.C. Lewis, 22 Jan. 1858, Labouchere, n.d. [Jan. 1858], Cranworth, n.d. [Jan. 1858], 'W.M.', n.d. [Jan. 1858], PP, CAB/91, 95, 97 and 100. In a similar vein, also memoranda by R. Vernon Smith, n.d. [Jan. 1858] and George Grey, n.d. [Jan. 1858], PP, CAB/96 and 98.
157. G.C. Lewis, diary, 29 Jan. 1858, Harpton Court Ms, NLW, Ms 3572.
158. G.C. Lewis, diary, 1, 2 Feb. 1858, ibid.
159. Ashley, ii, pp. 144–5.
160. G.C. Lewis, diary, 19 Feb. 1858, Harpton Court Ms, NLW, Ms 3572. On the earlier stages of the debate see also ibid., 9 Feb. 1858.
161. Palmerston's diary, 19 Feb. 1858, PP, D/18.
162. Palmerston's diary, 20 Feb. 1858, PP, D/18; Palmerston to Emily Palmerston, 20 Feb. 1858, PP, BR23AA/1/25; G.C. Lewis, diary, 20 Feb. 1858, Harpton Court Ms, NLW, Ms 3572.
163. G.C. Lewis, diary, 21, 26 Feb. 1858, Harpton Court Ms, NLW, Ms 3572.
164. Palmerston to Emily Palmerston, 20 Feb. 1858, PP, BR23AA/1/24.
165. Aberdeen to Guizot, 28 Feb. 1858, Papiers Guizot, Archives Nationales, Paris, 42 AP 211/68 [163 MI 51].
166. Mike Sampson, *A History of Tiverton* (Tiverton: Tiverton War Memorial Trust, 2004), p. 247.
167. G.C. Lewis, diary, 24 Feb. 1858, Harpton Court Ms, NLW, Ms 3572.
168. Palmerston's diary, 1857 (notes at the end of the journal), PP, D/17.
169. Lady Jocelyn to Palmerston, 28 Aug. 1857, Lamb Papers, BL, Add Ms 45548, ff. 177–8.
170. Palmerston to Laurence Sulivan, 22, 29 July, 2, 4, 9, 24 Aug. 1856, *PSL*, pp. 311–12.
171. Palmerston to Emily Palmerston, 24 Aug. 1856, PP, BR23AA/1/18.
172. R.F. Burnett to Palmerston, 4 Sept. 1856, PP, BR31/1; Frederick Nicholl to Palmerston, 4 Nov. 1856, PP, BR31/2; Palmerston to Elizabeth Sulivan (daughter of Laurence; niece of Palmerston), 29 Sept. 1856, *PSL*, p. 313 and n. 1.
173. James C. Sharp to Palmerston, 21 Oct. 1858, PP, BR207/1/1; Palmerston's diary, 25 Oct. 1858, PP, D/18; James Rawlines [?Rawlence] to Palmerston, 14 June 1859, PP, BR207/1/1.
174. Palmerston to Emily Palmerston, 5 Aug. 1858, PP, BR23AA/1/27.
175. Palmerston to Emily Palmerston, 5 Aug. 1858, PP, BR23AA/1/28.
176. Palmerston's diary, 7 Aug. 1858, PP, D/18.
177. Palmerston to Emily Palmerston, 8 Aug. 1858, PP, BR23AA/1/31.
178. The following figures, detailing the dividends received by Palmerston from the Welsh Slate Company between Apr. 1857 and Dec. 1864, are derived from notes made by Palmerston in his diaries for 1857–64, PP, D/17–24.

		1	2	3	4	5	Total
1857	Yield per share (£)	80	100	120			
	Income on 24 shares (£)	1,920	2,400	2,880			7,200
1858	Yield per share (£)	60	60	60	130	130	
	Income on 24 shares (£)	1,440	1,440	1,440	3,120	3,120	10,560
1859	Yield per share (£)	70	90	110	110		
	Income on 24 shares (£)	1,680	2,160	2,640	2,640		9,120
1860	Yield per share (£)	100	200	150	110		
	Income on 24 shares (£)	2,400	4,800	3,600	2,640		13,440
1861	Yield per share (£)	70	100	120	100	100	
	Income on 24 shares (£)	1,680	2,400	2,880	2,400	2,400	11,760
1862	Yield per share (£)	100	100	100			
	Income on 24 shares (£)	2,400	2,400	2,400			7,200
1863	Yield per share (£)	100	100	100	100		
	Income on 24 shares (£)	2,400	2,400	2,400	2,400		9,600
1864	Yield per share (£)	100	100	100	100		
	Income on 24 shares (£)	2,400	2,400	2,400	2,400		9,600

Payments received: 1857 (Apr., July, Oct.); 1858 (Jan., Apr., July, Oct., Dec.); 1859 (Apr., June, Aug., Dec.); 1860 (Apr., July, Aug., Nov.); 1861 (Feb., May, July, Aug., Dec.): 1862 (June, Aug., Nov.); 1863 (Mar., Apr., Aug., Nov.); 1864 (May, July, Sept., Dec.).

179. Palmerston to Emily Palmerston, 14 Aug. 1858, PP, BR23AA/1/35.
180. See, for example, his comments to G.C. Lewis in March 1858 (PP, GC/LE/202): 'I doubt whether the Irish generally would like to lose the local court which serves to gratify the vanity of many who could not come to St James's. Scotland is not quite an example for Ireland, it is so much smaller a country. Moreover Scotland is homogenous [sic] while Ireland is split into Catholic & Protestant, north & south & these divisions give rise to a great many small questions to which there is nothing similar in Scotland.'
181. Palmerston to G.C. Lewis, 26 Dec. 1859, PP, GC/LE/212.
182. For example: Southgate, p. 408.
183. Shaftesbury to Evelyn Ashley, 28 Feb. 1855, Edwin Hodder, *The Life and Work of the Seventh Earl of Shaftesbury*, 3 vols. (London: Cassell, 1886), ii, p. 505.
184. Shaftesbury to Edward Baines, 12 May 1856, Edward Baines Papers, WYAS, Leeds, WYL 383/52/2.
185. John Wolffe, 'Lord Palmerston and Religion: A Reappraisal', *EHR*, 120: 488 (2005), 936.
186. For example: Ridley, pp. 499–501; Nigel Scotland, *'Good and Proper Men': Lord Palmerston and the Bench of Bishops* (Cambridge: James Clarke, 2000), esp. ch. 2.
187. Hodder, *Shaftesbury*, iii, p. 197.
188. Wolffe, 'Lord Palmerston and Religion', 929.
189. Steele, p. 167.
190. Palmerston, House of Commons, 23 Mar. 1855, Wolffe, 'Lord Palmerston and Religion', 917.
191. Palmerston, House of Commons, 15 Apr. 1856, ibid., 919.
192. Hodder, *Shaftesbury*, iii, pp. 194–5. Palmerston made the following appointments during this period: (1) English Archbishops. Canterbury: Longley (1862); York: Longley (1860), Thomson (1862). (2) English Bishops. London: Tait (1856); Durham: Longley (1856), Villiers (1860), Baring (1861); Carlisle: Villiers (1856), Waldegrave (1860); Gloucester and Bristol: Baring (1856), Thomson (1861), Ellicott (1861); Ripon: Bickersteth (1856); Norwich: Pelham (1857); Rochester: Wigram (1860); Worcester: Philpott (1860); Ely: Harold Browne (1864); Peterborough: Jeune (1864); Chester: Jacobson (1865). (3) Irish Archbishops. Armagh: Beresford (1862); Dublin: Trench (1863). (4) Irish Bishops: Cork: Fitzgerald (1857); Gregg (1862); Killaloe: Fitzgerald (1862); Kilmore: Verschoyle (1862). (5) English Deans. Christ Church, Oxford: Liddell (1855); Westminster: Trench (1857), Stanley (1863); Canterbury: Alford (1857); Carlisle: Close (1856); Ripon: Garnier (1859); Goode (1860); Lincoln: Garnier (1860), Jeune (1864), Jeremie (1864); Gloucester: Henry Law (1862); Exeter: Ellicott (1861); Midleton (1862).
193. Hodder, *Shaftesbury*, iii, p. 192.
194. Shaftesbury to Evelyn Ashley, 6 Jan. 1876, Ashley, ii, p. 319.
195. Wolffe, 'Lord Palmerston and Religion', 920–1.
196. For examples of Shaftesbury's suggestions for Church appointments, see the memoranda for 1856 collected in PP, HA/H/4–7.
197. The phrases are Hodder's: *Shaftesbury*, iii, p. 198.
198. Palmerston to Prince Albert, 3 Aug. 1856, Wolffe 'Lord Palmerston and Religion', 921–2.

199. Shaftesbury to Palmerston, 20 Dec. 1856, PP, GC/SH/34.
200. Shaftesbury to Palmerston, 18 Feb. 1857, PP, GC/SH/35.
201. Wolffe 'Lord Palmerston and Religion', 930, also 924–5.
202. Shaftesbury's diary, 1 Nov. 1865, Hodder, *Shaftesbury*, iii, p. 196; Steele, p. 171.
203. Steele, p. 172; Wolffe, 'Lord Palmerston and Religion', 918.
204. Wolffe, 'Lord Palmerston and Religion', 933–4.
205. Palmerston to Queen Victoria, Apr. 1864, *LQV II*, i, pp. 178–9.
206. *The Times*, 24 Mar. 1857.
207. Ridley, pp. 471–3.
208. Charles Dickens, *Little Dorritt* (1857), esp. book i, ch. 10.
209. See, for example, Palmerston's comments on possible candidates for peerages in 1856. Of those he rejected, Palmerston singled out Lord Edward Howard MP as being 'not rich enough' and Charles Townley as 'not distinguished enough', while Sir Edward Tiering was turned down on account of his being 'a ruined man'. Memo on 'Candidates for Peerage, 1856', PP, HA/H/8.
210. For a very useful summary of these issues, see J. Parry, *The Rise and Fall of Liberal Government in Victorian Britain* (New Haven and London: Yale University Press, 1993), pp. 180–3.
211. W.L. Burn, *The Age of Equipoise: A Study of the mid-Victorian Generation* (London: George Allen & Unwin, 1964), p. 18.
212. For a revisionist assessment of Palmerston as a democratic reformer, see Steele.
213. *The Times*, 7 Nov. 1856.
214. Ibid., 8 Nov. 1856.
215. See, for example, Palmerston's comments on a discussion of universal suffrage with Napoleon III while visiting Paris in Nov. 1858 (Palmerston's diary, 16 Nov. 1858, PP, D/18).
216. Palmerston to Charles Wood, 7 May 1857, Hickleton Papers, BIY, A4/63/80.
217. Nassau Senior to George Bancroft, 19 Jan. 1859, Nassau Senior Ms, NLW, Ms C/85.
218. For example, Hawkins, *Parliament, Party and the Art of Politics*, ch. 6.
219. W.E. Gladstone to John Bright, 22 Feb. 1858, Bright Papers, BL, Add Ms 43385, ff. 5–6.
220. G.C. Lewis, diary, 22–27 Oct. 1858, Harpton Court Ms, NLW, Ms 3572.
221. Charles Wood to Palmerston, 26 Dec. 1858, Hickleton Papers, BIY, A4/63/97–9.
222. Russell to James Graham, 16 Jan. 1858, Russell Papers, TNA, PRO 30/22/13E, ff. 175–7.
223. G.C. Lewis, diary, 6, 7 Mar. 1858, Harpton Court Ms, NLW, Ms 3572; Palmerston's diary, 6 Mar. 1858, PP, D/18. Quotations from Lewis's diary.
224. G.C. Lewis, diary, 10 Mar. 1858, Harpton Court Ms, NLW, Ms 3572.
225. Palmerston's diary, 25, 31 Mar. 1858, PP, D/18. The dinner at the Duchess of Sutherland's was on 31 Mar.; on the 25th Palmerston and Russell had spoken in the House of Commons.
226. Palmerston to G.C. Lewis, 30 Mar. 1858, PP, GC/LE/203.
227. Palmerston to Charles Wood, 31 Mar. 1858, Hickleton Papers, BIY, A4/63/91–2.
228. G.C. Lewis, diary, 13 Apr. 1858, Harpton Court Ms, NLW, Ms 3572. See also ibid., 31 Mar, 5–8 Apr. 1858.
229. Thomas Milner Gibson to John Bright, 1 Apr. 1858, Bright Papers, BL, Add Ms 43388, ff. 75–6.
230. Thomas Erskine Perry to G.C. Lewis, 18 Apr. 1858, Harpton Court Ms, NLW, Ms C/2198.
231. G.C. Lewis to Palmerston, 5 Apr. 1858, PP, GC/LE/111.
232. Palmerston to G.C. Lewis, 16 Apr. 1858, PP, GC/LE/206.
233. Charles Wood to Palmerston, 2 Apr. 1858, Hickleton Papers, BIY, A4/63/93–4.
234. Thomas Milner Gibson to John Bright, 20 May 1858, Bright Papers, BL, Add Ms 43388, ff. 80–1.
235. Charles Wood to Palmerston, 23 May 1858, Hickleton Papers, BIY, A4/63/96.
236. Nassau Senior to Tocqueville, 2 Aug. [1858], Nassau Senior Papers, NLW, Ms C/441.
237. See G.C. Lewis, diary, 21 May, 2 July 1858, Harpton Court Ms, NLW, Ms 3572.
238. G.C. Lewis, diary, 31 July–2 Aug. 1858, ibid.
239. G.C. Lewis, diary, 15 Nov., 7 Dec. 1858 (and cf. 17, 23 July), ibid.
240. G.C. Lewis, diary, 22–27 Jan. 1859, Harpton Court Ms, NLW, Ms 3573.
241. See, for example, letters collected in the Russell Papers, TNA, PRO 30/22/13G.
242. G.C. Lewis, diary, 3, 4 Mar. 1859, Harpton Court Ms, NLW, Ms 3573; Palmerston's diary, 7 Mar. 1859, PP, D/19.
243. G.C. Lewis, diary, 25 Mar. 1859, Harpton Court Ms, NLW, Ms 3573.
244. Emily Palmerston to Goderich, 19 Mar. 1859, Ripon Papers, BL, Add Ms 43512, ff. 80–3.
245. Palmerston's diary, 2 Apr. 1859, PP, D/19; Aberdeen to Guizot, 23 Apr. 1859, Papiers Guizot, Archives Nationales, Paris, 42 AP 211/77 [163 MI 51].
246. Charles Wood to Palmerston, 4 May 1859, Hickleton Papers, BIY, A4/63/107–9.
247. Memo in Palmerston's hand, 7 May 1859, ibid., A4/63/111.
248. Thomas Erskine Perry to G.C. Lewis, 9 May 1859, Harpton Court Ms, NLW, Ms C/2200.
249. G.C. Lewis, diary, 15, 20, 22 May 1859, ibid., Ms 3573.

NOTES to pp. 428-38 549

250. Palmerston's diary, 29 May, 2 June 1859, PP, D/19; Palmerston to Granville, 29 May 1859, Granville Papers (2nd Earl), TNA, PRO 30/29/18/15, ff. 9–10; G.C. Lewis, diary, 30 May 1859, Harpton Court Ms, NLW, Ms 3573.

251. G.C. Lewis, diary, 6 June 1859, Harpton Court Ms, NLW, Ms 3573.

252. *The Times*, 7 June 1859; G.C. Lewis, diary, 6 June 1859, Harpton Court Ms, NLW, Ms 3573.

253. Palmerston's diary, 6 June 1859, PP, D/19.

254. Ashley, ii, pp. 154–7 (including Palmerston to Queen Victoria, 11 June 1859, pp. 155–6).

255. Clarendon to Granville, Granville Papers (2nd Earl), TNA, PRO 30/29/18/15, ff. 13–16. Granville's unsuccessful attempt to form a government is outlined in the following correspondence preserved among his papers (ibid., ff. 17–32): Granville to Russell, 11 June, G.C. Lewis to Granville, 'Sunday' [12 June], George Grey to Granville, 12 June, Granville to Russell, 12 June, Russell to Granville, 12 June, Granville to Palmerston and Russell, 26 June 1859.

256. Palmerston to the electors of Tiverton, 20 June 1859, PP, BR23/1/21.

Chapter 12 The Prime Minister, 1859–1865

1. PP, BR195/106. The verse is undated but is most likely to date from Apr. 1862. The first Romsey Exhibition was held on 23 Apr. 1862 (see *The Times*, 24 Apr. 1862). In the first verse of the 'Ode', omitted above, are the lines: 'Guide and Guardian of our Queen, / Comfort in her widow'd hour'; Prince Albert died on 14 Dec. 1861.

2. Ridley, p. 485.

3. Palmerston to Argyll, 20 Aug. 1858, Ridley, p. 483.

4. Disraeli to Palmerston, 3 May 1859, *BDL*, vii, 3343.

5. Disraeli to Derby, 10 June 1859, ibid., 3366.

6. Bright's warning to Palmerston had been reported to Disraeli who repeated it in a letter to Derby, Sunday [12 June 1859], ibid., 3369.

7. Disraeli to Sarah Brydges Willyams, 16 June 1859, ibid., 3376.

8. Palmerston to G.C. Lewis, 13 June 1859 (two letters), PP, GC/LE/209 and 210.

9. John Morley, *The Life of William Ewart Gladstone* 3 vols. (London: Macmillan, 1903), i, p. 585 (Memo by Gladstone submitted to Aberdeen and Sir James Graham, 22 May 1858).

10. H.C.G. Matthew, *Gladstone, 1809–1898* (Oxford: Oxford University Press, 1999), pp. 104–5.

11. Quoted ibid., p. 105.

12. Gladstone to Sir William Heathcote, 16 June 1859, Morley, *Gladstone*, i, p. 628.

13. Southgate, p. 460.

14. Gladstone to Sir John Acton, 1864 (explaining his decision to join the government 1859), Morley, *Gladstone*, i, p. 628.

15. George Shee to Palmerston, 17 June 1859, Shee Papers, BL, Add Ms 60342, ff. 73–4; Palmerston to George Shee, 23 June 1859, Shee Papers, BL, Add Ms 60341, f. 245.

16. Palmerston to Richard Cobden, 27 June 1859, Ridley, p. 490.

17. Shaftesbury to Palmerston, 30 June 1859, PP, GC/SH/38.

18. Richard Cobden to Catherine Cobden, 30 June 1859, Cobden Papers, WSRO, Add Ms 6017, f. L223.

19. As reported by Richard Cobden to W. Sale, 4[?] July 1859, Cobden Papers, BL, Add Ms 43669. See also Richard Cobden to Henry Ashworth, 10 July 1859, Cobden Papers, BL, Add Ms 43653.

20. Richard Cobden to Catherine Cobden, 12 July 1859, Cobden Papers, BL, Add Ms 50749, ff. 241–2.

21. Ashley, ii, p. 157.

22. For a succinct summary of the Italian question (and on which this discussion draws heavily), see Derek Beales, *England and Italy, 1859–60* (London: Nelson, 1961).

23. Cavour to Contessa di Circourt, 21 June 1857, Beales, *England and Italy*, pp. 3–4.

24. Beales, *England and Italy*, pp. 3–7.

25. Ibid., pp. 36–7.

26. For a recent assessment of the Conservative's foreign policy, see Geoffrey Hicks, *Peace, War and Party Politics: The Conservatives and Europe, 1846–59* (Manchester: Manchester University Press, 2007).

27. Malmesbury to Cowley, 13 Jan. 1859, Beales, *England and Italy*, pp. 42–3.

28. Ibid., pp. 43, 45.

29. Nassau Senior to Whaley, 18 Jan. 1859, Nassau Senior Papers, NLW, Ms C/810.

30. Ridley, p. 486.

31. Palmerston to Granville, 30 Jan. 1859, Granville Papers (2nd Earl), TNA, PRO 30/29/18/6, ff. 69–72.

32. Malmesbury to Palmerston, 10 Apr. 1859, PP, GC/MA/195.

33. Charles Wood to Palmerston, 8 Jan. 1859, Hickleton Papers, BIY, A4/63/102.

34. Charles Wood to Palmerston, 4 May 1859, ibid., A4/63/107–9.
35. Ridley, p. 486.
36. *Greville Memoirs*, vii, p.426 (26 June 1859); Beales, *England and Italy*, p. 68.
37. Prince Albert to the Prince Regent of Prussia, 15 June 1859, Beales, *England and Italy*, p. 92.
38. Beales, *England and Italy*, pp. 98–9. The phrase 'pro-Italian triumvirate' is Derek Beales's, ibid., p. 92.
39. Palmerston to Russell, 6 July 1859, Ashley, ii, pp. 158–60.
40. Palmerston to Persigny, 13 July 1859, Ashley, ii, pp. 161–3.
41. Palmerston to Cowley, 22 Aug. 1859, Ashley, ii, pp. 164–5.
42. Ridley, p. 492.
43. Beales, *England and Italy*, pp. 110–24.
44. Memorandum by Palmerston, 5 Jan. 1860, PP, CAB/103. The memo is also printed in Ashley, ii, p. 174–80.
45. Palmerston to G.C. Lewis, 6 Jan. 1860, PP, GC/LE/214.
46. Palmerston to Charles Wood, 7 Jan. 1860, Halifax Papers, BL, Add Ms 49531, ff. 181–3.
47. G.C. Lewis to Palmerston, 7 Jan. 1860, PP, GC/LE/123.
48. Shaftesbury to Palmerston, 17 Jan. 1860, PP, GC/SH/41.
49. Ridley, p. 495.
50. Charles Wood to Palmerston, 23 Sept. 1860, Hickleton Papers, BIY, A4/63/118.
51. See Palmerston's margin comments on an article cut from *The Times* [19–21?] Oct. 1860, PP, BR206/1.
52. Palmerston's endorsement, dated 30 Apr. 1862, on a letter from Edward Walter Bonham, 23 Apr. 1862, forwarding an address from Capua, PP, MM/IT/52. Palmerston received numerous addresses during the spring and early summer of 1862 from across Italy commending his efforts to secure freedom from Austria and unification – see PP, MM/IT/50–78.
53. Beales, *England and Italy*, p. 131.
54. Palmerston, 'Memorandum of a conversation with Count Flahault on Tuesday 27 March 1860', written 29 Mar. 1860, PP, MM/FR/29.
55. Cowley to Clarendon, 10 Dec. 1855, Sir Victor Wellesley and Robert Sencourt, *Conversations with Napoleon III* (London: Ernest Benn, 1934), pp. 101–2.
56. Palmerston to Charles Wood, 29 July 1856, Hickleton Papers, BIY, A4/63/69.
57. The following extracts from a report by M. le Général Randon, Ministre de Guerre on the importance of Cherbourg in the event of war with Britain were extracted from the *Moniteur* of 2 Mar. 1851 and circulated among ministers in Britain: 'Depuis plus d'un demi-siècle, le Département de la Marine travaille avec persévérance à la création de ce vaste établissement, qui, par sa position géographique à trente lieues de l'Angleterre, par les ressources qu'il offrira à la navigation, en paix comme en guerre, et par les sacrifices mêmes que le pays s'est déjà imposés, afin de tirer parti des avantages naturels de son site, peut être à bon droit, aujourd'hui, considéré comme le point militaire le plus important de nos côtes. . . . Cherbourg est donc parfaitement propre au rassemblement d'une flotte; c'est le seul point qui, en cas de guerre, nous donne le moyen de tenir en échec une Puissance voisine et rivale, pour laquelle il deviendra de plus en plus un objet d'envie, et qui, sans aucun doute, tâchera de le détruire si l'occasion s'en présente. . . . En seconde lieu, aujourd'hui que l'enceinte du port militaire est sur le point d'être terminée, il n'est pas douteux qu'une attaque par terre ne soit infiniment moins probable qu'une attaque par mer. . . . (PP, MM/FR/21).
58. Memorandum on the Defence of Cherbourg, [c.Mar.] 1851 (Copy, in Palmerston's hand but author not identified, poss. Sir John Burgoyne), PP, MM/FR/23/enc.1 (1–2).
59. Crédits accordés au Ministère de la Marine (in francs) – 1846: 140,247,101; 1847: 158,093,515; 1848: 153,615,777; 1849: 128,137,418; 1852: 117,215,804; 1853: 117,181,001. See R. Edwards to Palmerston, 29 Nov. 1852, PP, MM/FR/25 and MM/FR/25/enc.1.
60. Palmerston's comments on France were reported by Clarendon to Lord Cowley in late Sept. 1857: see *The Paris Embassy during the Second Empire. Selections from the Papers of Henry Richard Charles Wellesley, 1st Earl Cowley, Ambassador at Paris, 1852–1867*, ed. F.A. Wellesley (London: Thornton Butterworth, 1928), p. 131.
61. Cowley to Clarendon, 15 Nov. 1857, ibid., pp. 139–40.
62. Aberdeen to Guizot, 19 Mar. 1858, Papiers Guizot, Archives Nationales, Paris, 42 AP 211/69 [163 MI 51].
63. A.D. Lambert, 'Politics, Technology and Policy-Making, 1859–1865: Palmerston, Gladstone and the Management of the Ironclad Naval Race', *Northern Mariner*, 8:3 (1998), 10.
64. Ibid., 13–14.
65. *The Parliamentary Diaries of Sir John Trelawny, 1858–1865*, ed. T.A. Jenkins (London: RHS/Camden Fourth Series, Vol. 40, 1990), pp. 141 (23 July 1860), 146 (24 Aug. 1860).
66. Palmerston's diary, 6 Mar. 1860, PP, D/20.

67. Aberdeen to Guizot, 19 Mar. 1858, Papiers Guizot, Archives Nationales, Paris, 42 AP 211/69 [163 MI 51].

68. Palmerston to Clarendon, 18 May 1858, quoted in Steele, p. 246.

69. Palmerston to Clarendon, 18 May 1858, quoted ibid., p. 249.

70. Richard Cobden to Eugene Rouher, Archives Nationales, Ministry of Commerce, F^{12} 2482 (copies exist in the BL, Misc. Corresp., Add Ms 43670, and Gladstone Papers, BL, Add Ms 44135).

71. Richard Cobden to Michel Chevalier, 24 July 1859, W. S. Lindsay, *Incidents in the Life of Richard Cobden Esq.* (privately printed, 1869) with manuscript continuation, Cobden Papers, WSRO, CP290 ff. 55 (first para.) and 103–5.

72. Richard Cobden to Henry Ashworth, 16 Oct. 1859, Cobden Papers, WSRO 103, ff. 64–6.

73. Richard Cobden to Palmerston, 29 Oct. 1859, PP, GC/CO/1.

74. Richard Cobden to W.E. Gladstone, 29 Oct. 1859, Gladstone Papers, BL, Add Ms 44135.

75. Richard Cobden to Palmerston, 12 July 1860, PP, GC/CO/4.

76. P.T. Marsh, 'The End of the Anglo-French Commercial Alliance, 1860–1894', in P. Chassaigne and M. Dockrill (eds), *Anglo-French Relations 1898–1998: From Fashoda to Jospin* (Basingstoke, 2002), pp. 34–43.

77. Malmesbury's account (from his unpublished diary) quoted from and discussed in Steele, pp. 267–8.

78. Palmerston in House of Commons, 13 Mar. 1860, ibid., p. 267.

79. C.J. Bartlett, *Defence and Diplomacy: Britain and the Great Powers, 1815–1914* (Manchester: Manchester University Press, 1993), pp. 64–5.

80. Alfred, Lord Tennyson, 'The War'. This call for volunteers was published in *The Times*, 9 May 1860.

81. Queen Victoria to the King of the Belgians, 8 May 1860, *LQV*, iii, p. 399.

82. Palmerston to Clarendon, 4 Nov. 1859, quoted in Steele, p. 249.

83. Palmerston to Somerset, 27 Aug. 1865, quoted ibid., p. 254.

84. Quoted in Lambert, 'Politics, Technology and Policy-Making', p. 28.

85. Ibid., p. 30.

86. *Trelawny Diaries*, p. 188 (22 July, 1861).

87. Palmerston to G.C. Lewis, 22 Nov. 1860, PP, GC/LE/221.

88. G.C. Lewis to Palmerston, 23 Nov. 1860, PP, GC/LE/132.

89. Palmerston to G.C. Lewis, 1 Dec. 1860, in reply to Lewis's letter of the same date, PP, GC/LE/222 and 134.

90. Palmerston to G.C. Lewis, 25 Sept. 1856, Ridley, p. 548.

91. G.C. Lewis to Palmerston, 14 Jan. 1861, PP, GC/LE/139.

92. Palmerston to Edward Ellice, 5 May 1861, Ashley, ii, p. 209.

93. Palmerston to G.C. Lewis, 26 Aug. 1861, PP, GC/LE/230.

94. Ridley, p. 549.

95. See Duncan Campbell, *English Public Opinion and the American Civil War* (Woodbridge, Suffolk: Boydell and Brewer/RHS, 2003) and *idem*, 'Palmerston and the American Civil War', in David Brown and Miles Taylor (eds), *Palmerston Studies II* (Southampton: Hartley Institute, 2007), esp. pp. 168–71.

96. G.C. Lewis to Palmerston, 27 Aug. 1861, PP, GC/LE/143.

97. G.C. Lewis to Palmerston, 3 Sept. 1861, PP, GC/LE/144.

98. Note by Palmerston, 20 Oct 1861, Layard Papers, BL, Add Ms 38987, f. 301.

99. G.C. Lewis, diary, 27, 29 Nov. 1862, Harpton Court Ms, NLW, Ms 3575; Ridley, pp. 552–3.

100. Palmerston to G.C. Lewis, 27 Nov. 1861, PP, GC/LE/236.

101. G.C. Lewis to Palmerston, 27 Nov. 1861, PP, GC/LE/149.

102. Palmerston to Granville, 29 Nov. 1861, Granville Papers (2nd Earl), TNA, PRO 30/29/18/8, ff. 44–5.

103. Palmerston to Granville, 26 Dec. 1861, ibid., ff. 50–1.

104. Palmerston to Sir Robert Gore-Booth, 10 Jan. 1861, Lissadell Papers, PRONI, D/4131/H/1.

105. Ridley, p. 553.

106. Palmerston to Russell, 6 Dec. 1861, Ridley, p. 554.

107. Palmerston to G.C. Lewis, 31 Dec. 1862, PP, GC/LE/251.

108. Palmerston to Earl de Grey, 7 Sept. 1863, Ripon Papers, BL, Add Ms 43512, ff. 158–9.

109. Palmerston to Earl de Grey, 16 Oct. 1863, ibid., ff. 162–3.

110. Ridley, p. 554.

111. Palmerston to Earl de Grey, 27 Sept. 1860, in Lucien Wolf, *Life of the First Marquess of Ripon* (London: John Murray, 1921), p. 202.

112. Campbell, 'Palmerston and the American Civil War', 162.

113. Steele, pp. 304–5.

114. On Cobden's attitude towards the American Civil War, see two letters he wrote to Samuel Lucas at this time. On 25 Sept. 1861 he wrote: 'Are you not, both in your American correspondence &

your leading articles, taking too much the tone of belligerents in this wretched American war? *All my sympathies are with the North*. . . . I think you should throw in a word for peace, or at least to show that war is not in this case without its gravest dangers to both sides' (Cobden Papers WSRO, 134). On 16 Jan. he wrote: 'It is of course not easy for you in your line to avoid appearing to be the champion of the North & to be also in a certain degree pledged for its success. Yet I should like you to keep as independent a position as you can' (ibid.).

115. Sir Henry Drummond Wolff, *Rambling Recollections*, 2 vols. (London: Macmillan, 1908), i, p. 55. Richard Mellish had retired from the Foreign Office in 1855 but did not die until 29 Dec. 1865: Ray Jones, *The Nineteenth-Century Foreign Office: An Administrative History* (London: LSE/Weidenfeld & Nicolson, 1971), p. 178).

116. Memorandum, 2 Feb. 1864, PP, MM/DE/20.

117. *Hansard*, 3rd ser., clxxii, 1252 (23 July 1863).

118. Memorandum by Palmerston, 25 July 1863, PP, MM/DE/16.

119. Palmerston to Russell, 13 Feb. 1864, Russell Papers, TNA, PRO 30/22/15A, ff. 147–9.

120. Palmerston to Russell, 1 May 1864, Russell Papers, TNA, PRO 30/22/15B, ff. 75–8.

121. Palmerston to W.E. Gladstone, 3 July 1864 in P. Guedalla (ed.), *The Palmerston Papers: Gladstone and Palmerston, being the Correspondence of Lord Palmerston with Mr Gladstone, 1851–1865* (London: Victor Gollancz, 1928), p. 290.

122. Palmerston to the King of the Belgians, 28 Aug. 1864, Ashley, ii, p. 256.

123. Note by Palmerston, 2 Jan. 1865, Layard Papers, BL, Add Ms 38991, f. 1.

124. *Hansard*, 3rd ser., clxxiii, 27–9 (4 Feb. 1864).

125. According to Bulwer, in discussing the shortcomings of Aberdeen's foreign policy in 1842: '"Why," he [Palmerston] used to say, "every state would be disposed to give up three out of every four questions sooner than go to war to maintain them" . . .', Bulwer, iii, pp. 64–5.

126. A. Tilney Bassett (ed.), *Gladstone to his Wife* (London: Methuen, 1936), p. 126 (17 Sept. 1859 and 28 Oct. 1859).

127. See Matthew, *Gladstone*, p. 108.

128. E.J. Feuchtwanger, *Gladstone* (London: Macmillan, 2nd edn, 1989), pp. 116–17.

129. Steele, p. 24.

130. Morley, *Gladstone*, ii, p. 171.

131. Quoted in Matthew, *Gladstone*, p. 137.

132. G.C. Lewis, diary, 31 Jan. 1860, Harpton Court Ms, NLW, Ms 3574.

133. Ridley, pp. 495–6.

134. Gladstone to Palmerston, 25 Nov. 1859, PP, GC/GL/20.

135. Gladstone to Palmerston, 7 Feb. 1860, in Guedalla (ed.), *Gladstone and Palmerston*, p. 123.

136. As reported by John Bright to Richard Cobden, 3 July 1860, Steele, p. 101.

137. Steele, p. 102.

138. Palmerston's diary, 5 May 1860, PP, D/20.

139. G.C. Lewis, diary, 8 May 1860, Harpton Court Ms, NLW, Ms 3574.

140. G.C. Lewis, diary, 21 May 1860, ibid.

141. G.C. Lewis, diary, 21, 22, 25 May, 30 June, 2 July 1860, ibid.

142. Steele, p. 103.

143. G.C. Lewis, diary, 21 July 1860, Harpton Court Ms, NLW, Ms 3574.

144. Palmerston, diary, 25 Jan. 1861, PP, D/21.

145. G.C. Lewis, diary, 11, 12, 13 Apr. 1861, Harpton Court Ms, NLW, Ms 3575.

146. Steele, pp. 104–5.

147. Palmerston's diary, 14 Apr. 1861, PP, D/21.

148. Quoted in Steele, p. 33.

149. Tilney Bassett (ed.), *Gladstone to his Wife*, p. 162 (7 Oct. 1864)

150. W. E. Gladstone, 'The Declining Efficiency of Parliament', *Quarterly Review*, 99 (1856), 557.

151. Gladstone's third Midlothian speech, 27 Nov. 1879, in Kenneth Bourne, *The Foreign Policy of Victorian England, 1830–1902* (Oxford: Oxford University Press, 1970), p. 422.

152. Matthew, *Gladstone*, p. 139

153. Steele, pp. 23–42.

154. George Jacob Holyoake, *Sixty Years of an Agitator's Life*, 2 vols. (London: T. Fisher Unwin, 1902), ii, p. 76.

155. Summary notes on the constitution by Lord Palmerston, based on the work of J. Hatsell, n.d., BL, Add Ms 60753, ff. 51–2. According to the BL catalogue entry for this manuscript: 'The notes bear a watermark date of 1859 and probably date from the House of Lords' rejection of Gladstone's budget of 1860, and the subsequent crisis; [1860–1861?]'.

156. John Hatsell (1733–1820) was appointed clerk assistant of the House of Commons in 1760 and succeeded as clerk in 1768; he retired in 1797 but retained his title and emoluments and

continued to take an active role in parliamentary affairs. He was widely acknowledged as a leading authority on parliamentary procedure, a reputation founded in large part on his works *A Collection of Cases of Privilege of Parliament* (1776), *Rules and Standing Orders of the House of Commons* (1809) and *Precedents of Proceedings in the House of Commons*, 4 vols. (1776–96). His work continues to be widely referred to, both in Britain and elsewhere. See Thompson Cooper, 'Hatsell, John (1733–1820)', rev. Clare Wilkinson, *ODNB*.

157. Palmerston to Granville, 26 Mar. 1857, Granville Papers (2nd Earl), TNA, PRO 30/29/19/22, ff. 13–14.

158. Palmerston to Granville, 26 Dec 1859, Granville Papers (2nd Earl), TNA, PRO 30/29/18/17, ff. 3–4.

159. Palmerston's diary, 9 June 1860, PP, D/20.

160. For example Steele, pp. 220–4.

161. G.C. Lewis, diary, 17 Nov. 1860, Harpton Court Ms, NLW, Ms 3574.

162. Palmerston to G.C. Lewis, 1 Jan. 1860, PP, GC/LE/213.

163. Memorandum by Palmerston, 15 May 1864, PP, HA/N/13.

164. Holyoake, *Sixty Years of an Agitator's Life*, ii, pp. 78–80.

165. *The Times*, 10 Aug. 1864.

166. Richard Monckton Milnes to C.J. McCarthy, 21 Oct. and 21 Dec. 1860, T. Wemyss Reid, *The Life, Letters, and Friendships of Richard Monckton Milnes, first Lord Houghton*, 2 vols. (London: Cassell, 1891), ii, pp. 62–3.

167. *The Times*, 31 Oct. 1860.

168. *The Times*, 1 Nov. 1860; Richard Monckton Milnes to C.J. McCarthy, 21 Dec. 1860, *Life, Letters, and Friendships of Richard Monckton Milnes*, ii, p. 63.

169. *The Times*, 26 Oct. 1860.

170. Ibid., 27 Oct. 1860.

171. Ibid., 29 Oct. 1860.

172. 'An address to the Prize Holders of the Labourers' Encouragement Society, delivered at the Town Hall, Romsey, on Wednesday, December 21st, 1859, by the Viscount Palmerston, President of the Society. Published by request'. PP, BR 199/12. Gladstone thought this speech 'excellent' (Gladstone to Palmerston, 23 Dec. 1859, PP, GC/GL/21).

173. *The Times*, 29 Oct. 1860.

174. For details of the election contest, see: [Open letter] 'To the Students of the University of Glasgow', by the Liberal Association, 11 Nov. 1862, contained in a collection of squibs, petitions and other ephemera relating to the Rectorial election at the University of Glasgow at the NLS, 6.692 (18).

175. The text of Palmerston's speech can be found in the *Illustrated London News*, 4 Apr. 1863, p. 386.

176. Lord Palmerston's Address, Music Hall, Edinburgh, March 1863, quoted in *'England' versus 'Great Britain'. . . . on the question, whether the practice of imposing the name 'England' on the United Kingdom is legitimate in itself, or injurious to Scotland?* (Glasgow, 1865), p. 9.

177. [William Burns], *Address by William Burns to Glasgow St. Andrew's Society . . . Delivered 4th February, 1869* (Glasgow, 1869), p. 19.

178. Ashley, ii, p. 233.

179. Palmerston to Emily Palmerston, 30 Mar., 1 Apr. 1863, PP, BR23AA/1/42 and 43.

180. From the 'Address to the Right Honourable Viscount Palmerston', given by James J. Grieve, Provost at a 'Banquet in Honour of . . . Palmerston . . . in the Town Hall of Greenock on occasion of presenting an address from the Provost, Magistrates, Councillors and Inhabitants, 31 Mar. 1863', PP, BR 27/12.

181. *North British Daily Mail*, 1 Apr. 1863 (cutting in PP, BR207/2/5).

182. *Weekly Review*, 5 Dec. 1863, pp. 979–80 (cutting in PP, BR27/13).

183. From the 'Address to the Right Honourable Viscount Palmerston', given by James J. Grieve, Provost, PP, BR 27/12.

184. Palmerston's diary, 8 Nov. 1863, PP, D/23.

185. On this theme, see Antony Taylor, 'Palmerston and Radicalism, 1847–1865', *Journal of British Studies*, 33:2 (1994), 157–79, esp. 160–1.

186. A full account of the fight can be found in *The Times*, 18 Apr. 1860.

187. Palmerston to G.C. Lewis, 20 Apr. 1860, Harpton Court Ms, NLW, Ms C/2149.

188. Abraham Hayward to W.E. Gladstone, 11 Aug. 1856, *A Selection from the Correspondence of Abraham Hayward, QC, from 1832 to 1884*, ed. Henry E. Carlisle, 2 vols. (London: John Murray, 1886), i, p. 293.

189. Clarendon to Cowley, 2 Oct. 1861, *The Paris Embassy*, p. 221.

190. Abraham Hayward to Broughton, 21 Dec. 1861, *A Selection from the Correspondence of Abraham Hayward*, ii, p. 65; Ashley, ii, p. 219.

191. Clarendon to Abraham Hayward, 31 Jan. 1862, *A Selection from the Correspondence of Abraham Hayward*, ii, p. 72.

192. Holyoake, *Sixty Years of an Agitator's Life*, ii, p. 77.
193. For a biographical note on Timothy O'Kane, see: www.adb.online.anu.edu.au/biogs/A050416b.htm (valid link as at March 2010).
194. Clarendon to Cowley, 4 Nov. 1863, *The Paris Embassy*, pp. 253–4.
195. Palmerston's diary, 13 Nov. 1863, PP, D/23; Clarendon to Cowley, Nov. 1863, *The Paris Embassy*, pp. 254–5.
196. Ridley, pp. 531–2.
197. Palmerston's diary, 4 Feb. 1864, PP, D/24.
198. Ridley, pp. 531–2.
199. PP, BR22(ii)/20.
200. Gordon Winter and Wendy Kochman, *Secrets of the Royals* (London: Robson Books, 1990), p. 24.
201. Copy of post-mortem report on Palmerston's body by Protheroe Smith as sent to the Editor of the *Lancet* on 21 Oct. 1865, PP, BR22(ii)/22/1; 'The Last Illness of the Late Premier', *Lancet*, 4 Nov. 1865, 521–2.
202. Palmerston to Lord Fitz Hardinge, 8 Sept. 1865, PP, BR25/2/2.
203. Protheroe Smith to Palmerston, 30 Aug. 1865, PP, BR22(i)/1/114.
204. As reported in Abraham Hayward to Stirling of Keir, *A Selection from the Correspondence of Abraham Hayward*, ii, p. 115.
205. Albert Edward, Prince of Wales to Viscount Hamilton, 15 Oct. 1865, Abercorn Papers, PRONI, T/2541/VR8/17.
206. Copy of post-mortem report on Palmerston's body by Protheroe Smith PP, BR22(ii)/22/1; 'The Last Illness of the Late Premier', *Lancet*, 4 Nov. 1865, 521–2; *Earl Cowper, KG: A Memoir*, by his wife (printed for private circulation, 1913), p. 135.
207. 'The Last Illness of the Late Premier', 522. The 'Necropsy of the body of Viscount Palmerston, at 81, made at Brocket Hall, Oct. 19 1865' is appended to Protheroe Smith's report sent to the *Lancet* (BR22(ii)/22/1) but did not form part of the published account.
208. M.J.D. Roberts offers an interpretation of Palmerston's death as 'an episode in Victorian cultural history', in which Palmerston is himself almost incidental: see 'The Deathbed of Lord Palmerston', *Cultural and Social History*, 5:2 (2008), 183–96.
209. Protheroe Smith, 'Notes of Conversation with Lord Palmerston in his last illness', PP, BR22(ii)/22/1.
210. Protheroe Smith, 'Lord Palmerston's last moments', PP, BR22(ii)/22/1.
211. Edwin Hodder, *The Life and Work of the Seventh Earl of Shaftesbury* 3 vols. (London: Cassell, 1887), iii, pp. 185–7.
212. The estimate for Palmerston's probate duty valued the estate at £96,789 11s. 4d. PP, BR22(ii)/4.
213. Ridley, p. 583.
214. Palmerston to Shaftesbury, 19 Sept. 1860, PP, BR22(i)/1/104.
215. Notes on the 'Disposal of Broadlands Estate after 3rd Viscount Palmerston's death in 1865', PP, BR22(ii)/4.
216. *Earl Cowper, KG: A Memoir*, by his wife, p. 136.
217. Lady Westmorland to Comtesse Pauline Neale, 24 Oct. 1865, *The Correspondence of Priscilla, Countess of Westmorland*, ed. Lady Rose Weigall (London: John Murray, 1909), p. 466.
218. Sir Henry Drummond Wolff, *Rambling Recollections*, i, pp. 195–6.
219. Condolence book from the City of Manchester, PP, BR22(ii)/22/3.
220. Gladstone to Anthony Panizzi, 18 Oct. 1865, PP, BR22(ii)/22/6.
221. M. Drouyn de Lhuys to Baron Baude (French chargé d'affaires in London), 20 Oct. 1865, expressing the French Emperor's condolences and formally communicated to the British government, 23 Oct. 1865, PP, BR22(ii)/22/2.
222. *Pall Mall Gazette*, 27 Oct. 1866.
223. W.L. Burn, *The Age of Equipoise: A Study of the Mid-Victorian Generation* (London: George Allen & Unwin 1964), p. 18.
224. Guedalla, p. 405; Steele, p. 367.
225. Walter Bagehot, *The English Constitution*, ed. Paul Smith (1867; Cambridge: Cambridge University Press, 2001), p. 118.
226. *The Times*, 27 Oct. 1860.

Legacy

1. *The Parliamentary Diaries of Sir John Trelawny, 1858–1865*, ed. T.A. Jenkins (London: RHS/Camden Fourth Series, Vol. 40, 1990), p. 221: entry for 7 Aug. 1862.
2. *The Journal of John Wodehouse First Earl of Kimberley 1862–1902*, ed. Angus Hawkins and John Powell (Cambridge: Cambridge University Press/Camden Fifth Series, 1998), p. 176 (18 Oct. 1865).

3. See, for example, Reginald Brett, 'The Queen and Lord Palmerston', *Nineteenth Century* 35:208 (June 1894), 912–21. 'First and foremost', writes Brett, Palmerston 'was lucky, and there is, in the view of the average Briton, Cato notwithstanding, no more glorious attribute' (p. 912).

4. John Charmley, 'Palmerston: "Artful Old Dodger" or "Babe of Grace" ', in T.G. Otte, *The Makers of British Foreign Policy, from Pitt to Thatcher* (Basingstoke: Palgrave, 2001), pp.75–97; quotations from pp. 79, 81, 86 (quoting Roger Bullen, *Palmerston, Guizot and the Collapse of the Entente Cordiale* (London: Athlone Press, 1974), p. 57), 93.

5. *Hansard*, 3rd ser., clxxxi, 915, 917 (22 Feb. 1866).

6. E. Latham, *Famous Sayings and their Authors* (London: Swan Sonnenschein, 1904), p. 12.

7. *The Collected Works of Walter Bagehot*, ed. Norman St John-Stevas, 15 vols. (London: Economist, 1965–86), iii, p. 278.

8. *The British Empire with essays on Prince Albert, Lord Palmerston, Lord Beaconsfield, Mr Gladstone and reform of the House of Lords by Dr Geffcken*, trans. S.J. Macmullan (London: Sampson Low, Marston, Searle and Rivington, 1889), p. 185.

9. *Materials for the True History of Lord Palmerston . . . reprinted from the 'Free Press,' from May to November 1865* (London: Robert Hardwicke, 1866).

10. *Annual Register* (1875) p. 319, quoted in James Gregory, 'Protecting the Legacy of Lord Palmerston', unpublished paper (2007), p. 6.

11. Gregory, 'Protecting the Legacy', p. 8.

12. Ibid., p. 2.

13. Anthony Trollope, *Lord Palmerston* (London: Wm. Isbister, 1882), p. 1.

14. Marquis of Lorne, *Viscount Palmerston, KG* (London: Sampson Low, Marston, 1892), esp. ch. xii: 'Some Personal Characteristics of Lord Palmerston'.

15. *The Collected Works of Walter Bagehot*, iii, pp. 214–15; *The Times*, 19 Oct. 1865.

16. Guedalla, p. 405.

17. Contemporary reviewers mocked Guedalla's florid style; see, for example, *Saturday Review*, 27 Nov. 1926, 648–9; *Bookman*, 71:424 (Jan. 1927), 211–12. See also: Southgate, p. xv; Chamberlain, p. 3.

18. Bell, *passim*.

19. A.J.P. Taylor, *Essays in English History* (Harmondsworth: Penguin, 1976), pp. 113–14. This essay was first published in 1954.

20. Bell, ii, pp. 424–8.

21. Southgate, p. 544.

22. David Steele, 'Temple, Henry John, third Viscount Palmerston (1784–1865)', *ODNB*.

23. W. E. Gladstone, 'The Declining Efficiency of Parliament', *Quarterly Review*, 99 (1856), 557.

24. Robert Blake, *Disraeli* (London: Eyre & Spottiswoode, 1966), p. 570.

25. *Endymion* was written in the late 1870s and published in 1880.

26. John Charmley, *Splendid Isolation: Britain and the Balance of Power, 1874–1914* (London: Hodder & Stoughton, 1999), p. 17.

27. M.E. Chamberlain, *'Pax Britannica?': British Foreign Policy, 1789–1914* (Harlow: Longman, 1988), p. 8.

28. Paul Smith, *Disraeli: A Brief Life* (Cambridge: Cambridge University Press, 1996), p. 184.

29. *Hansard*, 3rd ser., xcvii, 121–3 (1 Mar. 1848)

30. A. Bullock, *Ernest Bevin: Foreign Secretary, 1945–51* (Oxford, 1985), p. 89.

31. Kitaoka Shin'ichi, 'Reform in Japanese Foreign Affairs: Policy Review Long Overdue' [trans. Dean Robson from the original, 'Gaiko kaikaku to Gaimusho kaikaku: Machigatta "seijika shudo" o aratameru tame ni'], *Gaiko Forum*, 167 (June 2002), 3–12, here p. 3: 'Since the end of World War II, some observers suggest, Japan has not had what could be properly called a foreign policy. Such an assessment is hardly surprising if one compares postwar Japanese foreign policy with that pursued in other times and places under such leaders as Viscount Palmerston, Otto von Bismarck, Winston Churchill, or even Japan's own Mutsu Munemitsu (foreign minister 1892–96).'

32. See Irwin Stelzer, 'Nailing the Neocon Myth' (based on his *Neoconservatism*, 2004), in the *Sunday Times Review*, 3 Oct. 2004.

33. James Chace, 'The Balance of Power', *World Policy Journal*, 15:4 (winter 1998/99).

34. *Hansard*, 3rd ser., clxxxi, 914 (22 Feb. 1866).

35. *The Times*, 12, 14, 18, 22 Aug. 1936.

36. E. H. Carr, *The Soviet Impact on the Western World* (London: Macmillan, 1946), pp. 82–3.

37. A. Howe, *Free Trade and Liberal England, 1846–1946* (Oxford: Oxford University Press, 1997), pp. 240–1.

INDEX

Question, as he sees that I was
right in maintaining that if we
only held our ground, the French
Fury would End in Bluster,
and would not lead to any
unpleasant Results. Talleyrand
is quite come round upon that
Subject, swears that so far from
having blown the Coals, as we
happen to know he did, he
always preached Temper &
Moderation aparib, and instead
of demanding the Demolition of
God knows how many Fortresses
if we wish to avoid War,
(The Language held by Belliard
& Louis Philippe) he hopes
we will write him a civil
note assuring him that our